CW00522520

Home Builders: Glasgow Corporation direct labour staff at the Pollokshaws Unit 2 redevelopment site in 1963; the first 16-storey 'Bison' system tower block is visible behind. (Boswell, Mitchell & Johnston)

Front cover (left): 1937 watercolour of Mactaggart & Mickel's first full-page colour newspaper advertisement for Orchard Park Estate. (Sunday Mail, 24 October 1937; DMS Menzies Advertising)

Front cover (right): 1998 watercolour (by Sandy Bell) of Roan Rutherford's design for Mactaggart & Mickel's housing contribution to the 1999 Homes for the Future project, Glasgow. (MMC)

Back cover (top): Detail from 1965 promotional brochure for Wimpey multi-storey flats. (George Wimpey Ltd)

Back cover (bottom): Steel-framed 31-storey tower blocks of council flats under construction at Red Road in 1965 by Glasgow Corporation's direct labour department, working with steel fabrication subcontractors.

HOME BUILDERS

First published in 1999 by

The Royal Commission on the Ancient and Historical Monuments of Scotland, John Sinclair House, 16 Bernard Terrace, Edinburgh EH8 9NX, Scotland.

Telephone: 0044-131-662-1456
Fax: 0044-131-662-1477/1499

Crown Copyright: RCAHMS, 1999.

ISBN 1-902419-08-1

British Library Cataloguing in Publication Data:
A CIP catalogue record for this book is available on request from the British Library.

All rights reserved.
No part of this publication may be reproduced or transmitted in any form or by any means, electronic or mechanical, without permission in writing from the publisher.

Book design by Kate George @ Finiflex.
Printed in Scotland by Bell and Bain Ltd, Glasgow.

The publisher gratefully acknowledges the sponsorship of Mactaggart & Mickel, which has made possible the publication of this volume.

CONTENTS

ACKNOWLEDGEMENTS

This book forms the first stage of an extensive RCAHMS research and archival project, initiated and generously funded by Mactaggart & Mickel. It sets out an introductory history of the company and of the wider Scottish housebuilding industry in the modern era, together with a selection of supporting historical source material; later stages in the project will include the archival accessioning of the firm's extensive architectural records, and the formation of a company cine film archive.

The vision which first inspired this project in early 1998, and which has since sustained it over a period of a year and a half, stemmed from three people. Within the company, Anne Mickel and Iain Drysdale have given the book their constant support; and outside the company, Charles McKean conceived the original idea of a volume in this form, building on his own pioneering researches into 1930s architecture. Other individuals within Mactaggart & Mickel who have provided valuable help and information have included directors Derek and Bruce Mickel; Douglas and Marjorie Mickel, who provided access to their personal papers, including historic material handed down by company co-founder Andrew Mickel; chairman John Craig, who analysed the financial history of the firm for us; and other staff members, including Pauline Stewart and Jennifer Freeman.

Several RCAHMS colleagues contributed significantly to the publication: Sir William Fraser and Professor Roland Paxton read through and commented on draft text; Gareth Wells carried out extensive documentary and picture research; Matthew Fawcett and Lynn Johnson sorted and listed the Glasgow office drawings; Rob Duncan assisted with the collection listing. Help was also received from Tahra Duncan, David Easton, Simon Green, Angus Lamb, Anne Martin, Diana Murray, Derek Smart, Geoffrey Stell, John Stevenson, Jane Thomas, and Steven Thomson. The book was designed by Kate George and copy-edited by Ruth Freestone King.

In addition to the named authors and editors (see below for biographical details), and the interview subjects and illustration copyright holders who kindly allowed their recollections or pictures to be reproduced, a number of other individuals contributed with research, advice and other help, including Matthew Dickie, Eilidh Donaldson, Roger Emmerson, Nigel Fender, Anne Laird, Charles McKean, Aonghus MacKechnie, Susan Millar and Julie Poole (on Mickel family history), Nicholas Morgan, Stefan Muthesius, David Page, Ian Paterson, Peter Robinson, Roan Rutherford, Fiona Sinclair, Robin Urquhart, David Whitham and Dorothy Young.

Unless otherwise specified, illustrations are the copyright of RCAHMS. The negative numbers are given in brackets at the end of the captions, as are the names of non-RCAHMS/Mactaggart & Mickel copyright holders, to assist reference and the ordering of prints from the NMRS; 'CN' denotes a colour original. RCAHMS gratefully acknowledges permission from copyright holders to reproduce illustrations. Every effort has been made to trace copyright holders; RCAHMS wishes to apologise to any who may have been inadvertently omitted from the caption acknowledgements.

The authors

Kenneth Gibb is a lecturer in the Department of Urban Studies at the University of Glasgow. A housing economist, he has been interested in the workings of the contemporary Scottish housebuilding sector for several years and has carried out a number of research projects in this area, most notably for Scottish Homes.

Miles Glendinning is head of the Threatened Buildings and Topographical Surveys at RCAHMS. He has co-authored and edited a number of books on architecture and the city, including *Tower Block* (1994, with Stefan Muthesius), *History of Scottish Architecture* (1996, with Aonghus MacKechnie and Ranald MacInnes), *Rebuilding Scotland* (1997), and *Clone City* (1999, with David Page).

Annette O'Carroll is a freelance researcher with an interest in urban development, and is currently focusing on the social history of the Old and New Towns of Edinburgh. Her PhD thesis examined the development of owner-occupation in Edinburgh between 1918 and 1939. She has taught planning and housing history at undergraduate and postgraduate levels.

Richard Rodger teaches economic and social history at Leicester University. He has written and edited several books on the economic, social and business history of cities, including *Scottish Housing in the Twentieth Century* (1989), *European Urban History* (1993) and *Housing in Urban Britain 1780-1914* (1995), and since 1987 has been editor of *Urban History*. He is currently completing a book entitled *Land, Property and Trust: Edinburgh 1800-1920*.

Diane Watters is Threatened Buildings Survey Liaison Officer at RCAHMS. An author and researcher specialising in 20th-century architecture, and an active participant in the international Modernist heritage organisation DOCOMOMO, she wrote the 1997 RCAHMS book, *Cardross Seminary: Gillespie, Kidd & Coia and the Architecture of Postwar Catholicism*.

List of RCAHMS Commissioners

Sir William Fraser, GCB MA LLD FRSE (Chairman)
Professor J M Coles, MA ScD PhD FBA FSA FSA Scot
Professor Rosemary Cramp, CBE MA BLitt DSc FSA FSA Scot
Dr Barbara E Crawford, MA PhD FSA FSA Scot
Dr Deborah J Howard, MA PhD FSA FSA Scot Hon FRIAS
Dr Margaret A Mackay, BA DipScotStud PhD FSA Scot
Professor Roland A Paxton, MBE MSc CEng FRSE FICE AMCST
Miss Anne C Riches, OBE MA FSA FSA Scot
Mr James Simpson, BArch RIAS RIBA FSA Scot
Professor T C Smout, CBE MA PhD Dsc FBA FRSE FSA Scot

Secretary
Mr R J Mercer, MA FSA FRSE FSA Scot MIFA

INTRODUCTION

The Tortoise and the Hare?

This book contains an introductory overview of the history of housebuilding in 19th- and (especially) 20th-century Scotland, together with a detailed case study of one of its most important specific elements: the work of the firm of Mactaggart & Mickel and its immediate predecessors since the 1880s. Most architectural debates in this year of Scottish political change have been preoccupied with the culturally prestigious issues of parliament-building. But the story of Scotland's home builders is in many ways even more central to the definition or redefinition of our collective identity. It is an important story in plain quantitative terms, because houses form such a large part of the modern city and of the total building stock. And it is also significant because of the uniquely symbolic role played by 'the home' as the front line in the constantly shifting conflict between the world of the private and individual on the one hand, and that of the public and collective on the other.

A book of this size, even if in general overview form, can only tackle one aspect of this vast subject. Some recent volumes have addressed the home mainly from the perspective of those who inhabited it or commissioned its construction. (1) But this book focuses on a different aspect: the contribution of those whose job it was to build it. Or, put more impersonally, it focuses on the 'supply' rather than the 'demand' side of housing production. Of course, during the period under review, the two repeatedly overlapped - we need only to think of the role of 1930s speculative builders in fomenting public demand for home-ownership, or the zeal of 1960s contractors in encouraging small local authorities to commission tower blocks.

One key area of overlap between supply and demand concerns the point at which the dwelling is actually 'paid for'. Most products in modern society are made first, at the risk of the producer, and are then put on the market for sale blind to the consumer. That rule, with its constant disciplining effects on productivity, applies even to large, complex objects such as cars. And it applies to speculative houses, which formed the overwhelming majority of Scottish dwellings before World War I. Most 'special' or elite buildings, however, have been produced in a different way; they have been ordered and paid for beforehand at the command of the client. What does not apply to Scottish urban buildings is another option, where the dwellers themselves, rather than 'someone else', commission the houses. The key issue dominating this book is the question that faced Scots at the beginning of the 20th century. How were the vast numbers of new dwellings demanded by modern society to be built: in the first way, or in the second?

Where some countries, such as the United States, simply perpetuated and extended the speculative building system into the new conditions of the 20th century, in Scotland and (to a lesser extent) in the rest of Britain, the mass housing of this century was built very much to order. The approach previously used for elite buildings was generalised across the entire urban environment. It is not perhaps a coincidence that building, during that period, showed the lowest productivity gains of seven major sectors of the economy: for example, only a quarter of that within manufacturing between 1924 and 1973. (2) Housebuilding became used as a stabilising buffer against economic turbulence, an instrument with which governments could 'regulate the economy'. Yet as we shall see, this position did not amount, as in post-1945 eastern Europe, to an exclusion or abolition of the private building industry.

In this short introduction to *Home Builders*, we have two main tasks. First, we attempt to identify the overarching structures and trends of Scottish housebuilding during our period - the story dealt with in Part B of the book. Then we define the relationship of the work of Mactaggart & Mickel to those general themes. What we will discover is a striking contrast, even a conflict, between the two. The general course of Scottish housebuilding since the late 19th century has been dominated by a vast and impetuous drive of social housing dictated or directly provided by the state. But Mactaggart & Mickel, after an initial dalliance with this programme, resolutely abstained from it, and instead pursued the less spectacular approach of speculative building for sale. In the 1980s and 1990s, that conflict between the values of Mactaggart & Mickel and those of the wider housing system ended, when the force of the state housing programme disappeared, returning us to a market-ruled situation not unlike that of the 19th century.

The organisation, technology and built form of housing

'[It is] the duty of the nation to undertake the great work of providing decent homes for the citizens of a great Empire.'
Ballantyne Report, 1917 (3)

On the whole, it was in the organisation of building that demand-side influences made themselves directly felt. Here the dominant trend, from the late 19th century to today, has been the startling growth, and equally startling decline, of the collective and aggressively 'political' framework for the organising of housing production.

On the face of it, this story of rise and fall could not have been more dramatic or clear-cut. In Richard Rodger's essay (Chapter

CITY TENEMENTS

GLASGOW tenement of fine red sandstone built in 1907. On each floor above the ground floor is a pair of two-roomed houses with a one-roomed house sandwiched between, all sharing the same w.c. on the stair. No baths. Sink in each living-room. Poor storage space (paras. 128-135).

There are many thousands of these 2-1-2 tenement houses in Glasgow.

Suggestions for combination and modernisation in Plan 4.

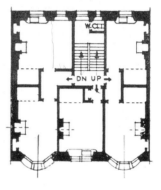

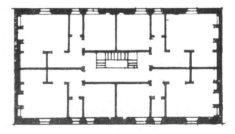

EDINBURGH's typical tenement block has two pairs of " back-to-back " houses on each floor (paras. 128-134).

Note the 16 door bells at a single entrance. No scullery or bath. Bed recesses common. Some houses have w.cs. of their own ; sometimes one w.c. serves two houses.

Suggestions for combination and modernisation in Plan 7.

*INT.1. Market demand, market supply: standard turn-of-century Glasgow and Edinburgh working class tenements, showing the influence of official ('police') controls in encouraging ventilation and basic internal amenities. Reproduced from a pioneering Scottish Housing Advisory Committee report of 1947, **Modernising our Homes**, which advocated tenement rehabilitation. (SHAC)*

B1), the highly decentralised and fragmented mechanisms of housebuilding in the 19th century are outlined. Despite the growing agitations of reformers, and in contrast to some of the more urgent crises of public health, housing was still not generally seen as a matter of national 'political' importance. Reacting against these, the 20th century insisted that the building of housing, especially working class housing, should be driven by collective ethical-political values of democratic equality and national cohesion. This, it was hoped, would help the nation and the state fight its external enemies and emancipate its own citizens. In Scotland, as in the remainder of western Europe, it was the trauma of World War I which allowed those ideas to suddenly triumph, and joined them up with practical administrative structures to give them effect. The foundation-stone of this revolution was the influential 1917 report of the Ballantyne Commission into Scottish working class housing, which demanded that the state should take charge of housing as a branch of 'public administration'. From then on, housing became a matter of political goals and targets, and of warlike campaigns.

The way in which Scotland (and, partly, England) set about this became dominated by direct building and ownership of social rental housing by local authorities. The financing of housing was shaped more and more by government subsidies, grants, loans and other manipulations of the market. The Scottish system of direct municipal building diverged strikingly from the mainstream European pattern. On the Continent, state intervention took the form of sponsorship of the existing private or quasi-private agencies, rather than paying for and owning the housing itself. Countries such as Germany or Belgium placed almost complete reliance on policies that played only a minority role in Scotland, such as the state subsidies or loans to private building for rent or sale which Mactaggart & Mickel exploited between the wars, as we see in Chapters A2 and A3. And Scottish housing diverged even more dramatically from the position in North America, where housing continued to be seen as a consumer good rather than as a social right.

But, although organised in larger blocs of demand than the individual small developers of the 19th century, the 20th century's new patrons of Scottish housing were hardly unified in their outlook. There was constant conflict between different groups of 'public patrons', between planners and housers, councillors and officials and so forth. And although discipline and the collective seemed so dominant, in fact those programmes also continued to have the effect of emancipating individuals. Finally, with the decline of state intervention since the 1970s in all western European countries, there has been a re-convergence around themes of increased owner occupation and general loosening of controls. (4)

What were the effects on the building process of this drive for collective organisation of housing provision? The early and mid-20th century, with its 'total' warfare and 'mass' society, saw growing attempts to organise housing production in a way which would be dictated by an ethos of social discipline rather than that of individual competition. The harsh market cycle of boom and slump was increasingly replaced by command production mechanisms; the state tried to control and spur on the entire 'building industry' in accordance with the Taylorist and Fordist ideas of scientific management, mass production and ever-increasing pace and scale of activity. The crises of this system were those of resource shortages, price inflation and rationing. But the effects of these interventions, especially in the interwar period and the years of the 'mixed economy' in the later 1950s and 1960s, were much more complex than suggested by the

simplistic rhetoric of mass building. There were some attempts, especially in Glasgow, to organise direct housebuilding by the state - 'direct labour' building. But in general, the private building industry was retained as the state's preferred partner, working usually as a contractor rather than as an autonomous speculative builder.

The way in which the building industry set about this task was characterised by a constant tension between tendencies of integration and security on the one hand, and initiatives of dispersal or specialisation on the other. (5) It was the initiatives of concentration that grabbed the headlines. These included the gradual replacement of fragmented 'separate-trades' contracting by the 'Anglo-American' pattern of the single or main contractor; the extension of the latter's authority into the field of design in the 'package deal' or design-and-build contract; the preference of many public authorities for the continuity of serial or negotiated contracts rather than open competitive tendering; and the growing security of employment and trade union power in the industry. However, some of these trends were a little deceptive. For example, in the 19th century the separate-trades system applied mainly to contracted work under the control of an architect, rather than to speculative housebuilding, where the master builder-cum-land speculator was more prominent - a type of developer exemplified by Robert Mickel, whose work (as we see in Chapter A1) was the springboard of the Mactaggart & Mickel story. Thus the 'disappearance' of separate-trades from housing was not quite what it seemed! (6) And no sooner had it 'disappeared' in the 20th century, than separate-trades was immediately replaced by a proliferation of specialist subcontractors: by the early 1970s, half of all building firms were subcontractors. The replacement of speculative building with little architectural input by public housebuilding under the name of a municipal designer was sometimes something of a misnomer. For example, the apparently homogeneous housing programmes built under the official design aegis of Glasgow city architect Archibald Jury in the 1950s and 1960s were actually 'designed' by a wide range of groups with little in common, ranging from road engineers to town and country planners.

All these tensions between unifying and fragmenting trends sometimes left medium-sized firms torn between different priorities. Companies such as Mactaggart & Mickel, as we see in Chapter A2, repeatedly faced the dilemma of whether to commit their resources to grandiose state-sponsored programmes, given the track-record of disunity, policy changes and extended chains of decision-making on the part of the patron organisations.

The technology of building, and the built forms or architecture of housing, were shaped indirectly by these pressures of demand and building organisation. But they also reflected a more self-contained set of influences, in the form of a Scottish tradition of urban housing technology and architecture which stretched back to the 'Age of Improvement' in the 18th century. The result was a less clear cut and dramatic picture than in the field of patronage and organisation, with its dramatic rise-and-fall sawtooth profile.

Like England and America, but unlike most European countries, the physical expression of Scottish housing production had developed on highly repetitive, ordered lines. This principle was exemplified by the unified 'terrace' of identical dwellings, an idea popularised largely by Robert Adam, and the grid plan town extension, as seen in the Edinburgh New Town and in countless British colonial settlements; vernacular or 'craft' traditions had been expunged early from Scottish housing. In the 19th-century Scottish city, with its homogeneous street facades of industrially

3

produced masonry ashlar blocks and timber sash windows, there was already a well developed tension between collective exterior and the individual life and aspiration for betterment concealed within. However, as Richard Rodger's essay makes clear, the extent of systematisation in the building industry, and of individualisation of domestic life, both had their strict limits.

The 20th century, with its pressures for accelerated collectivisation, accentuated these conflicts into a glaring disparity between sudden and extreme bursts of change, endorsed by official organisations for the purposes of their own campaigns, and the underlying piecemeal evolution of building techniques and architectural forms. In building construction, the revolutionary changes were focused on the issue of prefabrication, or 'system building', in response to periods of resource shortages. Spaced out between the 1920s and 1970s, there were several intense systems crazes, each of which blossomed and faded after a handful of years. But alongside these there was a slower evolution from systematised stone construction, which became too expensive after around 1910, to a variety of composite methods of on-site and selectively prefabricated building. Architecturally, the old, 19th-century tenement city was rejected in two bursts of dramatic innovation-the embrace of low-density garden suburbs from around 1910, powerfully endorsed by the Ballantyne Report, and the enthusiasm of the 1950s and 1960s for Modernist tower blocks in free-flowing space. But at the same time the old patterns

continued to develop unobtrusively in a modest and evolutionary way, as seen in the terraced villas built by Mactaggart & Mickel in the 1920s and the four-storey tenements built by Glasgow Corporation in the 1950s.

In general, those evolutionary developments were attended with the least controversy at the time, whereas the radical innovations, despite their usual Taylorist rhetoric of rationalism and efficiency, often descended into muddle and acrimony. As we will see in Chapter B4, this disparity was exemplified in the Red Road skyscraper project of Glasgow Corporation, in which soaring architectural form and highly experimental construction were combined with the collectivist patronage and organisation provided by Glasgow Corporation's 'crusading' housing convener, Councillor David Gibson, and the council's direct labour force - the result being one of the most chaotic housing projects ever built in Scotland!

The exception or the rule?
the significance of
Mactaggart & Mickel

'When the history of the building industry of the present century is written, I think it will be found that the two most important contributors to the housing of the people were private enterprise

INT.2. *Public consumption, state and private production: this 1989 view of Castlemilk, one of Glasgow Corporation's enormous peripheral schemes, shows the contribution of public production agencies, in the form of the four-storey 1950s tenements built largely by direct labour, and that of private contractors, in the form of the Wimpey tower blocks added to the landscaped edge of the scheme, at Ardencraig Road (five blocks, 1963-65) and Bogany Terrace (one block, 1966-67). (RCAHMS B21565)*

builders and the building societies, most of whose members are the prudent and saving members of the working and lower-salaried classes'.
W S Cruickshank, *The Scotsman*, 1950 (7)

The overall trends in the organisation and built form of modern Scottish housing, sketched out above, are reviewed at greater length in Part B (Chapters B1-B5) of this book. But first, in Part A (Chapters A1-A5), we begin by tracing the company history of Mactaggart & Mickel. Our account places special emphasis on the firm's 'historic' period between 1880 and the late 1950s, and reviews more summarily its modern phase since around 1960.

How does that story relate to the wider themes we have just set out? What we witness is a business which was, from its earliest roots in the late 19th century work of Robert Mickel, highly 'modern' in its mobility and its versatility, and which eagerly exploited the 20th century's mechanisms of public propagandising. Yet this business stood deliberately aside from the dominant theme of Scottish housing in those years: that of state collectivism. That position was only arrived at after a period of experimental involvement in the new state programmes of council building and subsidised private housing, as is related in Chapters A2 and A3. But by the 1930s, the company's orientation towards owner occupation had become resolute and irreversible. As Chapter A4 demonstrates, it was, on the whole, maintained during the years of severe government restrictions on private building in the 1940s and early 1950s. In the area of building technology and architectural form, the company also moved from an initially revolutionary position, of enthusiastic endorsement of the Ballantyne Commission's rejection of tenements for cottage housing, towards a more cautiously evolutionary stance, developing its output steadily from terraced villas to bungalows and modestly sized service apartment blocks, and infiltrating prefabricated elements gradually into its everyday construction methods.

That position began to seem in some ways an aberration during the 1950s and 1960s, when other companies such as Crudens and Wimpey were eagerly exploiting the high-rise boom - an era whose heady opportunism is described in Chapters B3 and B4, and in the Appendix interviews with building-industry and housing figures from the time. But from around 1970, with the progressive collapse in status of mass housing, and then of all public housing - a collapse graphically charted in the output table in the Appendices, and in Chapter B5 - Mactaggart & Mickel's consistent adherence to the ideal of speculative building for owner occupation began to take on, retrospectively, a new legitimacy. That position gained additional force in the context of the political endorsement and subsidising of that ideal by post-1979 governments.

Of course, mass building in separate single-family dwellings for owner occupation was just as 'modern' a housing form as public rental flats in tower blocks; in some countries, such as Belgium or the United States, it was the dominant method throughout the 20th century. And across the western world, even in countries where rental flats had been prominent, the 1970s and 1980s saw an inexorable trend towards owner occupation and detached dwellings. In many ways, the turn of the 21st century seemed to have returned full circle to the turn of the 20th, towards a generally capitalistic system encompassing islands of social provision and concern. But the reversal of the state housing juggernaut in Scotland, where it had been specially dominant, seemed a particularly staggering result. And as the decline in state provision

was not accompanied by a general 'de-politicisation' of housing, but rather by a new twist in its political polarisation, the reaction was not a chastened caution but a new phase of unrestrained polemic. This was strongly reminiscent of the Ballantyne Report's attacks on 'bad Scottish housing' in 1917 - even though the targets were now almost exactly the opposite. For example, Tom Begg's 1996 book, *Housing Policy in Scotland*, argued that Scottish public housing programmes were 'huge engines for generating and perpetuating poverty', which had crushed individuals' freedom in the same way as had the Soviet domination of postwar Poland, and had 'hung a huge millstone around the neck of the Scottish economy'. (8) Already, there had been a foretaste of that general revaluation in the architectural field, where the attacks on tower blocks spurred a revaluation of the previously unfashionable bungalow suburbia, beginning in the 1970s. (9) In 1975, Cathcart MP Teddy Taylor had applied that argument to Mactaggart & Mickel's work, asking why 'local authorities, with all the resources available to them, have built so many major housing developments which lack the planning sense and vision which were demonstrated fifty years ago by Mactaggart & Mickel?' (10)

In the light of that reversal of the political polemic of housing, it would be tempting for us today to interpret the story of Mactaggart & Mickel and Scottish speculative housebuilding, and its relationship to the vast 20th-century state housing drive, as a story of the tortoise and the hare: the hare furiously and erratically racing ahead, but finally collapsing exhausted; the tortoise steadily and methodically carrying on, and finally waddling across the finishing line to rest in triumph. Such a view, although satisfyingly dramatic, would disguise the true complexity, and open-endedness, of this subject. It is our hope that the rich variety of experiences, opinions and other historical evidence contained in this volume will contribute to a more multi-faceted perspective on these years of flux in Scottish housebuilding.

From today's deregulated capitalistic perspective, for instance, the criticisms directed in the 1940s by Douglas Mickel at the excesses of state housing and the command economy may seem to have been strikingly prescient warnings. But to go on to argue that they should have been heeded at the time would be a clear historical anachronism, given the then overwhelming bias of political and public opinion towards ideals of national cohesion, in the aftermath of a major war. A polarised political evaluation, whether from today's capitalist viewpoint or from the socialist perspective of the 1940s, also risks concealing the constant interplay between the public and private sectors. We can see examples of the latter in Mactaggart & Mickel's operations of the 1920s and early 1930s, or, later on, in the mutually beneficial exploitation of 'no-fines' concrete building by the Scottish Special Housing Association (a government agency), and George Wimpey Ltd. Clearly, the venture by the municipal state into the building process itself, through direct labour building, was a very chequered one. But the private building industry showed itself able to prosper whether it built public housing as a contractor or speculatively for itself; both were equally examples of 'modern', 'mass' housing. What was important was a combination of opportunistic mobility and efficiency. The Taylorist and Fordist slogans so dear to 20th-century 'socialist' mass building were, after all, invented by American capitalists.

The temptation to pass judgement in hindsight on the great adventure of the public housing 'drive' also assumes that the story is now complete. After the enormous aberration of tower blocks and new towns, we might seem to have have arrived conclusively back where we started, there to remain. But the late 19th century, as Richard Rodger makes clear in Chapter B1, was a time of urgent discontent with the laissez-faire status quo, and of demands for the state to intervene in limited and discrete areas to remedy the worst injustices. Today, as criticisms of the unfettered global market spread across the world, here in Scotland there are calls for publicly sponsored action in housing, to combat both the problem of social exclusion and the crisis of 'Clone City' - the architectural anarchy which results from market-driven housing and building policies in our Scottish towns. (11) In their participation in the Glasgow 'Homes for the Future' project - a bold attempt to fight the fragmenting effects of unplanned city development - Mactaggart & Mickel and other private building firms have signalled their commitment to this new phase of social housebuilding. If the private speculative builder, during this century, has been a tortoise racing the 'hare' of mass public housing, what is now clear is that, although that race has now ended, the tortoise is still out there on the road, continuing its course into the far future.

Organisation of this book

Home Builders is arranged in the form of two parallel 'stories': a company history of Mactaggart & Mickel, contained in Part A, and a general history of the modern Scottish housebuilding industry, in Part B. The overall chronological correspondence between the two Parts is not exact: while the Mactaggart & Mickel business began only in the 1880s, with the work of Robert and Thomas Mickel, the first chapter of Part B (by Richard Rodger) stretches back to provide a more general background to the housebuilding of the 19th century as a whole. The chapters of Parts A and B are weighted in order to highlight the particularly dramatic contrast between the speculative building approach emphasised by Mactaggart & Mickel, and the mass public housing which dominated mid-20th century Scottish housing as a whole. The longest chapter of Part A is A3, dealing with the company's 1930s halcyon years of private building, while the longest chapters of Part B are B3 and B4, covering the mass public housing of the three post-1945 decades. Both Parts A and B are concerned above all with the organisation of the building process, and the relationship of that organisation to the built results. It should be emphasised that Part A is not a conventional business history, but a case study in urban history.

The chronologically arranged accounts in Parts A and B are supplemented by a range of source material in Part C, the Appendices. Part C comprises the following elements: an interim summary of the Mactaggart & Mickel archival material currently being accessioned into the National Monuments Record of Scotland; a collection of edited interviews, including a 1937 discussion between Douglas Mickel and Edinburgh Corporation officials, and recent interviews with a range of figures involved in the postwar housing programme; statistics of 20th-century housing production arranged by tenure (to emphasise the dramatic rise and fall of the public housing drive); and statistics and a gazetteer of post-1945 multi-storey flats and mass housing production, with contractual information. Explanations of frequently used abbreviations and full bibliographic details of publications listed in the Notes to each chapter are given in the Abbreviations and Bibliography at the end of the book.

The complex plan of *Home Builders*, with its overlapping strands of historical accounts in Parts A and B and supporting documentation in Part C, is designed above all to emphasise the many conflicting motives and forces which lay behind the apparently homogeneous facade of 'mass housing' production. It is intended to act not as a final authoritative account of this vast subject, but as an introductory source-book, and a stimulus to further research, archive-gathering, and recording.

Notes

1   A Carruthers (ed.), *The Scottish Home*, 1996; S Damer, *A Social History of Glasgow Council Housing*, 1991; M Glendinning and S Muthesius, *Tower Block*, 1994.

2   E W Cooney, 'Productivity, conflict and order in the British construction industry', *Construction History*, 9, 1993, 77; R C O Matthews, C H Feinstein and J C Odling-Smee, *British Economic Growth*, 1982.

3   *Report of the Royal Commission on the Housing of the Industrial Population of Scotland, Rural and Urban* (Ballantyne Report), Cd 8371, 1917, 6.

4   A Power, *Hovels to High Rise*, 1993, 2-4.

5   C G Powell, *An Economic History of the British Building Industry*, 1980, 181.

6   For an earlier 19th-century example than Robert Mickel, see for example the builder-developer-land speculator William Henderson of Glasgow: *Alexander Thomson Society Newsletter*, May 1998, 10-11.

7   W S Cruickshank, letter to *The Scotsman*, 18 May 1950.

8   T Begg, *Housing Policy in Scotland*, 1996, 135, 163.

9   P Oliver, I Davis and I Bentley, *Dunroamin - the Suburban Semi and its Enemies*, 1981.

10 *Fifty Years of King's Park, 1925-1975*, 1975.

11 M Glendinning and D Page, *Clone City*, 1999.

Part A

Mactaggart & Mickel

A Company History

○ Diane Watters

○

GROWTH OF A PARTNERSHIP

The Prehistory of Mactaggart & Mickel, 1880-1925

Introduction

In this chapter, we gather together the threads that were to lead to the foundation of the present firm of Mactaggart & Mickel in 1925. We begin with the late 19th-century work of Robert and Thomas Mickel, which established a highly mobile and flexible business approach, balancing building and development activity with profits from property and land ownership. Robert Mickel's firm acted as an incubator for two younger entrepreneurs, John Auld Mactaggart and Andrew Mickel, who would lay the foundations of the present business. Both at first worked separately as developers in pre-1914 Glasgow, the more flamboyant Mactaggart concentrating on building tenements for rent while Mickel built self-contained dwellings for sale.

After World War I, with its heavy blows against the old laissez-faire housing system, the two men at first combined forces under Mactaggart's leadership, to exploit the two main strands of housing policy in the new era of state intervention: municipal building for rent, and subsidised private building for rent or sale. The firm leapt to the forefront of the municipal building field by taking on the largest single interwar contract in Glasgow, a garden-suburb development at Mosspark that established the single-contractor system of building in Scotland for the first time. And they avidly exploited the 1923 Housing Act's subsidies of private housebuilding, using a 'ladies syndicate' of the wives of directors to accumulate a secure land-bank. Eventually, in 1925, to cope more effectively with this increasingly complex situation, the business was separated into two more specialised arms: the Western Heritable Investment Co., dominated by Mactaggart,

A1.1. 155/159 High Street, Linlithgow, the home and early business base of Robert Mickel, whose timber production and construction company laid the foundations of Andrew Mickel's and John Mactaggart's 20th century entreprenurial building ventures. The photograph was taken by Andrew Mickel's son, Douglas Mickel, around 1955. (Mactaggart & Mickel Collection, RCAHMS; hereafter MMC)

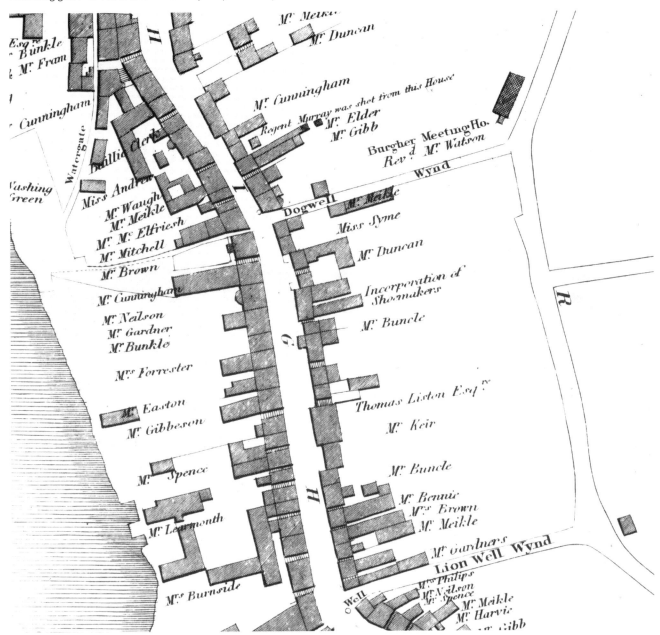

A1.2. Detail of John Wood's Plan of Linlithgow (1820), showing the Meikle (Mickel) family home (above Lion Well Wynd). The family had been settled in the burgh since the late 17th century; for generations, the male members had worked as wrights, joiners or builders in the historic town. (National Library of Scotland)

which concentrated on rental housing development and management; and Mactaggart & Mickel, directed by the Mickel family and by John Mactaggart's son, Jack, which concentrated on building work and development for owner occupation.

Laying the foundations
Robert Mickel & Co.

The Mactaggart & Mickel story began not in 1925, when the present firm was founded, but in the late 19th century. And it started not in one of Scotland's great industrial centres, with their burgeoning belts of working-class housing, but in one of the oldest royal burghs, the small county town of Linlithgow - located, significantly, almost midway between Edinburgh and Glasgow, between east and west. We commence our story with the work of two brothers, Robert Mickel (1845-1923) and Thomas Mickel (1865-1954), first in the local building industry and then on a wider stage. Of the two, it was Robert Mickel who played the much more significant role in establishing the fundamental

business principles that would later govern the work of Mactaggart & Mickel. Robert and Thomas came from a family that had been settled in the burgh since the late 17th century, and whose male members had worked as wrights, joiners or builders, generation after generation, ever since that time. Robert and Thomas Mickel's great, great, great grandfather, James Meikle (who died in 1717) was the deacon of the Incorporation of Wrights in Linlithgow in the late 17th century, while their grandfather, Robert Meikle (1763-1868) was a wright and 'proprietor of houses' in the town, and their father, Andrew Mickel, was recorded as a builder.

The story begins in earnest in 1881, when Robert Mickel, working until then as a timber merchant in Linlithgow and living at 159 High Street, suddenly decided to launch into an energetic phase of business expansion. In 1883, perhaps taking advantage of the beginnings of recovery from the building trade depression following the crash of the City of Glasgow Bank in 1878, he opened a timber and sawmilling business at Broomloan Saw Mills, Govan, moving to live in the city at 6 Woodville Place and, subsequently, 10 Burnbank Gardens. In 1887, he spread his

A1.3. View of the port town of Bo'ness in the late 19th century. In 1887, Robert Mickel opened a large sawmills and steam joinery works, the Victoria Sawmills, as the first stage of his business expansion. (RCAHMS D44980)

A1.4. Detail of an aerial view of Maryhill, Glasgow, taken in 1940 as part of a survey by the German airforce. At the centre of the view, on the north side of Gairbraid Avenue, are two massive, near-rectangular street-blocks constructed by Partick builder Thomas Morgan on land feued out by Robert Mickel in 1893-7. The blocks were redeveloped in the mid 20th century. (RCAHMS D47632)

focusing mainly on the north side of the city, but also ranging as far afield as Hamilton. A number of feu contracts issued by Mickel in the 1890s are recorded in the Register of Deeds. Most of them relate to sales of land to two Partick builders, Thomas Morgan and John Duncan; an 1892 feu of land at Old Kilpatrick to a joiner, Richard Kerr, was also recorded. The feus of land to Morgan were concentrated in an area of ground at the Gairbraid Estate, Maryhill, by the Forth & Clyde Canal; following several feus of 1893-97 in this industrial area, two massive street-blocks of working class tenements were constructed north of Gairbraid Avenue (demolished in post-1960s redevelopments). (1)

Robert Mickel's range of work was highly significant for the future. What it showed was a business in transition from the old, piecemeal and muddled-together activities typical of the 19th-century building trade, and described in Richard Rodger's account in Chapter B1 of this book, to something more industrial, mobile and modern. The close interrelationship of the building of houses and the manufacture of building materials would be important especially to 20th-century firms which specialised in the building of housing as contractors, above all during the 'systems' booms. And for the future work of Mactaggart & Mickel in particular, the way in which Robert Mickel's land speculation supported speculative housebuilding would provide a vital precedent.

Between 1892 and 1899, Robert Mickel moved his home back from Glasgow to Linlithgow, where he had continued since 1880 to maintain a busy life as a town councillor, freemason, justice of the peace and Free Churchman; after his return, he resided first at Bonnytoun and latterly at Rivaldsgreen. But the firm continued its growth in Glasgow, and the business address of Robert Mickel & Co. remained in that city, at 65 Bath Street (followed by 162 Buchanan Street). Robert and his wife, Janet Perry Dougal, had five daughters. Their only son, Robert, died in 1902 at the age of five in an electrocution accident on a tram in Rothesay - a personal tragedy which was, at first glance, seemingly unrelated to the story of Mactaggart & Mickel, but which, as we will see shortly, may in fact have made a decisive contribution to it. (2)

geographical base by opening a large sawmills and steam joinery works, the Victoria Sawmills, at Bo'ness (the port town nearest to Linlithgow); by the 1890s, he was busy working as both a wood merchant and a builder, constructing around 1,500 tenement houses in the Glasgow area during that decade, ranging in size from single-ends (one-apartment flats) to seven-apartments. This work was not purely speculative, but also had contractor-like aspects; in 1890, for example, he was paid £1,300 by George Kerr to complete a tenement in Montague Street, Woodlands.

Alongside his own building work, Robert Mickel also engaged in land speculation on a substantial scale in the Glasgow area,

Robert Mickel's opportunistic readiness to travel did not stop at the Central Belt of Scotland. Attracted by the breakneck expansion of Edwardian Imperial London, he opened a branch in that city, specialising in building development and property management. Between 1909 and 1914 the Robert Mickel & Co. building business was located at 182 Great Portland Street. In that reconstructed thoroughfare and nearby Clipstone Street, he erected several blocks of offices and flats, including Portland Court. They were of the standard five storeys and attic permitted by the 'envelope' of early 20th-century Central London building regulations, and followed a normal Edwardian Baroque stylistic format, comprising ground-floor shops, first floor with channelled masonry, plain Portland stone ashlar upper storeys, and mansarded attic; perhaps reflecting the conventions of Glasgow tenements and offices, the upper floors had canted bay windows. Other blocks were located in Wardour Street and Cavendish Square (Harcourt House).

After the turn of the century, the firm also built a wide range of other projects, including office blocks elsewhere in London and in Glasgow, and prefabricated station waiting rooms. Its activities were strengthened by the work of Robert's youngest brother, Thomas, who also became a master builder (after a period working as a mining inspector in California in the 1890s) and, in 1900, moved to London, returning to Scotland only on his retiral; in 1918 he was recorded as living in one of his own London apartment blocks, at 10 Portland Court. The two brothers co-owned a wide range of London properties, including blocks in Wardour Street as well as Great Portland Street, and Robert at his death in 1923 owned many tenements in inner Glasgow suburbs, Hamilton, Clydebank and Bo'ness. After his death, Robert was hailed by his local newspaper, the *West Lothian Courier*, as a 'fine example of a persevering Scot'. (3)

All in all, the two Mickels' activities already seemed to point beyond the scattered, small operations typical of the 19th-century housebuilding industry, towards something more forceful and fluid. Interestingly, the most meteoric Scottish success story of a much later building boom, the 1960s high-rise contracting drive, was another firm - Crudens - which sprang not from orthodox building but from the timber trade.

1889-1918: John Mactaggart and Andrew Mickel

At the end of the 19th century the initiative within the firm, and its governing ethos of dynamism and mobility, began to pass to two younger men, from whose activities the Mactaggart & Mickel business would directly coalesce: John Auld Mactaggart (1867-1956) and Andrew Mickel (1877-1962). The former was born in Glasgow, and was the son of a Campbeltown coppersmith, Neil Mactaggart, who had moved to the city in the 1830s. The latter was Robert Mickel's nephew; his father, Andrew Mickel, was a Glasgow draper and clothing manufacturer, who married Helen Weir and had six children, of whom Andrew was the eldest. Both Mactaggart and Mickel were educated in Glasgow, where Mactaggart at one stage studied for the civil service. (4) They might have ventured down different business paths if it had not been for an opportune meeting in the 1880s through Robert Mickel.

John Mactaggart joined Robert Mickel's firm as a mercantile clerk (after a brief period working at his own uncle's sawmill in Pollokshields) prior to the move to Bo'ness, and remained in the Glasgow office in Waterloo Street, where he rose to the post of

A1.5. 1925 portrait view of John Auld Mactaggart (1867-1956). Mactaggart joined Robert Mickel's firm as a mercantile clerk in the mid 1890s, but left soon after. He established his own successful building firm, J A Mactaggart & Co., in 1901, and became one of the most prominent figures in Scottish housing. His son, Jack Auld Mactaggart, was co-founder of Mactaggart & Mickel, with Andrew Mickel, in 1925.

chief accountant, and dealt increasingly with the building and property side of Mickel's business. Andrew Mickel joined his uncle's firm in his late teens, initially as an apprentice joiner, but he too was soon elevated to the role of manager to several of Robert's building projects. The rapid progress of his career may have been caused not just by his own efficiency at work, but by the consequences of the death of Robert's only son just at that time, in 1902. It appears that Robert thereafter increasingly looked to his nephew, rather more than to his brother Thomas, as his male heir; following Robert's death, for example, Andrew acted as the latter's executor. John Mactaggart had already left Robert Mickel & Co. in 1898; the younger Andrew Mickel would only have been in contact with Mactaggart (ten years his senior) for a short time, but this meeting established a future Mactaggart and Mickel partnership in the building industry which would last over fifty fruitful years. (5)

At first, the two men concentrated on separate, clearly demarcated activities, all in the Glasgow area. John Mactaggart built mainly tenements, for sale and rent; Andrew Mickel built self-contained dwellings for sale, and speculated in land. The differing paths of the firms established by the two were influenced not only by their personal preferences but by the external constraints posed by the complexities and difficulties of the Glasgow housing market, from the turn of the century up to the outbreak of war. Irrespective of their individual skills and entrepreneurial flair, two other important factors were at play in this story: the timing of each new venture in a period of both boom and slump in the building trade; and the tenurial possibilities and obstructions in Glasgow at that time.

On leaving Robert Mickel, Mactaggart at first worked in a productive partnership with Robert Pollock between 1898 and 1901. They set up workshops in Kelvin Street, in which they stored plant and materials and manufactured concrete steps, and between 1898 and 1900 the partnership built twelve tenements in the Springburn area. In 1901, Mactaggart established his own independent firm, J A Mactaggart & Co. The firm specialised in building, plastering, and the manufacture of concrete steps, pipes and lintels. Between 1901 and 1914, Mactaggart constructed a number of tenemental developments in Glasgow's South Side (mainly in the Pollokshaws area) and West End. These ultimately totalled 2,300 houses, ranging between one and five apartments, primarily for middle class tenants, and boasting an unusually high standard of internal amenities; before the war, he boasted that he was building on average 'two stone houses per day'. (6) Through force of character and a gift for publicity, Mactaggart became

established in those years as one of the most prominent figures in Scottish housebuilding.

J A Mactaggart & Co.'s earliest speculative tenemental scheme, the development of the north-west corner of Hyndland in Glasgow, was undertaken in 1901. Dudley Drive, Hyndland, was developed from that year onwards; Mactaggart employed the 24 year old Andrew Mickel to design fourteen four-storey tenemental blocks over a period of two years. The houses were mainly of three and four apartments, but some of six, seven and eight apartments were built. Mactaggart continued to employ Andrew as an architect throughout the decade, at Clarence Drive (five tenement blocks of 1902), Aitken and Walter Streets (five tenement and shop blocks of 1905), and Appin Road (six tenement and shop blocks of 1907). The internal accommodation of these houses was typical of the middle class apartments of the

A1.6. Novar Drive and Dudley Drive, Hyndland, seen c.1913: one of J A Mactaggart's earliest speculative middle-class tenemental developments in Glasgow's west end. In 1901, Mactaggart employed the young Andrew Mickel to design the two most distant flanking blocks in Dudley Drive. (Bill Scobie, Hyndland Bowling Club)

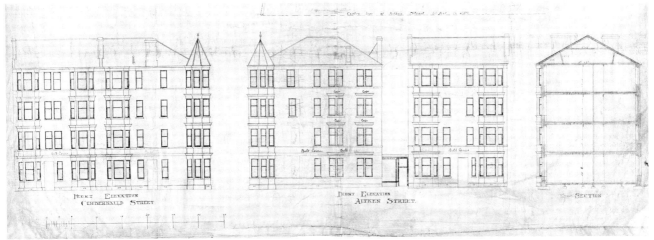

A1.7. Undated and unsigned drawing, presumably by Andrew Mickel, for proposed tenements at Aitken Street and Cumbernauld Street, Glasgow, to be built by J A Mactaggart & Co. (MMC D44834)

A1.8. Airlie Street, Hyndland, c.1907; in the distance, J A Mactaggart's Novar Drive (designed by J Nisbet in 1905) is seen under construction. (Ann Laird)

turn of the century, with a growing trend towards self-contained domestic amenities, including internal bathrooms, and attempts to provide segregated sleeping accommodation, either in bedrooms or (for servants) in bed recesses; the large and relatively undifferentiated spaces of earlier 19th-century tenements were now giving way to more complex and intricate plans. Construction conformed to the hybrid traditional methods that had evolved for tenement-building over the 19th century, exploiting industrialised techniques in a selective and unobtrusive way, with masonry outer walls of dressed ashlar (made possible on this scale by machine finishing techniques) and a complicated mixture of load-bearing internal masonry walls, timber floors and partitions, and iron or steel strengthening joists; numerous components such as joinery elements and stone lintels were mass produced off-site.

Between 1901 and 1911, Mactaggart appears to have employed only one architect other than Andrew Mickel, namely John Nisbet; the latter designed well over fifty tenemental blocks for him, including a number of blocks in Queensborough Gardens (1902), Allison Street (1903), and Bute Gardens (1906). J A Mactaggart & Co. not only built tenements speculatively, but also embarked on contracting work for housing in the late 1900s, in tandem with land speculation. As part of complex land and building transactions, they were contracted by J W Gordon Oswald to build 44 cottages on the Scotstoun estate for incoming English workers. These were constructed of brick, and, unusually for that period, had flat concrete and asphalt roofs. The firm also built a number of large villas, and four eight-apartment 'self contained lodgings' in Bute Gardens (1907). Villas designed by Nisbet included Mactaggart's own house, Kelmscott, 110 Springkell Avenue, in the middle-class suburb of Pollokshields (1902-3). Kelmscott, its name suggesting an admiration for the English Arts & Crafts reformist William Morris, is a prominently situated thirteen-room villa in a Scots Baronial style with some free Renaissance elements. (7)

Andrew Mickel's activities in the early 20th century, although clearly not on the same scale as Mactaggart's, nonetheless displayed a youthful entrepreneurial flair and adaptability inspired by the work of his uncle. He remained with Robert until 1909, when he set up his own firm in Glasgow, Andrew Mickel & Co., Builders and Contractors; this firm was based initially at Byres Road, moving later to 4 Bath Street. (8) During the period prior to the establishment of his own firm, he not only worked as an architect for Mactaggart, but was also recorded in the Renfrewshire Sasines for 1906-7 as buying and selling six plots of land in Southbrae Drive, Jordanhill (an area he was later to build on himself). After the establishment of his own firm, his land transactions increased rapidly, in Renfrewshire and elsewhere; he began selling land at Ashburn, Gourock, in 1910, and his selling and buying activities reached their peak in 1915. He also continued his involvement with his uncle's business, providing security for a loan of £550 for the purchase of land in Southbrae Drive. Following his marriage to Agnes Frances McWhirter, Andrew Mickel had three children, Frank (born 1908), Douglas (1911) and Eileen (1916).

Alongside his successful work of land speculation, Mickel's building operations in Glasgow during the prewar period included tenements, villas and cottages, but with special emphasis on cottages. In 1914-15, for example, the company built a villa and offices in Southbrae Drive, Jordanhill, and constructed streets and sewers in Campsie Street, Glasgow. Activity in landward areas which were then outside Glasgow, such as Clarkston, is more difficult to assess, owing to the scarcity of local records, especially in Renfrewshire. In 1913, John Lawrence (born 1893) was engaged as Mickel's foreman; he subsequently left to establish a joinery contracting firm (working on the Corporation's Knightswood housing scheme in the late 1920s). From the mid-1930s, Lawrence would become the primary competitor to the Mactaggart & Mickel speculative-building market in the west, and would subsequently diversify widely into contracting and building-materials manufacture. (9)

A1.9. *The Mickel family, seen* c.*1917. From left to right: Mrs Agnes Frances Mickel, daughter Eileen Mickel, Andrew Mickel (standing, in military uniform), and sons Douglas and Frank Mickel. (Derek Mickel)*

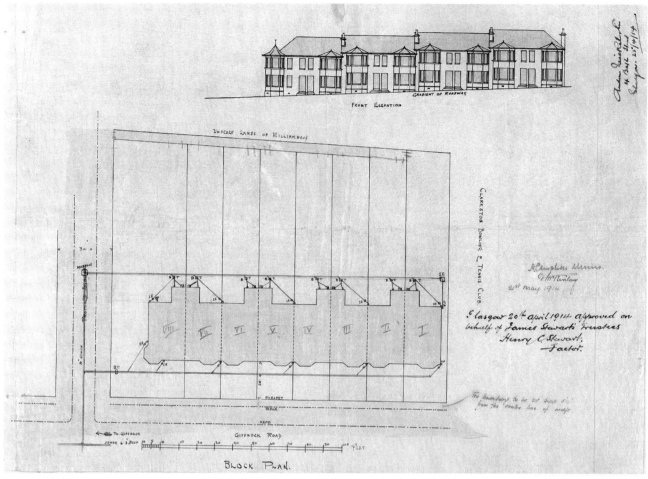

A1.10. Block plan of proposed terrace of houses at Giffnock Road, Clarkston, by Andrew Mickel, 1914. This development of middle-class villas is typical of Andrew Mickel's suburban speculative housebuilding activities just prior to the outbreak of war. (MMC D44829CN)

While it might have seemed a considerable risk for Mactaggart to abandon the relative security of his post at Robert Mickel & Co. in 1901 (at the age of 31) to establish his own building firm, in fact housebuilding in Glasgow was at its peak at the turn of the century. Although the city's building industry had suffered during the slump which followed the 1878 banking crisis and the accusations of malpractice in the bankruptcy courts which followed, in the late 1880s a recovery began, and a new generation of better-organised speculative housing developers began to emerge. One key example was the firm owned by J C McKellar, who designed tenements and employed separate contractors to build them; in 1896 he formed Glasgow's first limited liability building and property-ownership company, and between 1900 and 1906 he built between 80 and 100 tenements. The recovery from the 1878 slump reached a climax around 1900. Mactaggart's venture was therefore started in the middle of a building boom. Counterbalancing this was a sharp rise in price of labour and materials between 1899 and 1902; by the mid-1900s a trade depression had begun to set in. Mactaggart's company continued to fare reasonably well, however; between 1904 and 1909 he continued to develop tenemental areas in Pollokshaws Road, Springkell Street, and Bute and Kelvinside Gardens. (10)

Andrew Mickel's solo venture, by contrast, began in earnest during the mounting building recession, in 1909. Almost immediately afterwards, the 1909-10 budget worsened the position further by taxing feu duties and ground rents with a new 'increment duty', undermining builders' most lucrative source of income and finance for their speculative future ventures; the building industry, according to Morgan, had been 'assassinated by the budget of 1909-10'. Many large building firms suffered, including J C

McKellar and Archibald Stewart (a large-scale builder of working class tenements in Govan), who both ceased business as a result. The loss of McKellar, who was a key figure in the property-owning lobby, must have sent out an early warning signal to Andrew Mickel. The latter's venture differed from Mactaggart's above all else in its relationship to one of the key issues of the early 20th-century private housing market in Scotland, namely renting versus home ownership. Whereas Mactaggart both sold and rented property, Mickel was fully committed to home ownership from an early date. Prior to 1914, the private rented sector was by far the most important tenure in Scotland as a whole, and the level of owner occupation was low. In 1900 only 12% of housing in Glasgow was in owner occupation; the 1914 figure for Edinburgh was 12.4%. (11) The 'customers' of housing developers and builders in this period were mainly landlords and existing owners; the management of the majority of this private rented sector was carried out by house factors, and in 1911, 43% of all houses in Glasgow were managed this way. In the wake of the 1909-10 budget, however, many builders turned to property development and management. In 1911 Mactaggart augmented his own cash flow with a portfolio of 83 tenements worth £200,000, which provided a total annual rent of £14,000; his average rent in 1911 was £19, well above the Glasgow average of £13. Mactaggart used this as security for raising loans to finance building and land purchases. His views on rents, rates, and owner occupation, which came to public prominence in the early 1920s, will be examined in the next section. (12)

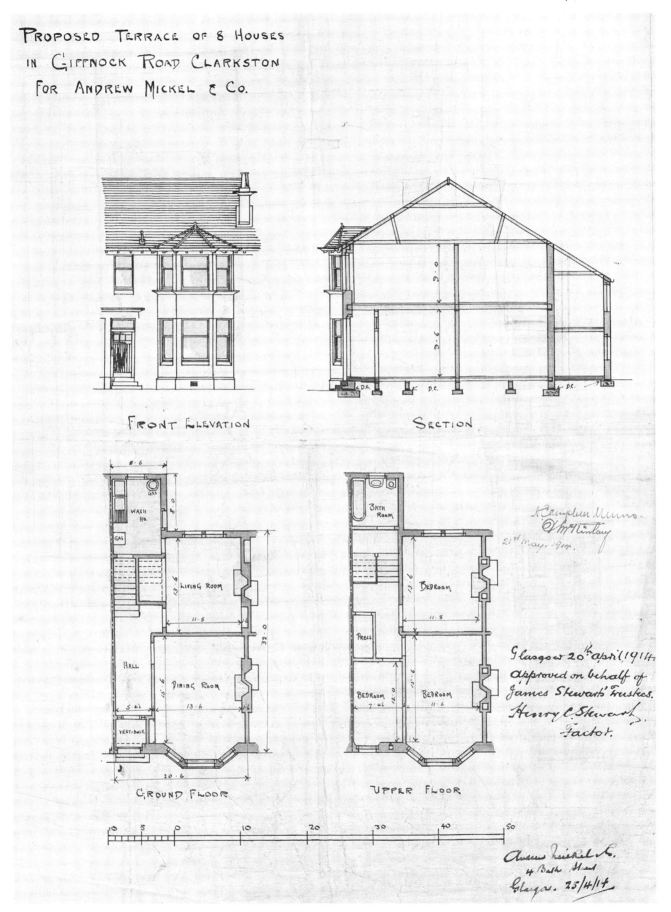

PROPOSED TERRACE OF 8 HOUSES
IN GIFFNOCK ROAD CLARKSTON
FOR ANDREW MICKEL & CO.

FRONT ELEVATION

SECTION

GROUND FLOOR

UPPER FLOOR

A1.11. Detail drawings of the Giffnock Road terrace. (MMC D44828CN)

Mickel had very different views on this issue; his ultimate objective was to provide housing for owner-occupation. The housing and business objectives of both men were made clear in the evidence they gave to the Ballantyne Commission (the Royal Commission on the Housing of the Industrial Population of Scotland), set up in 1912 to investigate working class housing conditions and suggest reforms. In its vastly influential report of 1917, which largely set the guidelines for Scottish social housing over the next sixty years, the Ballantyne Commission concluded that the status quo had failed to deliver both quantity and quality in housing, and therefore should be replaced by radically new policies. Organisationally, it argued that the free-market system should be replaced by state intervention, including regulation and even direct provision - although a minority report (the Lovat Report) argued for caution, and warned against revolutionary change. Architecturally, Ballantyne argued that the tenements of 19th-century Scottish towns were too dense and unhygienic, and should be replaced by garden suburbs of cottages - a solution by then growing in popularity among reformists all over Europe. (13)

In his 1913 evidence to the Commission, Andrew Mickel wholeheartedly endorsed the architectural preference for cottage building over tenemental design, but not the advocacy of violent organisational change. Instead, he showed a thorough commitment to private enterprise and owner occupation, and an antipathy to the idea of extensive housebuilding directly by local authorities. He argued that 'the party who has his own house takes a certain amount of pride in it' - a commitment that, he believed, could not be matched in other tenures, even the experimental co-ownership arrangements of pioneering projects such as the Westerton Garden Suburb (1912-15, by J A W Grant). The most efficient means of government support, he felt, would be a state-backed 'housing loan fund' empowered to distribute cheap loans of up to 75% of houses' value to builders. The loans were needed, in Mickel's view, not least because if cottages were to be built to Scottish standards, rather than the lightweight construction of English terrace houses, they would be far more expensive to construct than tenements. (14)

Mickel conceded that, to overcome excessive land costs, it might be necessary for the state to introduce compulsory purchase powers. But in general, his attitude to state intervention was more cautious than the sweeping Ballantyne prescriptions. This caution resulted not from a reactionary conservatism, like that of the small, fragmented builders of the mid-19th century, but from its opposite - an outward-looking and more intellectually ambitious attitude on Mickel's part. From his extensive pre-1914 study of the housing and land question, including a trip to Canada for international comparative purposes, Mickel would have become aware that the municipal interventionism charted out by Ballantyne was not a policy favoured in any other modern overseas country as a solution to the problem of providing low-cost housing with state help. Elsewhere, the state set out to intervene by helping or loosening-up the existing private system with loans or tax breaks, with the aim of encouraging either low-cost social renting or mass home ownership. The establishment of a state housing loan fund, for example, was the centrepiece of the pioneering social housing support measures of 1889 in Belgium - the first in Europe. Mickel enthusiastically embraced the latter policy, which was typical of North America and a few European countries (including Belgium), and remained, by and large, committed to the ideal of owner occupation until the day he died; only in times of a slump in the owner-occupier market would he enter other fields of activity on a large scale. In his commitment to strong social and political ideas about housing, Mickel was thoroughly representative of the new, 20th-century attitudes to the housing

problem - even if his own favoured recipe was not the one which established an ascendancy in Scotland!

Mactaggart, by contrast, adopted a more neutral and eclectic approach, not biased against any particular tenure or building type. Between the wars, he would show an opportunistic readiness to adapt to the changing policy climate, by balancing contracting for municipal housing with speculative building, mainly for rental. In his evidence to Ballantyne, Mactaggart severely criticised the bias of the Commission's membership towards housing-reformist zealots, and its exclusion of representatives of the building or property-owning interest. Among the economic factors which in his view impeded the private builder, he singled out especially the 'penal' local property tax (the rates), which until 1956 was imposed on both owners and occupiers, creating a double burden on home ownership and varying between different municipalities; he argued that 'few Scots would opt for larger houses until rates were reduced, making them a more economical proposition'. In contrast to Mickel's emphasis on cottages, Mactaggart extolled the design and management benefits of modern tenement housing, of the kind that he had built in large numbers prior to the war for both skilled working class and middle class tenants. (15)

The disruptive effects of World War I itself hammered further nails into the coffin of the old housing system, already creaking under the impact of the 1909-10 tax reforms. In 1915, the government attempted to appease striking munitions workers by introducing restrictions on rents, and on mortgages to housebuilders - crippling the viability of both existing rented property and new building. The building of new houses largely came to a halt, and disrepair of existing houses mounted. The rent and mortgage restrictions in no way increased the attractiveness of building for owner occupation as an alternative, and after the war the rates increases needed for large-scale local authority housebuilding would in many ways make the position worse. At the outbreak of war in 1914, Andrew Mickel, a lifelong supporter of the volunteer movement, enlisted in the Royal Scots and Royal Engineers for the duration of hostilities. He wrote to the firm from northern France in December 1916 asking them to send him a 'simple text book on Road making', as 'I may be taking up this class of work here soon'; Mickel added that since returning from leave a month previously, 'we have had hard frost or incessant rains, and we are all under canvas, so it is no picnic'. Mactaggart set aside his past differences with central government following the Ballantyne Commission debate, and obtained a number of lucrative wartime contracts, including work for the Admiralty at Gourock. For the moment, the housing activities of both were suspended; but a postwar future of opportunity and innovation lay ahead. (16)

1919-1925: Private or public?

The period from 1919 to 1925 saw the beginnings of a revolution in Scottish housebuilding, with the growing shift in emphasis from the free market towards direct provision by the state. But that decline in private housing *provision* did not mean a decline in work for the private house *builder*. Far from it - the decline in work for builders as speculative developers was matched by a growth in opportunity for them to build for local authorities as contractors. That opportunity was eagerly seized by John Mactaggart's firm, and by Andrew Mickel, who joined Mactaggart, his former employer, in 1919, at the age of 42. In the remainder of this chapter, we follow their joint story up to 1925, a crucial year in the development of their business - or businesses. It was early in 1925 that John Mactaggart's company was liquidated, and the two went their separate ways. In September, Mactaggart formed a new business, the Western Heritable Investment Company, and in March of the same year Mactaggart & Mickel was founded. In terms of actual building policies and patterns, the two new companies at first diverged very little, either from each other or from Mactaggart's pre-1925 business. However, as the 1920s progressed, and the generous government subsidies began to shift to rehousing and slum clearance, clear differences opened up between the portfolios of John Mactaggart's new firm and Mactaggart & Mickel; we will consider the consequences of those differences in the next chapter.

On the whole, the primary focus of housebuilding following the 1919 Housing Act was the production of municipal housing for rent - the revolution called for by Ballantyne. In the first years after the war, there was almost no return to tenement building by private developers, and little opportunity for speculative cottage, villa or terraced house building. The failure to rescind the wartime rent restrictions, which made it uneconomical for private enterprise to build unaided by the state, in combination with high postwar building material costs, resulted in a poor market for both private rented and owner-occupied housing. This period of crisis and transition also saw substantial change in the organisation of housebuilding. The prewar pattern of small-scale speculative tenement-focused operations faded, and large-scale firms began to emerge which were focused on cottage-type developments and were able to switch between contracting and speculative building. Such firms included John McDonald in Glasgow and James Miller in Edinburgh. It was paradoxical that it was the state-subsidised municipal housing programmes unleashed by the generally anti-private-enterprise Ballantyne Report which kick-started this transformation, creating and safeguarding a new pivotal role for the private builder.

The Ballantyne Report, although it attacked the private housing system and argued that working class housing should be seen as a branch of 'public administration', did not specifically prescribe direct local authority building and ownership of low-rent housing. Local authorities, it declared, should control and subsidise new housing. This distinction between control and production left the door open to private builders, operating either as contractors or as regulated private developers. (17) The 1919 Housing Act,

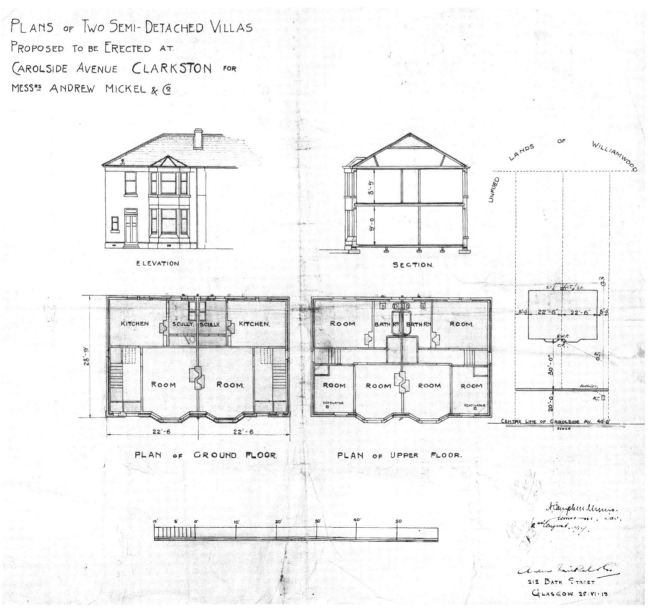

A1.12. *Plans of two semi-detached villas in Carolside Avenue, Clarkston, for Andrew Mickel & Co. Despite joining the firm of J A Mactaggart & Co. in 1919 (and subsequently becoming a director), Andrew continued with his own speculative projects until the end of that year. (MMC)*

A1.13. Mosspark Boulevard, Glasgow, seen in 1925. This, the largest interwar council housing contract in Glasgow, was awarded to the new limited company of J A Mactaggart & Co. in September 1920. Mosspark represented a landmark for the 20th century Scottish building industry, because it introduced for the first time the single-contractor system to municipal housing. (Glasgow City Libraries and Archives)

A1.14. Among Glasgow citizens in the 1920s, the Mosspark project became synonymous with innovation in social housing; here it is mentioned along with experimental steel systems in a 1926 cartoon in the Bulletin. *(Bulletin, 14 January 1926; Glasgow City Libraries and Archives)*

in response to the postwar building production crisis, required local authorities to conduct a survey of existing housing conditions, and to make estimates to the Scottish Board of Health for the 'making good' of any unsatisfied needs. The central state in turn offered to generously subsidise the local authorities, through an open-ended deficit subsidy which made up the entire excess cost of schemes over and above a four-fifths penny rate (local taxation) charge. This was envisaged only as a stop-gap measure during the inflationary postwar aftermath, until private building could recover. That hope was made explicit in the Housing (Additional Powers) Act, introduced some months later in 1919, which aimed to encourage private builders to provide housing by offering subsidies ranging from £230 to £260 per house.

The local authority which embraced the new powers most eagerly was Glasgow Corporation. In the late 19th century, the Corporation had built up a formidable international reputation of 'municipal socialism' in a range of public utilities, especially those concerned with health. This was driven not by 20th-century style socialism, but by a pragmatic desire to protect business and ratepayer interests from disruption. The council had already intervened in working class housing before the war to a limited extent, focusing on slum redevelopment, and now it responded to Ballantyne and the 1919 Act with a far more ambitious programme, arguing that no less than 57,000 new houses were required. But it had few professional and organisational resources with which to do this. Peter Fyfe was appointed first director of housing in 1919, and gradually built up a staff of architects, engineers and others. (18) There were also, from 1921, experiments with council action in the building process itself, in the form of direct labour schemes; but only with the rise of the Labour Party to control over the council in the 1930s would the direct labour organisation (DLO) assume a major, even dominant role in the Corporation's programme. For the moment, therefore, private housebuilders, working as contractors, had an unparalleled opportunity to carve out a pivotal role in the new housing programmes of Glasgow and other municipalities. J A Mactaggart & Co. proved to be a key player in this development, and came increasingly to dominate housing production in Glasgow and the west.

In October 1919, Mactaggart, then aged 53, prepared his firm for this period of activity by converting it into a limited company, with a capital of £30,000. John A Mactaggart became the managing director; his son Jack Auld Mactaggart and Andrew Mickel were the two other directors. Jack and Margaret Mactaggart held 5,000 shares each; John Mactaggart held 4,000, Isa Mactaggart held 1,000 and Andrew Mickel 1,000. Mickel apparently joined the firm in 1919, although he was clearly still in business himself at that date; in August, Andrew Mickel & Co. was still selling properties, including, for example, a house at 47 Carolside Avenue, Clarkston, sold for £650 to a Mr Poole-Jones. (19)

From the earliest date, Mactaggart attempted to put himself and his company at the forefront of the debate over state-assisted housing, ever ready to propose new types of government and municipal assistance. In his evidence of 1918 to the Tudor Walters Committee (an official housing inquiry which forcefully endorsed low-density cottage layouts), his main concern was the revival of the private sector by the lifting of taxation burdens and anti-competitive practices. He attacked price-fixing rings in the industry, and returned to the issue of rents and rates, arguing that the housing problem could only be solved by 'dissociating house rental from local authorities', to halve rents and put building

for the rented sector back on an economic level. His self-styled image as a housing specialist reached its peak in this period; in November 1920, the pro-business Glasgow newspaper, *The Bailie*, claimed: 'Like all men of ideas and pioneering methods, Mr Mactaggart has his critics and detractors ... he has the courage of his convictions and is not afraid to bring his theories into the fullest blaze of publicity ... Mr Mactaggart is a practical dreamer'. (20)

Following the formation of the new limited company in 1919, Mactaggart and his younger fellow-directors plunged head first into the new world of local authority contracting. In September 1920, they successfully tendered for the largest single interwar council-housing contract of all, for over 1,500 dwellings to be erected for Glasgow Corporation at the new Mosspark garden-suburb scheme. Quite apart from its importance for Mactaggart and the housebuilding industry, Mosspark occupies a pivotal place in the social history of interwar Scottish housing, as the largest and most prominent of the 1919 Act schemes. It was the leader in the movement to establish 'general-needs' council housing, under that law, as something new and different from the old 'city improvement' sanitary redevelopments, something much more like prewar middle class houses with several dedicated bedrooms and lavish internal amenities, but now in the form of garden-suburb cottages rather than suburban tenements. In Glasgow, this distinction was made explicit in the two-tier system made up of 'Rehousing' tenements for unskilled slum displacees (an updated version of City Improvement) and lower-density 'Ordinary' schemes such as Mosspark, reserved largely for middle class Protestants. (21)

From a building industry viewpoint, Mosspark represented a landmark for quite a different reason: because it introduced to Scottish municipal housing the single-contractor system favoured in England and North America, and did so, furthermore, in a contract which covered a 1,500-dwelling scheme in its entirety. And for Mactaggart's firm, it was significant above all as a decisive, lucky break into the world of large-scale council contracting for Clydeside authorities. It was followed by other smaller Corporation contracts awarded to Mactaggart in the early 1920s, at Riddrie, Greenhead, Baillieston, Bellshill, and the first parts of Knightswood - the largest interwar Glasgow Corporation scheme of all. None of those was for single-contractor work, but, as we will find in the next chapter, following the 1925 separation, Mactaggart & Mickel shared with John McDonald Ltd an all-trades contract for 1,000 dwellings at Knightswood No.3, awarded in February 1926. As far as the early 1920s are concerned, the fact that J A Mactaggart & Co. was directly involved in the two largest municipal housing schemes in Glasgow in the interwar period - Mosspark and Knightswood - is in itself evidence of its pivotal role in the west.

The triangular and hilly site of Mosspark, bordered to the south by the Pollok Estate and Bellahouston Park, was bought by Glasgow Corporation in 1908. The Corporation originally planned to use the 175 acres as a municipal-run golf course, but the war prevented that plan from being realised. Instead, Mosspark became Glasgow Corporation's largest municipal development of the early interwar period; the contract originally specified 1,502 houses on the site, but 1,510 houses were actually built. Perhaps because of its size, the scheme was treated as an experiment in single contracting; 1919/20 had seen incessant disputes between the Corporation and builders about the protracted processes of valuation and other lengthy procedures prior to the awarding of contracts. An unsolicited single-contract bid for Mosspark from Robert McAlpine had been turned down prior to the awarding of the contract to Mactaggart in February 1921; the contract schedules were prepared for tender by June 1920, but Mactaggart's winning and lowest bid of £1,818,977 19s 7d, accepted in September, had to be checked and approved by the Scottish Board of Health in October. (22) In some ways, McAlpine would have been a logical choice for this contract, with its extensive prewar experience in single-contractor building in civil engineering projects, and its track-record of innovative use of construction techniques, including the construction of over a thousand flat concrete roofed tenements at Radnor Park, Clydebank (from 1904). (23) But during the war, the firm had moved its headquarters and the focus of its operations to England, and its experience of garden-suburb building was not extensive.

The single-contractor system gave the responsibility for all elements of the construction of the site to one builder. In Scottish building contracts, as in most other European countries, each of the separate trades normally made a specific tender for mason work, joiner work, plumbing, and so forth; the single-contractor system was largely confined to work of a civil engineering character, such as railway building. In the other anglophone countries, by contrast, most building contracts, including housing, were organised on that system. However, the pre-1914 system of speculative housebuilding had not belonged unambiguously to either single- or separate-trades building, or to either contracting or builder-developer work. Many of the builders were so small that these categories became artificial: even if they themselves had originated in one specific trade, they took responsibility for the others in their projects. In the turn-of-century tenement-building work of J A Mactaggart or J C McKellar, or James Steel in Edinburgh, we seem to witness a division between developer and separate-trades contracting. In Mactaggart's successful bid for Mosspark, the single-contractor system was applied to large-scale house contracting in Scotland for the first time; the key difference was that of scale. Naturally, this stirred up controversy from the beginning. Mactaggart was able to benefit from direct negotiations over piecework and overtime rates, but at the cost of greatly antagonising the separate-trades associations; in defence, admirers of Mactaggart claimed that Glasgow could now 'take fuller advantage of his un-doubtable genius'. (24)

J A Mactaggart & Co. began work at Mosspark in February 1921, and had completed 500 houses by November 1922, at which time the company estimated that a further 1,000 would be completed by November 1923. The dwellings were all finally completed in June 1924, but seven and a half miles of new roads still remained to be built. (25) In addition to the incessant trade disputes, the contractors had to face increasing shortages and subsequent high costs of materials. Building costs had only recently reached a postwar peak, in 1920, and while masonry construction in stone was now prohibitively expensive, the alternative of harled brickwork was also problematic, as it was insufficiently developed in Scotland to be easily economic. In response, Mactaggart and his colleagues made strenuous efforts to find alternatives to brick construction; 252 experimental houses were built of concrete blocks, which increased production and cut the cost of each house (on average £1,150) by £17. Brick shortages eased somewhat in 1923, and at that point brickwork construction was reinstated on the project. The pattern of convulsive, short-term use of non-traditional building systems, during emergency periods only, would perpetuate itself over the next fifty years. Mactaggart's company also worked on ways to utilise the unskilled labour of former servicemen, who were employed to help in the construction of walls. Further delays also stemmed from the inherent topographical problems of the hilly Mosspark site. (26) Drainage disposal in particular posed significant difficulties, and

Mactaggart engaged an engineer working in France, John C C Munro, to resolve them, through the construction of a pumping station. Munro remained in Scotland and played a significant role in the early years of Mactaggart & Mickel, including, for instance, the drawing up of the survey plans of the Kelvinside estate.

Despite all these problems, the three directors eventually successfully carried through the completion of 1,510 houses at Mosspark (593 of three apartments, 644 of four, and 273 of five). There were thirteen different house-types, each containing a bathroom, scullery, gas cooker, gas boiler, washing tub, and electric lighting; designed by the architects of the newly established Housing Department, they comprised two-storey cottages and flats set in lavish greenery, on a contoured garden-suburb street layout. With the aid of the lavish state subsidies of the 1919 Act, even the smallest of the houses was substantially larger and better equipped than the compact modern tenements for skilled workers built by Mactaggart before the war. At the peak of activity, Mactaggart employed a workforce of 1,300 on the scheme. The large-scale single-contracting pioneered at Mosspark was to become the favoured approach of both John Mactaggart and Andrew Mickel in future building ventures, and in that they were running somewhat 'ahead' of Glasgow Corporation; for a time, single-contracting in the city was even known as 'the Mactaggart principle', and *The Bailie* hailed his efforts in steadily developing 'the English system of employing workmen on all branches, from street making to painting'. Although the company, as explained, was to be awarded further local authority contracts, none of them, until Mactaggart & Mickel's Carntyne contract of 1927-29, involved the building of entire houses by either Mactaggart or Mickel. In 1921, for example the company was awarded the Riddrie No.2 contract for brickwork worth £87,000, and Riddrie No.4 for joiner work worth £27,000; in total 400 houses were worked on within that scheme. Joiner work worth £70,000 for 350 houses at Greenhead was awarded in 1922. The contract for brick, mason, joiner, and glazier work (worth in total £176,074, including painter work) at Knightswood No.2 in 1923, was the closest that the company came during those years to full house construction other than at Mosspark; it actually defeated Mactaggart & Mickel's future rival, John McDonald Ltd, for the Knightswood work. (27)

Despite this resurgence of separate-trades contracts in Glasgow work of the mid-1920s, the role played by large private contractors did not diminish overall. In the same years, Lanark County Council awarded Mactaggart & Mickel large single-contractor jobs at Baillieston, 1923, 250 houses; Bellshill, 1923, 200 houses, and Carnbroe, 1923, 48 houses. The issue stirred up controversy: in 1922, for example, the *Glasgow Herald* attacked the Corporation for not providing the new communities of Riddrie and Mosspark (anticipated at that time as having an eventual population of 4,000 and 6,000 respectively) with basic utilities such as schools, but hailed 'private enterprise' for 'proving eminently efficient in looking after the commissariat of the communities'. (28)

The physical form of the Mosspark scheme, with its sweeping garden suburb layout, two-storey cottages and flats, and profuse greenery, corresponded closely to the ideal advocated by Andrew Mickel in his evidence to the Ballantyne Commission. Perhaps Mickel's support for this pattern, and his personal experience of low-density single-family housing on his visit to Canada, may have encouraged Mactaggart to engage him as a director prior to the Mosspark contract. Although Mickel's (and to a certain extent Mactaggart's) ultimate vision of large-scale state-aided home ownership and limited local authority rental housing had not yet taken shape in their minds, the political and financial forces that might underpin such a vision were beginning to emerge.

It is also interesting to note that the Mosspark contract was supervised by the Corporation's director of housing, Peter Fyfe. Fyfe appears to have been instrumental in obtaining John Mactaggart the contract. Both men shared an enthusiasm for standardisation of construction, and experimented with non-traditional housing-types (including, as we saw above, the substitution of concrete blockwork for the now normal rendered common brick in later sections of Mosspark) in an attempt to circumvent the shortages and high costs of materials and labour in the postwar housing market crisis; the sudden turn to brick construction in response to the prohibitive postwar rise in stonework costs had highlighted the shortage of bricklayers, not a trade previously common in Scotland. (29) Fyfe left Glasgow Corporation in 1923 to establish his own firm, Fyfe Stone Limited, which aimed to produce low-cost artificial stone concrete blocks based on an American model. Fyfe tried to raise £30,000 to obtain the production plant for the venture, and amongst his backers were the three directors of J A Mactaggart & Co. However, the project was eventually abandoned due to lack of capital. It should be distinguished from the 'Fyfestone' with which we are familiar today, a different type of blockwork construction promoted under the same name after World War II by an Aberdeenshire firm (see Chapter B3).

Fyfe's unsuccessful proposal was intended to address the key organisational problem of the post-1919 municipal housing programme, that of rising costs and low production levels. (30) As local authorities began to pursue subsidised municipal housebuilding with vigour (with Glasgow Corporation, for example, producing a total of 4,744 houses under the 1919 Act), costs rose dramatically and production suffered from the resulting shortages and delays. Two years after the 1919 Act, therefore, private contractor/builders such as Mactaggart found themselves playing a linchpin role in a supposedly temporary municipal housing programme which was riven by clear internal contradictions. Responding to these stresses, in 1921, the government finally called a halt to the 1919 Act programme, and abolished its open-ended subsidies, which the Treasury was no longer prepared to support. From now on, Mactaggart and his directors would have to pursue a different path if they wished to exploit the new climate of state support for housing.

In 1923 and 1924, a number of new solutions, primarily aimed at encouraging private enterprise building and introducing competition to lower costs of labour and materials, were introduced through legislation. John Mactaggart, of course, had his own ideas, which he voiced (through the press) to his fellow citizens and politicians; the 1924 legislation formulated by the Labour minister for health, Shettleston MP John Wheatley ('Partnership with Private Enterprise'), may have benefited from detailed help from Mactaggart. The previous year, he had argued that unaided private enterprise building could not solve the housing problem at a time of extremely high costs and labour shortage; he claimed that the cost of labour had doubled since 1914, with tradesmen receiving 1s 8d per hour compared with 10d in 1914. Mactaggart's ongoing battle with the trade organisations continued; in January 1923 the Federation of Building Trade Operatives wrote to complain to Glasgow Corporation about his company's activities relating to output bonuses on Corporation schemes. (31) The financial hardships facing those who chose home ownership (as opposed, for example, to subsidised rents in new local authority housing schemes) held

out little opportunity for growth in that area. It is difficult to establish what Mactaggart's company envisaged for its future in the early 1920s, but with the benefit of hindsight, it would appear that it was motivated by a combination of a short-term, opportunistic approach to subsidies, and an anticipation of long-term growth potential for both the private rented sector and home ownership, under the auspices of private enterprise builders like J A Mactaggart & Co. This may well have motivated the company's voluntary liquidation in early 1925, allowing two more specialised successor firms to be formed: the Western Heritable Investment Company, dominated by John Mactaggart's commitment and faith in the private rented sector; and Mactaggart & Mickel, imbued with Andrew Mickel and Jack Mactaggart's ultimate commitment to home ownership. The fact that both families were financially involved with both companies following the split (a situation which continued up to the 1940s), and that Mactaggart & Mickel continued to build Western Heritable's new houses, suggested a degree of hedging of bets against the eventual success or failure of one type of tenure or the other. Behind these complicated policies ultimately lay the uncertainty and flux of housing policies in the early 1920s.

During those years, the firm's public face was dominated by its efforts in local authority contracting. These would secure its short-term cash flow. Behind the scenes, however, an equally important and longer-term strategy was under way, to acquire a 'land-bank' for use either in future building for rental or sale, or for speculative resale - continuing the pattern begun at the end of the previous century by Robert Mickel. The years of economic slump following the war had depressed land prices, creating a golden opportunity for far-sighted firms. Steadily, the Mactaggarts and Mickels expanded their holdings by purchasing land on the outskirts of Glasgow. The mechanism through which this was done was the so-called 'ladies syndicate' - a grouping which comprised Margaret Mactaggart (John Mactaggart's wife); their daughters Isa and Jeanie Mactaggart; the wife of Jack Auld Mactaggart; and Agnes Frances McWhirter Mickel (wife of Andrew Mickel). The reason for setting up this indirect mechanism was to insulate the land-bank from the short-term fortunes of the main business, especially the risk of bankruptcy.

From around 1923, the syndicate began buying and holding large amounts of land, mainly on the south-eastern and north-western edges of the built-up area of Glasgow. A large part of the Kelvinside estate was bought for £22,000 in May 1923, followed in July by a substantial part of King's Park, at a cost of £6,600; further King's Park purchases included '100 Acre Hill', bought in 1926. Lesser acquisitions included a site at Bankhead, Rutherglen, purchased in October 1923 for £7,150, and a site in Carmunnock Road, in May 1927, for which Mrs Mickel's share was £1,250. Morgan records that King's Park, together with a 114-acre section of the Kelvinside estate, was purchased for £33,000. (32)

During the early 1920s, these land-acquisition policies, so vital for any eventual upturn in the market, were paralleled by Mactaggart's public proselytising work. He continued to put forward a profusion of proposals for the revitalisation of the private building market, including home ownership - looking beyond the depressed conditions that then prevailed. In 1919, he initiated a complex scheme which offered 25-year terminable annuity bonds to rented tenants in seventy of his Broomhill houses (in Beechwood Drive, etc.), to avoid rent rises; only those renting at over £30 per year were eligible. The bonds would have cost £225 for 'a modern four-apartment house with bathroom'. Tenants had possession of the house for 25 years at prewar rents, but were responsible for rates and repairs - the latter now an onerous burden, with postwar inflation. Capital repayment was annual and interest-free, and additional loans of up to £150 were available, leaving only £75 to be found by purchasers. However, the proposal met strong tenant resistance, as it gave no extra security of tenure or ownership rights; one tenant described it as 'a very skilfully camouflaged plan to get a very large increase in rent out of the tenants', and it was withdrawn by the company. (33)

Mactaggart and his fellow directors were well aware that state and local authority intervention in some form was by now inevitable, to increase the supply of small dwellings, whether in the private rented, local authority rented, or owner-occupied sectors. Their argument was a more restricted one: that economy demanded, to a certain extent, free competition. The clearest indication of Mactaggart's views can be found in a 1923 article which he wrote for the *Sunday Mail*: 'How To Get Houses Built'. Writing as a 'recognised authority on housing', he restated views on the housing problem which were essentially similar to those he voiced in 1920. He argued that 'The housing shortage in this country will never be alleviated to any appreciable extent by unaided private enterprise', although 'many persons still cherish this idea'; this, he claimed, was an 'economic impossibility'. But at the same time he launched an attack on the very state-subsidised system which had allowed his company to build Mosspark: the 'fatal weakness' of the economics of these schemes had 'helped to raise the cost of construction to four times what it was in 1911'. The government's 1919 Act formula of an open-ended direct subsidy combined with attempts to fix prices of material and labour through centralised bureaucratic controls, he argued, had provided no incentive for economy on the part of the contractor, and as a result the government had eventually had to 'back out' under the 'terrific strain', and 'quit the building field'. The escalation in prices had been made far worse, in his view, by price-fixing rings among building material supplies firms, which he mercilessly attacked. (34)

The government's most recent response to the 1919 Act problems, the 1923 Housing Act, proposed to stimulate a private-enterprise revival through government or municipal subsidies, given in a lump sum or annually for 20 years, calculated to compensate for low rents. The state gave the local authority an annual grant of £6, half of the assumed yearly loss of the economic rent of the average house; the local authority made up the other half, and handed on the combined payment to the private builder. Direct municipal housing was now to be confined to slum clearance and other restricted cases. Although Mactaggart believed that this legislation 'might work fairly well in connection with the very cheapest class of house erected by the local authorities', he firmly believed that it 'would not encourage private enterprise'. Instead, he proposed a system of indirect stimulation through tax breaks, as in many other countries in Europe and America. He argued that the 'insuperable barrier that stands in the way of private enterprise' (that is, the fact that building costs had risen by almost 100% from 1914, whereas rents had only increased by 25%) should be overcome by exempting new houses from local taxation (rating) for ten years. In New York City and in Italy, he explained, this model had recently and successfully been adopted; New York had, as a result, recorded an increase in housing output of 413% over the preceding two years. On a house worth £500, he claimed that these policies would save £200 over the ten tax-free years, stimulating demand and thus, in turn, the private building industry. Local authorities could supplement these tax breaks by offering loans of up to 5% to encourage home ownership. Mactaggart's dual commitment to private renting and owner

occupation alike was highlighted in his view of rent restrictions. 'As a large owner of property', he explained, he was firmly against the decontrol of rents because this would 'accentuate the housing crisis'; houses which were currently rented would, he argued, be offered for sale and this would 'spoil the new market'. (35)

Despite Mactaggart's personal reservations, J A Mactaggart & Co. immediately set about making the fullest use of the provisions of the 1923 Act. The firm initially approached Glasgow Corporation to ask if it would provide subsidies and loans for houses which the company planned to build at King's Park; the enquiry related to houses which were proposed outwith the city boundary. In January 1924 the loans were approved, but the question of direct subsidy was deferred. (36)

The 1923 Act, in addition to its grant provisions, contained another element which closely resembled Mactaggart's suggestion that local authorities should provide low-interest loans to encourage home ownership. This was done by increasing the powers of the Small Dwellings Acquisition Act of 1899. Local authorities were now allowed either to provide advances or loans (up to £300 or 85% of cost) to private builders for housing which could ultimately be sold by the authorities at favourable terms, or to provide loans direct to individuals to purchase housing. In Glasgow Corporation, the former plan was adopted under the heading of the 1923 Assisted Purchase System; the Kelvindale scheme of 52 houses, whose roads and sewers had already been laid out under an unemployment assistance scheme, became the pilot. The three-, four- and five-apartment houses, which cost between £500 and £670, were sold by the Corporation for a cash payment of £110, followed by six-monthly instalments. In Edinburgh, the second scheme, which Mactaggart preferred, found greater favour: the Corporation provided loans for house purchase at lower rates of interest (4.5%) than the Edinburgh building societies (which, of course, antagonised the latter) or any other local authority. In total, Edinburgh Corporation provided almost three times as many loans as Glasgow Corporation between the wars. (37)

The differing interpretation of this 1923 legislation highlights the power wielded by individual local authorities in shaping housing policies at a municipal level. (38) Although the central government formulated housing policy, the local authority had a large degree of autonomy in implementing these policies. The differences in approach between Glasgow and Edinburgh Corporations from 1919 onwards (as a result of their pursuit of different political-economic objectives) clearly affected housing development, and, in particular, housing tenure. Within this period, Edinburgh Corporation was dominated by the Progressives (broadly non-socialist) whose main priority was to keep local property taxes low. This, of course, meant restraining expenditure on working class housing at a low level, in order to prevent rises in business and owner-occupier rates. Throughout the 1920s and 1930s, Edinburgh Corporation encouraged private enterprise housing for sale and (to a lesser extent) rent, while trying to restrict municipal housing to slum clearance, and ensuring that suburban building land was reserved, as far as possible, for private developers. The Corporation saw slum clearance building (which received a 50% subsidy under the 1923 Act) as no direct threat to private enterprise, in terms of the labour market, because the clearance programme would primarily utilise unskilled labour rather than tradesmen. (39)

Local authority aspirations in the early to mid-1920s had a direct effect on the activities of builders, such as Mactaggart's firm. Mactaggart, who was very much based in the west, appears neither to have involved his company in the Assisted Purchase System nor to have built houses in anticipation of low-interest loans from local authorities. The differences between the Edinburgh and Glasgow municipalities' approach to housing tenure even more clearly affected the later development of Mactaggart & Mickel after the split of 1925, as we will see in the next chapter. While Western Heritable Investment Co. became more entrenched in the private rented sector in the west, Mactaggart & Mickel moved east to capture the loan-dominated Edinburgh market, and then, of course, moved into building for home ownership.

The 1923 legislation, as Mactaggart anticipated, did not produce a high supply of, or demand for, private enterprise building. On the demand side, the property rates system, and the high levels charged, hit owner occupiers hard; even attempts to sell 1919 Act houses had not been at all successful, despite being pursued actively by Edinburgh Corporation. O'Carroll's recent research into interwar housing tenure in Edinburgh and the east has suggested that owner occupation there was 'not considered an especially superior or high status tenure'; indeed, even when income levels could permit home ownership, it was not preferred, even by white-collar workers, when there was satisfactory access to good quality newly built housing in the public or private rented sector. (40) Such a 'tenure neutrality' could hardly have been encouraging to the pro-home-ownership lobby in Edinburgh Corporation, or on the supply side, to builders such as John Mactaggart and Andrew Mickel - who were still compelled to pay local rates for new unoccupied houses, and faced stiff competition from new high-quality local authority rented properties.

The 1924 (Financial Provisions) Act attempted to solve this dilemma by increasing state subsidy to £9 per house per annum, with the local authority contributing £4 10s, and extending the eligibility for subsidy to new housing for private rental (the rentals being set at pre-1914 rent levels); the period of subsidy was also extended to 40 years. Although it was claimed that Mactaggart was instrumental in this piece of legislation, it incorporated none of his 1923 suggestions. The subsidy to private builders became more generous, and the new law extended its scope, importantly, to the private rented sector (introducing competition in this area); but it did not tackle the onerous rating system which Mactaggart believed lay at the heart of the problem.

Almost immediately, in late 1924, J A Mactaggart & Co. made an application for subsidies and loans to build a development at King's Park under this new legislation. But by then the internal organisation, or rather reorganisation, of his own business was a more immediate concern: in October of that year the company decided to go into voluntary liquidation. (41) As already indicated, it was succeeded in early 1925 by the two new companies: the Western Heritable Investment Co., specialising in management of rented property, and Mactaggart & Mickel, specialising at first in building work. Mactaggart's company had simply become too unwieldy, but there was no intention at first to segregate its component parts from one another; the aim was a rationalised partnership, with overlaps where necessary. For example, Mactaggart & Mickel, the new building-contracting venture, worked as a single contractor to build new Western Heritable developments. They also overlapped in housing tenure. Mactaggart & Mickel, as we will see, focused on subsidised housing for sale, but continued with local authority contracting work; it eventually entered the private rented market in Edinburgh in the early 1930s, and also introduced rented service flats in the mid-1930s. Western Heritable also made moves to sell some of its subsidised property, although much later, in the early 1950s.

The strong financial and organisational links between the two successor firms, including cross-ownership of shares, underlined the level of uncertainty about the future of the housing market and tenure in interwar Scotland.

The financial prosperity on which that division was based was very clear. The surplus assets of the old firm as at 12 October 1925 were £134,484. In 1924 and 1925, £25,000 of stocks and shares were bought, and £74,000 was spent. At the point of dividing up of the old firm's capital in September 1925, the total number of shares was 25,945. Of these, John and Margaret Mactaggart owned 4,000 shares each (at a value of about £5 per share, compared with £1 for the new Mactaggart & Mickel business), Isa Mactaggart owned 4,800, and Jack Mactaggart 6,000; further shares were also held by the Mactaggart family. Andrew Mickel owned 2,000 shares, and had, during the intervening period, allocated 400 shares to each of his children, Frank, Eileen and Douglas. The capital pay-out to the Mickel family (including a portion of all other shares and dividends held on other companies by J A Mactaggart & Co.) was approximately £35,800, almost exactly the same amount as the total capital raised to convert the venture into a limited company in 1919. The Mickels' number of shares in the firm had increased over that five-year period from 1,000 to 3,200, and the Mactaggart family had increased its share total by a quarter. Thus the Mickels had increased their share allocation sharply, although the Mactaggarts still remained dominant overall. (42)

All in all, Andrew Mickel's growing contribution to the activities of the J A Mactaggart business during the early 1920s had paid off handsomely. Although little evidence exists to outline his own thoughts on housing solutions in this early period, his commitment to home ownership from the 1930s is clear and well documented. Could it have been that Mickel found these views increasingly incompatible with Mactaggart's preoccupation with the private rented sector, and that a separation into two linked businesses was an ideal way to resolve that tension? Certainly, within the new Mactaggart & Mickel company, Andrew Mickel, at the age of 48, was able to establish, for the first time, a near-equal partnership (in terms of share control) with the younger Jack Auld Mactaggart.

Notes

1   Information from Susan Millar; Registers of Scotland, Register of Deeds, feu contracts, references (specimen numbers) Glasgow 3059/132/16, 2435/51/16, 2451/101/18, 2027/58/18, 2059/3/15, 2115/141/18, 1997/23/13, 1997/47/14.

2   Research reports by Julie Poole, 1998.

3   West Lothian Courier, 10 August 1923. London: research reports by Julie Poole and Simeon Clarke, 1998.

4   The Bailie, November 1920.

5   N J Morgan, 'Sir John Mactaggart' and 'Andrew Mickel', in A Slaven and S Checkland (eds), Dictionary of Scottish Business Biography, Volume 2, 1990 (hereafter Morgan, DSBB).

6   Morgan, DSBB; The Bailie, November 1920 (containing claim that he was responsible for building 4,000 houses at, primarily, Hyndland, Broomhill, Alexandra Park, Shawlands and Gourock).

7   On Scotstoun see Morgan, DSBB; Glasgow Dean of Guild Court Minute Books. Mactaggart buying and selling of land in 1908-1915 (Dumbarton Road, Balshagray, Scotstoun: Renfrewshire Sasines.

8   Royal Commission on the Housing of the Industrial Population of Scotland, Minutes of Evidence (hereafter Ballantyne Commission Evidence), 1913, 876.

9   Ballantyne Commission Evidence, 12 November 1913, 876. Mactaggart & Mickel Archives (hereafter MMA), letter of 11 July 1997 from John Sinclair of Peter A Menzies Ltd to Mactaggart & Mickel (hereafter MM).

10   Morgan, DSBB.

11   Morgan, DSBB; N J Morgan, '£8 cottages for Glasgow citizens', in R Rodger

(ed.), *Scottish Housing in the Twentieth Century*, 1989

12   Morgan, *DSBB*.

13   M Glendinning, 'The Ballantyne Report', in D Mays (ed.), *The Architecture of Scottish Cities*, 1997.

14   Ballantyne Commission Evidence, 876-85.

15   On owners' rates, see A O'Carroll, 'The influence of local authorities on the growth of owner occupation', *Planning Perspectives*, 11, 1996 (hereafter O'Carroll, ILA).

16   Morgan, *DSBB*; MMA, letter of 10 December 1916 from A Mickel to Mr Cowan.

17   Glendinning, 'The Ballantyne Report'.

18   Morgan, '£8 Cottages'.

19   Morgan, *DSBB*; MMA.

20   *The Bailie*, November 1920.

21   Morgan, '£8 Cottages'; S Damer, *A Social History of Glasgow Council Housing 1919-1965*, 1991.

22   Damer, *Social History*; *Glasgow Herald* (hereafter *GH*), 22 September 1920.

23   I Russell and G Dixon, 'Sir Robert McAlpine', in *DSBB*, 149.

24   *The Bailie*, November 1920; Morgan, *DSBB*.

25   *GH*, 20 September 1922; Damer, *Social History*.

26   Morgan, *DSBB*; *The Bailie*, November 1920; Damer, *Social History*.

27   Morgan, *DSBB*; MMA; *The Bailie*, November 1920; Glasgow Corporation Minutes (GCM), Housing Committee Sub-committee on Sites and Buildings Minutes (hereafter Sites), 6 March 1925; GCM, 24 October 1923 and 1 November 1923.

28   Morgan, *DSBB* and MMA; *GH*, 22 December 1922.

29   Morgan, '£8 Cottages', 143-45; Morgan, *DSBB*.

30   Morgan, '£8 Cottages'; National Archives of Scotland, file BT2/12983, Fyfe-Stone Ltd.

31   Morgan, *DSBB*; *Sunday Mail*, 16 February 1923; Sites, 4 January 1923.

32   MMA, letters of 28 May 1923 (to Agnes Frances Mickel), 31 July 1923, 15 May 1926, 23 January 1925 (on the liquidation), 14 May 1927, and 15 September 1927; Morgan, *DSBB*.

33   *GH*, 19 and 20 February 1919.

34   *Sunday Mail*, 16 February 1923.

35   *Sunday Mail*, 16 February 1923.

36   GCM, 12 December 1923; GCM, 10 January 1924.

37   *GH*, 19 May 1923; O'Carroll, ILA.

38   For fuller discussion, see O'Carroll, ILA.

39   O'Carroll, ILA.

40   O'Carroll, ILA.

41   MMA, 1924 accounts.

42   Report by William H Martin, Liquidator, September 1925. MMA, letters relating to J A Mactaggart & Co. voluntary liquidation from 5 September 1925.

THE FIRST FIVE YEARS

Building for the Corporation and Citizens of Glasgow, 1925-30

Introduction

In this chapter, which deals with the new firm of Mactaggart & Mickel following the division of J A Mactaggart & Co. in 1925, we trace a transitional period in the affairs of the business, at the end of which its eventual owner-occupation focus began to emerge. At first, its operations in the Glasgow area had a three-fold emphasis, divided among building houses for sale under the provisions of the 1923 Act, building as a contractor for Western Heritable under the provisions of the 1924 Act, and building council houses (including experimental construction types) as a contractor for Glasgow Corporation. By the end of this period, changes in the state subsidy arrangements to disadvantage the rented sector, and the increasingly self-contained building organisation of Glasgow Corporation, would destabilise this balance, and begin to encourage a move by the firm towards building for owner occupation. We discuss in this chapter some of the methods that would later be used in that programme, including the beginning of advertising, the use of secure methods of acquiring a land-bank, and the devising of a range of new house-types.

The new company
contracting work, 1925-27

The newly formed firm of Mactaggart & Mickel commenced trading on 1 March 1925 at 65 Bath Street, Glasgow, with a share capital of £20,000; the shareholders paid an initial instalment of one shilling on each £1 share, with a commitment to make up the remainder in the future. On 11 March the statutory meeting of the shareholders established Jack Auld Mactaggart, son of John Mactaggart, and Andrew Mickel as directors of the firm. Mactaggart, as the chairman, held the controlling allocation of 10,002 shares, and Andrew Mickel held 8,000 shares; in addition, Betty and Ian Auld Mactaggart had 999 shares each. Later in 1925, Walter Grieve was appointed company secretary. (1) As a limited company, responsibility for its financial wellbeing lay with the directors alone. Although still at a share disadvantage in terms of control of the new firm, Andrew Mickel's continued efforts and increasing contribution to the activities of J A Mactaggart & Co. during the early 1920s had enabled him to construct a near-equal partnership with the younger Mactaggart in the new firm, in 1925. Mickel's salary was set at £1,400 per annum and Mactaggart's at a lower level of £1,000. The former was presumably paid more in anticipation that the largest share of the work would be carried out by him rather than by the chairman; Jack Mactaggart may also have been receiving a salary from other business activities, such as through his father's new venture,

Western Heritable. At the end of 1925, Andrew Mickel changed the new firm's telephone number to 'DOUglas 1' (coincidentally the name of his son, Douglas), a number which was to become synonymous with Mactaggart & Mickel in later years. (2)

As we saw in the previous chapter, Mactaggart & Mickel was established in a period of both instability and opportunity, from the perspective of housebuilding contractors. The central focus of the new firm was clearly house production, as opposed to Western Heritable's housing management activities, and every opportunity to build new houses was grasped and pursued with vigour. During the first five years of business the firm pursued three main strands of activity: first, separate-trades and all-trades contracting for Glasgow Corporation; second, building houses of its own for owner occupation sale under the subsidy of the 1923 Housing Act; and third, acting as single contractor for Western Heritable's private rented housing schemes, built under the subsidy of the 1924 Wheatley Act. In fact, the only large-scale programme of housebuilding in Glasgow with which Mactaggart & Mickel was not involved was the Corporation's 'Rehousing' programme of tenement-building for slum clearance. But, by 1925, this only totalled 4,600 houses constructed or under construction in Glasgow - less than half the corresponding total (9,398) for housing under the 1923 and 1924 Acts. (3) The scale of Mactaggart & Mickel's activity in this period was vast in comparison with the pre-1925 production of J A Mactaggart & Co; in the years between 1926 and 1933, Mactaggart & Mickel built no less than 8,260 houses of all types and tenures, as compared with 3,258 between 1919 and 1924.

From 1925 to mid-1927 Mactaggart & Mickel's business focused solely on Corporation contracts and the construction of houses for sale under the subsidies package of the 1923 Housing Act. Single-contractor (or all-trades) and separate-trades contracting for the local authority had formed the core of J A Mactaggart & Co.'s business before 1925; Mactaggart & Mickel continued this tradition, but only as one strand of its activities. The principal J A Mactaggart & Co. contract inherited by the new firm, in March 1925, was a contract for brick, joiner, lath and glazier work at the second section of the vast Corporation 'Ordinary' garden-suburb scheme at Knightswood, involving 602 houses. All in all, Knightswood No.2 proved to be a difficult contract for the new company. In June 1925, for example, Mactaggart & Mickel wrote to the Corporation to complain that the dumping of waste soil from road and sewer works had obstructed their access to the building sites, but the Corporation refused liability; there were also grave shortages of plastering labour and materials, leading the firm to complete the scheme in a new method of 'hard wall plaster'. The scheme ran seriously over schedule, beginning in 1924 and eventually being completed in spring 1927. Mactaggart

A2.1. Glasgow Corporation's vast, multi-phase Knightswood housing scheme seen under construction in the summer of 1925; Mactaggart & Mickel carried out both single and all-trades contracts at Knightswood in its formative years. (Glasgow City Libraries and Archives)

& Mickel was clearly unwilling to accept responsibility for that delay, arguing in February 1927 that the 'contract has been very seriously delayed through difficulties with plumber, slater and plaster work, all outwith our contracts, and while there has been no complaint as regards delay on our section of the work, the scheme has taken more than twice the anticipated time to complete ...' (4) The difficulties at Knightswood No. 2 only deepened Mactaggart & Mickel's antipathy towards separate-trades contracting; it had never been the favoured system of John Mactaggart or Andrew Mickel, and from that point onwards Mactaggart & Mickel tried to avoid it at all costs.

As the new business grew in confidence, the directors focused their attention on obtaining large all-trades Corporation contracts for the construction of houses; the distinction was still maintained between this and the preparatory roads and sewers work. Within Glasgow's ongoing council house building programme of the late 1920s, the centrepiece remained the vast Knightswood scheme. Mactaggart & Mickel remained quite aware of its continuing importance, whatever the delays and difficulties they had experienced at Knightswood No.2. Hailed, in 1925, as the 'greatest enterprise of the kind yet undertaken by the Corporation', the Knightswood scheme was planned with the aim of bringing a great sweep of farmland within the city boundary, and building on it a total of 3,386 houses of the high-rent 'Ordinary' category - more than double the size of the Mosspark Ordinary scheme. By September 1925, 1,140 dwellings, exclusively comprising two-storey cottages and 'four-in-a-block' flats, were under construction. (5)

Late in 1925, the Corporation invited tenders for the next stage of the project, the 1,000-dwelling Knightswood No.3 development. Perhaps because of the delays experienced with the different trades at Knightswood No.2, this was to be an all-trades contract, on a negotiated rather than competitive basis. After a number of firms submitted bids, the contract was eventually divided almost equally, in January 1926, between Mactaggart & Mickel, with 506 dwellings, and John McDonald Ltd, with the remainder (McDonald was also involved in the contract for Knightswood Nos 1 and 2 at that time). The scheme consisted of largely of three- and four- apartment four-in-a-block two-storey flats, and cottages of three, four and five apartments, costing between £414 and £505 to build. It was to be constructed under the government subsidy established by the 1924 Act; for each dwelling the government was to contribute £9 for 40 years and the local authority £4 10s 'towards the economic rent'. What were the advantages and disadvantages of this kind of all-works negotiated contract, from the builder's point of view? In Mactaggart & Mickel's judgement, the firm had obtained at Knightswood No.3 'more favourable conditions ... more rapid payments to account of work done, substantial advances on the value of materials on the site ... consequent saving of interest charges, and unusually favourable terms as regards final payments'. They felt, however, that the company had 'probably gained no great advantage in price over a competitive contract'. (6)

Despite the greater security and stability offered by the contract method, the Knightswood No.3 project soon encountered familiar difficulties of labour and materials shortages. In August 1926, for example, Mactaggart & Mickel offered, because of the shortage of plasterers, to finish friezes and ceilings with board, and to plaster lower walls as normal. The Corporation turned down this suggestion, perhaps because it was under pressure to continue supporting the 'wet' plaster method; the production of plasterboard, which had begun as a wartime emergency measure around 1917, was opposed by the trade association. There were also protracted disputes over costs, as for instance when, in January 1927, the company unsuccessfully tried to persuade the Corporation to offset some materials costs stemming from the recent coal dispute. The firm tried to alleviate timber shortages for Knightswood No.3 by importing timber from Riga in Latvia, including a consignment worth £1,974 obtained from from the Latvian Timber Company in December 1926. This deal was preceded by complex negotiations, in which Mactaggart & Mickel investigated the standing of the Latvian firm, while the latter sought a financial guarantee in return; an extremely large advance of £5,000 was deposited by Mactaggart & Mickel with Sir James Calder, London, prior to delivery. (7)

All in all, the firm was increasingly finding Corporation contracts to be uneconomic and frustrating, in terms of control and decision making. Although it continued to explore the possibilities of further negotiated work for the council, Mactaggart & Mickel did not tender for any further Knightswood contracts; the only other Corporation work in this period was for a scheme at Carntyne in 1927. Further programmes at Knightswood, by other contractors, continued to involve both single- and separate-trades contracting. John McDonald maintained prominence with an all-trades contract to build 510 four- and five-apartment cottages at Knightswood No.6, 496 houses at Knightswood Nos 8 and 9, and a project for Knightswood No.4 involving his own patent house designs, which were to be constructed in fourteen months. In 1928 the Corporation again returned to separate-trades contracts at Knightswood, with Contract No.4, for 842 houses; this included a contract of joiner work to John Lawrence. Of these two contractors, McDonald was closely involved in the Assisted Purchase System and Corporation contracting, but not in 1923/24 Act private housing; and John Lawrence was soon to follow along the path pioneered by Mactaggart & Mickel. (8)

Although Glasgow Corporation contract work dominated Mactaggart & Mickel's first three years of business, the construction of houses for sale under the provisions of the 1923 Housing Act (with its annual £6 subsidies to builders from

A2.2. 1991 view of King's Park (top) and the post-1945 Simshill estate (centre) from the air, showing the simplified garden suburb low density layout; between 1925 and 1934, Mactaggart & Mickel built almost 6,000 houses at King's Park for sale and rent. (RCAHMS B71782)

A2.3. King's Park under construction in 1925. (MMC)

councils and central government on completion of houses) formed a strong, and growing, minority element in its work. Unlike Western Heritable, whose first successful application to build subsidised housing would come in June 1926, Mactaggart & Mickel made its first application to Glasgow Corporation to build houses under the 1923 Act as early as October 1925 (while in the midst of the difficult Knightswood No.1 contract). This first Mactaggart & Mickel application was for the development of King's Park, an area on the south-eastern edge of Glasgow which had been brought into the territory of the city through the 1925 Boundaries Act. This project was to become one of the firm's largest owner-occupied developments of the interwar period, eclipsed only by Carolside Park, Clarkston. The first application covered houses costing between £750 and £860 for brick and roughcast construction, and £800-£910 for the synthetic stone-fronted version. Mactaggart & Mickel received a lump sum subsidy of £21,000 and the opportunity of an 80% loan totalling £101,132. Further applications for King's Park No.1 in late 1925 and early 1926 included eight five-apartment houses at Kinmount Avenue, each valued at £940, and receiving a 1923 Act loan of £752 each (totalling £6,016), and a further 34 two-storey houses, awarded a total subsidy of £4,590 and loan of £21,592. The number of houses built at King's Park No.1 finally totalled 208; Mactaggart & Mickel estimated that they represented a total gross selling value of £190,000, of which £28,000 was covered by subsidies, and, when capitalised, £7,000 in feu duties. The first house at King's Park was sold on 3 December 1925 for £500; it was probably still under construction at the time. By April 1927 the development was complete, and all the houses were sold. (9)

Running parallel to the construction and selling of the King's Park project was that at Kelvinside, located on the opposite, north-western edge of the city. The first phase, built by Mactaggart & Mickel between 1926 and 1932, comprised 415 houses for owner occupation; these were followed in 1932-33 by 390 Western Heritable houses for letting. Again this development was staged. The first application for 164 two-storey terraced houses at Cleveden Road in January 1926 attracted a total subsidy of

£22,140 and loan of £106,292; this was based on two house-types, type 'A', selling at £755, and type 'B', at £820. The gross value of the development was £154,000, of which £22,000 represented government and local authority subsidies. It was on site by May 1926, and by February 1927 was mostly complete, with 113 houses out of the 162 already sold. These two first-phase developments, at King's Park and Kelvinside, laid the foundations of Mactaggart & Mickel's 1923 Act work. Sales were good, and confidence reasonably high; but later in 1926, in view of 'rumours ... that the Board of Health were about to modify subsidy conditions', Mactaggart & Mickel very quickly managed to get a further instalment of projects approved. (10)

King's Park No.2, which consisted of 210 five-apartment two-storey houses, was approved for subsidy in August 1926. The estimated gross selling value, subsidy and feu duties were identical to King's Park No.1. The project went on site in December 1926, and 31 houses had been sold by February 1927, with completion scheduled for later that year. The application for King's Park No.3 followed soon after: 226 two-storey, five-apartment terrace and semi-detached houses were approved for a lump sum subsidy of £30,510 and loan of £146,932. Work on the development started late in 1927; following the application approval at the end of 1926, Mactaggart & Mickel anticipated starting work at the end of 1927 'if our sales during this year justify this'. Kelvinside No.2 consisted of a further 182 houses and attracted £24,570 in subsidies and a loan of £123,892. In early 1927, Mactaggart & Mickel estimated that its gross value would be £180,000, and anticipated beginning work in early summer 1927 and completion in October 1928; Kelvinside No.2 would not be 'placed before the public' until Kelvinside No.1 had been 'substantially sold'. (11)

The above projects exhausted all the firm's land which was immediately 'available' for development at the end of 1927,

(opposite) A2.4. An early illustrated advertisement for a Mactaggart & Mickel semi-detached five apartment showhouse at 46 Manchester Avenue, Kelvinside. (Bulletin, 6 September 1930, 15; MMC)

ONLY THREE LEFT *!*

If you are paying from £60 to £70 in rent and taxes, you can get better value!

For a cash payment of only £50 and a total annual cost of £80 (including ALL rates and taxes, feu-duty, interest, and repayment of loan, etc.) **you can** actually own a five-apartment villa —
A BEAUTIFUL HOME AT KELVINSIDE

Each house contains:

**TWO PUBLIC ROOMS
THREE BEDROOMS
TILED BATHROOM
TILED KITCHENETTE**

and all modern conveniences, **including Easiwork Kitchen Cabinet in Kitchenette.**

Only Three Houses left for Sale.

Call any time between 1 p.m. and dusk at 46 Manchester Avenue, Kelvinside, and inspect our Show House.

MACTAGGART & MICKEL
LIMITED
65 BATH STREET, GLASGOW
Telephone: Douglas One

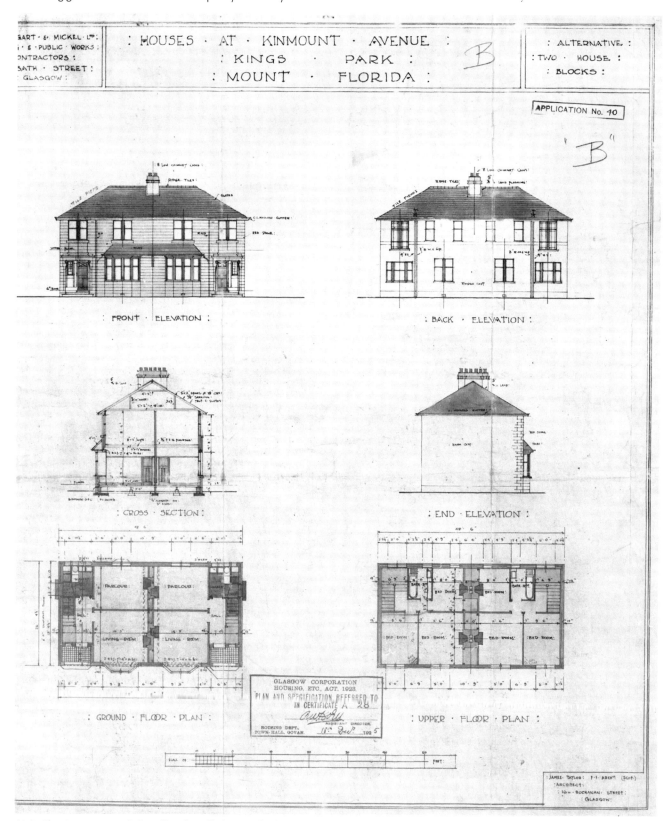

A2.5. Elevations, sections and plans of 'two house blocks' (semi-detached pairs) at Kinmount Avenue, King's Park, designed c.1925 by James Taylor. (MMC D33469/CN)

although the activities of the ladies' syndicate (under the company's direction) were attempting to piece together new sites to follow them. The government subsidies were central to the company's activities at that time. In early 1927, for example, all of its built and proposed houses for sale (644 at King's Park and 346 at Kelvinside) were subsidised at an average of £135 each. The company attempted to speed up progress by taking up a Corporation offer of 80% loans to 'builders or purchasers' prepared to take on any of these houses, and to complete them

by October 1928; as a fallback position in case of a decline in public demand for the houses, the company reserved the right to take 'advantage of the Corporation loan and thereafter hold them for sale'. In general, Mactaggart & Mickel eagerly exploited the financial assistance offered by the local authority. In February 1927 the directors agreed to take advantage of Glasgow Corporation loans (offered at a 5% interest rate) on houses in course of erection as part of the 210-house project at King's Park No.2; on that security they borrowed £75,000. (12)

In late 1927, only weeks after a batch of Mactaggart & Mickel projects was approved for subsidy, the conditions of eligibility of these state and local authority subsidies were made more restrictive by the government. They limited the existing subsidy and loan levels to houses of gross value of £750 or less (including any interest which the builder had in feu duties); overall subsidy reductions followed in 1929 and 1933. The 1927 change made Mactaggart & Mickel, as an early starter in this sector of housebuilding, more confident of its own position in relation to potential competitors. In a letter to its bank in early 1927, the firm claimed that it had a virtual monopoly in this field of building in Glasgow and the west. According to the directors, the average gross value of the company's King's Park and Kelvinside houses approved for subsidy was £940, and, as a result, any dwellings approved for subsidy and loan after October 1927 'would require to sell at approx. £200 less than the houses we are building'. The directors had acted quickly and shrewdly in obtaining subsidies and loans under the old conditions, and confidently claimed: 'As no other Firm in or around Glasgow has any substantial number of houses approved under the old conditions, we consider that this constitutes a very valuable monopoly for us'. (13)

The activities of its first two years of trading, and in particular the building of houses for sale under state and local authority subsidies, afforded Mactaggart & Mickel 'a satisfactory profit'. A dividend of 10% of the share capital was paid to shareholders in May 1926 (the dividend involved the sharing out of profits which were, of course, heavily taxed), and the company established an overdraft facility of up to £50,000 to finance future housebuilding operations. The outlook was buoyant. Less than a year later, with 'excellent prospects of securing another large negotiated contract' for council housing, and in anticipation of increasing its turnover in 1927/28 from 30% to 50%, the company raised its overdraft limit to £60,000. (14) The financial gains of the following two to three years would reflect the growing scale and complexity of Mactaggart & Mickel's business ventures.

1927-30: Diversification and the partnership with Western Heritable

The latter half of the first five years of Mactaggart & Mickel, in other words from mid-1927 to 1930, was dominated by three main building activities. The first involved the completion of the proposed 1923 Act housing, and further extension to King's Park and Kelvinside on newly acquired land. The second comprised a large negotiated Glasgow Corporation contract to build 1,000 Corporation-type houses at Carntyne. The third, and largest, activity was closely bound up with the King's Park development, and involved the construction of housing for private rental on behalf of Western Heritable under a large-scale single contract: between 1927 and 1944, some 4,424 houses were built by Mactaggart & Mickel for Western Heritable).

For the first of these activities, the continuing work of the ladies' syndicate was vital, as the firm claimed to have exhausted its land-bank in early 1927; now the target was to buy more land adjoining the existing developments at King's Park and Kelvinside. As before, the syndicate allowed the land assets to be kept two steps away from directors, as a precaution against insolvency, since Mactaggart & Mickel did not own the land, and did not feu the land until the houses were complete and ready for sale. Surviving documentation has indicated complex transfers of shares over ground, including that at King's Park and Kelvinside. It appears that Agnes Frances Mickel, Andrew's wife, was in the process of buying Isa Auld Mactaggart's share of the syndicate for King's

Park, Kelvinside, Bankhead and Meikle Aikenhead (farmland adjoining King's Park) by September 1927. (15) This transfer of land may have allowed for the smaller ad hoc developments made at both schemes in the following two years. Shortly after this transfer of land, Mactaggart & Mickel received Dean of Guild approval for two cottages and 70 dwelling houses, plus roads and sewers, at Meikle Aikenhead, King's Park No.3; the existing farm was demolished in 1928. Further small applications followed: in January 1928, 74 two-storey four-apartment cottage houses for King's Park No. 4 received a grant of £125 per house (with the Corporation valuer estimating selling values of £605 for a mid-terrace and £620 for an end house) totalling £9,280 in subsidy, and an 80% loan of £36,512; and a joint subsidy of £9,750 and loan of £38,400 was approved in May 1928 for 30 four-apartment cottages at King's Park and 48 four-apartment cottages at Kelvinside. In the late 1920s, Mactaggart & Mickel again took advantage of Glasgow Corporation's 5% loan rate for houses under erection; it was agreed in May 1928 to borrow a sum not exceeding £36,512 and 'grant to the Corporation in security' 74 houses which were in the course of erection at King's Park No. 4 scheme. (16)

Mactaggart & Mickel made only two further applications for subsidy in Glasgow under the 1923 Act. In February and April 1929, 39 four-apartment cottages (valued at £645 for 'double bungalow' and £650 for 'single') and a further 32 four-apartment houses, all for King's Park, received a total subsidy of £5,538, calculated at only £78 per house (as compared with an average of £135 per house in 1926-27). These applications were granted on the 'understanding that any incomplete houses at the time of reduction of government subsidy or corporation subsidy to the applicants will be redeemed'. The 1929 (Revisions of Contributions) Act, which attempted to reduce the 1923 Act level of subsidies in line with reductions in building costs, marked a downward turning point for subsidised housing for sale. (17) Mactaggart & Mickel had envisaged this downturn in early 1927 and had taken steps to exploit its financial potential at the time, but by the end of 1929 the financial assistance which afforded the venture 'a satisfactory profit' had been almost cut in half. Inevitably, Mactaggart & Mickel's ad hoc small applications in the late 1920s (listed above) were gradually replaced with other building commitments and ventures. The partnership with Western Heritable was to be the most financially lucrative.

The Western Heritable Investment Company was not, strictly speaking, a new company at all. Originally established in 1896, it was a small concern with a capital of £5,000 when John Mactaggart took over, and remodelled the business in September 1925. Mactaggart initially increased its capital to £30,000, and by 1931 the issued capital of the firm had risen to £130,000. (18) By this time, Andrew Mickel had become a substantial shareholder in the firm; in 1938, some of the Mickel shares were sold on to Jack Mactaggart. It is difficult to establish when Mactaggart & Mickel started working for Western Heritable, but it would appear that its involvement began in early to mid 1927; the firm did not mention contract work for Western Heritable in its business programme for 1927. From late 1924, J A Mactaggart & Co. had been receiving Dean of Guild approval for roads and sewers at King's Park; Mactaggart & Mickel may possibly have been involved with this. Western Heritable's extensive building programme began in earnest when it received Corporation approval, under the 1924 Housing Act (which John Mactaggart reportedly helped Wheatley to formulate), for 100 flatted dwellings; the houses were estimated at a cost of £450 each, and a loan of £336 was offered. This was followed by a number of large-scale applications in 1927 and 1928 under the terms of the

1924 Act, as part of a highly ambitious building programme which continued into the early 1930s. Between 1927 and late 1929, Mactaggart & Mickel built approximately 2,900 houses for Western Heritable, at a estimated cost of £2,000,000, on ground purchased in the 1920s by the ladies' syndicate. (19)

In 1927 an application was made and approved by Glasgow Corporation for 712 four-apartment four-in-a-block flatted dwellings at King's Park, although the committee disapproved of the form of construction, which was duly amended. The 'Cottage Houses for £32 Rent', built on land at Meikle Aikenhead, King's Park, were eagerly anticipated by the press, and established the model for future Western Heritable development. Applications in 1928 included one for 700 flatted houses (with an average selling price of £470 and £352 and 'agreed' recommended rent of £30 and £32), and one for 1,308 (later extended to 1,350) four-apartment houses for letting, of which 552 were located within the Glasgow boundary. The latter application was, according to the Corporation, made prior to the downward revision of the terms of subsidy, so the 1924 Act approved annual grant of £13 10s, and loan of 75% (repayable over 40 years) of the estimated value, were awarded for those houses within the city boundaries. (20)

It was at this point that the generous state and local authority subsidies, which Western Heritable had clearly exploited in a monopolistic way within Glasgow, really started to falter; we saw above how reduced subsidies had already begun, from October 1927, to curtail Mactaggart & Mickel's building activities for owner occupation. However, John Mactaggart, displaying his extensive negotiating skills, increasingly and openly challenged Glasgow Corporation's reluctance to subsidise his business activities - in contrast to the Mactaggart & Mickel directors, who chose to work and lobby more quietly. (21) Western Heritable's application for a 756-house extension to the previous application at King's Park in February 1929 proved the flashpoint for an outbreak of controversy. This application was initially accepted at the higher rate of subsidy (£13 10s) and 75% loan by the Corporation, although with a caveat that if government subsidy was reduced, it would be redeemed on houses still to be completed. But Mactaggart was unable to obtain land within the city boundaries, and found an alternative site within the landward territory of Lanark County Council. Falling back on an unsubtle attempt to intervene in local authority boundary issues, Mactaggart suggested that the county council should cede the land to the city and the Corporation should then provide the subsidy. Unsurprisingly, Lanark County Council refused, and Mactaggart then suggested, as a compromise, that the Corporation subsidy be reduced from £4 10s to £3 10s; in addition to state assistance, Mactaggart actually succeeded in obtaining a total Glasgow Corporation subsidy of £2,646 and loan of £266,112, for housing that was actually outwith the Glasgow boundaries. This proved to be a contentious decision by the Corporation's sub-committee on finance. The Housing Committee stepped in to stop Western Heritable obtaining Corporation subsidies for this development. Councillor James Welsh, later Lord Provost, called a special meeting to vote on the matter; Welsh won his case, and the subsidy was duly withdrawn.

Welsh was one of Mactaggart's fiercest critics within the Corporation at that time (and later, for example writing a letter of complaint to the Secretary of State for Scotland when Western Heritable tried to sell some subsidised housing in 1953). In response to Mactaggart's objections to the Corporation's methods of estimating rents, and subsequent subsidies, he wrote in September 1929 that 'Mactaggart's method of controversy is to

treat every comparison, other than his own, with contempt ... [he] drags in methods of valuation adopted in pre-war days, when there were no Rent Restriction Acts or subsidies to complicate matters'. Welsh estimated that Glasgow Corporation had subsidised Mactaggart's business venture to the sum of £105,640, and was clearly against further assistance. (22)

Mactaggart appeared unperturbed by this criticism and continued apace with his housing programme. In August 1929, Western Heritable and Mactaggart & Mickel purchased the 250 acres of what then constituted the 'greater part of Aikenhead estate' through a 'private syndicate' (presumably the ladies' syndicate). The two firms, working together in partnership, planned to build a development similar in overall numbers to the 2,900 units already erected on the King's Park site. The new houses were to be completed within one year, and a total expenditure of £1,500,000 was anticipated. Although Western Heritable was confident of achieving this envisaged programme, the nature of Glasgow's future housing tenure was clearly still unpredictable; this next section of King's Park, according to Western Heritable, would be let or sold 'depending on the market.' (23) As we noted above, Mactaggart & Mickel did not make any new applications for subsidised housing for owner occupation after 1929, and so it would appear that the remaining building activity at King's Park, up to early 1930, involved, on the one hand, new dwellings contracted by Western Heritable (which may have experienced a fallow period following the refusal of the May 1929 application for subsidy) and, on the other, completion of any unfinished Mactaggart & Mickel housing prior to further reductions in subsidy.

The Carntyne scheme

The other large-scale activity of the second half of the 1925-30 five-year period was Mactaggart & Mickel's negotiated contract for the Glasgow Corporation housing scheme at Carntyne. This municipal contract witnessed the firm's first large-scale venture into non-traditional materials and methods of construction (although both directors had had experience of low-cost concrete block construction at Mosspark in 1921); and it prompted the erection of the firm's Carntyne concrete works in 1927, which was to become an important element in its building programmes of the 1930s.

In late 1926, Glasgow Corporation representatives visited the 210-acre Carntyne site, situated between Shettleston and Parkhead, and proudly announced the intention to build a 'big scheme' of 2,000 houses for Glasgow's east end, which would eclipse Mosspark in scale. The houses were to be of the high-rent Ordinary category, with rents of approximately 12s per week, and would be chiefly of three and four apartments, for which, reportedly, there was an 'exceptionally high demand'. In January 1927, Glasgow Corporation bought the site from Watt, Son & Co. for £23,330. (24) One month later, Mactaggart & Mickel wrote to the Corporation formally tendering for the contract to build the scheme; it proposed to construct the houses using the patented Winget system of prefabricated pier and panel concrete construction. Mactaggart & Mickel provided 'prepared plans and prices for this system, applied to several of the types of houses which the Corporation are presently erecting'. The firm attempted to sell the proposal to the Corporation by stressing the constructional speed of this system, the durability and look of the finished product, and the reputation of the company's directors; the latter explained that they had an experience of housebuilding in Glasgow 'unequalled by any other firm in the

A2.6. 1990 aerial view of Glasgow Corporation's Carntyne housing scheme, showing the similarity to the private King's Park layout. (RCAHMS B37532)

United Kingdom'. The directors claimed to understand the 'necessity of having the maximum number of houses completed before the expected alteration of the Government subsidy conditions after October 1928'. They declared that they were 'convinced with regard to labour and material, that this system offers the best method of getting houses completed rapidly and in large numbers, on a system of construction which is orthodox, permanent and normal in appearance and which is structurally sound in every respect.' (25)

The costings and schedule were based on building the entire 2,000-dwelling scheme, and after 'careful investigation' of the system in England and consideration of 'local conditions as regards the supply of labour and materials', the firm estimated that within nine months 20% of the housing would be completed, within 12 months 50%, within 15 months 80%, and that after 18 months the whole scheme could be completed. Mactaggart & Mickel based its costings on the house-types which it had constructed for the Corporation at Knightswood No.3. These included: type C (£407); type D (£474); type N3 (£408); type N4 (£432). The

costing assumed an all-trades contract at a similar standard to those at Knightswood No.3, except for 'modifications usual to this system', and underbuilding, drains and footpaths. Mactaggart & Mickel concluded that if its offer was accepted, this would 'result in a very substantial addition to the housing programme of the city ... which will appeal both to the Corporation as owners and to the citizens as occupiers.' (26)

Mactaggart and Mickel had been in correspondence since early 1927 with Winget (1924) Limited, a firm based in the northern English town of Wakefield, with the intention of obtaining the exclusive patented licence to the system of concrete block construction for the anticipated contract at Carntyne. In return, Mactaggart & Mickel would be contractually obliged to purchase from the Yorkshire firm all cement-, block- and slab-making machinery, pallets, crushers, elevators, concrete mixers, screen for grading aggregate, and other machinery required 'for the manufacture of concrete material used in the erection of houses built under the Winget Patented Systems'. In addition, royalties on all the houses built using the system were to be paid to the company; the amount paid would fall as the actual number of houses constructed rose. For up to 100 houses, £3 per house would be payable; up to 900, £2; and up to 1,000, £1. Despite the financial obligations of the licence, Mactaggart & Mickel believed that the 'special advantage' of the system was that walling could be erected very rapidly; it was anticipated that the new machinery could provide manufacturing material for 20 to 40 houses per week. Speed was clearly the prime motivator for using this system; when comparing the costs of the patented system (per Corporation house built), with those using traditional material at Knightswood No.3 in 1926, the Winget system only saved on average £4-£5 per house. Mactaggart & Mickel surely saw the subsidised construction of a new concrete works as an advantage. (27) Here we see, already emerging, the polarisation between the advantages of prefabrication in expanding and accelerating output, and the disadvantage, from the contractor's perspective, of the capital investment required for prefabrication (factory-building, etc.) - a polarisation that was to recur in all the 'system building' episodes of the 20th century.

Prior to the official letter of tender for Carntyne in late February 1927, Glasgow Corporation's Housing Committee, at the invitation of Mactaggart & Mickel, sent Bailie Livingston and Councillors Logie and Welsh (Mactaggart's old adversary) of the Sites and Buildings Sub-committee to Wakefield to inspect the system, which had been used extensively throughout England. In England, as a result of falling cement prices from the mid-1920s, concrete construction also became cheaper (by 30% between 1924 and 1938) and underwent extensive technical developments; competition within manufacturing was strong and the production of concrete was increasingly captured by a small number of manufacturers. (28)

Glasgow Corporation was clearly interested in Mactaggart & Mickel's Winget proposal, but following the report by the deputation who visited Wakefield and by the director of housing, it cautiously offered the firm a contract to build only 1,000 of the Carntyne houses. The Corporation also set down two main contract conditions: firstly, that the Corporation could terminate the contract when 500 houses had been erected if it was dissatisfied with the construction or speed of erection, and, secondly, that the firm should pay workmen in accordance with agreed national wages and conditions for the building industry. Mactaggart & Mickel accepted the reduced contract, at adjusted, slightly higher costs, and estimated that 75% of the housing would be four-in-a-block flats, and 25% cottage dwellings; 75% of the housing would consist of three apartments, and the remainder would be of four apartments. Soon after, the firm ratified its patent agreement with Winget (which now stipulated that Mactaggart & Mickel could only use this system for the construction of Glasgow Corporation housing schemes), and began construction of the plant. In total, the cost of the machinery, which included pan mill, mixers, power presses, tamping machine, and palettes, was £1,000; Mactaggart & Mickel estimated that for 1,000 houses this would work out at 5d per square yard. (29)

In early 1928, in accordance with the Corporation contract, Mactaggart & Mickel had to sign an agreement with the National Federation of Building Trade Operatives, which prohibited 'piece-work' or 'payment by results'; instead Mactaggart & Mickel was to offer a uniform hourly rate, and not employ labour in any way which would differentiate it from 'any other building contractor'. By May 1928, Mactaggart & Mickel had successfully completed 500 of the Winget houses and the Corporation agreed to the remaining 500 being built. (30)

In awarding the contract for Mactaggart & Mickel's patented concrete construction, Glasgow Corporation showed itself willing to accept the responsibility (encouraged by central government from 1924) to introduce and experiment with new materials and methods of construction in an effort to reduce building costs for local authority schemes, without lowering construction standards or affecting the generally 'traditional' appearance of the housing. By the late 1920s, the chronic shortage of materials witnessed in the early postwar period had lessened; Mactaggart & Mickel's system clearly did not offer substantial cost reductions, but the cheapness and availability of cement in 1927, and the guarantee that Winget concrete blocks would be 'normal in appearance' and 'structurally sound' clearly met with the Corporation's approval. The Corporation had been utilising concrete in early direct labour housing schemes, such as Drumoyne in 1922; the production of concrete bricks was carried out at Corporation and Board of Health sponsored plants, and of course, J A Mactaggart & Co.'s concrete block construction at Mosspark had made a significant reduction in cost per house at that scheme. (31)

But cost reduction, although an important issue, was not the Corporation's main concern when it proceeded to the matter of awarding the remaining contracts for Carntyne. In May 1927, a contract for a further 1,000 houses was awarded to Mactaggart & Mickel's main contracting rival in the late 1920s, John McDonald, and an extension contract for 1,000 houses was awarded to the Balshagray Building Company. In August of that year, the Scottish Board of Health complained to the Corporation that all the tenders for Carntyne were in fact, higher in cost than those recently contracted for the Balornock area. At Carntyne, McDonald used his own patented system of flat-roofed 'Sunlit Homes' which, according to McDonald, took 12 days to construct (in the case of a three-apartment house); Glasgow Corporation justified the awarding of this contract as a 'practical experiment'. The costs of all the dwelling types included were almost identical to those of the same types in the Mactaggart & Mickel section: for example, the type 'C3' three-apartment flatted house for £405 and the 'NA' four-apartment flat for £430. The Balshagray Building Company provided 1,000 'C3' flatted blocks in the more traditional brick roughcast (£400) and terrazzo (£409) construction methods. The cost of these two later contracts alone (which brought the total housing for the scheme up to 3,000) was estimated at £945,483; they received Dean of Guild approval in October 1927 and work began shortly afterwards, proceeding with some delay through mining subsidence. (32)

The 'Million Pound Scheme at Carntyne' was officially opened one year later, in October 1928, although a considerable proportion of the houses was still in construction. Lord Provost Sir David Mason praised the scheme for its 'restriction of building density', which 'had secured for these houses the maximum of sunlight and fresh air'. In reply to the complaint (which had also been voiced concerning the Mosspark scheme in 1921) that Carntyne, as an 'Ordinary' category scheme, provided housing for 'people who were quite able to get houses for themselves', Mason claimed that this had 'never been proved'. (33)

The beginnings of reassessment

At the offical opening ceremony for Carntyne, the contractors were represented by John McDonald, who had focused his building activities primarily on contracting for the local authority. Mactaggart & Mickel's directors, in contrast, kept a low profile. Could this have indicated a growing disenchantment, on the company's part, with contracted local authority work? That much was certainly suggested by the policies it actually followed during the decade that followed. During the 1930s, it turned sharply away from contract work to speculative building for owner-occupation, and its directors, especially Andrew Mickel, began to participate in public debates surrounding housing production.

By the end of the 1920s, local authority contracting was beginning to seem unattractive for a number of diverse reasons. On the one hand, there was competition from more economical small firms. Andrew Mickel's son Douglas (who joined the firm in 1932) later recalled to Edinburgh councillors that 'we have done schemes for some of the largest authorities, but there were so many smaller people coming in and cutting prices to such an alarming extent ... that we let the thing dry up a little bit.' (34) On the other hand, there was the way in which the involvement of the state in housing was used to discourage old-style competitive practices and encourage more 'corporate' and 'social' ways of organising production. Although the company welcomed the security implicit in the negotiated form of the Carntyne contract, other departures from free-market conditions were more disagreeable: for example, the company's lack of managerial control (including compulsory trade agreements with the NFBTO), and limited financial return. And the process of 'socialising' the housebuilding process in Glasgow had not stopped there. Even during the 1920s, when the Corporation was still under the non-socialist control of the Moderates, it was increasingly experimenting with building by direct labour. And by 1935, two years after the Labour Party gained control of the council, 65% of Glasgow Corporation's programme was being built, or partly built, by direct labour. The central role of the private contractor in 1920s Glasgow housing suddenly began to seem a transient episode which was about to be superseded by a new and aggressive phase of municipal controlled housing production. Among citizens as a whole, confidence in the 'gigantic achievements of Glasgow Corporation in the provision of housing' was growing. The *Glasgow Herald* claimed that this achievement was 'probably not fully appreciated by the general body of the citizens'. (35) There was an increasing public appetite for a radical municipal interventionism in housing. While Andrew Mickel, following the earlier example of John Mactaggart, was quite prepared to accept the 20th century's politicisation of the housing question, and to engage in vociferous ideological campaigns through the mass media, the solutions he put forward differed radically from the emerging social-democratic consensus, with its demands for ever tighter public control over the means of production (including housing production).

By the end of the 1920s, therefore, it was becoming more and more clear that Mactaggart & Mickel's immediate future did not lie in the building of housing as a contractor. That applied not only to contracts for Glasgow Corporation but also to private sector building on behalf of Western Heritable. The system of subsidised housing under the 1923 Act, which had helped finance the operations at King's Park and Kelvinside, had been revised in the 1929 (Revisions of Contributions) Act, and Western Heritable's programme of new subsidised housing for the private rented sector was meeting with increasing opposition within Glasgow Corporation. Although Mactaggart & Mickel continued to act as a single contractor for Western Heritable into the early 1930s, the long-term prospects did not look good; the financial provisions of the 1924 Act were ultimately annulled by central government in the Housing (Financial Provisions) Act of 1933. Nor was there any opportunity for Mactaggart & Mickel to exploit the 1924 Act directly itself to build for the private rented sector. Western Heritable held a very firm monopoly on this activity in Glasgow, as part of its partnership arrangement with Mactaggart

& Mickel and the consequent allocations of building activities and housing tenure.

What, then, were the future prospects for Andrew Mickel and Jack Mactaggart's company as it stood on the brink of the 1930s? The period of generous state and local authority subsidies for general-needs housing to let or sell, although not stopped until 1933, was entering its last phase in the late 1920s. The opportunities for growth in home ownership still seemed bleak: the heavy rating system, discussed in the previous chapter, still financially burdened the owner occupier and private builder, who would have to pay rates until the housing had been sold. Glasgow Corporation still appeared opposed to promoting home ownership on a large scale. In 1927 the Corporation rebuffed a letter from a junior government minister urging it to 'encourage the purchase of houses for occupation by owners' under the Small Dwellings Acquisition Act 1899-1923; the Scottish Office had received complaints that Glasgow was not participating in the scheme and was only providing subsidies. In addition, the apparent 'tenure neutrality' between potential owner occupiers and those wanting to rent was at that stage still strong; Mactaggart & Mickel and Western Heritable, planning the next phase of King's Park in late 1929, claimed that the housing, if approved, would be let or sold 'depending on the market'. (36)

But there were also signs of change, signs of a brighter future for owner occupation. In the medium term, the decline of council general-needs building, and the redirection of council efforts to slum clearance, would undoubtedly redirect middle class demand towards the private sector. (37) The chronic shortage of building materials was no longer hampering progress; local authority low-interest loans were becoming available (although they were not popular with Glasgow Corporation), and building societies were operating on an increasingly large scale in Scotland.

Mactaggart & Mickel had been attempting to coax tenants in private rented property away from that tenure towards home ownership as early as 1928. One of the most important means of both responding to and influencing the home ownership market was advertising. In the 1930s, this was to become a powerful tool for both Mactaggart & Mickel and its competitors. In the late 1920s, by contrast, no other firm posed any real competition to Mactaggart & Mickel in the home ownership market. Early classified adverts for King's Park and Kelvinside publicised showhouses in Cleveden Road, Kelvinside and Third Avenue, Mount Florida for 'little more than the cost of rent' at a cost of £750. Modernity of fittings and equipment, a central Mactaggart & Mickel selling point in the 1930s, was first highlighted as early as 1929: the five-apartment showhouse (furnished by Wylie & Lochhead) at 45 Leicester Avenue, Kelvinside, was hailed as 'The Most Modern House in Glasgow'; rental was equal to £50 per annum, repayment of the loan was to be made twice yearly (£6 6s 9d), and a £50 down-payment was required. Similar conditions were offered at King's Park, and a five-apartment showhouse at 171 King's Park Avenue had a total cost of £750. As early as 1926, Mactaggart & Mickel spent as much as £400 on advertising which, it claimed, resulted in 'building up a very valuable good-will'. In 1927, approximately £1,200 was spent on advertising; Mactaggart & Mickel estimated that if the anticipated annual sales rate of 250-300 houses was achieved, advertising would represent 'less than half of 1%' of the total profit. (38)

The unwritten 'gentlemen's agreement' between Mactaggart & Mickel and Western Heritable, which allowed the former to concentrate on subsidised owner occupation and the latter on subsidised private rented housing within Glasgow, shut

YGORRA!

NOT

A HOUSE TO LET

BUT A "HOME" FOR SALE AND MOST OF THE MONEY TO BUY IT!

Painted and Decorated to Purchasers' Choice

Complete Ready for Furniture

TERRACE OF FOUR HOUSES

At KING'S PARK and KELVINSIDE

Each house consists of :—Two Public Rooms, Three Bedrooms, Tiled Kitchenette, Perfectly fitted Bathroom, Two large Wardrobe Presses, Electric Light, Gas Cooking

COMPLETELY FINISHED HOUSES

CAN BE SEEN TO-DAY

THEY WILL INTEREST YOU!

Mount Florida or Cathcart car within Five Minutes, or Bus from Botanic Gardens to Cleveden Road

PRICES from £750 complete

NO EXTRAS

TERMS : £25 when you buy your house

£125 when your house is ready

Balance repayable over a period of 25 years if desired

EARLY OCCUPANCY ON BOTH SCHEMES

Full Particulars of Houses, Lay-out, and Purchase Agreement from

Telephone : DOUGLAS 1

MACTAGGART & MICKEL, LTD.
BUILDERS OF FINE HOMES

Telegrams : "CONTRACT, GLASGOW."

65 BATH STREET ———————— GLASGOW

A2.7. 1928 advertisement in Ygorra *(Glasgow University student magazine). (Glasgow University Archives)*

A2.8. Douglas Mickel seen surrounded by a crowd of Ygorra *sellers in January 1930. (MMC)*

Mactaggart & Mickel out of the private rented sector in Glasgow and the west. Partly as a result of this, and possibly as early as 1930, the company's attention began to shift eastwards, to the potential of the private rented sector in Edinburgh, which it finally pursued in 1933. In the capital, the home ownership market had begun to be exploited in earnest by the young James Miller. In 1927, his first large venture of semi-detached bungalows for sale on Queensferry Road had sold for £840 each. Like Mactaggart & Mickel in Glasgow, Miller had established a head-start with the owner-occupied market in Edinburgh - although in Glasgow some competition was beginning to emerge from

Mactaggart & Mickel's ex-employee John Lawrence. The potential for both the owner-occupied and private rented sectors, as opposed to local authority housing, appeared generally stronger in Edinburgh than in the west. Edinburgh's Progressive-controlled council, as we saw above, was actively encouraging private enterprise building and, in particular, owner occupation throughout the interwar period; Mactaggart & Mickel was poised to exploit these opportunities in the early 1930s. (39)

The company was also beginning to look in more unorthodox directions in order to keep up the pace of innovation. In August 1929, Mactaggart & Mickel received Corporation approval for a group of multi-storey blocks of 'service flats' on Great Western Road, Glasgow. The unbuilt classical design, probably by W A Gladstone (who later became the company's in-house architect), was exhibited at the Town Clerk's Department in the City Chambers. It exemplified this new, modern type of apartment complex, so consciously different from the pre-1914 tenements; placed 100 feet apart, and shielded from the main road by a line of trees, the blocks would be accessed by a 'private carriageway'. Local Kelvindale residents voiced concerns over the proposed flats and urged the Corporation to withhold consent. In its defence, Mactaggart & Mickel claimed that it had 'no intention of proceeding immediately' with the scheme and described it as 'a mere vision of the future'. (40) This vision of the future was very distinct from the previous and current activities of the company. It highlighted an interest not only in the private rented sector, but in the more exclusive (and of course unsubsidised) provision and management of service flats. This proposed scheme indicated

A2.9. Displaying a keen interest in building: Douglas (far right) and Frank Mickel (second from right), on board a 'Help Build the Hospital Fund' float at the January 1930 Glasgow University students' day. (MMC)

one particular change in the outlook of the young company, and although the scheme for Glasgow's west end was unrealised, by the mid-1930s Mactaggart & Mickel was building service flats in the exclusive owner-occupied estate at the Broom, Whitecraigs, Renfrewshire. The 1930s witnessed some significant changes in the company's activities; in particular, Andrew Mickel's commitment to home ownership was finally about to bear fruit.

Despite the uncertainty over future housing tenure and the falling subsidies, the financial state of the company at the end of the decade was sound; throughout this period of intense activity it made financial gains. The profits on the share capital were divided amongst the shareholders; in 1927 a dividend of 15% of the share capital was awarded, and in 1928 it rose to 50%. (41) The dynastic family structure of Mactaggart & Mickel, which has been a significant feature throughout its history, was also beginning to emerge in these early years. In 1927, Andrew Mickel's eldest son, Francis (known as Frank, born in 1908), joined the business, and in 1934 he became a director. Also during the 1930s, Andrew's second son, Douglas (born 1911) would take responsibility for the firm's venture into the Edinburgh housebuilding market, as we will see in the next chapter. And eventually, in turn, their respective sons Derek (born in 1935) and Bruce (born 1945) would join the firm and the board of directors.

Architecture and building

Having traced the general sequence of the new company's building projects in its first five years, we now return to review more briefly their organisation, construction and architecture.

In the field of construction, the new Glasgow housing programmes of the 1920s were, as we have seen, a field of considerable innovation; but this dramatic pattern of innovation was emphatically confined to the public sector. In 1924, the first of several experimental 20th-century housing areas in the city was begun by the Corporation at Langlands. Here, contractors could try out their proprietary methods; the aim of the Corporation was to speed up production, pinpoint non-traditional methods of construction to alleviate any shortages in traditional materials, and satisfy central government's requirements to experiment with new technology and reduce subsidised building costs. In all, 56 houses of 13 different types were built there. Mactaggart & Mickel contributed to the Langlands experiment with two three-apartment 'Mansard' timber-framed houses in 1925. They were arranged as a semi-detached pair, which featured a concrete slab floor at the base, roughcast and breeze-slab-clad ground storey, and asbestos slate-hung attic mansard with low-pitched felted roof; at the front was a canted oriel. (42) And the firm also, as we saw above, adopted the patented concrete block Winget system for its four-in-a-block houses built from 1927 at Carntyne. But in general, Mactaggart & Mickel seems to have been relatively opposed to the non-traditional methods of construction being introduced through prefabrication in the 1920s.

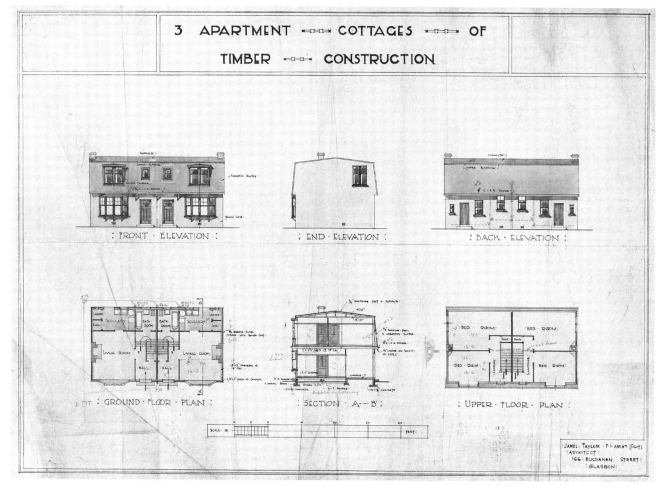

A2.11. *Experimental three-apartment Mactaggart & Mickel cottages of timber construction, designed for the Langlands site by James Taylor c.1925. (MMC D44832CN)*

(opposite) A2.10. The young Douglas Mickel seen at his desk, 1931. (MMC)

A2.12. Semi-detached pair seen almost complete at King's Park, 1925. (MMC)

Despite contemporary claims that prefabrication would make site work less dependent on weather and alleviate shortages of skilled labour, the company maintained a generally traditional approach to house construction and, to the same extent, supported these tested methods and materials. (43) But it was more directly interested in a gradual change in traditional techniques through the introduction of selective mechanisation to the site. In addition to the concrete production plant built at Carntyne in 1927 (which later produced kerbs, lintels, sills and paving slabs before the works moved to Orchard Park in the 1970s), Douglas Mickel later recalled seeing 'a wonderful piece of machinery' which was used to build King's Park. This, the 'steam navvy', was a mechanical excavator which had 'a cabin the size of a small bungalow, belched steam all around, and had a huge bucket which scooped out a cartload of soil at one time'; the 'truly monstrous piece of equipment' was the pride of the firm. (44)

However, the majority of site work remained heavy and manual. On-site transport was mainly carried out by horse and cart; one former plumber recalled horses and carts, supplied by Peter Hastie's Stables, transporting concrete blocks from the Carntyne plant to King's Park. The physical nature of the job posed inherent dangers. King's Park, for example, witnessed two fatalities in this period: at King's Park No.3, Joseph McEwan, a 55 year old painter, fell fourteen feet to his death in November 1928, leaving the firm to settle a claim of £130 by his sister, including funeral costs; and at King's Park No.5, Felix McGuinness, a 16 year old slaters' apprentice (whose wages were 16s per week), fell 15 feet from scaffolding and died in late December 1928. It is difficult to establish the scale of Mactaggart & Mickel's workforce in these first five years. In 1932 the company was employing over 2,000 workers on its sites; the figure for the late 1920s would probably have been similar, if not greater than that in 1932. Douglas Mickel recalled that his father visited the sites to pay the workers' wages, in cash, each Saturday at 12 noon: 'For protection my father carried a revolver, but I never heard of it even being brought out of his pocket'. (45)

In the design of house-types, there was also a sharp division between Mactaggart & Mickel's contracted work for Glasgow Corporation on the one hand, and its own projects (including those of Western Heritable) on the other. The Corporation's house-types were usually designed by its own architects, although in the experimental Langlands Road project Mactaggart & Mickel's own retained architect was also involved. The company worked with the Housing Department in managing its building work, the supervisory role of the department's clerks of works obviously being greater in separate-trades schemes. On the whole, the Corporation's house designs for the 'Ordinary' schemes (in contrast to its more conventional tenements for its 'Rehousing' schemes) were direct offshoots of the garden-suburb tradition of cottages in greenery; the most common types were three- and four-apartment houses arranged either vertically, in the form of cottages on two floors, or horizontally, in 'four-in-a-block' flats. The latter were low and heavy in appearance, and treated in an austere, tenemental fashion, whereas the cottages often had small gables or dormers. House plans departed from the prewar villa pattern, with its front-to-back linear arrangement, towards a more compact and versatile layout, including in some cases side entrances and larger living rooms dispensing with separate parlours; kitchens were well equipped, with freestanding copper boiler, gas cooker, enclosed larder and coal store.

A2.13. Company staff outside a works hut at King's Park, c.1928. (MMC)

A2.14. King's Park supervisory staff on site in 1931. (MMC)

The company's own houses were dealt with in a different way. As an all-trades developer-builder, there was no need for an architect either in the old-fashioned sense of the overseer and organiser of the separate trades (something which to some extent continued among local authority architects), nor in the new, highly professionalised modern role of the problem-solving artist-scientist. (46) The company needed architects mainly to draw up type-plans, both for its own developments and for non-traditional construction types to be built in Corporation schemes. Where Andrew Mickel, as an (unqualified) architect, had been involved in design before 1925, after that date two private architects were engaged as consultants: James Taylor (born 1890) and Joseph Wilson. Taylor, a Fellow of the Institute of the Architects of Scotland, was first employed by the company in 1925 to design the timber-framed 'Mansard' type cottage for the

Langlands experimental housing area, and he was also involved in 1927 in design work on the Winget types built at Carntyne. He rapidly moved on, later in 1925, to design standard types of terrace houses for the company's own developments at King's Park. Shortly afterwards, Joseph Wilson became involved in design work for Mactaggart & Mickel; he was formally appointed in July 1927 to make designs for 'any and all building work, including layouts for any small areas requested by us'. For one year's work, he was to be paid £120 in monthly instalments, along with expenses; the firm would be 'at liberty' to employ any other architects 'to repeat with or without variation, any plans drawn by you for us ... all plans prepared by you for us to be our property.' He drew up a range of standard plans, including four-apartment cottages at Kelvinside in 1928; but he was also overwhelmed by a large number of small jobs, especially the addition of garages to existing houses. In response to his complaints, in 1928 his retaining fee was increased to £168, plus 10s for each Dean of Guild Minor Warrant handled and £2 2s for each garage plan; but the following year, again citing inadequate remuneration, Wilson finally resigned his consultancy. (47)

The standard types designed by Taylor and Wilson were, on the whole, more conservative than the layout of post-1919 council houses. The first developments were dominated by two-storey houses directly descended from the prewar terraced villas, with their strongly linear front-back layout, but at the end of the 1920s there was a move towards bungalows, whose more compact, centralised plans seemed more closely related to prewar tenement plans. A typical example of the mid-1920s two-storey norm was the standard four-house terrace designed in 1925 by Taylor for use at Kelvinside and King's Park. Built of rendered 12" cavity brick walls, the house was dominated by a full-depth staircase

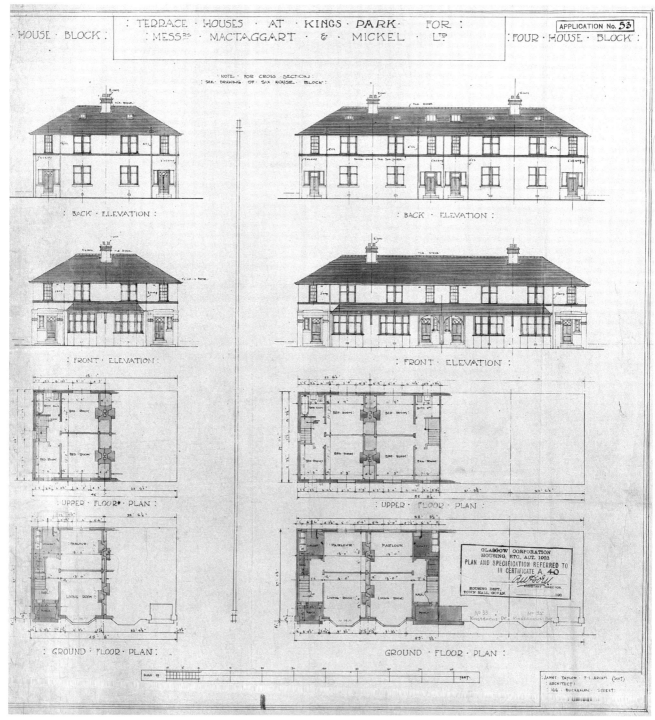

A2.15. *Mid-1920s design by James Taylor for two-house and four-house terraces at King's Park. (MMC D33471CN)*

hall, giving direct access to a front living room and rear parlour and scullery on the ground floor, and three bedrooms and bathroom on the first floor; a council house of corresponding size in the 'Ordinary' category, for the same social class of occupant, would have sacrificed the parlour, with its connotations of middle class status and display, for a larger living room and bedrooms. Externally, the terrace house was distinguished from the architecturally 'respectable' simplicity of the council cottages by a somewhat more busily ornamented front facade, including ground floor oriels and paired timber-arched doorways linked by a tile-hung canopy roof. It was advertised in 1926 for sale at prices 'from £750 complete', with accommodation and fittings including 'two Public Rooms, Three Bedrooms, Perfectly fitted Bathroom, Two large Wardrobe Presses, Electric Light, Gas Cooking'. In detail, the kitchenette fittings comprised a

freestanding boiler and tub, each with wood cover; a freestanding canopied gas cooker; a recessed dresser; a sink; a hinged wall-flap for baking and ironing; and a larder and coal house accessible from the hall.

The first mid-terrace example of this five-apartment type ('A') was sold for £775 in April 1926 in Southampton Drive, Kelvinside; end-terrace houses commanded a premium of around £50 or £60, while four-apartment houses were £130-£145 cheaper, costing as little as £605 at King's Park in 1928. By way of comparison, a four-apartment flat in a Western Heritable four-in-a-block in 1927 cost £470 to build and commanded a rent of £32, while a four-apartment flat on the Carntyne council scheme commenced that year cost £479 to build. Taylor and Wilson continued to revise these types, in terraces of up to eight houses

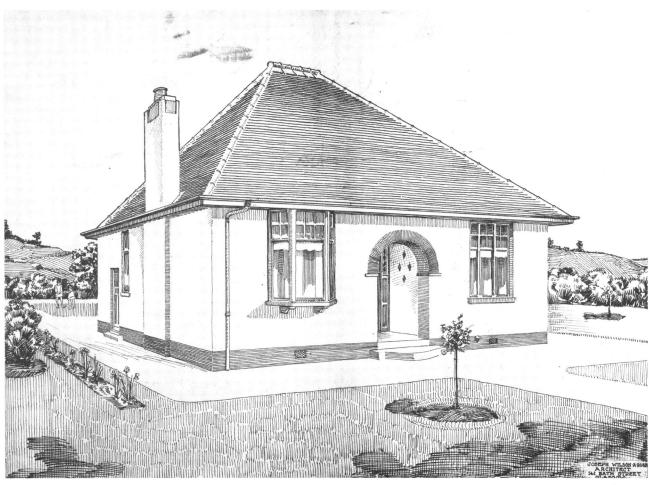

A2.16. Perspective of a bungalow drawn by Joseph Wilson in the late 1920s; this was presumably conceived as an initial presentation drawing for Mactaggart & Mickel. In reality, the detached Mactaggart & Mickel bungalow only 'took off' in the early 1930s. (MMC D33465)

A2.17. King's Park c.1929, showing Mactaggart & Mickel's earliest semi-detached bungalows under construction. (MMC)

45

in length, during the late 1920s. By 1929, reflecting a general reduction in housebuilding costs, there had been a slight drop in prices; a Mactaggart & Mickel five-apartment house at Kelvinside would sell for approximately £750 and command an estimated annual rental equivalent to £50. (48) In 1929, however, the company signalled a move away from these relatively dense and old-fashioned formulas towards the more spacious and self-contained pattern of the detached bungalow, by unveiling the 'F' type, designed by Joseph Wilson, initially for use at King's Park No. 3 development. From now on, the contrast with the two-storey house-types and relatively mixed-use space patterns of the higher-class council schemes would become much sharper, allowing the competition between the two to be stepped up in the 1930s.

Notes

Readers are referred to the Notes section of Chapter A1, and the Abbreviations section at the end of the book, for an explanation of the abbreviated forms used in this list.

1   Minutes of the Statutory Meeting of the Shareholders, 11 March 1925 and 11 December 1925.
2   Minutes of the Statutory Meeting; information from John Craig; MMA, letter of January 1926.
3   *GH*, 24 August 1925.
4   MMA, letter from MM to James Ledingham, North of Scotland Bank, 24 February 1927; Sites, 6 March 1925, 26 June 1925, 14 April 1926; MMA, letter of 24 February 1927.
5   *GH*, 24 September 1925.
6   GCM, 15 January 1926; *GH*, 25 February 1926, 6; MMA, 24 February 1927; MMA, letter from MM to James Ledingham, 24 February 1927. House costs for Knightswood as calculated by Mactaggart & Mickel: type C, £414; D, £470; E4, £450; F3, £505; N3, £415; N4, £446 (including fencing and hollow walls): MMA, letter from MM to Glasgow Corporation, 25 February 1927.
7   C G Powell, *An Economic History of the British Building Industry*, 1980, 124; Sites, 22 September 1926; GCM, 5 January 1927; MMA, contract of 9 September 1926 and various papers relating to the Latvian Timber Company Ltd, Riga.
8   Sites, 3 August 1927; *GH*, 17 May 1928, 7; Sites, 10 August 1928.
9   GCM, 7 October 1925, 2 December 1925, 27 January 1926; *50 Years of King's Park*; MMA, 24 February 1927.
10 GCM, 27 January 1926, 3 March 1926; MMA, 24 February 1927.
11 'Terraces and tenements', *GH*, 21 August 1926, 11: 'All the houses in this scheme are for sale', as distinct from other applications approved by the Corporation at that time. MMA, 24 February 1927; GCM, 2 September 1926, 17 November 1926.
12 MMA, 24 February 1927; MM Minutes, 21 February 1927.
13 MMA, 24 February 1927.
14 MMA, 24 February 1927; MM Minutes, 13 July 1926 and 31 May 1926.
15 MMA, 24 February 1927; information from J Craig; MMA, letter of 15 September 1927.
16 *GH*, 22 October 1927; *50 Years of King's Park*; GCM, 4 January 1928; Sites, 30 May 1928; MMA, Minutes of Extraordinary General Meeting, 14 May 1928.
17 GCM, 6 February 1929 and 17 April 1929.
18 Morgan, *DSBB*; information from J Craig.
19 GCM, 21 June 1926 and 9 August 1929, 10; figures may include Mactaggart & Mickel's own developments.
20 Sites, 24 August 1927; *GH*, 12 November 1927; GCM, 25 January 1928 and 27 June 1928.
21 Morgan, *DSBB*.
22 GCM, 27 February 1929, 13 February 1929, 3 April 1929, 10 April 1929, 26 April 1929; *GH*, 14 September 1929.
23 *GH*, 9 August 1929, 10.
24 *GH*, 15 December 1926, 14; *GH*, 13 December 1927, 9; GCM, 7 January 1927.
25 MMA, letter from MM to Glasgow Town Clerk, 25 February 1927.
26 MMA, letter from MM to Glasgow Town Clerk, 25 February 1927.
27 MMA, letter from MM to Glasgow Town Clerk, 25 February 1927; MMA, Winget Agreement, 30 March 1927.
28 Sites, 4 February 1927, 25 February 1927; Powell, *Building Industry*.
29 Sites, 25 February 1927, 15 March 1927. MMA, letter from MM to Glasgow Town Clerk, 25 February 1927; MMA, Winget Agreement, 30
March 1927 (Joseph Wilson designed the concrete plant).
30 MMA, letter from National Federation of Building Trade Operatives, 19 January 1928; Sites, 18 May 1928.
31 MMA, letter of 25 February 1927; Morgan, '£8 Cottages' (for fuller discussion of Glasgow Corporation's approach to new building methods and materials in the interwar period).
32 Sites, 13 April 1927, 12 August 1927; *GH*, 24 September 1927, 3; 22 October 1927, 7; 18 December 1929, 8 ('alleged delay through subsidence' at No.2 scheme).
33 *GH*, 26 October 1928, 7.
34 Douglas Mickel, 'Statement to Edinburgh Corporation', 3 February 1937.
35 O'Carroll, ILA; *GH*, 24 September 1925.
36 GCM, 5 January 1927 SCF. For general discussion of this period see A O'Carroll, 'The development of owner occupation in Edinburgh' (hereafter O'Carroll, DOO), PhD thesis, Heriot-Watt University, 1994, 57-8.
37 O'Carroll, DOO.
38 *GH*, June 1928, 22; *GH*, 4 August 1929, 12; MMA, 24 February 1927.
39 Morgan, *DSBB*.
40 Information from Iain Drysdale; *GH*, 9 May 1930, 10.
41 MM Minutes, 14 July 1927 and 12 July 1928.
42 Morgan, '£8 Cottages'; Sites, 15 May 1925.
43 Powell, *Building Industry*, 123-4.
44 *50 Years of King's Park*.
45 *50 Years of King's Park*, and MMA; discussion of how best to pay site-workers continued until the 1950s.
46 E Cooney, *Construction History*, 3, 1987.
47 MMA, letters from MM to Wilson, 8 July 1927, 5 July 1928; letter from Wilson to MM, 5 June 1929.
48 MMA, sales books and drawings.

THE GOLDEN YEARS

Home Building West and East, 1930-39

Introduction

In this period, at last, Andrew Mickel's longstanding ideal was realised, as building for owner occupation finally became the largest element in the company's output. However, its dominance was precarious, reflecting its still uncertain status within Scottish housing as a whole. A total of 3,808 houses was built for sale by Mactaggart & Mickel during the 1930s, only 10% more than a new and burgeoning element in the firm's portfolio, the building of houses to let in Edinburgh (totalling 3,356 units). What had declined sharply was the contractual building of letting properties for Western Heritable; the two partner-firms were drifting inexorably apart, and Mactaggart & Mickel was acting with increasing autonomy and strategic boldness.

In this chapter, the firm's 1930s work is grouped into four overlapping phases, or parts. Part I is concerned with its work in Glasgow in the early 1930s, including continued building for Western Heritable (up to 1933) and of its own houses for sale with 1923 Act subsidies (up to 1934), but increasingly dominated by a boom in unsubsidised building, especially in new developments outwith the city boundaries. We examine both the supply-side and demand-side reasons for that boom, including cuts in building costs and interest rates, and rises in real incomes and lower-middle class aspirations; and we trace the mechanisms used by the company to exploit those trends, including sophisticated marketing campaigns, and mechanisms of easy finance for house-buying, including the 'pool' system of co-operation between building societies and builders.

Part II traces the firm's eastwards move into the Edinburgh private housing market, exploiting the capital's relative immunity from the economic slump, and the attempts of its city council to support the private sector in opposition to a Glasgow-style hegemony of council housing. At first, constrained by the market dominance of the firm of James Miller, Mactaggart & Mickel concentrated on building for rent, especially in East Pilton, but later it branched out into extensive developments for sale. In Part III, we discuss the firm's mid-1930s strategy of moving upmarket into more individualised and high-status developments, including some service apartment blocks (Sandringham Court) and villa designs acknowledging stylistic aspects of the architectural Modern Movement, at projects such as the Broom Estate, outside Glasgow, and Hillpark, Edinburgh. Finally, Part IV outlines the major developments of the later 1930s around Glasgow, including suburban projects such as Orchard Park, Carolside Park and Merrylee Park, as well as Ayrshire seaside developments in Largs and Stevenston, and traces the

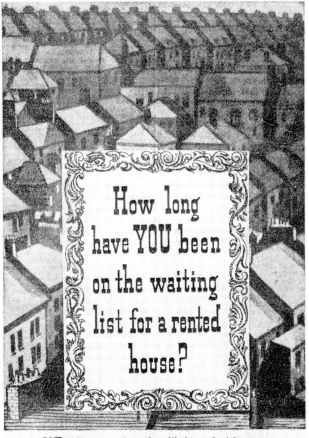

A3.1. *1938 advertisement for Orchard Park Estate, emphasising the problems of rented accommodation.* (Evening Times, *3 June 1938; MMC*)

A3.2. Four generations of the Mickel family, seen c.1938. From left to right: Frank Mickel, Andrew Mickel senior, Derek Mickel, and Andrew Mickel. (MMC)

organisational difficulties that began to gather force in the years immediately leading up to the outbreak of World War II.

All in all, in this period Mactaggart & Mickel established itself as a large-scale building firm executing contracting, housebuilding for sale, and ultimately housing management. It is important to understand that all these activities ran in parallel, and the construction of one new owner-occupied suburban scheme often overlapped with a concentrated sales push for a number of established developments. Added to the contracting commitment to Western Heritable, the business activities of Mactaggart & Mickel in this period were diverse and extremely challenging for its directors. By the early 1930s, Andrew Mickel had over 40 years' experience in the building industry. In conjunction with his partner Jack Mactaggart, Frank Mickel (who became a director in 1934) and the newly recruited Douglas Mickel (who joined the firm in 1932), he steered the firm through one of the most productive and successful periods in its history. (1)

In 1932, to support these activities, the borrowing powers of the directors were increased to £120,000, underwritten by the North of Scotland Bank. (2) In November 1933, the firm attempted to make a bonus issue of 30,000 shares, but this was discovered to have been *ultra vires* and the Articles of Association were changed on 15 March 1935 to allow the bonus issue to be regularised. There was some rearrangement of shareholdings (with Neil and Alastair Mactaggart, for example, becoming shareholders) and 2,000 shares were renounced by Jack Mactaggart in favour of Walter Grieve; these were transferred back in 1939. Financially, the Mactaggart family continued to control Mactaggart & Mickel, although that control was not secured by Jack's holding in isolation. Various shares were transferred to trusts for the three sons of Jack Mactaggart, mainly in February 1941, and at the

end of the war the Mactaggart holdings totalled 29,900 out of 50,000 overall (comprising 20,003 by Jack, 2,499 by Ian, 1,000 by Neil, 500 by Alastair, and 5,898 by four trusts). One hundred shares had been transferred to James Ledingham in 1939 to give him his director's share qualification. It appears that the company traded profitably in the 1930s, and that it was prepared to borrow money to enable it to hold heritable property. From 1925 to 1938, the total share capital subscribed by shareholders rose from £20,000 to £390,703; at the latter date, loans secured over Edinburgh letting properties totalled £826,000, the bank overdraft was £50,000, and £30,000 was borrowed from Western Heritable, so the gross assets were in excess of £1,300,000. (3)

In a memorandum of *c.*1933, Jack Mactaggart and Andrew Mickel summed up the activities of the business during this period as follows: 'This firm is engaged in the erection of dwelling houses in Glasgow and district, and Edinburgh. During the past seven years they have erected approximately 8,000 houses and were responsible for the work in all trades, including the construction of roads and sewers. In the same period, and included in this number, they built and sold approximately 3,000 houses at an average selling value of £600 ... Their present work includes the erection under one of the Government Subsidy Acts of 1,200 houses at Cardonald, Glasgow, 500 houses in Edinburgh and a scheme of their own in Netherlee, Renfrewshire of 400 houses, which they are selling ... They sell on average over the past five years 400 houses per annum ... They have over 2,000 men of all grades on their pay roll, which amounts in cash to over £6,000 weekly. They pay their accounts regularly each month, one day being set aside for this purpose per month; for the past year this amounted to approximately £50,000 per month, and taken over five years averaged £35,000 per month.' The two directors listed numerous firms of 'considerable importance in Scotland' with which they did business, including the Carron Company and the Caledonian Portland Cement Company, and concluded that 'the Directors have been associated with the Building Trade for many years, one in particular for over 40 years'. (4)

Part I: Glasgow, 1930-35

Contracting for Western Heritable
King's Park, Kelvinside and Cardonald

The period from mid-1930 to 1934 witnessed a steep reduction in the contracting work which Mactaggart & Mickel carried out for Western Heritable, and a remarkable growth in its own programme of housebuilding for owner occupation (which will be discussed later). Despite this, the ongoing business arrangement with Western Heritable still played a dominant role in the firm's activities up until 1934, when the two firms parted company. Contracting for Western Heritable provided a reliable alternative source of income, which was ploughed into Mactaggart & Mickel's increasingly important house-selling activities. Mactaggart & Mickel carried out three main contracts for Western Heritable in this period: at the latter's King's Park, Kelvinside and Cardonald developments; this final contract was completed in 1934. By 1934, the bottom had fallen out of the subsidised private rented market in Glasgow, a sector within which Western Heritable had held a comfortable monopoly. The 1933 Housing Act reduced the 1924 Act annual subsidy from £9 to £3 per house until 30 June 1935; after this date the central government subsidy was withdrawn completely, although some local authorities, including Edinburgh but not Labour-controlled Glasgow, continued to support private enterprise building for sale or rent. (5) A decisive financial segregation of the two companies followed four years later, in 1938, when Mactaggart & Mickel sold its considerable shareholding in Western Heritable back to the Mactaggart family.

In late 1929, Western Heritable and Mactaggart & Mickel had confidently anticipated building another 2,900 houses at King's Park. In reality, Western Heritable was destined to build only another 1,552 new approved houses on this site (although a large number of previously approved houses were under construction in the early 1930s); Mactaggart & Mickel had built and sold the vast majority of its approved houses on this site before 1930. Mactaggart had, as we saw in Chapter A2, already experienced a certain reluctance on Glasgow Corporation's part to finance his private building projects at King's Park, and the Corporation had begun in 1929 to reduce its subsidy contribution given to Western Heritable under the 1924 Act. Despite opposition within the council, Mactaggart (who at 62 years of age showed no signs of retiring) was determined to continue his housing programme, for which, he argued, demand was still 'buoyant'. (6) In 1930, Glasgow Corporation was still under the control of the anti-socialist Moderate Party, but despite being encouraged by central government (under the 1923 and 1924 Acts) to support private enterprise housebuilding, even the Moderate council leadership showed a growing reluctance to finance the activities of builders such as Western Heritable. As we saw previously, subsidy reductions by the Corporation had deterred Mactaggart & Mickel from making any further applications to the Corporation for subsidy under the 1923 Act; the firm had decided instead to focus its 1923 Act housing on the territory of the traditionally Progressive (non-socialist) controlled county council of Renfrew.

In 1933 the socialists took control of Glasgow Corporation, and in the same year central government withdrew the 1923 Act subsidies to private builders and sharply cut the 1924 Act subsidy.

In direct consequence, the Corporation forged ahead with vast general-needs and slum clearance housing programmes, built primarily by its growing direct labour force, and the provision of private-enterprise-built general-needs housing took a back seat. The opposition already experienced by Western Heritable, in its lengthy and complicated negotiations with the Corporation, grew more vociferous, and ultimately curtailed, in quantitative terms, Mactaggart's activities. However, Mactaggart again persisted with his plans, and appears, on the whole, to have achieved his short-term building objectives. Mactaggart & Mickel, as an all-trades contractor, was of course shielded from these difficult proceedings, but as a significant shareholder the company must have contributed to the negotiations, and of course benefited financially at both levels. However, it is worth bearing in mind that, despite all the tensions between Mactaggart and Glasgow Corporation, he gifted Aikenhead House and its grounds to the City of Glasgow for recreational use in May 1930. (7)

In March 1930, Western Heritable applied to Glasgow Corporation for subsidy and loans to build 1,364 four-apartment flatted houses for letting at King's Park. Anticipating Corporation reluctance to award the maximum annual subsidy available (£13 10s per house), Mactaggart's company sent an indirect warning to the Corporation, using the press; the firm argued that unless the project proceeded, 'a number of the men at present employed on building work will require to be dismissed'. In the early 1930s, Mactaggart estimated Western Heritable's labour requirements at around 900 men; working as all-trades contractors to Western Heritable, Mactaggart & Mickel had a workforce of approximately 2,000 men in 1932, and just under half of this workforce appears to have been working on Western Heritable schemes. By October 1932, Western Heritable had been granted a subsidy of £10 15s per house for 40 years and a loan of 75% of the valuation of £383 per house; £9 of the subsidy came from the state, and £1 15s (instead of the maximum £4 10s) from Glasgow Corporation. Further Corporation reluctance and debate ensued: councillors squabbled over rent levels, in an attempt to lower Western Heritable's proposed annual rental from £32 to £30. One councillor, Bailie McSkimming, proposed that no local authority subsidy be given at all; the authority, he argued, would then be unable to 'interfere' with the rent levels for this application. By late 1932, Western Heritable's application for a further 188 flatted four-apartment houses at King's Park received only the £9 central government subsidy and a loan of two-thirds of the estimated value of £324 (approximately £60 less per house for what the Corporation believed to be 'similar' houses). (8)

The second of Western Heritable's schemes, Kelvinside, attracted further attacks in the council; in this instance, objections were levelled at the construction techniques, the value of the loans that might be made, the rent levels, and ultimately the wisdom of the local authority's approving such a scheme at all. Western Heritable did not anticipate any direct local authority subsidy; its application for the 423 'tenement houses' on Dorchester Avenue, off Great Western Road and adjoining the Mactaggart & Mickel development at Kelvinside, envisaged a central government subsidy of £9 per annum and a loan of 75% of the estimated value of £353 per house. Although the building density (19 houses per acre) was in 'conformity with the town planning scheme for that area', Corporation officials advised the members that the designs deviated from the 'methods of construction which are at present prescribed for houses to be erected with subsidy by private enterprise'. The construction actually comprised 16.5" cavity outer walls with an outer face of roughcast brick on a base of concrete blocks, and decorated with timber-framed, slate-hung oriels. The area of each house was 770 square feet, with ceiling heights of 8' and 8'6". Supported by a strong undercurrent of disapproval of this scheme, Councillor Swan argued for a 'restricted' loan of 66% of its total value, Councillor Winning proposed that the rents should be restricted to £25, and Councillors Hood and Storrie (of the Sub-committee on Sites and Buildings) urged that the entire application should be dropped. Eventually, however, permission was narrowly granted for reduced subsidy for the tenement flats: at a Corporation meeting in May 1934, 32 councillors voted for the development, and 29 for Hood's hostile amendment. (9)

Councillor Hood continued to voice his objections to Western Heritable applications, as support for private enterprise building of general-needs housing within Glasgow's city boundaries diminished. In late 1932, Hood proposed that the new subsidised private development at Cardonald for 2,512 general-needs dwellings, of which Western Heritable was to build just under half, should be abandoned, and a council scheme in the new 'Intermediate' category (midway between 'Ordinary' and 'Rehousing') should be built there instead; his proposal was only just defeated. The Cardonald project was the last all-trades contract which Mactaggart & Mickel carried out for Western Heritable, and it introduced, for the first time in Glasgow, a procedure under which private builders and property factors feued ground directly from the Corporation for the purpose of building private rented houses - a procedure already adopted in Edinburgh earlier the same year by Mactaggart & Mickel, as we will see later. In December 1931, Glasgow Corporation received offers from both Western Heritable and Glasgow Estates Development Ltd (John McDonald's new company) to feu the ground at Cardonald for the erection of four- and five-apartment houses with subsidy under the 1924 Act. A special sub-committee was set up to consider the Cardonald applications, and in May 1932 it agreed to offer Glasgow Estates Development Ltd Area No.1 (totalling 101.5 acres) and Western Heritable Area No. 2 (97 acres) on the basis of a feu of £4 per house, subsidy of £9 per house, and loan of two-thirds of the value; Western Heritable sought unsuccessfully to obtain exactly 50% of the land. Overriding objections from Hood, the project proceeded apace. In November 1932, Western Heritable employed Joseph Wilson, former consultant architect of Mactaggart & Mickel, to design the eight different house-types for use at Cardonald, including two-storey flats and terraces, the designs being rendered and embellished with thin bay windows. (10)

After various alternative layouts and allocations of ground had been discussed for the Cardonald scheme, the detailed feu agreement between the Corporation and the two companies was finalised in December 1932, one year after the initial proposal had been made. Area No.1 was divided into four sections, with each company taking two alternately placed sections, and Area No.2 was divided into two sections, with one section for each builder. In each area ground was reserved for schools, public areas and open spaces; originally both schools were in the Western Heritable area, but this was altered. In Area No.1, Western Heritable was to erect 608 and 572 houses, and Glasgow Estates Development 680 and 652 houses. It was anticipated that a quarter of these houses would be ready for occupation by November 1933, and that the two companies would then each pay an advance instalment of feu duties to the Corporation (£608 by Western Heritable, and £680 by Glasgow Estates). It was estimated that Area No.1 would be finished by May 1934, and that feu duties of £1,216 and £1,360 would then be payable; a 'like' sum was to be paid twice yearly thereafter. For Area No.2, the respective companies were to pay £1,144 and £1,304 on the anticipated completion of their 527 and 652 houses in November

1934; similarly a 'like' sum was to be paid thereafter. Throughout these year-long negotiations the valuation of the houses, for loan purposes, was reduced from £357 to £319. (11)

Despite the finalisation of the Cardonald contract, and the fact that foundation work had begun in autumn 1932, two socialist councillors, George Smith and Jean Mann, made a late attempt to block the project and, when that failed, tried to significantly increase the proposed feu duties, by nearly doubling them. Their amendment was disapproved by 56 votes to 36, but the episode further underlined the likely course of council policy should the socialist grouping win control. Once construction began, the Cardonald scheme appears to have progressed well, and by early 1933 Western Heritable was requesting permission to build more houses in areas feued for shops, the latter being moved to a site on Mosspark Drive. (12) The development was completed in late 1934.

Cardonald was the final contract that Mactaggart & Mickel carried out for Western Heritable. It was also Western Heritable's final subsidised housing scheme under the 1924 Act. The Housing (Financial Provisions)(Scotland) Act of 1933 finally put an end to Western Heritable's activities in this sector; it reduced government subsidy to £3 per house up to 30 June 1935, and after that date all subsidy was stopped. Andrew Mickel later argued (in 1945) that by abolishing the 1924 Wheatley Act private subsidy, 'the Conservative government had caused the projected building of thousands of letting houses to be abandoned'. (13) Between 1926 and 1934, Mactaggart & Mickel had built, in total, 6,042 houses for Western Heritable under the 1924 Act. Throughout this period John Mactaggart had developed the Western Heritable firm as an impressive property development, management, and maintenance organisation. Now he responded to the increasingly inimical economic-political circumstances in Glasgow by moving the emphasis of its activities to southern England, exploiting the economic recovery there. In 1935, it built luxury flats in Park Lane, London, again employing Joseph Wilson as architect; and in the late 1930s two new companies, the London Heritable Investment Company and Grove End Gardens Ltd, were formed to build and manage luxury flats in St John's Wood. Mactaggart extended his proselytising on housing and social issues to an international level, providing, for example, a memorandum on housing for President Roosevelt's advisers in 1936, and financing the building of a classical 'Peace Pavilion' (designed by Prime Minister Ramsay MacDonald's architect son Alister) at the 1938 Glasgow Empire Exhibition. (14)

Mactaggart & Mickel, of course, remained a substantial shareholder in Western Heritable until 1938. Its close involvement with that firm's activities doubtless equipped both Andrew Mickel and Jack Mactaggart with experience and knowledge of the private rented sector, which they themselves entered in 1932. Their activities in this area were equally productive; between 1932 and 1939 Mactaggart & Mickel built, in total, 3,356 houses for rent in Edinburgh, as we will see below in Part II of this chapter. Not only did contracting for Western Heritable provide capital which could be ploughed into Mactaggart & Mickel's own housebuilding ventures, but in addition, the company benefited directly, as a shareholder in Western Heritable. It is difficult to establish the exact quantity and value of these shares; the earliest Mactaggart & Mickel balance sheet traced dates from 30 April 1938, but some earlier sources indicate that Mactaggart & Mickel was keen to increase its shareholdings in the early 1930s and to remain involved in this profitable venture. In May 1931, Mactaggart & Mickel purchased from a Mrs A Campbell 500 Western Heritable £10 shares at

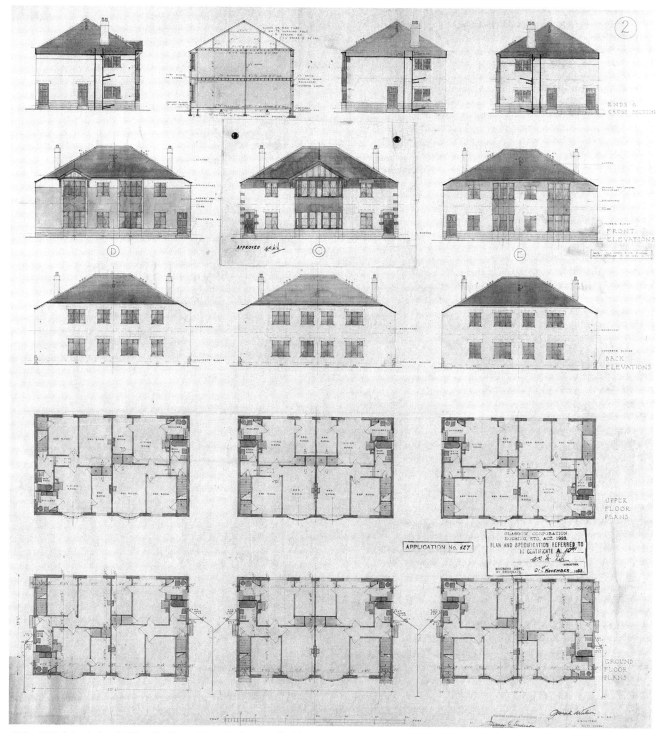

A3.3. 1932 design by Joseph Wilson for Western Heritable four-in-a-block houses at Cardonald. (MMC D33263CN)

£12 10s each (a total of £6,250). Financial dealing between the companies continued after the final contract at Cardonald; in September 1935, Mactaggart & Mickel loaned £30,000 to Western Heritable. By 30 April 1938, Mactaggart & Mickel owned 5,000 Western Heritable £10 shares; this investment appeared in the balance sheet at cost £50,312 10s (the value was £100,000 - the price paid shortly after for them by Mactaggart). The total share capital of Western Heritable at that time was £130,000; Mactaggart & Mickel therefore owned about 38.5% of the company's shares. (15)

In June 1938, the two companies were financially separated. Mactaggart & Mickel agreed to sell its 5,000 shares to Jack A Mactaggart or his 'nominees' for £100,000; the capital gain on the sale for Mactaggart & Mickel was £48,687 10s. From then

on, Western Heritable was wholly owned by the Mactaggart family (since 1971, it has been owned via Mactaggart Heritable Holdings Ltd). The mutually beneficial relationship which the two companies had fostered, in a period where both had enjoyed a monopolistic role in Glasgow, had come to an end. Western Heritable had begun to focus its activities on property development in England and, of course, property management back home; and the end of subsidised private building, and the relative boom in owner-occupation, was increasingly forcing both firms to refocus their activities and broaden their horizons in the 1930s. (16)

King's Park and Kelvinside in the 1930s
the suburban bungalow

For Mactaggart & Mickel, the first years of the 1930s, in terms of building houses for owner-occupation, were some of the most productive in the company's history. Prior to beginning the innovative Glasgow 'district' suburban developments at Merrylee Park, Linn Park and Rouken Glen in 1931, Netherlee Park in 1932, and the ambitious Carolside Park in 1934, the firm focused its own housebuilding activities on new land purchased through the ladies' syndicate at King's Park; strenuous efforts were also made to sell the remaining houses on the Kelvinside site. In demand terms, this early period witnessed more assertive selling and advertising, in an attempt to both shape and tap into prospective home-buyers' ownership aspirations. Architecturally, it saw a move away from the terraced and semi-detached two-storey designs and the introduction of the ubiquitous bungalow on a large scale. By 1934, James Taylor was appointed architectural consultant for the firm for all projects other than in Edinburgh, where Stewart Kaye was used; by around 1936, W A Gladstone was also used as an architect for some projects, and by 1939 he was listed as an in-house architect on a yearly salary of £750. In supply terms, the early 1930s also witnessed, as a result of falling labour and material costs, the revolutionary introduction of a £500 house - a three-apartment bungalow - at King's Park. Mactaggart & Mickel also made strenuous efforts to reduce building times and costs. Although two-thirds of the King's Park development was already sold before 1930, some important innovations, setting the pattern for future Mactaggart & Mickel

schemes, were introduced now in the remaining part of the area. (17)

As we saw in Chapter A2, King's Park sales had begun in 1925, with four-apartment terraced cottages selling later for as little as £620. In 1929, Mactaggart & Mickel unveiled and sold its first detached bungalow for King's Park, selling it at £650. In September 1930 its first five-apartment semi-detached bungalow, selling for £825 was built, at plot 10, Menock Road. (18) Soon after, smaller, significantly cheaper bungalows, such as three-apartment semi-detached units, were sold for £500. Within the remaining land available to it at King's Park, Mactaggart & Mickel built, advertised and sold seven different house-types (many of which were amended at a later date) between 1930 and 1934. King's Park set the pattern for the typical development of the 1930s, with its range of house-types and plans at various price levels (including semi-detached and detached bungalows, and villas). These developments were associated with a broader range of prospective buyers; now each development would have to be constantly reviewed, with new advertising angles, fresh showhouses, and keener prices (and eventually the new, amended types would have to compete with the 'second-hand' market in Mactaggart & Mickel bungalows).

The earliest existing bungalow-type designs within the Mactaggart & Mickel archive are by Joseph Wilson; these undated designs must have been prepared by Wilson prior to the termination of his contract in June 1929. As we saw above in Chapter A2, it was Wilson who designed Mactaggart & Mickel's first bungalows; the 'F' type single and double bungalows were designed specifically for King's Park. These distinctive designs were built of brick and

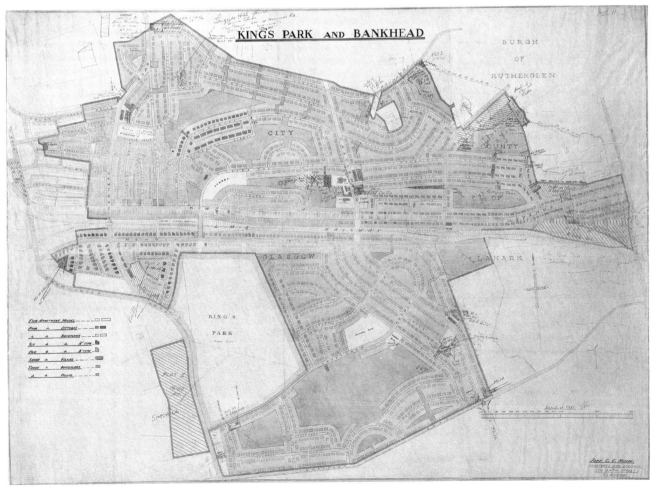

A3.4. Layout plan (as eventually executed) of c.1935 for King's Park and Bankhead developments by John C C Munro, engineer. (MMC D44975CN)

A3.5. 315-317 King's Park Avenue, King's Park; these four apartment semi-detached bungalows each sold for £650 in 1930-31. (MMC)

A3.6. Third day of construction of a demonstration bungalow in Menock Road, King's Park, in 1930. (MMC)

A3.7. The Menock Road bungalow seen on its completion, on the tenth day of construction. (MMC)

roughcast construction, with bay window and long verandas to the front; the internal arrangement consisted of two bedrooms and two public rooms. At first, between 1929 and 1931, the company concentrated mainly on building the detached version at King's Park, selling at £650, with a £30 down-payment; the semi-detached version sold for £645 in 1930. In an effort to reduce building time (and perhaps to create publicity and interest), Mactaggart & Mickel built one of Wilson's 'F' type detached bungalows on a site at Menock Road in only ten days. Douglas Mickel recorded the various stages of construction of the bungalow, but it is not known on which plot this experiment was carried out. An amended four-apartment bungalow introduced in 1932 was based on the same layout, but with the front parlour turned into a bedroom; the company promoted this through a 'startling' financial package which would entail a weekly outlay of only 26s. (19)

The 'F' type was the only bungalow at King's Park designed by an outside architect. Mactaggart & Mickel was now beginning to develop its own staff of architectural technicians, who produced all the other bungalow designs for the development using similar standards of space and amenity. The first of these in-house designed bungalows built and sold at King's Park was the five-apartment semi-detached 'H' type, built at Menock Road and selling for approximately £825, with a £95 down-payment. Walter Grieve, appointed secretary to Mactaggart & Mickel earlier in the 1920s, was one of those who bought this early bungalow-type in 1931. In early 1932 the semi-detached 'H' was relaunched, followed by the 'D' type three-apartment semi-detached bungalow, at a cost of only £500 (Mactaggart & Mickel's

cheapest house to date) with a down-payment of only £25. The first development of these very simple bungalows (which had their entrance on the side) was sold quickly from the sales office at 428 King's Park Avenue in 1930, but small 1931 amendments to the plans introduced a new wave of 'D' type bungalows. (20)

In November 1932, Mactaggart & Mickel introduced a 'startling offer' of new reduced terms for the 'D' type bungalow, 'which may never be repeated'. This involved a £25 down payment (which had, in fact, been featured previously) and a weekly outlay of 20s. This enticement immediately proved effective. By the next month only a few of the King's Park semi-detached bungalows were available for immediate occupancy, and by July 1933 only four 'D' types were left for sale. (21) Mactaggart & Mickel's King's Park advertising introduced a new element of immediacy, announcing once-only offers and providing a countdown on remaining houses. This approach was thereafter employed on all Mactaggart & Mickel developments.

In 1931, the 'E' type four-apartment semi-detached bungalow, which provided a small bedroom off the living room, was introduced. The type was to prove one of the company's most popular. This plan-feature had been employed in the four-in-a-block flats which Mactaggart & Mickel had built for Western Heritable at Cardonald and can be seen as a logical development of the bed-recess commonly favoured in the prewar modern tenements built by Mactaggart and others. These bungalows sold for £521, with a £25 down-payment and weekly outlay of 21s 6d. By 1934, the availability of cheap labour and materials had reached its 1930s peak, allowing Mactaggart & Mickel to sell the

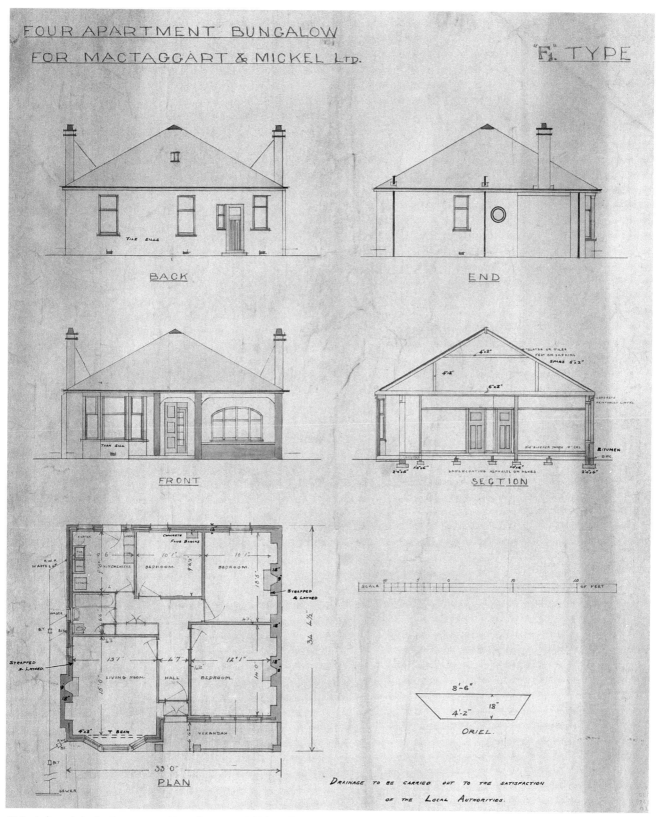

FOUR APARTMENT BUNGALOW
FOR MACTAGGART & MICKEL LTD.

"F" TYPE

BACK

END

FRONT

SECTION

PLAN

ORIEL.

DRAINAGE TO BE CARRIED OUT TO THE SATISFACTION
OF THE LOCAL AUTHORITIES.

A3.8. In-house design by the company architects for an amended 'F' type bungalow, c.1932. (MMC D39725CN)

four-apartment 'E' type at a reduced cost of £500. It is interesting to note that the three-apartment 'D' semi-detached type had cost £500 four years previously, in 1930. (22) These popular small bungalows were all sold by the end of 1934. Mactaggart & Mickel was very keen, however, to provide different price levels for prospective buyers.

In 1931, attempting to capture more affluent prospective bungalow purchasers, the company began building new and larger

'A' and 'B' type bungalows at Menock Road. The six-apartment detached 'A' type bungalow had flanking bay windows on either side of a deep inset porch. The spacious plan provided four bedrooms (one of which was in the roof-space, with a dormer window), two public rooms and a typically small kitchenette. The first 'A' was sold in early 1931 for £1,090, with a substantial down-payment of £334. The 'B' type had the same layout as the 'A', without the attic bedroom and with pared-down architectural detail. It sold for £925 with a £227 down-payment. The

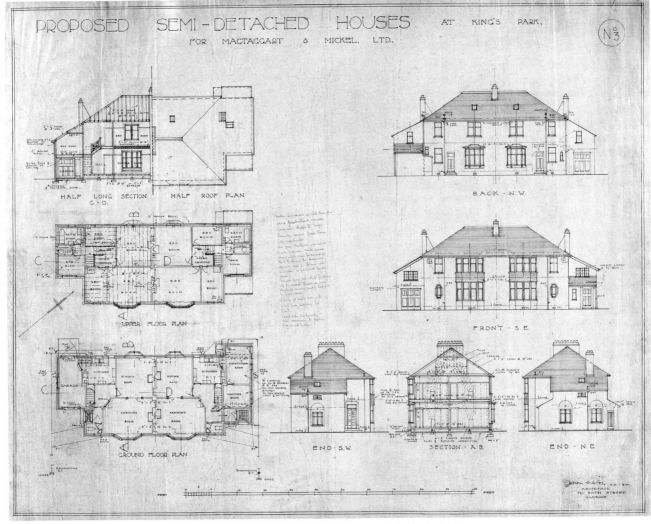

A3.9. Design by Joseph Wilson, probably in the late 1920s, for semi-detached houses at King's Park. (MMC D44723)

traditionally high-status Glasgow suburban double villa type (a large and stately kind of semi-detached pair) also featured at the King's Park development. In 1931, Mactaggart & Mickel built a small number of seven-apartment semi-detached villas with side wings at the King's Park No.3 site. Designed by Joseph Wilson, the original drawings illustrate an extremely grand double villa with large public rooms on the ground floor, and four bedrooms, box room, and linen room on the first floor; the wing on one villa included a garage, and that on the other villa a doctor's consulting room and waiting room. In 1931, a small number of villas built to this general design sold for £1,275, with a down-payment of £370, but by 1933 the three remaining 'ultra-modern' villas of this type at the corner of Aikenhead and Carmunnock Roads, with four bedrooms and a maid's room, were being advertised as requiring only £100 cash deposit. Mactaggart & Mickel also employed William Ross to design a four-apartment double villa for planned use at King's Park in 1931, and a four-apartment terraced villa with the same layout in 1934; the public rooms and bedroom of this design were roomy and high-ceilinged. By late 1934 (with the assistance of a number of repetitive 'countdown' press advertising campaigns), Mactaggart & Mickel had successfully sold all its existing houses on the King's Park site. A clubhouse was designed for the estate by James Taylor and built in the early 1930s. (23)

A cost calculations booklet for King's Park in the company archives, dating from 1931-33, gives a more detailed insight into the actual yearly cost of home ownership for Mactaggart & Mickel's house-types. At King's Park, the cheapest bungalow in

1931, the 'D' type, cost £500, with a cash down-payment of £25; a loan of £493 over a period of 25 years was required, and the assessed notional rental was £25. Yearly outgoings would include £4 5s for feu duty, £35 10s for interest and repayment, £12 13s 2d for owners' rates and taxes, and 7s 6d for insurance. The most expensive bungalow, the six-apartment 'A', costing £1,090, required a £334 cash payment, a total loan of £756 over a period of 23 years and three months; its notional rental was £48-£52, and annual expenditure included £8 15s for feu duty, £58 10s for interest and repayment, £14 2s 7d for rates and taxes, and 16s for insurance. Seen in the light of these figures, the demand of some Glasgow councillors for an £8 feu duty for the four-apartment Cardonald Western Heritable houses appears a little confrontational!

The Kelvinside scheme of the early 1930s was clearly a survival from the late 1920s era of subsidised housing for sale under the 1923 Act. As we saw in Chapter A2, the pre-1930 developments at Kelvinside had consisted of five-apartment terrace houses, designed by James Taylor, which sold for £775 and £835; by 1930 their prices had risen to £820 and £860. In June 1930, designs were prepared for substantial semi-detached houses at Kelvinside, and a showhouse was built at 46 Manchester Avenue. By September 1930 only three of these five-apartment 'Beautiful Homes at Kelvinside' were left for sale. For the first time, Mactaggart & Mickel's advertising directly targeted the rented sector in an attempt to lure them into home ownership: 'If you are paying from £60 to £70 in rent and taxes, you can get better value!' With 'a cash payment of £50 and total annual cost of

£80, including ALL rates and taxes, feu-duty, interest, and repayment of loan', the prospective renter was urged to reconsider. However, the middle class social aspirations associated with the traditionally exclusive 19th-century west-end suburbs, such as Hyndland, clearly had an effect on housing costs and rates in the newly emerging 1930s owner-occupied schemes in that part of the city. This was presumably also the case with the rented sector. Not only did Mactaggart & Mickel build two of its most expensive villas of the early 1930s at Kelvinside (seven-apartment villas, which sold for £1,400 in late 1930), but its newly introduced bungalow at Kelvinside cost significantly more than if it had been built at King's Park. The firm's new six-apartment detached bungalow at Kelvinside (the majority of which were sold by autumn 1930) cost £1,180, whereas the same house-type at King's Park cost almost £100 less; in addition the rates and taxes at Kelvinside were double those at King's Park. To buy a six-apartment Mactaggart & Mickel bungalow in 1930 involved a yearly outlay of £123 4s at Kelvinside, but only £82 4s 4d at King's Park. (24) The high owner occupier rates at Kelvinside may have discouraged Mactaggart & Mickel from further development on this site in the 1930s, although work for Western Heritable was continuing on the adjacent site.

During the early 1930s Mactaggart & Mickel increasingly, but not exclusively, tried to exploit and enhance the demand for bungalows in the £500-£650 price range. With affordable loans, this price range could realistically tempt those who could afford to buy, away from renting. Taxes, rates and loans, of course, had to be accordingly low for Mactaggart & Mickel to achieve this at an acceptable profit level. For this purpose, and to exploit cheaper land and escape the increasing bias of Glasgow Corporation against private housing in allocation of sites and in the high level of rates, the company began, in the early 1930s, to focus its activities on new suburban sites outwith the Glasgow city boundary.

To understand the significance of Mactaggart & Mickel's early innovations at King's Park, Kelvinside, and the new Glasgow suburban schemes (discussed below), we must first set this boom in the context of its home ownership building activities and the growing consumer popularity of the low-cost bungalow-type house. By 1933, in terms of supply, building materials were cheaper and more plentiful, and building workers' wages were at their lowest, since the outbreak of World War I. Mactaggart & Mickel's bungalow at Menock Road, King's Park, which was built in ten days, and the introduction of its low-cost 'D' type bungalow for £500, clearly illustrated a substantial cut in costs from the late 1920s, and highlighted the suitability of the bungalow-type to exploit increasingly cheap materials and labour. In addition to this, the emerging building societies of the 1930s were, in conjunction with large-scale speculative builders, offering favourable loans and for the first time providing a realistic financial option to renting, in terms of weekly outlay. (25) The pre-arranged house-purchasing loan agreement between builders and building societies offered to prospective buyers became known as the 'pool system'. Mactaggart & Mickel exploited this opportunity and established such a system in 1932, initially in relation to the Netherlee Park scheme.

The circumstances surrounding demand for home ownership in general, and for the bungalow type in particular, were more complex and contradictory than implied above. In the early 1930s, it was clearly difficult for the speculative builder to measure popular taste or the housing preferences of prospective house-buyers. And as explained in the previous chapter, there was continuing uncertainty in Scotland about the balance of perceived advantage between buying and renting. Recent research by Annette O'Carroll has suggested that a mixture of favourable financial circumstances in the early 1930s, including falling building costs, a rise in real wages, and building society loans allowed, for the first time, certain socio-economic groups (skilled manual workers and medium-grade white-collar workers) to buy their own home. However, only the best-paid skilled manual workers in steady employment could have afforded to purchase even the cheapest house in the mid-1930s (£475 in Edinburgh), and purchasing a house at £650 would have proven extremely difficult for most manual workers. O'Carroll argues that owner occupation was not considered an especially superior or high status tenure between the wars, nor was it considered more appropriate for white-collar workers than for manual workers. Rather, modernity and location were deciding factors which determined whether those who could afford to buy chose a new home or a good quality rented house in the public or private sector. (26)

Mactaggart & Mickel was, however, increasingly targeting and actively pursuing prospective buyers away from the rented sector. Initially this took the form of securing financially reasonable weekly outlays (with the assistance of the pool system) and cheaper houses for those who could afford to buy. As the new suburbs at Merrylee Park and Carolside Park opened up, prospective buyers were offered free legal fees and removal, and ultra-modern amenities. At the same time, Mactaggart & Mickel exploited the widespread anti-landlordism on Clydeside by campaigning against the supposedly selfish and neglectful landlord, emphasising the merits of ownership for the prospective owner and his/her family. This theme was reinforced later in the decade by propaganda advocating the open, civilised surroundings and activities of the suburb, as compared with the dense congested inner city. In exactly the same way that the socialist advocates of public housing attacked the old landlords and argued for modern, healthy housing schemes set in greenery, so equally Mactaggart & Mickel used the same general ideas as a way of tapping into, and trying to exaggerate, a status distinction between home ownership and renting; the firm's advertising and marketing strategies throughout the 1930s, as we will see, highlight this point. Both 'capitalist' and 'socialist' housing of the 20th century shared an opposition to 19th-century free-market housing, which they attacked as an obsolete muddle.

The housing tenure path followed by one surviving original King's Park resident highlights the progression from local authority general-needs housing towards home ownership in the early 1930s. Mrs Dorothy Young moved as a young child to King's Park in late 1930 with her parents. Her father had previously been a sales representative for the *Daily Express* in Edinburgh; the young married couple had 'progressed' from a three-roomed Corporation house in the early 1920s to their first owner-occupied house at 67 Boswall Drive in 1927. Dorothy Young did not recall 'feeling any better or grander' than those who lived in municipal housing at that time, but there was a marked sense of 'moving up in the world' when her parents purchased a bungalow at King's Park in Glasgow. Originally, her mother had had her hopes set on buying the six-apartment 'B' type showhouse on Menock Road, but it was thought too costly at over £900; she settled for a £645 four-apartment bungalow at 64 Kingslynn Drive. Despite the premature death of Dorothy's father in 1933, the purchase of the bungalow, according to Dorothy Young, was never 'financially difficult for the family'. (27)

Increasingly, the company attempted to emphasise the differences between its houses and council general-needs schemes. That task was made easier by the Housing (Financial Provisions) (Scotland)

WHOSE KEY DO YOU CARRY IN YOUR POCKET..

YOUR OWN OR YOUR LANDLORD'S

Are you whiling away the years in a home owned by another man? A home which, even if you stay in it for 20-25 years, will be no more your own than it is now? Are you handing a considerable portion of your hard-earned income to a landlord for a house that will always just be on loan?
If you are, then study the proposition offered by Mactaggart & Mickel. Give due consideration to the points which made you first decide on a flat, then consider the advantages of one of the modern type Bungalows or Villas. You will find that a Mactaggart & Mickel home offers you everything you have now and lots more, with the added advantage that you stop paying rent and start investing in Home Ownership.
Study the figures set out below—then come and see the Show Houses this week-end.
Remember, missive time is drawing near. Now is your opportunity to make a fresh start.

Silverknowes
DAVIDSON'S MAINS

4-APARTMENT DETACHED BUNGALOWS
A total deposit of £50, payable £25 down and £25 upon occupancy, secures possession, and the inclusive weekly outlay is only 25/-. Also Villas at £605 (22/2 per week) and £700.

HOW TO GET THERE
S.M.T. or Corporation 'Bus from Hope St. Post Office (West End) to Craigcrook Rd. or Davidson's Mains Cross respectively. Trains from Caledonian Station (L.M.S.) to Davidson's Mains. The journey only takes 12 minutes from Princes Street.

Hillpark Estate
CRAIGCROOK

A fine, picturesque estate of distinguished Villas, each designed with due regard to the amenities of the setting. These Homes are priced from £1000 to £1300, which includes road charges.

HOW TO GET THERE
S.M.T. or Corporation 'Buses from Hope Street Post Office (West End) to Craigcrook Rd., or Davidson's Mains Cross respectively. Trains from Caledonian Station (L.M.S.) to Davidson's Mains.

SHOW HOUSES FURNISHED BY BINNS LTD., PRINCES STREET, EDINBURGH.
SHOW HOUSES OPEN DAILY, Including Sunday, from 12 noon till Dusk.

MACTAGGART & MICKEL LTD.
67, YORK PLACE   EDINBURGH
TELEPHONE 21717

A3.10. *1938 advertisement for Silverknowes and Hillpark developments in Edinburgh, exploiting hostility to landlords of rented houses. (Edinburgh Evening News, 28.1.1938; MMC)*

(opposite) A3.11. *1939 advertisement for the 'sunny sites' at Carolside Park and Orchard Park. (Bulletin, 26 June 1939; MMC)*

Act 1933, which ended government support for general needs housing and channelled public housing into slum clearance. The task of differentiation was more complex in the case of the high-amenity general-needs housing built by councils prior to that. As early as 1932, Mactaggart & Mickel had begun to call King's Park an 'estate' (with all the aristocratic and elite urban residential connotations of that term) rather than 'scheme'. Mactaggart & Mickel directly targeted Mosspark and Knightswood residents as potential house-buyers through mail-shots in 1935; this proved successful and an increasingly significant number of Mosspark residents moved into Mactaggart & Mickel bungalows in the mid to late 1930s. By the mid-1930s Mactaggart & Mickel's estates were also attracting house-buyers from the rented properties owned by Western Heritable at King's Park, particularly to Carolside Park. It was the introduction of the low-cost modern bungalows in the owner-occupied sector which provided the most arresting distinction. Despite the generally middle class character of the first residents of Mosspark and other early 'Ordinary' council schemes in Glasgow, it would appear that by the early 1930s the prospective lower-middle class house-buyer was beginning to associate the simplified cottage-style house and sweeping garden-city layouts of much 1920s general-needs council housing with a subtly lower social status. From the early 1930s, home-buyers increasingly wanted their prospective houses to be visually distinct from council housing. (28) The showhouse and its on-site sales team was crucial in gauging these subtle changes in public taste and aspirations. Mactaggart & Mickel could also look to the success of earlier small bungalow developments, such as James Miller's at Blackhall, Edinburgh (1927).

Various theories have been expounded about the interwar popularity of the bungalow in Scotland; in addition to the visual difference from 1920s cottage housing, the popularity of the suburban bungalow has been attributed to its quasi-rural context, and its class associations with country or holiday residences. At a practical level, however, there were also strong links of convenience and convention between the bungalow and the traditional tenement. The single-storey bungalow was, of course, on one level, and resembled the compact planning of the tenement form; arguably the massive, bay-windowed bungalow of the interwar period was a continuation of the tenement flat in a 'separated rather than stacked form'. (29)

Mactaggart & Mickel's building and advertising activities of the early 1930s, as we will see, supported both of these theories. Initially, the key selling strength of its bungalows was modernity, and although the planning of these new houses strongly echoed the centralised, compact layout of the tenements (including, in the case of the 'E' type bungalow at King's Park, a small room like a bed recess, leading off the living room), it was above all through modern bathrooms and 'kitchenettes' that the prospective buyer was tempted. By the mid-1930s, Mactaggart & Mickel was urging prospective buyers to consider the health benefits of moving out of the city, into the clean air of the suburb and an ultra-modern Mactaggart & Mickel bungalow or villa. These dwellings would perpetuate the convenience of single-storey living with modern conveniences, but in the salubrious and spacious setting of the suburb.

The layouts of the new estates played a less important role in differentiating them from council schemes. In fact, they were very similar to the garden-suburb plans of the Ordinary schemes, although in a slightly more simplified form, avoiding culs-de-sac in favour of through roads. The southern suburbs, especially King's Park and Merrylee Park, consisted of fairly steeply graded

TO THE CITY.... *and smoke and grime!*

To THE COUNTRY... *and Health and Cleanliness!*

WHICH SHALL IT BE?
Mactaggart & Mickel have built magnificent homes in the country which cost no more than the rented flat in the city. They have fitted them with every conceivable convenience and modern labour-saving idea. These homes are situated amidst magnificent suburban surroundings—and all around is fresh air, sunshine, and cleanliness, yet they are only 15 minutes from the heart of Glasgow.

Remember, your Mactaggart and Mickel home calls for no greater outlay than your present rent. At Orchard Park the total weekly outlay is only 18/10—at Carolside Park 23/6 per week covers all expenses, and in each case a small initial deposit secures the house.

HOW TO GET TO CAROLSIDE PARK
These houses are well served by frequent 'buses, trains, and tram to Clarkston Terminus, and S.M.T. run a service from Clyde Street right into the Estate.

HOW TO GET TO ORCHARD PARK
The Estate is at the foot of Orchard Drive, off Kilmarnock Road. A Corporation 'bus, or tram, an S.M.T. 'bus, or train to Giffnock Station will take you within 2 minutes of the site.

SEE THE SUNNY SITES AT

CAROLSIDE PARK CLARKSTON **ORCHARD PARK ESTATE** GIFFNOCK

MACTAGGART & MICKEL Ltd.
63-65 BATH STREET, GLASGOW, C.2
TELEPHONE - DOUGLAS ONE

sites, for which irregular contoured layouts, employing cut-and-fill construction methods, were the most economical solution, in view of the company's lack of heavy earthmoving plant. (30)

Suburbs beyond the city
Merrylee Park, Linn Park, Rouken Glen, Netherlee Park and Carolside Park

Merrylee Park was the first in a succession of new large-scale suburban home-ownership sites developed by Mactaggart & Mickel in the 1930s; it was preceded only by the small development at Linn Park. Over a period of only two years the firm built and sold 479 houses on this site; from mid-1931 to the end of 1932, the site generated total sales of £275,460. It was at Merrylee Park that Mactaggart & Mickel's advertising and marketing techniques were refined into their most mature and effective form; in June 1931 the company proudly announced a new (world) record in house sales. As a result, Merrylee Park provided an immensely significant test-bed for future Mactaggart & Mickel home-ownership schemes of the 1930s. (31)

The Merrylee Park site fell outwith Glasgow City boundaries and within the jurisdiction of the Renfrew County Council's First (or Upper) District. This move outside the city was prompted by a complex mixture of financial and organisational factors. Although Glasgow Corporation was increasingly opposed to funding private enterprise housing (as Western Heritable's experience showed in its 1930s schemes at King's Park and Kelvinside), Mactaggart & Mickel could not have realistically hoped to obtain substantially more favourable subsidies by looking to another housing authority. But the generous subsidies offered under the 1923 Housing Act were, as outlined in the previous chapter, being gradually reduced prior to their abandonment by central and local government under the 1933 Housing (Financial Provisions) (Scotland) Act. In late 1927, Glasgow Corporation had altered private builders' eligibility for 1923 Act subsidies: only houses costing £750 or under would receive subsidy. Mactaggart & Mickel hurried through the approvals for the remaining housing at King's Park and Kelvinside. The Housing (Revision of Contributions) Act of 1929 further revised 1923 subsidies, reducing them in line with falling building costs. By early 1930, only houses costing £600 or under were eligible for the reduced subsidy.

Local authorities could manage these declining subsidies with some freedom, and the landward authorities around Glasgow did so in a more builder-friendly manner than Glasgow Corporation. In 1931, at the time of Mactaggart & Mickel's first applications for subsidy at Linn Park and Merrylee Park, Renfrew County Council was operating a 'District Committees Scheme', which aimed to assist the provision of houses by private enterprise under the 1923 and 1924 Housing Acts, by providing a neat lump sum grant of £100 per house after completion; no loans were offered. The council kept a running total of houses being built in the county under this subsidy; by March 1932, 304 certificates had been granted for 2,790 houses; 958 were completed and 496 were under construction. (32) The lengthy procedures of house-type approval and housing evaluation, which were inherent in the approval of grants and loans by Glasgow Corporation, were absent in the county. Mactaggart & Mickel, and fellow builders such as John Lawrence, and James Y Keanie Ltd of Johnstone, obtained subsidies on a regular basis, from an authority aiming to maximise private enterprise building, and this applied once again in the case of Merrylee Park.

Preparations for the new site at Merrylee Park began in spring 1931; Mactaggart & Mickel initially applied for county approval for 32 bungalow-type houses and associated sewers at Kilmarnock Road, Giffnock, established the entrance to the site between Braidholm Road and Kilmarnock Road, and finalised the first house-type in April that year. The new 'G' type four-apartment semi-detached bungalow, which sold for £555 and a down-payment of £25, was to provide Mactaggart & Mickel with its biggest marketing coup to date. The first bungalow, at 24 Briarlee Drive, was sold in June 1931. The semi-detached 'G' type dominated the Merrylee Park scheme, and further applications were made to the county for approximately 300 of them during the summer and autumn of 1931. Throughout 1931, construction of roads, sewers and houses proceeded apace. The steam digger employed at King's Park was also utilised at Merrylee Park to speed up activity; the county council instructed Mactaggart & Mickel to connect the machine to a metered water supply at the height of its activity, and by November 1931 Mactaggart & Mickel had applied for water mains throughout the entire scheme. Sales were buoyant throughout 1931, and by early 1933 all of the first section of Merrylee Park was sold. (33)

The success and speedy sale of these low-cost bungalows at Merrylee Park was heavily reliant on advertising and marketing. On Friday 26 June 1931, Mactaggart & Mickel, according to the popular newspaper *The Bulletin*, displayed a new 'Originality in Bungalow Salesmanship' by erecting a 'specimen of their four roomed "super" bungalow' as a showhouse and sales office at Eglinton Toll, Glasgow: it claimed that 'such an advertising at a busy crossing is unique.' The showhouse, as explained, was extremely important for the 1930s speculative builder. Not only could the popularity of the specific house-type be measured, but more general owner-occupier preferences and aspirations could be gauged; the opening of a showhouse 'in the heart of one of the city's busiest traffic ways' was, of course, a shrewd marketing ploy. Mactaggart & Mickel again deployed this marketing tool in 1934 when it erected another, similar showhouse in Central Station, Glasgow. The Eglinton Toll showhouse was an unprecedented success for Mactaggart & Mickel, and the company made sure that fact was not lost on the citizens of Glasgow! Following the opening of the showhouse on Friday, 26 June 1934, there was 'a tremendous rush of visitors from all parts' to see the 'bungalow home of unique charm and distinction' with its 'little trim gardens of colourful flowers'. As a result, over 130 houses were sold in an 'actual working time of 24 hours'. Mactaggart & Mickel announced events as a 'World Record in House Sales'. The Eglinton Toll site was closed three years later in May 1934. The 'G' type was redecorated, reopened, and repromoted throughout this period, and was replaced by the 'famous' Netherlee Park type 'K' house in August 1934. (34)

Prospective buyers were encouraged to visit the Merrylee Park site and partake in an 'amazing financial proposition'. Merrylee Park was hailed by Mactaggart & Mickel, through extensive advertising, as 'the only all-in-one house purchase scheme in Scotland'. In an attempt to strip away the complicated and off-putting aspects of house buying, which may have prejudiced those accustomed to the private rented sector, Mactaggart & Mickel offered a simple down-payment of £25, no road charges, no legal fees, free removal, and estimated a weekly outlay of 21s for the 'G' type bungalow at Merrylee Park. In addition, Mactaggart & Mickel urged on prospective buyers that building costs were likely to rise; this, it argued, would inevitably increase house costs. Mactaggart & Mickel also began, for the first time, to focus its advertising towards particular professions and groups of individuals. The Merrylee Park 'all-in-one house purchase scheme'

ORIGINALITY IN BUNGALOW SALESMANSHIP

The bungalow erected at Eglinton Toll, Glasgow, by Mactaggart and Mickel, Ltd., as a specimen of their four-roomed " super " bungalows at Merrylee Park, Newlands. Such an advertising building at a busy crossing is unique. An announcement on another page gives details of the company's house purchase scheme.

A3.12. Semi-detached bungalow showhouse at Eglinton Toll, Glasgow, in 1931 (Bulletin, 27 June 1931; Glasgow Herald; MMC)

was advertised in the *Scottish Educational Journal* in January 1933; in the two months following the advertisement, seven teachers bought bungalows at Merrylee Park. Making house purchasing simpler and economically more viable attracted growing numbers of purchasers from general-needs council housing schemes; throughout 1931 and 1932 skilled manual workers (plumbers, electricians) and white-collar workers from Mosspark, Knightswood and Riddrie, bought low-cost four-apartment semi-detached bungalows at Merrylee Park. By November 1932, only eleven 'G' type bungalows were left for sale. Mactaggart & Mickel proclaimed that 'over 500 hundred of these wonderful bungalows' had been sold already in the last year at Merrylee Park and Rouken Glen (see below): 'It may prove the finest investment you have ever made, as well as providing you with a home of singular charm and distinction'. (35)

The increasing amount of money Mactaggart & Mickel allocated to advertising throughout the 1930s bears witness to advertisements' central role in attracting buyers. In 1927

Mactaggart & Mickel was spending 1% of its total yearly sales on advertising. By 1932 this had increased to nearly 10%; between January and December 1932, £1,000 was spent on advertising, while total sales were £120,294. During the early 1930s, Mactaggart & Mickel shrewdly enlisted the services of 'one of the great pioneering advertising firms of Scotland': Peter A Menzies Advertising Ltd. Peter A Menzies, described as 'a giant of the old school', had formed his own company in 1904 in a one-room office at 54 Gordon Street, following a brief period as a junior with one of Scotland's first advertising agencies, C P Watson; the company subsequently moved to 111 Bath Street, and is today based at 2 Newton Place, Glasgow. Peter Menzies, who often wore full Highland dress (Menzies tartan, of course), developed a highly successful family-run business at a transitional and opportunistic time for advertising. In the late 19th century, advertising agents existed solely as agents for newspapers, who sold space to prospective advertisers in column inches, and in turn received commission from the paper. By the early decades of the 20th century, advertising agencies began to establish

A3.13. 1930s photograph of Peter A Menzies. (DMS Menzies Advertising)

themselves as businesses in their own right. The 1930s witnessed a flourishing in the creativity and imagination of these agencies. Peter Menzies was joined by a future partner, James E Hastings, in 1928, and by R N MacDonald Menzies in the 1930s. The firm was a founder member of the Glasgow Advertising Agents' Association, which 'set their own ethical standards', and served as a precursor to the Institute of Practitioners in Advertising. Menzies's clients included the financially lucrative 1930s account with 'Paterson's Clensel', and Henry Boot Ltd, builders. (36) Its most creative attributed work for Mactaggart & Mickel was produced for the Orchard Park and Broom estates in the mid to late 1930s, but it is probable that all the latter's advertising in the 1930s was provided by them, including the early promotional material for Merrylee Park.

Although the first development at Merrylee Park did not have the extensive variety of house-types found at King's Park, a number of other bungalow-types were introduced. In June 1931, the first of 42 'F' type detached bungalows was sold at Thornlea Drive. This Wilson design, which was so popular at King's Park, sold here for £650 with a down-payment of £36 16s. Although the selling price was above the £600 limit for 1923 Act subsidy, Mactaggart & Mickel nevertheless appear to have received a £100 county council grant for each of these bungalows. The 'new' five-apartment semi-detached 'H' type bungalow (which had been introduced at King's Park in 1931) sold here for £830 and £95 12s down (and an annual outlay of £70), the first example being at 2 Ashlea Drive. For cost reasons, the 'H' did not receive any subsidy from the county council. Only two other non-subsidised houses were built at Merrylee Park: the exclusive 'B' type five-apartment detached bungalows at 25 and 27 Merrylee Avenue; these sold for £925 and a down-payment of £227 16s. (37)

All in all, Mactaggart & Mickel was awarded £38,000 in subsidies under the District Committees Scheme, after completion of the Merrylee Park site in early 1933. Relations with the county council were less harmonious concerning the adoption of estate roads as public highways; the firm unsuccessfully pressed the County Roads Surveyor to adopt some roads prior to their completion. (38)

Two small southern suburban estates were developed at the same time as Merrylee Park: Linn Park and Rouken Glen. Linn Park, which consisted of 52 bungalows on a six-acre site at Oakley Drive and Linn Drive, was begun in the autumn of 1930. Utilising the bungalow-types built at King's Park, Mactaggart & Mickel applied for £100 grants from Renfrew County Council for 26 'D' type, 24 'E' semi-detached type, and two 'F' type detached bungalows. In return for consent to build, Mactaggart & Mickel had to give the county a 'necessary undertaking that the development would not go on unless the subsidy was forthcoming'. The first bungalow was sold in November 1930, and by early 1931 all had been were sold; the firm received a total local authority grant of £52,000 in late 1931. The smaller estate at Rouken Glen, Thornliebank, was started in summer 1931. Mactaggart & Mickel applied for Renfrew County Council grants for 46 houses, and built both 'G' and 'J' type four-apartment semi-detached bungalows, which sold for £555 and a £25 down-payment. In marketing terms, the Rouken Glen 'G' bungalows benefited vicariously from the extensive Merrylee Park advertising campaign, and, of course, the Eglinton Toll showhouse. A similar 'all-inclusive' sales deal (including free removal and legal fees) also attracted a number of purchasers from 1920s local authority housing schemes, towards this 'amazing proposition'. The first bungalow was sold in March 1932; by October that year only 18 houses remained unsold; by the new year the whole scheme was sold, with accumulated sales revenue of £25,530. (39)

The Netherlee Park scheme, which began in spring 1932, was important in the history of Mactaggart & Mickel for several reasons. It was the last state-subsidised scheme under the 1923 Housing Act (a fact which Mactaggart & Mickel tried to turn to its own advantage); it introduced the mutually beneficial pool system of financing loans for house-buyers; and it was the first outer suburban scheme to offer purchasers markedly lower owners' rates and taxes. In addition, Mactaggart & Mickel exploited every potential marketing and advertising angle to lure prospective purchasers away from renting. Perhaps anticipating the imminent withdrawal of state subsidy, Mactaggart & Mickel made a large-scale application for consent and subsidy to Renfrew County Council in January 1932; the project was to comprise 353 bungalows of four apartments and either 880 or 816 square feet floor space, and eight three-apartment bungalows of 700 square feet, on new roads off Clarkston Road. In the event only 342, rather than 361, were built and sold on the site over a three-year period; the first 'K' type bungalow, at 15 Netherburn Avenue, was sold in August 1932, and by early 1935 Netherlee Park sales had totalled £215,095. (40)

Netherlee Park primarily consisted of four bungalow house-types, although a small number of larger bungalow-types were built in late 1934. The scheme opened triumphantly with the new 'K' detached bungalow. This had, in fact, been designed by Joseph Wilson in the late 1920s, but that had no bearing on the way it was presented in the company's marketing as a triumph of modernity. Selling at £675 with a £50 down-payment (and a weekly outlay of 26s), this compact bungalow utilised the roof space, as had the 'A' type bungalow in Menock Road, to provide an extra bedroom. The 'K', at Netherlee Park, was marketed as a

When carpets get that worn and lifeless look give them a rub over with one or two tablespoonfuls of Paterson's Clensel in one pint of luke-warm water using a soft cloth wrung out in this solution. See how the colours are restored as if by magic.

PATERSON'S CLENSEL TO REVIVE FADED COLOURS

WHATEVER THE SHADE — WHATEVER THE MATERIAL

RENOVATE WITH CLENSEL

No matter how soiled and dirty your garments become . . . . whether suit or costume . . . blouse or jumper . . . Clensel will quickly and economically make them like new, provided the colours are fast.

SOLD EVERY.WHERE.   1/- LARGE BOTTLE.   7½d. HALF-SIZE BOTTLE.

SEE OVERLEAF

A3.14. Peter A Menzies' other main client of the 1930s, cleaning firm Paterson's Clensel, was also focused on the domestic market. (DMS Menzies Advertising)

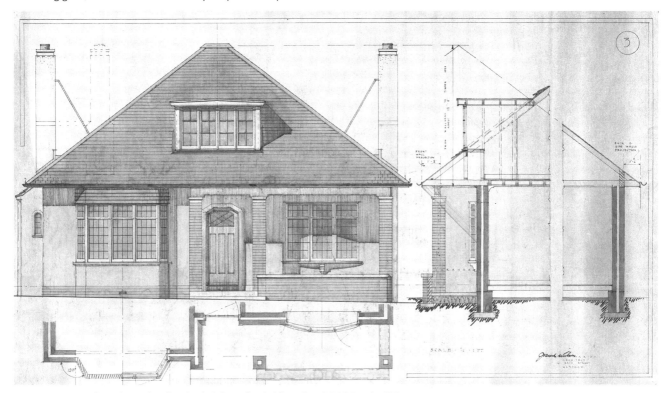

A3.15. Late 1920s design by Joseph Wilson for the 'K' type detached bungalow. (MMC D39699CN)

house which combined up-to-the-minute mod cons with visual individuality. Promoted as 'The House that the Housewife Built', it introduced a more 'spacious' kitchenette design than Mactaggart & Mickel's 1930s bungalow designs, and the new feature of a dining alcove. The Netherlee Park advertisements argued that 'for too long now the housewife has had to adapt herself to the home instead of the home being adapted to her needs'; over 5,000 housewives had been asked to give 'their views on the Ideal Home', and the 'self-contained' 'K' type was 'the result'. Its external ornamentation would individualise the house 'as surely as if it had been specially built for you': leaded windows gave 'a charming effect in keeping with the rustic brick exterior', while the spacious verandah provided 'a pleasant spot for sunny days in the suburbs, and a feature which lends character and dignity to the frontage.' Prospective purchasers were invited to 'choose their own site for erection' at Netherlee Park, but only after visiting the Eglinton Toll showhouse, which would, they claimed, 'delight every house-proud woman'. The assistance of the traditional wage-earner was enlisted, too: 'Husbands! Tell your wives to go and see the housewives' ideal house'. The 'K' showhouse at Eglinton Toll, of which, Mactaggart & Mickel claimed, there were 'many imitations, but no equal', provided £6,750 in sales in its first week, and the type continued to sell well throughout 1933 and 1934. The Eglinton Toll house was closed in May 1934, and by then only a few 'K' types were left for sale. (41)

One new bungalow-type ('J'), and two tested types ('G' and 'F') quickly followed the introduction of the 'K' type. The semi-detached four-apartment 'J', with its attic room, was also a late 1920s Wilson design. (42) The four-apartment, semi-detached 'G', which had provided Mactaggart & Mickel with its record sales at Merrylee Park, was introduced in September 1932. Both semis sold for £555, with a down-payment of £40 which included legal fees, and had a weekly outlay of 22s 6d. Showhouses were quickly built on-site; by the end of 1932 the company boasted that its 'range' at Netherlee Park provided the 'finest proposition in the housing market today'. The detached 'F' type, Mactaggart & Mickel's first bungalow design, was introduced to Netherlee Avenue in early 1933 and sold throughout 1934 and 1935 for

£650, with a down-payment of £50, and weekly payments of 25s. (43)

Alongside the marketing of these four bungalow-types, which highlighted their individuality and modern amenities, broader advertising campaigns, which focused on contemporary housing issues, were also employed. Mactaggart & Mickel worked hard to exploit public awareness of certain key housing issues, such as the removal of state subsidies, anti-landordism, and the growth of the interwar suburbs. Mactaggart & Mickel's advertising at Netherlee Park focused not on competition with other builders, but on encouraging those who were renting to buy instead - a situation which was to change in the late 1930s. In February 1932, the firm produced a circular which tried to turn the potentially financially damaging removal of state subsidy to marketing advantage. It warned that 'soon you will be receiving a notice from your landlord asking you to retake your flat', and advised tenants to 'read this letter carefully ... Since the introduction of the new housing bill all subsidies on houses built for sale have been withdrawn ... [and] even those houses which were granted subsidy may not receive subsidy unless built and completed before 30 September this year. As the whole of the subsidy on our houses has always been passed on to our new purchasers by deducting it from the actual cost of the house, we will have no option but to increase the selling price of our houses to the value of the subsidy when state aid withdrawn'. 'What does this mean to you?' Mactaggart & Mickel asked rhetorically. The firm argued that a house worth £650, on which subsidy could be in the region of £50-£100, would cost the purchaser £50-£100 more after September, and that as a result, 'if you order your house now in time for us to complete by September, you may save £100 on the deal ... there is not much time to lose'. (44) Five houses were sold as a result of the circular, which cost £13 to produce.

To enhance forward sales of the 200 newly released bungalow sites at Netherlee Park, a further circular was sent which again

(opposite) A3.16. 1932 advertisement for Netherlee Park Estate, featuring the 'K' bungalow. (Daily Record, 17 August 1932; MMC)

THE HOUSE THAT THE HOUSEWIFE BUILT!

For too long now the housewife has had to adapt herself to the home instead of the home being adapted to her needs. Realising this, *we asked over 5000 Glasgow Housewives to give us their views on* the Ideal Home, and this New 4-Apartment Self-Contained Bungalow is the result. Every feature which was in popular demand has been embodied — at last a moderate price will purchase a house that will meet your every requirement as surely as if it had been specially built for you.

FIVE OF THE NEW FEATURES IN THIS MOST ORIGINAL HOUSE:—

- **LEADED WINDOWS** give a charming effect in keeping with the rustic brick exterior.

- **DINING ALCOVE IN KITCHENETTE.** A new innovation providing a small dining-table which folds up to the wall when not in use. Mothers will understand how handy this is for children's meals.

- **SPACIOUS VERANDAH.** A pleasant spot for sunny days in the suburbs, and a feature which lends character and dignity to the frontage.

- **LARGE SITTING-ROOM** with **INGLE-NOOK FIREPLACE** and fireside seats. A room of unusual charm and distinction.

- **TWO FULL-SIZED BEDROOMS.** One for those who prefer to sleep upstairs.

Space forbids a more detailed account of the many interesting points of this house. Sufficient to say that it will be Painted, Papered and Decorated to your own taste and everything is just as it should be. You may choose your own site for erection in the beautiful suburb of Netherlee Park.

TO BE BUILT AT NETHERLEE PARK CLARKSTON ROAD

£50

DOWN INCLUDES

LEGAL FEES
ROAD CHARGES
FREE REMOVAL
THE ONLY
CASH PAYMENT

26/- PER WEEK COMPLETES PURCHASE AND COVERS ALL OUTLAYS

Don't miss seeing this most interesting house whether you contemplate purchase or not. You will find it full of novel features

Open daily at Eglinton Toll from 1 p.m. till 9 p.m.

Mactaggart & Mickel Ltd

SALES OFFICE & SHOWHOUSE EGLINTON TOLL

Telephone:- Queens Park 1669

HEAD OFFICE 65 BATH STREET - 'PHONE DOUGLAS ONE

A Typical View from our Netherlee Park Estate

"G" TYPE £25 the only cash payment. 22/- per week covers all outlays.

"J" TYPE £25 the only cash payment. 22/- per week covers all outlays.

"F" TYPE £50 the only cash payment. 25/- per week covers all outlays.

"K" TYPE £50 the only cash payment. 26/- per week covers all outlays.

HOUSES WILL COST MORE AFTER SEPTEMBER!

Secure yours before it is too late!

OUR houses have always been good value. To-day they are the finest proposition in the Housing Market. Each house shown here is a subsidised house. The subsidy varies from £50 to £100.

All subsidies have now been withdrawn; therefore, after September similar houses will cost from £50 to £100 more.

This is one of the reasons why we are experiencing such a demand NOW.

We must have your order now if we are to complete your house in time

GO OUT TO NETHERLEE PARK— CLARKSTON ROAD—THIS WEEK-END AND SEE THESE HOUSES FOR YOURSELF!

4 Show Houses open on the site every day (including Sunday) from 1 p.m. till dusk

When we state that your cash payment is the *only* cash payment we mean *the only* cash payment; and when we state that your weekly payment covers all outlays we mean *all* outlays!! We are the only builders in Scotland giving free removal.

SALES DEPARTMENT EGLINTON TOLL

MACTAGGART & MICKEL, LTD.

SALES OFFICE AND SHOW HOUSES OPEN USUAL HOURS ON MONDAY

A3.17. *Advertisement of 1933 for Netherlee Park, highlighting the subsidy changes of that year.* (Bulletin, *1 April 1933; MMC*)

Saturday, March 4, 1933. £42·0·0 *The Bulletin*

Building Costs will rise?

1914   1923   1933   1934

Before you sign your missive read this—

"Since the introduction of the new Housing Bill all subsidies on houses built for sale have been withdrawn, and even houses on which subsidy has already been granted may not receive this subsidy unless built and completed before 30th Sept. of this year—"

When those houses already approved for subsidy have been disposed of similar houses will cost from £50 to £100 more

To those who are interested in securing a modern Bungalow on the most advantageous terms there is need for immediate action.

On our Netherlee Park Estate, Clarkston Road a number of houses presently under construction are available over the whole area of the scheme.

The present low rate of money has enabled us to secure specially favourable terms for our "G" & "J" type Bungalows at Netherlee Park and these can now be purchased for one inclusive payment of £25 and a weekly outlay (which includes everything) of 22/

Before you sign your missive we strongly urge you to see these houses. At present day prices they offer an opportunity which once they are sold cannot be repeated.

Mactaggart and Mickel Limited

Sales Office Eglinton Toll
Saturday 4th March.

A3.18. 1933 advertisement highlighting the effects of the subsidy changes. (Bulletin, 4 March 1933; MMC)

STATION NOVELTY.—The show house in the Central Station, Glasgow, for Mactaggart and Mickel's new houses at Clarkston. It is furnished by Bow's, of High Street, and is attracting large crowds

A3.19. 'Unit' showhouse at Glasgow Central Station in March 1934, promoting Carolside Park Estate and 'attracting large crowds'. (Bulletin, 5 March 1934; Glasgow Herald)

highlighted the removal of subsidy, but added to this the claim that Mactaggart & Mickel had been able to effect a 'substantial reduction in terms of purchase'. Down-payments for 'G' and 'J' type bungalows were reduced from £40 to £25, and weekly outlay from 22s 6d to 22s. Mactaggart & Mickel cited reduced building society interest rates as the reason for this particular new offer; and by late 1932 the company had gone further, entering into a formal agreement with the Halifax Building Society whereby it placed £10,000 with the society as collateral security for all loans to be granted by the Halifax to purchasers of Mactaggart & Mickel houses. Similar agreements were made in March 1933 with the Abbey Road Building Society (with £3,000 deposited as collateral), and in September that year with the Leeds Building Society (with £2,000 deposited). The vast majority of Netherlee Park was sold under the pool agreement with all three of the societies. With these favourable financial circumstances in place, Mactaggart & Mickel mounted a 'deadline' advertising campaign for Netherlee Park as the last houses built under government subsidy. In a full-page advertisement, it warned that 'building costs will rise', and throughout 1933 purchasers were urged to go to Netherlee Park 'now', as this offer would 'never be repeated'. (45)

The landlord and the rented tenement flat also became a focus, or more accurately a target, of Mactaggart & Mickel's advertising campaigns for Netherlee Park. Renting was criticised initially on a financial basis: 'more and more people recognise the fact', Mactaggart & Mickel argued, 'that paying rent for an old or inferior house is a positive extravagance when, for the same money a better up-to-date bungalow can be actually purchased ... the important thing is to secure your site now!' It claimed that living was 'cheaper out there ... building costs are rising but rates at Netherlee Park at low ... and purchase is even easier than renting', and of course, it concluded that 'the money that goes on rent is gone forever.' The autonomy and freedom of home purchase was also promoted. Mactaggart & Mickel asked prospective buyers: 'Are you master of your own house? Do you live under allegiance to the landlord? Or are you free from hindrance and restriction in your own house?' The 'freedom' of house purchase was presented in terms of a kind of Covenanting egalitarianism: 'As subjects we cherish our national freedom, and as housewives we prefer freedom and ownership to tenancy and restrictions'. (46)

It was also at Netherlee Park that Mactaggart & Mickel's advertising began to take on a strongly anti-urban and pro-suburban character, using language remarkably like the polemic of socialist advocates of garden cities, such as Jean Mann. In the tradition of the Ballantyne Report, the first target was of course the tenement: 'Only the other day houses were without baths and owed their charm to concealed beds and funny plaster. Now it's goodbye to all that at Netherlee Park'. The alienated stone hardness of the inner city was contrasted with the outer-suburban closeness to nature, which allowed dwellers to experience the changing seasons to the full: on a 'bright day in spring, when you feel the need for a change', housewives were urged to board the 'yellow tram ... leaving the smoky old city, whirring up into the clean air of the country' to arrive at the new bright and sunny Netherlee Park. Suburban life allowed residents to enjoy the 'clear, clean, tonic air' without having to give up city amenities: 'the country is at your back door, yet the town is within a short tram ride'. The soaring idealisation of the suburb reached its apogee in a Netherlee Park advertisement of May 1933: 'To-night the tennis and bowling and golfing are in full swing. In the garden the peony rose is making a fine show ... the hawthorn smells sweet down the road. Yes, it is pleasant in the suburbs these days ... living undisturbed in a bungalow of one's own, where everything is fresh and colourful and modern. Yet it is curious how people will go on paying good money on rent - money that could be buying a new home'. (47)

The culmination of the firm's unsubsidised work on the Glasgow periphery in the first half of the 1930s was the Carolside Park estate, Clarkston, commenced in 1934 and developed right through to 1960, with only a brief break between 1941 and 1946; the total number of houses there by 1960 was 1,561. From the beginning, it was used as a location to build prototypes of a number of the house-types prominent in the later 1930s, two of which were linked closely to showhouses built on the concourse of Central Station.

The first of these was the 'Unit House', a new semi-detached villa-type of four or five apartments. The four-apartment house contained, on its ground floor, a living room, kitchen and dining room and, on the first floor, two bedrooms. An example was built at Central Station in February 1934 and opened with much press fanfare on 3 March, as 'a strange erection ... the most amazing house ever built!' The next day an advertisement apologised to the queues who had been 'unable to gain admission' to the showhouse. Train tickets to visit Carolside Park, 'a popular Easter excursion', could be bought at the showhouse, and by April the company boasted that the Unit had been 'definitely the most popular house in 1934', with over 150 houses sold so far; the first had been sold at Carolside Park on 3 March, at a price of £500, with £25 down-payment. Purchasers came from a wide variety of tenures and locations across Glasgow, including the Ordinary Corporation schemes at Riddrie and Mosspark, Western Heritable's rented Cardonald houses, and earlier Mactaggart & Mickel owner-occupied houses at King's Park. In November 1935, the type was developed into the four- or five-apartment 'Super-Unit', designed by James Taylor; from July 1936, it was offered for sale at Carolside Park for £605, including £30 deposit and 21s 2d weekly payment. (48)

The Unit showhouse in Central Station was demolished on 1 September 1934, and was immediately replaced by a showhouse of the company's next major type, the more expensive 'Colour Home': a five-apartment, semi-detached villa, just designed by Taylor, which was to be built in considerable numbers at Carolside Park, at a price of £690, with £50 down-payment and 24s 6d

GLASGOW'S NEW SHOW HOUSE

The Colour Home—the new show house of Mactaggart and Mickel, Ltd., in the Central Station, Glasgow. The house is modernistic in design, special attention being given to health and sunlight. It has been furnished by Bow's Emporium, Ltd.

A3.20. 'Colour Home' showhouse in Central Station, September 1934: 'The house is modernistic in design, special attention being given to health and sunlight'. (Bulletin, 13 September 1934; Glasgow Herald)

DAILY RECORD AND MAIL, WEDNESDAY, SEPTEMBER 12, 1934 — Cost £64.

WE ASKED OUR ARCHITECT FOR HIS IDEAL HOUSE—AND SO HE DESIGNED THE COLOUR HOME!!

THE HOUSE OF THE FUTURE—BUILT FOR THE NEEDS OF TO-DAY!

Here is a Home different to anything ever attempted before—giving Colour, Sunlight, and Modernistic design—a house that is ahead of its time. Well-balanced design and harmonious blending of well-chosen colours gives this house a dignified and pleasing appearance from all angles. The rear of the "Colour" Home actually compares more than favourably in appearance with the front of most modern houses.

THE "COLOUR" HOME HAS ACTUALLY THREE TIMES MORE WINDOW SPACE THAN THAT DEMANDED

Health and sunlight go hand in hand—therefore the Colour Home has been designed so that the whole interior is flooded with light. There is actually three times more window space than regulations demand, and the window design has been planned to enhance the appearance of the house

EXPERIENCED PLANNING AND DESIGN GIVES COMFORT AND CONVENIENCE

All the accumulated experience of Scotland's largest builders went into the design of the Colour Home. In design and construction it simply cannot be compared with any other type of house—it is the biggest advance of the century in Scottish Housing.

SEE THE NEW SHOW HOUSE IN THE CENTRAL STATION —THEN VISIT THE SITE AT CLARKSTON

The furnished Show House at Central Station is open daily from 11 a.m. till 10 p.m. After your visit see the beautiful countryside where this home is being erected. The site is only a few minutes from the Clarkston Tram Terminus.

● **SPACIOUS AND WELL-DESIGNED PORCH.** The entrance porch is just one of the features which makes this house distinctively different. It will be seen that its design blends perfectly with the rest of the house to form one harmonious whole. Steel windows add further attraction to the design.

● **PANEL FIRES AND BUILT-IN WARDROBE.** Two of the three bedrooms incorporate the latest design in panel electric fires which fit flush into the wall—a feature entirely in keeping with modern furnishing technique. A unique feature of one of the bedrooms is a built-in wardrobe of exceptionally commodious proportions.

● **WELL-EQUIPPED AND TILED KITCHENETTE.** The sparkling brightness of the kitchenette will appeal at once to the housewife. Twin sinks with porcelain surrounds and soap trays eliminating all wood—new improved gas cooker—wash boiler—a brush cabinet—utility kitchen cabinet and larder.

● **METICULOUS ATTENTION TO DETAIL.** The small things (which really matter such a lot) receive careful attention in the Colour Home. Taps and Toilet fittings are chromium-plated, window-sills are of slate and therefore non-absorbent and waterproof, the staircase window floods the hall with light— everything for convenience and comfort has been carefully planned and executed.

● **TERMS THAT MAKE PURCHASE EASY.** Finally comes the biggest surprise of all. The Colour Home is obtainable on terms actually lower than many five-apartment houses of ordinary design. These terms cover rates, taxes, legal fees, feu-duty, etc.— even free removal.

£50
DOWN AND
PER **24/6** WEEK
COMPLETES PURCHASE

MACTAGGART & MICKEL, LIMITED

SHOW HOUSE CENTRAL STATION——HEAD OFFICE, 63-65 BATH STREET, GLASGOW

TELEPHONE DOUGLAS ONE

A3.21. Full-page advertisement of September 1934 for the 'Colour Home'. (Daily Record and Mail, 12 September 1934; MMC)

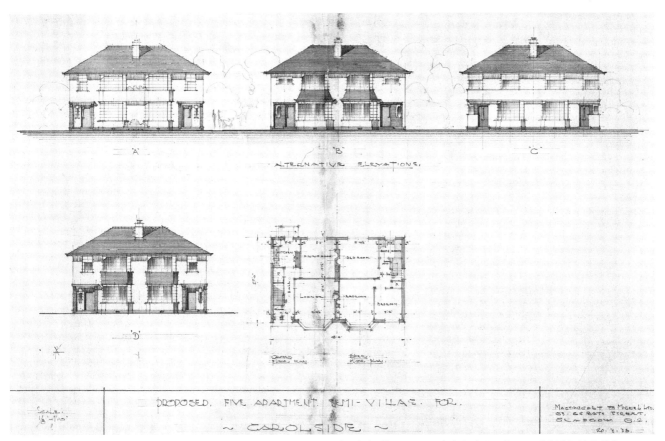

A3.22. Plan and alternative facade variants for 'Colour Home' five-apartment semi-detached villa type at Carolside Park, March 1938. (MMC D44753CN)

weekly outgoing. It contained ground-floor front living room and rear dining room, and bathroom and three bedrooms (one very small) on the first floor. Concessions to Art Deco modernity included the metal window-frames and triangular-plan stair windows on the side walls, but the traditional motif of thin, individual tile-hung bay windows for each house was perpetuated, now in a curious tapered form; there was a double bay window on the ground floor of the rear elevation, too. The house was built in a number of alternative material and detail treatments; some had glazed green columns and roof tiles, others had natural green roof slates, and red rustic bases and dressings. In September 1934, a company advertisement enthused that 'We asked our architect for his ideal house - and so he designed the Colour Home!! The house of the future - built for the needs of today ... different to anything ever attempted before ... giving colour, sunlight and modernistic design'. The Central Station showhouse was 'modernistic in design, special attention being given to health and sunlight'. Late 1935 saw the design of a 'Super Colour' villa by Taylor, including a lavatory and maid's room, and selling for £850. Other new types built in the first development of Carolside Park included a four-apartment bungalow, developed by Taylor from the older 'E' type, its 'artistic exterior' being rendered, with central doorway flanked by a bay window and corner window, and obtainable for £685, with a £50 deposit and 23s 4d weekly payment. There was also a handful of large, custom-designed bungalows, costing up to £1,775. (49)

By 1936, as we will see later in this chapter, there was increasing concern in the company about sales levels and profit margins, and Jack Mactaggart demanded the immediate start of 'an intensive building programme in order that as many houses as possible be made available for May 1936'; 30 five-apartment Colour Homes (of the 'new Edinburgh type', with splayed bay windows), 20 four-apartment bungalows, and 50 four- and five-apartment Super Unit houses (costing £605 each, with £30 down-

payment) were to be started. On one site along Greenwood Road, twenty lower-cost semi-detached 'D' type bungalows, along with some Super Units, were to be started. Following complaints from Frank Mickel that the £75 down-payment demanded for the larger £850 villas was excessive and hampered sales, it was reduced to £50. There were rhetorical warnings that prices were about to go up: 'After November your new house will cost £40 more!' However, by 1938, with the beginning of rearmament-stimulated rises in materials and labour costs, price rises had become a reality at Carolside Park, as in the company's other developments; by that time, some houses on the estate were being sold through a pool arrangement with the Co-operative Building Society. The shadow of war, as more generally, brought a slump in building progress at Carolside Park, with a reduction of the bricklaying squad and a slow-down in bungalow building in April 1939. Building stopped altogether after the outbreak of war, and did not resume until 1946; sales by that date totalled £537,660. (50)

The marketing of the Carolside Park development, and the name of the 'Colour Home' type itself, emphasised the now well-established contrast of fog-bound, grey Glasgow and sunny suburb: 'Substitute a bright modern kitchenette ... and clean, fresh country air for the drudgery and smokiness of the old-fashioned flat, and you have the new Colour Home at Clarkston.' 'While Glasgow was wrapped up in the thick fog yesterday, some of the higher suburbs were remarkably clear. At Clarkston ... housewives were able to hang out clothes in the forenoon, in the sunshine, while a spot of gardening was indulged in by some menfolk ... if you are living in the city in a rented home you surely cannot see your way clear ... you can own a modern sun-lit home in the beautiful suburbs of Clarkston - happy in the healthy surroundings of this suburb'. In 1935, a circular was sent to 2,898 households in Mosspark and Knightswood advertising the Colour Home and arguing that 'renting has been rendered obsolete'. Most of Carolside Park was sold through a pool

A3.23. *Advertisement of 1936 for Carolside Park. (*Evening Times, *16 May 1936; MMC)*

agreement with the Abbey Road Building Society. Although a London Midland & Scottish railway station was nearby, motor bus transport was also vital for marketing; in February 1937, the company announced that an SMT service was now running from Clyde Street to Carolside Park. (51) Carolside Park, with its protracted development, straddles the early and late 1930s; we will deal in Part IV of this chapter with those developments in the west which were entirely built in the late 1930s.

Part II

The move east
Edinburgh, 1932-39

In late 1932, Mactaggart & Mickel extended its operations eastwards to Edinburgh. Such a move, given the favourable circumstances nurtured for private enterprise builders by Edinburgh Corporation, might have seemed a simple and logical matter, but the firm was fully committed at the time to its extensive and demanding schedule of work in the west. By this date it was poised to begin building for Western Heritable the Cardonald scheme of over 1,228 houses, and the remaining 188 1924 Act houses at King's Park. And, in its own housebuilding programme for sale, while Merrylee Park was already complete, the ambitious Netherlee Park scheme was in full swing by late 1932. Despite these distracting commitments, the potential to build, rent, and sell houses in interwar Edinburgh eventually proved an irresistible lure even for a traditionally west-based company; and at the height of its busy house-selling programme in the outer suburbs of Glasgow, the firm began operations in the capital, building there for the first time, for itself, houses under the 1924 Housing Act subsidy scheme. Between 1932 and 1939, Mactaggart & Mickel built a total of 3,356 houses for rent, and, in an arrangement with the house factoring company Gumley and Davidson, came to dominate the private rented sector in Edinburgh well into the 1970s. Building houses for sale only followed, very tentatively, in 1934, and in quantitative terms was a significantly smaller concern: in Edinburgh, Mactaggart & Mickel built only 268 houses for sale between 1934 and 1939.

The particular path which Mactaggart & Mickel followed on entering the housebuilding sphere in Edinburgh was strongly shaped by the existing local housing market. Nationally, as we saw previously, state subsidies for building for sale were drying up, in the face of the 1929 reduction and 1933 withdrawal of the 1923 Act grants. The 1933 legislation also put an end to the 1924 Act subsidies by reducing state input from £9 to £3 per house and withdrawing state assistance completely in 1935. Despite this legislation, autonomous local authorities continued their support of private enterprise housebuilding, by providing post-subsidy schemes: as we have seen, Renfrew County Council in the early 1930s were providing one such alternative subsidy for private housebuilding. Of the cities, Glasgow Corporation focused its efforts on a municipal direct labour building programme; but it was Edinburgh Corporation which displayed a continued support for the private sector despite central government withdrawal.

Edinburgh Corporation was dominated by the non-socialist Progressive members. They had, throughout the interwar period, displayed both a willingness to support and enhance private enterprise (with or without central government assistance), and to keep public sector municipal building to a minimum. In addition to this, the council had maintained relatively low owners' rates, in comparison with Glasgow and the rest of Scotland.

Between the wars, Edinburgh, despite having a population only 40% of Glasgow's, had a significantly greater number of houses built by private enterprise (letting and selling) than Glasgow: 28,708 compared with 19,769. Edinburgh appears also to have concentrated its subsidised activities on the 1923 rather than 1924 Act. (52)

By late 1932, with central government subsidised housing for sale being increasingly withdrawn, Edinburgh Corporation was poised to take advantage of the remaining 1924 Act government subsidies for the private rented sector, which were ultimately to stop in 1935. Mactaggart & Mickel was similarly poised to exploit this opportunity. By moving east into the subsidised rented sector, Mactaggart & Mickel, in a sense, re-created the monopolistic situation which it and Western Heritable had formed in 1925. But whereas, in Glasgow, Mactaggart & Mickel had 'cornered' the subsidised owner-occupied market and Western Heritable the subsidised private rented sector, in Edinburgh Mactaggart & Mickel's role was reversed; there, as explained in Annette O'Carroll in Chapter B2 of this book, the well established James Miller had already monopolised the production of housing for sale, building 1,922 houses between 1927 and 1934. In 1937, Douglas Mickel recounted the move east five years previously: 'We came over here on the Wheatley Scheme [1924 Act] to begin with, because we had been the only people in Scotland who had been developing the Wheatley Scheme at all. We and our associated company have done 6,000 houses under the Wheatley Act, and it was that which first attracted us to Edinburgh'. (53)

Between 1932 and 1939, Mactaggart & Mickel developed three large new private rented schemes in Edinburgh - East Pilton, Carrick Knowe, and Colinton - and began another, at Broomhouse. Although the basic arrangement between the Corporation and Mactaggart & Mickel remained constant - that is, Mactaggart & Mickel feued land from the Corporation and employed a factor to collect rents and service the estates - the subsidy levels shifted with new legislation. In comparison with Western Heritable's trouble-dogged experiences in obtaining approval, and negotiating plan types, for 1924 Act subsidies from Glasgow Corporation, Mactaggart & Mickel nurtured a very good working relationship with Edinburgh Corporation, and in particular with the city architect, Ebenezer J MacRae. Evidence of this mutual respect can be found throughout this period. From the beginning, Mactaggart & Mickel stressed the company's long established tradition of housebuilding. All the Edinburgh activities were managed by the young and recently-recruited Douglas Mickel, then aged 21. In 1937, Douglas reaffirmed the firm's commitment and reliability: the firm was 'not a mushroom growth, and anything we take in hand we can see it through', he argued to the Sub-committee on the Progress of the Housing Programme. (54)

East Pilton

Mactaggart & Mickel's first Edinburgh development was at East Pilton, Granton; it was developed over five years in three main phases. Following negotiations in late 1932, the company finally proposed to build 500 houses on 31 acres feued from Edinburgh Corporation (at a duty of £50 per acre per annum, i.e. £3 5s per house), at East Pilton No.1. Edinburgh Corporation subsequently 'agreed to grant facilities for the erection of houses for letting under the 1924 Housing Act'. The conditions of this agreement required the Corporation to build roads and sewers, and the financial assistance was by way of loan (75% of the value of each house, repayable by 40 six-monthly instalments at 4% interest)

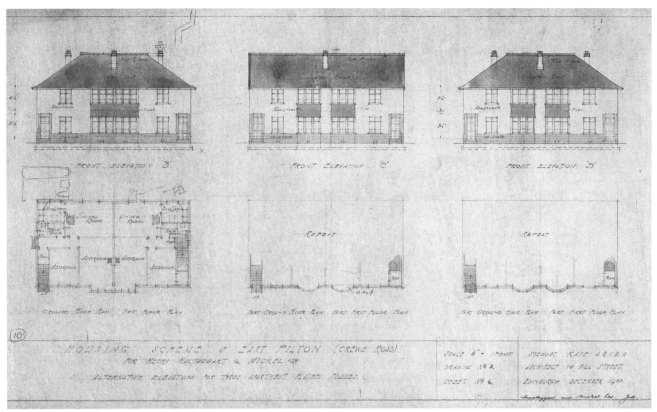

A3.24. Three alternative facade designs by Stewart Kaye for East Pilton housing scheme, Edinburgh, December 1933. (MMC D44942CN)

A3.26. East Pilton scheme, Edinburgh, built from 1932; 1930s view. (MMC)

A GRANTON HOUSING SCHEME

Part of the East Pilton Estate housing scheme of Messrs Mactaggart & Mickel (Ltd.), Glasgow, comprising 500 houses of three and four apartments, which is nearly completed at Granton. The houses, which are of the flatted villa type, four in a block, were started early in the year. Nine shops are included, and there is a seven acres park in the centre. The scheme employs upwards of 400 men. The houses are available to rent.

A3.25. East Pilton Estate seen under construction in August 1933. (Evening Dispatch, 26 August 1933)

and subsidy (£9 per annum for 40 years). This arrangement was similar to that which Western Heritable secured at Cardonald, Glasgow. Mactaggart & Mickel took advantage of the loan and arranged to borrow £160,500 on the security of the houses, but could not obtain any advance until it had first spent £10,000. This arrangement had an overriding condition attached to it that the work had to be completed by 30 September 1933 to fulfil the subsidy requirements. (55)

In the shadow of subsidy withdrawal, work on East Pilton No. 1 began almost immediately. In order to speed up production, Mactaggart & Mickel urged the Corporation to build the roads and sewers by direct labour, using the city engineer's own workforce rather than putting the work to contract. The roads and sewers work was costed at £16,000, of which £13,000 was applicable to the ground feued to Mactaggart & Mickel. By December, City Architect MacRae was able to report on type plans for four- and five-apartment houses. The four-apartment houses were approved with some amendments (e.g. that windows were to be provided in the hallway and natural slates from approved quarries were required) but the proposed five-apartment house was refused on the grounds that it did 'not yet conform to the conditions of the subsidy scheme'. This was probably on grounds of cost, because it was above the £600 limit for subsidy.

No sooner had the five-apartment been abandoned than Mactaggart & Mickel submitted, and obtained approval for, a type-plan of three-apartment 'flatted villas' in four-in-a-block groups. (56) These two types of two-storey flats (three- and four-apartment), and the various layouts for all phases of East Pilton, were designed by the Edinburgh architect Stewart Kaye. Kaye was to become Mactaggart & Mickel's consultant architect in the east, and designed almost all layouts and house-types for the 1930s Edinburgh estates. His two house designs for East Pilton No.1 were adopted as a standard for the remaining extensions of East Pilton, and were also employed later at Carrick Knowe. Construction comprised roughcast 11.5" cavity outer brick walls with brick or breeze inner walls. Internally, as in council four-in-a-block dwellings, the ground- and first-floor flats were identically planned, other than the staircases and halls; two bedrooms were at the front, and a living room (with scullery and coal bunker off) were at the back; the bathroom was at the side. Externally, the blocks were distinguished fron council designs by their full-height tile-hung window bays; the arrangement of the doors and windows at the front resembled that of a semi-detached villa. The pedigree of this kind of design included Robert Lorimer's Colinton cottages of 1902, which employed slates between the different floors, but it could also simply be read as an adaptation of the projecting bays of 19th-century tenements.

In 1937, Douglas Mickel defended the decision to adopt only two house-types at East Pilton on grounds of construction, organisation, and popular taste: 'We have variations in the construction of the oriel windows and the roofs, and you will find that our schemes have a considerable amount of sparkle about them in colour schemes. We have found that these two types of houses have been very attractive wherever we have gone, and people have clamoured to get them. So we stuck to these particular types; there was no use experimenting with other types. It allows us to go ahead, our people get into the way of working, and it becomes, as we say, a trick to get on with us'. He argued, more generally, that because the firm built for sale and rent, 'we have to have a proper organisation otherwise we would be in a state of chaos. I have an organisation here which I instituted when I came through to start in Granton first'. (57)

Evidence of Douglas Mickel's organisational powers can be found in the Mactaggart & Mickel archives in the form of a progress chart which meticulously records all the building activities carried out at East Pilton No.1. The detailed chronological development of each block is traced (including all trades separately and the date of occupation); the time taken to carry out each activity, and which 'squad' of workers was allocated to them, is also recorded. The first block, for example, was begun on 23 February 1933; all brick and joiner work was completed by the beginning of March; throughout April and May all plumber, plaster, slater and painter work was completed; and following final wiring checks and drainage, the first occupant took possession on 1 June 1933. This detailed schedule of work done at East Pilton not only functioned as a check-list for all activities, but proved crucial in supporting Mactaggart & Mickel's costing and scheduling of the labour requirements of further feuing agreements from Edinburgh Corporation. The chart was presumably pinned on the wall of the original temporary site office at Pilton Avenue. (58)

Despite approval of the two house types at East Pilton, negotiations over density levels, and in particular the stipulations of the central government Department of Health (DHS), ultimately changed Mactaggart & Mickel's original design layout and extended the land built upon, and subsequently increased the level of feu charge to £4 per house. Mactaggart & Mickel had estimated for a density of 16 houses per acre, but DHS opposed this 'because of imminent change in legislation', and insisted on a reduction to 12 per acre. Mactaggart & Mickel revised its plan, but the DHS then had a change of heart. However, in view of 'the attractiveness of their revised layout of 12 houses per acre', Mactaggart & Mickel, with the support of MacRae, preferred to 'adhere to the layout even though it will involve an additional feu of almost £1 per house'. The revised layout comprised 100 houses less than the original, and it was agreed that Mactaggart & Mickel should be feued an additional area adjoining, on which it could build the 100 houses. In early 1933, Mactaggart & Mickel applied for Corporation advances, as the layouts of the remainder of East Pilton No.1 were being planned. By February, MacRae had approved the layout plan for 124 additional houses (32 of three apartments and 92 of four) west of Pilton Drive, which were, he explained 'in keeping with the larger layout' of 376 houses already approved; these were laid out in one small and two large areas. As regards rent, Mactaggart & Mickel was forced to reduce the annual rent form £26 per annum (for the the apartment) to DHS's approved rate of £24 14s. (59)

The only significant problem which Mactaggart & Mickel encountered in its negotiations with the Corporation concerning East Pilton was the thorny issue of building labour rates. One of the conditions of central government subsidy was that private builders working on subsidised schemes should adhere to DHS standard wage rates; unsubsidised building, was, of course, exempt from this. In addition, the Corporation insisted that 75% of labour employed at East Pilton should be local; a number of councillors wanted this raised to 90%, but this amendment was out-voted. Mactaggart & Mickel was therefore unable to bring its own Glasgow labour to Edinburgh, and was also unable to offer rate inducements to tempt experienced labour from owner-occupied programmes current in the east at that time. As outlined, Edinburgh Corporation had pursued a policy of minimal municipal house building; one of its concerns at the time was that local authority building would drain the labour available to private enterprise building. In the early 1930s, as part of the move towards a more 'social' concept of all housebuilding, DHS standard rates were adopted for municipal developments and subsidised private enterprise alike. It was only the companies which carried out unsubsidised building programmes which could offer inducements; however, this situation was to change for a while after the withdrawal of central government subsidies in the second half of the decade (to be discussed below). These labour cost restrictions were opposed with increasing vehemence by Douglas Mickel. In April 1933, Edinburgh Corporation received letters of complaint from DHS and the District Master Builders Association regarding the labour wages being paid by Mactaggart & Mickel at East Pilton; according to these letters, bricklayers on the site were being paid in excess of the standard rate 'contrary to the conditions upon which subsidies are paid'. Despite the town clerk being 'in communication with Mactaggart & Mickel who are now paying the standard rate', complaints were still being received the following month, but the issue was soon resolved. Mactaggart & Mickel began to build up a team of reliable workers in Edinburgh, who could be employed on all the subsequent schemes; some workers stayed with the company well into the postwar period. Amongst them were Jimmy Lees, who was appointed manager for East Pilton in 1933, and Stanley Sutherland, bricklayer. Sutherland later recalled: 'When I served my time with Mactaggart & Mickel I got a good grounding. When I started on my own in 1947 I had 28s capital. It was a hard battle ... but worth it'. By August 1933, Mactaggart & Mickel was employing approximately 400 men on the site. (60) The firm's first Edinburgh office, opened in 1933, was in Shandwick Place; in November 1934, it moved to 67 York Place, remaining there until 1962.

The 500 houses of East Pilton No. 1 were completed in November 1933, one year after the feuing agreement was approved. Mactaggart & Mickel clearly had no experience in housing management; Andrew Mickel, for example, had from the beginning of his career distanced himself from this activity. The company therefore came to an arrangement with the large Edinburgh house factoring firm, Messrs Gumley and Davidson, to factor East Pilton and all subsequent rented property. It is interesting to note that Louis Gumley, head of the factoring company, was treasurer of Edinburgh Corporation in 1933. Indeed, Edinburgh Corporation appears to have viewed private builders and factoring arrangements as a direct substitute for general-needs municipal housing: an applicant for a Corporation house in February 1933 was advised to apply instead to Gumley and Davidson, who were also factoring for the Scottish National Housing Company at that time. (61)

East Pilton No.1 was followed in 1934 by Phase 2 of the scheme, a 17-acre site comprising 260 houses, and in 1936 by Granton (Phase 3), comprising 276 houses. In 1933, Stewart Kaye had explained the firm's 'desire' to extend the existing scheme with two further phases, partly in order 'to keep their men in employment'. He argued that 'Mactaggart & Mickel are prepared to extend the existing East Pilton scheme by 200 additional houses of three apartments'; a 'further area of land to accommodate 200 houses of the same type' was also required. Mactaggart & Mickel intended this development to come under a scheme outlined by the Corporation at a recent conference with building societies and others. Despite the removal of central government subsidies, Edinburgh Corporation was still keen to support private enterprise building. The Corporation made assisted building programmes a priority; it was believed that by 'giving a once and for all subsidy, they avoided the deficit which would be incurred in the building of general needs housing'. The conference highlighted Edinburgh Corporation's willingness to adopt a post-subsidy scheme, and in September 1934 such a scheme was adopted, allowing advances of 90% of the estimated cost of a house, at an interest rate of 3.75%, to be made to feuars. The mechanism was referred to as the Treasurer's Committee Scheme, after the council committee that administered it. The company was not allowed to sell the houses for twenty years after construction; the first sales, of vacated properties, occurred from 1953. (62)

The new advances may not have actually been available to Mactaggart & Mickel for East Pilton No. 2. In December 1933, the company secured a loan from the Halifax Building Society of £93,656 (repayable over 30 years) on the 260 houses planned for the scheme; that loan was reduced to £70,000 in 1934. As in the case of East Pilton No. 1, negotiations over the size of plot, the proposed density, and the actual number of houses built, proved to be complex. Originally it was proposed to feu land for 224 houses in East Pilton No. 2, and 320 in East Pilton No. 3; in reality, 260 and 276 houses respectively were built, all from the same range of types as in the earlier development. In December 1933, the Corporation approved the layout for a 17-acre site west of the current feu, stipulating a maximum rent level of £27. They

also granted a feu option for an additional area of the same size, for 284 houses. The density of the extended area was fixed at 16 houses per acre, the same as the original concept for Area No. 1; the Corporation valued the houses at £307 each, and recommended a 90% loan. There were lengthy negotiations over the feuing arrangements; Mactaggart & Mickel successfully proposed the insertion of a provision that it should be allowed to transfer some or all of the houses to a holding company. The non-residential amenities of the development were considered too, with debate about land and feu duties for shops and garages at Boswall Parkway, Wardieburn Drive, Pilton Drive and elsewhere, and an offer by the company to transfer a seven-acre area to the Corporation for use as a public park, as well as other small plots scattered throughout the estate. The Superintendent of Parks estimated that clearing and levelling would cost £240, the planting of small plots £95, and maintenance £25. In early 1935, the company successfully objected to a Corporation plan to build a three-storey tenement block on Boswall Parkway, overlooking its estate; the council agreed to restrict its housing to two storeys on this frontage. (63)

Post-1934 Edinburgh estates

Following the extensive developments at East Pilton, Mactaggart & Mickel turned its attention to a project for the building of over 1,000 houses for rent at Carrick Knowe, in Edinburgh's western suburbs. Mactaggart & Mickel had previously approached the Corporation in late 1933, claiming it was 'ready to build houses for letting under the scheme outlined at the recent conference with builders'. It offered to take on feus for an area adjoining Carrick Knowe Golf Course. The town clerk reported that the area being proposed by Mactaggart & Mickel formed part of Saughton Mains Farm, which was at that time being purchased by the Corporation; he proposed to serve notice of removal upon the current tenant, Sir James Davidson, for the

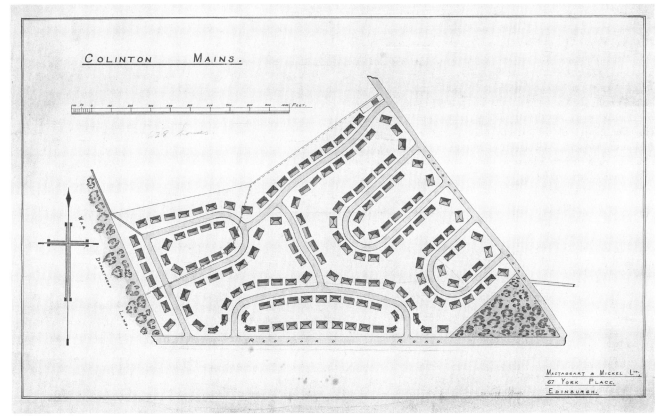

A3.27. Original proposed layout of Colinton Mains Estate, Edinburgh. (MMC D44939)

purpose of feuing the land to Mactaggart & Mickel; but the matter was deferred for a time. (64)

Eventually, in 1935, a first development of 856 houses on a 52-acre site was approved, followed the next year by a 292-house extension on 16 acres to the east; this comprised 73 blocks of three-apartment dwellings. As in the case of East Pilton and the later Colinton Estate, the Corporation loan was so structured that, as each house was built, part of the loan was repaid, and the title was granted by the council with the consent of Mactaggart & Mickel. Eventually, in 1976, when the loans had been repaid in full, the remainder of the estate was conveyed to the firm. The houses were to be similar two-storey 'flatted villas' to those at East Pilton, mostly containing three-apartment flats but with a minority of four-apartments. Most were to be in blocks of four, but some were to be arranged in rows of eight, with four-apartment units extending above a central double pend. In a report to the Corporation in October 1935, the city architect stated that 'no effort had been made to give interest or variety to the scheme, one type of block being used through the whole scheme with only slight variations, and suggested that some arrangement might be made whereby some of the blocks should be arranged in larger groups than four, so as to give less jerkiness of layout, and, if possible, some real variation in design'. Ebenezer MacRae was working with Kaye at that very time on a grand council-housing scheme of his own, at West Pilton, incorporating far more varigated planning devices, including a giant circus; the East Pilton No. 2 designs had already been modified at his suggestion in 1934 to give more 'variety'. In response to these criticisms, the Carrick Knowe layout was adjusted slightly, and Kaye produced a final set of elevations in November, showing double-width tile-hung bay windows and piended roofs of varying heights; construction began in 1936. (65) A block of shops was authorised by the Corporation at an annual feu duty of £60.

By 1937, construction of Carrick Knowe was well under way, with an average block of four houses being erected for £1,600. Bricklayers were paid 1s 6d per hour and hod carriers 1s; a newspaper article on the building work reported that 'the hod carriers took ten bricks a time on the ground level, on the upper floor they carried only nine'. However, by that date, building work on Edinburgh private housing was beginning to suffer from a new and unwelcome source of direct competition: Glasgow Corporation's council house building drive, and the mushrooming Glasgow direct labour force, which offered a guaranteed 51-week employmemt. In reply, private builders could offer inducements over and above the standard building rates specified by the Department of Health for local authority and subsidised housing; there was also fierce competition for casual building labourers. (66)

Carrick Knowe was followed by a project of almost the same size at Colinton, comprising 920 'flatted villa' dwellings and built in 1937-38. The council had drawn up in 1933 its original development proposals for the Colinton Mains estate, adjacent to Redford Barracks in the less socially exclusive zone of Colinton; of the nearly 200 acres, 35 were to be set aside for civil and military hospitals, and the remaining 163 for residential feuing. In 1936, Mactaggart & Mickel successfully proposed that it should be allocated 28 acres for development with 320 Corporation-assisted dwellings, of similar two-storey flatted types to Carrick Knowe. Typical houses in the development comprised four rooms, kitchenette, bathroom, for a £32 annual rent; three-apartment flats commanded a £27 rent. (67) At the same time, the firm was negotiating for a substantial extension at the southern end of the Colinton Mains development, comprising the 20-acre Oxgangs

Farm site; in July 1936 Edinburgh Corporation agreed to feu the area to Mactaggart & Mickel for a development at 16 dwellings to the acre, with a feu duty of 15s per house for 30 years, and to grant a Treasurer's Committee Scheme loan at 3.75%. This area, along with another extension, was developed with 592 houses, largely of three apartments, and was augmented in 1938-39 by a further 16 houses. These extensions were argued for by the company 'in order to meet the further demand for working-class dwellings at Colinton Mains' and to 'maintain a continuity' of building. Stewart Kaye wrote to the Corporation in February 1938 that Mactaggart & Mickel 'have a waiting list of tenants for letting houses which cannot be met with the number of houses contained in the present development. The prospective tenants are of the artisan class, similar to those already being housed in this area, and include tradesmen, Corporation employees, civil servants, warehousemen and the like ... if our clients are to maintain their organisation and employment of labour your sanction to the allocation of land, at an early date, is desirable'. (68)

All of the Edinburgh rental schemes were marketed by Mactaggart & Mickel's Edinburgh factors, Gumley & Davidson, along with private rented housing owned by other firms in locations such as Calder Road and Sighthill. In terms of social class, the above quotation from Kaye's letter indicates clearly that they were an almost exact private equivalent to the Glasgow Ordinary schemes, with their preponderance of artisan tenants; Edinburgh's success in substantially bettering Glasgow's per-capita building rate very much depended on these large developments. Advertisements of 1938-39 promoted them as offering a combination of suburban health and rented flexibility, with freedom from maintenance costs and owners' rates: 'Houses to let away from the smoke' ... 'Country Freedom, Town Convenience ... Rent A House at Colinton Mains ... it gives you your own garden, freedom, healthy environment, and greater safety for your children ... well served by Bus and Tram ... you are not committed to buy - you RENT your house at a modest rate'. As in the case of the Ordinary schemes, there were efforts to foster community spirit and a sense of self-regulating order: the interest on the £1 deposit paid by tenants to the factors was used to finance gardening prizes for tenants on each of three schemes, East Pilton, Colinton and Carrick Knowe. (69)

By 1936, the firm was looking onward to a further extension of this rental programme, by proposing a new development of 252 houses at Broomhouse Farm, beyond Carrick Knowe on the western edge of Edinburgh. In 1938, the company proposed to feu from the Corporation a 16-acre site off Broomhouse Road, valued at £175 per acre, and to build 260 three- and four-apartment houses for letting, assisted by a loan of 90%; construction was to be the same as at Colinton Mains, but the separate blocks of housing, designed by Stewart Kaye and Walls, were to be similar to the adjoining scheme. By December, it had been decided to build only three apartment houses, as four or five apartments were 'hard to let'. A preliminary layout for Phase I of the estate, comprising 256 houses, was approved in 1939, and work was started on 72 houses on a three-acre section of the site; but the outbreak of war forced the curtailment of the scheme. The complex later history of the estate will be dealt with in more detail in Chapter A4. (70)

Having established the company in the new Edinburgh housing market, Mactaggart & Mickel began building houses for sale there in 1934. The social and economic circumstances now appeared sufficiently favourable for the directors to be able to risk such a move. In addition to low owners' rates, and a council which was

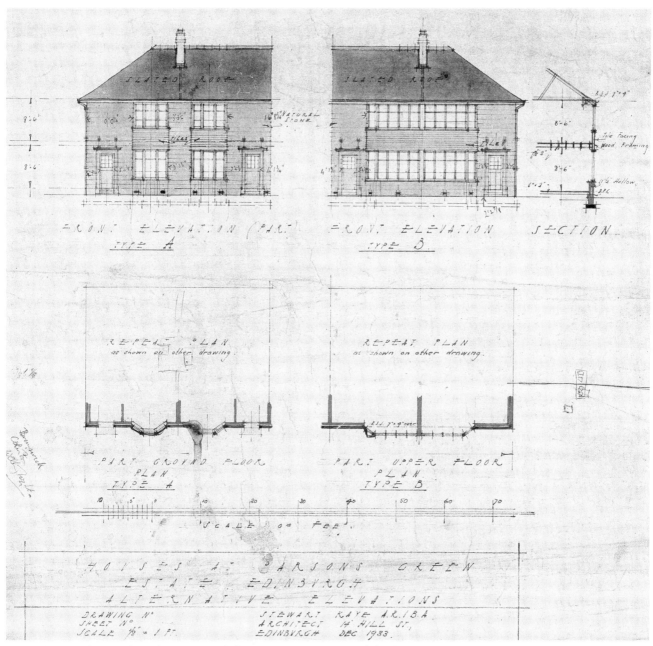

A3.28. Alternative elevations of 1933 by Stewart Kaye for houses at Parsons Green Estate, Edinburgh. (MMC D44733CN)

well-disposed to private enterprise and home ownership, Edinburgh also had a plentiful supply of land, in contrast to Glasgow, where the council's own low-density general-needs building had largely exhausted potential large sites. Its economy was proving reasonably resilient in the face of the economic depression, as it was dominated by the service industries and, unlike Glasgow, had no reliance on core manufacturing industries. This broader and more stable economic base, with its large middle class, supported the highest and fastest-growing level of owner occupation of any local authority area in Scotland. (71)

Mactaggart & Mickel was well aware of these differences between the Edinburgh and Glasgow housing markets. Its owner-occupation developments in the east began tentatively, with a small estate of 69 houses at Parsons Green, Willowbrae. In late 1933, Stewart Kaye designed the layout and house-types. The regularly disposed terraced villas, in rows of four and six houses, were set in straightforward lines along new side streets at right angles to the main Willowbrae Avenue. This conservative pattern harked back to the mid-1920s villa developments at King's Park and Kelvinside and even to pre-1914 terraced villas, rather than

to the more sweepingly dispersed and curving bungalow estates now being built by the firm in the west. The 'soundly built ... ingeniously planned and amazingly equipped' houses themselves were also rather old-fashioned terraced villas, similar in their linear front-back hall and staircase layouts to the 1925 King's Park and Kelvinside designs; the four-apartment houses had a front living room and rear kitchen and bedroom on the ground floor, and two bedrooms and bathroom on the upper floor. Construction comprised cavity brickwork; on the front facade, each house had a full-height canted and tile-hung bay window, and Kaye provided a 'modern natural stone front' to distinguish the houses from the rented version. The first mid-terrace house, in Glenlea Gardens, was sold in April 1934 for £560; end-terraces sold for £600 and a cash down-payment of £45. A pool system was established with the Abbey Road Building Society; the vast majority of the houses were sold quickly in 1934, with only three left for sale in February 1935: the total sales for this small site were £19,290. (72)

In Edinburgh, with its absence of combative politicisation of the housing problem, the harsh anti-landlord and anti-urban

The most amazing house value ever offered.
Four apartment stone-fronted villas with
Kitchenette and Bathroom.

£45 THE ONLY CASH PAYMENT INCLUDING ALL LEGAL FEES   **22/-** A WEEK COVERS ALL OUTLAYS Including All Rates and Taxes

See the furnished Show House at Willowbrae
Avenue, opening To-day (Saturday) and every
day thereafter from 2 p.m. till dusk.

Revolutionary new design, incorporating
the very latest ideas in Home Planning and
Equipment, *Economically Devised, ingeniously
planned and amazingly equipped.*

To those who are interested in securing a
modern Villa on the most advantageous
terms, there is need for immediate action.
Every house painted, papered, and decorated
to purchaser's own taste free.

*A NUMBER OF HOUSES WILL BE
READY FOR OCCUPANCY NEXT MAY!*

See the Show House to-day and select your site now!

MACTAGGART & MICKEL LTD.
Builders of Fine Homes
9 SHANDWICK PLACE, EDINBURGH
TELEPHONE 30800

A3.30. 'Two Tickets to Health and Happiness': Silverknowes and Carolside Park advertisement, 1937. (Edinburgh Evening News *and* Daily Record, *17 April 1937; MMC*)

(opposite) A3.29. Advertisement of 1934 for Parsons Green Estate, Edinburgh. (Scotsman, *17 March 1934; MMC*)

advertising rhetoric employed in Glasgow would have been counter-productive. Thus the Parsons Green houses were sold primarily on their 'exceptional terms', and Mactaggart & Mickel's housebuilding reputation: 'It is no coincidence', the company claimed, 'that Mactaggart & Mickel offer the finest house value in Scotland - it is a logical result of their experience and initiative over many years. The Edinburgh housewife demands more from her house today!' The 'Edinburgh housewife' was to be attracted by an 'inclusive' sales deal, decoration to 'her choice', and a year's free maintenance - all only a '1d car ride from the General Post Office'. Although Mactaggart & Mickel did not itself directly act as a property manager in Edinburgh, its early advertising there (up to around 1938), conspicuously avoided open attacks on the private rented sector and the supposed futility of renting. It was only when sales began to slow down in 1938 that its advertising in the capital adopted a more assertive angle. In its fixing of house-prices for Parsons Green, Mactaggart & Mickel may have been initially guided by a report issued in 1932 by city architect MacRae. This report estimated that the most prevalent house price in Edinburgh was £600, just inside the 1923 subsidy limit. MacRae also concluded that the £900-£1,000 range was the next most popular, followed by the £750-£850 range; there were, he reported, very few houses selling for under £500 at that time. (73)

The second of Mactaggart & Mickel's three interwar owner-occupied schemes in Edinburgh, and the one which established the firm securely in the city's owner-occupied market, was the 137-house estate at Silverknowes, near Davidson's Mains. This 'Garden Estate of Edinburgh', as it was later called, was 'only 12 minutes from Princes Street', and lay west of the future local authority scheme of Muirhouse and east of Lauriston Farm. The surviving drawings suggest that the layout was acquired and developed piecemeal, to the designs of Stewart Kaye, from late 1934. The land was feued to the firm by the Corporation at a price of £200 per acre for the initial five-acre site. The feu conditions specified that houses erected should be of no less value than £450, and of two storeys maximum; the first 18 houses to be built were mostly three-bedroom semi-detached villas. The north-western boundary of the site (Silverknowes Terrace and Avenue and Loan, adjoining Lauriston Farm Road) was set out in culs-de-sac and terraces, and the distinctive circular layout of the Silverknowes estate was developed at a later date, after the purchase of additional ground in 1936. The house layout and the disposition of the different house-types was determined by the proximity of surrounding residential areas. In late 1935, salesmen had reported to the directors that the showhouse site on Lauriston Farm Road was particularly problematic on Sundays. 'Excursionists of a very noisy and undesirable type', they reported, had given the wrong impression of the new estate. Arising out of this stimulus, the whole layout of the site was reconsidered. It was decided that the more expensive houses should be built on the 'Edinburgh side', and that the cheaper houses should face Lauriston Farm Road, with bungalows in the centre, 'thus obtaining a suitable price grading combined with aesthetic balance'. Construction began on site in early 1935 and the first five-apartment 'Colour Home', at 14 Silverknowes Terrace, was sold for £700, and a down-payment of £25, in March 1935. Showhouses were built on the triangular site between Silverknowes Drive and Terrace throughout 1935, with constant feedback from on-site sales staff about popularity of different house-types, and the entire first phase of the estate was sold by 1940, with total sales of £76,335. (74)

Several different house-types were utilised on the 1930s phase of the Silverknowes site, but it was the clean, white, harled semi-

detached villas that dominated the 1930s development. With its £600-£800 price range, this medium-cost development was the eastern equivalent to Carolside Park. Four basic house-types were built on the site: the five-apartment semi-detached 'Colour Home'; the bungalow; the semi-detached 'Unit' (later 'Super-Unit'); and the detached villa. The Colour and Unit designs, had already, of course, been successfully built and sold at Carolside Park, and the same plans were reproduced here, but with their facade designs slightly altered by Stewart Kaye for the Edinburgh market. Kaye's adapted version of James Taylor's original Colour Home, including shallow curved Art Deco projecting bays, metal-framed windows and a distinctive 'V' shaped stair window, dominated the estate. This 'sunny home on a healthy site' proved particularly popular in Edinburgh, and sold well throughout 1936; by late 1937, despite several cost increases, only six Colour Homes were left for sale at the original price of £700. Kaye's design for a detached five-apartment villa, which initially sold for £725, but by 1939 was priced at £830, was basically a detached version of the Colour Home. In plan, the villa devoted its ground floor to living areas (with a living room and spacious dining room), while a small box-bedroom was squeezed into the upper level to allow the design to claim three separate bedrooms. The cheaper semi-detached Unit Home, simply a copy of the Carolside Park design, was introduced, and sold, for £650 in mid-1935. These lower-price houses were situated along Lauriston Farm Road. In terms of bungalows, Kaye appears to have provided both alternative facade designs for existing Mactaggart & Mickel bunglaows, and designed new proposed types; for example, a variant of Joseph Wilson's 'K' type was produced, with steel framed windows, while others were given alternative brickwork details which wrapped around doors and corners. What was actually built on the site, however, was the four-apartment detached bungalow, selling at between £685 and £725. By late 1939 all the existing bungalows had been sold, and a final eight were built to 'clean up' any possible remaining sales. (75)

The Silverknowes estate was marketed above all as a 'sunny' garden suburb, but without the anti-urban edge of the Glasgow advertising. Its high standard of domestic modernity was particularly emphasised. An article in the SMT bus company magazine, for example, heralded Mactaggart & Mickel's 'super efficient kitchenette of 1937' as a vehicle for female domestic liberation: 'Why do Scottish women put up with such bad kitchens?... Many factors in post-war life have helped to sweep away such conditions; first and foremost women's own desire for healthy leisure, a generation labelled as "selfish", preferring wisely to spend more time in the open air and less time bending over an oven ... and the servant problem, too has underlined the need for simplified domestic arrangements'. The answer to those demands was Mactaggart & Mickel's 'oblong' kitchenette at Silverknowes, with its cooking and storage arrangements on one side and washing on the other. (76)

The fact that it had taken approximately five years to develop and sell only 137 medium-cost houses on the Silverknowes site (as compared with 130 low-cost houses in 24 hours at Merrylee Park, Glasgow, in 1931) clearly highlights the differences between the Edinburgh and Glasgow markets, and of course the strength of local competitors such as Miller, and the private rented sector alternatives (which Mactaggart & Mickel was developing at that time). By the late 1930s, the rate of sales in Edinburgh slackened off further, and, in response, elements of 'hard-sell' advertising appeared. Despite being a landlord itself, Mactaggart & Mickel asked prospective purchasers: 'Whose keys do you have in your pocket ... your own or your landlord's? Are you whiling away years in a home owned by another man? Are you handing a

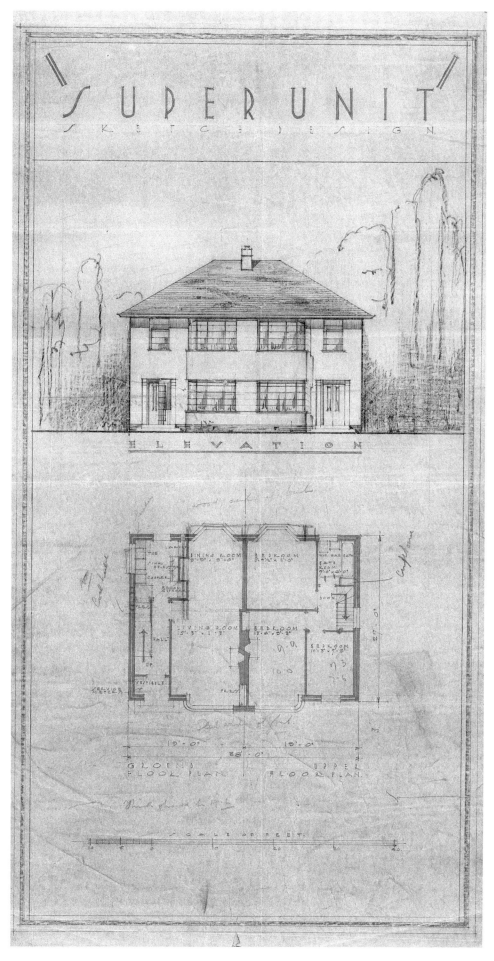

A3.31. Undated sketch design for 'Super-Unit' semi-detached type. (MMC D39727CN)

considerable portion of your hard earned income to a landlord for a house that will always just be a loan?' (77)

This slowing down of sales points to the more general difficulties which Mactaggart & Mickel, and other builders, encountered in the later years of the decade. These difficulties were, in part, the result of general industrial and economic constraints: growing competition for customers and resources, increased materials and labour costs, and in the later stages the threat of war. Those overarching constraints, as well as more specific background on the company's position in Edinburgh, were extensively dealt with in an interview of 1937, reproduced in the Appendices to this book, between Douglas Mickel and Edinburgh councillors and officials. It is worth summarising here some of the themes of that interview, which have bearing not only on the Mactaggart & Mickel story but on the wider building industry issues dealt with in Chapter B3.

The council had called the meeting principally with the aim of finding ways to maintain its own municipal housebuilding programme, in the context of the cost rises and resource shortages of the late 1930s, without damaging the progress of private enterprise building in the city. Its suggestion was that Mactaggart & Mickel should build up to a thousand Corporation houses each year as contractor, in addition to its existing private output. What was clear was that the rising cost of materials and growing competition for labour, especially bricklayers, were forcing firms to employ all sorts of expedients, such as importing non-local labour and sourcing materials from abroad. As far as any return to council contracting was concerned, the company's attitude was one of extreme caution, and insistence on the security of negotiated, fixed-price contracts and assured programmes over several years (a role that James Miller would, in the end, play for Edinburgh Corporation in the postwar years), rather than competitive building to trades schedules. The issue of single-contractor versus separate-trades was now in the past, and the new challenge, in the age of 'mass housing' and 'national planning', was that of negotiated and serial contracts. Overshadowing all else was the growing sense of emergency and of the need to consider 'the building industry as a whole' (in the words of the Edinburgh city chamberlain). Whatever the counter-arguments of market efficiency, even anti-socialists such as Douglas Mickel and the Edinburgh Corporation Progressives were finding themselves forced into the acceptance of ever greater co-ordination and political intervention in housebuilding.

The uncertainties experienced by Mactaggart & Mickel were also, however, exacerbated by a factor specific to the firm's own business: their bold attempt in the second half of the decade to refocus its owner-occupation building from low/medium to medium/high cost housing. This strategic reorientation, as significant in its own way as the eastward move of the early 1930s, brought with it both financial benefits and pitfalls, and created substantial tensions within the organisation. These can best be witnessed in the firm's two most significant 'upmarket' developments of the late 1930s, at the Broom, Whitecraigs (near Glasgow), and, to a lesser extent, Hillpark, in Edinburgh.

A3.32. 1938 view of 29 Broompark Drive, Broom Estate (sold in 1936). (MMC)

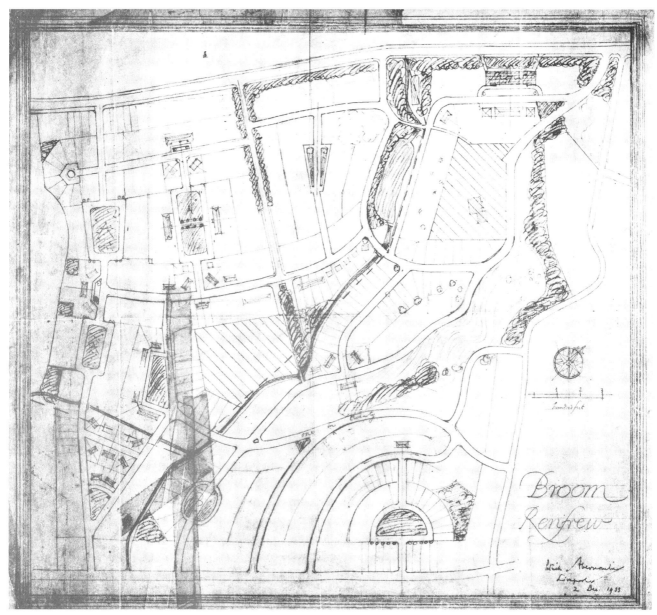

A3.33. Proposed plan for Broom Estate drawn up in December 1933 by Patrick Abercrombie. (MMC D33472)

Part III

Moving upmarket
the Broom and Hillpark

In late 1933, in the midst of selling a large number of low/medium cost houses in the Glasgow suburbs, Mactaggart & Mickel began to develop the idea of a radical departure from this pattern. It began to contemplate the idea of building a housing estate which targeted the more affluent house purchaser. Its aspiration was to provide a planned environment with architect-designed villas and bungalows. These would be clearly distinct from both general-needs local authority housing and its own earlier bungalow developments with their standard house-types and use of mass-produced ornamentation to give 'individuality' - an approach, typical of all speculative housebuilding, that had been the subject of architectural critiques since the late 19th century. Similar attempts to refocus the market positioning and general ethos of interwar speculative housing had been made by some English builders, but Mactaggart and Mickel's initiative was unique in interwar Scotland. The leading figure in the English efforts had been John Laing, who attempted over a number of years to

establish himself as a Maecenas of speculative building, employing, and deriving prestige from, mainstream housing architects. In 1932, he set aside a small estate (Sunnyfields, Mill Hill) for an architectural competition. The garden-city architect-planners Arthur Kenyon and T Alwyn Lloyd, produced an estate plan and designed 78 out of 92 houses. Laing's difficulty was that these garden city ideals of tastefully plain design had become associated in the public mind with council housing schemes, and Sunnyfields proved to be the slowest selling estate that Laing ever built; the firm's on-site salesmen vainly tried to encouraged it to add bay windows and other common speculative motifs in an attempt to sell the houses. (78) Mactaggart & Mickel's slightly later experience at the Broom Estate, although envisaging a 'modernistic' Art Deco rather than cottage-vernacular style for its houses, would prove strikingly similar in its outcome. The initial high design and planning aspirations of the directors would be increasingly undermined, and subsequently modified, by the pressing practical realities of the market - in addition to the inhibiting effect of the looming threat of war.

The Broom Estate is situated in Whitecraigs, adjacent to the Kilmarnock trunk road on one of the strands of suburban development stretching southwards into the Renfrewshire countryside for some miles beyond the Glasgow municipal boundary. In December 1933, Mactaggart & Mickel commissioned the town planner Patrick Abercrombie to design a layout for the newly purchased estate. (79) By that date, Abercrombie had already become one of the leading figures in the burgeoning movement of state-sponsored town and country planning, producing numerous town plans and particularly associating himself with the movement for population decentralisation from crowded old cities to completely new towns with different functions separately 'zoned' rather than mixed together - a philosophy whose major impetus in Scotland would come from his later Clyde Valley Regional Plan of 1946-49, co-authored with Robert Matthew.

One of the key concerns of the interwar planning movement was to stop the sprawl of unstructured suburban growth, especially in the form of 'ribbon development' alongside major roads. On the Broom site, Abercrombie's plan envisaged a small, largely self-contained garden suburb. In contrast to the uniformity of much normal speculative planning, he attempted to use the zoning idea to create clearly differentiated areas of natural irregularity and formality, each with a specific price-band connotation. The layout combined a sinuous central area of naturally contoured roads, running from the entrance at Kilmarnock Road to the south-western boundary of the site, and a number of more regular layouts on the western and south-eastern sections. The main route through the development (Broompark Drive) shadowed the layout of the estate before its purchase by the firm, connecting two gate-lodges. The western area (Area 'A', intended for the highest-priced houses) would consist of three grand central squares flanked by large detached houses in spacious gardens; its street plan was clearly derived from the Gretna and English garden city civic plans, with their wide boulevards or elongated squares of greenery flanked by terraces. At the Broom, Abercrombie adapted this formula to suit a residential scale: larger houses would run parallel to the square, whilst smaller (bungalows) would be set at angles to the crossroads. These open squares would be flanked at each axis by a house. The focus of the southernmost area ('C') would

be a triangular wedged section (another adopted garden city formula), and the 'B' area would be centred on an oval green. The remaining larger area (intended as the cheaper 'D' area) would consist of long, curved, sweeping roads, flanked at some points by long stretches of greenery; an oval 'lake' was retained near the Kilmarnock Road entrance. At the south-eastern corner, Abercrombie envisaged a grand half-moon crescent with radiating house-plots.

Abercrombie's layout was increasingly altered during the initial planning stages of 1934. The basic zoning concept was, however, still in place by late 1934, when the minimum selling value of houses in each of the four 'zones' was fixed as follows: £1,200 in 'A', £950 in 'B', £740 in 'C', and £600 in 'D'. At this point, James Taylor and the engineer John Munro were instructed to lay out the plots in Area 'A'. The project was first introduced to the public in an advertisement of December 1934: it reported that 'operations have commenced', and that 'a layout has been prepared by an expert in town planning, and a well known Glasgow architect will design houses to individual requirements'. In 1934, the newly-married Frank Mickel moved into and modernised a two-century-old, whitewashed cottage on the estate: Broom Cottage, in Broom Road. (80)

In a burst of publicity in spring 1935, Mactaggart & Mickel's suggested designs for the four areas of Broom Estate were strikingly illustrated in *Glasgow Herald* advertisements. Whereas Abercrombie's plan had seemed to point to an Arts and Crafts cottage formula of architecture, it now became clear that something more modish was the aim. Taylor's perspectives, with their sharply contrasted white villas and brooding, dark backgrounds, emphasised the firm's commitment to introduce a new architectural style for speculative housing. The flat-roofed, white-harled, and cubic form of the sample design for the exclusive Area A, in particular, proclaimed an affiliation to the commercially stylish world of Art Deco cinema modernity, with its eclectic assemblages of motifs culled from skyscrapers and European Modernism. Other sample designs for the 'A', however, mostly

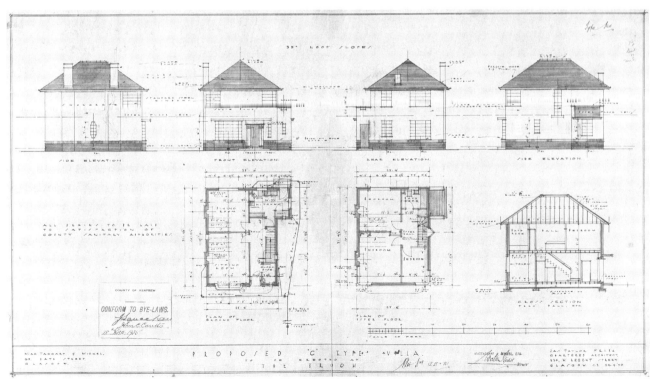

A3.34. April 1935 design by James Taylor for 'C' type villa to be erected at Broom Estate. (MMC D44749)

THE BROOM ESTATE WHITECRAIGS

IN NO OTHER SPHERE OF LIFE IS THE PROGRESS OF THE CENTURY
BETTER EXEMPLIFIED THAN IN HOUSING ● THE DEVELOPMENT OF
THE BEAUTIFUL BROOM ESTATE IS THE CULMINATING TRIUMPH OF
AN ORGANISATION WITH A RECOGNISED TRADITION FOR DOING THINGS
WELL ● HERE IN A NATURAL SETTING THE PINNACLE OF ACHIEVE-
MENT HAS BEEN REACHED IN HOUSE DESIGN ● WITH THE AID OF
OUR ARCHITECT, FULL EXPRESSION CAN BE GIVEN TO INDIVIDUALITY
IN DESIGN AND ACCOMMODATION, WHILE HE ENSURES THAT THE
EXTERIOR BLENDS HARMONIOUSLY WITH THE SURROUNDINGS ● THE
ABOVE IS AN ILLUSTRATION OF A SUGGESTED HOUSE FOR "A"
AREA ● FURTHER DESIGNS, TOGETHER WITH A MODEL OF PART
OF THE ESTATE, CAN BE SEEN AT THE ADDRESS BELOW

ANNOUNCEMENT OF

MACTAGGART & MICKEL LTD
63 BATH STREET GLASGOW
TELEPHONE DOUGLAS ONE

A3.35. *Broom Estate advertisement of May 1935, showing suggested modernistic house-type for use in Area 'A'. (Glasgow Herald, 4 May 1935; MMC D43297)*

THE BROOM ESTATE WHITECRAIGS

THE PERFECT BLENDING OF BOTH HOUSE AND SITE HAS BEEN ACHIEVED AT BROOM ESTATE. THIS LOVELY COUNTRY ESTATE HAS BEEN CHOSEN AS A SETTING FOR A LIMITED NUMBER OF EXCEPTIONALLY FINE HOUSES.

EACH ONE IS THE DESIGN OF A LEADING ARCHITECT AND THERE IS A STRICT INSISTENCE ON A CERTAIN HARMONY OF STYLE, AND A RESPECT FOR THE NATURAL AMENITIES OF THE ESTATE.

THE ABOVE ILLUSTRATION IS A SUGGESTION FOR "C" AREA, AND IS TYPICAL OF THE MANY DESIGNS AVAILABLE. THE INTERIOR OF THE HOUSE FULLY JUSTIFIES ITS OUT-WARD APPEARANCE. WELL PLANNED, AIRY AND EQUIPPED WITH EVERY MODERN FITMENT.

FURTHER DESIGNS, TOGETHER WITH A MODEL OF PART OF THE ESTATE, AT—

MACTAGGART & MICKEL LTD
63 BATH STREET GLASGOW
TELEPHONE DOUGLAS ONE

A3.36. Broom Estate advertisement of April 1935, showing bungalow type for use in Area 'C'; the advertisement cost £28 10s to place. (Glasgow Herald, 12 April 1935; MMC)

pictured large box-like villas with shallow pitched roofs, and only occasional flat-roofed extensions. The language of socialist and scientific progress, which made up many avant-garde Continental Modernist manifestos, was simplified into slogans of advertisement: 'In no other sphere of life is the progress of the century better exemplified than in housing. The development of the beautiful Broom Estate is the culminating triumph of an organisation with a recognised tradition'. 'The adoption of Modernism does not always bid good-bye to beauty ... the striking modern architecture is well expressed without losing anything of the dignity of house design'. To ensure the architectural 'harmony' of the estate, all designs were to be vetted by one architect to avoid a 'clash'. (81)

At this early stage, however, the main selling point of this estate was not its design modernity but its natural beauty and the 'individuality in design and accommodation', that Mactaggart & Mickel's 'leading architect' could offer for every purchaser within the higher price range. The Broom was to be a 'novel experiment which would silence critics of modern housing schemes ... When is a housing scheme not a housing scheme? When the houses are built to meet the buyer's special requirements and when they are placed in an unusually attractive setting by experts in estate planning'. The Broom was heralded as an alternative to the existing profusion of bungalow suburbs: 'criticism has always been publicly voiced against the builder of the bungalow and modern villa.' One journalist wrote that the speculative builder 'as a class ... is accused of having no eye for natural amenities and natural beauties, of having thought for nothing beyond the number of houses he can erect on any given number of acres, and of generally despoiling the countryside with long lines of little houses, all the same type and all lacking in architectural imagination ... but it is refreshing in the middle of an era in housing schemes to find builders who are departing from the contemporary orthodoxy and branching out into something different ... here is a future colony of modern houses each in a setting equal to that of the finest mansion in the land'. Despite the fact that the Broom site, according to Mactaggart & Mickel, could accommodate over 1,000 houses, the company stressed that only half of that number would actually be built; to erect houses on the estate in the ordinary way would, according to one article, 'approximate very closely to vandalism'. The 'charming lake banked by rhododendrons', the preservation of landscape, the fact that a system of footpaths would ensure that no children need 'go on any main road at all', and its overall 'quiet, peace and charm', would clearly distinguish the Broom from all 'modern conceptions of a housing scheme'. (82)

However, the built reality of the Broom Estate would prove to be very different from this airy vision. Some of the changes that occurred in the development of the estate, including the abandonment of Abercrombie's zoned plan and Taylor's exaggeratedly Art Deco house designs, can be, in part, attributed to the taste and preferences of central Scotland's house-buyers. More important in shaping the final outcome, however, were the company's own organisational and financial circumstances. The year 1935 marked the beginning of an organisational review at Mactaggart & Mickel; the following years would see a break in business relations with Western Heritable, a debate over a possible further split of the functions of the company, and an increasingly adverse business environment, overshadowed by the threat of war and its associated labour and cost problems. Although sales, and to a lesser extent profits, continued to grow, the post-subsidy building trade was growing increasingly difficult; Mactaggart & Mickel's monopolistic control of the house-buying market in the west of Scotland was, for the first time, being challenged. In

1939, Andrew Mickel claimed that 'never before in his experience had he seen so many houses advertised for sale'. And Sir John Mactaggart recalled at the end of the war that, in 1939, the value of his housing properties had been 'very low, owing to a slackening of demand'. (83)

Initial suggestions of organisational review had already begun in the more prosperous years of the mid-1930s. During the initial discussions concerning the Broom development, the chairman, Jack Mactaggart, had been absent from the company for a lengthy period, mostly in America; he had been increasingly suffering from ill health, and had been advised by his doctor to live in a warmer climate. From across the Atlantic, Jack attempted to keep track of all the business's activities, but in January 1935 (in the midst of the planning of the Broom), matters reached a head and a crisis meeting was called in New York. Directors Frank Mickel and Walter Grieve were asked to 'proceed immediately' to America. In Grieve's absence, Douglas Mickel was appointed a director, and was given a qualifying share allocation to make this possible. On their return, Grieve reported on 'conversations he and Mr Frank Mickel had had with Mr Mactaggart in New York' in which the latter had 'outlined a scheme for the re-organisation of the complete personnel of the firm' in a bid to boost production and sales. At an administration level, this would include the appointment of a chartered accountant as secretary, a sales manager, and a sales inspector; there should be a tightening up of on-site organisation, including employment of 'ex-policemen as timekeepers and watchmen', a system of status reports on foremen and superintendents, and a system of training existing suitable employees as possible foremen and superintendents'. The directors were split on the best course of action. Andrew Mickel did not believe that 'the present time was suitable for this reorganisation, as work on hand did not warrant it', but he agreed to appoint an accountant, James B Cunninghame, as secretary, and to promote a number of existing staff to the posts of sales manager and sales inspector; the other suggestions were deferred until a later date. In a list of salaried staff drawn up in c.1938, 46 Clydeside-based staff were listed (earning an annual total of £8,930), and 12 Edinburgh-based staff (earning an annual total of £2,164). All but one were paid weekly, including Douglas Mickel in Edinburgh (£6 weekly); the exception was the architect W A Gladstone, based in Glasgow, who was paid the substantial sum of £750 annually. Gladstone had already been used to supplement the work of Taylor, and of Stewart Kaye in Edinburgh, but now became a company architect. Much of the company's architectural work by this stage involved reworking or restyling of standard designs. (84)

During this period of growing concern over sales and profit margins, the development of Area 'A' of the Broom Estate had begun. Discussions over prices ensued: in Andrew Mickel's opinion, they were 'too low', and he subsequently questioned the estimates of the company surveyor (R Galbraith). The cost of £1,135 for a bungalow and £1,300 for a villa yielded a profit of 17.5-20%, but it was decided to 'up the prices' by £50. The display of a specimen Area 'A' house at the company's office in Bath Street resulted in the first real sales feedback. There were a number of enquiries about the likelihood of inclusion of five-apartment houses selling in the region of £1,000 (which was originally the Area 'B' price range); the viability of Area 'B' was queried, but they agreed to push ahead. The writing was now also on the wall for Taylor's flat-roofed cubistic Art Deco designs. Following Jack Mactaggart's return from America in late 1935, Taylor had been instructed by him to prepare sketch plans for villas and bungalows for five proposed plots 'with elevations more approaching period design than the existing houses'; it was at

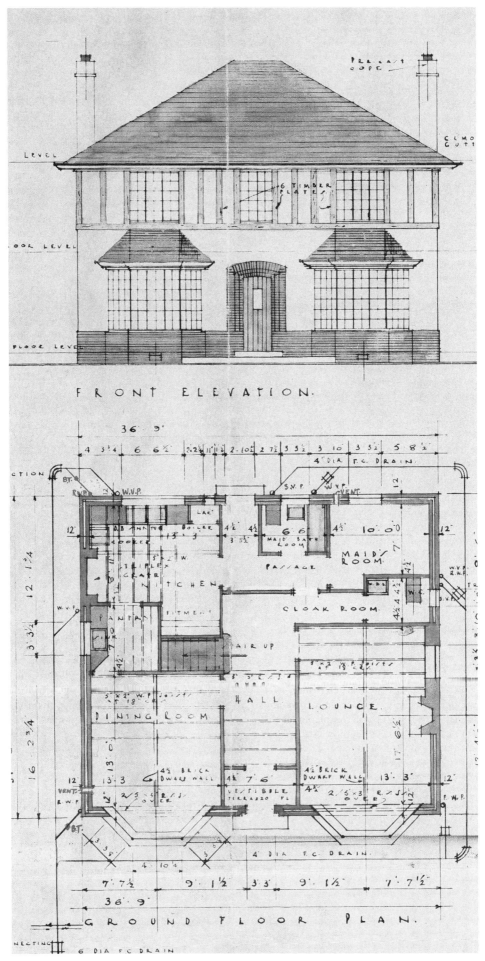

FRONT ELEVATION.

GROUND FLOOR PLAN.

A3.37. 1936 elevation detail and plan of detached villa proposed for Broom Estate; drawing by James Taylor. (MMC D44731CN)

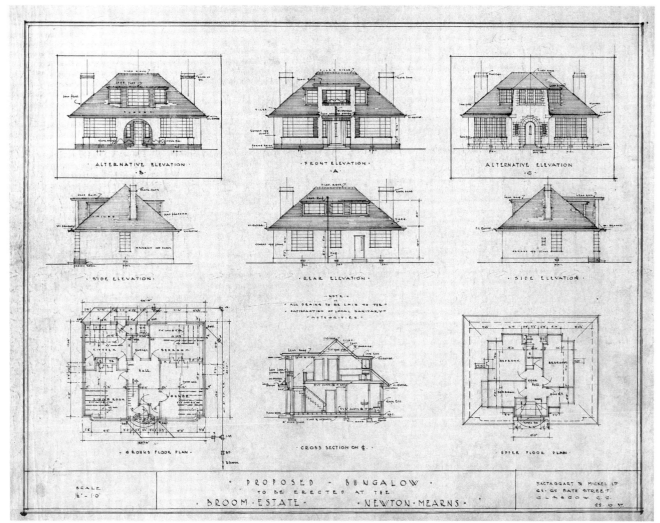

A3.38. Three alternative elevations for proposed bungalows at Broom Estate, October 1937. (MMC D44728)

this point that James Taylor's consultancy was renewed until 31 July 1936 at a monthly fee of £90, plus daily attendance fees of around £3. (85)

During 1935, a number of events resulted in the final abandonment of the original four-zoned concept for the Broom. Jack Mactaggart's return coincided with an 'intensive building programme' which was planned to produce 'as many houses as possible' by May 1936. Broom was to be a central part of this programme, and it was 'made clear by the chairman that immediate steps must be taken to counteract or remove any apparent difficulties which might prevent the completion of the work in the time stated'. An output of 12 houses in Area 'A' and 50 in Area 'C' was planned. Area 'B' was cancelled, and 'A' was extended accordingly. The Area 'A' prices were now to range from £1,200 to £1,750 (for villas of five to seven apartments). Area 'D' was to consist solely of Colour Homes. It was around this time that the final amendments were made to Abercrombie's plan for the Broom. A plan of 1938 shows the eventual layout: the sinuous road plan and picturesque planting which characterised the original concept for the northern zone was extended throughout the site, and the quasi-classical regular layouts were largely abandoned. The flat section that was to have been Area 'A' was now used for the compactly planned lower-cost Area 'C' (to the west of Broompark and Cavendish Drive), and the upmarket Area 'A' was moved eastwards to surround the loch, occupying the whole of the remainder of the site. (86) The proposed lower-priced Area 'D', with its minimum selling price of £750, was abandoned altogether.

It should be emphasised that the thrust of the changes to the Broom was not a move downmarket, but a simplification of the complicated zoning structure, and the replacement of the most individualistic architectural and planning elements by somewhat more standardised formulas, to speed progress. But despite the abandonment of the two zones and Taylor's flat-roofed designs, the Broom remained unique in offering speculative housing designed to meet the requirements of the individual purchaser, and it did much to foster the development of a more distinctly architectural approach to appeal to the sophisticated purchaser. As finally constructed, the Broom contained a great variety of individual and modified standard designs for rendered and metal-windowed detached bungalows and villas, mostly with tiled or slated pitched roofs, and set in lavish landscaping. The development was celebrated in 1937 in a sumptuous booklet by Peter Menzies, of which 1,100 were sent out to selected houses in the Glasgow valuation roll; this hailed the estate as 'indeed a world of its own - rich alike in history and natural beauty, a place which has defied desecration in the past, and whose future is now assured'.

Because of the requirement for individuality, the process of construction turned out to be much more complicated than on estates designed in a completely standardised way. The heavy reliance upon the architect was often difficult for Mactaggart & Mickel to accept; in the tradition of the single contractor, it had an ingrained scepticism about the effectiveness of architects in general. In late 1935, for example, the directors complained about the delay in obtaining plans from James Taylor, which was

BROOM ESTATE

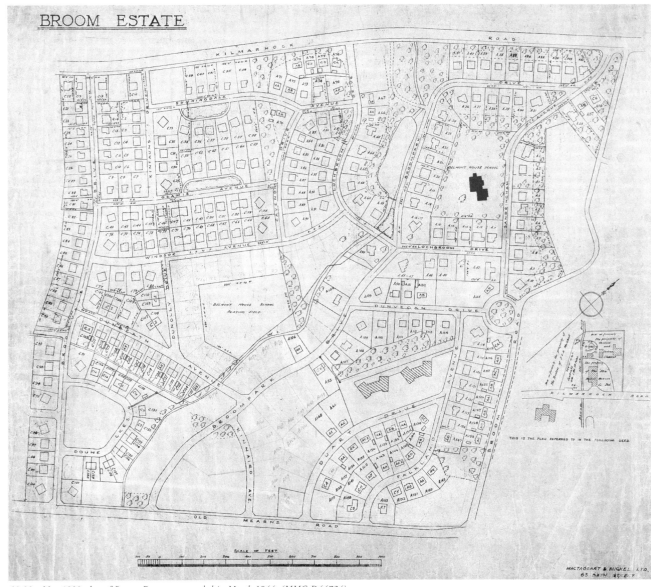

A3.39. May 1938 plan of Broom Estate, as amended in March 1944. (MMC D44724)

'hampering the building programme'; they speculated that 'unless better service could be obtained from his office, the whole question of his contract would be required to be reviewed'. Problems were also encountered on-site, as Mactaggart's new system of superintendents and inspectors proved difficult to enforce. A superintendent for Broom was appointed, as was an inspector (both on a weekly salary of £6); the latter was to report 'on matters of construction only'. The superintendent was to oversee the work of the site foreman and his men. One month after launching this system the Broom superintendent resigned, following demarcation disputes with the inspector. It was the practical-minded Frank Mickel who was burdened with the responsibility of dealing with these staffing problems. (87)

In total, 76 houses were built in Area 'A' before the outbreak of war, and 102 in Area 'C', whose dwellings, although cheaper, were still in an elite category by comparison with most speculative housing. By the date of the first wave of publicity, in May 1935, eight houses were under construction, and by the following month two showhouses for both areas were open. A 'temporary' sales office was constructed, to Taylor's design, at the entrance to the estate. It consisted of a timber frame with cement rendering on chicken netting; despite this makeshift construction, and lack of insulation, the building still remains in use today as an office for the Eastwood branch of the Scottish Conservative Party. Because

of the changing circumstances of the Broom's plan, and the tailor-made aspects of the estate, sales did not take off until mid-1935. Showhouses were crucial in the marketing of such a heterogeneous estate; a further nine plots were reserved for showhouses in late 1935, and the on-site sales staff based in them were regularly consulted for advice. (88)

The first house in Area 'A', a six-apartment bungalow costing £1,250, was sold in May 1935. The average cost of a villa or bungalow in Area 'A' was £1,500, although a small number sold for over £2,000, and one house at 25 Sandringham Avenue sold for £3,000. The high cost of this particular house was probably not determined by the building itself, but instead by the fact that it was built on a double feu, leaving two adjacent plots unbuilt upon. The majority of Area 'C' was sold before the war; sales began in March 1936, when a house on Kinfauns Drive was sold for £950. The average Area 'C' price was £1,000, inclusive of garage. Interwar purchasers of Broom houses primarily came from Glasgow, with some moving direct from council schemes such as Mosspark. There was a lull in advertising in late 1935, but after resumption of promotion in early 1936, further showhouses of five-apartment bungalows (selling for £975) and villas (£950) were opened. By late 1938, prices had risen markedly: a six-apartment bungalow in Area 'A' was selling for £1,375, and Area 'C' five-apartment bungalows for between £1,050 and £1,180. (89)

A3.40. Nicknamed the 'Clutterbucks House' (after the owners), this villa on Broom Road, Broom Estate, was sold for £1,390 in 1936. The caption in the estate brochure of 1938 reads: 'No better example could be given of the care which is taken to harmonise houses with their natural surroundings ... This photograph shows an ultra-modern six-apartment Detached Villa with special Roof Garden'. (The Book of Broom Estate, 1938, MMC)

A3.41. View of a specimen kitchen on Broom Estate, from the 1938 estate brochure. The caption reads: 'The Kitchen ... designed to eliminate as much work as possible, and a separate Maid's Sitting Room has been provided'. (The Book of Broom Estate, 1938, MMC)

A3.42. The original Broom Estate sales office at 69 Ayr Road, seen in 1997. (RCAHMS D01432)

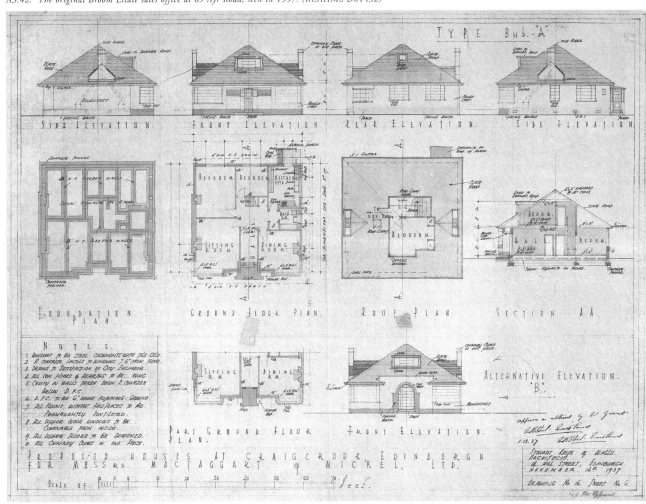

A3.43. Two alternative bungalow designs for Hillpark (Craigcrook) by Stewart Kaye & Walls, November 1937. (MMC 44843CN)

In December of that year, the repackaging of the Broom Estate was carried a stage further, when Mactaggart & Mickel opened Sandringham Court, a group of two blocks of rental service apartments. Although this had not been included in Abercrombie's original concept, working drawings for it, dated as early as 1933, survive in the company archives. Designed by W A Gladstone, the blocks were of three storeys and similar Art Deco style to the remainder of the estate, with concave-splayed frontage, metal-framed windows, some curved or swept-round, brick and render finish, and low-pitched roof. Each block contained twelve flats, consisting of a lounge, dining room, two bedrooms (one with built-in wardrobe) and tiled bathroom and kitchen. Great emphasis was given to lavish mod cons, including full central heating, vitriolite-lined bathroom, and stainless steel sinks and electric refrigerator in the 'laboratory style' kitchen. The annual rent of £250 was to include rates, tax, heating, hot water, external cleaning, lock-up garage, and the services of a uniformed porter. (90)

Sandringham Court formed part of a limited movement in late 1930s Glasgow and Edinburgh to build high-rental, highly serviced apartment blocks on the model established in London and in American cities; the most prominent example of these was the multi-storey Kelvin Court at Anniesland, 1937 (designed by J N Fatkin of Newcastle). The marketing of Sandringham Court exploited the established theme of technological modernity combined with suburban greenery, but in a heightened form: these were 'luxury flats in country surroundings' ... 'country flats for city people'. They targeted mobile professional people, '£1,000-a-year people' who wanted highly serviced accommodation 'without the responsibility of house ownership'. The superimposed bay windows on the sides were described as 'the highest glass wall in Scotland'. The development was marketed throughout early 1939, but by July, with the war crisis looming, the rents had fallen to £200-£225. (91)

In 1936-40, the Broom concept of an individualistic and exclusive detached villa development was exported to Edinburgh, where the Hillpark development was built in a similar landscaped outer-suburban setting, on the eastern side of Corstorphine Hill, and adjacent to the main Queensferry Road leading out of the city to the north. The development was smaller than the Broom, with only 51 houses sold by 1941, and it was less self-contained in its planning, as it abutted main roads directly. But it was more consistent in adopting a white-rendered, metal-windowed 'modernistic' Art Deco style. The finalised plan of March 1936

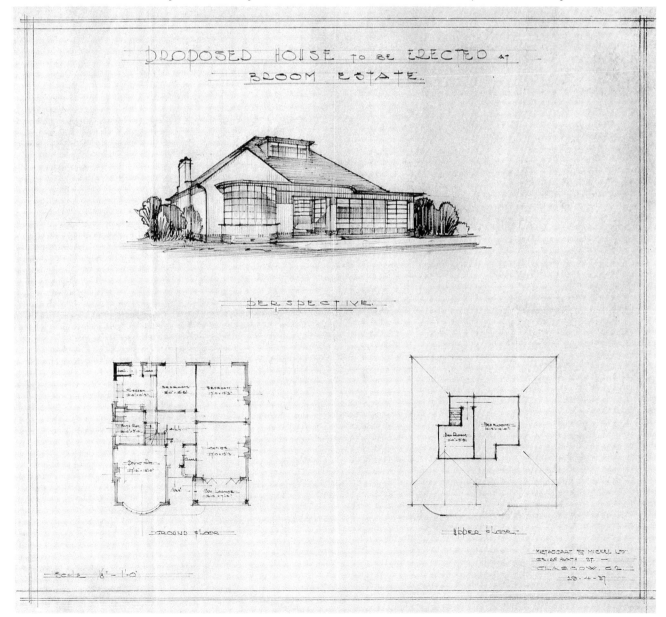

A3.44. Proposed house to be erected at Broom Estate: ground floor and upper floor plans, dated 29 April 1937. (MMC D44754)

HILLPARK ESTATE

OVERLOOKING THE BEAUTIFUL WOODLANDS OF DAVIDSON'S MAINS & CORSTORPHINE HILL PARKS.   THE FINEST RESIDENTIAL DISTRICT IN EDINBURGH, YET ONLY 12 MINUTES FROM PRINCES STREET.

This picturesque estate in the Queensferry Road has been chosen as the site for a limited number of distinguished Bungalows and Villas.   Each design has been prepared with due regard to the amenities of its setting and the architecture is dignified and practical. Every house has a charming aspect and many have an uninterrupted vista of magnificent parkland.

The above illustration shows a 5-apartment Bungalow for which the price is £1100.   There are also other types of houses ranging in price from £900.   Prices include road charges.

Show Houses are now open daily (including Sundays) from 1 p.m. until dusk and inspection is cordially invited.

HOW TO GET THERE.   S.M.T. or Corporation 'Buses from Hope Street Post Office (West End) to Craigcrook Road or Davidson's Mains Cross respectively.   Trains from Caledonian Station (L.M.S.) to Davidson's Mains.

Mactaggart & Mickel Ltd

67 YORK PLACE - - - - - - EDINBURGH
TELEPHONE — EDINBURGH 21717

by Stewart Kaye for the first development, then under construction, envisaged 78 plots arranged along the main Queensferry Road and Craigcrook Road frontages, and along Hillpark Avenue and two connecting spur roads behind to the west. Three villa-types and two bungalow-types were envisaged, costing between £900 and £1,390; the two most prominent plots at the north-east corner of the site, facing the Queensferry Road junction, were marked as 'reserved'; there were also plans of November 1935 for erection of up to 12 semi-detached 'Super Colour Homes' on an adjacent site. (92)

Both of the Hillpark bungalow-types, the £1,180 'Lh' and the £1,300 'Bh' (the 'h' denoting a specially styled version for Hillpark) were of five apartments, with two public rooms, two bedrooms, kitchen and bathroom on the ground floor and bedroom and boxroom in the high roof space. The 'Bh', entered by a brick archway, was slightly larger, with a fitted kitchen rather than a kitchenette, and a 'sitting room' rather than 'lounge'; the hall had a small cloakroom adjoining it. The villas included the £1,390 'Jh', with ground-floor staircase hall, drawing room, dining room and kitchenette, and three bedrooms, bathroom and maid's room on the first floor. Construction of these houses comprised roughcast 12" cavity brickwork with 4.5" and 3" internal breeze block walls; there were facing brick dressings and base, and metal Art Deco windows, some curved round on bay windows. The foreman and chief bricklayer on the job was Charlie Lees. (93)

The first sale on the development was 409 Queensferry Road, a six-apartment detached villa with garage (presumably a former showhouse) sold in late March 1936 for £1,485, with £75 down-payment. Then followed a pause until the main sales commenced in 1937, mostly for five- and six- apartment houses, some purchased through the Eastbourne Building Society, and some outright. In April 1937, three five-apartment type 'Bh' bungalows facing Queensferry Road were sold (here for £1,150), and in August two five-apartment-type 'G' villas at 2 and 4 Hillpark Drive for £900 and £925. These represented the cheaper end of the spectrum of Hillpark properties, and more expensive villas and bungalows followed. The estate was marketed in a similar manner to the Broom, emphasising its combination of landscaped, rural exclusivity with accessibility. A 1937 advertisement showed a perspective of white showhouses against the broad sweep of Queensferry Road: 'The finest residential district in Edinburgh, yet only 12 minutes from Princes Street', it was described as a 'picturesque estate ... the site for a limited number of distinguished bungalows and villas ... the architecture is dignified and practical ... uninterrupted vista of magnificent parkland'. (94) As on other estates, sales plummeted in 1939 with the threat of war, and in April 1940 Douglas Mickel himself bought one of the six-apartment villas, 20 Hillpark Avenue, for £1,375. He and his wife Marjorie have continued to live in the house since then, and raised their family there. Sales at Hillpark continued intermittently into 1941, with one of the showhouses, 385 Queensferry Road, a five-apartment detached bungalow with garage, being sold in February 1941 for £1,300, with £200 deposit.

(opposite) A3.45. 1937 advertisement for Hillpark Estate. (SMT Magazine, December 1937; MMC)

Part IV

Orchard Park and the build-up to war

In the years of economic and political uncertainty leading up to the outbreak of World War II, there was a perceptible shift in the firm's policy away from the adventurous departure represented by the Broom, back towards the selling of medium-cost speculative housing, quickly and well, using the same general marketing approaches as in the early 1930s.

The debates within the firm about policy direction continued in these years. On the one hand, Jack Mactaggart continued his attacks on declining profits, claiming that these resulted from the company's own excessively high selling prices rather than from the soaring materials and labour costs of the time; but he attended fewer and fewer directors' meetings. In practice, the separation of the 'Mactaggart' and 'Mickel' elements in the firm continued, with the severance of the relationship with Western Heritable, after the latter's cessation of building, and the transfer of 5,000 Western Heritable shares to Jack Mactaggart for £100,000 in 1938. In 1939, Walter Grieve resigned his directorship to take up a similar position in a company formed by Sir J A Mactaggart. During the mid and late 1930s, as part of this restructuring, some consideration was also given to a further subdivision of the firm to segregate the building activity from the Edinburgh letting stock, probably for taxation purposes. One proposal, later withdrawn, was to create a holding company with building and property-management subsidiaries, the building company having a capital of £50,000. (95)

During the late 1930s, as we have already seen from Douglas Mickel's discussions with Edinburgh Corporation, the company continued to keep at a distance from local authority contracting. In 1935, it had got as far as pricing a schedule for the 160-house first development of Paisley Town Council's major Ferguslie Park development, but it decided not to return the schedule. In 1938, a reluctance to exclude future local authority contracts in the burgeoning field of 'non-traditional' or prefabricated construction led the company to pursue development of its own patented method of construction, comprising timber-framing clad in 2" breeze-block concrete, incorporating a diaphragm of bitumen sheeting (patent 5075/38). In 1939, a proposal to build demonstration houses in experimental construction in Saughton Mains Road, Carrick Knowe, was put forward, followed (in consultation with Sir John Mactaggart) by a more ambitious plan for a 'four-in-a-block' at King's Park, on a site in Carmunnock Road adjoining Croftfoot Garage, to be taken over on completion by Western Heritable but made available for inspection by local authorities; these were complete by April 1939.

The most concerted attempt by the firm to return to large-scale local authority contracting, on an all-trades basis, was made in conjunction with Sir John Mactaggart in 1938. It concerned Castlemilk, a large outer-suburban Glasgow scheme which the Corporation planned to build following a major boundary extension. A handwritten memo of March 1939 by Andrew Mickel described what happened: 'About a year ago, Sir John and I discussed the possibility of helping the Corporation of Glasgow with their Housing Programme and most particularly as to the development of Castlemilk Estate. Together we went over the Estate to enable us to be acquainted with the site. After two visits we decided that Sir John would send in an offer to the Corporation to build Castlemilk through an association. He was to be one of the associates, and Sir Alex Swan's name was mentioned as another. In the event of the offer being successful,

Mactaggart & Mickel were to get the contract from the association to build the houses. We also discussed the possibilities of alternative methods of construction for speedy output. The offer was considered by the Corporation and turned down'. In December 1938 Andrew Mickel and Mactaggart had met George Smith, convener of the Corporation's Housing Committee, but 'he let us know in no uncertain manner that no offer such as had been submitted or contracts with private firms would be entertained by his committee; under no circumstances would work go out to private enterprises. So that finished for the time being'. Castlemilk was eventually built in the 1950s by the Corporation as one of its giant schemes of tenements.

In those same years, the owner-occupation sector was also beginning to throw up its own specific problems, such as the growing difficulties of the pool system. In an April 1937 comparison of building societies, the Halifax was said to be retaining too much pool money and demanding an excessively large deposit and guarantee (£20 and £100 respectively on a £500 house); the Abbey Road, National, and Leeds were much preferable, and in 1938 it was recommended to do no further business with the Halifax unless it was 'prepared to release unconditionally' a substantial portion of the pool money it held. In May 1939, the Dunfermline Building Society reported 'appalling' levels of arrears among pool borrowers. (96)

But alongside all these difficulties and debates, in Mactaggart & Mickel's heartland of the west the late 1930s nevertheless saw substantial building progress. Throughout the middle of the decade, the firm had been continuing to build up its land-bank in the west. These acquisitions would make possible a new drive of large-scale speculative building in the Glasgow hinterland, including sites in towns some distance down the Clyde estuary. To help focus on these sites, from 1935 the company began searching for a site on the south side of Glasgow suitable for a yard, stores and works, then still housed in cramped conditions adjacent to completed houses. (97) The largest development

which began in the late 1930s was in the company's established building zone south of Glasgow: Orchard Park, an extensive estate on a site stretching eastwards from Thornliebank Main Street to Orchard Drive, Giffnock.

Orchard Park was built on the site of the former Eastwood Golf Course, an 82-acre site bought from Giffnock Estates by the company in February 1937; the purchase price, which also included a 1.6 acre site at Thornliebank, was £11,000, amounting to £132 per acre. That was relatively inexpensive for land in that area (for example, 23 acres had been bought just over a year previously at Kirkhill, Newton Mearns, for £220 per acre). However, 18% of the site was occupied by quarry workings and was unsuitable for development, while only 38% of it was level ground completely suitable for building. (98) Extensive papers on the negotiations leading up to the purchase survive in the company archives, allowing it to be examined in some detail as a case study.

Negotiations for the site had begun in mid-1935, leading up to an initial purchase offer in August. The conditions set out in the draft agreement perpetuated the centuries-old tradition of restrictive guidelines on suburban development, designed to ensure a strictly residential character at a controlled density and appearance; they represented a somewhat watered-down version of the elite feuing specifications for developments such as the West End terraces of Glasgow or Edinburgh. The houses were to be of a minimum value of £800 and a minimum size of five apartments, constructed of stone, concrete or roughcast brick, and not exceeding two storeys and attic. Streets were to be of 36' minimum width, and the houses were to be set no closer than 18'6". The annual feu duty was to be £30, and houses of a minimum total value of £12,000 were to be completed within one year of sale of the land. All plans were to be approved by Giffnock Estates before building; in contrast to the pre-1914 'terrace' tradition of repetitive units, there was now (doubtless in reaction to council schemes) a concern that 'the front elevation

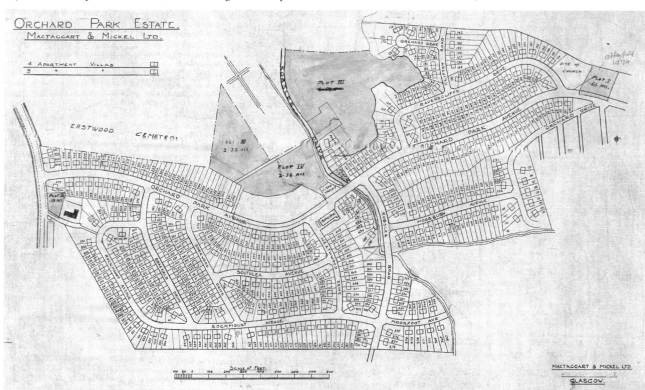

A3.46. Undated plan of Orchard Park Estate. (MMC D44735)
(opposite) A3.47. 1937 advertisement for Orchard Park. (Evening Times, 15 October 1937; MMC)

RE-OPENING OF ORCHARD PARK ESTATE

AT THORNLIEBANK ROAD
ONE MINUTE FROM THE STATION

First 36 HOUSES FOR £525 ON BASIS OF £25 DOWN & 18/10ᴰ WEEKLY

Owing to the phenomenal success of our previous 4-Apartment Housing Offer (we sold 60 houses in 12 hours), we were forced to cancel all advertising until further sites were prepared to meet the demand. NOW we are ready once again, and to celebrate the opening of the Thornliebank end of the Estate we are offering the first 36 houses at £525 on basis of £25 down and 18/10 per week. Here is an offer you simply can't afford to miss. Remember, when these 36 are sold the price MUST rise to £550. So be in at the beginning—save £25 and avoid disappointment. We are booking from to-day onwards.

A HOUSE OF DREAMS.

- The airy hall, with staircase lit by a big window at the extreme end, connects the upstairs rooms.
- The large front room is equipped with a beautifully tiled sitting-room fireplace, and cleverly concealed is a water-heating control.
- The Dining-room, spacious and airy, overlooks a generous garden.
- All windows are of the French type and are designed to admit a maximum of sunshine and fresh air.
- Of especial appeal to the housewife is the sparkling kitchenette with its twin sinks, new improved gas cooker, cabinet with glass doors, and well-ventilated larder.
- Now, the Bathroom. . . . All taps are chromium-plated, and the bath is panelled to eliminate awkward sweeping. Walls are lined with glistening tiles, and the ceiling is finished with a special plaster boarding which cannot crack or fall.
- Beautifully enamelled paintwork eliminates the drudgery of old-time cleaning. . . . Veritably a HOUSE OF DREAMS.

HOW TO GET THERE.—The Estate is on the main Thornliebank Road one stop past Thornliebank Station. Take a tram or bus right to the door, or train to Thornliebank Station takes you within one minute of the Estate. Show Houses open daily, including Sunday, from 12 noon until dusk.

MACTAGGART & MICKEL LTD

63-65 BATH STREET   **GLASGOW C.1**

TELEPHONE DOUGLAS ONE

GIVE YOUR BABY
A PLACE
IN THE SUN

Why be content to raise your family in the smoky atmosphere of the city when you can, for the same weekly outlay, be living in the clear, sunny atmosphere of the country.

Mactaggart and Mickel homes are as easy to own as a city flat is to rent. They are modern in every respect, have big airy rooms, and are equipped with every conceivable comfort and labour-saving device.

Then there's the garden where the kiddies can frolic in the clear fresh air, safe from the dangers of city traffic.

Please come out this weekend and look over the Show Houses.

Carolside Park
4-APARTMENT DETACHED BUNGALOWS

A total deposit of £50, payable £25 down and £25 upon occupancy, secures possession, and the inclusive weekly outlay is only 25/3. No Legal Fees or Road Charges. (Cash purchase price, £770.)

Also 5-Apartment Bungalows.

HOW TO GET THERE

These houses are well served by frequent 'buses, trams, and trams to Clarkston Terminus, and S.M.T. run a service from Clyde Street right into the Estate.

Orchard Park Estate
4 AND 5-APARTMENT VILLAS

These homes, offered at special low terms of £575 for the 4-apartment or £30 down and 20/2 per week, and £725 for the 5-apartment or £35 down and 22/4 per week, have entailed a substantially low outlay. No Legal Fees or Road Charges.

HOW TO GET THERE

The entrance to the Estate for the 5-apartment house is at the foot of Orchard Drive, off Kilmarnock Road, just past Tudor Cinema. Take a Corporation 'bus or tram, an S.M.T. 'bus or train to Giffnock Station.

For 4-apartment houses take a tram or 'bus to Thornliebank Road, one stop past Thornliebank Station, or train to Thornliebank.

MACTAGGART & MICKEL, LTD.
63-65 BATH STREET --------- GLASGOW.
TELEPHONE—DOUGLAS ONE

A3.48. March 1938 advertisement for Carolside Park and Orchard Park. (Daily Record, 12 March 1938; MMC)

of each house shall be essentially different in design so as to prevent the houses presenting a uniform appearance'. Of course, the private feu-restriction system was now supplemented by growing state controls through town planning mechanisms, and in January 1936 the firm applied to Renfrew County Council for planning permission under the Town & Country Planning (General Interim Development Order) (Scotland) 1933, submitting a layout plan and indication of zoned density; permission was granted in August. (99)

It was not until February 1937 that the disposition of the land by Giffnock Estates to Mactaggart & Mickel was finalised and work could begin. By then, the conditions of the sale had subtly changed, as the firm was no longer taking on a feu, with its subordinate status, but buying the superiority of the land as well - that is, acquiring it outright and becoming the superior itself, in order to simplify its control over development and subsequent amenity. In the prewar section of the estate, up to 1940, 636 houses were built, with a total sales figure of £387,675. The development was dominated at first by four- and five-apartment semi-detached villas. The first house sold, in May 1937, was a four-apartment, costing £500 (with a weekly outlay of 18s 3d); the price of that type rose in late 1937 to £525, in 1938 to £550 and in 1939 to £575, at which date a five-apartment villa cost £685.

The estate was marketed from the beginning in terms of economy rather than luxury; the inaugural advertisements in May 1937 praised the four-apartment homes as heralds of a new era of 'bargain houses' of 'plain but effective design' ... 'within the capacity of ordinary wage earners'. But there was equal emphasis on the estate's landscaped, suburban amenity, exploiting particularly its golfing heritage: 'Whose house will be the 19th? ... [It] may now be possible for a married golfer to go into his back garden and point proudly to the green on which he won with a "birdie" ... [From] a comfortable armchair in his sitting room, he may view the bunker which ruined his chance of whacking the professional on his own course'. A week later, advertisements apologised to the 'hundreds disappointed' by queues at the Orchard Park showhouses; the first 60 houses, priced at £500, had been sold in twelve hours, and a second instalment of 60 was now on offer for £525 each, and £25 down. The advertising campaign for Orchard Park was high-profile and costly; for example, Peter A Menzies Advertising produced Mactaggart & Mickel's first ever full-page colour advertisement in the Sunday Mail of 24 October 1937; the newspaper claimed that this was 'the first full-page colour advertisement to be carried by any Sunday newspaper . (100)

Given the emphasis on output at this estate, it was especially hard hit by the rearmament-led resource shortages of the late 1930s. There were appalling difficulties in obtaining workmen, particularly bricklayers: a report of August 1937 claimed 'we were very far behind with our building programme, especially at Orchard Park ... no matter what inducements we offered in regard to hourly rates, the bricklayers were leaving us to go to employers who were guaranteeing payment for bad weather'. (101)

However, by October 1937, 250 houses had been sold, and the company claimed to have had to postpone its advertising again because of the excess demand and 'public furore'; labourers were working on Saturdays marking up plots and erecting 'sold' signs. Further marketing of Orchard Park linked criticism of urban rental housing with a new emphasis of greater health and safety for children: 'Every child should have a place in the sun. To-day medical authorities emphasise the health benefits to be derived by children from fresh air and sunshine, and deplore the artificial life that even children whose parents are in comfortable circumstances are subjected to in the big cities ... the crowded streets of the city may offer adventure and fascinate the young child with their lights and glamour, but no mother can rest happily at home knowing that their children are exposed to the increasing dangers of road traffic'. And, 'This man once paid rent ... just as you do! He's a happier man, with a happier wife and a healthy kiddie. In a house where both he and his family are healthier, more contented, and secure!' And, 'Her garden's her guardian ... your child too can have this opportunity, you too, can have her mother's peace of mind ... buy a Mactaggart & Mickel house'. (102)

A surviving log book which details the firm's sales department costs from March 1936 to October 1938 provides a detailed insight into the significant advertising costs, the seasonal sales fluctuations (tied, of course, to the housing production cycle) and the relative success of estates in terms of sales. In the financial year March 1936 to February 1937, the total sales income was £214,732. The sales department costs, including salaries, for this period were £4,018 and the advertising costs £1,752; the peak months for advertising costs were February-April (corresponding to the peak sales period of January-May). The greatest number of sales of that year was at Carolside Park (144 houses); Orchard Park dominated the following year's production, prompting a 50% increase in advertising costs (to £3,545) and sales. Between March 1937 and February 1938, 543 houses were sold (including 318 at Orchard Park) for a total of £382,325.

At the end of the 1930s, the revival of the company's high-output strand of production was continuing. A few estates were started towards the upper end of the market, such as Muirburn Avenue, Muirend, 'one of the city's most select districts', where 15 houses ranging from a £900, five-apartment type 'B' bungalow to a six-apartment £1,240 bungalow were sold in 1936-37; and a new development near Eaglesham Road in 1938, ranging from £850 five-apartment semi-detached villas to four £1,390 detached houses. (103)

As part of its average-priced developments, from 1936 the firm ventured further down the Clyde coast to its first seaside resort estates, in Largs. Its first development there was under construction by November 1935 in a 'intensive building programme', and was complete by 1938, while a second and smaller development was built in 1939. This development was built without a building society pool arrangement, with 85% rather than 80% loans offered, and feu duties providing £300 revenue per annum. Its construction was hampered by chronic labour shortages, especially of bricklayers, leading to discussions about the possibility of offering 'premium' pay or drafting in a squad from Glasgow; the foreman was paid £5 weekly. Prices of completed houses at Barrfields and Beachway in 1937 ranged from £850 for a mid-terrace villa and £900 for an end villa to £950 for a bungalow; in 1939, four-apartment bungalows and terraces were being offered in Blythswood Crescent, off John Street. Further up the coast, in the burgh of Stevenston, 1939-40 saw the building of a development of 36 houses in the small Ardeer Estate, on the Kilwinning Road. In 1939, it was first decided to build four- and five-apartment villas of a type selling at Carolside Park, but after slow sales cheaper bungalows and four-apartment terrace houses selling for £600-£630 (with £30 down-payment and all-in weekly outlay of 22s 8d) were added. The same year saw a medium-sized development in a suburban area of the North Clyde burgh of Dumbarton: the Overtoun Estate, in Round Riding Road. Fifty houses were built, including three- and four-

A3.49. February 1938 advertisement for Carolside Park and Orchard Park. (Sunday Mail, 13 February 1938; MMC)

LIVE AND LET TO LIVE

WHY NOT LIVE ON THE GLORIOUS FIRTH OF CLYDE

Mactaggart & Mickel have built a number of magnificent Bungalows and Villas at this bracing seaside resort, and there are a few still available for immediate occupancy. You **AT LARGS?** can live here in surroundings of seaside, country, and town, more cheaply than you can in the city.

Then again you can "let" your house for the summer months and in this way partly pay for its upkeep.

These houses are tastefully designed and strongly built. The rooms are large and airy, and the beautiful tiled kitchenette is fitted with every modern labour-saving idea. In the case of the Bungalow an extra bathroom is provided.

Spend a day in Largs and look through the Mactaggart & Mickel houses.

Prices from £850 to £950. Small deposit and very easy terms.

Show Houses off Beachway Avenue, Esplanade, open daily 12 noon till dusk (Sundays included).

MACTAGGART & MICKEL LTD
63-65 BATH STREET, GLASGOW
TELEPHONE DOUGLAS ONE

A3.51. Andrew and Agnes Frances Mickel seen at Largs in 1931. They were later to buy a Mactaggart & Mickel built home at 2 Beachway, Largs in 1937, at a cost of £1,100. (MMC)

(opposite) A3.50. 1937 advertisement for Largs houses. 'Live and Let to Live at Largs': 'let your house for the summer months and in this way partly pay for its upkeep'. (Evening Citizen, 16 July 1937; MMC)

apartment semi-detached villas, and four-apartment detached bungalows for £50 down and 29s 8d weekly outlay; to speed up sales, showhouses at Merrylee Park were disposed of to free a salesman for redeployment, and local firms were contacted to bring the houses to employees' notice. (104)

The international crises of 1938-39 cruelly snuffed out this increasingly confident programme of the late 1930s. The fluctuating uncertainty hit sales hard, with peaks and troughs corresponding to the public perception of threat. Where 1938 saw a total sales turnover of £200,000, in 1939 the rate of sales dropped off further, although there was a brief recovery in the spring, the May figure of £11,910 being the best since August 1938. With the exception of a single house at Hillpark, all sales were of the less expensive houses, and in July the Broom and Carolside Park were 'dead at present' as the crisis had become 'more serious'. By August, there were numbers of cancellations of sales. Responses included the possibility of renting out unsold houses; in April and May, there had already been abortive discussions with the Hillington factory Pigson Ltd, about the possible renting out of six houses to employees for a year, with the option of buying at the end. (105)

The trajectory of the crisis was mirrored in the internal debates within the firm. In January 1939, Andrew Mickel highlighted the 'serious state of affairs which existed at Broom, where 19 houses in Area 'A' and 25 in Area 'C' have been built for some time and remained unsold'; the sales manager, Mr McFadyen, 'must institute an extensive campaign for the disposal of these', possibly by reducing cash down-payments in Area 'C' to £100 and cutting selling prices in area 'A'. Andrew Mickel had 'never before in his experience seen so many houses advertised for sale'. One sales manager, Miss Rule, argued that the company should concentrate on 'producing a cheap four-apartment house selling at approximately £600'; Andrew Mickel declared that although the September 1938 crisis had severely affected sales, the 'present crisis, coming on as it has just at the letting and selling season, would prove more serious for the company', and thus it should be 'everyone's endeavour to do his or her utmost to reduce the stock of houses on hand'. John Mactaggart had advised the engagement of an outside letting agent, R B Wilson & Co., to help sell houses in the Broom and to let Sandringham Court; its 'best salesman', a Mr Summers, had been transferred to the Broom. Five pounds would be paid to the salesmen for every house sold in the Broom, and £2 10s for every flat let. In April, it was decided to scale down promotion of Sandringham Court until the 'international crisis had passed', and rents were cut by up to 20%; the size of work-squads was reduced, for example to only four men at the Broom. In a paper, C Douglas Calverley argued that 'most people are discouraged from embarking on the great event of buying a house, when the dark clouds of war loom so heavily over us'. (106)

As it became clear that war was inevitable, the rhetoric of dispersal from bombing and of wartime scarcity began to infiltrate advertising: 'Live in a safe area and stop worrying. Modern bungalows and villas can quickly be made available for occupancy ... outside the danger zone', at Carolside Park, the Broom, and Orchard Park. 'Why part with your children when you can move from your city dwelling and take your family to live in a safe area?' 'Notwithstanding the Emergency which has arisen, we are still in a position to sell houses at prewar prices - although previous Building Society terms can not be arranged ... loans can be arranged'. But even if prices could be held at prewar levels, everything else was to change completely for the Scottish housebuilder during the next decade, as we will see in the next

A3.52. 'East & West - Mactaggart & Mickel Homes are Best!' Advertisement for houses in Edinburgh and Clydeside, 1939. (Daily Record, 2 April 1939; MMC)

chapter. Whatever the views of its directors on the desirability of state intervention in the housing market and the building industry, building in a highly regulated command economy would be the only outlet open to Mactaggart & Mickel. (107)

Notes

Readers are referred to the Notes sections of Chapters A1 and A2, and the Abbreviations section at the end of the book, for an explanation of the abbreviated forms used in this list.

1   MMA, document signed by Jack Mactaggart and Andrew Mickel, *c.*1933.
2   MM Minutes, 13 April 1932.
3   Information from John Craig.
4   MMA, document signed by Jack Mactaggart and Andrew Mickel, *c.*1933.
5   1933 subsidy withdrawal: information from A O'Carroll.
6   *GH*, 9 August 1929, 10; Morgan, *DSBB.*
7   Morgan, *DSBB.*
8   *GH*, 8 March 1930, 7; Morgan, *DSBB*; *GH*, 3 October 1930, 6; GCM Subcommittee on Finance (hereafter GCM SF), 19 November 1930, 11 December 1930, 14 January 1931; 12 March 1931; 12 October 1932.
9   GCM SF, 3 February 1932, 11 March 1932; Sites, 5 February 1932 and 11

10   Sites, 7 October 1932 and 5 February 1932; GCM, 18 May 1932; Sites, 7 October 1932. On Cardonald: MMA drawings of eight different types C, D, E, F, G, H, I, J.

11   GCM, 4 August 1932 and 16 November 1932; GCM SF, 21 December 1932.

12   GCM, 23 December 1932 and 16 January 1933; GCM SF, 29 March 1933; Sites, 5 May 1933.

13   Andrew Mickel, *The Citizen*, 9 November 1945.

14   Mactaggart: Morgan, *DSBB*.

15   MMA, letter from Mactaggart & Mickel to Trustees of Mrs A Campbell (Breeze, Paterson & Chapman), 22 May 1932; MM Minutes, 22 May 1931 and 18 September 1935.

16   MM Minutes, 20 July 1938; MM balance accounts, 30 April 1939 (information and analysis by John Craig).

17   MM Minutes, 17 August 1934.

18   MMA sales books (hereafter MMASB) for King's Park, 27 February 1928, 18 May 1929, 2 September 1929. The size of houses for sale or rent in the 1920s and 1930s was described in terms of numbers of 'apartments'; an apartment could be a public room (living, drawing or dining room) or a bedroom, but it excluded the kitchen and bathroom.

19   MMA drawings (hereafter MMAD), undated; MMASB; MMA, estate prices book, 1931-32 (hereafter MMAEPB); MMAD, 11 March 1932; *Daily Record* (hereafter *DR*), 10 September 1932.

20   MMAEPB; *DR* and *Bulletin*, 6 February 1932; MMAD, June and December 1930 and November 1931; MMASB.

21   *DR*, 10 September 1932; *Bulletin*, 22 October 1932; *GH*, 6 May 1933; *Bulletin*, 16 June 1933.

22   MMAD, June 1930 and 11 March 1932; MMAEPB, advertisements of 30 January 1932; MMASB, 14 September 1934.

23   MMAD, 1931; MMAEPB; MMASB, 23 April 1931; *GH*, 12 April 1933; MMAD, 1929 and 22 October 1934.

24   MMAD; *Bulletin*, 6 September 1930; MMASB, 22 August 1930; MMAEPB.

25   Central Housing Advisory Committee, *Private Enterprise Housing*, 1944, cited in O'Carroll, ILA.

26   O'Carroll, ILA.

27   Interview with Mrs Dorothy Young, 28 January 1999; Mrs Young still lives in King's Park, at 73 Kingslynn Drive, with her husband Robert, who moved into that house when he was four years old.

28   Advertisement, 30 January 1932; M G Horsey, *London Journal*, 11, 1985, 147-59.

29   On bungalows, see C McKean, *The Scottish Thirties*, 1987; M Glendinning, A MacKechnie, and R MacInnes, *A History of Scottish Architecture*, 1996, 392.

30   Contoured layouts: information from Iain Drysdale.

31   MMASB.

32   Renfrew County Council Minutes (hereafter RCM), Public Health Committee, March 1932.

33   RCM, Sub-committee on Building Works, 8 March 1931, 8 June 1931, 13 July 1931, 14 September 1931, 12 October 1931, 9 November 1931; MMAD, April 1931; MMAEPB; MMASB. Mactaggart & Mickel also built 11 shops to service the new development.

34   *Bulletin*, 27 July 1931. In 1933, Laings followed Mactaggart & Mickel's example at Eglinton Toll, when it leased a plot in front of King's Cross Station, London, and erected a 'Rona' type showhouse: M G Horsey, *London Journal*, 11, 1985, 147-59; *Bulletin*, 29 June 1931 and 17 June 1933; *Citizen*, 26 May 1934.

35   *Bulletin*, 29 June 1931; *DR*, October 1932, 16 January 1932 and 25 March 1932; 1 October 1932; *Scottish Education Journal*, 29 January 1932, MMASB.

36   MMA, advertising books, 1932; 'Peter A Menzies Advertising: The Lively Ones', *Glasgow Illustrated*, May 1967; information courtesy of Peter Menzies.

37   MMASB, 27 June 1931; MMAEPB; RCM, Sub-committee on Building Works, 16 January 1933 and 12 October 1931; *DR*, 6 February 1932; MMAD, July 1931; *Bulletin*, 4 February 1933.

38   RCM, Sub-committee on Building Works, 16 January 1933 and 13 March 1933; Sub-committee on Finance, 23 January 1933 and 20 March 1933, RCM, County Roads Board, 19 June 1933.

39   RCM, Sub-committee on Sites, 8 December 1930 and 8 June 1931; RCM, Sub-committee on Building Works, 9 November 1931; MMAEPB; *DR*, 1 October 1932.

40   RCM, Public Health Committee, 11 January 1932; MMASB, 7 August 1932.

41   MMASB; MMAEPB; *Bulletin*, 17 September 1932 and 2 December 1933; *GH*, 3 September 1932; *Evening Times*, 3 September 1932; MMASB; *DR*, 16 December 1933; *GH*, 27 February 1934 and 21 May 1934; *Citizen*, 26 May 1934.

42   *Bulletin*, 21 January 1933.

43   MMAEPB; MMASB, 7 January 1933 and 13 September 1932; *Bulletin*, 19 November 1932 and 1 April 1933; MMASB. Two further house-types

44   introduced in 1934 and 1935 were sold as follows: type 'A' bungalow, two units sold for £1,200; type 'M', one sold for £900, MMASB, 14 January 1935 and 2 July 1934.

Circular of February 1932.

45   Circular of March 1932; MM Minutes, 23 November 1932, 23 March 1933, 29 September 1933; *Citizen*, 26 May 1934; *Bulletin*, 4 March 1933.

46   *DR*, 1 July 1933 and 4 November 1933; *Evening News* (hereafter *EN*), 19 September 1933; *Bulletin*, 21 October 1933.

47   *EN*, 6 May 1933; *Evening Citizen*, 20 May 1933; *Bulletin*, 27 May 1933.

48   *Citizen*, 26 February 1934; *DR*, 2 March 1934, 3 March 1934, 10 March 1934; *Sunday Mail*, 4 March 1934; *Evening Citizen*, 31 March 1934 and 16 June 1934; *EN*, 17 April 1934 and 29 August 1934; *Daily Express*, 28 April 1934; *GH*, 9 June 1934.

49   MM Minutes, 17 August 1934; *EN*, 29 September 1934; *DR*, 12 September 1934; *Bulletin*, 13 September 1934; MM Minutes, 28 November 1935; *Sunday Mail*, 31 August 1935, 8 September 1935. Variations: McKean, *Scottish Thirties*, 168.

50   MM Minutes, 8 November 1935, 14 November 1935, 28 November 1935; MM Minutes, 17 April 1936; *Sunday Mail*, 25 October 1936; MM Minutes, 27 March 1939, 31 March 1939, 21 April 1939, 4 August 1939.

51   *DR*, 12 November 1934 and 27 February 1936; *Bulletin*, 21 November 1934; *Evening Citizen*, 20 February 1937.

52   Glasgow Corporation Housing Department, *Review of Operations 1919-1947*, 1948; O'Carroll, ILA and DOO.

53   D Mickel, 'Statement to Edinburgh Corporation', 3 February 1937.

54   D Mickel, 'Statement to Edinburgh Corporation', 3 February 1937.

55   ECM, Treasurer's Committee (hereafter ECMTC), 15 November 1932 and 28 November 1932; MM Minutes, 14 November 1932.

56   ECMTC, 7 December and 28 December 1932.

57   D Mickel, 'Statement to Edinburgh Corporation', 3 February 1937.

58   MMA, Granton Progress Chart, 1933.

59   ECMTC, 19 December and 28 December 1932, 30 January 1933; Edinburgh Corporation Minutes, Properties Sub-committee (hereafter ECMPS), 17 January 1933, 30 January 1933, 20 February 1933.

60   ECMTC, 28 November 1932; O'Carroll, DOO; ECMTC, 3 April and 1 May 1933; ECMPS, 24 April 1933; MMA, letter from Stanley Sutherland to Douglas Mickel, 26 March 1990; *EN*, 26 August 1933.

61   ECMPS, 9 November 1933; O'Carroll, DOO.

62   ECMPS, 9 November 1933; O'Carroll, DOO; ECMPS, 12 October 1936; ECMTC, 11 December 1933; Elliot and McCrone, 1972.

63   MM Minutes, 28 December 1933, 7 August 1934; ECMTC, 11 December 1933; ECMPS, 18 December 1933, 17 January 1933, 15 January 1934; ECMTC, 1 June 1936, 3 December 1934, 7 January 1935, 4 February 1935.

64   ECMPS, 9 November 1933, reference to letter dated 7 November 1933. ECMTC, 11 December 1933.

65   ECMPS, 15 January 1934, 25 February 1935, 22 April 1935; ECMTC, 28 October 1935, 4 March 1935; letter of 11 March 1999 from Connell & Connell, Solicitors, to MM.

66   1937 building squad picture: *EN*, 8 February 1990; O'Carroll, DOO. For discussion of labour rates, bonuses, etc., see MM Minutes, 16 December 1936.

67   ECMTC, 29 June 1936; ECMPS, 22 June 1936; Gumley advertisement, *EN*, c.1938/9.

68   ECMPS, 20 July 1926, 12 October 1936; MMA, letter from Stewart Kaye & Walls, Architects to Edinburgh Corporation Town Clerk, 22 February 1938.

69   MMA, cutting from *EN*, c.1938/39; MM Minutes, 8 July 1938.

70   MM Minutes, 20 January 1936; MMA, file on Broomhouse developments; ECMPS, 27 June 1938, 15 September 1938, 17 October 1938; ECM, 11 July 1938, 28 December 1938; MM Minutes, 15 December 1939.

71   A O'Carroll, *Urban History*, 24 (2), 1997.

72   *The Scotsman*, 17 March 1934, 19 May 1934; MMASB, 26 April 1934; MMAEPB; *EN*, 22 February 1935.

73   *EN*, 23 June 1934; *The Scotsman*, 19 May 1934, 23 June 1934, 13 October 1934; ECMTC, 25 October 1932, Report by City Architect.

74   ECMPS, 19 February 1934; ECMTC, 15 October 1934; *EN*, 7 March 1936, 18 April 1936; MM Minutes, 20 January 1936, 14 November 1935; MMASB, 9 March 1935; MM Minutes, 8 November 1935.

75   *EN*, 3 December 1937, 10 December 1937 (only three houses left); MMASB, 12 June 1939; MMAD; MMASB, 25 June 1935; MMASB, 24 June 1938, on 'Super Unit', 43 Silverknowes Terrace, £615 for five-apartment, £605 for four-apartment in 1938; *EN*, 18 April 1936; MMAD; MMASB, 11 May 1935, 12 August 1935, 11 June 1938; *EN*, 14 September 1935; MM Minutes, 18 August, 1939.

76   *EN*, 17 April 1937; *SMT Magazine*, October 1937.

77   *EN*, 28 January 1938.

78   Horsey, *London Journal*, 157; *DR*, 17 May 1935: initial publicity for the Broom claimed that there was 'only one other estate like it in England'.

79   MMAD, 2 December 1933.

80   MM Minutes, 1 October 1934; *GH*, 21 December 1934, 26 December

March 1932; GCM, 14 April 1932.

1934.

81   *GH*, 29 March 1935, 30 March 1935, 12 April 1935, 26 April 1935.
     Advertisement for 'B', 'C' bungalows, *GH*, 12 April 1935; *GH*, 4 May 1935;
     Evening Citizen, 17 May 1935.

82   *GH*, 4 May 1935, 12 April 1935, 17 May 1935; *Bulletin*, 17 May 1935;
     Glasgow Evening News, 17 May 1935.

83   MM Minutes, 31 March 1939; *The Times*, 24 October 1944.

84   Interview with Tom Rollands, Secretary of Western Heritable Investment
     Company, 19 February 1999; MM Minutes, 7 January 1935; 18 February
     1935, 1 April 1935.

85   MM Minutes, 19 June 1935, 25 June 1935, 5 September 1935.

86   MM Minutes, 8 November 1935; MMAD, 25 May 1938.

87   MM MInutes, 14 November 1935, 8 November 1935, 11 December 1935.

88   *Bulletin*, 17 May 1935; MMAD, 27 October 1934; MM Minutes, 11
     December 1935.

89   MMASB, 16 March 1936; MM Minutes, 20 January 1936; *GH*, 18 April
     1936, 19 December 1938; *DR*, 4 June 1938.

90   MMAD, 20 April 1933; *GH*, 13 December 1938; *Daily Express*, 13
     December 1938; *Bulletin*, 16 June 1939.

91   *Bulletin*, 16 June 1939; *EN*, 4 July 1939.

92   MM Minutes, 11 December 1935.

93   Letter from Stanley Sutherland (workman on project), to MM, 26 March
     1990.

94   *The Scotsman*, 18 September 1937; *DR*, 10 September 1938, 8 April 1939;
     SMT Magazine, November 1937.

95   MM Minutes, 18 September 1935, 20 June 1938, 7 July 1939; ECMPS,
     15 January 1934; MM Minutes, 20 June 1938, 8 July 1938.

96   On the Castlemilk issue, see MMA, note by Andrew Mickel, 10 March
     1939. On the building society problems, see MM Minutes, 31 March 1939,
     28 April 1939; MMA, letter from DHS, 10 March 1938; *Sunday Post*, 2
     August 1939; MMA, letter to Andrew Mickel, 9 August 1939; MMA, report
     by Mr Grieve, April 1937; MM Minutes, 8 July 1938, 5 May 1939.

97   MM Minutes, 8 November 1935.

98   MMA, letter from MM to Robert Barr, 1 November 1935; MMA, sale
     disposition for Orchard Park dated 15 February 1937; MM Minutes, 14
     November 1935.

99   MMA, letter from A R Craig to Giffnock Estates, 5 August 1935; MM
     Minutes, 17 June 1935.

100 MMASB; *Citizen*, 6 May 1937; *The Times*, 6 May 1937; *Daily Express*, 6
     May 1937; *Bulletin*, 6 May 1937; *EN*, 6 May 1937; *DR*, 8 May 1937; *DR*,
     11 May 1937, 18 September 1937; *Bulletin*, 25 September 1937; *Sunday
     Mail*, 24 October 1937.

101 MM Minutes, 25 August 1937, 28 April 1939.

102 *Sunday Mail*, 15 October 1937; information from Iain Drysdale; *DR*, 16
     October 1937; *Daily Express*, 5 February 1938; *DR*, 19 February 1938;
     MMA, Property Register 1938.

103 MMA, Sales Department log book, 1936-8; MMASB; *Sunday Mail*, 28
     March 1937; *DR*, 4 June 1938.

104 MM Minutes, 8 November 1935, 14 November 1935, 11 December 1935;
     GH, 10 December 1937; *DR*, 8 April 1939; MM Minutes, 21 April 1939,
     26 May 1939, 7 July 1939, 4 August 1939; *Ardrossan and Saltcoats Herald*,
     4 August 1939; *Lennox Herald*, 3 June 1939; MM Minutes, 5 May 1939;
     DR, 8 April 1939; MM Minutes, 31 March 1939; *DR*, 8 April 1939.

105 MM Minutes, 21 April 1939, 19 May 1939, 2 June 1939, 1 July 1939, 4
     August 1939, 1 September 1939.

106 MM Minutes, 27 January 1939, 31 March 1939, 7 April 1939, 11 April
     1939, 21 April 1939, 28 April 1939, 5 May 1939, 2 June 1939, 30 June
     1939.

107 *DR*, 25 November 1939; *GH*, 13 September 1939; *Evening Citizen*, 3
     November 1939, 10 November 1939; MM Minutes, 4 September 1939.

YEARS OF WAR AND REASSESSMENT

1939-60

Introduction

The financial and organisational difficulties which Mactaggart & Mickel encountered prior to the outbreak of war proved to be insignificant in comparison to the frustrating circumstances which it experienced during and immediately after the conflict, along with other traditional private housebuilders.

The cessation of almost all private enterprise (and local authority) building in wartime was followed by a virtual postwar ban on private building for sale or rent until 1954. Throughout this difficult period, Mactaggart & Mickel reluctantly returned to its previous role as all-trades contractor for the central state and local authorities. With the continuation of the war, Mactaggart & Mickel became increasingly dependent on wartime non-housing work, and actively sought it out; but it remained ready to exploit any housebuilding opportunity which presented itself in the challenging times of building rationing. By the time of deregulation in the early 1950s, the firm was poised to exploit the owner-occupied market, which it had built up so vigorously in the 1930s, by commencing new estates in the Glasgow area at Simshill and Braehead in 1952-3. An additional difficulty was caused by the rent restrictions imposed throughout this emergency period. These undermined the viability of the company's Edinburgh rented properties, whose maintenance had also proved financially and practically difficult. Accordingly, Mactaggart & Mickel started to dispose of these houses, through sale, from 1953 onwards. The firm also underwent a significant organisational change. Following Jack Mactaggart's long period of absence from the firm during the difficult wartime years, the entire Mactaggart family interest in the firm was bought out by the Mickels in early 1947.

In this chapter, taken up by a fast-moving mixture of issues and debates on the one hand, and building activity on the other, we follow a single, generally chronological account. The first part of the story, up to 1952, is dominated by talk and writing rather than action, athough with the emphasis already beginning to shift after 1950; the mid and late 1950s saw a return to large-scale building work. Because of the smaller scale of the later developments, by comparison with the interwar estates, and their basically traditional construction and design, the individual house-types and estates are described in a more summary form in this chapter and in Chapter A5. After 1960, the company would embark on a fresh phase of innovative policies.

Part I

The wartime years: 1939-45

Mactaggart & Mickel's normal building programme, for sale and letting purposes, came to a virtual standstill in late 1939 - a situation found across the building trade. Following the outbreak of war in September, Scotland's local authorities were ordered to complete all municipal houses under construction, and cancel any proposed new developments. This 'regrettable necessity of war', had, in fact, been badly affecting the building industry for some months prior to September 1939; private enterprise and local authorities alike had suffered from calls made on the building industry to erect armament factories, and the 'cessation of commercial building activity' was anticipated. The lack of skilled labour, owing to the enrolment of men to Air Raid Precaution (ARP) rescue and repair squads, had begun to 'starve' the private building industry, and brought experimentation into alternative methods of building to a standstill in the public sector. The private rental and owner-occupied market suffered immediately, and by late September the property world was said to be in a 'chaotic condition', with prospective purchasers withdrawing from sales and tenants surrendering leases. Building societies automatically felt the effect of the building industry collapse in September 1939. The National Building Society, for example, witnessed a reduction in loans from £6,188,309 to £3,837,381, and expressed its sympathy with the speculative builder, arguing that 'it needs confidence to build a house in the expectation of finding a buyer'. The diversion of resources increased further in early 1940, and severe shortages of brick and concrete forced the private and public sector to lay off many workers. (1)

Private housebuilders were forced to switch their activities to war contracting. For some firms, such as James Miller, this brought a new diversification into specialist contracting, and a significant expansion of their building activities. State control of all building operations was introduced on 7 October 1940, and a system of licensing was established in twelve UK 'regions'; building was forbidden without a licence. The controls were intensified through building registration in September 1941, in an attempt to mobilise the 'national building industry' as a whole for war production. A *Glasgow Herald* editorial welcomed this attempt to organise builders, civil engineers and all branches of the building industry for essential war work: 'No attempt has hitherto been made to assess the potentialities of so important an industry'. Some small or medium-sized firms, critical of the way in which contracts had been allocated prior to the new registration scheme, expressed hopes that this new move would help reverse an imbalance which had seen large firms 'receiving an undue

A4.1. The Mickel family at war. From left to right: Eileen (WRNS Transport Driver), Andrew (Home Guard Colonel), Frank (Captain), Agnes Frances, and Douglas (2nd Lieutenant, later Captain). (MMC)

proportion of work'. This issue had nationalistic overtones; one industry critic claimed that 'we in Scotland have had good reason to complain over the large volume of work given to English contractors'. (2)

The growth of state control and regulation through licensing and registration was emphatically not welcomed by the entrepreneurial Andrew Mickel; as we will see later, it brought him much personal frustration. Despite this, Mactaggart & Mickel's commitment to the war effort throughout this period was enthusiastic. Andrew Mickel, as a volunteer colonel in the Home Guard, contributed a great deal of time and effort to his wartime duties, and both Frank and Douglas Mickel joined the armed forces in 1942; Eileen Mickel became a Wren. Mactaggart & Mickel made the first of its many supportive gestures to the war effort in October 1939. Under the central government 'Dig for Victory' banner, it set aside a stretch of unsold plots alongside its scheme at Carolside Park for 100 wartime allotments. According to Andrew, the firm was 'throwing a war handicap into a means of helping the Government's appeal to the nation to grow more vegetables'; a nominal rent of 5s per year was to go towards making paths, and any excess to Red Cross funds. Here the imposition of severe government restrictions on new building, with inspectors visiting all estates to make inventories of completed houses, was turned to both public good and marketing advantage, as an extension of the traditional philanthropic element in estate development. (3)

Following the outbreak of war, the most urgent task facing the directors was that of financial stabilisation. Drastic steps were immediately taken to conserve Mactaggart & Mickel's liquid resources. As a 'considerable amount of the company's total assets was represented by ground and feu duties ... not readily converted

into cash', all activity that could tie up cash was to be severely cut back, to keep the firm 'as liquid as possible'. There was discussion among the directors, including a meeting attended by Mactaggart on 5 September. While the latter urged a total stop of work on all houses except those nearly completed, the Mickels urged greater caution, in order to retain men until agreed government work could be secured. Threatening factors included the ever-greater materials and labour shortages; it was now virtually impossible to obtain bricklayers and joiners, as government work was 'absorbing available men ... the company can not face the inducements being offered to them'; work on the Broomhouse and Hillpark sites was hit hard 'owing to demand in Fifeshire', although an arrangement with the trade unions allowed a squad of bricklayers to be kept at Broomhouse, and to work overtime. More generally, there were the problems of the virtual standstill of civil building, the collapse of the property market and the threat of a possible withdrawal of pool advances by the building societies. It was estimated that the cost of completing all houses under erection would be £96,000, and the company had a current bank overdraft of £95,000; however, £20,000 payment was due for Edinburgh Corporation for lands at Broomhouse, and it was suggested that a £20,000 loan could be raised on Sandringham Court, by then three-quarters occupied. By November 1939, Andrew Mickel (in the continued absence of Jack Mactaggart) was taking energetic steps aimed at 'conserving the company's resources': the company's credit balance on profit and loss account at the end of 1939 was £341,889, and fell only to £287,931 by 1941. It seemed clear that the way forward lay in a return to the world of all-trades, and single contracting - only now not for housing but for war works. In the ongoing debate among the directors, Frank Mickel suggested urgent steps to 'get in the class of work which would be regarded as protected trade'; Andrew would contact the Department of Health about materials supply. (4)

Mactaggart & Mickel's wartime work fell into four main areas: extensive ARP and security construction for local authorities and private companies; emergency hospital contracts for the Ministry of Works; home defence works for the Admiralty and the Ministry of Aircraft Production; and single-trade contracting for local authorities. It was the first three areas which occupied the majority of the firm's early wartime production. Although ARP work was continuous, it was not as financially lucrative as the other areas of contracting. Payment for this local authority work was made on a 'time and material basis'; the firm charged the client for their time plus 17.5%, and for material plus 15%. Continuing the pattern already established before September 1939, Mactaggart & Mickel was contracted to build numerous air-raid shelters and warden posts for Glasgow and Edinburgh Corporations, and for Renfrew County Council. These ranged from 'single' shelters (such as a batch of nine shelters in Newhaven, Edinburgh, for a total price of £924) to larger Communal Domestic Surface Shelters, such as a Port Glasgow contract for 59 communal shelters at a cost of £90 18s 3d for a 'two unit house'. Domestic shelters were usually described as 'single units' and 'double units'. Education authority contracts for shelters were also undertaken. Mactaggart & Mickel built five air-raid shelters for Glasgow Education Authority in May 1940 at a cost of £1,195, and 184 school shelters of reinforced brickwork and flat cement roof type, each for 50 pupils, at Paisley; the latter contract earned the company approximately £27,500. Shelters were also built for companies participating in the 'war effort': twelve air-raid shelters, costing £1,645, were built for R & W Watson, at Linwood Paper Mills, and three double and one single shelter, at a cost of £2,460, for Yarrow & Company Ltd. Material-only contracts, for supply by Mactaggart & Mickel's Carntyne works, were also received from all three local authorities. The firm supplied concrete roofing slabs for shelters, and cement blocks for the production of 300 police boxes in Glasgow, at a cost of £5 17s 6d per block. In addition, Mactaggart & Mickel built a control room at Renfrew Burgh Police Station, and an auxiliary fire station at Hillington Industrial Estate. (5)

Contracts for the Office of Works (later, the Ministry of Works) to build hospitals under the government's emergency programme brought the company some financial security in difficult times; in contrast to heavy civil engineering work, hospitals were not dissimilar in scale to suburban housing. The first proper wartime contract, secured in late 1939, was for an extension to the Princess Margaret Rose Hospital, Edinburgh, at the value of £18,290. This contract was quickly followed by one for an emergency hospital at Killearn, to the value of £42,935. Mactaggart & Mickel then successfully secured the much larger Buchanan Castle emergency hospital contract, for £133,860, using Portland blast furnace cement for construction. Other Ministry of Works contracts included the construction of Ministry of Food storage accommodation at Lauder, Berwickshire, costing £11,640. Home defence contracts for the Admiralty and the Ministry of Aircraft Production included the building of retaining walls at the RAF Station Prestwick, costing £1,386, roads at Eaglesham, worth £1,571, and concrete fencing for Blackburn Aircraft Ltd, Dumbarton (which later built AIROH prefabricated housing). The largest such contracts were to build oil storage tanks for the Admiralty at Old Kilpatrick and Dalnottar; this work included excavation and bricklaying, and construction of blast walls around the tanks. Materials were supplied for these jobs, and payment was received on a 'time plus percentage basis'. The War Office's ultimate control of these contracts was clearly defined: Mactaggart

& Mickel was 'instructed' to 'supply as much labour as possible' for the contracts. (6)

The building of houses for sale was now prohibited, but Mactaggart & Mickel had a number of houses completed, but not yet sold, at Carolside Park (six-apartment bungalows costing £1,275), Orchard Park (five-apartment semi-villas for £725), Silverknowes (villas and bungalows from £830), Hillpark and the Broom. A large number of these houses had been provisionally sold, but hesitant purchasers had withdrawn and cancelled just prior to the war. Following the outbreak of war, only one or two houses were being sold each week, but this soon increased to approximately five each week by 1941, as the situation settled. In 1942, sales reached a wartime peak, when 14 houses were sold in one week for a total of £11,200. In a move to encourage sales (and in turn free the liquid assets of the company), and in view of the withdrawal of building society advances, Mactaggart & Mickel offered purchasers loans (in the form of bonds) on similar terms to those previously provided by the building societies: a 20-year loan, with an interest level of 5%. Despite the withdrawal of its pool facility, the firm maintained regular contact with all the building societies involved during the war. Mactaggart & Mickel's high profile prewar advertising was reduced to the occasional classified advertisement, which primarily stressed the firm's 'prewar prices' for its remaining houses. By 1941, its advertising had petered out almost completely, as almost all remaining homes on estates such as Carolside Park were finally sold. The company tried to entice block purchases for unsold houses at Stevenston and Dumbarton, and held discussions with the Rolls Royce aero engine plant at Hillington over the possibility of housing a number of its employees. Approaches were made to ICI's explosives works at Ardeer, near Stevenston, because it was known locally that a number of Ardeer technical staff were 'living in hotels'. Although ICI was not interested in this offer, the Ministry of Supply purchased 23 houses in Dumbarton 'en bloc' for workers at the Royal Ordnance Works, Dalmuir, at a significantly reduced cost of £575 15s each. The firm's anxiety to sell all remaining houses as quickly as possible was accentuated by the threat that unsold houses might be requisitioned by the government to house war-workers. When six such houses at Stevenston were 'commandeered' by the government in 1941, Andrew Mickel instructed remaining sales staff to list enquiries about these, for the purpose of 'having the houses released'. Rather than risk the requisitioning of empty houses, Mactaggart & Mickel provided them for short-term rental; these houses were sold when the tenancy was terminated. Mactaggart & Mickel's Edinburgh rented properties also faced the threat of requisitioning: Gumley & Davidson informed Mactaggart & Mickel in November 1940 that all unlet properties were liable for requisitioning by the Admiralty. (7)

In addition to the need to diversify into non-housing contracts, and the threat of requisitioning, the war also had more dramatic effects on the firm. The evening of 29 September 1940 saw the first bombing damage to Mactaggart & Mickel houses, when a four-in-a-block at 21-27 Crewe Place, Edinburgh (Granton No.3) was wrecked by a direct hit from a high explosive bomb; one other block was badly damaged. Douglas Mickel immediately set about rehousing the dispossessed tenants, notified Edinburgh Corporation and the District Valuer under the terms of the Housing (Emergency Powers) Act 1939 and the War Damage to Land (Scotland) Act 1939, and the damaged block was 'completely razed to the ground' by the Corporation's demolition squad. This unfortunate incident provided Mactaggart & Mickel with an opportunity to display its continuing building efficiency, by building replacement houses on the site in six weeks. 'How's that for a record?' one national newspaper asked. Douglas Mickel explained that he had started work 'the next day' after the bombing, and set out the company's policy on the need for speedy repair and reinstatement of war damage: 'We do not intend to leave it to the local authorities to do this sort of thing ... we do not intend to have people sitting in the ruins of their homes or to have their neighbours gazing at ruined houses every time they look out. That is not good for morale'. Further damage was caused during the nights of heavy bombing of Clydeside on 13 and 14 March 1941. A number of houses on Mactaggart & Mickel's Kelvinside site were affected; 24 were made uninhabitable, and a further 50 damaged. In such cases, the local authorities were responsible for co-ordination and financing of bomb damage repair work, along similar lines to the ARP system. (8)

These various contracting and selling activities occupied the majority of Mactaggart & Mickel's early wartime business. In organisational terms, as the war developed, and its demands on staffing took effect, the management of these activities became increasingly difficult. The chairman, Jack Mactaggart, attended only one board meeting in these five years, and owing to his 'prolonged absence abroad' the quorum for the transaction of the business of the directors was reduced from three to two. In late 1942, Andrew Mickel came under pressure by shareholders and senior staff to consider Mactaggart's 'automatic disqualification' from continued membership of the board, but continued to support the latter's position within the firm. The duties falling on Andrew became more onerous following Frank Mickel's call up to military service (Air Transport Auxiliary) in June 1941; additionally, his father, Andrew Mickel (senior), had died at that time, in Glasgow, at the age of 94. Andrew's duties with the Home Guard added to the pressure on him, but 'some measure of relief' came in the appointment of Douglas Mickel as a director in May 1942; he already had the necessary share qualification for that position. This relief proved to be short-lived. Douglas Mickel's period of deferment from conscription expired in 30 September 1942, and his wish to secure a commission in the Royal Engineers was realised when he was released from company duties to join the Garrison Engineers in August 1942. Frank Mickel returned to work for the company in November 1942 (although continuing with some ATA duties until 1945), and finally, in late 1943, Andrew was appointed chairman of Mactaggart & Mickel. There were increasing constraints on the firm's employment of professional staff; Andrew Mickel agreed in 1940 to continue to pay half of the wages of office staff called to war service, but in early 1942, in view of the 'present changed nature of the company's business and the prolonged nature of the war', supplementary payments to staff on service were suspended; in June 1943, architect W Gladstone wrote to the directors thanking them 'for what had been done for him in this direction' and expressing hope that he could 'renew his association with the company on his return to civil life'. (9)

By early 1942, Mactaggart & Mickel, aware of the longer-term financial importance of obtaining war contracts, stepped up a gear in its pursuit of them. Andrew Mickel declared that 'all concerned should make every effort possible to secure further contracts ... either by approaching Government departments or by contacting individuals or firms who might be in a position to influence work'. The context within which firms were working was mainly one of negotiated rather than competitive contracts, again for the sake of security and continuity. In view of the prevailing 'keen prices', Andrew Mickel also urged staff to reduce costs to a minimum and employ 'the greatest possible degree of efficiency'; for this purpose he proposed to offer inducements to

the superintendents and others, while accepting that these would have to adhere to 'current legislation'. This contracting 'call to arms' appears to have worked, and Mactaggart & Mickel secured larger home defence jobs in the later years of the war. Contracts were obtained from the Air Ministry for the first of a number of accommodation blocks for female Balloon Operators in summer 1942, and a substantial Admiralty contract for the extension to the camp at HMS Scotia, Doonfoot, Ayr, worth over £40,000, was secured in May 1943. One further Admiralty contract was won in wartime: at a naval barracks in Port Glasgow, Mactaggart & Mickel built in 1943-44 a complex of huts, canteen buildings, officer quarters, guard rooms, gymnasium, cinema and a church, at an estimated total cost of £50,000. (10)

Preparing for peace

With the approaching end to hostilities in Europe in early 1945, Mactaggart & Mickel's defence contracts were greatly reduced. There were only a handful of directors' meetings held during this period. In spring and summer 1945, the firm took on, with some pleasure, contracts for the dismantling and demolishing of wartime home defence construction. Andrew Mickel reported in July 1945 that a 'considerable amount of work, on time and materials basis, had been secured for the Corporation of Glasgow, Civil Defence Section, consisting of demolishing baffle walls and removing stratting'. Mactaggart & Mickel had, of course, constructed many of these defence works; this satisfyingly rounded off the company's wartime work. In August 1945, Andrew Mickel urged that unfinished wartime contracts be 'finally completed and wiped off'. (11)

With the winding down of war work and the increasing focus on postwar reconstruction as a new area of 'national effort', inexorably housing began to return to the forefront of the company's attention. It had already taken advantage of the limited revival of local authority housebuilding for war workers by returning to the house contracting field, and securing a number of traditional separate-trades housing contracts. In September 1943, Port Glasgow Town Council contracted the firm to carry out brick work and painter work for 50 houses at its Broadfield site, for £30,000; a further 20 houses were added to this contract in late 1944. No activity was considered too small; a slater work contract worth £1,476 was secured for a Dumbarton council housing scheme in 1945. Mactaggart & Mickel also obtained contracts for repairing bomb-damaged tenements in Port Glasgow; brick work and plumber work worth £1,409, for instance, were carried out at 18 Woodhall Terrace, Port Glasgow, in April 1944. (12)

However, in these closing years of the war, the main activity in the field of housing in Scotland was not building, but debate about future policies. That debate focused on two main issues. The first was a revisit of the main issue of the Ballantyne Report: everyone accepted that large numbers of new houses were needed, but who should build them, who should channel that demand - private agencies or the state? The second was a technical issue: to what extent would new construction methods be needed to achieve the desired output? Mactaggart & Mickel continued to stay at the forefront of these often heated debates. Through the medium of the local and national press, Andrew Mickel became more vocal than ever in his criticism of the increasing bias towards public rather than private housing which was, by 1943, beginning to take shape. It was clear from the vast wartime complexity of state regulation and control of the building industry, and the acute shortage of materials and labour throughout the war, that the relatively loose regime following World War I, and the prominence of the private housebuilder in the 1930s, would not be revived in the short term. But Mactaggart & Mickel clearly hoped that there would still be an important state-sponsored role for the private builder. As the coalition government began to consider this question at the end of the war, builders such as Mactaggart & Mickel began to make known their views. Sympathetic voices of support for private builders, and their prospective role in the postwar housing programme, grew in the later months of the war. But the election of a Labour government in July 1945 brought that support to an abrupt end.

The eventual (and, some argued, inevitable) postwar 'strangulation' of the speculative builder's activities had been presaged as early as 1941, when the reconstruction minister, Lord Reith, brought in measures to curtail speculative purchase of land in bombed areas. He strongly argued that rebuilding after the war 'should not be hampered or prejudiced in any way by speculative transactions ... carried out in advance!' Mactaggart & Mickel had begun, as early as 1942, to investigate the resumption of land acquisition for postwar development, but with inconclusive results; in conjunction with Gumley and Davidson, sites at Harvieston (10 miles from Edinburgh), and Hilltown Farm (four miles from the city) were investigated, but they proved suitable only for 'workers' cottages'. Interest was also shown in the grounds adjoining Inch House, Liberton, Edinburgh - eventually used for a large Corporation housing scheme. (13)

In early 1944, there was a parliamentary debate concerning the likely level of private enterprise building in postwar Scotland, and the Poole Committee was set up, with a UK-wide remit, to consider the question. Sir John Mactaggart, then based in London, may have had some direct input into the committee. In November 1944, Mactaggart claimed that Sir Felix Poole's forthcoming report would recommend that 'private enterprise should be brought in to assist local authority housing by building both owner occupied and letting houses'. Mactaggart saw this as the only practical solution, at a time when building costs had doubled from prewar levels. If this policy was not followed, he argued, the returning soldier would have to wait three years for a home: 'Is this his recompense for fighting the country's battles?' In early 1945 the government also set up a committee to consider the practicability of controlling or regulating the selling prices of

postwar houses. The debate reached a climax in May 1945, when the Poole Committee's findings were issued. It recommended that private enterprise developments which met the same needs as local authorities should be eligible for similar Exchequer subsidy (subject to regulation of price, size and construction). The subsidy should be either an annual payment over a number of years or lump sum after completion; a related parliamentary bill proposed the same level of subsidy for private and local authority building alike. Whilst central government was contemplating what housing policy to adopt, English and Welsh local authorities received a circular from the Ministry of Health encouraging them to 'make full use of all agencies, and, in particular, builders' so as to facilitate an 'early start'. Where builders had sites ready for development, the circular urged local authorities to use their 'best endeavours' to encourage housebuilding. (14)

In May 1945, as a result of these developments, Andrew Mickel optimistically set out his own predictions. 'There is going to be another invasion of this country', he declared, 'but it will be by our men and women released from the forces who are coming home in the expectation that, in return for their war sacrifices, they will get a house to live in'. He was convinced that if the housebuilders were allowed to start, 'even in a small way', they would find sufficient ordinary materials or substitutes to begin work. In unusually conciliatory language, he concluded: 'Let us all play our full part in providing houses for the homeless, be it by state enterprise or private enterprise'. On 7 June 1945, the government announced new plans for 'bringing in private enterprise', in an effort to speed up Scottish housebuilding; both owner-occupied and letting construction was to be 'facilitated' within the existing framework of the Housing (Scotland) Act 1935. (15)

One month later, the entire situation had changed completely. The Labour Party replaced the wartime coalition government, and the new administration began to formulate a new housing policy, which would allow private enterprise a very limited role in postwar reconstruction. Although some of the policy formulation was led by the English Ministry of Health, in Scotland the policy was given distinctive shape by junior Scottish housing minister George Buchanan. In October 1945, Andrew Mickel met with Dr Taylor, a DHS civil servant, and 'submitted his views

A4.2. December 1944 sketch of war memorial cottages for RAF 603 (City of Edinburgh) Squadron, gifted by Andrew Mickel and Sir John A Mactaggart. (MMC)

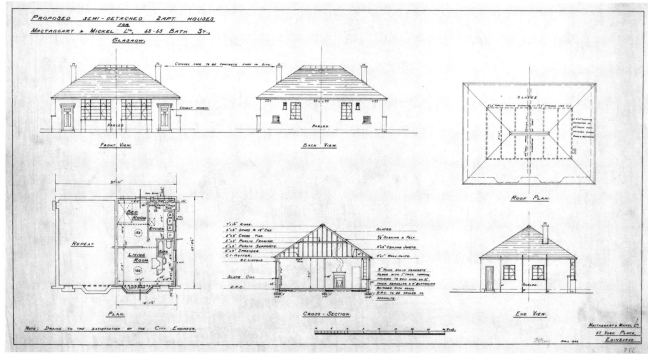

A4.3. April 1944 drawing of proposed semi-detached two-apartment houses for Mactaggart & Mickel. (MMC D44841)

and ideas on building houses by private enterprise for owner-occupiers'; regarding letting properties, Dr Taylor advised Andrew to 'communicate with London'. It would appear that Andrew drew very little from this meeting, but with the help of Sir John Mactaggart, he pursued correspondence with the Ministry of Health in London. But all was in vain, for in September, despite all these representations to the new administration, Labour dropped a 'bombshell for builders' when it decided to provide no subsidy whatever for postwar private enterprise housing. (16)

To Mactaggart & Mickel this was, of course, a very disagreeable turn of events - especially as the firm had, over the previous year, invested considerable practical effort in an ingenious demonstration project, intended to show its preparedness for rapid postwar building of social housing. In a period of exceptionally tight building controls, such private initiatives proved difficult, but not impossible. In early 1944, Andrew Mickel hit on the idea of building, and gifting, small houses for disabled ex-servicemen returning from the war, and using these at the same time for demonstration purposes. The firm applied to Edinburgh and Glasgow Corporation for permission to build a pair of two-apartment semi-detached cottages at its own expense in each city; the cottages had steep pitched roofs, metal-framed windows, and a plan with a front living room and rear bedroom and kitchen, with bathroom leading off the front entrance lobby. Whilst Edinburgh eventually approved the application, Glasgow rejected the offer on the grounds that the cottages were 'too small'; Glasgow Corporation had, at that time, adopted a policy not to build any houses which had less than three apartments. Andrew Mickel was 'indignant at the refusal', and explained that 'my reason for not increasing the size ... is that I hoped my gift would be only the start of a large scheme in which individuals and organisations would give memorial houses to Scottish units of the forces, and so help in a practical way to solve the service man's problem of accommodation after the war! If the presentation house is too costly, people would refuse to take up the scheme'. Under Andrew's 'War Memorial Cottages' scheme, all charges for the construction of the houses would be met by the donor, and the titles of the houses would be passed 'without restriction' to the trustees of the particular squadron; the trustees would then have

'full powers in connection with administration and occupation'. Each house was to contain a living room, bedroom, kitchen and bathroom. Andrew envisaged that a house of such a size would require a minimum of maintenance, would fall outwith the terms of the Rent Restriction Act, and that the disabled men would only have to pay occupiers' rates. (17)

The two houses for 603 (Edinburgh) Squadron, gifted by Andrew Mickel and Sir John Mactaggart, were approved by Edinburgh's Dean of Guild Court in December 1944, and rapidly built on a site at 80-82 Broomhouse Road. Later in 1945, donors were found for a further two ex-servicemen's houses to be erected on the adjoining site at 84-86 Broomhouse Road; Jack Paterson, a former sports star, donated one to the 'maimed Royal Scots', and the houses were passed to the Royal Scots Regiment. In typical fashion, Andrew used the handing over of the first pair of houses in May 1945, in the presence of the Lord Provost (John Falconer) and assembled councillors and journalists, as an opportunity to showcase the benefits of private enterprise building using traditional methods. The houses, he claimed, cost £1,100 to build, and were constructed in 20 days of 'traditional methods, harling, brick cavity walls, external roughcast, slated roofs, internal walls plastered ... and ordinary joiner, plumber, and painter work!' Because of this, he 'wanted to demonstrate to the public that by having material made available and the work carried out under ordinary conditions, permanent houses could be built as quickly and as cheaply as temporary houses, and cheaper than some types, with much more satisfactory and lasting results'. In an interview with the *Daily Express*, which described him as 'brisk, 60-ish and brimful of confidence', Andrew Mickel set out his views on the changing circumstances of postwar building. Prior to the outbreak of war, Mactaggart & Mickel had built houses in Edinburgh at 'nearly two a day', but only these two houses had been built so far in the first five months of 1945. From the bedroom of the demonstration house, looking out over the 170 acres of open land at Broomhouse, which Mactaggart & Mickel had planned to build on prior to the war, Andrew 'exploded on the subject of housing': 'Why don't they give the housing job to the builders? Let us get on with it and have done with merely talking and writing about it'. (18)

However, the period of 'merely talking', to the frustration of Andrew Mickel and other traditional housebuilders, was destined to continue for an extended period. For what actually began to unfold in the late 1940s, under Buchanan's oversight, was a massive state-sponsored housing programme which placed almost exclusive reliance on the municipal sector; not only was the private speculative sector not helped, but it was actively choked off through the use of building licensing. Building for the private rented sector was almost abandoned, and those who had housing stock in this tenure area, such as Mactaggart & Mickel and Western Heritable, began to dispose of it. But despite the large programme now allocated by Glasgow Corporation and some other councils to their direct labour organisations, this was a revolution only in housing demand, not in supply, which remained overwhelmingly with the private sector; there was no general nationalisation of the building industry. A vast programme of contracting work was open to building firms, and Mactaggart & Mickel soon began to investigate its potential. What seemed clear was that open competitive tendering was unsuitable for the emergency conditions. Some kind of negotiated contracting would be needed. At the end of 1945, for example, the firm offered to build Edinburgh Corporation municipal houses at an 'inclusive lump sum per house of a particular type'. Edinburgh Corporation had made it known to the company that it wanted 'speedier methods for obtaining tenders for houses', and Douglas Mickel responded quickly with his suggestion. (19)

The prefabrication issue

As indicated by his praise of traditional building methods at the opening of the Broomhouse cottages, Andrew Mickel also sharply disagreed with the official consensus on the other key issue of postwar housebuilding: traditional versus 'non-traditional' construction. We trace in Chapter B3 how, in response to the severe wartime shortages of labour and materials and the anticipation of continuing shortages after the war, prefabricated methods using alternative materials were developed by government housing bodies such as the Scottish Special Housing Association, formed in 1937. This course was reinforced by the wartime Burt Committee, which examined and recommended various non-traditional methods. The next logical step, authorised by the Housing (Temporary Accommodation) Act 1944 in response to the emergency housing problems of the end of the war, was a programme of not just non-traditional but temporary houses: the 'prefabs'. Prefabrication on the large scale envisaged was a threat not only to traditional building operatives (whose working conditions had in fact improved during wartime centralisation) but also 'traditional' housebuilders such as Mactaggart & Mickel who were jostling for a position in the postwar building drive. And although, as we will see, it developed its own non-traditional forms of construction, Mactaggart & Mickel remained opposed in general to temporary prefabricated housing and suspicious of non-traditional building in general.

Following the announcement in December 1942, by the Secretary of State for Scotland, that an estimated 50,000 houses per year would have to be built after the war, debate quickly turned to the

MEMORIAL HOUSES. — Lord Provost John I. Falconer accepting from Colonel A. Mickel the title deeds for two memorial houses at Broomhouse Road, Edinburgh, presented by himself and Sir John MacTaggart to the 603 (City of Edinburgh) Squadron Auxiliary Air Force Trust. Among those who attended the ceremony were members of Edinburgh Town Council.

A4.4. The official handing over of the memorial cottages at Broomhouse Road, Edinburgh, in May 1945. (Edinburgh Evening News, 30 May 1945; Scotsman)

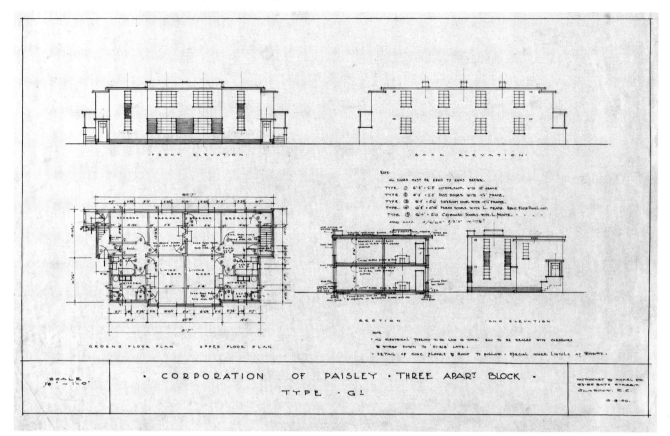

A4.5. May 1940 design for concrete-built four-in-a-block houses for Paisley Corporation (Type 'G', three-apartment flats). (MMC D44836)

question of whether these houses should be 'prefabs or traditional'. Despite the 'stupendous' scale of the proposed programme, many 'solid Scottish builders and architects' were opposed to the use of prefabrication. Andrew Mickel was among the first to make his opposition clear: 'Prefabrication enthusiasts who talk of completing a house in 12 to 14 days don't mention the prosaic but essential points of roads, sewage and services ... Surely it's the falsest economy to embark on such a scheme simply as a tide-over?' He was convinced that prefabricated houses using highly composite materials and methods in their make-up were unsuitable for Scotland: 'Both the Scottish climate and the Scottish character are against prefabrication. Let us get our brick and concrete works going and our skilled men back from the Services. With organisation and continuity, I am sure that we can keep pace with the building programme - and provide the solid, long lasting homes which Scotsmen want'. (20)

However, the firm hedged its bets by pursuing its own patented non-traditional construction method, which continued to rely essentially on timber framing, clad externally with 2" thick roughcast breeze blocks, separated by a bitumen damp-proof layer - itself a highly composite method. In 1939, following the completion of the demonstration units in King's Park and Carrick Knowe, it had offered to build 52 of these flat-roofed houses at West Pilton for Edinburgh Town Council, at a unit cost of £441, with the 'same solid appearance as brick houses'. During the war, there was a flirtation with an almost opposite approach, in the form of flat-roofed houses that dispensed with timber altogether, using in-situ reinforced concrete for walls, floors and ceilings, and metal for details such as sills. In 1940 there was a proposal to build a block of four such 'timberless houses' at Broomhouse in Edinburgh, and an experimental flat-roofed block of this construction, containing four three-apartment flats, was built in that year for Paisley Corporation at their Gallowhill 3rd Development. The firm also tried to develop a cavity wall system

of blockwork. After the war, the emphasis returned to the timber-framed method. In March-April 1948, an experimental semi-detached pair of four-apartment pitched-roofed demonstration bungalows, constructed of a frame of prefabricated timber panels in 7' sections and coke-breeze cladding slabs, was built by the company at Broomhouse Road, using Stewart Kaye as architect; it was later passed to the Scottish Veterans' Garden City Association. This bungalow type was intended not to compete directly with prefabricated building in urban areas, but for use in remote or agricultural locations, and the company emphasised its traditional external appearance. However, the government Burt Committee on non-traditional building methods refused to certify its construction as sufficiently solidly built or fireproof to merit a 60-year loan, pointing to numerous design problems. (21)

Andrew Mickel continued in his criticisms of large-scale prefabrication, but it was not until the introduction of steel and aluminium prefabs, planned from 1944, that he was joined by other builders in condemnation of these houses. The Federation of Master Builders, not unexpectedly, condemned the prefabs as a 'ghastly mistake'. In 1945, from his base in England, Sir John Mactaggart entered the debate. He pronounced himself 'yet to be convinced that, on new or old sites, prefabrication will prove speedier and cheaper in the final result than traditional building', and argued that because most prefabricated systems involved the handling on site of large panels and fitments, they were 'too heavy for men to lift into position'. Because of this problem, 'moveable cranes' had to be used, but, he explained, these would be unable to work in wet weather 'through the churning up of ground'. Although Mactaggart believed that mass production did have a limited role to play in the construction of houses (about 25% per house), he concluded by asking: 'Are some brickfields, timber yards, and factories to be scrapped, and war factories converted at great expense to fabricate flimsy walls and combined metal units?' (22)

A4.6. The Mactaggart & Mickel patent construction timber houses at Broomhouse Road, Edinburgh, under construction on 29 March 1948; here the coke-breeze cladding is being attached. (MMC)

A4.7. The patent houses, photographed almost completed on 6 April 1948. (MMC)

By late 1945, Andrew Mickel was criticising the ongoing prefab programme in increasingly harsh terms, as excessively costly and inefficient, and arguing that the government should instead develop methods of mass production suitable for traditional construction. In a letter to the *Glasgow Herald* in September, he alleged that the 'delivery timetable seems to have gone out of gear', and questioned the financial logic of spending millions of pounds of taxpayers' money on 'costly preliminaries' such as 'jigs, templates and machinery'. Permanent traditional houses, he claimed, did not require these, and the government should therefore do everything possible to facilitate their construction. His suggestions included the release of all building trade personnel at present in the forces, the stimulation of brick and cement manufacturing, and a 'clear cut policy' on financial assistance. As a result, the 'costly, unwanted temporary or prefabricated house would quickly disappear as it did after World War I'. John Lawrence, writing as 'another practical builder', eagerly endorsed these views. In a letter to the *Scotsman*, he highlighted the inherent problems of prefab construction by relaying his own company's frustrating experiences. Lawrence had taken on a contract in January 1945 for the construction of number of prefabs. In his view, if the company had been asked to build traditional houses, 'we could have had many ready for occupancy by now, but it will be months yet before we can have one of the prefabricated type completed'. Lawrence claimed not to be alone in this experience: 'We have received about a hundred drawings and many hundreds of letters regarding the contract, but they, I regret to say, represent almost the only results of eight months' effort'. But the momentum of the programme continued: for example, two months later, the Department of Health for Scotland allocated a further 1,150 aluminium temporary houses to Glasgow. (23) As we will see below, in an effort to enhance his company's profile in the permanent non-traditional market, Lawrence developed and patented the compacted gypsum-based 'Gyproc' construction slab in 1944, and after the war encouraged other builders (including Mactaggart & Mickel) to join the Scottish Builders Group cartel.

Whereas the prefab programme, because of its lightweight construction, was associated with suburban sprawl, Andrew Mickel argued that the solidity of traditional construction could make possible a greater variety of solutions, including blocks of modern flats of six to eight storeys height, 'erected in the heart of the city'. In 1942, he elaborated this vision: 'My idea is that there are many areas of Glasgow which will have to be cleared after the war. They already possess streets, sewers and services - an important economy effect. I visualise in these areas blocks of one, two, or three room and kitchen flats, served by elevators and with a strip of green in front, possibly a sandpit for the children and certainly a lock-up for the prams'. These modest flats would have no built-in furniture; 'Scots people', he argued, 'prefer to have their own things'. He drew on his own extensive practical experiences in housebuilding to back up his claims: 'In some houses where we provided fitted and built-in wardrobes in the bedrooms, we've found that the people brought in their own wardrobes as well, though there of course wasn't room for both. We have found too that ordinary Scots people aren't anxious to have refrigerators - probably because it is rarely warm enough to make them necessary'. Such flats would have been not dissimilar to the simple low-rise tenement blocks of public housing which were eventually built in large numbers in the 1950s, using modified traditional methods, in schemes such as Glasgow's Drumchapel or Dundee's Fintry. All in all, Andrew concluded that there was a 'modified place for prefabrication in the building trade ... But I don't believe it is a big, or important, or permanent place'. (24)

Part II

The years of rationing: 1946-52

Despite the new government's move away from the private housebuilding cause, the immediate postwar years began optimistically for Mactaggart & Mickel, with the hope that speculative housing would be allowed a limited field of operation. But in the event, political shifts at both the central and local levels, and tensions between the two, combined with the most acute shortages of materials and labour, forced the firm to continue its existing policy of contracting and diversifying.

Let us first briefly review the company's organisation in this period. In the immediate aftermath of the war, the main need seemed to be to get the workers back from the war, to recover the company's strength. Between November 1944 and July 1946, for example, the office staff numbers recovered from 8 to 24. The company architect, W A Gladstone, returned from the navy in September 1945, but left Mactaggart & Mickel in March 1946 to set up his own private practice. Compelled to vacate its Edinburgh office at 67 York Place, the firm moved into new premises at 12 North St. Andrew Street in May 1946. The Mactaggart family withdrew completely from the firm in 1947. In February, Jack finally resigned from the board of directors; in a letter to Andrew Mickel a year previously, Sir John Mactaggart had criticised his son's lack of commitment to the family business. Andrew Mickel immediately purchased his holding of 20,003 shares, and the other Mactaggart holdings (belonging to Jack's sons) were transferred to Frank (4,599 shares) and Douglas Mickel (5,298 shares). These purchases were financed by bank borrowings of £50,000 each by Andrew, Frank and Douglas, and £41,000 by

Andrew's wife; further loans totalling £134,955 were taken out later in 1948-49. The remaining family directors all received pay rises: Andrew, to £2,000; Frank, to £1,075; and Douglas, to £875. (25)

During 1948, there was further consolidation, when the company purchased 12-13 North St. Andrew Street, Edinburgh, for £5,250, and 105-107 West Regent Street/120-122 Wellington Street, Glasgow, for £18,000. The Glasgow building had been the office, in the early 1870s, of the architect Alexander 'Greek' Thomson, who had remodelled it himself *c*.1872; Thomson's own work, one should remember, had astutely combined design with building development and property speculation. In the same year, on the recommendation of James Ledingham, Andrew Mickel was given a further £500 pay rise 'in view of the very strenuous and wanting nature' of his 'present duties due to the vast amount of legislation introduced into the building industry'. (26) However, from that point, he began to become increasingly distanced from the day to day running of the firm, and Frank progressively assumed oversight of the Glasgow office. In January 1949, Andrew travelled abroad for several weeks and George Lawrence was appointed as a deputy director, and in November 1949 he transferred 7,951 shares to Frank and 8,052 to Douglas.

Private versus public

The government's new housing drive, heralded by the 1946 Housing (Financial Provisions) (Scotland) Act, clearly favoured local authorities to an even greater extent than the 1919 Act after the previous war, doubling the existing 1938 subsidies to councils. Now Glasgow Corporation and the large Labour-controlled city councils could become almost sole providers of new housing in their areas - a situation unparalleled in any other Western country - and the scope of mass council housing was extended into the remotest rural areas.

Major obstacles now stood in the way of any firm wishing to resume speculative housebuilding. The system of building licensing was made up of overlapping local and national restrictions. To qualify for a building licence, the selling price had to be approved by the local authority (including a provision forbidding resale by the owner at a higher price), certificates for timber, steel and iron had to be obtained from the Ministry of Works and other relevant departments, and priority permits for labour were to be arranged. Also, the normal peacetime requirements of Dean of Guild approval, Town & Country Planning Act approval, and Restriction of Ribbon Development Act approval all still applied. In the view of the Master Builders Association, the low level of private-enterprise output attained by 1947 (3,000-5,000 houses under construction, as against 70,000 by local authorities) was substantially caused by these price controls: it was 'hardly worthwhile trying to erect a reasonable dwelling at the restricted price of £1,300'. (27)

This policy shift was accompanied by constant debate. At first, there was still much talk of united effort, and of all sectors of the housing industry pulling together. As late as November 1945, for example, Hector McNeill, the Labour Lord Provost of Glasgow, tried to 'appeal to every agency concerned with the building of houses to go out in one great crusade to end the present condition of affairs, and so earn the thanks of the whole community'. And Tom Johnston, the former Secretary of State for Scotland, hoped housing, as 'a service', would be outside 'the orbit and strife of partisan policy ... both our major political armies are busy whipping up their followers into believing that

the other fellow can give no advice, guidance, or assistance in housing, that he is incompetent and foolish, and that all the wisdom and ability in the construction of dwellings resides and abides on his own side of the fence'. (28) But in practice, debate polarised on party-political lines, with the anti-socialist camp arguing against the rising tide of mass council housing. That debate was at its most heated in Glasgow. There the Labour administration was building up its ambitious housing drive and its direct labour force, under pressure from the strong ratepayer interest on the right, and the more radical socialist force of the Independent Labour Party on the left.

Andrew Mickel contributed constantly to these discussions in the press, directly and under pseudonyms. The theme of his writings was the inefficiency of the state and the unfulfilled potential of the private sector. For example, in February 1946, writing to the *Evening Times* under the pen-name 'Builder No.2', he argued that Glasgow Corporation, in the years of Labour control since 1933, had built only 3,000 houses per annum. Contrasting this with pre-1914 private output, he asked, 'How long will it take direct labour to build 1,000,000?' In his view, the shortage of houses was caused not by evil landlords but by the 'disappearance of the private investor ... bedevilled by rent restrictions and other forms of state intervention'; he argued that price controls tended to keep prices higher, citing the fact that an average three-apartment Glasgow Corporation house cost £821 in 1919-21, when price controls were in force, compared with £351 when they were not, during the following twelve years. In the United States, by contrast, controls on housebuilding, including price restrictions, rent controls and materials controls, were ended in 1946 to open it 'to all citizens'. For Mickel, the solution to the Scottish housing problem lay in a more free-market approach, with trade unions left to arrange a standard minimum wage, and private enterprise receiving the same subsidies and loans as local authorities. As a man of military disposition, he saw a more immediate opportunity in the vast numbers of combatant men displaced by the fighting, suggesting that the hundreds of thousands of Polish troops in Britain, 'showing no anxiety to return to their own country', should be sent to relieve Royal Engineers in Germany, that German prisoners should be employed in building material production, and that German timber output should be requisitioned. German prisoners of war were already earmarked for the advance preparation of Edinburgh Corporation housing sites; squads would be organised by the City Engineer, working under armed guard and housed under canvas, with no contact allowed with other workmen. (29)

These ideas were linked to a strong desire to resume building of speculative housing, tempered with an equally strong realism at what could actually be achieved in the face of the local authority and central government controls. In March 1946, Douglas Mickel reported that Edinburgh Corporation had agreed to grant the firm building licences for 120 houses at Hillpark and Silverknowes (at the same time as giving Miller permission for 100 houses). An engineer, John Gray, would provide a layout for Dean of Guild purposes, and the first instalment would comprise 20 three-apartment houses at Silverknowes. From May 1948, 17 three-apartment type 'I' bungalows were built at Hillpark, selling for £1,270. Following the initial 120 houses at those two sites in 1946, the firm built 146 more in 1947-51, and 150 in 1951-54. The house-types, with their metal framed windows and generally Art Deco appearance, were simplified variants of those built in the late '30s. In the west, 48 houses were begun in 1946 at Clarkston, and others were to be erected in Giffnock and Orchard Park when a licence was procured. However, in August 1946, Renfrew County Council refused to grant further licences to private enterprise 'at the present time', and so proposed development at Merrylee Park and Orchard Park was postponed; licences for 24 houses at the former were granted in November, and in August 1947 the county council granted permission for roads at Broom Estate, Carolside Park, Kilmacolm (Woodrow Avenue), Orchard Park, Giffnock and Merrylee Park. (30)

Added to these organisational difficulties facing the company in any speculative building revival were new political ones. Many of the large Labour burghs were now determined to use the increasing powers given them by planning legislation as a way of shutting out the private builder and to create scope for their own building programmes. In April 1946, for instance, the company emerged victorious from a battle with the burgh of Dumbarton. The council wanted to compulsorily acquire a section of its land at Garshake Road and tried to refuse Mactaggart & Mickel permission to build a road and 38 houses; the Department of Health overturned the council's decision on appeal. Even in the relatively favourable climate of Edinburgh, the council was on the lookout for sites for its allocation of several thousand prefabs, the largest in Scotland; the resumption of building at Silverknowes and Hillpark had been prompted by this threat, which encouraged the firm (in Andrew Mickel's words) to 'take action to protect our amenities and ... proceed with the building of permanent houses on both sites'. (31)

In an attempt to avoid this confrontation of private ownership and state letting, Mactaggart & Mickel also tried to re-enter the letting market, using a new mechanism: the housing association. In general, the private rented sector was now experiencing a crisis of confidence and viability. The 1940s saw an increase of complaints about the continuing burden of rent control, and claims that it was killing the private rented market: for example, in 1948, the Edinburgh District Property Association bemoaned the effects of this 'freezing process', with rental values the same as 28 years ago but the cost of repairs increased by 200%. Even higher-rental properties experienced this shortfall; a £40 rent rise by Mactaggart & Mickel at Sandringham Court was said to have generated an insufficient return. In a letter of May 1946 to Colonel J R H Hutchison MP, Andrew Mickel blamed owners' rates for this situation. He stated that the 1924 Act rental houses built by the firm and by Western Heritable were 'still being let at £30, with tenant's rates being paid by the tenant. This rent is perhaps £2 to £4 less per annum than the rents of Glasgow Corporation's houses of four rooms'. It would 'pay the community' if owners' rates could be stabilised at the 1919 level of 3s 3d in Glasgow and 2s 7d in Edinburgh, as Western Heritable's Glasgow rents could be cut to £21, and Mactaggart & Mickel would 'gladly try to build similar houses to the four rooms, kitchen and bathroom ... at the subsidies stated in the Housing (Financial Provisions) (Scotland) Bill presented on 6 February 1946, and let them at £26 per annum, leaving the tenants to pay all the rates'. Mickel explained that the firm had prepared two schemes for working class rental housing in the Lanarkshire burgh of Rutherglen (just outside socialist Glasgow), comprising 134 houses at Mill Street and 162 houses at Bankhead Road, but that these 'cannot proceed without financial assistance'; of the total 1946 annual state subsidy of £30, only the central government element of £23, and not the local authority subsidy of £7, would be needed to make the schemes viable. (32)

The idea of forming a housing association for rental building in Edinburgh stemmed not just from these general problems but also from the difficulty experienced by the firm in proceeding with its Broomhouse development, which had been cut short by the war and afterwards was bogged down in disputes with the Corporation. The latter was now less favourably disposed to unrestrained speculative building. This was not because of any political opposition to the private sector but for planning reasons, with the onset of green belt and zoning restrictions. In 1943, Douglas Mickel suggested that the 'plans for the future' should be 'crystallised', and that the engineer John Gray's layout plan for the area should be put to the council, to allow it to be co-ordinated with the development of the Corporation's lands at South Gyle. In 1946, after indecisive exchanges, a plan was submitted to develop a 27-acre site at Broomhouse with 432 houses for rent, in accordance with DHS circular 59/1946; the firm would 'build our own type houses on our own land for the Corporation at an agreed price per house'. Eventually, as no action had been taken by the council, the firm decided to form a housing association, the St. Andrew Housing Association, to get the houses built. The main obstacle was the Corporation's consultant planner, Derek Plumstead, who had been engaged to prepare the city's advisory plan (with Patrick Abercrombie) in 1945, followed by the full development plan. After a succession of refusals, on the grounds that the layout clashed with 'the principles of good planning', a proposal was put forward that the association should build 76 houses for letting to 'key workers' and 'key executives' on a site north of the main railway line, already zoned for housing. Despite supporting letters from firms requiring employee houses, Plumstead tried to delay the project further, and to reduce its density to 12 houses an acre, but a 73-house development was eventually approved in 1948. Plumstead eventually abruptly resigned in 1951 over delays in the implementation of the development plan. The years 1947-48 also saw an abortive proposal to form a housing association to build dwellings for let on a site in Renfrew County just outside the city boundaries, east of Hillington Road, with 90% loans from the council and with tenants substantially drawn from its housing list. (33)

Alongside these largely frustrated attempts to re-enter the speculative or rental building market, Mactaggart & Mickel recognised the need to continue its wartime reliance on contract work, including non-housing jobs in various locations across the Central Belt. In 1945-47, these included a Building Trades Training Centre for the Ministry of Labour at Granton, Edinburgh, built for £107,000 (but already redundant by 1948 owing to the resources crisis!); removal of air-raid shelters; temporary offices and hutting for the Ministry of Works at Sighthill, in Edinburgh, for £144,000; a £32,000 Ministry of Works contract for temporary classrooms at four Glasgow schools; and a temporary classroom for Renfrew County Council at St Joseph's RC School, Clarkston. Work also began to rebuild 14 of the 16 war-destroyed houses at Kelvinside, following the usual protracted negotiations with the government's war damage commission. (34)

Crisis of production

In 1947, the position of Scottish housebuilding worsened, with the deepening national economic crisis. As we will see in Chapter B3, the extensive range of controls was not enough to prevent the eventual emergence of a materials shortage and price inflation as serious as that of 1937. By 1947, building costs in Edinburgh had nearly trebled since before the war, and the Housing Committee was receiving tenders for its new Inch and Liberton schemes at £600 above the £1,250 limit laid down by DHS; some houses would cost over £2,000 each! The cost of prefabs, too, had seen a steep rise, to £1,610. The government's first response was to impose a blanket ban in August 1947 on all new licences for housing projects. As a result Renfrew County Council, for example, refused permission for 20 houses in Orchard Park in October. Andrew Mickel, returning from the Building Exhibition, in London, declared that 'it would be some considerable time before the government policy would be altered to allow private enterprise to build houses for sale', so the company would have to continue to 'concentrate meantime on contract work ... every effort should be made to ensure an even flow of orders'. (35)

In August-October 1947, the labour and materials shortages had reached such a level that it was also proposed to freeze work on all private housing projects in progress across the UK, other than those certified for key workers or agriculture. Andrew Mickel responded that the ban would mean 'dearer homes'. Such an 'endeavour to eliminate building by private enterprise if not permanently, at least temporarily' was misguided, as private builders could 'produce the goods', including new houses for letting if they received the same financial help as local authorities: 'The Government should be prepared to provide for all its constituents. A large proportion of people wish to own their house'. In the end, the ban was not applied to Scotland because of the low level of private building here. The government also responded to the crisis by stepping up the drive for permanent non-traditional building. Against this, Andrew Mickel argued that resources should be biased towards expanded brick and concrete production in Scotland, rather than foreign prefabrication. Claiming that the Swedish timber houses imported by DHS from 1945 were temporary houses, Mickel wrote that '11,737 builders are idle waiting for bricks' ... 'instead of erecting costly and unsightly steel prefabs, build houses of concrete ... in Scotland 250,000 tons of concrete are produced yearly ... the concrete business is screaming out for orders ... why bring temporary houses made of Swedish timber to this country? Why not bring the timber and let us use it to build permanent houses?' (36)

These building rationing measures continued in force into 1948, with a ban on new contracts in September, and ongoing restraints on speculative building. In England, the restriction of speculative building to 20% of total housing output and the controls on maximum selling prices were both abolished in June, but Scotland was excluded because of the continuing number of unfinished houses on Scottish schemes. The only outlet for private building was building for key workers. In response to the report of the Laidlaw Committee on excessive housebuilding costs, the Secretary of State encouraged a move to single contracts to push prices down. This situation continued to provoke frustrated reactions from Andrew Mickel. In bold letters, he wrote the word 'LIES' across a newspaper claim by Secretary of State Arthur Woodburn that state-dominated housing production in Scotland had beaten all previous records. Woodburn argued that as a survey in Edinburgh had shown that less than 5% of the people wanted to buy a house, it was 'not the government's place to give anybody authority to jump the queue by taking material and labour from their schemes for somebody who could buy a house - in other words to get a privilege'. The 1949 Housing Act's deletion of the words 'working classes' from the legal definition of the purpose of council housing underlined the government's determination that 'housing needs, as distinct from ability to pay, should be the determining factor in the allocation of houses'. (37)

At this most depressed period of the rationing era, political calls arose for the state involvement in housing demand to be extended into supply, by nationalising the building industry and the building materials industry. Building trade workers advocated it on grounds of greater efficiency, and groups within the Labour Party advocated it as a way of ensuring that building for private

ownership was kept to a maximum of 25%. These arguments were countered by Andrew Mickel and an Edinburgh Tory councillor, Robert Bell, who opposed any further extension of 'Socialism and Bureaucracy', arguing that 'men and women should not be condemned to stand forever in a Corporation housing queue while the Socialist Government muddles along in a sea of forms, regulations, and reports which no person ever reads'. A Portobello bricklayer wrote in reply that, from the 'violence' of Bell's language, one would expect to learn that he had 'discovered a government plot to strangle all builders at birth'. (38)

Collaborative ventures of the late 1940s

Despite the strong arguments on both sides, the role of the private industry in housing production was preserved even during the government-directed command economy of the rationing years. At the Labour Party conference of 1950, for example, the Minister of Health, Aneurin Bevan, rejected nationalisation of the building industry, while still maintaining that 'we are trying to interpose a piece of socialist planning and sanity into the jungle of private enterprise'. And increasingly in practice, in both speculative and contracted housing, the way for Scottish builders to combat the difficulties of the 1940s seemed to be through collaboration, both with each other and with the government agencies they sometimes criticised in public. Here again, we see in practice the watering-down of competitive ideas and the making of concessions to the overall collective climate of those years. Solidarity also had another aspect - to protect Scottish economic interests against firms from outside. All these ideas were reflected in two related initiatives of the mid-1940s, in both of which Mactaggart & Mickel played a prominent role: for speculative housing, the Scottish House Builders' Association (SHBA, which Mactaggart & Mickel pioneered); and for contracted work, the Scottish Housing Group.

The SHBA, founded in November 1945, brought together a range of speculative builders from different areas of Scotland. In keeping with the relatively marginal status of speculative building, it was mainly a lobbying organisation, targeting central government to preserve the profile of the sector. Its inaugural meeting in November 1945, chaired by Andrew Mickel, was attended by John Lawrence, Norman Keanie, James Miller, R S Bisset and R S Gray - builders who accounted for over 80% of current Scottish speculative output. Mickel argued that housebuilders, in approaching government departments, 'could make very little progress as individuals', and Lawrence had even had a personal discussion with Secretary of State Westwood, 'without result'. Because of this, as Keanie put it, 'there is a great deal of misunderstanding ... our part as providers had been obscured, but large numbers of people were getting the benefit of our activities. How many people living in our houses today are not delighted that they had secured them?' With the exception of Miller, who strongly advocated a London-based approach to the problem, all the other builders were insistent on the need to differentiate Scottish from English building conditions, and to keep the SHBA separate from the Housebuilders Association of Great Britain. Mickel reported that he had raised the question of the different conditions in England with DHS, and claimed that an average English house cost £120 less to build. He pointed out that, paradoxically, the 1920s private enterprise subsidies had been formulated by Labour MPs, but scrapped by the non-socialist National governments of the 1930s, and advocated the use of German and Italian prisoners to turn out concrete blocks from gravel deposits in the north, to save brick transport costs. After discussion of the merits of Edinburgh and Glasgow as headquarters for the SHBA, Glasgow was selected, as the largest population centre, and Mickel was appointed president, with John Lawrence as vice president; Miller was offered the treasurer's post but turned it down. The SHBA subscription invitation letter emphasised the commitment to traditional building in opposition to prefabrication: the maximum price of a 'sound traditional house' was £1,200 (including land, roads, services) whereas a 'temporary house of limited life and unproved quality' would cost £1,350 for the shell only: 'this tendency is contrary to the public good'. (39)

The Scottish Housing Group (SHG) was a cartel of housing contractors, under Lawrence's chairmanship, which was built up in the mid-1940s with DHS and Building Research Station help. Its aims were to exploit non-traditional construction and resist the incursion of English firms, especially by acting as main contractors for systems emanating from outside Scotland; its importance declined after the government allowed local authorities to negotiate non-traditional contracts directly with promoters in 1948. For an overall account of its work, see Chapter B3. Mactaggart & Mickel joined the group in May 1946, and almost immediately began receiving contracts for SHG work, under the system of allocation co-ordinated by the DHS; even the metal-based building systems castigated by Mickel required substantial general builder work. A selection of these contracts illustrates the mobility and diversity needed to participate in non-traditional building, which included both all-trades and separate-trades work, and a mixture of large local authority and small philanthropic projects. The contracts included the erection of 150 BISF steel houses at South Markinhill site, and 50 Whitson-Fairhurst houses at Pennyfern, both for Greenock Corporation; 150 BISF houses for the SSHA at Bellsmyre, Dumbarton; brick and joiner work for 100 Atholl steel houses at Loanhead, Midlothian, and another 100 at Danderhall; brick work and joiner work for 108 Atholl steel houses at Balornock, Glasgow; all-trades builder work (other than steel fabrication and plastering) for 120 Atholl steel houses for agricultural workers on various sites in the counties of Dumbarton, Stirling and Renfrew; and the erection of the Mk III house-type of the Blackburn Aircraft Company at Dalkeith, Auchenback (Barrhead) and Barmulloch (Glasgow); ten houses at King's Park, and two at Stevenston, for the Scottish Veterans' Garden City Association; 14 houses for Earl Haig Homes at Stenhouse, Edinburgh; further veterans houses at Paisley, and eleven shops at Old Saughton and Moredun for Edinburgh Corporation. (40)

The SHG and Andrew Mickel also involved themselves in Lawrence's efforts in non-traditional building materials manufacture, especially in his 'Bellrock' patent walling system of gypsum panelling, which removed the need for nails or plaster. The SHG lobbied the government and, after a visit to the works by Andrew Mickel, it was agreed to associate with the proposed syndicate to manufacture the walling locally. More generally, its members, with their substantial overlap with the SHBA, fuelled the housing debate with press correspondence and lobbying letters to government. The main concern of this lobbying was the allegedly greater cost and the inefficiency of the state-controlled system. For example, in February and April 1948, Andrew Mickel, backed up by John Lawrence, sent off a barrage of letters criticising the government's restrictions on use of timber flooring and its promotion of more expensive concrete precast floors. He bemoaned the plight of the 'harassed housewives who are condemned to tread these solid floors for 16 hours of the day!' (41)

Harbingers of change

The dawning of 1950 saw the first hints of a change in the position of private building. With the election in 1949 of an anti-socialist Progressive Party administration to power in Glasgow Corporation, both Glasgow and Edinburgh were briefly united in general opposition to mass housing by the state. In the event, this would turn out to be a false dawn for the private sector, as the Progressives would lose power again in Glasgow in only two years, and Labour would then begin an even larger housing drive. But it showed that the position was at least potentially fluid. (42)

Within Edinburgh Corporation, the beginning of 1950 saw calls for a relaxation of the restrictions on private building: the Housing Committee Chairman argued that 'surely it is time that Scotland was getting some measure of liberty comparable with England', provoking a response from a socialist member, Councillor Ball, that anyone who wanted to buy their house was an 'enemy of society'. At a meeting of Clydeside builders in January, Andrew Mickel argued that private builders had been 'able to build anywhere but Glasgow', including Lanarkshire, Stirling, Dundee and Ayrshire. Support came from traditionalist architects such as J Steel Maitland of Paisley, who attacked the prefabs as a mistake that 'future generations will have to suffer ... in our despoiled countryside ... in the near future what was not so long ago considered cheap jerry-building will be held up as models of excellent craftsmanship, compared with the derelicts that will disgrace our civilisation'. W S Cruickshank, a *Scotsman* correspondent, put it more colourfully: in a few years, 'most of the architectural monstrosities being erected today will probably be lying in heaps of broken asbestos and twisted sheet metal'. In response, Secretary of State Hector McNeil announced that private builders would be allocated 10% of output; further small concessions, focusing on priority housing cases such as key workers, followed in the autumn, with centralised licensing controls ending in early 1951; at the same time, Glasgow Corporation announced that 500 new speculative houses would be allowed in the city. Mactaggart & Mickel immediately began promotional attempts to capture this limited new market, with an advertisement which pointed out that 'under new regulations, there is a possibility of a limited number of houses being built for sale to persons in priority classes such as industrial key workers, doctors, nurses, teachers, transport workers, and persons requiring accommodation for reasons of ill health, etc. If you are interested, send details of your case, in writing, to Mactaggart & Mickel'. (43)

In its building activity during this period, Mactaggart & Mickel gradually expanded its output in both the speculative and contracting fields. In Edinburgh, a group of 47 four-apartment bungalows, cottages and flats for sale was commenced in early 1950 at Silverknowes Avenue, Road, Crescent and Hill, costing a total of £75,000. At the same time, the firm won a contract from Edinburgh Corporation for 172 council houses at Old Saughton, commencing in March 1950, as part of a 365-house scheme which the City had divided into two sections; the use of competitive tendering for the project had cut prices by 15%, or £243 per house. In an illustration of the way in which Mactaggart & Mickel preferred to modernise its building processes in gradual steps, construction of this scheme was carried out using extensive electric floodlighting, but its overall construction was in 'traditional' rendered brick. Further council housing contracts won by the firm in 1950 were, however, largely for non-traditional building, including 20 Blackburn and 58 Atholl houses at Bo'ness, and 128 Atholl houses at Gorebridge. (44)

A4.8. Floodlit building on an autumn evening: the Old Saughton contract for Edinburgh Corporation (172 houses) in progress in October 1950. (MMC)

With the election of a Tory government in Westminster in 1951, the demands to free the housing market became more prominent. Newspaper campaigns began to 'free the builder': the *Sunday Mail* declared that there were 'too many long-haired young men planning away in Government offices, quite out of touch with the realities of the situation'. In another *Sunday Mail* campaign, 'How to Get More Homes', John Lawrence argued for the building of economic private-sector terraced houses, and 'tenements and flats on present-day slum sites', using elements of prefabrication and abandoning separate-trades contracting: 'When a man has waited seven weary years and is still without a house for his family, he doesn't care whether his house-to-be is built by local authority or by private enterprise'. In November, the new government raised the proportion of total output allocated to speculative building to 20% (for sale only), although maximum prices and sizes were still fixed (the maximum size being raised from 1,000 to 1,500 square feet); 'bulk licences' could now be issued for larger developments. Scottish Office junior housing minister T D Galbraith explained that the government wanted houses to be 'within the reach of many of modest means, including artisans, who were willing to make sacrifices to own their own home'; the aim was to foster a 'sense of responsibility and dignity'. Douglas Mickel, now emerging as a housing spokesman alongside his father, acclaimed the new policy: 'It is exactly what I expected would happen. This will increase the rate of housing. We have 700 people waiting to buy houses now, and the corporation have about 500 on their waiting list to buy - we can certainly provide them!' He dismissed the Labour opposition's warnings that liberalisation should be phased, in order to prevent chaos: 'We are ready, willing and able, and we are champing at the bit!' This optimism did not extend to rental housing: in view of the low levels of rents in existing housing, it would be economically possible only if 'private enterprise got a subsidy similar to that which local authorities were getting because rents would be far too high'; both Glasgow and Edinburgh housing committees welcomed the development. (45)

The company followed up these words of welcome with immediate building activity. Already, they had exploited the 500-dwelling private housing allocation by Glasgow's Tory administration, by commencing a large development of semi-detached and terraced homes of three, four and five apartments at Braehead, Cathcart; 326 dwellings were originally planned. The Corporation housing convener, Councillor Macpherson-Rait, hailed these as a 'welcome addition' to the estates already being built by Lawrence at Broomhill and Scotstounhill; these developments would be ready by August 1951, with selling prices of £1,550-£1,680. Macpherson-Rait claimed that Glasgow was the first city in Scotland to issue a bulk licence, saving the government £23 annual subsidy for each house. In Edinburgh, 29 more houses were started at Silverknowes in mid-1951, at a total cost of £61,230. In reply to criticisms from inhabitants of emergency hutted accommodation at Duddingston that these houses for sale at Silverknowes were not helping the housing problem, Andrew Mickel responded that they were built only for priority cases under present regulations, and some of them were freeing rented properties. Council contracting work in the capital continued actively, with site preparation starting for a large estate of 1,300 mostly non-traditional houses at Drylaw Mains South and Ferry Road, and 1,000 traditionally built houses at Drumbrae and Clermiston Road. (46)

By early 1952, the full consequences of the partial relaxation of control on private building had become clearer. From the perspective of Mactaggart & Mickel, who, like Miller, had been able to secure bulk licences under the new system, it had strengthened the firm's commitment to build more. Douglas Mickel claimed that 'at the moment we are building for private purchasers at only one-tenth of what we could be doing'; in the past five years they had sought permission to build 1,000 houses in the Edinburgh area, but only 200 had been sanctioned. As a result, with an average building time of seven months from foundation-laying to occupation, there were still 750 people on the company waiting list for new houses. Their most popular types were five-apartment villas and cottage types, completely decorated and ready for occupation at £2,000. But the situation looked very different for firms who had not secured bulk licences, such as Hepburn Brothers. It took them a year to build each house, and they had to charge £1,750-£2,200 for three or four apartments. From their perspective the situation was one of 'discrimination'. In response, Douglas Mickel argued for greater deregulation: 'housing should be a social and not political issue. Those able to afford them should be offered houses let at economic rent, or for purchase, and the subsidised houses reserved for those unable to cope with a high rent'. In May 1952, the private building cause suffered a major reversal, when the anti-socialist Progressives lost power again to Labour, after three years, at the Glasgow council elections. Since 1950, Labour had complained of the handing out of bulk licences to private firms in the city, with 1,500 dwellings being distributed mostly to Mactaggart & Mickel and John MacDonald. A controversial bulk licence for 356 houses at Jordanhill and Drumchapel, awarded by the Progressives just before the election, was cancelled, and a new application for 46 private houses at Crow Road, by builder William S Gordon, was refused. In Edinburgh, the awarding of private licences continued unabated, with 305 given out in mid-1952, despite Labour claims that they were slowing the housing programme. (47)

Almost immediately, however, central government moved decisively in the other direction from Glasgow Corporation. It signalled the abolition of its own regulation of local authority controls over private building, including the 20% quota rule; in England, housing minister Harold Macmillan went further and promised the early lifting of all licensing controls. Accordingly, 1952 saw, for the first time since the war, the beginnings of a full range of private building for sale by Mactaggart & Mickel, including large and small developments. The Braehead project, as built, comprised 307 semi-detached villas of four and five apartments; erected in 1952-54, these houses sold readily for prices between £1,944 and £2,091. The final 150 of the Braehead houses were authorised by Glasgow Corporation in March 1952 on a single bulk licence, interestingly without any overt opposition from the Labour members. At the same time, the first of a number of small developments intended for occupation by police staff was built at Dorchester Avenue and Ripon Drive, Kelvinside, at a unit cost of £1,751. The year 1952 also saw the start of large-scale building elsewhere on Clydeside, with an estate of over 100 houses at Stevenston. In the Edinburgh area, the large Broomhall development was inaugurated, as we will see later in this chapter; and a development of larger villas and cottages at Balerno was started, selling at 'controlled prices'. The firm continued to accept local authority contract work, although it was still making general criticisms of the public sector. In February 1952, Douglas Mickel complained in a *Scotsman* letter that every council house in Edinburgh 'is subsidised to such a degree that the tenant pays less than one third of the economic rent, no owners' rates, or maintenance costs ... and now we learn that even the beautiful western slopes of Clermiston Hill, Barnton, are going to be swallowed up by a Corporation housing scheme' which would

'bring down the value of the surrounding houses and put the Corporation further into debt!' Yet the firm actually took contracts in due course to build some of this development, a carefully designed garden suburb by J A W Grant. Other contracted work in Edinburgh at this time included a 14-dwelling memorial group for the Royal Artillery and Royal Engineers, designed by L C Powell of Chesham, near London; and 66 Lawrence houses at Drylaw. (48)

While they were showing increasing confidence in building for sale, the firm was moving in precisely the opposite direction within the private rented sector, by beginning to vacate it altogether. In 1952, Douglas Mickel explained that it was 'uneconomic to continue to let the houses. The rents are still as they were in 1932, but repair costs have bounded up, and rates and property tax have increased'. From 1953 onwards, as soon as the terms of the original Corporation loans allowed it, when each house at Pilton, Carrick Knowe, Colinton Mains and Broomhouse became vacant, it was offered for sale. Soon 'hundreds' were on the market, at prices of between £1,200 and £1,400 for cottages and flatted villas of three and four apartments; the £1,200 price corresponded to a £170 down-payment and £2 weekly loan repayment, a cost subsequently reduced further when the government guaranteed loans of up to 95% of the purchase price. L S Gumley & Davidson handled the sales, which could mostly be done by word of mouth, except for 'the East Pilton area, a congested area that holds little appeal for prospective buyers'. (49)

Mactaggart & Mickel's actions should be seen as part of a wider movement of political and social polarisation within Scottish housing from the 1950s. Renting became more and more exclusively identified with the local authority sector, while the private sector began to focus only on owner occupation. The result was a growing trend to sell houses that had originally been built for rental with subsidy. Mactaggart & Mickel's sales of its loan-subsidised Edinburgh stock were followed rapidly in 1953 by the more heavily subsidised earlier stock of Western Heritable in Glasgow. The issue of house sales in Glasgow had already been raised in November 1951, in a slightly different form, when the then Progressive administration began a short-lived attempt to build council houses for sale. The Housing Committee's decision, by 18 votes to 15, to make a previously planned scheme of 622 houses at Merrylee (a generally middle class suburban area) available for sale, was fiercely opposed by the Labour group and by tenants' groups. Their demonstrations and protests, including a mass 'storming' of the City Chambers on 6 December 1951, delayed the proposal until May 1952, when Labour was able to cancel it. (50)

In general, the early 1950s in Glasgow saw growing alarm among owners at the state of the private rented stock, and the effects of low rents and high owners' rates, in combination with the spreading problem of slums and inner-city dereliction. In April 1952, the Property Owners Association went so far as to argue that a 'housing disaster faces Glasgow'. In 1953, therefore, Western Heritable proposed to do the same in Glasgow as Mactaggart & Mickel was doing in Edinburgh: to begin selling its interwar rental stock, which amounted to 5,314 houses at Kelvinside, King's Park, Cardonald and Hillington. The houses would be sold for an average of £950 each, with 31s annual feu duty, relieving the company of a total of £66,000 annual maintenance expenditure. This would inevitably be a more contentious and difficult proposal than Mactaggart & Mickel's house sales programme in Edinburgh, owing to the more generous (and more closely regulated) subsidy regime enjoyed by Western

Heritable, and the more hostile attitude of the council. Members of the ruling Labour group in the Corporation opposed the proposal, arguing that the houses had been built with public subsidy, and so to sell them now amounted to profiteering. Dr James Welsh, Mactaggart's old opponent at King's Park, pointed out that the subsidies paid under the Wheatley Act since 1927 had amounted to over £1,225,000, and that each of the first batch of 1,356 houses had already received £337 10s subsidy against its original valuation of £470, leaving only £132 10s to be paid over the remaining 14 years of the subsidy term; he summed up the proposals as a 'selfish exploitation of the needs of the people'. Unlike the Merrylee case, the Corporation could not veto the proposal. Welsh warned that, if it was approved, the Secretary of State would 'soon be asked to grant the same freedom to the Glasgow Estates Development Company [McDonald's firm] for the 1,332 houses they own and let in Cardonald and Hillington. There is also a large estate in Edinburgh which you might expect to hear about at an early date'. After an initial refusal by the Scottish Office, the proposal was ultimately approved by the House of Lords, in a case heard on 1 March 1956. (51)

Part III
Return to 'normalcy': 1953-60

The mid-1950s, with its lifting of the remaining restrictions on private building, seemed to herald a return to the conditions of the 1930s 'golden years'. Not only was there no restriction on the number of houses the firm could build, but the lifting of materials rationing meant that this could be done in the 'traditional' rendered brick construction they favoured - albeit with various refinements of detail. However, the large-scale output of low-rental council housing by Glasgow Corporation and other authorities, and the beginnings of area slum clearance, had created a very different general context in housing compared with the 1930s. On the one hand, there was an overall rise in housing standards, as increasingly everyone had access to a home with basic facilities: there was no longer a big gulf between housing of the rich and housing of the poor. But alongside this, there was the growing political opposition, touched on above, between two 'sectors' - the council rented and the owner-occupied sectors - which actually built quite similar houses to each other, as we will see in the case of Mactaggart & Mickel's 'economy' houses of the mid and late '50s.

For Mactaggart & Mickel, this was a time of growing confidence, as it was able to look on itself primarily as a speculative builder once more: a 1953 advertisement presented the company above all as 'Scotland's most experienced house builders', and only secondly as a contractor to government and local authorities, builder of hospitals, offices and industrial installations. The firm's internal management saw the completion of its first generational change, with day to day direction in effect divided between Frank Mickel in Glasgow and Douglas in Edinburgh, although Andrew Mickel remained very much the firm's overall authority-figure. By 1952, the salaries of the family directors were: Andrew, £2,500; Frank, £1,700; Douglas, £1,500. From 1953 to 1960, the only formal directors' meeting was the annual general meeting. Andrew involved himself in non-commercial and philanthropic work; already a justice of the peace (since 1929), in 1953 he became Deputy Lieutenant of the City of Glasgow, and in the same year persuaded the company to build a hall for the elderly in Clarkston, named 'Mickel Hall'; he also served as a deacon of the Incorporation of Gardeners, convener of the Glasgow Discharged Prisoners' Aid Society, and a captain in the Boys' Brigade. In

1957, he undertook a six-month journey to New Zealand and Australia to investigate the possibility of the company extending its activity to either country, but the result was inconclusive. Overall, it is important to remember that the firm's family directors were all people who lived in the suburbs (in most cases in houses actually built by the firm) and who participated actively in the community life of those suburbs. On that participation was based their confidence in what they did, whether it was in the houses they built, the advertisements they produced, or the public statements on housing issues which they made. The dominant political opinion may have been flowing in the other direction, but they could nevertheless look on the communities, or potential communities, of house-owners as the 'constituencies' whose interests they legitimately represented. (52)

The early 1950s saw the appointment by Frank Mickel of a new company architect, Alexander Buchanan Campbell, who was a product of the Glasgow Beaux-Arts tradition of logical planning in architecture. Campbell's job was to design house-types and estate layouts, but not to supervise construction; the 'bread-and-butter' security provided by his hourly-paid work for the firm, until the 1970s, allowed him to design a range of major buildings elsewhere, including the vast, concrete-arched Dollan Baths in East Kilbride New Town (1965-68). He later recalled with affection the firm's 'strength in the practical side of building, and their good sense in bringing together and holding on to a team of sound craftsmen. They were a very supportive and friendly team to work with - there was never anything stinted!' Andrew Mickel's concept of the role of an architect was a traditional one: 'The first interview I had in the firm was with Colonel Mickel, who said "Remember this - if you're working with us here, there are no cocktails at lunchtime!"' (53)

The beginning of the 1960s, as we will see in Chapter 5, would mark a further generational watershed in the company's history. Following the deaths of Frank Mickel (in 1961) and J H MacHattie, Andrew appointed James D Goold as company secretary, to replace the latter, and J G L Wark joined the board of directors. Andrew also transferred 8,000 shares each to the next generation of the family, in the form of Frank's son Derek (born in 1935), and Douglas's son Bruce (born in 1945). In 1962, Andrew himself died in Largs. (54)

Within the company's housing work as a whole, its return to speculative building had already squeezed out building for rental. Now, what was also fading gradually from view, relatively speaking, was contracted housebuilding work. During the mid-1950s, the local authority contract work available in towns and cities was increasingly taking the form of low-rise flats in hybrid traditional and prefabricated construction. Here Mactaggart & Mickel differed from Miller, who exploited the change by developing its own 'new traditional' types of tenement block for Edinburgh Corporation, and from John Lawrence, who used his own precast concrete blockwork for crosswall tenements in Glasgow and Clydebank; instead, the company continued to build other firms' systems on licence where required.

During the mid-1950s, Mactaggart & Mickel's municipal housing contracts, although reasonably large by the standards of its own contemporary speculative building, remained modest in size by comparison with some of the enormous contracts for council housing being taken on by others. In 1954-57, for example, it took on slightly less than a one-tenth share (57 houses) of a grouped contract awarded by Glasgow Corporation for 624 tenement flats in Unit 4 (Drummore Road) of its Drumchapel peripheral scheme, using both traditional construction and

A4.9. Colonel Andrew Mickel in 1953. (MMC)

crosswall blockwork construction. The other contractors involved were A A Stuart & Sons, Melville Dundas & Whitson, Blackburn Ltd, and Atholl Ltd. From 1955, two groups of houses (totalling 92 and 66 respectively) were built at the Castlemilk scheme for the Corporation. A primary school was built in 1953 at one of Glasgow's other big schemes, Pollok. In Edinburgh, the company built 185 houses in 1953 at Clermiston 1st Development and

146 houses in 1955 at the 6th Development, as well as 16 Northern Lighthouse Board houses for the SSHA at Muirhouse, for occupation by the families of the keepers of the Inchkeith, Fidra and Bass Rock lighthouses. The only major contracting involvement during this period was a series of projects, almost a programme, in a new location for the firm: the shipbuilding town of Greenock. In the early '50s, the firm built 130 Lawrence houses

A4.10. 1954 portrait of Douglas Mickel in the Top Gear *motoring magazine; he was secretary of the MG Car Club from 1948, and also a keen cine-film maker. (*Top Gear, *March 1954)*

for the council at Larkfield, 100 houses at Auchmead and 14 houses for the Scottish Veterans' Garden City Association from June 1951. In 1953-54, the Pennyfern project of 252 dwellings was constructed on one of the steep and exposed sites characteristic of Inverclyde. Hailed by local newspapers as a 'new town ... built in ten months', the first 144 houses, half of three and half of four apartments and constructed of Lawrence crosswall construction

using Wilson blockwork, were begun in March 1953 under Frank Mickel's personal supervision, and completely occupied within a year; they were built for the SSHA, but the Corporation factored them and chose the tenants. Progress was so rapid that there were complaints that it had outpaced road construction. (55)

HOUSES FOR LIGHTHOUSE KEEPERS

A4.11. Lighthouse-keepers' houses at Muirhouse, Edinburgh, built by Mactaggart & Mickel for the Scottish Special Housing Association, and seen here newly completed in 1954. (Scotsman, 8 June 1954)

Building for sale in the mid 1950s

The year 1953 saw the next stage in the Unionist Party (Tory) government's strategy to 'resurrect' the speculative builder, allowing for the greater difficulties in doing so by comparison with England and Wales. During the year, the government announced the end of all controls on house prices and the virtual deregulation of bulk licences. Douglas Mickel welcomed the changes, and advised local authorities to issue bulk licences on demand, as this, in his view, would give better returns for labour and materials: 'Local authorities should try to forget they have ever been hedged round by restrictions, and get cracking with the job before there was a government change of mind! I have been trying to push the local authorities and convince them that there is this freedom, but they will not take it that way. They seem to have been caged in for too long!' (56)

Houses 'Grow' At Clermiston

Rapid progress is now being made on the Corporation housing scheme on the western slopes of Corstorphine Hill at Clermiston, one of the city's largest post-war building sites. The stone used for the foundations of the road in the foreground was obtained from old Saughton House *("News" photo.)*

A4.12. Mactaggart & Mickel contracting work in progress at Edinburgh Corporation's Clermiston garden suburb housing scheme, September 1953. (Scotsman, 15 September 1953)

A4.13. 1957 sketch design for company stand at Ideal Homes Exhibition, Edinburgh. (MMC D33275CN)

A4.14. Mactaggart & Mickel's stand at the 1959 Ideal Homes Exhibition, Edinburgh. (MMC)

For Mactaggart & Mickel, the time had now arrived to make ready its marketing and production machine again, with its showhouses, 'women's' features, courting of the press and promotion of home ownership in general. Whereas the attacks on landlords were largely abandoned, there were still efforts to lure buyers out of the depressed rented sector; the greatest emphasis was on a heightened, postwar sense of modernity, linking that to the ideal self-contained 'family'. For example, a 1955 advertisement for a five-apartment showhouse at Simshill, Glasgow, speculated about its ideal occupants: 'Mum is charming, young at heart, gay, imaginative about the job of homemaking. Dad is practical, knows value when he sees it, appreciates the cardinal virtue of efficiency in the house. Daughter ... inherits her mother's artistic streak ... The family likes people ... and it likes comfort ... yes, a delightful civilised family!!!' The firm enthusiastically participated in the Scottish 'Ideal Homes' shows from 1954 onwards, which celebrated this newly optimistic housebuilding climate. It contributed to the 1955 and 1956 events, at Edinburgh's Waverley Market, although it declined a proposal to build a wooden bungalow patented by a Birmingham firm at the 1955 event; Douglas Mickel supported the city's Lord Provost (Sir John G Banks) at the May 1956 opening ceremony. (57)

In contrast to the 1930s, there were few really big sites, with the major exceptions of Broomhall in Edinburgh and Simshill in Glasgow; the drive was to infill the suburbs with smaller

developments, and use up remaining land on the large interwar sites: an advertisement of January 1953 announced that 'Houses of Distinction are now being built at Braehead, Simshill, Carmunnock Road, Newton Mearns and the Edinburgh area'. However, steps were taken to replenish or adjust the company's land-bank; early in 1955, for example, 23 acres of land surplus to Edinburgh Corporation's requirements at Clermiston were acquired by the firm in exchange for a 19-acre section of the company's land at Broomhouse, required for a school. Although the firm would have preferred to resurrect its upmarket initiatives of the 1930s, compromise and measured change were still the overriding needs. Within mainstream speculative building, the requirement was above all for economical three-bedroom houses, costing as near as possible to £1,500. Following the building price inflation of the 1940s, such a price was of course far more than those of the 1930s. A 1954 advertisement emphasised that 'some of the least expensive houses are being built in Scotland to-day by the big Mactaggart & Mickel organisation', although house-types up to £5,000 were available. At the same time, there was the necessity for more specialised initiatives: the same advertisement praised Frank Mickel as 'a restless experimenter who tries out many of his best ideas in his own home, and learns from solid experience'. For example, while local authorities were beginning to react to land shortages and planning restrictions by considering use of multi-storey flats, Mactaggart & Mickel was returning to the concept of smaller-scale blocks of service

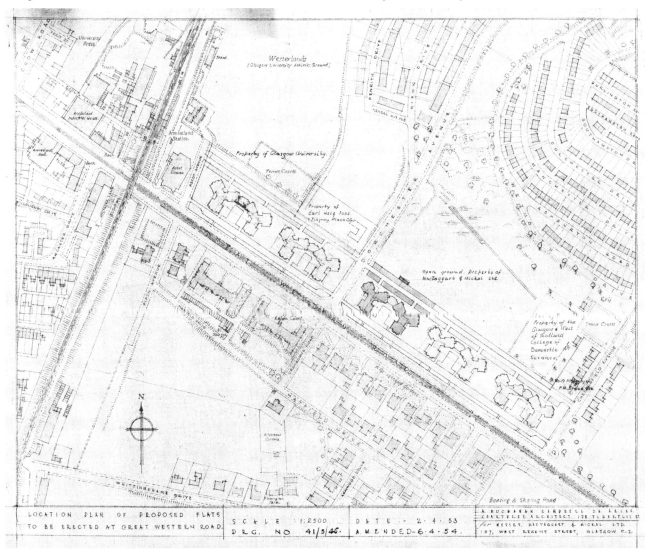

A4.15. April 1954 location plan of proposed six-storey flats at Great Western Road, designed by A Buchanan Campbell; these somewhat conservatively-styled blocks, with their complicated three-winged plan, were not built, but more modern medium-rise flats were constructed subsequently on the site, which is opposite the Kelvin Court interwar apartment blocks. (MMC D39748)

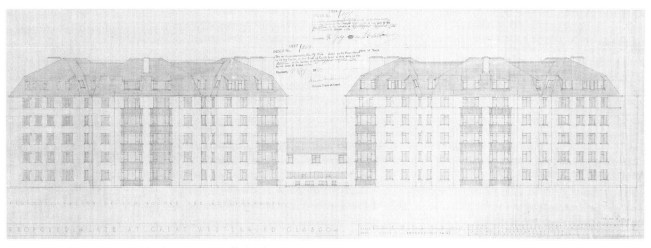

A4.16. 1953 elevation drawing of the abortive six-storey blocks. (MMC D39747CN)

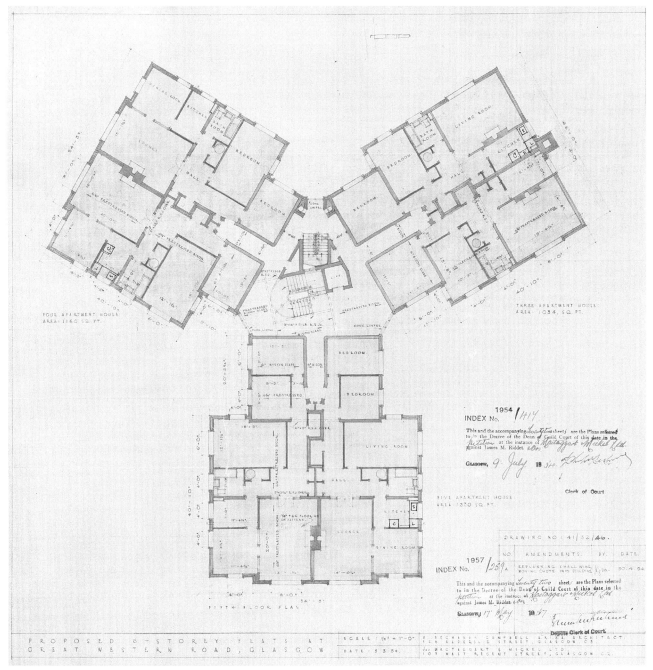

A4.17. 1954 first-floor plan for the six-storey blocks. (MMC D39756CN)

apartments in Glasgow: in August 1953, it announced its intention to make an 'early start' on five blocks of six or seven storeys on Great Western Road; Buchanan Campbell produced an abortive plan for linked pairs of three-winged blocks, six storeys high with massive mansard attics, containing six three-apartment flats on each floor. (58)

In the company's everyday estates of villas, Buchanan Campbell produced standard designs which were modified on-site as necessary. His practical, Beaux-Arts outlook allowed him to tolerate the inevitable on-site departures from his designs; there was no room for architectural artist-primadonnas on these pragmatic projects. 'When you saw your houses you often couldn't believe that was what you'd drawn at all. For example, when Frank Mickel took me out to look at some houses I designed for the Broom estate, all the windows and the other details had been completely changed!' In general, the mid and late 1950s designs fell into two broad categories, only subtly differentiated from one another. The smaller houses and blocks of low-rise flats emphasised a thrifty, sparing modernity, their plain rendered walls, metal-framed windows and pitched roofs creating an effect not at all unlike contemporary council housing. The mid-range and more expensive houses set themselves apart by using slightly more sober versions of the general features of the houses of the 1930s - bay windows, tile-hanging and so forth. Plan-types remained generally conservative, with Modernist ideas of flowing space exploited, as we will see, largely as a space-saving device in the smallest houses. For example, in a 1958 advertisement for the Kelvinside estate in Glasgow, the four- and five-apartment semi-detached villas follow the time-honoured linear plan, the five-apartment having a double curved bay window in the 1930s Art Deco fashion, while the three-storey blocks of flats have a conventional tenement plan, with flats flanking the staircase, and modest bay windows on the front facade. Thus, paradoxically, the more expensive houses were in some ways less architecturally 'advanced'. (59)

The new estate which got the company's new phase of speculative building off to a flying start in the west of Scotland was Simshill, a hilly site off Carmunnock Road on the south side of Glasgow. It was situated not far from King's Park, and also near the exactly contemporary Castlemilk, one of the Corporation's large peripheral schemes of tenements. Here we can see Mactaggart & Mickel's most economical postwar types in the process of evolving. Development of the Simshill estate got seriously under way in 1953, with bulk licences for 58 houses granted in October; these comprised 22 semi-detached five-apartment villas (selling at £2,091-£2,136), 30 semi-detached four-apartment cottages (£1,987), four mid-terrace houses of three apartments (£1,597), and two end terraced houses (£1,647), all attracting 90% building society advances. The initial target was to build 300 houses at Simshill, but it was anticipated that the development might eventually reach 900.

Glasgow's first fully furnished postwar showhouse was located on this new estate: 354 Carmunnock Road, a five-apartment semi-detached villa, was opened on 7 November 1953, with Frank Mickel 'towing' the press around it and cooking demonstrations available. A full-page newspaper feature praised the house as a sign of a full-blooded spec-building revival: 'Once more you can choose a dream home. It means more than just another exhibition - it means a return to the days when people can buy a house of their own choosing, instead of having to take anything that is offered'. Of the £2,091 price, the building society would lend £1,880 over 25 years, and annual outgoings would include £126 18s for interest and repayment of the loan, £5 10s feu duty, £41

13s 8d owners' and occupiers' rates, £2 7s 3d fire insurance - an annual total of £176 9s. The all-electric house had timber floors (including the ground floor), concrete block inner walls and solid concrete stair newel. Frank Mickel explained that 'we have cut down on extravagances to make the price of the house reasonable ... we wanted to give a popular price'. The type was designed to be suitable for variations of detail, although in acknowledgement of architectural modernism the emphasis was on different finishes rather than on stuck-on features such as gables: 'The architectural details of the houses are deliberately varied. Some have attractive porches with 'porthole' cut-outs in the cement surround. Some houses have sliding doors opening into a covered way, which is large enough to shelter a car'. Between November 1953 and March 1954, 48,000 people visited this showhouse. (60)

By June 1954, the development of Simshill was well under way, with a continuing emphasis on the more basic types of speculative dwelling, including 'cheap and lovely' terraces of 'cosy, compact, upstairs and downstairs houses' of three apartments. These now sold for £1,545, and featured metal window-frames and varied roof colours of grey, green and red, with some houses roughcast and others faced with 'Dorset pebbled concrete blocks of the firm's own manufacture ... treated so that they have the appearance of stone or random rock'. A blockwork-faced showhouse at 79 Carna Drive, furnished by Bows of High Street at a cost of £350 in an economical modern style, was opened on 26 June. Three-apartment houses might have been thought too small for large-scale speculative building before the war. What made them acceptable now was a planning innovation which reflected elements of Modern Movement open plans already well established in public housing. This innovation was the abolition of the formal separation on the ground floor between living room and dining room (or living room and parlour), and the merging of the two. The ground floor of the new three-apartment type comprised 'a long dinette running the entire depth of the house, and having a spaciousness and airiness that is singularly attractive'; there were two bedrooms upstairs. The advertisement description of the 79 Carna Drive showhouse referred to the 'back part of the room which, although not separated from the lounge, has all the air of a real dining-room'. As in the case of Castlemilk and the other big Corporation schemes, Mactaggart & Mickel's private houses at Simshill had been built first, with the promise of other amenities later; the firm stated that a cinema, restaurant, assembly hall and shops would be built soon on a 'central site'. (61)

By the end of 1954, a range of Simshill showhouses (furnished by Bows) lined Carmunnock Road, attracting thousands of 'house-hungry citizens' every week. 'Budget lines' for smaller families included a very small three-apartment semi-detached villa for £1,677, with a £177 down-payment and £2 15s weekly expenditure. Its 'simple, un-fussy plan', like that of the three-apartment terraces, included a 'through-and-through' living room (measuring 11' 3" by 20'), conveying 'a sensation of space and graciousness', and two bedrooms upstairs, one measuring 15' by 9'. The house was traditionally built with brick cavity walling, timber floors throughout, and roughcast-finish rendering. A three-apartment semi-detached showhouse at Seil Drive, Simshill, was offered for £1,750 in mid-1956. The original five-apartment showhouse at 354 Carmunnock Road reopened after refitting, with the expectation of 200,000 visitors; the type was now selling for £2,150. A journalist reported that she had 'walked like a queen through the hall of the Mactaggart & Mickel show house ... This is literally true. The carpet on which I trod is one of those the Queen admired when on her recent visit to Glasgow - she visited the place where they were made'. Internally, its modernity was expressed in its internal amenities, above all in its reliance on

AT KELVINSIDE

NEW

Glasgow's housing problem is being solved by Mactaggart & Mickel.

PLACES

Their grouped estates of well designed homes are a feature of modern Scottish towns and cities.

FOR

Internal planning takes account of the requirements of modern living. Traditional standards of workmanship are maintained.

NEW

They appreciate the financial difficulties of young home-builders. Deposits on estate houses range from £200.

FACES

Prices for individually designed homes are given on application.

4 Apartment from £2300

5 Apartment from £2500

Flats (including central heating) from £2335

Visit the Show Houses on the estate. By Bus No. 3, by trams 1 and 30.

MACTAGGART & MICKEL LTD.
Builders of Fine Houses

Mactaggart & Mickel Ltd. have sites available in these districts:
SIMSHILL ● CATHCART
CLARKSTON, RENFREWSHIRE
NEWTON MEARNS ● KELVINSIDE
GIFFNOCK ● STEVENSTON
DUMBARTON ● BURNSIDE
RUTHERGLEN ● AYR ● LARGS
and various sites on
EDINBURGH ESTATES

Sales Departments :

107 WEST REGENT STREET, GLASGOW, C.2

12 NORTH ST ANDREW STREET, EDINBURGH, 2

Telephones :

GLASGOW: DOUglas 0001   EDINBURGH: Waverley 3323

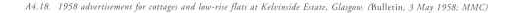

A4.18. 1958 advertisement for cottages and low-rise flats at Kelvinside Estate, Glasgow. (Bulletin, 3 May 1958; MMC)

The **Mactaggart & Mickel** 3 APARTMENT **Showhouse**

You are invited to visit this
NEW 3-APARTMENT
MACTAGGART & MICKEL SHOWHOUSE
which has been fully furnished by Messrs
Bows, of High Street, at a cost of £350.

**THIS IS THE BEST PLANNED AND
CHEAPEST NEW HOUSE BUILT TODAY**
at prices from £1,545. Easy Payment Terms
are easily arranged.

★ **OPENS SATURDAY, 26TH JUNE, 1954,
AT 2 P.M.**

79 GARNA DRIVE
OFF
CARMUNNOCK RD,
SIMSHILL
CATHCART
OPEN DAILY
Including Sundays
2 — 7 p.m.

*In sylvan surroundings—
but only 15 minutes from town*

Take a No. 5 Bus from St Enoch
Square to terminus.

MACTAGGART & MICKEL, LTD.
107 WEST REGENT STREET, GLASGOW, C.2. DOUGLAS 0001

By Special Arrangement with
J. D. FREW & CO. LTD.
Incorporated Insurance Brokers
200 ST VINCENT STREET GLASGOW, C.2
*Loans up to 100% Granted
in approved Cases*

A4.20. Broomhall Estate, Edinburgh, under construction in June 1955; here mechanical excavation for sewers is underway. (MMC)

(opposite) A4.19. Advertisement of June 1954 for three-apartment showhouse on Simshill Estate, Glasgow. (Evening Times, 24.6.1954; MMC)

electricity, 'the first essential in a modern home'. Externally, the abolition of formal front boundary walls in favour of low 'American style' kerbing was a modest concession to Modernist planning; Frank Mickel commented that 'It is in our own mind, a very fine looking style. It gives houses and gardens alike a new appearance ... it gets away from the stuffy closed in appearance of pre-war building'. Faced with the possible concern over children running in and out, Frank responded that this was 'a simple matter of discipline': 'Do you want to keep your barricades? Or can you imagine how pleasant your garden would look without its boundary battlements? Isn't it up to the parent or dog-owner to instil into children or animals this new discipline and respect for invisible boundaries?' All in all, the years 1953-60 saw the building of 856 villa-type houses and 12 low-rise flats at Simshill - not far off the original aspiration. (62)

In the Edinburgh area, the equivalent to Simshill was Broomhall, located immediately to the west of Carrick Knowe, and catering for the same general sector of the market, now via home-ownership rather than renting; Edinburgh was particularly receptive to this kind of low-cost private development as, almost uniquely, it continued to try to subsidise the private sector. It was another large, staged scheme comprising mostly economical and relatively small types. The development was begun in 1952, slightly earlier than Simshill, with the building of a group of 73 terraced houses in Broomhall Crescent, at a total cost of £109,500; 145 houses had been completed by 1955, 174 more houses were built between 1955 and 1957, and 537 more, in four phases, between 1957 and 1964. In July 1954, the company announced the opening of a three-apartment terraced showhouse at 2 Broomhall Crescent; costing £1,555, this was 'one of the cheapest houses being built in Edinburgh'. It featured a combined sitting-dining area, and extra cupboard space in the larger of the two bedrooms, gained

by utilising unnecessary headroom above the stairway. 'Carrying the budget-conscious theme through building to decorating', the showhouse was furnished in the simplicity of the 'contemporary style' for £400. Although a large estate overall, the development of Broomhall proceeded in relatively small sections at first: for example, 14 houses in Broomhall Place and Road, costing £24,000, in August 1954, and another 36 houses from December. April 1955 saw a more ambitious proposal for 116 houses at Broomhall, costing £139,200, and 42 more expensive houses at Hillpark, costing £126,000. (63)

In the evolution of the Broomhall estate, we can gradually trace a shift in demand from small terraced houses to slightly larger semi-detached dwellings. A full-page feature advertisement of early 1956 was devoted to a semi-detached, three-apartment showhouse at 29 Broomhall Road. With its living-dining room, kitchenette, two bedrooms and 'ample cupboards', it was dubbed the 'thrifty three', and praised for its 'sound economy, good planning, and attractive layout' ... 'highly finished, modern and economic'. It was furnished by Binns in a 'bright, adaptable, and modern - but not too modern' manner; the advertisement reassured readers that 'people who throw up their hands at "contemporary" furniture will not be shocked by the furnishings of the showhouse'. Its selling price was £1,735; a four-apartment semi-detached house in the same development cost £1,965. The company explained that owing to the growing customer resistance to mid-terrace houses, 'the builders now prefer to build semi-detached cottages and villas rather than terraced houses'; semis now cost around £50-£80 more than terraced houses. Three hundred houses were already built on the estate, and the plan was for 1,000. Despite these changes, the firm was obviously aware of the relative lack of variety of house-types at Broomhall, in comparison even to Simshill. In another full-page feature, 'Buying a Home of Your

A4.21. June 1955 view of the Highland Show car park at Ingliston, near Edinburgh, including advertisement hoarding for Broomhall Estate. (MMC)

A4.22. Newly completed houses in Broomhall Road, Edinburgh, in June 1956. (MMC)

*A4.23. Newly completed semi-detached pair at Broomhall, April 1960. (*Glasgow Herald*)*

A4.24. The living room of a three-apartment semi-detached villa at Broomhall, July 1954. (Glasgow Herald)

Own', it tried to circumvent this problem by highlighting the differences between individual houses, while claiming that the overall design principle was a moderate modernity which avoided showy novelty. The estate was 'different' from the usual 'forest of houses', because each house had its own individual features, including tiles, harling, different alignment in relation to the street; each house had space for a garage, and a front and back garden. But 'the house on sale is not aggressively modern. It is a point in its favour that there are no "sensational advances" over last year's houses'. (64)

By July 1956, 30,000 people had visited the company's two newest showhouses at Broomhall and Silverknowes; of these, over three-quarters were accounted for by the latter. That was hardly surprising, owing to the prominent location of Silverknowes by the 'seaside'; an advertisement of May 1956 even suggested that 'A HAPPY HOLIDAY could be spent this Week-end visiting Mactaggart & Mickel's Show House at Silverknowes (open 2.30 to 8 pm every day)'. In fact, the postwar development and extension of Silverknowes, with its distinctive curved street layout, had been steadily pursued ever since 1946, with nearly 300 houses built by 1954. On this somewhat more prestigious development, four- or five-apartment semi-detached villas, rather more cramped than their 1930s predecessors, but similar in Art Deco style, predominated. In spring 1953, this prominent estate, with its large number of summer day-trippers flocking to the Forth, was selected as the site for two marketing developments to mark the company's re-establishment of fully fledged speculative building: in April, the opening of the firm's first postwar showhouse; and the following month, the opening of the company's '4,000th house in Edinburgh'. (65)

The showhouse, a five-apartment semi-detached villa at 112 Silverknowes Road, was heralded in advertisements as 'a welcome return of a popular pre-war practice', in this case with 'just the type of small house people are looking for now'. It was reported that 'within half an hour of opening a queue had formed', and that over 500 visited it on the first day. Douglas Mickel reported that 'some appeared willing to sign there and then for a similar house, were it not for the need to have the sanction of the Town Council'; 15,000 had visited the house by the middle of May.

A4.25. November 1953 photograph of a type '1a' showhouse at Silverknowes, Edinburgh; this five-apartment cottage type sold for approximately £2,290. (MMC)

A Welcome Return

of a popular pre-war practice. It is with real pleasure that we suggest you visit

Mactaggart & Mickel's

first post-war

SHOW HOUSE

at 112 Silverknowes Road, Davidson's Mains

Open Daily, from To-morrow (Saturday), from 2.30 until 7 p.m.

This attractively-styled five-apartment, semi-detached, Cottage-type House has been fully furnished by

Here, in this charming home — just the type of small House people are looking for now — you'll be able to view, where they are seen to best advantage, well-chosen contemporary furniture with lovely furnishings and decorations at prices as moderate as possible consistent with good value. You can discuss, too, with the helpful representative who is at your service, any points which may interest you.

Binns Ltd. Princes Street West End Edinburgh 2 'PHONE 27041

A4.26. 1953 advertisement for showhouse at 112 Silverknowes Road, Edinburgh. (Scotsman, 3 May 1953; MMC)

4,000 HOUSES
Builder's City Record

The well-known firm of builders, Messrs Mactaggart & Mickel Ltd., yesterday handed over the keys of the 4000th house they have completed in Edinburgh alone for private sale.

The purchaser of this house uses modern electric labour-saving appliances and has installed the latest type electric cooker as recommended by PHILIP HARBEN, B.B.C. Television Chef.

This newly designed cooker may be seen at the

ELECTRICITY SERVICE CENTRES
127 George Street (West End)
Tel : CEN 6824 And

4 - 5 Crighton Place (Pilrig)
Tel.: 35600

A4.27. Advertisement about the completion of Mactaggart & Mickel's 4,000th private house, at Silverknowes. (Edinburgh Evening Dispatch, 13 May1953; MMC)

The type was advertised on the estate at an average price of £2,210. For the '4,000th house', at 25 Silverknowes Road, 700 company workers in the Edinburgh area 'downed tools' at 4 o'clock to attend the formal opening of the house they had 'helped to build'. Bailie J B Mackenzie, a Progressive Party ex-chairman of the Corporation's Housing Committee, declared in a short address that it was 'encouraging to find so comany people in this country still prepared to stand on their own two feet, and make the first claim on their wealth, the purchase of their own fireside'. Mackenzic used the occasion to argue for the further lifting of licensing regulations: it was unnecessary to investigate a prospective buyer's 'housing needs', or to ask them 'where their grandmothers lived', as these were purely 'private affairs'. Douglas Mickel backed him up by explaining that 'we have ... found it necessary to educate the public to a large extent in how and where to apply for licences ... The show House was a great feature of pre-war selling, and we are glad to return to this custom'. The purchasers of the house, a Mr and Mrs J A Morrison, received a toaster and hair-drier, and nursery bedlights for their two children, from the company as a memento, and received the keys of the house from Andrew Mickel and his granddaughter Angela. After the ceremony, the workmen were treated to refreshments, and

A4.28. Mactaggart & Mickel building operatives assembled on a nearby site at the opening of the 4,000th house, 25 Silverknowes Road, 12 May 1953. (MMC)

*A4.29. The handing-over ceremony of the 4,000th house. From left to right: the new owners; Andrew Mickel, presenting a gift (with Douglas Mickel behind him); and Marjorie Mickel, with family members. (*Scotsman/Evening Dispatch*)*

A4.31. *Bonney Parrot with purchasers and company staff, including Douglas Mickel (seated at right). (MMC)*

A4.32. *New roads and public transport links for the Silverknowes Estate, 1955. (MMC)*

(opposite) A4.30. 'The girl from Tennessee opens showhouse': Edinburgh student Charity Queen, Bonney Parrot of Knoxville, Tennessee, seen opening a new villa showhouse at Silverknowes on 17 April 1954. (MMC)

then 'turned back to their bricks and mortar to start work on another 500 houses'. On the Silverknowes site alone, development was still in full swing, with bulldozers clearing the roads and foundations, and over 70 employees at work. (66)

Building on the success of the first showhouse, visited by over 45,000 people, further showhouses were rapidly built at Silverknowes, including one five-apartment semi-detached villa opened in April 1954 by the Edinburgh Student's Charities queen, 21-year-old Bonney Parrot of Knoxville, Tennessee; it was priced at £2,290, with assessed rental of £45 and deposit of £250. By 1956, over 100,000 people had visited a showhouse at 116 Silverknowes Road built two years previously - another five-apartment semi-detached villa, priced at £2,400. In 1955, to serve the expanded estate, the No. 9 bus service from Greenbank to Davidson's Mains was extended to a new roundabout at Silverknowes Road, with a 4d fare into town. But, by then, some of the implications of the growing polarisation of private owner occupation and council renting, and the reflection of that in the residential class segregation of outer Edinburgh, had begun to emerge here. The Corporation had built a large estate of prefabs nearby, at Muirhouse, in the late 1940s, and in the mid-1950s it started adding permanent housing to these, in the form of tenements of up to five storeys, built by Scotcon in blockwork construction and with a marked 'slum-clearance' character. In 1956, as this development began to approach the Silverknowes houses, both Mactaggart & Mickel and the residents strenuously objected to a planned phase of 44 flats, arguing that the private 'houses will be dwarfed by the tenements with consequent loss of privacy and amenity'. Eventually, as in East Pilton, the Corporation responded by building mainly terraced houses at

that end of the site; in the 1960s, with the growing land shortages, the Progressive administration was compelled to raise the density of Muirhouse much more dramatically, by adding large numbers of multi-storey blocks in place of the prefabs. (67)

Elsewhere in the capital, the small interwar section of the rental Broomhouse estate was very considerably expanded by additional phases, now substantially featuring three-apartment terraced 'economy houses' for sale. By May 1953, the first houses, costing £1,490 each, were being completed in the first phase, and the second development was in progress, with prices at £1,515 (£1,545 for end terraced houses). These three-apartment terraced houses, 600 square feet in area, were built in traditional brick, with roughcast walls, steel windows, concrete-tiled roof, timber floors and staircase, and a kitchen with 'neat, purpose-made cabinet and store cupboards' (made by Mactaggart & Mickel). (68)

The recovery continues
housebuilding in the late 1950s

By the mid-1950s, speculative housing was getting back on its feet. As early as 1954, the government introduced a Treasury-backed local authority guarantee scheme to allow down-payments for houses costing up to £2,500 to be cut from 10% to 5%, in order to make it easier for those in the £8-£10 weekly wage group to buy their own home; however, the scheme was at the discretion of local authorities. But whereas the early 1950s had witnessed a sharp recovery in private building in Scotland from a very low base - from 3% of total output in 1950 to 17% in 1954 - the

A4.33. October 1956 view of new showhouse at Silverknowes. (Glasgow Herald)

remainder of the decade saw a much more gradual growth, to 23% in 1960. The reason for that lay largely in the established bias of subsidies towards the public sector, a situation that the Tory governments of the 1950s allowed to continue in order to avoid antagonising Glasgow Corporation and the other powerful large Labour authorities in the 'old' industrial centres. As it was now clear that the private industry would build the overwhelming majority of this public housing, and that direct labour building would only have a limited scope, many building firms began to commit themselves more and more to this public housing work. Mactaggart & Mickel drew exactly the opposite conclusion: that speculative building had now recovered enough to allow the firm to withdraw completely from contracting work. This it did in 1957, its last large jobs being war-damage reinstatement work in Newark Street, Greenock (1956), and two sections of Edinburgh Corporation's outer-suburban Gracemount scheme: the 3rd Development (91 houses, 1956) and the 5th Development (202 houses, 1957). (69)

The lifting of controls over private building allowed non-socialist county or burgh councils outwith those areas to encourage the private sector at will, regulated only by green belts and planning considerations. The result, especially around Glasgow, was an apparently random pattern of urban spread. In some places around the cities, there were council housing schemes on boundary extensions, while right next door to these there might be large areas of private estates, built in small burghs such as Bearsden or landward county areas like Newton Mearns. But there was an underlying logic behind this apparent confusion, based on the political control and social composition of each area. In Edinburgh, with its consistent Progressive Party control during

the '50s, this uneven pattern did not apply, and the city grew in a more orderly, radial fashion.

Increasingly, private building within Glasgow was virtually eliminated. This was not just because of socialist political hostility, but was also an indirect result of the new phenomenon of strong planning controls over land. The resulting land shortage put the housing faction within Glasgow Corporation under even more pressure, and from the late 1950s led to the policy of building tower blocks on any available site in the city. In this context the private developer came right at the back of the queue for land. In 1957, John Lawrence toyed with the idea of breaking with this pattern, by building private tower blocks himself. He proposed a 20-storey block of flats for sale in Pollok, designed by his consultant architect Sam Bunton, and containing four-apartment flats of 400 square feet, equipped with all mod cons, including lifts, dish-washers, washing machine, and underfloor heating. Of this 'Push-Button Skyscraper', Bunton argued that 'practically everything is included in the price of the flat!' and Lawrence insisted that 'it will be as attractive as buying a bungalow in the suburbs'. But the fact that council schemes were now taking up almost all available suburban land ruled out even this idea, and the block was not built. Gradually, the impact of planning and zoning restrictions began to make itself felt even in the landward, rural areas. In 1955, for example, a Mactaggart & Mickel proposal to build 900 houses at Newford and Housecraigs, on a 126-acre agricultural site between Clarkston and Eaglesham, was turned down by Renfrew County Council, who wanted it left open in order to separate built-up areas; the Scottish Office upheld the council's decision, adding that the site was also needed for a 'new arterial outer ring road'. (70)

A4.34. April 1958 aerial view of Silverknowes under construction. (MMC)

A4.35. 'House No.3' at the Bonaly development, November 1958. (MMC)

A4.36. Model of detached villa built at Broom Estate (in 1956, for £3,250),
Dollar (in 1957), and other locations. (MMC)

As the decade continued, Mactaggart & Mickel developments proliferated outside the Glasgow boundaries, while almost nothing was commenced inside them. Advertisements in 1955 listed three Glasgow sites at Simshill, Cathcart and Kelvinside, and eleven sites outside at Clarkston, Newton Mearns, Stevenston, Dumbarton, Busby, Largs, Burnside, Rutherglen and Edinburgh (three estates); in 1958, the same three Glasgow sites were mentioned, plus King's Park, but the number of non-Glasgow locations had risen to 25. These were: around Glasgow, the Broom Estate, Newton Mearns Village, Clarkston, Burnside, Rutherglen, Eaglesham, Giffnock, Kilmacolm and Waterfoot; around Edinburgh, Silverknowes, Hillpark, Cammo, Broomhall, Caiystane, Bonaly, and Balerno; in Ayrshire, Heathfield and Doonfoot (both in Ayr), Stevenston, West Kilbride and Largs; in Dunbartonshire, Helensburgh and Dumbarton; in Stirlingshire, Laurieston (near Falkirk); and in Clackmannanshire, Dollar. (71)

The 1950s also saw the first attempts to re-enter a more upmarket field of housebuilding - cautiously, in view of the chequered experiences of the 1930s - with dwellings costing around £3,000 or more. These houses were set apart from the economy houses not only by their extra size and number of rooms, but also by additional modern amenities, including not only the kitchen and bathroom fittings of the 1930s, but also now central heating and a garage, almost always, of course, seen at the moment as extras. In Edinburgh, alongside the continuing large-scale building of low-cost houses at Broomhall, the development of Hillpark continued with more expensive houses such as a five-apartment

A4.37. Hillpark under construction, May 1955. (MMC)

A4.38. Newly completed type 'Kh' house at Hillpark, 1955. (MMC)

A4.39. *Mechanised equipment in use at Hillpark, May 1955. (MMC)*

A4.40. *The site of Cammo Estate, seen in November 1955. (MMC)*

detached villa at 19 Hillpark Road, in 1954 (costing £3,550), and another 40 new houses built in the late 1950s. Some 44 houses were also built in the outer suburb of Balerno in the early 1950s. At a new 30-acre site, Cammo, on the edge of the exclusive suburb of Barnton, surrounded by trees to the south, an initial batch of 23 houses, costing a total of £100,000, were commenced in March 1956, and by the middle of the year 'a variety of distinguished houses' were under construction. Between 1957 and 1965, 160 houses were completed at Cammo, ranging from five to seven apartments, with selling prices between £3,000 and £4,500; the first houses included detached houses with integral garages and big, swept-down roofs. Douglas Mickel explained that Cammo was built speculatively, but with some bespoke elements: the firm 'had received many enquiries, but were not waiting for people coming along with orders. The houses would be reserved for purchasers at any stage of completion, even if it was just a peg in the ground'. Following on the heels of Cammo, as a landscaped, slightly upmarket outer-Edinburgh estate, was the Bonaly development. This was commenced in 1958, with the intention of building some 200-300 houses priced at £3,600-£4,800; eventually, 149 houses were built by 1970. Here, a slightly more Modernist styling was used for the £4,200 two-storey villas, with an integral garage and stone porch, and 'Swedish-designed' chimneypots: 'Because of the gently undulating nature of the site an entirely new design of dwelling has been chosen ... housewives will enjoy doing their chores in rooms looking out to the hills'. (72)

In the Glasgow region and the west more generally, there was a similar mixture of economical developments and more upmarket work. Within the city itself, there was still some room for continued building on the Kelvinside estate, where fairly small types were packaged as 'superior new homes'. These included a four-apartment semi-detached showhouse at Dorchester Avenue, opening on 23 March 1957, and advertised as the 'lowest-priced semi of this type'. It cost £2,050, with a down-payment of £210; five-apartment semis on this estate cost £2,465. Small flats were available from £2,300. As in the case of Sandringham Court, these emphasised a high level of services, including central heating, to differentiate their self-containment from the relative lack of amenities and privacy in older tenement flats. Many of the same services were provided in council tower blocks, of course, so marketing of these had to be carefully considered. Thirty-six three-apartment flats in three-storey blocks were built at Weymouth Court. A first-floor show flat at 4 Weymouth Court, Kelvinside, advertised as the 'Doorway to Domestic Contentment', was opened in October 1957, costing £2,440 plus £250 for a garage, with an assessed rental of £48. The company's advertising for this development emphasised a theme of social and civic responsibility: 'Glasgow's housing problem is being solved by Mactaggart & Mickel ... their grouped estates of well designed homes are a feature of modern Scottish towns and cities'. Further development at Kelvinside included semi-detached villas of four, five and six apartments, built in Dorchester Avenue and Weymouth Drive in 1957-59 for between £2,300 and £4,900. In Cleveden Road, twelve houses of £3,350-£3,800 were built at the same time. Elsewhere in Glasgow, a small group of ten four-apartment semi-detached bungalows was added to King's Park in 1952, selling for £2,225 each. (73)

In the Renfrewshire landward area on the south side of the city, the development of Carolside Park, Clarkston, had resumed at a rapid pace from the early 1950s. These included 22 houses in Area 10, 1951-52 (including five-apartment semis for £1,800-£2,150), 42 houses in area 11, 1953-54 (including some of the new three-apartment terraces), 90 houses in Area 12, 1954-56,

70 houses in Area 14, 1956-57, and 38 houses in area 15, 1958-59. In general, these were all standard types of a conservative character, but in July 1956, 24 new houses were customised for the benefit of 24 US families who had arrived to help set up the new Caterpillar tractor plant at Tannochside. An advertisement reported that, after fruitless attempts to find suitable rented housing, 'one of them spotted a private building estate in Clarkston. The Americans liked the layout there. The drives and terraces reminded them of home. They liked the houses too'. The plans, with suggested alterations and improvements, shuttled backward and forward across the Atlantic. In general, plan alterations enhanced the element of open-planning: in one case, for example, the wall betwen lounge and hall was removed, bringing the 'stair and front hall right into the room!' Oil fired central heating was installed, fuelled by massive oil tanks below the gardens, holding 500 gallons and filled by pipeline from the front of the houses. By August 1956, three families were already settled in villas in Beechlands Drive, 'cheek to jowl with houses of more orthodox Scottish character'. Above a new parade of shops on Eaglesham Road, a luxury flat, dubbed 'The Mercury', was laid out, with a top-level 'shared roof terrace'. (74)

Elsewhere in the Renfrewshire building area, the emphasis was on smaller and slightly more exclusive developments. On the Broom estate, some of the original houses were still on sale in the early '50s, and new development resumed in 1953/54, with six-apartment detached and semi-detached villas selling for about £3,850-£5,875. In Area C, 1953 saw the resumption of sales of four-apartment bungalows for about £2,800; 49 had been sold by 1958. The Broom No. 2 (South) development comprised 87 bungalows and villas, built in 1956-59, and selling for prices between £3,150 and over £5,000. The No. 4 development, 1959-62, was much larger, containing about 175 houses, bungalows and villas. The five-apartment semi-detached villa showhouse at 21 Castlehill Drive, newly opened in June 1962, remained faithful to the traditional front-back villa layout, retaining the two separate downstairs rooms, now called 'lounge' and dining room, and maintaining a generally interwar style outside, in its more sober postwar form, with bay windows marked off by contrasting brick panels. It was in the inside decoration and fittings that there were more signs of modernity. The interior, fitted out by D MacDonald & Bros of Glasgow, featured electric wall heating (an optional extra to the basic price of £3,150), and the beginnings of a revival of more flamboyant decorative eclecticism, for example in the 'Eastern' theme of the lounge, with its 'flame-coloured Oriental design curtains, and matching wallpaper'. (75)

The formula of high-amenity flats established at Sandringham Court was repeated on the estate, at Broom Court, a development of twelve four- and five-apartment flats selling at £2,480-£3,550. They were marketed as ideal for the person who wants to live in a suburb, but does not want a garden: 'His alternative - rightly dismissed - is to remain in outdated housing conditions within the dirt of the city ... now a much happier alternative is offered ... where many of the city's most successful businessmen have their houses'. This was 'country living without the spade-work'. Other groups of low-rise flats were built in this general area from the late '50s, all generally tenemental in their layout but marked off from the Easterhouse type of council tenement by features such as bay windows and tile-hanging. These included Broomburn Court (36 flats costing between £2,000 and £3,500, 1958-61), Greenwood Court, Clarkston (30 flats, from 1957), and Orchard Court, Orchard Park Avenue (1959), containing three-apartment centrally heated flats from £1,950. Further afield, the Kingsway Court development in Carmunnock Road (from 1959) comprised 24 similar four-apartment flats costing

A flat in Broom Estate...

EASILY RUN • CONVENIENT • LOVELY SURROUNDINGS • HEALTHY

A flat in this excellent residential estate offers country living without the spade work. Spacious reception rooms, central heating, more than adequate cupboard space all add up to yet another Mactaggart & Mickel "superbly planned home." Adjacent are modern shops and Golf Courses, Bowling Greens, Tennis Courts all within easy reach, making the purchase of one of these flats a most attractive proposition.

PRICES FROM £2480

VISIT THE SHOWHOUSE

PRICE £3550

on BROOM ESTATE. A newly completed flat has been luxuriously furnished by D. MacDonald & Brothers, to give you the feel of the place and to stimulate your imagination. The BROOM ESTATE is easy to find; the Mearnskirk bus from Clyde Street takes you direct to the Show House. Alternatively buses for Ayr, Kilmarnock, and Newton Mearns from Waterloo Street to Broomvale Drive. The Furnished Flat and the Show Houses are open 7 days a week from 2 p.m. to 7 p.m. from to-day (Saturday), 4th April.

Also at Broom Estate there are many different types of houses to see and two other Show Houses ready for your inspection.

MACTAGGART & MICKEL LTD.
Builders of Fine Homes

OTHER SITES AT: Newton Mearns, Clarkston, Waterfoot, Eaglesham, Giffnock, Simshill, King's Park, Burnside, Kelvinside, Kilsyth, Kilmacolm, Kilbarchan, Helensburgh, Ayr, Stevenston, West Kilbride, Mauchline; also Stirlingshire, Clackmannanshire, and the Edinburgh district

Glasgow: **107 WEST REGENT STREET**
Telephone: DOUglas 0001/2

Edinburgh: **12 NORTH ST ANDREW STREET**
Telephone: WAVerley 3323

A4.41. 1959 advertisement for Broom Estate flats. (Bulletin, 4 May 1959; MMC)

£2,380-£2,780, and the Overtoun estate saw three-five apartment flats on sale in 1959 from £2,425. (76)

The Broom estate was also steadily extended southwards beyond its original boundaries, firstly in 1956 by the building of a small group of relatively expensive houses in Beech Avenue; the five-apartment showhouse, a detached villa with built-in garage, cost £3,250, and its semi-detached equivalent £3,150, with assessed rental of £35, and 90% loan available. In 1956-57, 14 houses were built at the Shaw Estate, in Shawhill Crescent and Craigie Drive, comprising bungalows and villas of between five and seven apartments, costing between £3,150 and £5,213. And at Townhead, Newton Mearns, 56 houses, mainly five-apartment semi-detached cottages and bungalows, were built in 1957-59, at selling prices from £3,150 to £5,510. Responding to the established success of the Broom estate, or group of estates, the firm made energetic efforts to maintain and expand its land-bank in the area. In late 1958, for example, 223 acres of farmland were purchased from a major local landowner, the Fa'side estate, at a cost of £18,850 - approximately £85 per acre. (77)

Further afield, in the Ayrshire towns, reflecting their wide social mix, from industrial to elite residential, developments ranged from the basic to the luxurious. Stevenston, with its association with the Ardeer explosives works, continued to be orientated towards more economical types: a four-apartment showhouse villa at the Hillcrest Estate cost £1,995 in 1956, and two years later a similar house in Main Kilwinning Road was on offer for £2,300. In Largs, estates were far more exclusive: the 22-dwelling Danefield estate of 1955-56 included a seven-apartment villa with concave splayed front. In Ayr, there were developments of both types, including the relatively large Doonfoot estate (Abbots Way, etc.), with 66 houses built between 1958 and 1966 at prices starting from £3,530, and the 146-house Heathfield estate of 1957-66. At Seaforth Road, 22 houses, with 'each front ... finished differently to give individuality', were begun in early 1957. A £2,125 showhouse of four apartments opened in May; its claimed annual outlay of £198 included £10 feu duty, loan and interest charges of £158, owners' and occupiers' rates of £27 15s 10d, and fire insurance of £2 6s 1d. In January 1958, a four-apartment villa and several bungalows were open on the site. By contrast, in a small group of 17 houses within the Doonfoot estate, in Earls Way, opened in 1957 'under the constant supervision of Frank Mickel, a director of the firm', the seven-apartment splay-fronted type built at Largs was repeated. Costing £5,450, it was 'coloured white with rust-red roof tiling and turquoise painted-work'; the showhouse was refurnished by Afflecks of Ayr and reopened in March 1959. In 1959, there were houses of four to seven apartments on sale in Ayr, and the firm hoped soon to start work at Netherplace Estate, Mauchline. Other seaside housing of the period included a development of 43 houses at Helensburgh, in 1959-62. (78)

The end of this immediate postwar period saw the firm's affairs seemingly restored to normality and stability, in terms of its overriding ethos of speculative building for home-ownership. In the years after 1960, it would be able to expand even further its output of speculative homes, but that prosperity would be complicated by conflicting factors, especially the onerous impact of planning restrictions on suburban land, and the beginning of incursions by English-based volume builders - which would lead Mactaggart & Mickel increasingly to project itself as a traditional Scottish building firm.

A4.42. 154 Greenock Road, Largs, a six-apartment detached villa with splayed plan, sold for £4,500 in 1956. (MMC)

Notes

Readers are referred to the Notes sections of Chapters A1, A2 and A3, and the Abbreviations section at the end of the book, for an explanation of the abbreviated forms used in this list.

1   MM Minutes, 18 August 1939, 28 August 1939; *Bulletin*, 27 September 1939; *GH*, 11 September 1939; *Scotsman*, 23 December 1939; *GH*, 12 April 1940.

2   *Bulletin*, 25 September 1940, *GH*, August 1941.

3   *Bulletin*, 26 October 1939 (money from the allotments was given to the City of Glasgow Central War Fund, Red Cross Society, St. Andrew's Ambulance Association, with £30 being given to each); MMA, notice of 8 May 1942; *DR*, 25 November 1939; *GH*, 13 September 1939; *Evening Citizen*, 3 November 1939, 10 November 1939; MM Minutes, 4 September 1939.

4   MM Minutes, 18 August 1939, 28 August 1939; *Bulletin*, 27 September 1939; *GH*, 11 September 1939; MM Minutes, 17 November 1939; MM Minutes, 19 December 1941; MM Minutes, 5 September 1939 (meeting attended by Mactaggart), 8 September 1939.

5   MM Minutes, 21 March 1941, 2 October 1939, 17 November 1939, 12 July 1940, 4 July 1941, 19 April 1940, 28 March 1941, 16 May 1941, 28 June 1940.

6   MM Minutes, 2 October 1939, 23 February 1940, 5 April 1940, 19 April 1940 (on contract secured for isolation block and canteen hut, costing £2,505, at Buchanan Castle), 11 July 1941, 27 December 1940, 22 August 1941, 25 October 1940, 21 March 1941, 30 April 1942, 2 May 1941.

7   MMASB; MM Minutes, 24 January 1942, 2 October 1939; *Scotsman*, 30 March 1940; MM Minutes, 21 January 1941, 15 September 1939, 21 September 1939, 6 October 1939, 8 December 1939, 22 December 1939, 7 June 1940, 24 July 1942, 11 October 1940.

8   MM Minutes, 18 October 1940; *Daily Express*, 26 October 1940; MM Minutes, 21 March 1941.

9   MM Minutes, 14 November 1940, 30 May 1941, 21 February 1941 (on the transfer by Jack Mactaggart of 800 ordinary shares to Ian Mactaggart, 1,300 to Neil Mactaggart, and 2,799 to Alasdair Mactaggart, the shares in each case being held in trust), 6 November 1942, 30 April 1942, 19 June 1942, 28 August 1942, 6 November 1942, 26 November 1943, 22 November 1940, 14 May 1942, 11 June 1943.

10 MM Minutes, 30 April 1942, 30 June 1942, February 1943, 27 May 1943, 10 September 1943, 21 April 1944.

11 MM Minutes, 20 August 1945.

12 MM Minutes, 10 September 1943, 14 September 1944, 29 October 1945, 21 April 1944.

13 *EN*, 30 January 1941; MM Minutes, 19 June 1942, 21 April 1944.

14 MMA, cuttings book (hereafter MMACB), unidentified newspaper cutting, 1 March 1944; *The Times*, 24 October 1944, letter from Sir John A Mactaggart; *Scotsman*, 9 March 1945; *Sunday Times*, 20 May 1945; MMA, *Labour News*, undated cutting.

15 *Evening Dispatch*, 2 May 1945; *Scotsman*, 21 July 1945.

16 MM Minutes, 20 August 1945; *Bulletin*, 12 September 1945.

17 *Evening Dispatch*, 25 January 1944; *Daily Express*, 10 October 1944; *EN*, 1 December 1944.

18 *EN*, 2 December 1944; MM Minutes, 20 August 1945; *EN* and *GH*, 18 May 1945; *Daily Express*, 19 May 1945.

19 MMA, letter from Douglas Mickel to Andrew Mickel, 22 October 1945.

20 *Citizen*, 15 December 1942.

21 MMA, letter from Mactaggart & Mickel to Edinburgh Town Clerk, 3 April 1939; MM Minutes, 5 April 1940; *GH*, 2 July 1940, 1 March 1940, 15 March 1940; MMACB, 7 January 1949; MMA, correspondence with Building Research Station, December 1948.

22 *DR*, 7 March 1944; *EN*, 9 December 1944; MMA, letter from Sir J A Mactaggart, 4 September 1945.

23 *GH*, 5 September 1945; *Scotsman*, 6 September 1945, letter from John Lawrence; *GH*, 13 November 1945.

24 *Citizen*, 15 December 1942.

25 Information and analysis by John Craig; MM Minutes, 13 December 1945, 24 May 1946, 1 September 1946; MMA, letter from J A Mactaggart to A Mickel, 6 January 1946; MM Minutes, 27 November 1947.

26 MM Minutes, 2 April 1948; Historic Scotland, List Description, City of Glasgow, Item 3108.

27 MMA, letter from Douglas Mickel to Andrew Mickel, 29 April 1946; *EN*, 8 August 1947.

28 *GH*, 9 November 1945; *Sunday Mail*, 17 August 1947.

29 *Scotsman*, 21 June 1951; interview with A Buchanan Campbell, 12 August 1998; *ET*, 27 February 1946; *Daily Express*, 10 November 1945; *Bulletin*, 10 November 1945; *Express*, 16 December 1946; *GH*, 10 November 1945; *Scotsman*, 6 June 1945.

30 MMA, letter from Douglas Mickel to Andrew Mickel, 5 April 1946; MM Minutes, 24 April 1946; MM Minutes, 1 August 1946; MM Minutes, 8

31 MM Minutes, 24 April 1946; *Sunday Express*, 23 June 1946; MM Minutes, 24 May 1946; MMASB.

32 MMACB, 28 May 1948; MM Minutes, 24 May 1946; MMA, letter from Andrew Mickel to J R H Hutchison, 18 May 1946.

33 MM Minutes, 15 December 1939; letter from Douglas Mickel to Andrew Mickel, 28 October 1943; MM Minutes, 4 September 1946; *Scotsman*, 8 November 1948, 21 June 1951; MM Minutes, 30 October 1947; *Evening Dispatch*, 13 December 1950; *Scotsman*, 15 October 1948; *Renfrew Press*, 31 December 1947.

34 MM Minutes, 13 December 1945, 24 May 1946; *EN*, 10 June 1948; MM Minutes, 13 February 1947; MM Minutes, 30 October 1947, 1 August 1946; *Sunday Express*, 7 April 1946.

35 *EN*, 29 October 1947; *Daily Express*, 22 October 1947; *Scotsman*, 22 November 1947; MM Minutes, 30 October 1947; MM Minutes, 27 November 1947.

36 *Sunday Mail*, 17 August 1947; *EN*, 8 August 1947; *Sunday Express*, 7 April 1946; *Sunday Post*, 5 May 1946.

37 *Scotsman*, 2 October 1948, 25 October 1949, 8 November 1948, 2 December 1949; MMACB, 31 August 1949.

38 *Scotsman*, 28 May 1948; MMACB, 7 January 1949; *EN*, 17 February 1948; *EN*, 16 April 1948; MMACB, 28 May 1948 (Cllr Bell, at Scottish Unionist Party Conference).

39 *Scotsman*, 6 October 1950; MMA, Minutes of the Inaugural Meeting of the Scottish House Builders' Association at 35 Bath Street, Glasgow, 7 November 1945; letter of subscription to the SHBA, December 1946; *GH*, 27 February 1947; *Sunday Mail*, 17 August 1947.

40 MM Minutes, 1 August 1946, 13 February 1947; MM Minutes, 30 October 1947; MM Minutes, 18 March 1948, 28 November 1948, 4 November 1949.

41 MM Minutes, 4 November 1949, 29 November 1951; *EN* and *GH*, 27 February 1948; *GH*, 12 April 1948.

42 *GH*, 22 June 1949.

43 *EN*, 6 January 1950; *Evening Dispatch*, 11 February 1950; *Scotsman*, 21 March 1950; MMACB, 15 April 1950, 30 March 1950; *Scotsman*, 15 May 1950, letter from A T H Tilston; *Scotsman*, 18 May 1940, letter from W S Cruickshank; *Scotsman*, 4 November 1950, 21 December 1950.

44 *EN*, 27 February 1950; *GH*, 19 February 1950; *EN*, 2 March 1950; *EN*, 27 February 1950; MMACB, 27 October 1950, 24 July 1951.

45 *Sunday Mail*, 17 June 1951, 15 July 1951; MMACB, 28 November 1951; *EN*, 21 March 1952; *EN*, 28 November 1951.

46 *ET*, 22 March 1951; Edinburgh City Archives, Dean of Guild reference, 2 June 1951; *GH*, 6 June 1951; MMACB, 17 November 1951, 24 July 1951.

47 *Evening Dispatch*, 22 February 1952; *EN*, 8 March 1952; *GH*, 18 April 1952, 18 December 1952.

48 MMACB, 30 September 1952; *GH*, 5 January 1953; MMACB, 16 October 1952; *Scotsman*, 16 November 1952; MMASB; MMACB, 27 March 1952; *GH*, 17 April 1952; MMACB, 18 April 1952, 15 November 1953, 31 December 1952, 2 January 1953; *Scotsman*, 28 February 1952; MMACB, 21 March 1954, 22 October 1952.

49 MMACB, 5 December 1952; MMA, unidentified newspaper cutting of *c*.1953; *Sunday Express*, March 1954, L S Gumley & Davidson advertisement.

50 Donaldson and L Foster, *Sell and Be Damned*, *c*.1991; MMACB, 29 November 1951, 19 December 1951, 17 January 1952.

51 MMACB, 18 April 1952; *GH*, 15 August 1953; *Scotsman*, 21 August 1953.

52 MMA, certificate of office, Deputy Lieutenant of the County of the City of Glasgow, dated 2 March 1953.

53 Interview with A Buchanan Campbell, 12 August 1998.

54 MM Minutes, 18 March 1948; MM Minutes, 1 January 1949, 4 November 1949; MM Minutes, 21 May 1953; *Paisley and Renfrewshire Gazette*, 3 December 1955; MM Minutes, 25 October 1957; MM Minutes, 13 March 1959; MM Minutes, 11 October 1961; MM Minutes, 3 November 1961; interview with A Buchanan Campbell, 12 August 1998.

55 Glasgow City Archives, Dean of Guild reference 1954/393; *Scotsman*, 21 August 1953; *Industries of Midlothian*, 1953; *Scotsman*, 8 June 1954; *Greenock Telegraph*, 9 January 1954.

56 *GH*, 5 January 1953, 17 January 1953; *Times*, 5 November 1953.

57 *Evening Citizen*, 19 August 1955; MMA, letters from Herbert Daniel to Douglas Mickel, 16 November 1954 and 22 February 1956; MMA, memorandum of January 1956.

58 MMACB, 4 March 1955, 27 November 1954.

59 *Evening Citizen*, 24 January 1953; *GH*, 5 August 1953, 14 August 1953; Glasgow City Archives, Dean of Guild references 1954/417, 1957/259; interview with A Buchanan Campbell, 12 August 1998; *Bulletin*, 3 May 1958.

60 *Bulletin*, 7 November 1953; *GH*, 22 October 1953; *EN*, 30 October 1953; *ET*, 5 November 1953, 6 November 1953; *Bulletin*, 7 November 1953; MMACB, 10 April 1954; *Bulletin*, 10 May 1954.

61 MMACB, 24 June 1954.

62 MMACB, 27 November 1954; *Evening Citizen*, 19 August 1955; *Bulletin*,

20 August 1955; *EN*, 8 August 1956.

63   MMACB, 1 March 1952; MMASB; *Scotsman*, 7 July 1954; *EN*, 14 August 1954; *Scotsman*, 18 December 1954; *EN*, 30 April 1955.

64   *Bulletin*, 12 June 1956, 18 May 1956; *Evening Dispatch*, 12 June 1956.

65   *EN*, 19 May 1956; MMACB, 31 July 1956.

66   *Evening Dispatch*, 6 April 1953; *GH*, 13 May 1953; *Sunday Mail*, 10 May 1953; *GH*, 13 May 1953; *Evening Dispatch*, 13 May 1953; MMA, Mactaggart & Mickel press release, May 1953.

67   *Bulletin*, 17 April 1954; *Bulletin*, 18 October 1956; MMASB; *Evening Dispatch*, 26 May 1956; M Glendinning (ed.), *Rebuilding Scotland*, 1997; M Glendinning and S Muthesius, *Tower Block*, 1994, Chapter 25.

68   *Carpenter and Builder*, 11 July 1953; *EN*, 13 May 1953.

69   *Sunday Express*, March 1954; *Scotsman*, 21 March 1954; *GH*, 4 June 1954; MMACB, 21 October 1954.

70   *GH*, 26 March 1955; *Sunday Express*, 31 March 1957.

71   MMACB, advertisement of January 1955; *Daily Mail*, 4 March 1958; MMACB, advertisement of January 1955.

72   *EN*, 3 May 1956; *Bulletin*, 18 May 1956; MMASB, 2 March 1956; *Bulletin*, 29 November 1958.

73   *GH*, 30 October 1956; *Evening Citizen*, 22 March 1957; *Bulletin*, 19 October 1957, 3 May 1958; *ET*, 29 October 1957; MMASB.

74   MMASB; *DR*, 26 July 1956; *EN*, 4 August 1956, 15 November 1956.

75   MMASB.

76   *ET*, 2 April 1959; *Bulletin*, 4 April 1959; MMASB; *Evening Citizen*, December 1959.

77   *EN*, 19 October 1956; MMASB; MMA, letter from MM to Breeze, Paterson & Chapman, 10 November 1958.

78   *EN*, 19 October 1956; *Ardrossan and Saltcoats Herald*, 20 June 1958; MMASB; *Ayrshire Post*, 24 May 1957, 6 December 1957, 18 March 1959, 5 June 1959; MMACB, 31 January 1958; *Evening Citizen*, 12 November 1958.

THE MODERN COMPANY
Building on Tradition, 1960 to the Present Day

Introduction

In the years since 1960, the orientation of Mactaggart & Mickel's work changed gradually from large-scale housing development to more selective building activity, especially following the entry of large English-based housebuilders into the Scottish market in the most recent decades. What remained unaltered was its special concern with innovation in the speculative sector. That concern culminated in the company's enthusiastic participation in the Glasgow 1999 'Homes for the Future' experimental housing project, which would take the Mactaggart & Mickel story on into the new millennium.

During this period, the firm overcame a succession of tough challenges to its economic wellbeing. These mostly stemmed from nationwide recessions, especially those of the early 1980s and the early 1990s. But the first of these difficulties fell at the very beginning of the 1960s, and had a more immediate cause: the unexpected loss of Frank Mickel. This not only robbed the building programme in the west of his 'hands-on' approach but, as we will see shortly, also had serious financial consequences. Following the deaths of Frank and Andrew, the dominant members of the company were Douglas Mickel and James D Goold; the latter joined the firm in 1961 as assistant secretary, and became chairman in 1993; he died in 1997. Douglas Mickel was still heavily involved with the direction of the company until

A5.1. Mactaggart & Mickel's new offices at North St Andrew Street, Edinburgh, under construction in 1962; the block was redeveloped in the early 1990s. (MMC)

the 1990s, when he was forced by illness to retire from active involvement; from that point the direction of the business was increasingly in the hands of Derek Mickel (son of Frank) and Bruce Mickel (son of Douglas).

What was striking was the way in which, by negotiating these difficult years with prudence, this family business was able to survive and prosper when many others fell by the wayside. The key to its success was its safeguarding of its capital and land base. The net assets of the company grew steadily in real terms, from £1,804,000 in 1960 to £2,887,000 in 1970, £12,060,000 in 1980 and £31,921,000 in 1990, finally reaching a level of around £54,000,000 in 1999. Prior to the 1960s, the company's net assets had been relatively modest, but the income from sale of Edinburgh letting properties made an increasing contribution, especially from the 1970s. Almost 50% of the firm's net assets in 1990 (£15,270,000) derived from the cumulative income from these sales since 1953. Overall, the numbers of houses completed showed a decline compared with the years of consistent mass production, but the building programme, as we will see below, was a far more variegated and architecturally enterprising one. Annual new house sales in the west region, for example, averaged 217 in the 1960s and 193 in the 1970s (compared to 350-500 in the late 1930s), but dropped to 122 during the recession-blighted early and late 1980s.; the absolute minimum for the west was 55 during the economic slump of 1991, but the annual total had recovered to 160 (including a small contribution from the east region) by 1997. (1)

The commitment of the family-led management over generations also contributed to the firm's resilience. This contrasted markedly with some other companies. For example, John Lawrence's powerful business, founded in 1928, was progressively undermined by his own preoccupations as chairman of Rangers Football Club and as head of the ever-expanding John Lawrence housing group. After his death in 1977, his grandson, who had been groomed for the post of chairman, embarked on an expansion into the leisure trade, and purchased Rangers Football Club, as well as acquiring property in Carson City, Nevada. However, the Lawrence Group, as it was, overstepped the mark, and was eventually put into receivership in 1997 with debts in excess of £10,000,000. Another less dramatic casualty was the prominent family building and contracting business of James Y Keanie, originally founded in 1895; it was sold in 1971 to Melville, Dundas & Whitson, which was then itself absorbed in 1986 by Lilleys. (2) During the years from the 1970s, numerous Scottish family building firms were bought by larger English firms, but although Mactaggart & Mickel were approached on several occasions to sell the business in the 1980s and 1990s, these approaches were all refused. Now, at the end of the 1990s, the emphasis is increasingly on collaboration between firms rather than on laissez-faire acquisitions and takeovers.

In the company's general building programme, the affluence of the 1960s was reflected in a general increase in house size. The average 1960s Mactaggart & Mickel villa was about 1,000 sq ft in area; Edinburgh types included the three-bedroom detached '7E' and semi-detached '8E' villas, while a six-apartment detached villa might include 1,750 sq ft; Glasgow types were slightly smaller. (3) Already, however, there were the first signs of an opposite trend, of the downsizing of specific house types and rooms, possibly under the influence of English practice; the '7E' detached house was exactly the same area as the semi-detached '8E', and soon most detached houses would be built with floor areas previously associated with semis, while subsidiary bedrooms could become very small. The early 1970s years of economic crisis were

a kind of watershed, with a steady reduction of square footage in Mactaggart & Mickel houses, partly in response to competition from Lawrence. There was a wide spread between small houses such as the two-bedroom 'C53' (designed in 1970 by in-house engineer Iain Drysdale) and the 'C41' detached or semi-detached bungalow (698 sq ft; designed by Ayr architects Stevenson & Ferguson), and, on the other hand, larger houses, such as the 'C39' (1,498 sq ft) and the 'C38' (1,402 sq ft) at Eaglesham, both designed by Derek Mickel. Alongside this general output, the period also saw repeated attempts, just as at the Broom, to devise more architecturally complex patterns of speculative housing. These efforts were especially led by Bruce Mickel, who joined the firm in 1970 after an architectural training in Edinburgh, and consistently fostered more high-density, cluster-patterned layouts and a 'burgh vernacular' approach to housing design inspired by architects such as Basil Spence or Wheeler & Sproson. After a period, in the 1990s, when that more architecturally avant-garde approach seemed to have retreated from view, it was once more reasserted in the designs commissioned from Roan Rutherford for the Homes for the Future project, and a large scheme of houses at 'The Drum', Bo'ness.

In the remainder of the chapter, we trace this period in a broadly chronological sequence, beginning with the years of revived large-scale building in the 1960s.

The early 1960s
volume building revived

In this, the first decade since the 1930s with no significant government restrictions on housing production (other than the growing planning controls), the firm's output of houses for sale continued to grow, reaching a healthy postwar peak of around 500 dwellings per year in the early 1960s. This was almost equal to output levels of houses for sale in the 1930s (excluding, of course, output of houses for letting). The late 1960s saw another attempt to tap into a higher-priced market at the Broom Estate, under the direction of Derek Mickel (who qualified as an architect in 1959 at the Royal College in Glasgow - subsequently Strathclyde University). At the same time, the growing shortage of zoned housing land, especially in Glasgow, prompted both the building of flats on a large scale, including some modestly scaled tower blocks, and the further expansion of the Ayrshire and Renfrewshire suburbs on a small, ad-hoc scale. The land shortage around Edinburgh was not so acute, and so development there could be on a slightly larger scale.

In general, however, the climate was still not favourable to large-scale growth of home-ownership in Scotland, owing to the impact of owners' rates, the competition from low-rent council housing, and planning restrictions; the dominance of the market by relatively few firms also inhibited competition. Although Mactaggart & Mickel remained one of the biggest speculative builders in the middle of the decade, during the 1960s Wimpey increasingly began to exploit the Scottish market, as its huge local-authority housing workload declined. This was a harbinger of the entry of other English-based firms into Scotland in later years, and went hand-in-hand with the increasing Scottish influence of the National House Builders Registration Council (NHBRC; later NHBC), a London-based non-profit making organisation originally set up following the concern about 'jerry building' in south-east England between the wars. It laid down specifications of workmanship and materials, checked the developments of

A5.2. Douglas Mickel at his desk in July 1963; during the period immediately following Frank Mickel's unexpected death in 1961, Douglas oversaw all the company's activities in the east and west. (MMC)

registered firms during construction, and gave purchasers a ten-year warranty against faults. By 1962, eight Scottish firms were registered with the NHBRC; Mactaggart & Mickel eventually registered in 1967, and Douglas Mickel served on its technical panel, 'trying his utmost to stop English building practices from being employed in Scotland'. In response to this trend, the firm increasingly emphasised its reliance on tradition and its use of skilled craftsmen and local suppliers; its philanthropic outlook took on a new aspect with a growing concern with preservation of historic sites and artefacts. (4)

The deaths of Frank Mickel in 1961 and Andrew Mickel the following year prompted a far-reaching reorganisation, as well as posing the shareholders with financial difficulties. Following Frank's death, Andrew appointed Jim Goold as secretary in 1961 and transferred 8,000 shares to each of his two grandsons, Derek and Bruce. With J G L Walk as an additional director, and Derek actively joining the firm, Douglas Mickel now occupied the managing directorship, with Goold working in effect as his deputy. Goold, born in 1934, was a longstanding family friend of the Mickels; his early business career as an accountant had included a spell in Australia and New Zealand. After Frank's death, the family was hit by major estate duty liabilities, which took fifteen years to settle. But in 1963, the firm could look beyond those difficulties to the future, predicting that 'the traditions ... of this family business will carry on, as Douglas Mickel has now been joined by his nephew Derek Mickel, who is a qualified architect, and he hopes also to have with him in due course his son, Bruce, who is leaving school this year to take up the study of architecture and building. The future, therefore, of Mactaggart & Mickel and "Fine Homes" appears to be well assured'. (5) During his architectural training, Derek Mickel had worked for several substantial spells (including an entire year in 1959-60) with the renowned Glasgow practice of Gillespie, Kidd & Coia.

A more extended article published in a London building journal in late 1960, before the deaths of Frank and Andrew, gave a more comprehensive overview of the firm's activity and ethos at this time, although focusing in particular on the work of the Edinburgh office. The author declared that 'only two hours from London Airport and a short time spent with Douglas Mickel, managing Director, and I was convinced that here was a company which recognised the need to make a considerable contribution to the social problem of housing'. The company had 'not only succeeded in building up a strong financial company, but at the same time had built an enviable reputation for fine building. In the past years they have pioneered progressive developments in both building construction and architectural planning and design. A Mactaggart & Mickel house is recognised as a hallmark in Scotland.' The firm now built, on average, 500 houses a year, with more than 1,000 employees; a pension scheme was operated for chargehands and staff, and may be extended in future: 'On my visit to a number of sites, it was apparent that very good labour relations existed. This is clearly due to the fact that almost daily Douglas Mickel visits the sites and any disputes are dealt with on the spot'. The company's emphasis on tradition and on social responsibility was underlined: 'A further point of good citizenship is the laid-down policy of this company to utilise whenever possible local tradesman and materials ... on many houses local stone is used, and in all cases it is handled by stonemasons - craftsmen who are disappearing from the scene'. 'Construction is traditional and sturdy, brick built, rough-cast cavity walls, wood floors, and on the ground floors these rest on joists in all cases, and not directly on cement as a number of builders appear to be doing. The roofs are of timber boarding, felt, straps and tiles, making the houses both warm and substantial'. Although central heating was not yet a standard feature of Mactaggart & Mickel houses, and certainly not for the £2,010 two-bedroom semi-detached house, 'one of the most inexpensive houses in the United Kingdom', the company was considering installation of a gas warm air system as an optional fixture. The author concluded that 'I flew back to London with the thought that the Mickels are modest people doing a first-rate job for the community, but that they really do not have to sing their own praises - for the houses they are building will speak for them for many years to come'. (6)

The building programme in the east, which was spared the disruption experienced in the west following Frank's death, was able to maintain more continuity of output, and focused on a number of developments of several hundred houses; some 150-200 men were employed on these sites. Some were extensions of already established schemes, especially Broomhall where 500 further houses were added to the estate. A number of new house types were designed for these developments by Edinburgh architect William Vannan, a friend of Douglas Mickel (and a near-neighbour, at Hillpark); his designs had a quirky character with some Art Deco touches. In the arrangement of ground floor rooms, a limited degree of open planning was now emerging. The new '7E' and '8E' type villas of 1,053 sq ft, by Vannan, were available in either detached or semi-detached form. A detached villa of rendered 11" brick designed by Vannan in 1964 (based on a late 1950s type), type '9', featured a four/five-apartment plan turned at right-angles from the old front-to-back villa layout. Entered at one end by a feature porch of brick or artificial stone, it had an open-plan combined dining room and lounge; two of the three upstairs bedrooms had fitted cupboards.

At Silverknowes, 286 additional houses were built between 1963 and 1974. Construction began during the appalling winter conditions of early 1963, but owing to long-term planning of

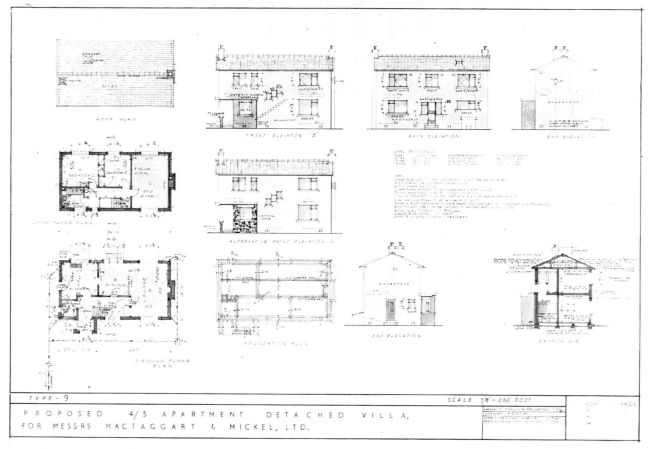

A5.3. William Vannan's type '9' design of 1964, for four and five apartment Mactaggart & Mickel villas. (MMC)

materials and manpower by Douglas Mickel some months earlier, and protective measures including felt to protect lower brickwork and mortar additives for low-temperature working, continuity of work could be maintained. A five-apartment semi-detached villa showhouse was built for this phase of development, at 44 Silverknowes Road East; costing £3,080, it opened in August 1963 and was expected to attract 1,500 visitors in the course of a month. It was described in an August 1963 article by Australian journalist Penny Sutherland: 'The standard minimum house block in Western Australia is a quarter acre, but Mactaggart & Mickel Ltd have had a space restriction of one-tenth of an acre per house. Within this restriction they have managed to build a house which is not cramped, and has a large enough garden to keep the husband of the house away from the golf course for many weekends'. She continued that 'Australia builds out, as a general rule, when Scotland builds up'. Later in the decade, building heights at Silverknowes did go up, when four-storey flats were built (costing between £4,312 and £4,537), along with a new three-apartment showhouse at Silverknowes Neuk. (7)

Other substantial Edinburgh suburban developments of this period included 149 houses at Bonaly between 1958 and 1970; a centrally heated 'smokeless' showhouse at Colinton, costing £4,875, was opened in May 1962, and within weeks had been visited by almost 10,000 people. At Caiystane, 124 houses were built in 1958-64, and 100 further houses in 1964-77; typical of this development was the type 'ST' five apartment terraced house with garage, selling for £7,951 in 1971. At Cammo, as already noted, 160 houses were built in 1957-65; 1962 saw completion of a showhouse at 18 Cammo Brae, which was again used to promote central heating, with a warm-air electric system by Airdun of Uddingston, exploiting off-peak tariffs: 'Welcome to the house which not only is ready for the Clean Air Act but one step ahead of it ... its central heating system filters clean warm air

to every room through ducts laid under the floors'. In February 1963, the house and its heating system were inspected by members and officials from Edinburgh Corporation, led by housing committee chairman Councillor Pat Rogan, who was at that time masterminding the council's ambitious programme of building multi-storey flats. In publicity of 1963, the company emphasised the social exclusivity of Cammo, as 'an exclusive residential district ... very conveniently situated for access to many good schools, such as Daniel Stewart's, St George's, John Watson's, Mary Erskine, etc'. Outwith the immediate Edinburgh area, Laurieston, near Falkirk, saw a modestly-sized development of 41 houses in 1961-63. This comprised cottages and villas of between three and six apartments, costing from £2,780; the development proved popular with staff of the new BMC factory at Bathgate. At this site, near the Antonine Wall, the firm's growing emphasis on preservation of the existing heritage, which already embraced trees, land contours and any small historic buildings incorporated in its estates, received a major boost, when thousands of pieces of Roman pottery were unearthed, and were passed to the National Museum of Antiquities for safekeeping. (8)

The firm's early 1960s developments in the west were slightly different in character to those around Edinburgh; there was a greater element of modernity, especially with the growing emphasis on flats, although this was counterbalanced by a programme of conservation-influenced development, designed by Derek Mickel, in the historic village of Eaglesham. The western programme was summarised in 1963 as comprising 'traditional detached and semi-detached bungalows from four to seven apartments, some with garage, and three-storey flats on some sites', along with an 'interesting development' of six-storey blocks of luxury flats at Anniesland, containing all-electric flats of two, three and four apartments with balconies; prices in the region varied from £2,495 for a three-apartment semi-detached villa in

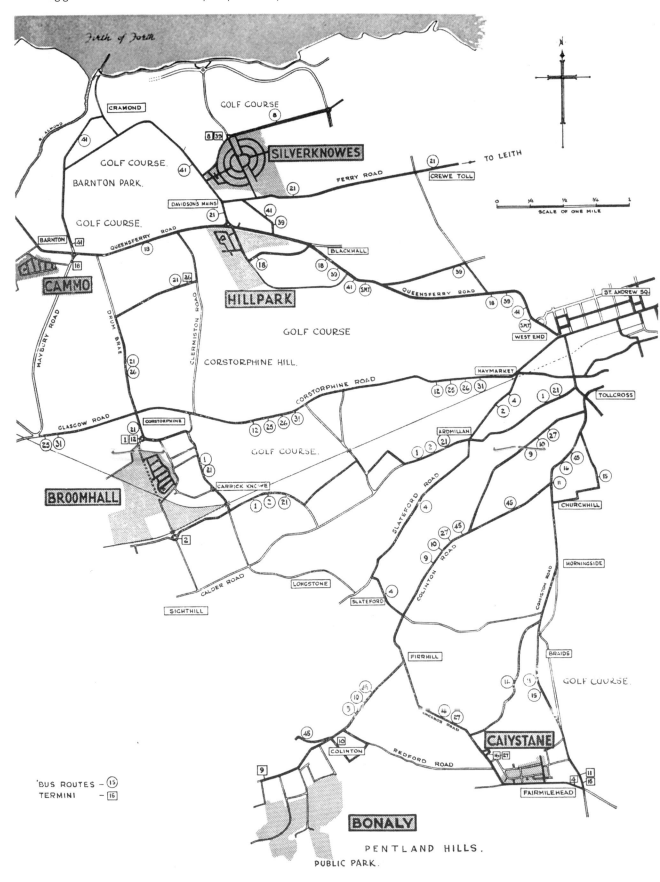

*A5.4. Map showing Mactaggart & Mickel's housing developments in the Edinburgh area in the early 1960s. (*Fine Homes by Mactaggart & Mickel, *brochure of c.1963)*

Love poem written on a brick

Mr Douglas Mickel shows folk-song collector Hamish Henderson a 150-year-old brick inscribed with a verse dug up on his building site at Broomhall Avenue, Corstorphine, just before the war. Now, after 16 years, workmen are back on the site, and Mr Mickel hopes that the mystery of the rhyming brick-layer may be cleared up.

"I never attached any literary importance to the verse," said Mr Mickel. "I thought it was just a romantically-inclined young man scratching out a ditty to his love. Now Hamish tells me it's a genuine folk-song."

Said Mr Henderson, who collects folk-songs for University Department of Scottish Studies: "I've collected songs from the inside of a family Bible and the back of a barn door, but it's the first time I've ever collected one from a brick.

"The song itself is almost certainly the first verse of an eighteenth century 'recognition' ballad which goes to the tune of the 'Lass of Glenshee.'"

THE VERSE

As I was a-walking one fine
 summer's evening
One fine summer's evening it
 happened to be,
There I spied a damsel—she
 appeared like an angel
As she sat neath the shade of
 a bonny green tree.
I stepped up to her as I seemed
 to view her
And said, "My pretty maid
 will you no marry me.
I'll make you a lady of high
 rank and houner
If you share me the half of
 your bonny green tree.

LUCKY ESCAPE

A housewife had a lucky escape when a neighbour's fireplace caught fire early to-day and fell through the ceiling into her kitchen. Mrs Alfred Shandly, of Hove, Sussex, was roused from bed by the neighbours upstairs. Had she gone into her kitchen at that moment the burning ceiling would have fallen on her.

A5.5. Douglas Mickel recognised the historic context of many of the development sites in the east; here, he and Hamish Henderson are shown examining a 150 year old brick inscribed with a poem, which was uncovered during construction at Broomhall Avenue, Corstorphine in February 1955. (Edinburgh Dispatch, 3 February 1955; Scotsman and Evening News)

Kilbarchan to £6,077 for a six-apartment house in Ayr. Flats in Kilbarchan and Eaglesham were on sale for around £2,900, and in Glasgow for prices ranging from £2,750 for a ground floor two-apartment flat to £4,550 for an upper-floor four-apartment flat. The firm argued that 'for generations we have pioneered progressive development in building construction, maintaining a lead in architectural planning and design, and providing unsurpassed refinements for reducing the daily burdens of domestic work ... At the same time we try to keep prices at the lowest level compatible with the rigid principles of sound building construction'. (9)

In the west, the firm faced considerable competition from a number of firms; the main competitors in 1962 were identified as Weir, Miller, Wimpey, Gordon, Lawrence and Ailsa. In a comparative table, the largest and most expensive four-apartment semi-detached house was that of Miller, at £2,980 for 1,110 sq ft, while Mactaggart & Mickel's 990 sq ft house cost £2,680. For five-apartment semis, there was competition only from Gordon, Wimpey and Lawrence, with the largest and most expensive being Gordon's (1,160 sq ft for £3,155, as against Mactaggart & Mickel's 1,104 sq ft for £3,035); Gordon and Ailsa were the only competition listed for six and seven apartment houses, with Mactaggart & Mickel's being larger and more expensive than the others. To maintain output in that context, David Cuthbertson, building manager in the west in 1960s, and his predecessor, Gordon Wright, judged his on-site staffing levels in accordance with a rule of thumb of, on average, one man employed for every house built; Cuthbertson kept in his office a graph which recorded these levels and, if staffing rose above production, he cut staff numbers accordingly. (10)

The biggest developments in the west during these years were concentrated in extensions to the Broom Estate, flats and terraces in Kelvinside, and developments in the Ayrshire and Renfrewshire suburbs. On the Broom Estate, an area of land south of Broom Burn, west of Mearns Castle and located around the old Blackhouse Farm was developed in stages (Broom 1-9) from 1956 to the mid 1970s, with over 500 houses and flats. This formed part of an even larger zone defined by Renfrew County Council, in a postwar development plan drawn up in its capacity as the planning authority; using the jargon of the reconstruction era, the zone was called the 'Kirkhill Neighbourhood'. Mactaggart & Mickel had an effective monopoly on land in this 'neighbourhood', in the same way as Lawrence had in the Crookfur neighbourhood immediately to the west, on the other side of the Ayr Road; in effect, the loose town planning framework for this landward area, outwith tighter burgh controls, followed the framework set by the developers, rather than the other way around. Embedded within the area of Broom 1-9 were a number of developments of flats; early 1960s groups included the 132-dwelling Castle Court (1961-62, in Broom 3) and the 36-flat Broomburn Court, Newton Mearns (1958-61, in Broom 1).

The area was marketed as a 'businessman's paradise' for a mobile middle class population, although there were, even here, references to the importance of tradition. In a 1963 article on a new five-apartment 'Breakaway Bungalow' showhouse at 49 Castlehill Drive, the 27 year old Derek Mickel claimed that the new house was 'getting back to the Scots style of building - it's a breakaway from the four-apartment with a door on the middle of the front and two bow windows on either side'. The article's journalist author compared it to the 1930s Broom houses, noting that it and its garden were smaller. By 1963, 200 villas and bungalows

A5.6. Whittinghame Court under construction in 1963. (MMC)

and 170 flats been built in this area since 1959, 100 flats were being actively planned and several hundred more villas and bungalows were envisaged during the following five years; fourteen shops had already been built and more were planned. Examples of house types under construction there at that time included the 'C32' five-apartment cottage, costing £4,345, and the 'C11' six-apartment cottage for £5,500; the 'C32', with its integral single garage, was one of the most ubiquitous types in the company's developments at the time. (11)

In the exclusive Glasgow west end suburb of Kelvinside, the 1960s saw construction of a range of higher-density developments, responding to the city's shortage of housing land, and the continuing hostility of the council leadership to private developers. Relatively conservative low-rise flats similar to the Broom blocks were built on three sites in Kelvinside: Dorchester Court (84 flats, 1960-61), Chesterfield Court (36 flats, 1962), and Highfield Drive and Cleveden Place, Kelvinside (1963-70), a mixed development of 74 flats and terraced houses. At Highfield Court, a steep fall in ground level to the rear allowed for 'spacious lock-up garages, one to each flat'. The flats, costing from £3,300, incorporated a 'special deadening introduced to the lounge floors [which] ensures that no one is likely to be disturbed unduly by the most spirited ceilidhs'. (12)

The use of terraced houses at Cleveden Place was prompted by the need for higher density, but it also foreshadowed an urban trend away from the universal popularity of semis and detached houses; a 1967 article in the *Evening Citizen* asked 'why young couples prefer these terrace houses', and concluded that it was because they were 'the ideal answer to many people's housing problems, whether it is one of the old red sandstone ... or one of the new imaginative home units constructed by builders like Mactaggart & Mickel Ltd'. These terraced houses were also of significance as they formed part of Mactaggart & Mickel's only dalliance with the system-building fashion of the 1960s (on which see also chapter B4), other than two Canadian timber-framed homes later built at Little Broom. The terraces were built in the 'Trusteel' system of rationalised-traditional construction, licensed by the Trusteel Corporation of Harlow, Essex. This was one of a great number of low-rise systems developed in England around 1960 in an attempt to extend the scope of industrialised methods beyond high-rise flats and heavy concrete prefabrication. These methods were little different from the 'new traditional' methods of the mid 1950s, in which conventional-looking two-storey houses might incorporate some prefabricated elements internally. The Trusteel system used a light-gauge steel frame, on which was attached an outer brick cladding, and internal plasterboard lining. As built in England, the type had experienced column corrosion, and so Mactaggart & Mickel strengthened it considerably, using a thicker outer cavity wall filled with concrete, and traditional timber, rather than solid concrete, ground floors. A number of standard Trusteel house types were modified in this way. In England, they had names such as the 'Cranbrook', 'Findon', 'Denham', and Oxhey', but Mactaggart & Mickel preferred at this time to use number-letter designations; at Kelvinside the Trusteel houses were referred to as type 'TT4', and were sold for between £4,495 and £4,820. Trusteel houses were also built by the company in the west during the mid 1960s at Largs, West Kilbride, Irvine, Greenbank, and the Broom. (13)

Whittinghame Court, Great Western Road, built in 1962-64, was an altogether more adventurous proposition. It was located near the site of the abortive three-winged blocks proposed in the early 1950s. The land facing Great Western Road here had been owned by the company since the building of the rest of Kelvindale

between the wars, but its development had been deferred. Eventually, with the growth of acceptance of high flats, it was decided to build three six-storey blocks, designed by A Buchanan Campbell, each containing 36 high-specification flats, costing between £2,400 and £4,200; twelve flats in each block were of two apartments, twelve of three apartments and twelve of four apartments. Construction, unlike some of the wilder projects of council tower blocks in the 1960s, was relatively conservative: load-bearing brick (faced with London bricks) with concrete floors capped with timber floating over-floors, for good sound insulation; Concrete (Scotland) Ltd, builders of 'Bison Wall Frame' high flats elsewhere, provided 13,500 square yards of prestressed Bison flooring planks.

In a 1962 article on 'Living High' at Whittinghame Court, Mactaggart & Mickel claimed that it was responding to the liking of many Glaswegians for two-apartment tenement flats: 'private builders are now meeting public demand by erecting blocks of modern flats whenever they can get sites in the city. Nowadays, of course, we don't talk about living in a tenement or "up a close". The 1962 idea is to own (not rent) a flat in a streamlined building which boasts a private, plate glass fronted entrance hall ... If, however, you want to achieve the ultimate in city living, you'll raise the money to buy a two, three, or four apartment flat in the first multi-storeyed block being erected in Glasgow by a private builder'. Derek Mickel explained that 'we're trying to ease the public gradually into the idea of living in, and buying, high flats. Flat buying is still a slightly alien thought to Glasgow, but we sold 12 of them before we started building and now have only five of the 36 left ... and that is without even a showhouse, which isn't due to open to the public until September'. The two-apartment flats had been especially popular among 'career people' without children, and could have been sold five times over, but it was 'economically impossible from a builder's point of view' to build only flats of that size: 'If people want to live in town where land is scarce, that is the only way to accomplish it'. The architect, Buchanan Campbell, himself lived in one of the blocks for a time. (14)

The company's building activity in the Renfrewshire and Ayrshire suburbs covered a wide range of development types. These ranged from the innovative to the relatively routine. With the planning-induced land shortages, developments were generally relatively small and scattered, with a growing element of flats. Some responded to the growing ethos of conservation, under the influence of Derek Mickel. In the historic village of Eaglesham, south of Glasgow, a succession of developments totalling some 255 dwellings, with a mixture of flats and cottages, was built in the Waterfoot area between 1960 and 1967. In January 1963, a showhouse at 25 Alexander Avenue was opened, forming part of a first development of 62 two and three bedroom houses and 72 flats; a journalist showed round by Derek Mickel noted that the designs had 'kept the simplicity of line and exterior colouring that will not clash with the old cottages in Polnoon Street'. Prices in 1964 ranged from £2,675 for a three-apartment ground floor flat to £6,093 for a six-apartment detached bungalow. Likewise, in the historic village of Kilbarchan, near Johnstone, 1963-67 saw construction of 131 flats and houses, costing from £2,425 upwards; a new cottage house-type, the 'C30', was built here at a price of £5,125. (15)

In some smaller estates, such as the 37-house Glenside development in the Ayrshire village of West Kilbride (1963-65, comprising 13 five-apartment semis, 18 three-apartment flats, and one three-apartment bungalow), the company turned small scale to advantage by promoting an image of rustic exclusivity:

"This is the house, tho' built anew,
Where Burns cam weary from the plough
To hae a crack wi Johnny Doo on nights ateen,
'And whiles to taste his Mountain Dew
Wi Bonnie Jean."

Thus a sign on the gable end of a building in the historic little town of Mauchline in Ayrshire. Nearby, on the Ayr road, Mactaggart & Mickel have acquired a beautiful wooded site on which they are building most attractive modern homes of 3, 4, 5 and 6 apartments. Mauchline lies within easy reach of Ayr and Kilmarnock and is less than an hour's run from Glasgow. Full particulars of this development will gladly be supplied, either at the Estate Office on the site itself, or at the Mactaggart & Mickel Glasgow Office, 107 West Regent Street.

FURNISHED SHOWHOUSE

OPEN DAILY

2 p.m.—4.30 p.m. WEEKDAYS

2 p.m.—6 p.m. SATURDAYS & SUNDAYS

Villas from **£2250**   Bungalows from **£3620**

MACTAGGART & MICKEL LTD.
Builders of Fine Homes

107 West Regent Street, Glasgow, C.2.
Telephone: DOUglas 0001

A5.7. Advertisement for Mactaggart & Mickel's Mauchline estate in Ayrshire, November 1960. (Ayrshire Post, 11 November 1960; MMC)

'With becoming modesty the Ayrshire coast has been moving steadily into the forefront of rural development, and builders with both eyes wide open for environmental selling points, have been exploiting many attractive areas pockets of land. Into them are poured small selective communities of home-makers to whom this pocket development is more exciting and more compensating than the comparative anonymity of living in a huge city suburb. One such development is that of Mactaggart & Mickel in West Kilbride, a secluded clachan of 37 homes which combine the highest standards of urban amenity with a delightfully picturesque rural framework'. In the Doonfoot suburb in Ayr, building continued on Earl's Way and Abbot's Way after 1960, followed by Knoweholm (1961-62, 30 houses), Greenan Road and Castle Walk (1969-78); in early 1960s literature, the company praised the 'charming sea-side development' with its 'wide imposing road which sweeps down to the sea, flanked with distinguished houses enhancing the natural beauty of an already magnificent landscape'. (16)

More routine developments further afield in Ayrshire included 88 houses in Stevenston, at the Mayfield estate (1962-69), with a four-apartment detached showhouse costing £3,700, five-apartment terraced houses for £3,690, and blocks of three-storey flats; at Mauchline, 20 villas and bungalows were built at the Netherplace estate in 1960-63. Infill projects in the company's established suburbs nearer Glasgow included 28 additional houses in Giffnock Park Avenue, Merrylee Park (1961). The company continued to expand its land bank immediately outside Glasgow by making strategic purchases wherever possible. In January 1963, for example, it outbid Wimpey and three other competitors to buy a 31-acre site at Flenders Farm, Greenbank, with the intention of building a 200-dwelling 'luxury' extension of Carolside Park estate, including villas, bungalows and flats. The owner, Ayrshire bachelor Jock Brown, was paid no less than £129,580 - £4,180 per acre - a price described as 'scandalous' by Glasgow Corporation's socialist housing committee convener, David Gibson. Further away from Glasgow, a typical purchase of the late 1960s was a 35-acre site at Rallies Farm, Largs, bought in 1969 for £2,500 per acre; land sales in the same period included 24.6 acres at Broomburn Drive, sold to Renfrew County Council for £20,910 (for use as a public park). (17)

The most ambitious development planned by the company on the outer Glasgow periphery in these years, however, was never actually built, partly owing to the same green-belt planning issue that blighted Glasgow's council building programme in the same years. At the end of the 1950s, the company bought a 300-acre swathe of farmland extending from Lennoxtown to Campsie Glen, along the foot of the Campsie Hills. Buoyed by the growing conviction of economic prosperity, their intention (in the words of J G L Wark) was to build a 'comprehensive development' of houses, flats, shops and playing fields. The initial proposal was deferred on appeal in 1959 by the Secretary of State, who advised the firm to apply again later, with houses to be built on the lower part of the Lennoxtown-Fintry road. In 1961, the firm received planning permission for a reduced development of 2,000 houses at Lennoxtown-Campsie Glen, but this was delayed by site difficulties and the site was eventually de-zoned in the 1970s from residential by Strathclyde Regional Council, which was anxious to curb housing in the Strathkelvin area and redirect attention to the redevelopment of Glasgow's east end. Unfortunately for Mactaggart & Mickel, the land remains undeveloped today. (18)

The late 1960s: competition and crisis

With the economic crisis and devaluation of the late 1960s, the optimistic era of postwar growth came to an end. House price inflation began in earnest, with values rising by half in five years from 1964, to an average figure of £3,336 for a new house. By late 1966, the government's 'credit squeeze' was beginning to bite into the private housing market, with a noticeable slackening in demand for buying houses. Competition intensified within the industry: Mactaggart & Mickel, Lawrence, Miller and Bett still remained dominant, but Wimpey was expanding rapidly; a 1968 article claimed that Lawrence was the 'largest private building organisation in Scotland'. With profit margins finely balanced, and higher taxes and the credit squeeze dealing a 'severe blow' to firms existing on borrowed capital, the feeling began to grow that some small or medium-sized firms might not survive, and indeed, by 1966, one small but well established Glasgow firm, L K Mackenzie & Partners, did indeed go into liquidation. Both Miller and Mactaggart & Mickel were now carrying out sales reviews at weekly rather than two or three monthly intervals; although there was little slackening of demand for new houses, people were finding it difficult to sell their old houses. During these troubled years, the firm saw a marked decline in output, to only 138 sales in the west in 1967, and, equally significantly, a gradual decline in its share of total new house sales, from 10% in 1966 to 7% in 1969. Of Mactaggart & Mickel's building output in 1968 and 1969, 25% comprised three-apartment houses, 30% four-apartment, 30% five-apartment, and the remainder six or more apartments; 7% of output comprised terraced houses, 36% semi-detached houses, 22% detached houses, 20% detached bungalows, and 4% flats and other types. (19)

The company's response was a mixture of internal reorganisation measures and changes to marketing and sales policies. In October 1966, reacting to the Labour government's introduction of a new company levy, Selective Employment Tax (SET) - a burden from which manufacturing companies were exempted - the business was reorganised so as to segregate its manufacturing aspects into a separate firm, Mickel Products Ltd. The latter took over responsibility for Carntyne Concrete Works (where precast concrete blocks were manufactured), the Broom workshop (where kitchen fitments and furniture were made), and the joinery workshop at Cartsbridge Farm, Clarkston. The latter eventually closed in 1968; its site was, naturally, developed for housing. It was decided not to sell the concrete products of the new firm on the market initially, as they did not conform to British Standards. The management of Mactaggart & Mickel was also substantially overhauled in 1966, with Derek Mickel, James D Goold and John Gray (an engineer who had joined the business in 1921 at Mosspark) brought on to the board of directors. Key managerial salaries were increased (that of Douglas by £5,000 per annum, J G L Wark by £1,500 and J D Goold by £2,500). Douglas Mickel represented the company in key external events, such as a 1968 Scottish National Federation of Building Trades' Employers study tour to Brussels - a party which also included Crudens and W S Gordon representatives. (20) In the late 1960s, in reaction to the adverse economic climate, Goold pared the technical-professional side of the Glasgow office down to the bare minimum, reducing the number of engineers and surveyors to five. (21)

Alongside these reorganisations, Mactaggart & Mickel publicised new arrangements for higher levels of loans, supported by the Building Societies Association, and, just as in the difficult years of the mid 1930s, adopted higher-profile sales techniques and a more comprehensive marketing approach. A bolder marketing

A5.8. Mactaggart & Mickel's fleet of works vehicles for the Edinburgh sites in 1968. (MMC)

A5.9. Three-storey flats at Forrester Park, Edinburgh, nearing completion in June 1966. (MMC)

opportunity was eagerly grasped in 1968: the 'I'm Backing Britain' campaign, an initiative spanning a wide range of industries across Britain, which packaged pledges to hold down prices in patriotic language. For Mactaggart & Mickel, this was a logical extension of their traditional philanthropic outlook, to include participation in the wider struggle against inflation. These years also saw the establishment of the Mickel Trust as a vehicle for the firm's long-established charitable donations; on its foundation in 1970, the trust was endowed with £20,000, and its assets in 1999 now exceed £1 million. (22)

Of the firm's participation in 'I'm Backing Britain', a newspaper article reported that 'five hundred Scots building workers will begin to help Britain back to greatness tomorrow, when their

firm [Mactaggart & Mickel] starts its bid to support the "I'm Backing Britain" campaign' ... 'A cross-section of the firm's workers in Edinburgh gave their backing yesterday to the drive, in which the firm risks thousands of pounds by keeping house prices down. In return, the men will be paid bonuses for increased output - although they are not expected to work longer hours'. Frank Knight, a site agent, argued that 'The lads are a good bunch and I'm sure we can expect even better results from them,' while bricklayer Andy Stewart declared that 'the firm can count on the men. It's a new challenge for us'. Jim Goold pointed out that 'the campaign is also meant for officials - I'm sure we won't be let down'. The 500 employees were first informed of the scheme by a letter inserted in their wage packets. In the east, a new six-apartment showhouse at 17 Bonaly Gardens was presented as a showcase of the new 'patriotic help-the-country' initiative. Priced at £8,047, its cost was to be pegged until July 1969, absorbing rising costs and saving prospective buyers over £150. In the west, the campaign was focused on the new six-storey block of luxury flats at Broom Cliff, Broom Estate, whose four-apartment flats were to be held to £7,980, and five-apartments to £9,900. Its buyers would enjoy 'magnificent vistas over the woods and meadows of the surrounding countryside' while helping the national economy at the same time. (23)

This initiative formed part of a succession of pledges to hold prices for fixed periods of several months. In mid 1968, for instance, the Mactaggart & Mickel staff bulletin contended that 'it is essential to keep house prices down' and called for 'an ever greater increase in productivity and efficiency', while warning that price increases from September would be inevitable, owing to the 'substantial increase in house prices from all builders' expected after that date. Jim Goold claimed that the co-operation and support of all staff and workers would be essential to conjure up that 'little extra effort' to build more economically: 'We're Still Backing Britain'. A further factor pointing to price increases, Goold explained, was a 50% rise in Selective Employment Tax due in September (amounting to 37s 6d per employee per week). He lamented the failure to allow traditional building firms any rebate, and warned that demand would probably increase over the next three months. Sure enough, a September 1968 advertisement for Edinburgh estates, including Hillpark, Forrester Park, Silverknowes Neuk (with its 'famous Thrifty Homes'), Bonaly, and Caiystane, proclaimed the company's success in holding prices since November 1967, but highlighted the impending SET increase, along with rises in health insurance and redundancy costs; the company would 'absorb' these for a limited period, but buyers must 'act now'. (24)

During 1969, the adverse economic situation prompted a further succession of sales promotion measures. For example, in October, the Forrester Park estate in Edinburgh saw a one-third reduction on all furniture, carpets and removals, and free carpets and removals up to £250 were offered at Silverknowes, Forrester Park and Caiystane the following month. At Greenbank, November 1969 saw a 'Do-it-yourself £250 reduction, given on terraced or semi detached houses ... if people will do their own interior decorating'. By mid December there had been a hundred enquiries about this scheme, and the directors 'resolved to continue these schemes indefinitely, but to make every endeavour to impress on the Government the need for subsidies or other help to the private house building sector of the industry'. Also in November, at all sites in the west, the company offered a trade-in scheme whereby 'we will take back in part exchange old houses at a value fixed independently by Messrs Walker, Fraser & Steele'. In itself, this scheme just broke even - by 1972, 30 houses had been taken over and resold, at an overall profit of £350 - but its overall aim was less to make a profit than to help new sales. (25)

The firm's building programme during the late 1960s continued the established balance of villa and flatted development, in competition with the low/medium cost efforts of Lawrence and Wimpey. But criticisms of the architecture and layout of the more conventional estates would lead in the following decade to a more innovative design policy. In the east, the major development of this period was Forrester Park, an estate of 464 villas and flats built in 1965-78 near Broomhouse. It included numbers of three-apartment flats, six to a block; a show flat selling for £3,683 was opened in August 1967. Three-storey blocks in the estate, designed by William Vannan, featured idiosyncratic butterfly roofs.

In the west, the most important new mainstream estate was Greenbank, an extension to Carolside Park built on the farmland purchased so expensively in 1963. Following an initial phase of development in 1966, including four-apartment terraced houses costing from £4,350, an extension of 370 houses was built in 1967-76. A new five-apartment showhouse in 1968 was described as 'modern in appearance, although it retains some of the character of the older Scottish type of dwelling, with its high-pitched roof and timber windows'. A 1967 price list for the estate listed six types ranging from the four-apartment mid-terrace Trusteel 'TT4' (costing £4,350, with £15 feu duty) to the six-apartment detached 'C39' cottage with garage (£8,659, with £26 feu duty), and by 1971 the 'TT4' cost had risen to £5,665, while a new 'Thrifty 5' five-apartment semi-detached villa was on offer for £5,613. House type particulars for Greenbank of c.1973 ranged from the 'C41' bungalow, a 'compact space saving country style' house with three apartments, no internal corridors (the living room serving as the main communication) and no central heating, to a five-apartment villa priced at £8,805 and including a full-depth living/dining area, attached garage and partial electric central heating as standard; a number of the Trusteel house types now retained their names (e.g. 'Birken', 'Heriot') in the promotional material, rather than adopting number/letter designations - one of the first

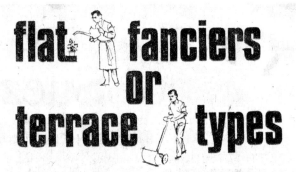

BROOM CLIFF, BROOM ESTATE, NEWTON MEARNS

The carefully planned elegance of Polished Italian marble, wood panelling and Swedish flooring in the entrance hall at Broom Cliff provides a luxurious prelude to the flats themselves, which are finished to a superb standard, with the most modern domestic facilities geared for effortless housework.

The furnished showflat at 30 Castleton Drive, Broom Cliff, Newton Mearns, is open every afternoon, including Saturday and Sunday.

4-APT. £7980. 5-APT. £9900.

LOANS AVAILABLE

GREENBANK ESTATE, CLARKSTON

These supremely comfortable terrace houses are set in rural surroundings, yet only 6 miles from Glasgow. Accommodation is spacious and well planned, with 3 bedrooms, bathroom, kitchen, and sizable lounge/dining-room, and ample storage space, hanging wardrobes, etc. There is partial off-peak central heating and a 'Sunhouse' flame effect fire.

The showhouse is situated at Hillend Road, just off Glendoune Road and is open every afternoon, including Saturday and Sunday.

PRICES FROM £4350

Mactaggart & Mickel LTD

107 WEST REGENT STREET, GLASGOW, C.2 Tel. DOUglas 0001
12 NORTH SAINT ANDREW STREET, EDINBURGH Tel. WAV 4747

A5.10. Advertisement for flats and terraces at Broom and Greenbank estates in 1967. (Glasgow Herald, 8 July 1967; MMC)

A5.11. Broomcliff, Broom Estate, seen under construction c.1965. (MMC)

A5.12. Advertisement for Broomcliff and other various late 1960s sites. (Glasgow & West College of Domestic Science Students Newsletter, 1967; MMC)

examples of the use of house-type names by the company. Further down the Clyde, the newly-designated Irvine New Town was the site of a 232-dwelling development at Mill Road in 1965-75, including a five-apartment showhouse opened in 1969 at a price of £4,921; 166 houses were built at Kirktonhall, West Kilbride, in 1966; 61 houses were built at Loans, near Troon, in 1969-72; and 70 houses were built at Humbie Road, Eaglesham, in 1966-72. (26)

At the same time as these estates, the development of the Broom Estate extensions continued steadily. A new factor was the beginning of criticisms of the Broom 1-9 extension, and unfavourable comparisons to the 1930s section. One 1968 newspaper article, for example, argued that 'the bit at the beginning of the Estate is without equal, but the further one penetrates into it the rot sets in and it becomes like most other suburban estates, and every bit as monotonous in houses and streets. It is a pity that they created a delight and let it merge slowly into mediocrity'. While a new extension development of nearly 200 houses, Broom North-East, was developed in very much the same manner, another smaller development started at the same time, Little Broom, was much more individualistic and exclusive, including a number of large, highly customised villas. A 1969 article reported that 'as soon as they finished number 14 Broom Road, they filed the plans away. Don't waste your time asking them to build another house the same - they won't'. Derek Mickel explained that 'We are determined that no two houses on this estate are alike. To make sure, we are having each house designed from scratch. We won't take out the plans of an existing house and adapt it slightly, because that wouldn't be a truly individual house. We're also using a variety of architects - again to make sure fresh ideas are constantly being brought in'. In one case, the firm agreed to build a house designed by the client's own architect. The £15,550 showhouse for this development was of seven apartments, faced in white roughcast, with Fyfestone decoration (multi-coloured granite aggregate blockwork) and grey-green concrete roof tiles; it had an integral garage, kitchens by the company's own joiners, and a layout which separated pedestrian and road access, emulating the contemporary 'Radburn' system. (27)

The major flatted development of the period at the Broom Estate also harked back in some ways to the estate's original exclusivity. Broomcliff, which formed part of the Broom 1-9 extension area, comprised one six-storey block of 34 flats, virtually identical in design to the Buchanan Campbell blocks at Great Western Road, including the yellow London brick facing. Built in 1966-71, and with the first show flats opening in mid 1969, it contained a mixture of four and five apartment flats, initially costing (as mentioned above) from £7,980 and £9,900 respectively. Its modern amenities were marketed in terms reminiscent of Sandringham Court, but with the additional heritage element of a view over to the ruins of Mearns Castle - ruins which were to be converted to a chapel, following the company's donation of the castle to the Church of Scotland. The firm hailed it as 'Your Own Castle ... luxury living "Mac and Mick" style ... it's not every flat that has a view like that!' (28)

1970-90: weathering the storms

During the 1970s, the economic troubles heralded in the late 1960s developed into a full-blown crisis of the system, and a period of inflation and instability was followed by two severe recessions, as the Scottish economy was restructured from a social-democratic to a capitalist form. In contrast to southern England, central Scotland enjoyed no intervening economic boom in the late 1980s. The result of this was the disappearance of most of the old private building firms that had emerged between the wars and the takeover of the emerging volume speculative building market by large English-based firms. However, to a family-owned business, market share is far less important than to a public company and its shareholders, and Mactaggart & Mickel was able to surmount these difficulties in robust financial health, and develop policies of architectural innovation that could be brought to bear once again in the more optimistic times of the late 1990s.

In the years of inflation during the 1970s, the company's net assets rose rapidly in value, from £2,900,000 million in 1970 to £3,200,000 the following year, while its liquid resources rose from £1,371,000 in 1972 to £1,740,000 in 1973. (29) It began to consider expansion through acquisition, taking over the Clydeside building form of E Ecrepont & Sons in 1974 at a price of one penny per share; all existing Ecrepont sites were taken on and completed, and the purchase of ten acres at Castlehill, Ayr, at a cost of £6,000 per acre was honoured. In 1971, a proposal to set up a new company, employing all the managers and staff of Trusteel Corporation, which had recently gone into liquidation,

had come to nothing, because the Trusteel system patent had already been bought by another company.

Throughout the 1970s, the firm's financial health fluctuated in response to the balance between its own internal activities, and to the wider economic climate, including inflation and recession. In the accounts for the year 1973-74, for example, a sharp fall in trading profit mainly resulted from a revision in the value of feu duties previously capitalised, and a sharp increase in staff pension costs. Two years later, a substantial increase in the housebuilding profit had been offset by a fall in ground sales. The 1976-77 accounts reported an increase of trading profit of £462,000 for the year, attributed to interest received (£234,000 higher), housebuilding profit (£120,000 higher), and gains on ground sales (£93,000 higher, including a £86,000 profit on land at Laurieston). There had also been large increases in work-in-progress (£979,000) and cash in hand on deposit (£1,090,500), and the company concluded that the building profit had been attributable to the Clyde coast and Glasgow sites, and that the improvement in the cash position had resulted from sale of Edinburgh letting properties. By the time the 1978-79 accounts were being considered, the position had changed again owing to the deepening recession: Douglas Mickel noted that over the past winter, 'output per man had risen by an estimated 20% due to better morale and loyalty, and also to good weather, but sales were disappointing due to the shortage of mortgages and to the fact that, in times of recession, people tend only to move house if they have to'. Such low sales increased substantially the work in progress at the expense of cash reserves; this would paradoxically leave the company in a strong position and generate a 'good notional profit' when sales eventually picked up again, as much of the unsold stock had been built prior to the June 1979 wage increase of 20%. (30)

Within the management, an April 1970 staff chart showed Douglas Mickel in full charge, with four directors (Derek Mickel, John Gray, Jim Goold, and Graham Wark) below him. Gray was in charge of the Edinburgh sites, with Bill Matthews as his deputy, managing the site agents, administrative staff and showhouse staff. In Glasgow, Goold had a similar role, but with a much larger staff, and six managers below him. These included Bill Gillies, surveyor, David Morris, chief engineer (assisted by Douglas Murray and Iain Drysdale), and sales manager Edith McKinlay (praised in an extensive Glasgow Herald feature of 1975 as 'Edith - at the top in a man's world'); Derek Mickel oversaw all designs plans and layouts in the west, and Graham Wark handled legal dealings. By 1970, there were only six design professionals in the firm. The early 1970s saw the growing prominence of Jim Goold, who became financial director in 1970 and was transferred 20,000 shares by Derek and Douglas Mickel in 1973. (31)

Although not a heavily unionised organisation, the firm was on occasion affected by the labour troubles of the 1970s. In mid 1972, for example, there was a wages strike, which was resolved through a 30% wage rise, to be paid for by adding 19% to the cost of houses not yet started. In a letter from Jim Goold to Douglas Mickel on the end of the dispute, Goold reported that 'in Glasgow we had a 95% turnout yesterday - the first day back - that is better than most Mondays! - but the main thing is, we are working again, and already morale is rising and people seem eager to forget what has happened'. Partly in response to these difficulties, the mechanisation of site operations proceeded steadily, but cautiously. In 1978, for instance, a '108S' excavator costing £20,915 was acquired, in view of the site conditions at Kingsburn and parts of Largs, which sometimes made work impossible for ordinary JCB type excavators; and a set of

A5.13. Castle Gate, Broom Estate, seen under construction c.1972; Broomcliff is visible in the background. (MMC)

'KwikForm system' scaffolding was bought for £65,000, especially for use on the Ascot flats at Anniesland. (32)

The tax-related decision to separate the company's manufacturing activities into the separate firm of Mickel Products began to seem increasingly problematic in the 1970s. In the accounts for the year ending April 1970, the subsidiary company had difficulty in showing a profit, and its net assets position was considerably poorer than in previous years. Goold pointed out that Mickel Products was charging Mactaggart & Mickel more for its Carntyne works concrete products than an outside company would charge, and claimed that the 'quality of the articles produced was usually inferior to that of other companies'. If the firm was to become profitable, its prices would have to be raised even higher. Goold argued that 'it appears that there is a general contraction in the pre-cast concrete business, and that more companies are specialising in one product only, and that no one seemed remotely interested in continuing with our type of business'. It was decided to stop concrete block production immediately, and to offer the workforce alternative site employment, but to continue with manufacture of specialist concrete items - copes, steps, rough lintels. The cessation of most concrete production at Carntyne had a stabilising effect on profits, and by 1974 it was proposed to build a new factory at Orchard Park, designed by A Buchanan Campbell, to replace Carntyne, at a cost of £95,000; the new factory at Robslee Drive, Giffnock, was completed in 1975. Eventually, in the 1980s and 1990s, taxation reforms removed the need for the separation between building and manufacturing, and Mickel Products gradually became a 'dormant' company. (33)

Throughout this period, the constant government interventions to regulate the economy made it necessary for the company to maintain political and lobbying connections in London. The accession of the Conservative Party to power in 1970 raised hopes for more business-friendly policies. Goold pressed the party for the abolition of the Land Betterment Levy and Selective Employment Tax, and for the introduction of direct subsidies for home-ownership. From July 1971, SET was reduced by 50%, and in response the firm decided to cut the prices of all houses by £50. In August 1971, the company also joined the London-based lobbying organisation, the Confederation of British Industry (CBI), which was currently urging companies to restrict their price increases to 5% over the next 12 months, in an effort to curb inflation. Throughout the 1970s, the firm regularly gave annual donations of £10,000 to the Conservative Party, but at the end of the decade that commitment increased sharply, as we will see later. The directors tried to balance these UK-wide concerns with policy developments specific to Scotland, such as the 1970 'Sidwell Report' on private housing costs (see also Chapter B4), which claimed that low productivity and monopolistic practices were artificially inflating Scottish prices by comparison with those in England. In 1971, the likely abolition of feu duties prompted a decision to raise house prices by £20, to compensate for the loss of revenue. In the same year, Jim Goold became president of the Scottish Building Contractors Association, where he argued that all wage-negotiation should be UK-wide, to iron out 'regional' differences. (34)

From 1973, growing political and industrial instability and the possibility of the return of a Labour government began to preoccupy the directors. Discussion of a possible land hoarding tax by the government began to focus attention, around 1973, on the need to build up land holdings at agricultural value; such land would not be subject to the proposed levy. In the opinion of Goold, even if the land did not eventually receive planning permission, it would still produce good investment return on agricultural values; Douglas Mickel agreed that this would be a 'sensible outlet for the company's considerable liquid resources', and all directors were encouraged to 'keep on the look out for suitable farmland'. (35) On the return of Labour to power in 1974, the possibility of land nationalisation began to throw a darker shadow over land acquisition policy. In 1975, for example, concerning a proposed agreement to buy 39.1 acres of ground at Erskine from Renfrew County Council for £260,000, Jim Goold expressed concern that 'in view of proposed legislation regarding the nationalisation of land, he was concerned about the wisdom of purchasing ground whose development potential was so long term'. In the end, the purchase was abandoned for that very reason. Land purchases proceeded at Balerno (for £69,325) and Castlehill, Ayr (for £65,530; the Ecrepont deal), and the company began discussing a land swap with Edinburgh Corporation at South Gyle, offering to part-exchange 40 acres of land suitable for commercial development for '20 acres of residential land in the same area, to allow for continuity at Forrester Park'. However, a dispute between Lothian Regional Council and City of Edinburgh District Council as to which authority should organise the exchange delayed the development for years. (36)

At one remove from the firm's 'political' concerns in the outside world, the charitable operations of the Mickel Trust continued apace during the 1970s. One major early initiative began in October 1973, when the trust bought Dalguise House, near Dunkeld, for £60,000 after a report that a residential centre run by the Scottish Association of Boys' Clubs might have to close. £50,000 was put into the Dalguise House Trust, the SABC was given 21 years' free rent, and Douglas and Jim Goold maintained a 'personal interest' in the continued well-being of the centre. An example of a smaller charitable initiative by the Mickel Trust, with a potentially beneficial spin-off effect for the company, was a £1,000 donation to the Greenbank Appeal of the National Trust for Scotland in 1976, to 'help to promote amenities in the immediate areas of our developments at Greenbank and Broom'. (37)

In their building activity in the west, the firm generally maintained its conventional pattern of low-density development of single-family houses, although with continuing elements of conservation-sensitive work, as we will see. Around Glasgow, there was still considerable competition, although Laidlaw Scothomes announced in 1971 their withdrawal from private housebuilding (and Mactaggart & Mickel attempted to obtain land from them). In the Eastwood area, Lawrence was building extensively at Crookfur, just adjoining the Broom extensions - a pattern of next-door competition which echoed earlier days, when Lawrence had built in Stamperland and Mactaggart & Mickel built in nearby Netherlee Park. However, the impetus of Lawrence's work was already beginning to taper off, and much of its land-bank was eventually sold to Wimpey, while the arrival of Newcastle-based Barratt in the later 1970s brought a new and brasher style of speculative building. In response, large numbers of showhouses were opened by Mactaggart & Mickel, and there was much debate among the directors about the relative benefits of classified advertising and posters; Jim Goold claimed in 1970 that advertising cost £100 per house sold. 18 new showhouses were opened on Saturday 28 March 1970, bringing the firm's total number of showhouses in the west to 24. In June 1970, a new 'H' type showhouse opened at Polnoon, along with two at Mount Charles and Irvine, and a further three at Broom 9 and other western sites. Later in the decade, annual sales in the west region fluctuated between 150 and 235. (38)

The company's 1970s development policies in the west became more sharply polarised between the remaining small gap sites in the Glasgow outskirts, including the 30-flat Robshill Court at Mearns Cross (the firm's only major incursion into 'Lawrence' territory west of the Ayr Road, commenced in 1978 and selling from £23,950) and a 79-house initial development at Kingsburn, King's Park (from 1979, on land purchased in the 1920s as part of the earlier King's Park schemes), along with larger sites in the coastal towns, and in Eaglesham. The commitment to Irvine New Town was expanded through a 240-dwelling development at Whitehurst Park, Kilwinning (1975-78), while 266 houses were built at Brisbane Glen, Largs (1976-86) and 66 at Castlehill, Ayr (1975-79). Even in these locations, the impact of planning

restrictions was beginning to be felt strongly. For example, at the Burton site in Ayr, bought for £273,918 in 1975, the local authority specified a low density layout, allowing only 147 plots and pushing up the cost of the finished houses. After about 40 houses, selling at about £27,000, had been built in 1976-86, the company decided that the rate of sales was far too slow, and resolved to sell the remaining plots unbuilt, for about £10,000-£15,000 each. The firm had never sold plots in such numbers before, and about 70 were eventually bought, mostly by Ayrshire people to build their 'dream homes' on the large sites. (39)

In Edinburgh and the east, the company's activity began to become more complex during this period. Two strands became increasingly prominent: the programme of sales of interwar rental property, and a more ambitious architectural approach to new housing development, which built further on some ideas adumbrated in the west.

In general, up until the Major government's introduction of short assured tenancies in the mid 1990s, the private rental market remained profoundly unattractive for commercial firms, owing to the continuing strength of rent controls and the political stigma still attached to landlords, and the undermining of its tenant-base by the availability of low-rent, high-quality council housing. At the same time, the demand for owner-occupation - a trend in all western countries, not just Britain - was steadily growing. With the increasing planning difficulties of building new private housing, it became obvious that Mactaggart & Mickel's large rental stock in Edinburgh was ripe for large-scale conversion to owner-occupation. This process, underway since 1953, had been facilitated by the lack of capital debt associated with 1923 and 1924 Act subsidised private housing, compared with council housing. The sales now continued apace, with 43% of all the rental stock disposed of by the early/mid 1970s; as we will see later, in 1996, with several hundred rental houses remaining, the policy was reversed following the government reforms of letting controls, and re-lets began in Colinton and Carrick Knowe, Broomhouse, and on a smaller scale in East Pilton. A decisive watershed in the policy came in the late 1960s and 1970s, when the houses began to shift into the more dynamic market typical of modern owner-occupation. Prior to that, almost all houses had been sold to sitting tenants, and had thus still remained within the system of residential stability characteristic also of council housing; after that, most were sold to incomers looking for starter homes, who then moved on after a few years.

In the early 1970s, the Conservative government policy of diluting rent controls by 'fair rents' was applied by the company to the remaining Edinburgh rental stock, and met with tenant protests. But the situation was thrown into reverse by Labour's 1974 Rent Freeze, described by Douglas Mickel as 'a hasty and ill-considered piece of legislation which has created some very odd anomalies, and which will seriously hinder the prospect of improvements which the 1969 and 1972 Acts had brought within the bounds of possibility by virtue of increased rental revenue'. A critical study of c.1975 argued that the population of these estates was 'increasingly being dichotomised between young, mobile owner-occupiers, and older, poorer tenants who have lived in the houses for 30 or 40 years'. But equally, the areas could be said to have played a valuable role, by filling a glaring hole in the Scottish owner-occupation market, and providing a first rung on the property ladder for skilled artisans and the clerical classes, at a time when the massive government subsidies for purchase of council houses by sitting tenants had not yet been devised. (40)

Alongside these innovations in the management of existing stock, the Edinburgh regional office also embarked on an innovative approach to architectural design during the 1970s and early 1980s - an approach which helped set Mactaggart & Mickel apart from other Scottish speculative builders in its sensitivity to advanced housing design trends. In many respects, the new policy was a development of the established conservation-sensitive work of Derek Mickel in Eaglesham and other sites in the west. However, it was also increasingly influenced by the ideas of Bruce Mickel. He joined the company in 1970 after completing his architectural training at Edinburgh College of Art. There, it is clear, he came under the influence of that important school of Scottish Modernist housing design, ultimately stemming from the turn-of-century Traditionalist work of Robert Lorimer and Patrick Geddes, which opposed repetitive mass housing and instead called for irregular 'vernacular' patterns reflecting the collective housing tradition of the Edinburgh Old Town and the east coast historic burghs. This had been introduced to postwar social housing in Basil Spence's influential infill group at Lamer Street, Dunbar (1949-52). But by the 1960s and early 1970s, the most important figure in this tradition was Anthony Wheeler of Wheeler & Sproson - an architect who was, coincidentally, at that time working on the redevelopment of Edinburgh College of Art itself, and who also exerted great influence through his teaching at Dundee School of Architecture. Most of the key works of this strand of Scottish Modernism were small groups of council housing, in historic towns, but it was also used for large new developments by the architects of the New Towns and the Scottish Special Housing Association, in places such as Cumbernauld, Irvine and Erskine. Mactaggart & Mickel attempted to apply it to speculative development, in effect using architectural form to bridge some of the gap between the public and private sectors.

Bruce Mickel explained these ideas at greater length in a significant lecture of 1983, and a 1981 article. In the 1983 lecture, appropriately at Edinburgh College of Art, he first recalled his own alienation from prefabricated mass housing through a spell (in 1968-69) spent working with a high-rise system building contractor, Reema Scotland of Bellshill. Of Reema, he recalled that they 'produced heavy mass concrete units and panels ... for some of the more spectacular social failures that now blot some of Scotland's major cities ... I was convinced that the way forward in housing lay in mass production of housing units on the factory floor'. But he had left Reema in 1970, 'finally convinced that my beliefs had been mistaken and my hopes a pipe dream'. The factory closed soon afterwards, when 'the desperate inefficiency of such production methods caught up with them'. He then joined the family firm, which 'for two generations ... had dominated the private housing market in central Scotland ... and had, along with the rest of the private industry, been producing the same tired old house types in the same old dull layouts, with no sense of place or identity and with a notable lack of design quality'. In the following years, the firm began 'to develop a clear regional company image through the use of more exciting forms of housing layouts and house types. We have tried to recognise the strong architectural heritage here in the east of Scotland ... Our housing has become the kind that people can live with as well as live in, which they can enjoy, identify with and feel that they have spent their money well!' Mickel criticised the polarisation between mass council housing, 'big, boarded up and ugly as hell', and mass private housing with its 'rows of tacky little boxes'; both extremes of this 'divided industry' relied on government subsidies, including mortgage tax relief in the private case. But he pointed to the first signs, since the late 1970s, that the two sectors might work together, prompted by cuts in government aid for council building and the drying up of cheap

greenfield land; cooperative ventures included joint new building ventures and private-led refurbishment of run-down council schemes. This polarisation of tenures was reflected in a polarisation of architecture, between developers and the design establishment. Such an oppositional pattern was clearly demonstrated in a Royal Incorporation of Architects in Scotland housing forum held in Livingston in 1975, at which representatives from Miller and Bovis argued that 'better design cost too much' and that 'bungalows and detached houses ... still ruled that market', while Robert Black of the Dundee-based vernacular Modernist architects Baxter, Clark & Paul argued that higher design standards were essential. (41)

In his 1981 article, Bruce Mickel outlined Mactaggart & Mickel's new architectural thinking in more detail. He lamented the fact that 'architects have long considered private house-builders the bogeymen of the industry', accused of 'carpeting the countryside with row upon row of little boxes, of producing vast developments with no real sense of place or identity and of failing to show any real recognition of our architectural heritage'. He expressed a hope that 'the developments built by this company over the last decade are tangible evidence that we, at least, are trying to produce housing that contributes to the environment, rather than detracting from it. Our intention has been to establish a new and stronger company identity, with real regional background and above all to prove that good design sells'. At the end of the 1960s, the company had anticipated the chronic land shortage which a decade later was 'crippling the industry in the Edinburgh area and elsewhere', and had realised it would have to 'considerably increase densities across the board'. Previously, Mactaggart & Mickel development had stressed detached properties and 'large blocks of low priced flats', while the sizes of the individual plots reached an 'irreducible minimum'. 'We felt that our approach was beginning to stagnate - one of the few times when our views had coincided with those of the planners - and decided that the time was ripe for a change of direction.' This was no simple attempt to move the company 'upmarket' by adopting more

A5.14. Hillpark Loan, Edinburgh, seen in 1976. (MMC)

A5.15. Hillpark Wood, Edinburgh, seen c.1976. (MMC)

A5.16. Bonaly Brae, Edinburgh, seen in 1974. (MMC)

ambitious architecture; in many ways, it represented a stylistic convergence with council housing, and was applied to low-cost and elite developments alike. (42)

In the west, these ideas were hardly new, as Derek Mickel's historic-context developments were continuing apace: in Eaglesham, for example, the 315-dwelling Polnoon estate, from 1970, combined a Modernist 'Radburn' layout (with vehicle/pedestrian segregation) and traditional elevations; and in 1973, the 15-house Townfoot development in Dreghorn was designed as an irregular, rendered group, with 'vernacular' dark window margins. In the east, the 'first experiment' of this policy was a small extension to Hillpark, built in two phases between 1973 and 1977. These two developments were tentative in style, and influenced not so much by the historic-burgh school of Scottish modernism as by some contemporary or slightly earlier work in England. Hillpark Loan (1973-75) was a 25-dwelling group of flat-roofed, buff brick houses in staggered terraces, punctuated by brick projecting garages and timber canopies, and heavily landscaped with rocks and shrubs. With its tile-hung detailing, it strongly resembled the medium-density 'Span' developments of private housing around courtyards, designed by Eric Lyons, built from the late 1950s in south-east London and elsewhere. Hillpark Wood (1976-77), designed by Bruce Mickel, was a 55-dwelling group of terraced houses and flats in one- and two-storey groups loosely arranged around courtyards. The blocks were an interesting hybrid of contemporary Scottish and English low-rise housing design, with upper-floor white timber cladding and dark brickwork recalling the East Anglian work of Tayler & Green or Norwich City Architect David Percival, and their areas of harled walling, pantiled pitched roofs and external staircases evoking the Scottish historic-burgh tradition. Hillpark Wood was the winner of the NHBC's award for the best-designed private housing scheme (higher-price category) in Scotland in the 1970s.

At the same time, however, in the middle of the 1970s, the fully-fledged Mactaggart & Mickel 'Scottish vernacular style' of Modern housing with harling and pitched roofs was also being developed. One of the pioneering examples in the east was the Bonaly Brae development (1974-75); here a style of harled courtyard vernacular, with swept down roofs, dormers, arched pends and dark window margins, was applied to a conservation-sensitive location on the edge of the Pentland Hills and the villa suburb of Colinton. The showpiece of this pattern was the multi-phase greenfield development at South Gyle, on the western outskirts of Edinburgh. This was a project of some 750 houses of relatively low selling prices, and in socio-economic terms differed little from Broomhall and Forrester Park. Its architectural and planning concept was very different, however. It was designed by L A Rolland and Bruce Mickel, Rolland being a Leven-based and Dundee-trained architect who was steeped in the historic-burgh school of Modernism, as applied to council housing (for example, at Provost's Land, Leslie, 1975, and housing at Newburgh in the early 1980s). The layout focused on a round 'village green', ringed by residential zones planned into culs de sac linked by paths.

The South Gyle housing itself, built from 1979 onwards, was arranged in irregular terraces in courtyard-like groups with a strong sense of visual enclosure, punctuated at the junctions by miniature four-storey 'tower houses' of small flats. Of the houses on sale in the 224-dwelling South Gyle Mains section, released in 1984, prices ranged from £19,924 for a one-bedroom 'compact flat' of type 'JV', which featured a bedroom, living room (with kitchen and dining recesses), bathroom and store, to £36,005 for a three-bedroom end terrace house of type 'HT', with kitchen and combined dining/sitting room on the ground floor, and three

A5.17. Sales brochure for South Gyle development, March 1984. (MMC)

bedrooms and bathroom on the first floor. Every house had its own parking space, most being in rear garage courts accessible through pends. The publicity for the innovative South Gyle project had much in common with contemporary writings about public housing and the new towns, in its concern with the fostering of collective social life: 'The development is situated in a rapidly expanding area of the city ... As the development grows to the east it will incorporate more and large play areas, a central "village green", shopping and other facilities; thus enhancing the feeling of community and bringing the whole development together as a "neighbourhood"'. The development of South Gyle continued in successive phases up until 1998, with the same emphasis on medium density development. (43)

**South Gyle Mains
Site Plan**

NORTH

VILLAGE GREEN

A5.18. *Layout plan for part of South Gyle development, March 1984. (MMC)*

A5.19. Hillpark Court, Edinburgh; photograph of c.1985. (MMC)

A5.20. 1985 view of the Ascot flats, Kelvinside, designed by A Buchanan Campbell. (Glasgow Herald & Evening Times, 16 May 1985)

The same general approach was reproduced in a less ambitious form and on a smaller scale in a number of later Edinburgh developments. Just as in and around Glasgow, large-scale peripheral housing around Edinburgh was now becoming subject to greater and greater planning pressure on land, and protests from conservationist groups such as the Cockburn Association. For example, 1983 saw vociferous controversies over Barratt and Wimpey proposals at Brunstane, Maybury and Craigmillar. These pressures were less of a problem for Mactaggart & Mickel's smaller-scale developments, especially in view of their more architecturally coordinated design. At Hillpark Brae (1981-84) and the adjacent Hillpark Green, designed by Bruce Mickel in collaboration with consultants Rayack Construction Ltd of Thankerton, Lanarkshire, the South Gyle layout of a central landscaped green ringed by vernacular-style housing was built in microcosm, on a scale of less than 40 dwellings. The one- and two-storey blocks, containing houses and flats, were harled in brown and grey, with grey and red tiled roofs and large, Modernist pivot windows; the garages, with pend-like openings, formed part of the overall design. At Hillpark Court (1984-87), also designed by Rayack and Bruce Mickel and backing on to a high retaining wall of the main Queensferry Road, the same general pattern was repeated, with picturesque terraces of grey and brown harling, contrasting window margins, red and grey tiled roofs, and pend-like garage openings. In response to the historicist trends of 1980s Postmodern architecture, there was a more explicit 'heritage' character, with small-paned PVC sash windows and corbelled detailing. The cul-de-sac layout was now broken up with traffic calming elements. (44)

At the same time as these projects, other developments of a more conventional character continued to be built in both the eastern and western regions, throughout the late 1970s and the 1980s. In the east, these included 42 more houses at Forrester Park (1974-78) and 130 at East Craigs (1980-82). In the west, the only large project within Glasgow itself was the Ascot development in Great Western Road, adjacent to Whittinghame Court. This, the last

A5.21. 1982 view of renovation work in progress at Lochbroom Court (former works building); here, original slates are being selected for re-use. (MMC)

A5.22. Lochbroom Court under renovation; slaters working on roof, 1982. (MMC)

element in the staged development of this site (much delayed by undermining), comprised 121 luxury flats in a complex of three and four-storey blocks designed by Buchanan Campbell, in a red brick pitched-roof style; earlier plans of the mid 1970s for tall blocks had been scaled down in the project as built (1983). Some of the group had garages underneath, and a number of the upper flats were maisonettes with an additional top floor. Around the Broom Estate, 1982-84 saw a conservation-orientated development in the form of Lochbroom Court, a conversion of the listed former country house stables of the estate to a group of 12 houses with landscaped central courtyard, to the designs of Derek Mickel. The complex comprised £38,966 two-apartment and £79,644 three-apartment houses. (45) In 1987, a 187-dwelling development began on land at Broomcastle, with initial prices ranging from £27,931 for small 'Cunninghame' houses to £72,933 for detached three-bedroom, two-storey 'Crofthouse' villas. At almost the same time (from 1986), the nearby Mearns Croft development included 87 houses, while the slightly earlier Orchardburn infill scheme (1982-83), near the Orchard Park factory, contained 40 houses and four flats.

These relatively substantial developments were, however, exceptions to the general climate of the early and mid 1980s. This was one of repeated economic recession, which depressed sales markedly, especially in the Clydeside region. However, the underlying financial soundness of the company soon began to exert a stabilising effect. In 1980, with the recession deepening, only 66 houses were sold in the west, and there were some worries

among the directors. Douglas Mickel reported the following year that the number of houses unsold was particularly high at Whitehurst Park, Burton and West Kilbride. He argued that 'the situation would not become dangerous and that, with its good labour force and reserves, the company would come through it all right'. By 1982 the position was little better. On several sites, such as Perceton and Kirktonhall, work had virtually stopped for lack of sales, and the on-site labour force was repeatedly cut back. Regarding the 1980-81 accounts, Douglas explained that the drop in trading profits resulted from 'reductions in interest received and profits on ground sales', while the level of work-in-progress had increased by 50% 'due to the recession'; the Major Ownership Scheme operated since early 1982 (see below) had had 'a large impact on work-in-progress and liquidity' and the first resale under the scheme had 'virtually broken even'. Douglas stressed that 'as the company had had very little labour trouble and only one industrial tribunal it was important, especially when men currently value their jobs so much, to keep confidence up by keeping building'. (46)

By 1983, it was becoming clear that the underlying position was secure. The 1982 trading profit was 'very satisfactory considering the recession', with liquid funds some £2 million higher, and the 1983 trading profit was increased by a third, owing 'entirely to a much improved position in the Coast and Edinburgh'. In the accounts year ending April 1987, there was a further increase in profits before tax of over £600,000, due mainly to gains on sale of ground and investments. Douglas believed that 'profit swings were partly attributable to planning delays on the minus side and improvements in efficiency on the plus side'. These improvements included a new computerised house costing system, first implemented in Glasgow in 1988 and then extended to Edinburgh. Changes among the directors included the death of Graham Wark, and the appointment of his son, J R C Wark, in his place. Attention also turned to the redevelopment potential of the company's Glasgow city-centre headquarters site, 107 West Regent Street. After five months of discussions, it was agreed in March 1989 to appoint Bett Developments to redevelop the site, and (in September of that year) to buy in its place, for £2,700,000, a smaller central property, 126 West Regent Street, which would be 'ideal for our head offices'. (47)

This combination of sluggish sales (owing to the recession and increasing competition in the west) with a sound underlying capital base prompted extensive discussions within the firm on how to proceed. It seemed essential to avoid any initiatives that might over-extend the company at the cost of higher tax liabilities. One possibility explored in the early 1980s was to invest some of the firm's resources in joint ventures with the public housing sector - the 'convergence' advocated by Bruce Mickel in his 1983 lecture. In 1981-83, Douglas Mickel became involved in the discussions about public-private upgrading of Edinburgh's troubled West Pilton scheme, a project which would of course indirectly benefit the company's own interests in the adjacent East Pilton area, where house sales had been much lower than at Colinton and Carrick Knowe. Encouraged by developer John Mackay, who had privatised the problem tower block Martello Court in 1991, Mickel entered the debate by advocating the 'homesteading' improvement method, then being developed by Glasgow District Council for its peripheral schemes, under which hard-to-let council houses would be sold piecemeal and at very low cost to

improving owners. He cited the success of the piecemeal sales policy of the company's own Edinburgh rental estates, and argued that this would avoid the 'ghetto situation' created by emptying entire council schemes at once. Douglas Mickel also made a tour of Swiss housing in 1980, where he noted the lack of obvious class segregation in housing, and the extensive mixed tenure suburbs and blocks of flats. However, at that stage the extensive 'partnership' mechanisms later created by the government to facilitate private investment in Scottish public housing regeneration did not yet exist. Another possibility explored was that of diversification, either into other companies, or into agricultural or commercial development: in 1987, for example, the board agreed to invest £75,000 in a new biochemicals company, Biomac Ltd, and in 1988 an £8,000 sponsorship deal of Stuart Gray in a Formula Ford 2000 car was arranged. (48)

But in the event, the main policy innovation of Mactaggart & Mickel in the 1980s was concerned with its traditional core activity of speculative building: the Major Ownership Scheme (MOS), introduced in 1982. This was essentially a scheme of staged purchase, under which the company retained 20% of the value of a new house on its initial sale. The purchaser paid no interest on that portion but agreed to pay back the percentage when the house was eventually sold or passed to anyone other than his/her spouse. Lord Goold explained in 1996 that the scheme had originated in the discussions about diversification during the 1980s: 'We looked at the possibility of taking over related companies and flirted with a biochemical, but we came out of that after five or six years because we just didn't have the management time to devote to it. So then we decided that what we'd really like to invest in was our own houses'. The scheme required a 'healthy cash flow to sustain, but it has enormous competitive benefits'. He estimated that, by 1996, over 85% of

A5.23. 1963 view of Mactaggart & Mickel's Glasgow headquarters at 107 West Regent Street, once the office of 19th century architect Alexander Thomson. (MMC)

purchasers were buying under MOS, and that 'over its 15 years of operation it has yielded certainly as much as it could have earned through bank interest'. His article concluded that 'to the customer, Mactaggart & Mickel is a company that puts its money where its mouth is, and shows confidence in the enduring value of the building and its location'; the scheme addressed any 'competitive weakness in the smaller comapany's cost base'. As an example of the savings in purchase price which were possible in the first years of the scheme, a £32,263 three-apartment semi-detached villa at Brisbane Glen, Largs, was reduced to £25,810 under the MOS. (49)

This policy was, in effect, a reinforcement of the traditional policy of mainstream speculative building, and the company made every effort, during the 1980s, to build up its land bank accordingly. In 1986, for example, it paid £800,000 for a flat, 40-acre site in Renfrew, suitable for a large development at the 'lower end of the market', convenient for the Glasgow motorway and the airport.

There were also complex negotiations about exchanges and part-exchanges of land - for example, with Cala Management Ltd over an exchange of a Cala equal option in land at Cammo for a Mactaggart & Mickel site at Johnsburn Road, Balerno. (50)

By the end of the 1980s, there was a growing consensus in the company that a modest but perceptible recovery in building and sales activity was underway. In the accounts for the year ending 30 April 1989, it was reported that 'trading had continued satisfactorily', with turnover increasing by over one-third, and profits more than doubling. The MOS was continuing to prove very popular, and company's investment in it was now almost £10 million. More generally, some of the excitement of the capitalist-led boom in southern England was reflected, in a more fragile form, among the business community in central Scotland. Those aspirations were bound up strongly with the confident ethos of Margaret Thatcher's government, and Jim Goold, who became chairman of the Scottish Conservative Party between 1983 and

MACTAGGART & MICKEL AT GLASGOW GARDEN FESTIVAL

Built by
Mactaggart & Mickel
as their contribution
to Glasgow Garden Festival '88
and managed by the
Scottish Milk Marketing Board

Glasgow Garden Festival 28th April - 26th September, 1988

A5.24. *The Broom Milk Bar: Mactaggart & Mickel's contribution to the 1988 Glasgow Garden Festival. (MMC)*

INSTRUCTIONS FOR BUILDING THE **MILK BAR** MODEL

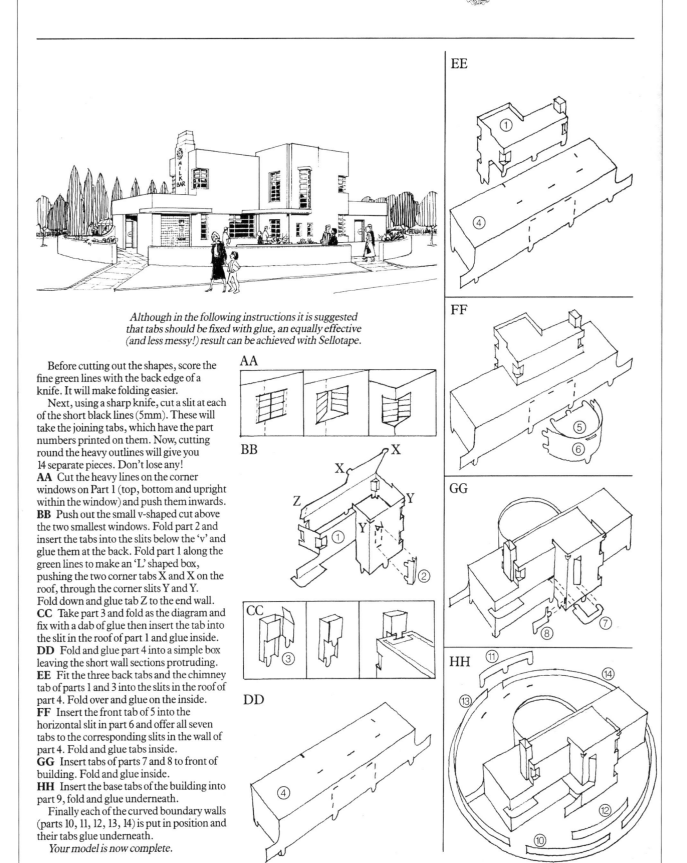

Although in the following instructions it is suggested that tabs should be fixed with glue, an equally effective (and less messy!) result can be achieved with Sellotape.

Before cutting out the shapes, score the fine green lines with the back edge of a knife. It will make folding easier.

Next, using a sharp knife, cut a slit at each of the short black lines (5mm). These will take the joining tabs, which have the part numbers printed on them. Now, cutting round the heavy outlines will give you 14 separate pieces. Don't lose any!

AA Cut the heavy lines on the corner windows on Part 1 (top, bottom and upright within the window) and push them inwards.

BB Push out the small v-shaped cut above the two smallest windows. Fold part 2 and insert the tabs into the slits below the 'v' and glue them at the back. Fold part 1 along the green lines to make an 'L' shaped box, pushing the two corner tabs X and X on the roof, through the corner slits Y and Y. Fold down and glue tab Z to the end wall.

CC Take part 3 and fold as the diagram and fix with a dab of glue then insert the tab into the slit in the roof of part 1 and glue inside.

DD Fold and glue part 4 into a simple box leaving the short wall sections protruding.

EE Fit the three back tabs and the chimney tab of parts 1 and 3 into the slits in the roof of part 4. Fold over and glue on the inside.

FF Insert the front tab of 5 into the horizontal slit in part 6 and offer all seven tabs to the corresponding slits in the wall of part 4. Fold and glue tabs inside.

GG Insert tabs of parts 7 and 8 to front of building. Fold and glue inside.

HH Insert the base tabs of the building into part 9, fold and glue underneath.

Finally each of the curved boundary walls (parts 10, 11, 12, 13, 14) is put in position and their tabs glue underneath.

Your model is now complete.

A5.25. Template for a model of the Broom Milk Bar - one of numerous advertising devices used to promote the pavilion. (MMC)

1990, was at the heart of the attempts to promote that message in Scotland, in combination with a trenchant opposition to parliamentary devolution. He was knighted in 1983 and made a life peer in 1987. During the Thatcher years, the message of revived laissez-faire capitalism seemed a very unpopular cause across Scottish society as a whole; ironically, it was only at the end of the 1990s and under a Labour government, almost a decade after both Goold and Thatcher had stepped down from their leadership positions, that the free-market system finally gained

consensus support across the Scottish political spectrum. Mactaggart & Mickel supported this position by stepping up their annual donations to the Conservative Party from £10,000 in the 1980s to £30,000 by 1993. However, in the later 1990s, and especially following Goold's death, the firm moved towards an apolitical stance, and discontinued its annual donations. (51)

One of the new ways in which the government promoted the idea that the economy was now on the mend, having been set on

A5.26. Jim Goold seen with Margaret Thatcher and Malcolm Rifkind at the Broom Milk Bar in 1988. (MMC)

a sounder, free-market footing, was the succession of garden festivals in various UK cities in the late 1980s. These were intended to stimulate regeneration of derelict former industrial areas, as well as to create a climate of public optimism. Glasgow was awarded the 1988 festival, which was built on an area of disused docks in Govan. To this festival Mactaggart & Mickel made a highly distinctive contribution, in the form of a pavilion based closely on the unexecuted flat-roofed villa type designed by James Taylor for the original Broom Estate. The reincarnated pavilion was a milk bar, commissioned by the Scottish Milk Marketing Board and designed (from October 1987) by the Edinburgh architect Roger Emmerson; he had been involved, earlier in the 1980s, in the pioneering 'Scottish Thirties' research project led by Charles McKean. The brilliantly white building, officially called the 'Broom Milk Bar', was a symmetrical block with a higher front facade and a single-storey, transverse rear section with projecting semi-circular window at its centre. It was not an exact facsimile of the original house type because, internally, the room dividing walls and upper floors of the original house design were left out. This allowed a flowing, open interior, which included serving counters and seats, along with a display case containing 1930s mementoes. Outside, the complex was ringed by a white circular boundary wall, with landscaping and canopied tables inside.

The Broom Milk Bar was opened to the press on 12 April 1988, and unveiled by Dr George Roberts, a retired pathologist, who had lived on the Broom Estate since his parents had first bought a house there in 1937. Dr and Mrs Roberts arrived at the milk bar in a 1930 Morris Cowley and toasted the festival with milk cocktails; they were joined by the chairman and chief executive of the Scottish Milk Marketing Board. A week later came the official opening, by Prince Charles and Princess Diana. On this occasion, all participants were dressed in 1930s period clothes, and the prince and princess stood on the milk bar terrace to watch a fashion show staged by Frasers and compered by Viv Lumsden of the BBC. In a contemporary article, the Broom Milk Bar project was hailed by its prime mover, company developments manager Iain Drysdale, in optimistic terms very similar to those used of the 1938 Glasgow Empire Exhibition. It was to be a tonic to the Glasgow and Scottish public, to help lift them out of the years of depression: 'We're looking at where Glasgow is today, and where Glasgow was in the '30s with the Empire Exhibition; and what one could say is that, but for the Second World War, Glasgow was going into the wide blue yonder'. (52)

The 1990s: from recession to recovery

But just as the late 1930s renaissance of Glasgow was cut short by the outbreak of war, so this late 1980s optimism also proved to be short-lived, as a fresh economic recession suddenly broke at the start of the following decade, and interest rates soared. For Mactaggart & Mickel, the difficult times began with the 1990-91 sales figures, which were just over half the 1988-89 level. In February 1991, Jim Goold reported that only one house had been sold in Edinburgh in the previous three months; cuts in production were ordered at a range of estates, including

A5.27. Mactaggart & Mickel's directors in 1996: (from left) Bruce Mickel, Ronald Wark, Jim Goold and Derek Mickel. (MMC)

THERE ISN'T A SINGLE DEVELOPMENT AS GOOD AS THIS IN EDINBURGH. THERE ARE TWO.

BONALY ROAD
EXECUTIVE LIVING
Colinton

At the foot of the Pentland Hills, a characterful development with one and two bedroom flats, and three and four bedroom houses. All with lock up garage, full gas-fired central heating, fitted kitchen.

**3 & 4 bedroom homes
Prices from £85,627 (MOS*)**

SOUTH GYLE
STARTER HOMES
South Gyle Wynd, Corstorphine

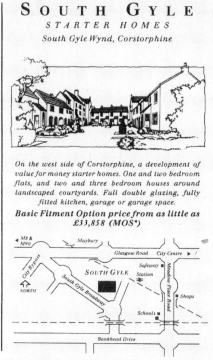

On the west side of Corstorphine, a development of value for money starter homes. One and two bedroom flats, and two and three bedroom houses around landscaped courtyards. Full double glazing, fully fitted kitchen, garage or garage space.

Basic Fitment Option price from as little as £33,858 (MOS*)

For such uncommonly distinctive develop-ments Bonaly Road and South Gyle have much in common. Both are considerately laid out around courts and courtyards. Both provide ready access to schools, shops and transport. Either one gives a splendid choice. Built in Mactaggart & Mickel's traditional, substantial manner, these are homes which draw upon local heritage for their styles. And our Major Ownership Scheme* helps you make the absolute most of your money. (You only pay 80% of the full price – ask for details.)

**18 ABERCROMBY PLACE
EDINBURGH EH3 6LB.
TELEPHONE: 031-556 4747**

**126 WEST REGENT STREET
GLASGOW G2 2BH
TELEPHONE: 041-332 0001**

Phone, write or call for Brochure and Availability/Price List.

Builders of Fine Homes

*ALSO BUILDING AT: HILLPARK PINES, CRAIGCROOK 4, 5 & 6 BEDROOM VILLAS FROM £360,000.
IN THE WEST OF SCOTLAND, NEWTON MEARNS, RUTHERGLEN, EAGLESHAM, MOUNT FLORIDA, AYR & ARDROSSAN.*

A5.28. *1991 advertisement for two Edinburgh estates: Bonaly Road (Colinton), and South Gyle. (Scotsman, 3 October 1991; MMC)*

Silverknowes, Bonaly and Hillpark. Goold expressed concern that some other builders, for example, Dickie at Giffnock, were still selling well, by offering better value for money. As the recession deepened, more cost-cutting measures were reluctantly agreed, culminating in January 1992 in the laying-off of all site operatives with the exception of trade foremen, site agents and sales staff, and any other workers urgently required. In March 1993, it was decided, as a stop-gap, to take on sub-contracted labour if required. In the middle of these tribulations, the increasing illness of Douglas Mickel forced a radical management reorganisation. Following Douglas's retiral in November 1993, Jim Goold took his place as chairman and managing director, while Derek and Bruce Mickel began to play an increasingly pivotal role in the company's affairs. In a valedictory statement of November 1993, Goold paid tribute to the 32-year chairmanship of Douglas Mickel, under whose 'immense leadership ... profits had increased virtually every year until the last one'. Four months later, a report by Goold summarised the current difficulties: '1993 was probably the most difficult the company had ever gone through. Many building companies had gone out of business, but due to measures previously taken and our tight control, we still made a small overall profit ... The fact that we are weathering the worst recession for over 50 years was in no small way due to Douglas's prudence over the years'. But once again, the underlying soundness of the company soon began to show itself. A 'respectable trading profit' of £1.4 million was reported even in 1992, and by October 1994 sales were 'progressing well'. 1995 showed a further 'tremendous improvement', with sales already up by 35% compared with the previous year, and almost all sites profitable once again. The MOS continued to prosper; by as early as 1991, the firm had sold 1,700 houses under the scheme and had made profits of £583,000 on the resale or redemption of 450 properties. (53)

A number of building projects were severely disrupted by this recession crisis. The most prominent casualty was the redevelopment of the company's old Glasgow headquarters site, 107 West Regent Street, which was cancelled in 1992. In the housing field, the drop in demand particularly affected the firm's flagship development in the east, Hillpark Pines, a luxury enclave group designed by Gray Marshall Associates and Bruce Mickel, and commenced in 1989. Hillpark Pines was located on a wooded site almost at the centre of the Hillpark group of developments. It comprised 19 large detached houses, with the first phase containing three houses of six bedrooms (costing £490,000), five of five bedrooms, and four of four bedrooms (costing £360,000); the six-bedroom houses had triple garages and the rest double garages. The layout was a cul-de-sac dotted with retained pine trees and heavy evergreen landscaping, bounded by a brick wall to emphasise the sense of privacy. Publicity described it as a 'private world ... a place of substance and character' ... 'a development of uncompromising luxury close to the heart of Scotland's capital city'. The houses themselves were explicitly historicist in style, generally recalling the turn-of-century Traditionalist villas of Robert Lorimer but with some details reminiscent of the houses of C R Mackintosh. Outside, they were harled, with complex piended and gabled patterns of steep tiled roofs, and small-paned windows. Inside, a classical columned hall was combined with a low-ceilinged crafts feel to other main rooms, including an ingleneuk and 'library corner' in the sitting room. The six bedroom house had a 'T' plan with the staircase hall at its centre, giving access to a transverse wing with sitting and dining rooms on the ground floor and guest bedrooms on the first floor; the other wing, forming the stem of the 'T', contained the family living accommodation and bedrooms. (54) During the early 1990s recession, it proved difficult to sell these luxurious houses, but with the economic recovery well underway by 1995, the estate began to sell much more readily. It received the 1995 *What House?* magazine award, and by May 1996 two more houses were being built and a fresh showhouse was opening.

The experience of the early 1990s recession had strengthened the company's determination to react prudently to the eventual upturn in the market. By the mid 1990s, numbers of large English building firms were seeking to enter the Scottish market, to exploit the government efforts to raise the (still relatively low) level of home ownership. These were mostly public rather than private companies, accountable to shareholders for continued growth, and ready to spend large amounts of (borrowed) money to obtain land. As a small but healthy private company, Mactaggart & Mickel had a more secure position than these mass builders, and greater scope for flexibility, so long as it followed cautious policies. One of the most prominent aspects of those large firms' output was their emphasis on an all-brick external style rather than the predominantly rendered exteriors of speculative housing up to the early 1980s. Part of the reason for that was architectural, with the popularisation of brick in the Postmodern buildings of the 1980s. But there were also industrial and constructional causes, in the form of the increasing industry-wide problems with roughcast from the 1970s owing to changes in materials, and the growing availability of English facing bricks to act as an alternative; the simultaneous move away from 'overhand' building from trestles inside the house carcase to the 'English' system of external scaffolding also made possible the accuracy necessary for facing brickwork. Mactaggart & Mickel's established experience in building in traditional architectural styles made them well placed to stay out of any market stampede towards all-brick styles.

In an extended interview in 1996, Lord Goold described in some detail the firm's fundamental ethos of stable growth, based on 'private ownership and conservative cash management', and on policies of 'good cash flow, careful land buying and retention of skilled manpower to produce a premium product'. Goold's overriding concern was to avoid a feckless attitude of expansionism, fuelled by debt. He argued that 'having experienced life in a private company and been a director of a few public companies, we will stay private as long as I've got anything to do with it. It's a highly desirable state to be in. Maybe

A5.29. Mactaggart & Mickel's most exclusive development of the postwar period, Hillpark Pines: view of the first six-bedroom showhouse, at 1 March Pines. (MMC)

THE DEVELOPMENT

At the foot of Corstorphine Hill, on the City side.

There's a strong sense of place to Hillpark Pines. It's a place with *atmosphere* and *personality* that speak volumes. A private place. A place of *substance* and *character*, echoing a more expensive past.

The development is sheltered from the road by a decorative boundary wall and entered from Craigcrook Road through a *fine pillared entrance*. Careful preservation of *sixty-year-old pine trees*, together with some highly imaginative new planting and landscaping, create a feeling of *real space* within this private world.

Hillpark Pines is an agreeably *low density development*. Gardens are *generously proportioned*, with walls and fences to front and rear. Each house has its *own garage:* a three-car garage for the six bedroom house and doubles for the others, with ample visitor parking.

SIX BEDROOM [TEN APARTMENT] VILLA

Six-bedroom, ten-apartment house with triple garage: a spacious and elegant family home.

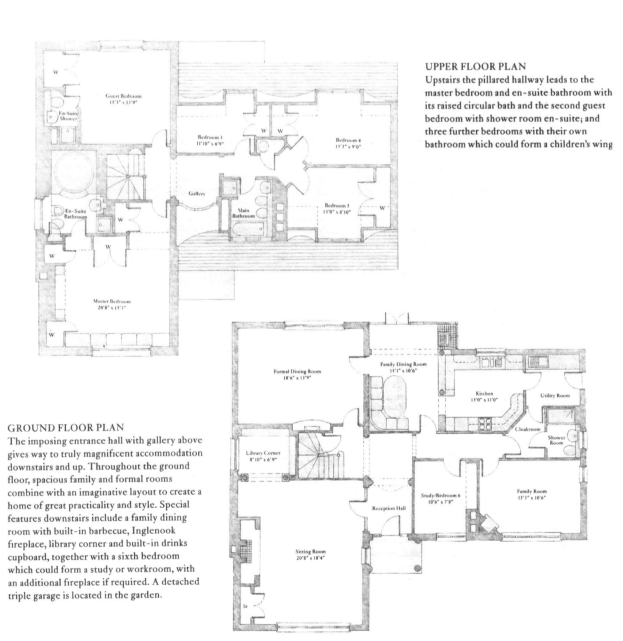

UPPER FLOOR PLAN
Upstairs the pillared hallway leads to the master bedroom and en-suite bathroom with its raised circular bath and the second guest bedroom with shower room en-suite; and three further bedrooms with their own bathroom which could form a children's wing

GROUND FLOOR PLAN
The imposing entrance hall with gallery above gives way to truly magnificent accommodation downstairs and up. Throughout the ground floor, spacious family and formal rooms combine with an imaginative layout to create a home of great practicality and style. Special features downstairs include a family dining room with built-in barbecue, Inglenook fireplace, library corner and built-in drinks cupboard, together with a sixth bedroom which could form a study or workroom, with an additional fireplace if required. A detached triple garage is located in the garden.

A5.31. 1991 sales brochure for Hillpark Pines: perspective and plans of the initial Pines showhouse. (MMC)

(opposite) A5.30. 1991 sales brochure for Hillpark Pines showing the layout of the first phase. (MMC)

IMAGINATIVE, WELL-CRAFTED DETAIL GIVES LIFE TO THE DESIGN OF THESE HOMES. IT IS THE ESSENCE OF THEIR STYLE. IT CREATES THAT VITAL DIFFERENCE BETWEEN A HOME OF CHARACTER AND THE MERELY ORDINARY, AND GIVES EACH INDIVIDUAL HOUSE A STRONG SENSE OF PERSONALITY.

SO AS WELL AS DOWNSTAIRS SHOWER ROOMS, SEPARATE CLOAKROOMS, REALLY USEFUL FAMILY ROOMS, PRACTICAL UTILITY ROOMS, LOTS OF BATHROOMS AND SOME STUNNING KITCHENS, THERE ARE SOME SURPRISES TOO. THESE ARE JUST A SELECTION:

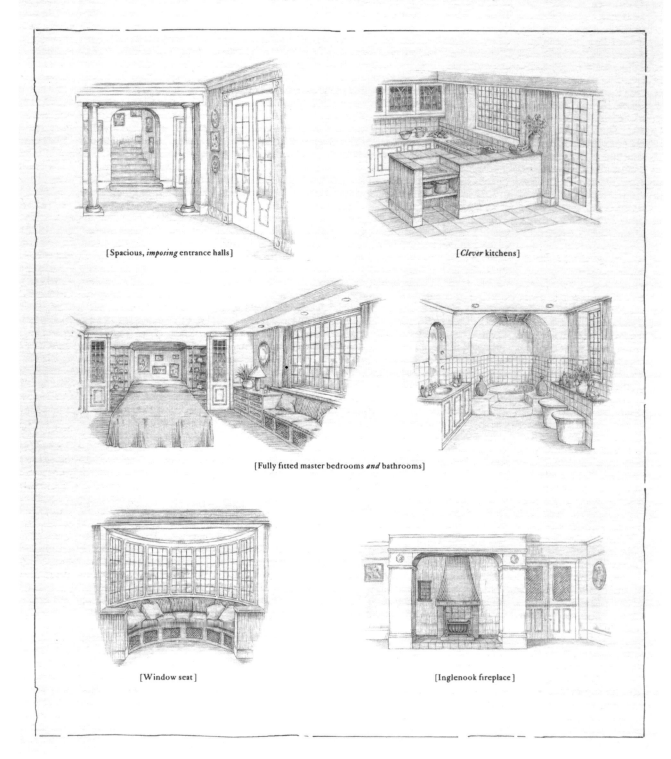

[Spacious, *imposing* entrance halls]

[*Clever* kitchens]

[Fully fitted master bedrooms *and* bathrooms]

[Window seat]

[Inglenook fireplace]

A5.32. Extract from sales brochure for Hillpark Pines, illustrating the 'luxury' interiors. (MMC)

some would say it's unadventurous but over the last 30 years I think we've been proved right time and time again'. With a 1995 turnover from house sales of around £9.5 million, and letting income adding just under £1 million, the firm was small by comparison with the London-based giants, but it sought to 'differentiate itself through quality and by taking advantage of its singular strengths'. Foremost among the latter was the insistence of traditional building methods, with timber-framing avoided completely. Land acquisition, in Goold's opinion, also had to follow a different course from the large firms, with the emphasis on steady turnover: 'Each year Mactaggart & Mickel tries to buy as much land as it has used during the same period, maintaining a bank of around five years worth of development land, and the policy has nourished the company through many ups and downs over the years'. But 'in recent years a lot of English builders have come in, paid what we consider very silly prices for land and put

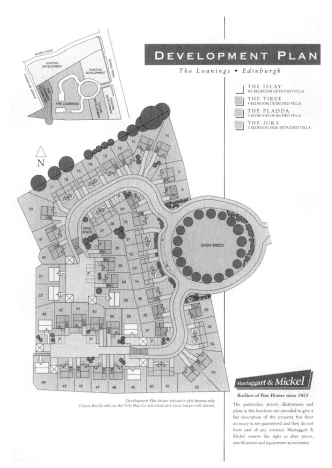

A5.33. Sales brochure layout plan for the Loanings development, Edinburgh, 1998. (MMC)

A5.34. Sales brochure for the Loanings, Edinburgh; view of the three-bedroomed 'Jura' type, 1998. (MMC)

prices up to what I think are unrealistic levels. As a result we haven't been as successful at replenishing our land stocks as we would like. We are very actively looking for land in the Edinburgh area and if we don't get some soon, then inevitably our output in the east will reduce. Again, we are in a fortunate position in that we have cash - if we see something we like we can pay for it - but we are not prepared to pay stupid prices'. As the cost of land was a major part of total cost of any development, 'by refusing to enter a bidding war Mactaggart & Mickel has been able to maintain its margins'. In fact, the firm was prepared to sell parts of its land bank that were in demand by larger firms: for example, a Murrayfield site in Edinburgh with planning permission only for flats was sold in 1991, because an excessive initial outlay would have been required, while sections of the Renfrew site bought in 1986 were resold at a profit in 1993, including one part bought by Wimpey for £1,740,000. The other main development cost, that of materials and labour, had been radically reduced by computer-led cuts in wastage. The materials needed for a site could be precisely inventorised and monitored, and plant could be scheduled centrally rather than allocated piecemeal to each site. Employee numbers had been cut by 60%, to a total of 250, over the three years since 1993, although the company was building almost as many houses as it did before. This allowed Mactaggart & Mickel to continue its policy, unusual in the 1990s, of employing most of its workers directly, including a number with service of over 25 years. The overall aim, Goold concluded, was a stability which would avoid 'the worst of the building industry's boom and bust cycle' ... 'It's the advantage of being a private company - we don't have to be continually growing and getting more and more return to pay a rising dividend every year'. (55)

The firm's activities during the mid 1990s were all attuned to that aim of stable growth. Following Lord Goold's death in July 1997, John Craig was appointed chairman; he had previously worked closely with the company as an accountant with KPMG. The accounts for 1997-98 showed a healthy increase in turnover, following good sales at estates in Clarkston and the coast towns. In Edinburgh, planning restrictions and an overheating market kept down the level of building, but ensured speedy sales of whatever was built. For example, the last of the original 19 houses at Hillpark Pines was sold in 1998, but over thirty people had already put their names down for a planned follow-on development; the drive for higher density in Edinburgh prompted a 1997 proposal for a further Hillpark extension including luxury blocks of flats. In 1995-98, an estate of 86 mews flats and terraced villas priced from £44,992 (MOS) was built at Gilmerton, and in 1998 a development of 56 houses was commenced at The Loanings, Bonaly, their harled 'vernacular' style echoing the earlier development there. The smallest house-type was the £106,471 three-bedroom 'Jura', a semi-detached villa. Perhaps the most dramatic policy development in Edinburgh during the mid 1990s was concerned not with new houses but with the remainder of Mactaggart & Mickel's rental stock. The move towards market rents and letting decontrol in the private rented sector led the company to the radical step of reversing its 40 year old policy of selling the Edinburgh rental properties. As early as 1990, Mactaggart & Mickel had been considering re-letting houses under 'assured tenancies', but the decision was deferred and the Edinburgh maintance squad was disbanded during the recession. By 1994, the decision was under review, and in 1995, it was decided to begin re-letting houses, initially at Carrick Knowe and Colinton, with an expected annual rent of £4,000 for each dwelling; by 1996 a heavy modernisation programme was underway on these estates. (56)

A5.35. *The marketing of tradition: advertisement for developments in Edinburgh in 1997.* (ESPC Newsletter, *25 July 1997; MMC*)

In the west, on the other hand, the emphasis was still on new development; standard types were still being developed for developments south of Glasgow and on the coast, some of a markedly up-market character; most sales in these areas were now through the MOS. Architecturally, there was a consistent concern to mark off these houses from the all-brick styles introduced by the English firms, either by stylistic adaptations to the conventional villa and bungalow types, or by introducing a more unified architectural approach influenced by the 1970s and '80s Edinburgh innovations. Extensions of the Broom Estate in the mid 1990s included a 132-house development at Castlefarm (1994-98) on normal detached and semi-detached lines, ranging from the £73,146 three-bedroom 'Jura' villa to the £133,600 five-bedroom 'Islay'. The Dell, Broom Road East (from 1998), was a very different cul-de-sac development of 69 houses, which in some ways resembled Hillpark Court or Bonaly, with its harling, window-margins, open access stairs and arched garage pends. This estate was a strong contrast to the massed brick ranks of some builders' developments in the central belt. It contained a combination of one and two-bedroom luxury flats and three-bedroom terraced houses. The smallest house-type, the £60,000 one-bedroom 'Skye', was offered in the alternative forms of a semi-detached or terraced cottage, and a mews flat above ground-floor parking. Internally, the 'Skye' was similar in plan to the one-bedroom 'JV' at South Gyle in the 1980s (with its lounge and kitchen/dining alcoves, and its separate small bedroom and bathroom), but all the rooms were rather larger.

A different type of distinctiveness derived from the way in which some standard types were restyled to evoke the 1930s speculative-building heritage. For example, the three-bedroom 'Easdale' bungalow selling for £131,330 on the Burnhouse Brae estate at Newton Mearns (1998; still part of the Kirkhill neighbourhood area), had a broad tiled roof with bracketed eaves and finials, a bay window and small panes, and was harled above a stone base; its internal plan, with central hall and corridor, was similar to interwar bungalows, but included an integral garage at one end. The same type, built in a plainer style at the Barassie development in Troon (1995-99), with brick plinth and harling above, cost

only £90,112. Increasingly, Mactaggart & Mickel interwar houses were acquiring a heritage cachet themselves, and commanded substantial prices; by 1998 the four-apartment semi-detached house-type at Orchard Park, originally sold for £525 (pictured on the cover of this book), cost £65,000. (57)

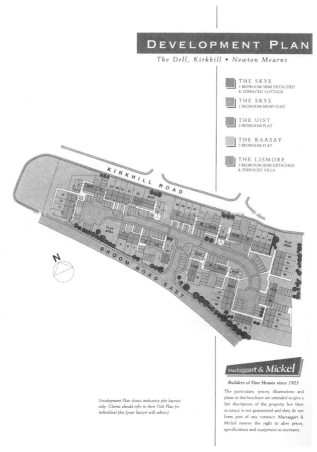

A5.36. *Sales brochure layout plan for the Dell, Kirkhill, Newton Mearns, 1998.* (MMC)

By the late 1990s, this picture of steady revival based on traditional speculative building was beginning to change, and Mactaggart & Mickel began to position itself to respond to the likely housing and planning challenges of the new century; in 1999/2000, a fifth generation of Mickel family involvement in the firm was anticipated, with Andrew (son of Derek), a qualified town-planner, due to join the company. As Kenneth Gibb explains in Chapter B5 of this book, the general governmental encouragement of private low-density housebuilding on new 'greenfield' sites outwith the cities during the 1980s and 1990s now began to give way to an environmentally-driven policy of re-using 'brownfield' land within urban areas, and to a socially-driven emphasis on collaboration (rather than competition) between public and private agencies; by 1996, it was estimated that 60% of new housebuilding in Scotland was on brownfield sites. Planners and architects also demanded that any new greenfield development should be architecturally coordinated, rather than built in repetitive lines. These were very similar ideas to those advocated by Douglas and Bruce Mickel back in the early 1980s - but now they had government backing. The firm's response was to embark on a new phase of innovation, including the prospect of involvement in urban regeneration and in a more architecturally sensitive method of greenfield building, fitting into overall 'masterplans' at a somewhat higher density rather than sprawling haphazardly together. (58)

The pioneer of the new greenfield approach was a development proposal for an extensive site named 'The Drum', situated on the southern outskirts of Bo'ness, looking across towards Linlithgow. Here the firm was returning to its 19th-century origins, and doing so in close co-operation with a local landowner (William Cadell) who himself had longstanding roots in the area. The proposed Mactaggart & Mickel development of 244 houses, which formed

the first phase of a wider masterplan by Alan Jeffrey of Anderson Jeffrey Associates, was designed by the architect Roan Rutherford (of the firm of Wren Rutherford ASL). As one of the principal designers of Irvine New Town Development Corporation from the 1970s to the 1990s, Rutherford had been one of the standard-bearers, in those decades, of the continuing 'Scottish vernacular Modernist' tradition of public housing design, following in the footsteps of Anthony Wheeler, Robert Hurd and others. In 1996, following the abolition of the last new town corporations and the effective end of public housing architecture in Scotland, Rutherford moved into private practice with George Wren. Now he was able to apply the lessons of coordinated architectural design and sensitivity to context, at reasonably high density, to private housing. From Mactaggart and Mickel's perspective, this project represented an updating of the 1970s and 1980s initiatives at South Gyle and elsewhere. (59)

The proposed layout at the Drum conformed to the masterplan requirement that the urban form should focus on an existing farm, sitting on the summit of the site; its density was a relatively high 46 houses per hectare. A network of four mixed vehicle/pedestrian roads radiated out from that focus, with car parking in rear courts accessed by pends. The design envisaged for the houses was composed of variegated street-groups dominated by two or three storey 'gateway' blocks of flats at either end, and emphasising a sense of enclosure in the vernacular Modernist tradition, as well as echoing earlier buildings in an adjacent village. The white and off-white harling and much of the detailing, including steep roofs, asymmetrical gables, chimneys and triangular bay windows, resembled Rutherford's Harbourside housing for Irvine New Town Corporation (1995).

A5.37. Sales brochure for the Dell, Kirkhill, showing the one-bedroomed 'Skye' type flat, 1998. (MMC)

A5.38. Sales brochure of 1998 for Burnhouse Brae development, showing the three-bedroomed 'Easdale' type bungalow. (MMC)

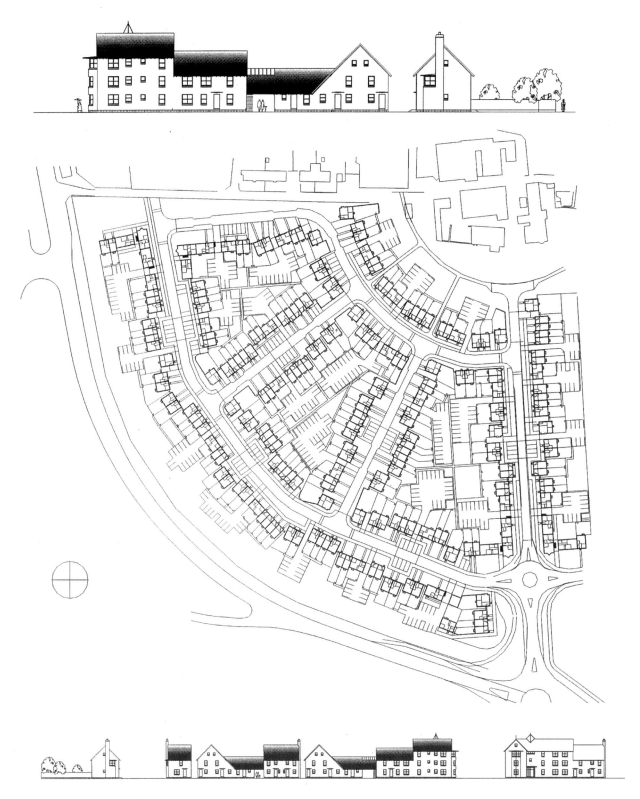

A5.39. Amended layout plan and sample elevations of 1999 for the Drum development, Bo'ness, by Wren Rutherford ASL. (MMC)

A5.40. 'Homes for the Future' 1999: early perspective sketch (c.1997) of site, seen from south, showing Mactaggart & Mickel's Wren Rutherford-designed block to the far right. (City of Architecture & Design: Glasgow 1999)

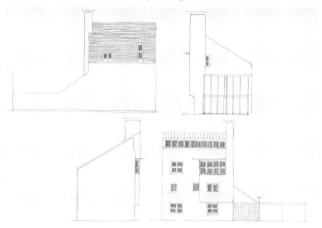

A5.41. 'Homes for the Future' project: early pencil sketch of c.1997 by Roan Rutherford, showing the elevations of the proposed block. (Wren Rutherford ASL)

Rutherford was also the architect for the firm's venture into the even more unfamiliar and exciting territory of inner city brownfield regeneration projects, at the 'Homes for the Future' experimental housing area built on the edge of Glasgow Green, as part of the 'Glasgow 99' architecture and design festival. Glasgow's successful bid to hold this international festival had specially emphasised the city's commitment to community-based housing initiatives, and the project's sense of collective social purpose made a telling contrast with the fun-loving frivolity of the Garden Festival eleven years earlier. Appropriately, Mactaggart & Mickel's contribution on this occasion was not a milk bar but a block of flats. It formed part of an irregularly-shaped, three-stage redevelopment area of medium/high density housing, funded by private and public regeneration agencies working together and masterplanned by David Page of Page & Park. Within this framework, each individual building was an experimental design by a different

architect, with the emphasis on innovative dwelling types to cater for new types of urban households and styles of living.

Most of the blocks in the 100-unit first phase of Homes for the Future were commissioned by development companies and housing associations specialising in urban sites. Architecturally, they mainly comprised flats or townhouses in compressed rows or towers, designed in the revived Modernist style that had become ascendant in the late 1990s. The Mactaggart & Mickel block, in Lanark Street, was rather different in character, although of the same height, four floors, as its neighbours. It was designed by Rutherford (who was appointed in October 1997) in the same geometric, white rendered style as the Irvine housing and the proposed Bo'ness estate, with prominent asymmetrical roof and chimney, and overtones of the 'Scottish vernacular' tradition. Inside were two experimental flats, intended to explore new ideas of energy sustainability and flexible living in the city in the 21st century. On the ground floor was a barrier-free house suitable for a disabled occupant, containing living room with kitchen alcove, bedroom, and shower-room, and including recharging facilities for a powered wheelchair. The upper floors, as eventually built, comprised a triplex house, with two bedrooms on the first floor, a living/work area above, and the kitchen located in the gallery above the lounge. A number of technologically innovative energy-saving features were included in the house, including highly insulated walls, special open flue fires, and photovoltaic roof tiles. It was ironical that this relatively modestly scaled and styled building should be more technologically advanced than all the other, more assertively Modernist styled blocks around it! (60)

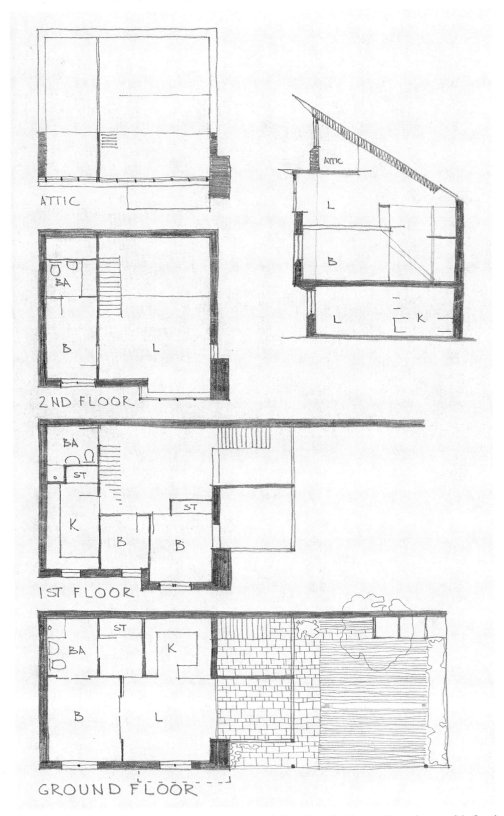

ATTIC

2ND FLOOR

1ST FLOOR

GROUND FLOOR

A5.42. 'Homes for the Future' project, early pencil sketch of c.1997 by Roan Rutherford showing plans and section of the flatted block. (Wren Rutherford ASL)

Conclusion

With its contribution to the Homes for the Future project, Mactaggart & Mickel had come full circle, returning to the denser, more urban contexts of the work of Robert and Andrew Mickel and John Mactaggart a century earlier - although the freestanding, tower-like form of the 1999 block, with its attached private courtyard for garden or parking, and its entrance conservatories to the houses, was very different from the wall-like inflexibility of the tenement, and was potentially just as suitable for suburban sites as for small urban infills. What had not changed throughout this entire story of over a hundred years was the readiness to embrace innovative solutions while keeping a firm footing in continuity and tradition - a formula which seemed well suited to the challenges and uncertainties of the coming century.

A5.43. 'Homes for the Future': visit to the construction site by delegates of the Royal Incorporation of Architects in Scotland Annual Convention, 29 May 1999. From left to right: the Mactaggart & Mickel block (designed by Wren Rutherford ASL); a block built by Dickie Ltd for Thenew Housing Association (designed by Ian Ritchie); and the stepped block by Ushida Findlay, architects, built for the Burrell Housing Co. by contractor Ballast Wiltshier. (M Glendinning).

Notes

1   Information from J Craig, May 1999; MMASB.
2   Information from Gordon MacInnes and Iain Drysdale, June 1999; interview with Matthew Dickie, 9 April 1999; information from J Geoffrey Keanie, May 1999.
3   MMA, memo of December 1962.
4   *Dispatch*, 8 November 1962; 'Trying his utmost': information from Iain Drysdale, March 1999; *The Edinburgh Tatler*, July 1963.
5   *The Edinburgh Tatler*, July 1963; MM Minutes, 11 October 1961, 3 November 1961; *Largs News*, 27 July 1962.
6   *Speculative Builder and Property News*, December 1960.
7   *Daily Mail*, 1 August 1963; *The Scotsman*, 1 August 1963; *EN*, 26 June 1968; *EN*, 29 March 1969.
8   MMA, MM memo of 19 May 1971; MMASB; *EN*, 20 September 1962; *EN*, 17 December 1962; *EN*, 22 November 1962, *Dispatch*, 23 November 1962; *EN*, 12 February 1963; *Fine Homes by Mactaggart & Mickel*, *c*. 1963; MMASB; *Grangemouth Advertiser*, 22 February 1963; *The Edinburgh Tatler*, July 1963.
9   *Scottish Field*, March 1963; *Fine Homes by Mactaggart & Mickel*, *c*.1963.
10 MMA, MM memo of December 1962; information from Iain Drysdale, March 1999.
11 *Evening Citizen*, 5 April 1963; *New Homes*, October 1963.
12 *Evening Citizen*, 31 October 1967.
13 *Evening Citizen*, 31 October 1967; MMA, MM memo of 22 May 1968; A F L Deeson (ed.), *The Comprehensive Industrialised Building Systems Annual*, 1965, 210-11.
14 *ET*, 14 June 1962, 12 October 1962; information from Iain Drysdale, May 1999.
15 *Evening Citizen*, 11 January 1963; MMAEPB, March 1964; *Paisley Pictorial*, 2 November 1961; *New Homes*, October 1963.
16 MMASB; *Fine Homes by Mactaggart & Mickel*.
17 *Ardrossan and Saltcoats Herald*, 23 March 1962; *Kilmarnock Evening Standard*, 12 November 1960; *Scottish Daily Mail*, 31 January 1963; MM Minutes, 17 December 1969.
18 *GH*, 18 October 1961; *Bulletin*, 3 November 1961.
19 MMA, Douglas Mickel paper, February 1964; *Glasgow Illustrated*, March 1968; *The Scotsman*, 30 August 1967; MMA, paper, 'A summary of some housing statistics for Scotland - sales, design and construction considerations', 26 October 1970.
20 MM Minutes, 22 August 1966, 30 September 1966, 20 February 1969, 18 December 1969, 5 September 1966, 29 November 1967.
21 Information from Iain Drysdale, March 1999.
22 MM Minutes, 28 January 1970.
23 *Scottish Sunday Express*, 7 January 1968, 11 July 1968; *Edinburgh Weekly*, 29 February 1968; *Glasgow Illustrated*, March 1968.
24 *Edinburgh Weekly*, 19 July 1968; *Bulletin*, 11 July 1968; *EN*, 13 September 1968.
25 MM Minutes, 17 December 1969, 8 June 1970, 19 June 1972, 30 October 1969, 13 November 1969, 19 November 1969.
26 MMASB; *Edinburgh Weekly*, 29 February 1968; *GH*, 27 October 1963, *Daily Express*, 19 June 1969; MMA, price lists for March 1967 and March 1971 and house particulars from *c*.1973.
27 MMA, undated 1968 cutting from *The Mercury*; *Scottish Daily Express*, 5 September 1969.
28 *Scottish Daily Express*, 5 September 1969.
29 MM Minutes, 19 June 1972, 27 June 1973.
30 MM Minutes, 5 March 1975, 8 September 1976, 18 May 1977, 12 April 1978, 9 June 1980.
31 MM Minutes, 29 December 1971, 18 November 1974, 27 November 1978; *GH*, 7 January 1975.
32 Letter from J Goold to Douglas Mickel, 19 September 1972; MM Minutes, 24 May 1978, 29 November 1978.
33 Mickel Products Ltd Minutes, 21 April 1971, 2 August 1971, 2 April 1973, 24 April 1974; MM Minutes, 12 May 1975; information from Iain Drysdale, April 1999.
34 MM Minutes, 13 July 1970, 23 July 1971, 4 August 1971, 11 August 1971, 16 July 1975, 30 June 1976, 24 October 1977, 30 April 1979, 11 May 1983, 1 March 1971; *Scottish Daily Express*, 6 August 1970.
35 MM Minutes, 27 June 1973.
36 MM Minutes, 20 July 1975, 16 July 1975; MMA, unidentified press cutting, *c*. 1977.
37 MM Minutes, 1 March 1972, 28 June 1975, 7 January 1976.
38 MM Minutes, 27 January 1971; *Daily Express*, 25 March 1970; MM Minutes, 29 April 1970, 8 June 1970, 13 July 1970.
39 MM Minutes, 18 May 1981; information from Iain Drysdale, April 1999.
40 MMA, private communication by Douglas Mickel; D McCrone and B Elliot, mid 1970s research notes for *Property and Power in the City*, published 1989.

41   Bruce Mickel, lecture to Edinburgh College of Art, 1983; *The Scotsman*, 23 August 1985; *Project*, 2 February 1975.

42   Bruce Mickel, *Prospect*, January 1981.

43   Hillpark Wood, NHBC: *GH*, 1 November 1979. MMA, South Gyle Road advertising booklet, March 1984.

44   *EN*, 18 September 1991; MMASB.

45   MM Minutes, 21 January 1975; MMASB.

46   MM Minutes, 18 May 1981, 1 October 1982, 15 October 1982, 3 November 1982.

47   MM Minutes, 22 July 1983, 22 February 1988, 30 November 1988, 6 February 1989, 6 March 1989, 29 September 1989.

48   MMA, letter of 9 December 1981 from John Mackay to Douglas Mickel; letter of 27 January 1983 from D Mickel to Edinburgh Director of Housing; MMA, Report by D Mickel, 27 April 1980; MM Minutes, 24 May 1987, 14 December 1987.

49   *Scotland in Business*, November 1996, 37-40; *Mactaggart & Mickel 1925-85: Sixty Years of Building*, 1985.

50   MM Minutes, 22 January 1986, 27 January 1986, 24 February 1986, 31 October 1988.

51   MM Minutes, 29 January 1990; Goold obituaries, *Daily Telegraph* and *The Times*, 1 August 1997; *The Herald*, 29 July 1997 and 2 August 1997.

52   W Jack, *What Home? Scotland*, June/July 1988; Scottish Milk Marketing Board, *The Broom Milk Bar*, 1988.

53   MM Minutes, 22 May 1990, 27 February 1991, 1 May 1991, 27 November 1991, 10 March 1993, 10 November 1993, 2 February 1994, 13 February 1991, 5 October 1994, 8 February 1995.

54   *The Scotsman*, 20 June 1991; MM Minutes, 24 June 1992.

55   *Scotland in Business*, November 1996, 37-40; MM Minutes, 27 February 1991, 27 March 1991, 18 September 1991, 5 February 1992, 3 March 1993, 17 December 1993.

56   *Scotland on Sunday*, 5 April 1998; MM Minutes, 22 January 1997; *EN*, 23 June 1997; MM Minutes, 11 February 1997, 8 December 1997, 30 November 1998, 29 January 1990, 12 September 1990, 13 January 1995, 10 August 1995; *The Scotsman*, 17 September 1998.

57   *The Herald*, 21 January 1998.

58   *The Herald*, 25 June 1996.

59   Letter about the Drum project, 2 June 1999, from Wren Rutherford ASL.

60   Glasgow 1999, *Glasgow's Homes for the Future*, 1999; information from R Rutherford, 1999.

Part B

The Modern Scottish Housebuilding Industry
● A Historical Overview

○

○

BUILDING DEVELOPMENT

Urbanisation and the Housing of the Scottish People, 1800-1914

Richard Rodger

Introduction

The Scottish urban system experienced considerable change in the course of the 18th century, as a result of seismic shifts in production, trade and political relations. (1) New towns, founded as part of the efforts to pacify the Highlands, and new estate villages, established in association with changed agricultural practices and improved productivity, both affected patterns of settlement in most areas. Important as these changes were, they were overshadowed by the spectacular growth of imports and re-exports as the effects of Scotland's admission to the Union, and native business acumen, combined to reorientate the commercial outlook of the country from the Baltic and North Seas to the Atlantic. (2) As the American colonies shipped rising volumes of cotton, sugar and tobacco to west of Scotland ports, so small burghs and county towns flourished from the ripple effects of economic growth enjoyed by Glasgow and its immediate hinterland. In the late 18th century, four of the five fastest-growing towns in Scotland were located in the Clyde basin. (3)

This mercantile transformation was complemented by an industrial one. Although Scottish industrialists and inventors made their own distinctive contribution to the technological developments which transformed textile and metal-working, many of the research and development costs were borne by English manufacturers. It is important not to make too much of Scotland as an industrial 'late-starter', but the lag was sufficient to enable Scottish industrialists to benefit from others' experience and to enjoy a period of rapid industrialisation when it did eventually materialise in the late 18th century. So, as the country entered the 19th century, significant productivity gains were enjoyed from the application of steam power to industrial processes, from economies of scale derived from a transition towards larger-scale factory production and from the increasing returns obtained by exploiting previously inaccessible coal and iron-ore fields. Agricultural productivity increases were equally crucial, not least since they generated sufficient food supplies for an increasing urban population. For the entrepreneur and investor, that is, for a rising group of middle class interests, the expanding burghs, notably of west-central Scotland, offered opportunities for profits, dividends and rents. For the labourer, employment in the ports, mining villages and industrial towns was a powerful magnetic force attracting those displaced successively by Hanoverian pacification, agricultural 'revolution', the Sutherland clearances, and across the Irish Sea, by famine.

Scottish industrialisation, therefore, had assumed a sufficient momentum in the early and mid-19th century to attract large numbers of migrants from highland and lowland Scotland, as well as many from Ulster and southern Ireland. (4) In short, the reorientation of trade and industry enabled otherwise moribund settlements to be reinvigorated, stimulated the foundation of new towns such as Motherwell and, later, Clydebank, and injected a new vitality into ancient burghs such as Paisley and Renfrew. The nature of urban settlement contributed to, but was also fundamentally reshaped by, the inter-related processes of mercantile and industrial change. The population of Glasgow quadrupled and that of Paisley doubled between 1801 and 1841; in Edinburgh and Leith, the increased population in these four decades was itself greater than the size of the burghs in 1800. Whereas in 1800, 20% of Scots lived in towns of 5,000 or more inhabitants, by 1861 the proportion was 40% and by 1901 almost 60%. (5) Although many smaller towns were transformed by the influx of population, predictably it was the cities which were most affected. In 1851, one in five Scots lived in the four cities, Glasgow, Edinburgh, Dundee and Aberdeen, and by 1911 the ratio was one in three. Put differently, the population increase of the four cities during the 19th century was equivalent to the creation of ten new Glasgows, five new Dundees and Aberdeens, and four new Edinburghs.

By 1911, with 50% of the population living in towns of 20,000 or more, Scots were a more urbanised nation than any other in the world, except for England. Together, natural increase and migration produced a 48% increase in the population of burghs with over 5,000 people between 1831 and 1861 and a further 113% increase between 1861 and 1901. In today's terms, this would be like raising the Scottish population to 8 million by the year 2030 and then to over 17 million by 2060.

In the 19th century an equivalent increase was absorbed with only sketchy powers governing building bylaws and planning controls. In the ancient royal burghs, residual powers governing 'nichtbourheid' interests - the infringement of light, ventilation or dangerous structures - were retained by the Dean of Guild Courts, but the terms of reference of these institutions rendered them unsuited to the scale and pace of 19th-century change. As a result, the Courts became arbiters of property infringements rather than a vanguard of environmental planning and building control. (6) Only with the Burgh Police Act of 1862 and subsequent legislation did the cities and larger burghs reinvigorate their Dean of Guild Courts, by adding to their powers over building standards. Thus the administrative vacuum was at its greatest precisely when Scottish urban population increase was advancing at unprecedented levels. (7)

To house the rapid population expansion of the 19th century put immense strain on existing accommodation. In the short term,

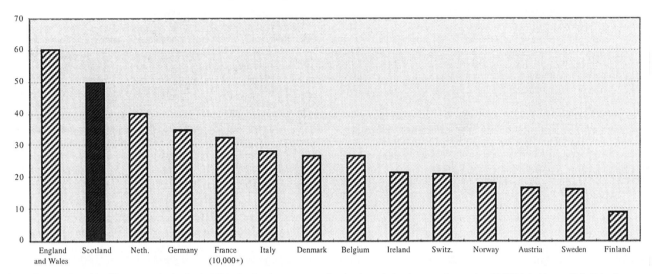

B1.1. *Comparative table of European urbanisation in 1911, showing the percentage of national population in towns of more than 20,000 inhabitants. (J De Vries,* European Urbanisation 1500-1800, *1984, 39-48)*

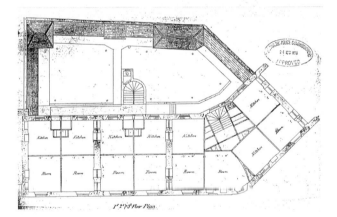

B1.2. *1873 plans for block of two working class tenements erected at Milnbank Road and Laurence Street, Dundee, by developer Reoch & Meldrum; plans by architects Young & Meldrum. The block contains two-apartment flats; the WCs are shared and located at staircase landings. In one tenement, the flats are reached by the typical Dundee external rear staircase and balconies. In contrast to the dense layouts of Continental tenements, this Scottish block occupies only the front strip of the site, leaving an open court to the rear, and allowing through ventilation of most flats. That type of layout was generally enforced following the Burgh Police (Scotland) Act of 1862 by the urban regulation authorities; in most towns, the responsible authority was the Dean of Guild Court, but in Dundee it was the Police Commissioners. (RCAHMS)*

flats were 'made-down' or sub-divided, floor space was shared, and common lodging houses originally intended as short-stay accommodation for single persons new to the city became long-term accommodation, often for families. For an emerging urban industrial working class with low and irregular wages new housing was both scarce and unaffordable; builders and developers, given the substantial capital and time required to build tenements, were unable to respond quickly, even if they judged it profitable. Consequently, in the first half of the 19th century the initial phase of urban expansion was met largely by a more intensive use of existing properties and plots within the ancient burghs. Merchants' houses were demolished and the plots redeveloped, as in Edinburgh's Cowgate; courtyards and gardens were built over. Two hundred year old houses were adapted by a process which meant that 'The large rooms of an earlier upper class were divided by wooden partitions into family apartments ...[so that] these inner cages had no direct communication even with a modicum of air and light that filtered in from the arms-breadth wynds'. (8) In the ports, sites adjacent to the waterfront commanded a sizeable premium for their proximity to warehouses and commercial offices, and in Leith and Dundee, as in many other burghs, existing land and buildings were developed intensively in the 1820s and 1830s.

Inevitably, as dwellings were subjected increasingly to overcrowding and sanitary arrangements shared by large numbers of occupants, there followed a progressive physical degradation of the housing stock. More seriously, at least in the minds of the urban middle classes, the closes and wynds of Scottish burghs, which as minor thoroughfares had contributed previously to the porous texture of Scottish urban life, were rendered by the 1840s into no-go areas as densely packed tenements blocked out light and air. With foul smells and concern for personal safety in these warrens of alleys and darkened passages, their instinct for survival told those who could afford to do so to quit the central areas. (9)

As the density of building increased to accommodate newcomers to the cities and major burghs, so the tenement backlands became badlands, riddled with structural faults and insanitary defects. Densely packed tenement dwellers were particularly exposed to epidemic disease and consequently to high mortality rates; cholera epidemics in 1832, 1848-49 and 1853-54 drew attention to the public health risks associated with the intensive tenement developments of Scottish towns and cities. (10) By national and international standards, housing standards in Scottish burghs stood indicted. In relation to Edinburgh, William Chambers, publisher, concluded in 1840 that 'the construction of the town is radically unfavourable to health' and the absence of water closets either within tenements or in back courts meant that the 'excrementitious matter of some forty or fifty thousand individuals is daily thrown into the gutters, at certain hours appointed by the police, or poured into carts which are sent about the principal streets'. (11) As part of his tour of British cities, Friedrich Engels commented in 1844 that the 'brilliant aristocratic quarter [of

Edinburgh's New Town]... contrast[ed] strongly with the foul wretchedness of the poor of the Old Town', (12) a view which only reinforced that of Dr Neil Arnott, the Edinburgh respondent for Edwin Chadwick's best-selling report (1842), who stated that the most wretched living conditions in the country were to be found in the wynds of Edinburgh, although those in Glasgow were also criticised severely. (13)

Amongst the residential responses to the escalating dirt, disease and depravity of urban life was the development of a new spatial arrangement, the suburb, of which the Edinburgh New Town, begun in 1767 but taking almost a century to complete, is the best known and most extensive example. (14) This was a middle and upper-middle class strategy which, by 1850 and in more modest forms, was replicated in Glasgow (Blythswood), Aberdeen (Bon-Accord) and in Leith's Charlotte Street and Hermitage

B1.5. The already highly segregated nature of late 19th century urban development is illustrated by this picture, in which a railway divides middle class housing at the top from working class housing below. By 1914, railways had acquired between 5% and 9% of urban land in the four Scottish cities. They generated employment and workers sought homes nearby. In Edinburgh, this was provided (in the foreground) by the Edinburgh Co-operative Company at Dalry (1868-71) and the private firm of James Steel at Caledonian Place, Road and Crescent (1869-74). In the background, more exclusive housing on the Coates Estate, feued by George Heriot's Trust, was built in the 1870s and 1880s. In the latter two cases, the layout is the normal perimeter street-block plan of the Scottish tenement; in the case of the Co-operative development, the layout is a hybrid of Scottish flatted and English terraced forms. (RCAHMS C10070)

B1.4. Allermuir, Colinton, Edinburgh (1879-82), home of the architect R Rowand Anderson, leader of the 'Traditionalist' movement, which championed the moral primacy of the individual home. Anderson built Allermuir and seven other villas on the Gillespie estate between 1878 and 1898. To ensure exclusivity, plot sizes of half an acre or more, and minimum prices averaging £1,125, were specified by the original landowners in their feu dispositions to Anderson. In this view, Anderson is visible playing golf in his garden. (RCAHMS ED/15556)

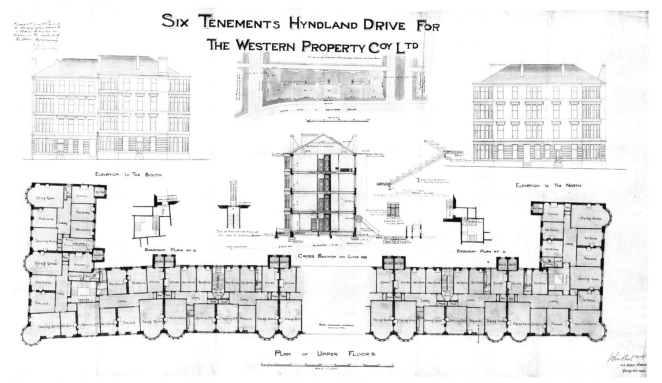

B1.3. A typical middle class tenement development of the turn-of-century, built in the exclusive Glasgow suburb of Hyndland by the Western Property Company, a development firm, and designed by architect John Short in 1898. The development occupies half of a street block, with the usual large court and an access lane at the rear. Built in a hybrid construction of stone outer and cross walls, brick inner walls, and timber floors, the flats are designed on the through-ventilation principle, with typical Glasgow internal centre-rear staircase positioning. The houses feature much greater segregation and specialisation of space than the small working class flats; they are of five, six or seven apartments, with specific public rooms (dining room, drawing room and parlour) and internal bathroom. (Glasgow City Archives; RCAHMS GWD/161/6)

developments across the Links. Indeed, for an emerging social and professional element in Scottish burghs determined to put space and clean air between them and the contamination of the inner cities, migration to the suburbs was an appealing prospect. (15) It was a trend which gathered pace in the last third of the 19th century as suburban villas gained in appeal over neo-classical Georgian terraces. The creation of Kelvinside and Morningside, genteel suburbs in Glasgow and Edinburgh, in the second half of the 19th century were survival strategies carefully worked out by a burgeoning urban middle class with sufficient purchasing power to buy themselves out of central areas perceived as hostile. (16) The cities extended their boundaries correspondingly to take account of such middle class housing preferences and discrete suburban settlements also developed in smaller towns to cater for middle class values and networks. Privacy, domesticity and the separation of work and home were valued increasingly by the middle class throughout urban Scotland, as they were elsewhere in the United Kingdom.

By the 1860s, the vertically segregated residential pattern of pre-modern urban Scotland, in which different social classes occupied the various storeys of the same tenement, had been largely replaced by a horizontally segregated residential pattern. Extensive areas of the city were by mid-century identifiable as working class, occupied by artisans, clerks and the *petite bourgeoisie*, or by the middle class. The inner city was abandoned to the poor; specific industrial districts developed, often with their skilled working class quarters carved out between the spaghetti of railway lines which developed in the 1840s and 1850s; suburbs inoculated the middle class against both developments.

The structure of the building industry

Qualitative improvements in housing were achievable by the middle class through their purchasing power. It was they who had the resources to buy outright or to obtain mortgages to finance the purchase of flats and villas, and in the last third of the 19th century, innumerable groups of individuals clubbed together, rather like terminating building societies, to finance a few tenements within a street. There were almost a hundred such building associations active in Edinburgh in the five years from 1869 to 1874, with a diverse membership mainly composed of managers, teachers, and annuitants such as widows and retired officers, but clerks, grocers and other members of the 'shopocracy' as well as dealers were also well represented. Had golfers on Bruntsfield Links in Edinburgh used their niblicks to hit balls in the direction of Drumdryan Brewery (site of the present-day King's Theatre), then they might have broken the window panes in properties built by any one of a dozen highly localised building associations.

Some housebuilders always managed to obtain secure contracts. Large numbers of Victorian gatekeepers and gardeners, coachmen and caretakers were commonly provided with a tied cottage, as were some railway workers, miners, water and gas officials. In the second half of the 19th century certain grades of employee in institutions - asylums, sanatoria, prisons and hospitals - and in government service, the army, customs and other inspectorates had accommodation made available to them. Churches, schools and parochial board officials, as well as golf clubs and societies like the Freemasons and Oddfellows were amongst other organisations which used a mixture of profits, subscriptions and benefactions to fund premises for their activities and accommodation for their paid servants. Often, of course, such

accommodation was 'above the shop' - built as an integral part of the works or a larger house. Whatever the nature of the tied accommodation, builders were guaranteed their interim and final payments since such prominent organisations rarely ceased to function and could not risk the opprobrium associated with non-payment. In a survey of building finance in the years

B1.6. Rockville, Napier Road, Edinburgh, was built in 1858 by James Gowans, railway contractor, quarrymaster, builder and architect as his own home. Gowans was 'obsessed by stone', partly as a result of the mid-19th century Edinburgh rationalist theories of 'harmonic proportion' in architecture, and partly as a result of listening to John Ruskin's Lectures on Architecture and Painting *in Edinburgh in 1853. Despite its fantastically picturesque appearance, the now-demolished Rockville was designed on a stone grid of two-foot squares of cyclopean rubble, supposedly designed to allow mass production of masonry components. During his era as Lord Dean of Guild, Gowans consistently rejected any proposal to build in brick in the capital. (RCAHMS A37556)*

B1.7. Relief sculpture of James Gowans at Rockville, showing him studying harmonic diagrams of triangles and circles. (Nicholas Groves-Raines, Architect)

1885-94, the extent of this assured source of building finance varied appreciably, but represented 6-7% of housebuilding in Aberdeen and Glasgow, and nearer to 10% in the larger Scottish burghs. (17)

Builders secured their working capital as both advances and instalments from wealthy individuals, and from shopkeepers and members of the *petite bourgeoisie* who combined in building associations to finance the construction of tenements in their preferred neighbourhood. These were customers who paid for their properties from their own savings, although if this was impossible, mortgage finance could be obtained through solicitors and their complex personal networks of trust and investment funds in search of annuities. (18) The management of funds in the form of legacies and bequests, as well as those portfolios from which solicitors sought to find suitable outlets to produce annuities, placed the legal profession in a pivotal position in relation to the provision of building finance, both directly as loans to builders and as mortgage finance to purchasers. Solicitors, therefore, acted not just as legal advisers but also as financial intermediaries, providing advances for the purchase of properties both by private individuals for their own accommodation and by landlords who used the advances to buy new or existing tenements from which they derived a rental income.

Only towards the end of the 19th century did building societies appear in significant numbers in urban Scotland, although they quickly established a foothold in the market for housing finance by offering favourable terms and requiring lower deposits than did solicitors. Building societies combined their conventional role of borrowing from, and lending to, private individuals with the more entrepreneurial activities of an investment society. That

is, they advanced depositors' money to speculative builders and developers, as was explicitly acknowledged in the many company names which included the description 'property investment company and building society'. The Amicable Property Investment Building Society, Edinburgh Mutual Investment Building Society, Fourth Provincial Property Investment and Building Society, Heritable Security and Mortgage Investment Company, Old Edinburgh Property Investment and Building Society, and Permanent Scottish Union Property Investment Society were just some among many Edinburgh companies who made loans available directly to builders and developers from the 1870s. (19) These companies were not content simply to act as a valve regulating the transfer of savings from one group of private individuals to the mortgages borrowed by others. Nor was it an approach confined to property investment and building societies: the Union Bank and the Life Assurance of Scotland were amongst other financial institutions which were active in lending directly to developers, and out-of-town companies which included the Kirkcaldy Property Investment Society and the Musselburgh Building and Investment Society also found it profitable in the last quarter of the 19th century to redirect local savings into the Edinburgh building industry. (20)

There was, therefore, no simple model by which housebuilding and property development was financed. A mosaic of different agencies emerged. Specialist intermediaries used share capital and deposits by investors to make loans available to house buyers, and the People's Bank, Co-operative Associations and a growing number of building, friendly and property investment societies emerged to fulfil a function which was well known in England but which until the last quarter of the 19th century had been stifled in Scotland because of the powerful leverage exerted on the mortgage market by the legal profession. When the Edinburgh Co-operative Building Company, a limited company formed in 1861 by a combination of Free Kirk campaigners for moral reform and disenchanted building trades workers, arranged in 1867 for a deposit scheme to assist future house buyers, and followed this in 1871 with a mortgage repayment scheme, it was as a direct response to the exclusion of significant social groups from housing finance. (21)

Feuing, the distinctive Scottish system of land tenure, was itself a critical contributor to building finance. (22) In Scotland, land was sold outright by the superior or vendor who relinquished all title to it, subject to the receipt of an annual or feu-duty, and other occasional payments (casualties). A key characteristic of feuing was that the annual duties were a first charge on an estate at death or bankruptcy. Accordingly, they were a highly desirable security; other creditors had to wait. With such armour-plated

B1.8. 1-23 Court Street, Dundee, a row of tenements built in 1874 by a local working men's housebuilding association. The block was unusual because it was constructed of mass concrete. (RCAHMS B17783)

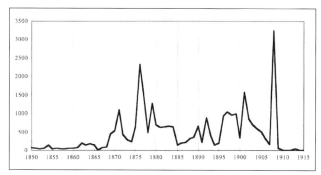

B1.9. Release of land for building purposes in Edinburgh, 1850-1914; statistics based on changes in the level of feu duty (in pounds) for major landowners. (Merchant Company of Edinburgh, Annual Reports, 1850-1909, cited by permission of the Merchant Company; Edinburgh City Archives, lists of superiorities belonging to the Governors of George Heriot's Trust, 1913-14; City of Edinburgh Superiorities, 1914)

B1.10. Piecemeal development in progress at Greenbank, an upper-middle class suburb on the south-west edge of Edinburgh. The area was feued out from the turn of the century in small groups of four or eight houses by the superior, Col. Algernon Richard Trotter of Mortonhall. In this 1910 view, 1-7 Greenbank Crescent are seen under construction alongside continuing agricultural activity and surviving farm cottages. The substantial stone semi-detached villas, with an insurance value of £950 each, were designed by W H A Ross of Castle Street, and erected by builder David Anderson of Morningside Road, as part of an eight-house development. (M Cant, The District of Greenbank, 1998, cover and 59)

assurances, future feu-duty revenues were a security upon which banks and individuals would lend, content in the knowledge that they would have first call on the assets or estate in the event of financial difficulty or death. Thus, future feuing income was the collateral used by landowners, builders and developers upon which capital was raised. As a basis for advances of capital, feus were themselves highly sought-after financial instruments, and no doubt increased in price as a consequence. But like any financial asset, the availability of building finance from the sale of future feu-duty revenue was influenced by yields on other investments, commonly municipal stocks, public utility stocks in gas and water companies, as well as railway and local mining firms. Wills and trust deeds were peppered with holdings in Scottish stocks, although British government as well as domestic and foreign municipal bonds together with overseas bank stocks were strong competitors for trust funds and private portfolios. Builders could not rely on a steady flow of capital for their activities, and when the building industry went into recession after 1905 there was a serious haemorrhaging of capital for local purposes, which drove the industry into even steeper decline, as investors looked very positively to Canadian investment opportunities in the decade before World War I. (23)

Of course, most of these sources of finance in 19th-century urban Scotland depended heavily upon the status and credit-rating of the building firm itself. In turn, this depended on a builder's ability to meet scheduled loan charges and repayments. Failure to do so resulted in the loan being recalled and ultimately, in fact all too precipitately, in bankruptcy. Indeed, once doubts were raised about a builder's ability to meet fixed charges and payments

then further deft financial footwork to keep a firm afloat was virtually impossible. The linkages between builders and their network of financial contacts - solicitors, building societies and associations, trusts and private contracts - depended heavily on the status of the building firm, and while that remained intact and the market buoyant, then the renegotiation of bonds and the extension of loans was unproblematic.

Many small firms, however, were under-capitalised. They were dependent upon personal contacts, family loyalties, advances in kind by suppliers of wood, slates, and plumbing materials as sources of working capital and trade credit. Lacking sufficient resources of their own and unable to establish the credit credentials to survive a downturn in the market, this hand-to-mouth existence to refinance their loans and evade the grasp of the trustee in bankruptcy often resulted in building firms simply ceasing to trade. In such cases, the founder would commonly be forced back to journeyman or jobbing builder status. Given their low capitalisation and susceptibility to fold or go bankrupt, formal links with banks were unusual amongst builders, and so, in periods of market difficulty, overdraft facilities were rarely available. The only financial cushion was that of personal and family contacts. This was the case, for example, with a Leith firm, A & W Fingzies, which borrowed from a relation, James Fingzies, a veterinary surgeon in Lochgelly, and a nephew, John Fingzies, a Kinross grocer who may have deliberately provoked his own bankruptcy by making loans to the Leith branch of the family in order to avoid repayments to his own creditors. Another family member, John Fingzies, often went many weeks unpaid during his six years working as a clerk with the family firm in the 1890s and, for 26

B1.11. Late 19th century medium-density suburban development on the outskirts of industrial Leith. The terraced development at the upper right, closest to Leith Links, was begun by the Industrial Co-operative Building Company, but was taken over by A & W Fingzies in 1875. In the same area are two other co-operative building initiatives: to the left, a large 'colony' development of terraces by the Edinburgh Co-operative Building Company (Restalrig, 1869 81) and to the right centre, the later petit-bourgeois Hermitage Park *(from 1885). (RCAHMS B71022)*

years, had made small amounts of money available to his Leith relations to keep the business afloat. Eventually Alexander Fingzies became so pressed that he mortgaged, illegally, the same property twice with different agencies, in order to keep his 53 creditors at bay. (24) Ultimately, in an effort to protect the family members over other creditors, Alexander Fingzies issued bonds to the veterinary surgeon, the erstwhile grocer and the clerk, albeit with doubtful substantiation of the debts, so that when his bankruptcy became irresistible, as bondholders they had first claim on the estate. The state of long-run uncertainty in the Fingzies family firm was no doubt unusual in some of its seedier details, but endemic cash flow and under-capitalisation were matters frequently recounted by builders.

Matching the repayment of maturing bonds given by builders for loans with the issuing of new ones was a skilful matter, and often made the difference between the survival and failure of a building firm. The inability to rearrange loans was the undoing of many firms, including an early venture of James Steel - who

B1.12. Brougham Place, Edinburgh, part of one of the first areas of Edinburgh largely developed by James Steel during his period of recovery from bankruptcy. The development was built in 1866-68 on James Home Rigg's Drumdryan feu, Tollcross. 1 Lonsdale Terrace, on the ground floor of the right-hand block in this view, was Steel's home and site office for some time. The pillars date from the Edinburgh International Exhibition, 1886. (Edinburgh Photographic Society; RCAHMS ED/9906)

B1.13. Edinburgh, Comely Bank Road. Beginning in 1890 and building continuously, it took James Steel almost twelve years to complete these tenements on land acquired from Lt Col. Alexander Learmonth, at the north-west edge of the exclusive West End residential area. The occupants were mostly clerks, shopkeepers and skilled artisans. The tram service from Stockbridge and Raeburn Place was extended along the street as the houses were completed. (R S Henderson; RCAHMS ED/10237)

later became one of Edinburgh's foremost developers. Born in 1829 to a tenant farmer and his wife at Buchts near Cambusnethan, Wishaw, James Steel was apprenticed as a mason in the 1840s. He accumulated £50 from his wages, started building in 1853 on his own account in Cambusnethan, and then in 1859 in Glasgow. (25) Together with his own resources, the accumulated capital for the business eventually ran to £230 from his brother, £80 from his brother-in-law, and almost £100 from his father. A buoyant housing market underpinned by urban population growth enabled Steel by 1861 to employ 26 men, to acquire plant and stock at three quarries to the value of £213, to receive an annual rental income of £300 from houses and shops built and owned in Wishaw, and to own two tenements he had built in Garnethill, Glasgow. Steel kept no accounts. Late in 1858 he lost £150 on two ventures. In one of these cases, a Wishaw draper who owed him money went bankrupt; then, a few months later, in 1859, Steel lost £600 over a contract at Lochgoilhead partly due to his under-estimation of the building costs and partly because his account was unpaid when the firm for whom he was working folded. He also lost £550 in two speculative building developments in Wishaw and Glasgow, and failed to dovetail the maturity of bonds. His brother, Thomas Steel, was owed £230 for joinery work and his cousin, Alexander Allan, a mason, was due £80 in unpaid wages since 1834 - over a quarter of a century in arrears! At his examination as a bankrupt, Steel acknowledged these unsystematic business practices and recognised that his assets of £543 were sufficient to offset only one-third of his liabilities.

To identify changes in the size and composition of demand based on trends in household income and demography seemed beyond the competence of most entrepreneurs, and builders were no exception. If, as in many instances, they were not prepared to keep their own accounting records, builders were hardly likely to undertake market research. Builders relied heavily on their own impressionistic perception of the 'state of trade', a vague term which encompassed the equally inexact gradations of 'dull', 'fair', 'good' and 'busy'. (26) Occasionally, newspaper reports from employers' associations or, after the 1860s, those of trade unionists such as the Associated Carpenters and Joiners of Scotland, were invoked to relay market trends. No builders referred to a quantitative analysis of immigration, natural increase, or household formation as a basis for decision making, despite the relative ease with which such components of demand were available in published form. A casual inspection of the censuses between 1861 and 1901, for example, would have shown that relative to the number of families one of the highest and sustained housing deficits in urban Scotland existed in Edinburgh. (27) In the same period, the contribution of the 20-44 age group to decennial population growth never fell below 30% per decade, but in the 1890s the expansion of this age group accounted for 52% of the increase in the population of Edinburgh, and it would not have taken a genius to deduce that household formation would rise for a time before resuming a more conventional level. Clearly, market knowledge was partial, or asymmetric, and business decisions were correspondingly risk-laden. (28)

In the absence of such market research, adjustments were always ex post, that is, once the trend was already evident, and even newspaper reports of the annual summary of building plans submitted to the Dean of Guild Court made little or no mention of broader demand and supply conditions. Thus the figures for changes in the numbers of houses and tenements came as something of a surprise to builders in the city, and not least to the members of the plans committee themselves. For example, in replying to the vote of thanks accorded to him in 1903 after

28 years public service and on the conferment of his baronetcy, the millionaire and former bankrupt Sir James Steel stated he was 'very much struck' by the statement by the Dean of Guild in which he said the 'building trade was reviving, because some of them had been under the impression that it was falling off. It was very satisfactory to hear that the opposite was the case'. (29)

To an extent, imprecise market analysis was a result of the small scale of production in the building industry. In the forty years before 1914, over half (52.9%) of the applications to build houses in 102 burghs in Scotland were on a 'one-off' basis (see Illustration B1.33, at end of chapter). Only one application in six (17.2%) was for a larger project of three or more properties. (30) In Edinburgh, 40% of Dean of Guild approvals for residential building in the decade 1885-94 were to builders; the majority, therefore, were for applications to build a single property and were made by private individuals on their own behalf, or for institutions, building associations and companies. Of those Dean of Guild Court permits applied for by Edinburgh builders, one-third were for single houses or tenements, and two-thirds of builders applied to construct three or fewer properties. This contrasted with Sheffield, the most detailed English comparison available, where planning permission granted to builders was in only 50% of cases for three or fewer houses. (31) On this basis at least, the building industry in Edinburgh was more fragmented than that south of the border, and while the theory of the firm indicates that this should have induced market equilibrium, this was counterbalanced by the imperfect information employed by builders, which removed a key condition of stability. (32)

Together these factors - small firm size, limited capitalisation, imprecise market analysis, lack of barriers to entry, limited book-keeping, and cash flow problems strongly associated with a product normally saleable only on completion - meant that builders were particularly vulnerable to bankruptcy should their sources of finance dry up. Collectively, these features of the Scottish building industry produced boom-to-bust cyclical fluctuations of unprecedented severity - at least 70% more pronounced than in the manufacturing sector generally. (33) Year-to-year variations in the Edinburgh building industry were 40-80% greater than those in English regional cities, such as Leeds, Liverpool, Manchester and Birmingham, and in many other industrial burghs in central Scotland levels of instability and uncertainty were far in excess of those in Edinburgh. (34)

To some extent, these fluctuations in the long-run experience of the Edinburgh housebuilding industry between 1850 and 1914 can be judged from changes in the feu-duty incomes received by major landowners in the capital, and also from the severity of year-to-year fluctuations in Glasgow, which was shadowed by many burghs in west-central Scotland. That other urban centres

B1.15. 25 Learmonth Terrace, Edinburgh, built in 1891-93 by spirits magnate Arthur Sanderson and decorated by Morton & Co. of Tynecastle: c.1900 view. Highly skilled artisans provided individualised homes for the middle and upper-middle classes. However, suppliers of art work and specialist plaster, wood and iron work gradually gained a foothold in the market, as in this house whose fitments came from Morton and Co. of Tynecastle. (RCAHMS ED/5844)

emulated the fluctuations of Glasgow, sometimes in even more exaggerated form, was in part a reflection of their dependency on the order-books of Glasgow's industrialists. Some indication of the pervasiveness of this instability can be judged from the annual variations in the level of approved housebuilding in burghs throughout Scotland.

The average annual change in the housebuilding index of 24 burghs is shown in Illustration B1.34 (at end of chapter), in descending order of instability. The volatility of housebuilding was greatest in Hawick (44.8%) where the annual variation in the levels of housebuilding activity were twice those of Edinburgh (22.1%). Compared with the years 1900-09, which form the basis for this comparison and have an index value of 100, in all of these burghs annual variations in the level of housebuilding averaged 19%; in half of the burghs annual changes in housebuilding levels were in the range 20-30%. These were market conditions which would have proved a formidable challenge to any business in the modern era when forecasting and commercial information is much more readily available. In the 19th century it is thus unsurprising, given this volatility in year-to-year activity and the strains imposed on builders' business ability, that builders were declared bankrupt in large numbers.

Modest financial resources and the absence of formal qualifications enabled anyone to style themselves as a 'builder'. No threshold existed in terms of plant and machinery in an industry which in Scotland retained essentially handicraft methods, even if in the 1870s some of the larger firms introduced steam-powered lathes for mass-produced joinery and, in the 1880s, alloy-steel drills to dress stone. Off-site preparation of materials and the development of mass-produced joinery, plaster-mouldings and plumbing materials, as well as specialist firms to supply grates, kitchen ranges, fireplaces, radiators and sanitary ware enabled an element of industrialised building to develop. But the small builder retained an important niche in the industry and did so on very modest levels of capital. Thomas Binnie, himself a builder and authority on the Glasgow building industry in the last third of the 19th century, explained the structure of the industry, its superstructure of debt, and its vulnerability to severe fluctuations. He noted how 'a man starting a building which would cost him £5,000' had only '£70 in the world and yet he managed to build and finish it'. Although such a builder might be successful, probably in the expansionary phase of the cycle, Binnie

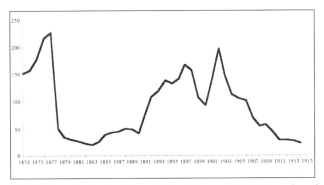

B1.14 Fluctuations in the Glasgow building industry, 1873-1914: numbers of linings in the Dean of Guild Court. (Glasgow City Archives, Dean of Guild collection)

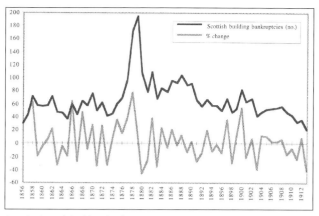

B1.16. Scottish building bankruptcies, 1856-1913.
(Edinburgh Gazette, 1856-1913)

B1.18. A delivery of window-mullions to 15-17 George Street.
(Mrs Esther Galbraith)

B1.17. A tenement of two-apartment houses under construction at 15-17 George Street, Whiteinch, in 1902 by P W & A Lightbody, a typical small housing developer of the Glasgow area. Under the direction of W Lightbody senior, the firm built many tenements in the area round Byres Road in the 1870s. It survived the City of Glasgow Bank crash of 1878, and by the time of the late 1890s boom was building in the burgh of Partick. Its output included these houses, probably for shipyard workers, designed by a John MacRae of Oran Street, Maryhill. The visible workforce seems to comprise ten men, operating with rudimentary hand winches and ramps, and horse-drawn deliveries of prefabricated components such as mullions, but also carrying out many skilled operations on site, including masonry preparations. Construction is 'overhand' from inside the building, without scaffolding; a general view of construction shows wooden cranes standing inside the shell of the building to facilitate this. William Lightbody junior is the bowler-hatted figure standing on the ramp. The business went bankrupt in the next market downturn in 1905; several firms of Clydeside materials suppliers were listed as creditors. (Mrs Esther Galbraith)

commented, knowingly, that this particular one 'had failed, of course'. (35)

If the informal financial networks lubricated the building industry in the expansionary phase, these could also bring the system to an abrupt halt. Personal loans and ad hoc advances were susceptible to immediate recall. By their very nature, they were not generally loans for a specified period. At least for those builders who had issued a bond in return for a capital advance, there was some breathing space to negotiate an alternative source of capital before the loan matured. Excluded from this formal financial arena, most small builders were highly vulnerable to any circumstances which might staunch the flow of private funds. Short term funding for long term projects, a factor central to the international depression of the 1930s, was also at the heart of the instability of the Scottish Victorian building industry. When Thomas Binnie drew attention to the calamitous effect of the failure of the City of Glasgow Bank in 1878, which resulted in two-thirds of the builders in Glasgow going bankrupt, he noted that this was not because the bank had suspended overdraft facilities. (36) Most builders could not have obtained such sources of finance. The bankruptcies occurred because the bank's own

liquidity problems forced up interest rates and induced a high degree of anxiety amongst lenders, who immediately recalled their own private loans to builders. Doubling the interest rate to 4% or 5% sent a signal of near-panic to savers and potential lenders, who then suspended their advances to builders. In an industry where small scale builders were so numerous and where so many had capital tied up in incomplete, and thus unsaleable, tenements, the cumulative effect of the bank failure was thus to begin a downward psychological spiral, which took a generation to repair. Housebuilding in Glasgow, as can be seen in Illustration B1.14, remained in the doldrums between 1878 and the early 1890s, despite new household formation and continued population growth. Rising levels of empty housing in the 1880s deterred landlords and builders from embarking on new housebuilding projects, and so structural factors in the building industry induced a paralysis, just as they could under different conditions galvanise production, on a scale rarely experienced in other industries.

Instability within the industry manifested itself in many forms. The annual variations in the 'linings' or plans approved by the Glasgow Dean of Guild Court provided one indicator of the volatility which faced builders. Another was the level of bankruptcy. Though there are considerable difficulties in interpreting this material - many firms simply ceased to trade, and after 1880 a streamlined process, cessio bonorum, diminished some of the knock-on effects of business failure on creditors - the annual percentage changes in the levels of bankruptcy illustrate some of the uncertainty with which small builders had to deal, and to which they themselves fell prey. (37)

The wreckage of excessive instability in the building industry was not only serious for the industry itself, but was also of considerable importance to Scots generally, who had to endure the consequences of instability in terms of the quantity and quality of their housing. The way in which the structure of production in the building industry had an impact on housing conditions is explored next.

Small flats and daily rituals

The block design of tenements was associated with distinctive patterns of daily behaviour. Many facilities were shared. Water-closets, running water and sinks, wash-houses and drying-greens for laundering and drying clothes, lime-washed common stair entries, and child-care within the inner tenement courts and alleys were an accepted part of everyday life for most urban Scots. The degree of proximity caused by living in densely packed one- and two-roomed houses imposed a degree of mutuality and co-operation which bonded a stair into an interdependent community. Behavioural codes, usually implicit, governed cooking and cleaning since access to water-supplies was shared. Negotiation over access and an awareness of the 'rights' of neighbours brought a level of discourse and daily gossip which ensured that Scottish women were engaged in defending their domestic territory while aware of infringements on the space and access of others. Rights were counterbalanced by obligations.

These routines, although by no means without friction between families over rotas and entitlements, nonetheless required an awareness of others which was rarely developed to the same degree in English terraced housing. The latter form of accommodation was more self-contained. Water and gas were piped and metered to individual houses. Back-extensions to houses from the 1880s commonly provided sculleries where washing and cooking could be undertaken without reference to other families' needs and if, as in many English houses, water-closets remained outside and an unappealing short walk away to the end of the back-yard, then they had the merit of being used normally by one family only, rather than shared by several. By contrast, water-closets in Scottish burghs were usually shared, as for example, in Clydebank, a new town of the 1880s and regarded as 'the best example of an almost entirely modern and tenement town', where WCs were shared in 40% of the accommodation; 35% of all WCs were shared by between 18 and 20 people. (38) Across the Clyde at Port Glasgow, 95% of all WCs were shared in 1914.

With a preponderance of one- and two-roomed houses, space and room function in Scottish housing were relatively undifferentiated. Sleeping, cooking, child-birth, nursing, children's games, sex, gossip, socialising, as well as rituals such as mourning, family celebrations, and visits from the minister or kirk elder, midwife, philanthropists, council and other officials were all conducted in the same room. Private business and confidentiality were difficult to sustain; openness and participation by other family members was accepted, if not always invited.

Floor space was at a premium with several competing uses. 'Hurley' or rollaway beds maximised floor space, since they could be stored under a fixed bed during daylight hours. 'Room and kitchen' houses often contained a 'bed-closet' - a bed hidden behind a closed door and, given the absence of ventilation, a cause for concern over the contraction of tuberculosis. In Glasgow from 1900, doors sealing these 'cubicles of consumption' were

B1.20. The lobby of a late 19th century terraced house in Leamington Terrace, Edinburgh. This photograph of c.1900 shows one of the nine-strong Mather family, who lived here along with two servants. Self-contained middle class houses reflected the importance attached to the moral and instructional role of the family and its privacy. Small gardens and exercise were part of that value system. (RCAHMS A3041; A Carruthers (ed.), The Scottish Home, 1996)

banned by local building regulations, and from 1913 legislation prohibited enclosed beds altogether, although it is doubtful how effectively these stipulations were monitored. The floor-plan of c.1945 (Illustration B1.19) prepared by council officials of a Glasgow 'single-end', as used by a married couple and seven children, would have been exceptional before 1914; more common was the two-roomed tenement flat. (39) Typical family sizes are difficult to identify, given wide variations according to class and occupation, but in 1911, two-thirds of all Scottish women aged 22-26 and with a marriage duration of at least fifteen years, had five or more children; 40% gave birth to seven or more children. (40)

Inevitably, given both low and irregular incomes, and limited floor and wall space, the furniture and furnishings of these tenement flats were modest. The absence of a range on which to cook food or heat water is conspicuous in this case, though these were gradually introduced towards the end of the 19th century. Given the floor space available, chairs, like most furniture, were roughly made and domestic comfort was difficult to obtain. Meals might be taken at the table, sitting on the bed, standing, or, often, in two sittings. Pictures, books, plants, curtains, linoleum, and furniture were minimal in the one- or two-roomed house, partly because of the limitations of floor and wall-space, but also because for many the uncertainty of tenancy and the likelihood of eviction and relocation put unencumbered removals at a premium. Midnight flits were best undertaken with few possessions. (41) As one contemporary observed, 'You really had to see a removal from a room and kitchen house in a Glasgow tenement to realise how few goods and chattels people owned. They usually filled a coal cart with room to spare for the bird cage and the two rolls of linolcum'. (42) Despite year-long leases, Scottish landlords

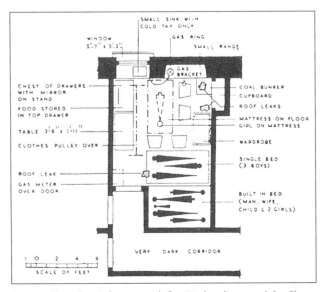

B1.19. Plan of typical one-roomed flat (single-end) prepared by Glasgow Corporation officials, c.1945. This plan shows the way in which older, larger flats were subdivided into multi-occupied one-roomed dwellings in the late 19th century and early 20th century.

increasingly sought to evict tenants. In London, the number of legal processes for this purpose was one-thirtieth of the level in Glasgow in the period 1886-90. From 1911, tenants who had only seven days of rent arrears could be evicted with only 48 hours notice. (43) The margin between security and homelessness was very slender if landlords sought to enforce their powers, which they did increasingly in the twenty years before 1914. Compared with self-contained English terraced housing, tenement accommodation was rudimentary and often lacked the bric-a-brac and memorabilia which added character and homeliness. The scope for individuality in decoration was limited not just by disposable incomes but by the manner in which a distinctive legal tradition operated to tenants' disadvantage, by providing for 'a form of privileged coercion' which was 'guarded jealously by proprietors'. (44)

An account of bereavement and mourning reveals something of the pressure of congested internal housing space and the daily rhythms of working class life. A table, for example, had multiple uses: 'The beloved is laid on the bed, and all the usual round of domestic duties, including the taking of meals, has to be done with ever that still pale form before their view. Night comes on and the household must go to rest, so the sad burden is now transferred from the bed and laid on the table, or it may be the coal bunker lid. In the morning, to admit of the table being used for breakfast, or to let coals be got for the fire, the body has to be lifted on to the bed again, and so on for the customary three days, the broken hearted relatives feeling it to be sacrilege thus to hustle the mortal remains of a much loved one'. (45) Thus 'the constant succession of lifting, folding and handing up constituted 'a very great deal of extra labour on an already overdriven class'. (46) Daily rituals - such as climbing several flights of stairs to obtain water, to hang out clothes on a drying line, to buy groceries, or to carry coal upstairs where it was stored within the flat, thereby creating considerable 'stour' (dust) which in turn took time to clean - were directly affected by Scottish housing form and required considerable physical effort, particularly from women, which spilled over into almost every facet of daily life.

In the management of the household budget, in dealing with the practicalities of the domestic conditions, in confronting the rent collector and the sheriff's officer, it was women who absorbed the greatest sources of stress. Part of this domestic management was concerned with the establishment of rhythms, of order. As Joan Williamson recalled her Glasgow childhood she observed, 'Even in the busiest house in the street there were limits to carelessness because there was simply no room for chaos ... everything had its place in the house. You would never find the hammer anywhere but in the kitchen drawer' and there was 'no hunting in attics for sledges, cricket bats or model railways ... because there was no attic and no old things'. (47) Spring cleaning was easy and simple and certain days were saturated with their own activities - washday Mondays, Friday nights for blackleading or brasso. Order extended to people: the male household head had his place at table or by the fireside.

Although lacking formal political representation and voting powers, women were not powerless, therefore, in the management of daily household concerns. Not surprisingly, then, it was they who used the housing issue to cut their political teeth and were active in the emerging Independent Labour Party of the west of Scotland. (48) Although women had only a modest input into two influential town planning reports in 1918 and 1919, their contribution in the west of Scotland to a broad coalition of political interests produced a political identity and cohesion unrivalled in the remainder of the United Kingdom. (49) Even

seventy years later, such alliances of women, co-operative and socialist politicians, trade unionists, and religious interest groups were able to produce a powerful political force resistant to Conservative onslaught.

Morality and morbidity

Despite the experience of intervention by public and philanthropic organisations, the Ballantyne Commission on working-class housing conditions commented in 1917 on 'the clotted masses of slums', and expressed 'amazement' at the streets of 'new tenements developed with the minimum regard for amenity' and the 'gigantic' proportions of the housing deficiency in Scotland. For turn-of-century Scotland, as the 'imperial partner', such complaints were most easily defined through comparisons with England. In 1911, one in twelve Scots lived single-roomed houses; two in five lived in two-roomed houses. Thus, every other Scot lived in a one or two-roomed house; in England the figure was less than one in fourteen. More than two-thirds of residents in Wishaw, Coatbridge, Kilsyth, Clydebank, Cowdenbeath, Airdrie, Govan, Hamilton, Motherwell, Barrhead, Johnstone, Port Glasgow and Renfrew lived at a density of more than two per room, the standard considered overcrowded by the Registrar-General in England and Wales. Forty-five per cent of all Scots were overcrowded in 1911 compared with 9% in England, and so stark was this comparison that the official standard of overcrowding was devalued to more than three persons per room. Even so, in the burghs mentioned above, some 30-40% still lived in overcrowded conditions. To achieve standards of accommodation comparable to those of English cities, 22.5% additional housing was required in Scotland in 1911. (50) This was the housing legacy with which Scots were faced after a century of industrialisation and rapid urbanisation (see Illustration B1.35, at end of chapter).

Although the percentage of overcrowding had declined between 1861 and 1911, the absolute number of overcrowded dwellings had increased from 1.7 million to 2.1 million. The equivalent of three Glasgows, that is 2.3 million Scots, lived in one- or two-roomed houses. Privacy was virtually an impossibility, and the behavioural standards of morality and propriety associated with separate sleeping arrangements for boys and girls, for parents and children, and for family members and lodgers, were difficult to achieve. Personal hygiene, sexual relations and family life were conducted in an atmosphere of communality. This was reinforced by the collective amenities of tenement houses - sanitary provisions, running water, and washing facilities were normally shared between several families. In contrast to the more self-contained space and privacy of the terraced house, Scottish tenement life was governed by confined, shared spaces, and this affected youth culture and patterns of child-care, just as it did games and gossip.

The impact of these living conditions on the Scottish physique was pronounced. Taller and indeed heavier children came from bigger houses, and the incidence of rickets, skeletal deformities, ear, nose and throat infections, heart defects and bronchial conditions was correlated strongly and inversely with the size of house. The more restricted and undifferentiated the housing space, the greater the frequency of physical deformities, and the higher the incidence of death. (51) For example, in a study in 1904 of 35,000 schoolgirls attending Glasgow Board schools, those from two-roomed houses were 6% lighter than girls of the same age from homes of four or more rooms. It was not an accident, one report commented, 'that children from one-roomed houses are lighter and smaller in stature ... than children from four-roomed houses'. (52) In the same year, a survey of schoolchildren attending Broughton School in Edinburgh showed that the offspring of shopkeepers, artisans and clerks were between one and three inches taller than children born to parents living in the poorest central area of the North Canongate, where labouring was the commonest occupation.

It was 'upon the children that the worst of the burden [of defective housing conditions] falls'. (53) The contrast according to house type and social class was apparent in Edinburgh where, in 1912, the infant mortality in middle class Merchiston was 46 per 1,000 and compared very favourably with 232 per 1,000 in the

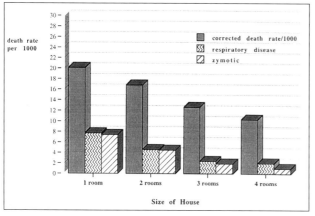

B1.21. Glasgow mortality according to house size, 1901. (Proceedings of the Royal Philosophical Society of Glasgow, 1902-3, 131)

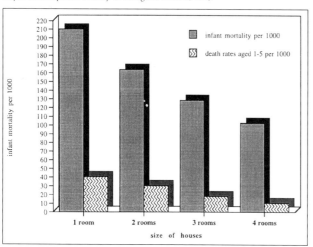

B1.22. Infant and child mortality in Glasgow, 1910. (Scottish Land Enquiry Committee, Scottish Land, 1914, 371)

B1.23. Double bed recess, Glasgow slum property, c.1910: living room of a subdivided tenement in the inner city, showing basic furnishings. (Glasgow City Archives)

Richmond Street area, close to the University and former site of the Infirmary, and to 277 per 1,000 in the Cowgate closes of the Old Town. The poorest, most overcrowded areas had infant mortality rates more than six times those of the suburban zones, a relationship which Dr. Chalmers, the Glasgow Medical Officer of Health, confirmed in his report for 1910. Although infant mortality in the first year of life for children in houses of three or four rooms was half that of infants from single-room houses, it was the relative change in the position for children aged one to five years which was most striking. Chalmers stated that: 'Under one year the four apartment [infant mortality] rate is still equal to one-half the rate for one apartment, but during the next four years of life the resistance of children in three and four apartment houses to fatal diseases increases so rapidly, or the risks of contracting infectious disease are so diminished, that the death rate among children in three-apartment houses is less than one half, and in four-apartment houses only one-fourth that of one-apartment children'. (54)

Faced with morbidity and mortality on this scale, Scottish municipalities and their administrators were not idle. An initiative from Glasgow City Council between 1871 and 1879 produced seven municipal lodging houses designed to offer shelter to those without permanent homes. (55) The Glasgow venture, which produced a return of 3.5% on the capital outlay and encouraged the Paisley, Perth and Aberdeen councils to follow suit by the end of the century, offered only a short-term palliative to the housing of the poor. More fundamentally, therefore, municipalities began to consider demolition and even direct council house building in the last half of the 19th century. In the larger Scottish burghs, municipal slum clearances developed in the 1860s in response to the seemingly intractable public health problems identified by prominent Medical Officers such as Henry Littlejohn (Edinburgh), J B Russell and later, A K Chalmers (both Glasgow), and associated with deficient housing. (56) This municipal intervention altered the townscape, even if the impact on health and housing varied from place to place. City Improvement Trusts in Glasgow (1866), Edinburgh (1867), Dundee (1871), Leith (1877), Greenock (1877) and Aberdeen (1884) demolished insanitary and overcrowded central sites, displacing significant numbers of their inhabitants as a result. While Glasgow City Council did little to build on cleared sites, Edinburgh City Council encouraged developers and stipulated designs and housing densities.

Although Scottish municipal slum clearance and improvement schemes have been considered as limited and even counter-productive in terms of their public health achievements, the Scotch Baronial style of St. Mary's, Blackfriars, and numerous other thoroughfares adjacent to the High Street in Edinburgh was one permanent result. (57) Edinburgh Town Council complemented the clearance campaigns, as did others, with a limited number of municipal housebuilding ventures of their own from the 1890s. In Edinburgh, the council's projects at High School Yards, Tynecastle, Cowgate, Portsburgh, Bedford Crescent, Potter Row, Pipe Street and Greenside produced an additional 600 flats in ten years between 1897 and 1907 at a cost of about £80,000 (or £5,000,000 in 1990s prices); almost £500,000, equivalent to about £30,000,000 in 1990s prices, had been spent by Glasgow City Council on just over 2,000 tenement flats by 1907. (58) Indeed, scattered throughout urban Scotland, many town councils accepted a responsibility to house their citizens, although still on a small scale. Perth, Greenock and Glasgow were amongst the most active in this respect, so that by 1913 their efforts represented 1.4% of the overall housing stock. (59) Edinburgh and Kilmarnock Corporations achieved just under 1%, and council house building in Clydebank, Aberdeen, Leith and Hamilton was equivalent to approximately 0.5% of the housing stock in these burghs. Small towns in semi-rural settings accepted this responsibility too; Bo'ness constructed ten flats, while Oban Town Council, with just 24 flats and thus 2.1% of its housing stock under council control, was proportionately the most active of all Scottish municipal housebuilders!

Philanthropists had made some efforts to build 'model dwellings' in an attempt to demonstrate both best practice and profitability. In most cases, though, the rents payable were consistent with regular employment and a steady income - something which at least a quarter of the Scottish working classes of the four cities could not command. About one in four of the male inhabitants of Dundee, Glasgow, Aberdeen and Edinburgh was susceptible to interrupted employment in the course of the year from cyclical, seasonal or casual work, and the proportion was only a little lower for women. (60) Private and philanthropic initiatives to build improved dwellings for the labouring classes foundered on the structure of the labour market, despite the buoyancy of the shipbuilding, marine and heavy engineering sectors throughout much of urban Scotland in the fifty years before World War I. Co-operative efforts by artisans made some headway in these years as building trades workers in Edinburgh and Glasgow formed Co-operative Building Companies, using their own skills to

construct the early properties. From its foundation in 1861, the Edinburgh Co-operative Building Company built 2,000 dwellings over the following fifty years and contributed up to 5% of the additions to housing stocks in the capital in these years.

Commenting in 1885 on the housing of the Scottish urban population, a Royal Commission concluded that 'we have no great anxiety about the large towns'. (61) Their recommendations were conservatively geared towards the introduction of standardised building regulations, cheaper property transfers including a reduction of stamp duty, and administrative reorganisation to defray municipal housing costs across a greater number of ratepayers. (62) It was assumed that if municipalities needed to intervene, it was as a short-term corrective to cater for those of the very poor or temporarily disadvantaged who needed accommodation. However, a combination of factors over the next thirty years ensured that Scottish housebuilding and the physical appearance of Scottish towns and cities would be transformed. By 1912, and in response to public opinion, the specific representations of Scottish Miners' Federation leaders and MPs from mining constituencies, the Secretary for Scotland, John Sinclair, reluctantly conceded the need for a through review of Scottish housing, both rural and urban - a review which led directly to the Ballantyne Commission and Report. (63)

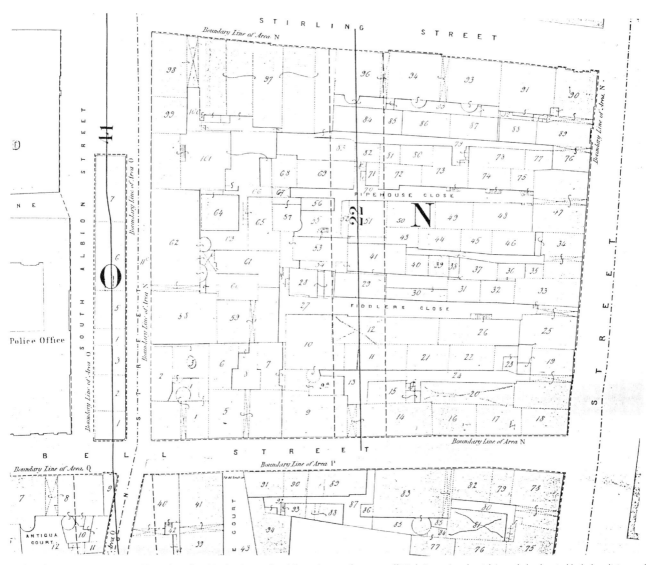

B1.24. Glasgow City Improvement Trust plan of 1865, showing medieval linear layout of an area off High Street (on the right), and the drastic block demolition and redevelopment plan, on a rationalist grid layout, proposed by the Trust. (Glasgow City Archives)

B1.25. Cockburn Street, Edinburgh, built in 1859-64. In contrast to the Glasgow patterns, Edinburgh's city improvement schemes deferred to the romantic imagery of Sir Walter Scott. While the Scott Monument itself (1840-46) had been neo-Gothic in style, the redevelopment projects introduced Scots baronial to the Old Town. Key phases of the programme included Cockburn Street (built in connection with the new railway station), Victoria Street (1860s), the City Improvement Scheme of 1867 (e.g. Blackfriars Street, St. Mary's Street), and adjacent streets such as Potterrow. (RCAHMS A74563)

The political agenda had changed. What had forced that change were essentially rural issues. The 'Irish Question' centred on fair rents and fixity of tenure, and this was easily translated to Scotland where the problems of tied cottages for crofters and miners, as well as the physical conditions in which they lived, were the subject of vigorous representation. The Scottish Secretary received deputations of miners about such issues in 1909 and 1911, and in both its reports for 1910 and 1911 the Local Government Board for Scotland criticised housing conditions in specific areas of Scotland. (64) The earlier propaganda war, influenced by such polemical lectures as 'Life in One Room' and 'Uninhabitable Houses' by J B Russell, the Glasgow Medical Officer of Health, was part of a late 19th-century campaign by social reformists to fan public concern about the lifestyles, life expectancy and living conditions of disadvantaged fellow citizens. Connected to this was the rise of the Independent Labour Party in the west of Scotland, which was concerned with issues of social justice, in which housing conditions figured prominently. Family and domestic issues gained in prominence, and as wartime rent controls were introduced to contain landlords' profits, a resumption of resource allocation in the building industry by means of a reliance on prices and profit motives was inevitably problematic. Inflation, supply shortages and public order combined to legitimate state intervention to regulate rent levels in 1915, and to remove them without addressing the fundamental problems of inadequate supply was to court trouble in 1919.

This is not to argue that council housebuilding in the form and scale which developed in interwar Scotland was inevitable; the experience of Edinburgh, and other burghs where a heavy reliance was placed on Treasury subsidies to private housebuilding, is indicative of alternative approaches to the provision of adequate housing accommodation in 20th-century Scotland. (65) However, where the problems of mortality and morbidity were

greatest and most intractable, then the balance of social benefits over private losses reinforced the cause of those advocating the building of local authority housing on a mass-produced scale. Whether this interventionism by local authorities was, as a London observer noted in 1924, 'a very big price' to pay to address the housing problems in 1919 is a subjective matter. From another perspective, council house building could be described as the direct 'consequence of disease [and] degenerate morals' amongst 'thousands of our fellow citizens ... condemned to exist in accommodation that in many cases has been declared to be unfit for human habitation'. (66)

B1.26. Urquhart Road, Aberdeen: on the left of this view is the first municipal housing project in Aberdeen, a group of sixteen tenements of one- and two-roomed flats built in 1897; on the right side are typical private Aberdeen tenements, with their top mansard storeys. Council housebuilding became generally permissible under the Housing of the Working Classes Act 1890. Aberdeen was one city council which made modest use of its powers, although the precedent was important for the years 1919-39, when Treasury subsidies became available. (RCAHMS B55654)

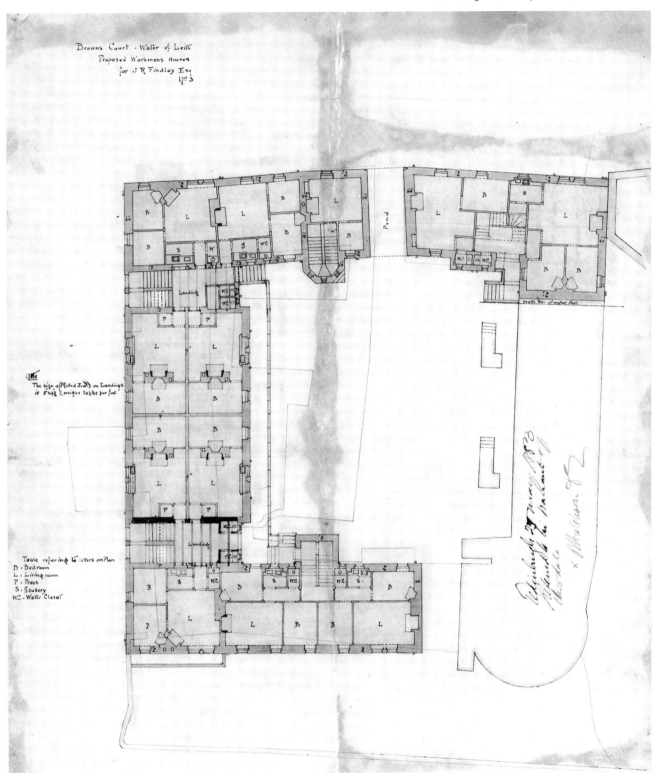

B1.27. *In 1883, the* Scotsman *newspaper owner, J R Findlay, commissioned the architect Sydney Mitchell to design for him a large terraced townhouse on a plot at 3 Rothesay Terrace, Edinburgh, part of the Walker estate originally sold by the Heriot Trust, and laid out by architect James Gillespie Graham in 1826. Findlay's house diverged from the New Town terraced norm only in its greater Renaissance sumptuousness. To its rear, and in the same year, Mitchell designed for Findlay a more overtly innovative project, down in the industrial Dean Village, where the publisher built for his own workers an 'artistic' development of two- and three-apartment flats: Well Court. This highly picturesque courtyard group was designed especially to be viewed from Findlay's own house. The project was extremely influential in the later phases of the Edinburgh Old Town redevelopment, including the work of Patrick Geddes. This plan shows the first phase of 1883; the following year, Well Court was completed by the addition of the towered club-house at the south-eastern corner, with landscaped gardens around. (RCAHMS EDD/78/4)*

B1.28. View of Well Court as seen from Findlay's own house at 3 Rothesay Terrace. (RCAHMS C43462)

B1.29. 3 Rothesay Terrace is the taller house at the centre of this row. (RCAHMS C43396)

B1.30. Walker Buildings, Hood Street, Kilmarnock: 1985 view prior to demolition. Many employers provided company housing for their workers, with mixed motives, combining good business sense with a desire to oversee and pressurise the employees. This group of three rendered, brick-built tenement blocks, with slightly Art Nouveau detailing, was built in 1904 by Alexander Walker, of the Johnny Walker Scotch Whisky Company, for his employees; it contained a total of 36 two-apartment flats, with shared WCs on the staircase landings. (RCAHMS A39944)

In Scotland, the scene for council house building in the 20th century was set by the nature of the labour market and the extreme instability of the building industry in the 19th century. Jointly, these demand and supply conditions created a yawning gap in provision into which public authorities could flow in the political context of an election conducted under the slogan of 'homes fit for heroes'. In England and Wales, deficient housing could be addressed by relatively modest municipal intervention, with a reversion to a private enterprise dominated provision of semi-detached villas in the 1930s; in Scotland, the 19th-century legacy was beyond the resources of an industry which had long been heavily dependent on the small-scale firm. The structure of the building industry in the 19th century, therefore, was organisationally and logistically unsuited to the conditions which prevailed in the 20th century.

Notes

1. T M Devine, 'Introduction' in T M Devine and R Mitchison (eds), *People and Society in Scotland 1760-1830*, 1989, 1.

2. C A Whatley, *"Bought and Sold for English Gold"? Explaining the Union of 1707*, 1994; and 'Economic causes and consequences of the Union of 1707: a survey', *Scottish Historical Review*, 68, 1989, XX.

3. T M Devine, 'Urbanisation', in Devine and Mitchison, *People and Society*, 27-52.

4. For a recent survey see M Gray, *Scots on the Move: Scots Migrants 1750-1914*, 1990.

5. M W Flinn (ed.), *Scottish Population from the 17th Century to the 1930s*, 1977, 313.

6. R Rodger, 'The evolution of Scottish town planning', in G Gordon and B Dicks (eds), *Scottish Urban History*, 1983, 71-91.

7. G Best, 'Another part of the island', in H J Dyos and M Wolff (eds), *The Victorian City: Images and Realities*, ii, 1978 edition, 389-411, previously published as 'The Scottish Victorian city', *Victorian Studies*, 11, 1968, 329-58.

8. A Wood, *Report on the Condition of the Poorer Classes of Edinburgh and of their Dwellings, Neighbourhoods and Families*, 1868, 53-4.

9. A Wood, *Report on the Condition of the Poorer Classes*, Appendix A.

10. An invaluable account of public health in Glasgow is contained in A K Chalmers, *Public Health Administration in Glasgow*, 1905; see also O Checkland and M Lamb, *Health Care as Social History: The Glasgow Case*, 1982. For accounts of public health conditions and administrative responses in Edinburgh see H P Tait, 'Two notable epidemics in Edinburgh and Leith', *Book of the Old Edinburgh Club*, 32, 1966, 21-31; B M White, 'Medical police. Politics and police: the fate of John Roberton', *Medical History*, 27, 1983, 407-22; C Hamlin, 'Environmental sensibility in Edinburgh 1839-40: the "fetid irrigation" controversy', *Journal of Urban History*, 20, 1994, 311-39; P J Smith, 'The foul burns of Edinburgh: public health attitudes and environmental change', *Scottish Geographical Magazine*, 91, 1975, 25-37.

B1.31. Late 19th century single-storey brick terraces for shale miners at Broxburn, West Lothian; contemporary view. Political agitation over Scottish housing conditions was associated especially with miners' dwellings, and with rural housing in the crofting counties. Miners' representatives from Broxburn and West Lothian were amongst those who lobbied the Scottish Secretary in 1909 to seek improvements. They succeeded in persuading Parliament to set up a comprehensive enquiry, in the form of the Ballantyne Commission, which reported in 1917 with the most far-reaching results. (RCAHMS WL/1007/32)

B1.32. During World War I, government restrictions limited large-scale housebuilding to such strategic centres as Rosyth and Gretna (new communities for munitions workers), or Greenock and Clydebank. These tenements in Castle Street, Clydebank, were built in 1915-17 for Beardmore Ltd's shipyard workers by the company's property arm, the Dalmuir and West of Scotland Estates Company; the houses could still be built of stone, but were given flat roofs for economy. (RCAHMS C45130)

Mercantile Land and Finance Company, 1966; W T Jackson, *The Enterprising Scot: Investors in the American West after 1873,* 1968; W G Kerr, 'Scotland and the Texas mortgage business', *Economic History Review,* 16, 1963, 91-103.

24   SRO CS318/49/67, Sequestration of A & W Fingzies, Sederunt Book, 1901, 39-58.

25   SRO CS318/325/1863, Inventory of estate, 27 Aug 1861; Census of Scotland, 1861; Enumerators books, village of Cambusnethan; SRO Register of Sasines (Glasgow), RS54 214.186; 214.192; 220.138; 220.191; 227.140; 242.117-8; 1558.256; 1559.28; 1559.51. The Glasgow properties were at 166 and 172 Bedford Terrace, Renfrew Street, and in Wishaw at Cambusnethan and Marshall Streets.

26   *The Builder* provides numerous examples of such terminology, as does the *Edinburgh Gazette.*

27   Censuses of Scotland, *City of Edinburgh,* 1861-1901.

28   For recent discussions on historical aspects of information costs to business see M Casson, 'Institutional economics and business history: a way forward?', and S Jones, 'Transactions costs and the theory of the firm: the scope and limitations of the new institutional approach', *Business History,* 39, 1997, 151-71 and 9-25.

29   Edinburgh City Archives, ACC 264, Guildry Cuttings file, Annual Report of the Dean of Guild, 1903.

30   Rodger, 'Speculative builders', 231-5.

31   P J Aspinall, 'The internal structure of the housebuilding industry', 91.

32   ECA Dean of Guild Court Registers, 1860-1914; Rodger, 'Speculative builders', Table 2, 228.

33   Rodger, 'Speculative builders'; 'Structural instability in the Scottish building industry 1820-80', *Construction History,* 2, 1986, 48-60; and *Housing in Urban Britain 1780-1920,* 1995, 20-2.

34   R Rodger, '"The Invisible Hand": market forces, housing and the urban form in Victorian cities', in D Fraser and A Sutcliffe (eds), *The Pursuit of Urban History,* 1983, Table 10.5, 206.

35   Glasgow Municipal Commission (hereafter GMC) on the Housing of the Poor, Evidence, 1904, Binnie, Q.6962.

36   GMC, Evidence, Binnie, Q.7011.

37   See R Rodger, 'Business failure in Scotland 1839-1913', *Business History,* 27, 1985, 75-99; M S Moss and J Hume, 'Business failure in Scotland 1839-1913', *Business History,* 25, 1983, 3-10.

38   PP 1917-18, XIV, *Report of the Royal Commission on the Housing of the Industrial Population of Scotland* (Ballantyne Report), Cd 8371 (hereafter *Report*), paragraph 373.

39   Census of Scotland, 1911, shows that in the Scottish burghs with a population of more than 2,000, 14% of all houses had only one room and housed 10% of the urban population; 42% of all accommodation was two-roomed and 43% of the population lived in these.

40   Census of Scotland, 1911, Table XLVII.

41   A system of 'ticketing' existed, most notably in Glasgow, but elsewhere too, whereby a ratio existed between the cubic capacity of the accommodation and the number of persons allowed in that domestic space. The system was 'policed' by municipal inspectors, and if not always effective was certainly a disincentive to overcrowding. See J B Russell, 'On the "ticketed houses" of Glasgow', *Proceedings of the Royal Philosophical Society of Glasgow,* 1888, 19.

42   Quoted in H Clark, 'Living in one or two rooms in the city', in A Carruthers, *The Scottish Home,* 1996, 69.

43   Presbytery of Glasgow, *Report of Commission on the Housing of the Poor in Relation to their Social Condition,* 1891, 96.

44   D Englander, 'Landlord and tenant', in *Urban Britain 1838-1918,* 1983, 30.

45   PP 1917-18, XIV, Evidence of Mary Laird, Q.23,066-67.

46   PP 1917-18, XIV, *Report,* paragraph 646.

47   H Clark, 'Living in one or two rooms', 70.

48   See for example, R J Morris, 'The ILP 1893-1932: Introduction', in A McKinlay and R J Morris (eds), *The ILP on Clydeside, 1893-1932: From Foundation to Disintegration,* 1991, 13; J Melling, *Rent Strikes: People's Struggle for Housing in West Scotland 1890-1916,* 1983, 27-34.

49   PP 1918, X, Ministry of Reconstruction, Women's Housing Sub-committee; and PP 1918 VII, *Report of the Committee appointed by the President of the*

11   W Chambers, *Report on the Sanitary State of the Residences of the Poorer Classes in the Old Town of Edinburgh,* 1840, 1.

12   F Engels, *The Condition of the Working Class in England in 1844,* 1936 edition, 34.

13   PP(HL) l842, XXVIII. The Edinburgh physician Dr Neil Arnott was Edwin Chadwick's personal physician and wrote the report on Edinburgh for the *Report.*

14   G Gordon, 'The status areas of early to mid-Victorian Edinburgh', *Transactions of the Institute of British Geographers,* 4, 1979, 168-91; J R Kellett, 'Property speculators and the building of Glasgow 1780-1830', *Scottish Journal of Political Economy,* 8, 1961, 211-32.

15   A J Youngson, *The Making of Classical Edinburgh 1750-1840,* 1966.

16   M A Simpson, 'Glasgow', in M A Simpson and T H Lloyd (eds), *Middle Class Housing in Britain,* 1977; M A Simpson, 'Middle class housing and the growth of suburban communities in the West End of Glasgow, 1830-1914', B Litt thesis, University of Glasgow, 1970.

17   R Rodger, 'Speculative builders and the structure of the Scottish building industry 1860-1914', *Business History,* 21 (2), 1979, 233.

18   J D Bailey, 'Australian borrowing in Scotland in the nineteenth century', *Economic History Review,* 12, 1959, 268-79.

19   Edinburgh Public Library (Edinburgh Room), annual *Post Office Directory.*

20   National Archives of Scotland/Scottish Record Office (SRO), Register of Sasines, RS108/4204.13, 3811.11, 2153.141.

21   R Pipes, *The Colonies of Stockbridge,* 1984.

22   R Rodger, 'The law and urban change: some nineteenth century Scottish evidence', *Urban History Yearbook,* 1979, 79-91, and 'The Victorian building industry and the housing of the Scottish working class', in M Doughty (ed.), *Building the Industrial City,* 1986, 172-4; N J Morgan, 'Building the city' in W H Fraser and I Maver (eds), *Glasgow 1830-1912,* 1996, 8-51.

23   A K Cairncross, *Home and Foreign Investment 1870-1913,* 1953, 37-64; J D Bailey, *A Hundred Years of Pastoral Banking: A History of the Australian*

		percentage of housebuilding in projects of 1, 2, or 3+ houses		
	number	*1 house*	*2 or more houses*	*3 or more houses*
cities	3	39.6	60.4	21.1
major burghs	30	53.9	46.1	20.4
small burghs	69	74.8	25.2	3.6
Scottish burghs	102	52.9	47.1	17.2

B1.33. Fluctuations in the building industry in selected burghs, 1873-1914. (R Rodger, Business History, *1985, 75-99)*

Local Government Board and Secretary for Scotland to consider questions of building construction in connection with the provision of dwellings for the working classes in England and Wales, and Scotland, and report upon methods of securing economy and despatch in the provision of such dwellings (Tudor Walters Report).

50   PP 1917-18, XIV, *Report*, paragraphs 46-50; PP 1912-13, XIV, Census of Scotland, parts 1-4.

51   Scotch Education Department, *Report on the Physical Condition of Children attending the Public School Board for Glasgow*, 1907; Dundee Social Union, *Report of Investigation into Social Conditions in Dundee*, 1905; City of Edinburgh Charity Organisation Society, *Report on the Physical Condition of Fourteen Hundred School Children in the City, together with some account of their Homes and Surroundings*, 1906.

52   Scottish Land Enquiry Committee, (hereafter SLEC), Report, *Scottish Land*, 1914, 369.

53   SLEC, 369.

54   SLEC, 371.

55   W Thompson, *Housing Up-to-Date*, 1907, 39.

56   J B Russell, 'On the sanitary results of the Glasgow Improvement Act', *Sanitary Journal of Scotland*, 1876, 137-8; J B Russell, *Life in One Room, or Some Considerations for the Citizens of Glasgow*, 1888; J B Russell, 'The house in relation to public health', *Transactions of the Insurance and Actuarial Society of Glasgow*, 5, 1887, 5-10; A K Chalmers, *Public Health Administration* (see also list of Russell's publications); H D Littlejohn, *Report on the Sanitary Condition of the City of Edinburgh*, 1865

57   P J Smith, 'Slum clearance as an instrument of sanitary reform: the flawed vision of Edinburgh's first slum clearance scheme', *Planning Perspectives*, 9, 1994, 1-27.

58   W Thompson, *Housing Up-to-Date*, 43.

59   PP 1917-18 XIV, *Report*, 387.

60   R Rodger, 'Wages, employment and poverty in the Scottish cities 1840-1914', in R J Morris and R Rodger (eds), *The Victorian City: A Reader in British Urban History 1820-1914*, 1993, 73-113.

61   PP 1884-85, XXX, Royal Commission on the Housing of the Working Classes, *Second Report*, Cd 4409, 4.

62   PP 1884-85, XXX, Royal Commission, *Second Report*, 7-8.

63   R Rodger, 'Crisis and confrontation in Scottish housing 1880-1914', in R Rodger (ed.), *Scottish Housing in the Twentieth Century*, 1989, 25-53; M Glendinning, 'The Ballantyne Report', in D Mays (ed.), *The Architecture of Scottish Cities*, 1997, 161-70.

64   PP 1911, XXXIII, *Annual Report of the Local Government Board for Scotland for 1910*, lxvii; PP 1912-13, XXXVII, for 1911, lix.

65   A O'Carroll, 'Tenements to bungalows: class and the growth of home ownership before the Second World War', *Urban History*, 24, 1997, 221-41; and 'The influence of local authorities on the growth of owner occupation 1914-39', *Planning Perspectives*, 11, 1996, 55-72.

66   B S Townroe, *The Slum Problem*, 1928, 19.

	av. index changes p.a.		av. index changes p.a.
Hawick	44.8	Motherwell	27.4
Irvine	43.7	Airdrie	25.5
Kilmarnock	43.6	Falkirk	24.8
Perth	39.2	Govan	23.5
Leith	38.3	Wishaw	22.8
Dunfermline	38.1	Dundee	22.1
Partick	35.7	Edinburgh	22.1
Port Glasgow	34.8	Paisley	21.6
Stirling	30.9	Glasgow	20.0
Rutherglen	28.6	Ayr	19.6
Kirkcaldy	27.7	Aberdeen	19.0
Coatbridge	27.7		

B1.34. *Fluctuations in housebuilding approvals in key burghs, 1873-1914. (R Rodger, Business History, 1985, 75-99) Note: in each burgh the average level of housebuilding approvals between 1900 and 1909 forms the basis of the index and thus equals 100.*

	Death Rate/ 1000	% of total houses having					% of population in houses having					% of population living more than		
		1 room	2 rooms	3 rooms	4 rooms	5 rooms	1 room	2 rooms	3 rooms	4 rooms	5 rooms	2 per room	3 per room	4 per room
Glasgow	20.4	20.0	46.3	18.9	6.6	8.2	13.8	48.7	21.2	7.2	9.1	55.7	27.9	10.7
Edinburgh	18.2	9.5	31.4	21.9	14.4	22.8	5.8	30.9	22.8	15.1	25.4	32.6	12.7	4.1
Dundee	20.0	16.9	54.0	17.3	5.2	7.6	9.9	53.2	21.5	6.4	9.0	48.2	20.0	6.1
Aberdeen	17.8	9.8	36.8	27.9	11.3	14.2	4.8	33.8	32.0	13.0	16.4	37.8	12.3	2.2

B1.35. *Housing, overcrowding and mortality in the Scottish cities, 1911. (Scottish Land Enquiry Committee, Scottish Land, 1914, 350-1; Board of Trade, Report of Enquiry into Working Class Rents, Cd 3864, 1908, 511, 516, 521, 535)*

SOCIAL HOMES, PRIVATE HOMES

The Reshaping of Scottish Housing, 1914-39

Annette O'Carroll

Introduction

The interwar period saw a huge increase in new-build housing construction, which changed significantly the physical appearance and social patterns of Scotland's towns and cities. This building activity was mainly commissioned by the city and town councils. However, there was also substantial speculative building activity by the private sector. Private housebuilding firms had a vital role in both kinds of provision, as they also constructed most local authority housing, working as contractors.

The new force of state intervention was not unified or homogeneous, but was divided between central and local municipal agencies. The result was a wide range of 'public' housing policies, including differing views as to how the private building industry might contribute. Because of the high price of housing construction immediately after World War I, central government intervention, in the form of the subsidy provisions of key interwar housing legislation, was of crucial importance both in assisting the revival of private sector building and enabling, for the first time, an effective programme of building by local authorities. Authorities had some autonomy in the directing of subsidies, and in most Scottish towns and cities the primary concern was to maximise the production of council housing. However, Edinburgh Corporation had a different priority, namely to encourage building by the private sector. In this chapter, we trace these contrasting policies, and conclude that the policy of concentration on building for owner occupation and private renting was more effective than that of local authority building for rent in maximising housing output at this period. After a discussion of the effects of housing subsidies, we consider not only how private sector housing was produced and marketed during this period but also how social, political and economic factors combined in the 1930s to produce an unprecedented demand for speculatively built owner-occupied homes. Demand was encouraged by sophisticated advertising, and facilitated by complicated arrangements between builders and building societies which made new-build houses available to consumers on easy repayment terms. Such arrangements extended owner occupation down the class structure to include skilled manual workers.

Although few accessible records of the building firms which were involved in constructing housing in this period have survived, other contemporary evidence indicates that the production of housing changed during the 1920s from a relatively small-scale operation to an important speculative enterprise. The physical form of the Scottish dwelling was also transformed, as housing developers ceased the production of the stone-built tenements which were the traditional housing type before 1914. Instead they now built mainly brick and harled cottage housing and flats for the public and private rented sectors, and bungalows for the owner-occupied sector.

The Ballantyne Report
turning-point of Scottish housing

The First World War revolutionised the processes of providing Scottish housing. At the outbreak of the war, around 90% of households rented housing from private landlords, about 10% were in owner occupation and less than 1% were housed by local authorities. During the war, however, the free market in private rented housing was radically undermined by the Rent and Mortgage Interest (War Restrictions) Act of 1915, which curtailed landlord profits by fixing rents at their 1914 levels for the duration of the war; the legislation was renewed and extended in 1919. This Act was passed as the result of political pressure from tenants, particularly on Clydeside, where hostility between landlord and tenant was especially strong. The government's action, together with the high price of housing construction in the immediate aftermath of the war, upset the always precarious equilibrium between supply and demand in the private rented sector, by discouraging the building of houses for rent. Into this wartime political crisis of housing production, in 1917, dropped a further

B2.1. Logie housing scheme, Dundee (designed by city engineer James Thomson and built in 1919-20): Scotland's first post-World War I council housing project. (RCAHMS B22130)

B2.2. Terrace of four-apartment cottages at Carter's Park, Kirkwall, the first 1919 Act scheme in Orkney, designed by T S Peace and built in 1920-21 by local contractor John Firth. The contract was changed from separate-trades to single-contractor when it was discovered that local stone would be too expensive, and harled brick was substituted. (M Glendinning)

bombshell: the report of the Royal Commission on the Housing of the Industrial Population of Scotland (the Ballantyne Commission), which had been set up in 1912 to answer criticisms of Scottish housing conditions by reformists and tenants.

The Ballantyne Report unequivocally rejected the private system of housing provision. It argued that private enterprise had failed to house adequately the working class population of Scotland, and that state intervention to provide housing was now necessary. Before the war, it claimed, the private industry had been 'practically the only agency that undertook the building of houses, and most of the troubles we have been investigating are due to the failure of private enterprise to provide and maintain the necessary houses sufficient in quantity and quality'. (1) It stated unequivocally that 'we have come to the definite conclusion that for the housing of the working classes the State must accept direct responsibility'. (2) This key recommendation led to the passing of the Housing, Town Planning, etc. (Scotland) Act in 1919. This Act no longer merely permitted, but actively required local authorities to conduct a survey of the housing needs of their areas and to build housing for the working classes with the help of central government subsidies. State involvement in the housing market was fuelled by the fear of insurrection, such as had threatened to occur on Clydeside in 1915 and had occurred in Russia in 1917. This was the first time that central government was prepared to subsidise the building of houses, a move that was intended to be temporary. It was hoped that when the high price of building materials and labour in the immediate postwar period (which had doubled the cost of building a house between 1914 and 1918) returned to 'normal', the private sector would be able to resume building working class rented housing and the role of the state could be reduced.

The most considered opposition to this snowballing momentum of state interventionism was offered by a dissenting faction within the Ballantyne Commission itself. Their minority report (the Lovat Report) claimed that the policy of radical but temporary state action was self-contradictory, as it would actually prevent a revival of the private sector: 'the need for the rapid supply of enlarged and improved houses [is] so great that no one form of enterprise is adequate to meet it ... to place the largest possible share of the responsibility for providing houses on the shoulders of Local Authorities would ... act as an actual obstacle in the way of the revival of private and co-operative enterprise in house building'. (3) As we will see, the experience of the interwar years to some extent vindicated Lovat's argument. Those Scottish cities

which prioritised council housebuilding failed to produce the largest volume of housing, when building for all three tenures was taken into account.

The effects of housing subsidies on housing supply

The progress of the housing market, in the interwar period as at present, is affected by both supply and demand factors. Interwar concepts of supply were conditioned by the fact that the building of housing by local authorities was intended to be temporary. Thus the legislation of most of the interwar period was directed not only towards the building of council houses but also towards the subsidising of housebuilding for both owner occupation and renting. Subsidies, and the manner in which they were operated by Scottish local authorities, had a significant influence on the differential rate of building for the private sector in Scottish cities. The Housing (Additional Powers) Act 1919 was intended to complement the Housing, Town Planning, etc. Act of the same year by reviving private housebuilding. However, the rate of building under this Act was disappointing because the subsidy did not fully compensate for the high costs of materials and labour at this period. The expansion of private sector housebuilding did not really begin until after 1923, in the aftermath of the Chamberlain and Wheatley Acts' subsidy provisions (see below), and the rate of building throughout the 1920s continued to be strongly influenced by the levels of subsidy available.

The first housing legislation which successfully provided subsidies for the private sector was the Housing, etc., Act 1923 (the Chamberlain Act), which was passed by a Unionist/Conservative government. While Section 1 (3) of this Act preserved a limited scope for direct local authority building within the sphere of slum-clearance rehousing schemes, the predominant slant of the new provisions was to deter general-needs building by councils, and redirect them towards a role as subsidising enablers of private enterprise. Here, because of pressure from the National Federation of House Builders, a subsidy for houses which conformed to government standards of space and design was paid as a lump sum to private builders. (4) Unlike the generous subsidies for local authorities under the Addison Act, any councils involved in this scheme were to be compensated by a payment from the Treasury of only £6 per house for 20 years. Local authorities were not permitted to build for general needs under this Act unless they could prove that it was impossible for private enterprise in their area to do so. Where houses were built by the private sector, the equivalent of this, expressed as a capital lump sum of £75, was to be paid to the builder on completion of the house; local authorities could provide extra funding in addition to this sum if they wished to increase the rate of building in their area. They were also allowed to lend money to builders to promote the building of houses for renting and to underwrite loans made by building societies. It was expected that this legislation would chiefly benefit lower-income would-be owner occupiers, since builders who obtained grants to build houses had to undertake to sell them at prices which would not make an unreasonably high profit. (5)

The Labour Party, with its stronger commitment towards direct provision of rented housing by the state, argued that this Act was a failure. In an attempt to improve the rate of production of houses to let, the first Labour government brought in the Housing (Financial Provisions) Act in 1924 (the Wheatley Act). This, like the Chamberlain Act, was a Britain-wide measure. However, the Chamberlain Act provisions were maintained in order that the subsidising of owner occupation would continue. Wheatley also attempted to stop restrictive practices in the building industry, which were slowing down housing production; for example, he managed to obtain an agreement which improved the ratio of apprentices to craftsmen. The Wheatley Act re-established the powers of the local authorities to provide houses for the working classes without first needing to prove that private enterprise was unable to build them. It increased the subsidy for each house; however, since it was not intended to help people become owner occupiers, the subsidy was not given as a capital sum but was paid annually to the landlord of the house.

By the late 1920s and early 1930s, the cost of both producing and financing housing had fallen to such an extent that in Scotland the average cost of building a three-apartment flatted house (which had been over £1,000 in 1920) was around £300 in 1932; this was said to be the lowest price since 1914. (6) The Conservative-dominated National government, which had replaced the Labour government as a result of the economic crisis of 1931, decided on the downward revision and eventual cessation of subsidies in England and Wales. In Scotland, although reduced, these were allowed to continue for a longer period, as an acknowledgement of the poorer housing conditions in this country. (7) The decision that local authorities would stop building for general-needs applicants after 1933 reflected the government's intention that, where possible, those in need of housing would be forced to buy with the help of a building society loan. (8) In future, government financial assistance was to be directed towards providing housing for those who were in special need of help, such as slum clearance tenants or those whose accommodation was overcrowded.

B2.3. Blackhill, Glasgow, a scheme largely of three-storey 'Rehousing' tenements built from 1935 using brick construction and synthetic stone (concrete blockwork) outer facing; the three-apartment flats each cost £248 to build.
(RCAHMS GW/3146)

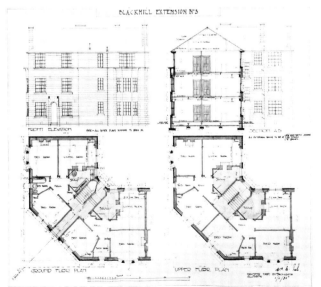

B2.4. Blackhill, plan of corner tenement.
(Glasgow City Council)

The boom in building for owner occupation

Although building costs had already begun to fall after 1921-22, owing partly to technological improvements in production methods, and subsidies were available for building small houses in Scotland until 1933, the rate of speculative housebuilding accelerated most strongly only after 1932. This suggests that the vital precipitating factors for the interwar housing boom were the low interest rates which followed Britain's withdrawal from the gold standard in 1931, and the fall in the retail prices index, which meant a rise in real wages for those in employment. By 1933, building materials were cheap and plentiful, the wages of those employed in the building trade were lower than at any time since the war, the output per worker (measured by the censuses of building production) was higher than in 1924, and funds for housing were easily available. (9) All these factors ensured that the cost of building houses was at a postwar low and, when combined with the cessation of general-needs building by local authorities after 1933, made possible not only an increase in the growth of owner occupation but also a temporary revival in

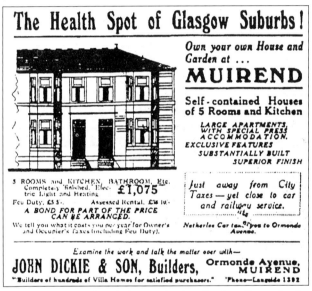

B2.5. Advertisement for suburban South Side villas, from Glasgow Evening News, 8 March 1927.

building for private renting. The rise in real wages also meant a rise in the growth of savings, and building societies were now in a period of rapid expansion. Indeed, part of the reason for the decline of private renting since 1918 had been the increasing capacity of the societies to provide a return for investors similar to that previously obtained from rented housing. The growing popularity of building societies with savers meant that the societies were forced to promote actively the extension of home ownership down the class structure in order to prevent the build-up of excessive funds. The societies also played an important role in providing finance for housebuilders, with completed houses remaining mortgaged to the societies until purchasers were found. These credit arrangements facilitated large-scale building operations without locking up too much capital. (10)

However, despite all the Ballantyne rhetoric of decisive national action, despite the high output of council housing and favourable treatment in the amount and duration of interwar housing subsidies, Scotland's housing output between 1918 and 1939, relative to population, was eventually only two-thirds that of England and Wales. The total of 311,500 houses built in Scotland was the equivalent of only 28% of the total number of houses that had existed there in 1911; the equivalent proportion south of the border was 52%. (11)

Table 1
Houses built per thousand of 1931 population in England/Wales, Scotland and the four main Scottish cities, 1918-1939

	Public Sector	Private Sector	Total
England/Wales	27.8	72.2	99.9
Scotland	43.9	20.4	64.3
Edinburgh	33.6	65.4	99.0
Aberdeen	38.5	29.7	68.2
Glasgow	49.5	18.1	67.6
Dundee	40.0	16.3	56.3

Source: Census, 1931

As Table 1 shows, this low overall output was strongly bound up with the issue of private versus state building, as it coincided with a relatively low rate of building by the private sector both in Scotland as a whole, and also in particular cities. England/Wales and Edinburgh (which had high housing outputs per head of population) had a relatively high rate of building for the private sector and a low level of council house building. Scotland as a whole, and the other three cities, had relatively low overall building levels; however, while their level of private sector building was low, their rate of public sector (council house) building was relatively high. Of the four million houses built in England and Wales between the wars, 72% were provided by private enterprise and only 28% by local authorities. In Scotland in the same period the percentages of private sector and local authority completions were virtually reversed, with 68% built by local authorities and 32% by private enterprise, the latter both for owner occupation and renting. In both cases, just over 10% of the total number of houses were built by *subsidised* private enterprise; this meant that the major difference between Scotland and the two southern countries was in the amount of unsubsidised building by the private sector. Unsubsidised housing constituted 61% of the total amount of house building in England and Wales, but only 21% of that in Scotland; the figures for Edinburgh and Glasgow were 40% and 12% respectively. (12) Most of the unsubsidised building between the wars was speculative housing built for owner occupation.

It is not possible to estimate the growth of home ownership in Scotland as a whole between 1914 and 1939, because there were no reliable statistics on this until the 1961 census, which included a question on tenure. However, figures are available for Glasgow in 1900 and Edinburgh in 1914, which indicate that both cities had owner occupation levels in the region of 12% by the outbreak of the First World War. (13) This is in line with an estimated figure of between 10% and 15% for owner occupation in England and Wales in 1914. (14) In 1946, as a result of the interwar boom in speculative housing for owner occupation and some tenure transfer from the private rented sector, the estimated overall British rate was 'somewhere below 35%' (15); at this time, 33% of Edinburgh houses were owner-occupied. (16) Census data for 1961 show that the figure for households in owner occupation in Scotland was 26%, compared with 41% in England and Wales. Where the four largest Scottish cities were concerned, the 1961 percentages were 43% for Edinburgh and 24% for Aberdeen, but only 16% each for Glasgow and Dundee. These tenure differences, together with the figures cited in Table 1, confirm that levels of private sector housebuilding between the wars were critical not only for the differential tenure development of

Scotland and the rest of Britain, but also for establishing differences between the Scottish cities.

Local authorities and the private housebuilding industry

The fact that a high level of building by the private sector was associated with a high overall building rate appears to vindicate the arguments of Lovat in 1917. It suggests that in order to maximise housing output at this period, the optimum policy would have been for local authorities to provide subsidies and other incentives to encourage private sector building. The results of this policy can be seen in Edinburgh, where, more than any other Scottish local authority, the Corporation was unenthusiastic about the long-term financial commitment involved in large-scale general-needs council provision, preferring rather to support building by private enterprise, even during times when national policy pointed in the other direction. Thus, of all the Edinburgh private sector housing constructed in the period between 1918 and 1932, around 75% was built with assistance from Edinburgh Corporation; the vast majority of this was for owner occupation. In addition to subsidies for building houses, the Corporation was prepared to provide loans for both building and purchasing houses at lower rates of interest than those offered either by other Scottish and English local authorities or by local building societies. (17)

Contemporary documents reveal that key officials of Edinburgh Corporation believed that it was important that the local authority should not, through competition resulting from an 'undue' amount of council building, raise the prices of building materials

B2.6. Saughton Golf Course housing scheme, Edinburgh, soon under construction in 1933, with the Dorset pea harling being applied to the common brick walls. This largely flatted development of over 650 dwellings, like most interwar Edinburgh council housing, was built on a separate-trades basis; the mason for most phases of the job was local Edinburgh contractor William Arnott McLeod.

B2.7. Blinkbonny estate, Edinburgh: unrealised feuing plan of 1875 for Trinity Hospital (the feudal superior), envisaging development with large villas, and terraces in the manner of the West End. (RCAHMS EDD/861/5)

and labour and thus damage the market for private enterprise construction. It was also alleged that this type of housing would act as a competitor to the private rented and owner-occupied sectors. Indeed, a 1925 report by the City Chamberlain maintained that 'in the best interests of the whole community it is undesirable that the Corporation should enter the market for housing labour and material in such a way as to raise the market against the enterprise of private persons'. (18) It was suggested that, after a seven year period, the private sector could resume the provision of general-needs rented housing for the working classes, leaving the Corporation to its 'real task' of providing only for the poorer classes. The Corporation should then aim to 'meet the needs of the insanitary areas'. (19) This could be done by building cheaper houses, as was currently being implemented under the slum clearance provision of the Housing, etc., Act 1923. Since building this type of house would engage a greater percentage of unskilled labour, there would not be competition for the same labour force between the public and private sectors. It was claimed that this policy would have the double advantage of both helping the unemployed and leaving building by private enterprise relatively unaffected. Indeed, although Glasgow Corporation built substantially more general-needs council housing than Edinburgh Corporation between the wars, Edinburgh succeeded in demolishing more substandard housing per head of population than Glasgow, and building more housing

for slum clearance under improvement and reconstruction schemes. (20)

In order to maintain a supply of general-needs rented housing after the subsidy provisions of the Wheatley Act expired in 1933, Edinburgh Corporation continued to provide help to firms prepared to build low-cost houses for renting, although there was no financial assistance from central government to compensate the Corporation for this. Building firms were helped by having land made available to them on favourable feuing terms and were provided with loans of up to 75% of the value of the houses at attractive rates of interest. Streets, main sewers and mains services were provided by the Corporation. In return, developers who built under these arrangements had to comply with limits on the rents that they could charge. In some ways, this policy represented an isolated municipal attempt to construct a system of regulation and cheap finance similar to those operated on a national scale in other countries, such as Germany. Of the total number of private sector houses built in Edinburgh after 1933, an estimated 25% were built for renting under such post-subsidy schemes. In the opinion of one recent urban historian: 'On balance this strategy represented an effective attempt by the local authority to reduce the scale of general needs demand on the local authority sector from the better paid "aristocracy of labour"'. (21) The effects of the policy stretched out beyond the city boundaries. For example,

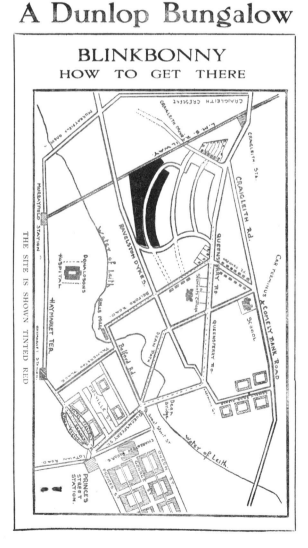

B2.8. The Blinkbonny area as eventually developed, with low-density interwar speculative bungalows for owner occupation: estate location map for a 44-bungalow development of 1932-33 by local speculative builder C H Dunlop. (James Miller Ltd)

B2.9. One of the types used by Dunlop at Blinkbonny: a four-apartment bungalow, built of harled brick and selling for £750 with £75 deposit and weekly outlay of 29s 3d. (James Miller Ltd)

B2.10. 1991 aerial view of C H Dunlop's Blinkbonny development.
(RCAHMS B62327)

as noted earlier in this book, it was largely because of these subsidies that Mactaggart & Mickel decided to transfer part of its operation from Glasgow to Edinburgh. Although the firm continued to build houses for owner occupation in Glasgow throughout the interwar period, from 1934 onwards all its building for the private rented sector was restricted to Edinburgh. In total the firm built or commenced over 3,400 houses for renting, at Granton, Carrick Knowe, Colinton and Broomhouse. (22)

The underlying reasons for Edinburgh Corporation's distinctive policy on housing provision were political, and these will be discussed below. In contrast to Edinburgh, other Scottish cities, and in particular Glasgow, developed housing policies, again for political reasons, which aimed to maximise the rate of general-needs council building. Were these two alternatives complementary, or conflicting? There is some evidence that the relatively large amount of general-needs council housing produced between the wars did affect both the supply of, and demand for, owner-occupied houses and, as has been indicated above, in Glasgow and Dundee owner occupation rates did not rise much above their probable 1914 levels until after 1961. Although research has shown that the number of households which had an income capable of supporting owner occupation was considerably higher in Glasgow than in Edinburgh between the wars, the potential demand for this tenure was not realised, certainly in part because of the availability of a plentiful supply of general-needs council housing in Glasgow. (23)

Factors influencing housing demand

When examining influences on the development and output of the private housebuilding industry in Scotland, it is important not only to look at the subsidy legislation, with its far-reaching effects on the supply of housing, but also to consider the factors which influenced demand. Here the economic and political background of the period was important. One reason for interwar Scotland's relatively low proportion of private sector housing and high provision of council housing was the economic performance of the country. In comparison with southern England, the Scottish economy, and especially the Clydeside military-industrial

complex, was particularly severely affected by the postwar economic crises; aspects of this which affected the demand for private house building included higher unemployment rates and lower real incomes. Where unemployment was concerned, a dependence on heavy industry made the country vulnerable to the economic depression of the 1930s. Scottish unemployment rates were higher than British rates in the 1920s and remained high until 1936; the gap increased after 1932 and especially after 1934, when unemployment began to decline in England. The 1930s saw a strong regional differentiation in employment and economic activity, especially between depressed Clydeside and Edinburgh, with its more broadly based industrial structure and expanding industries. By 1934, 16.6% of the population of Edinburgh was unemployed - an almost identical proportion to that of Britain as a whole - while the overall Scottish figure was 23.1%. In contrast to the capital, Glasgow's unemployment never fell below 25% in the period 1926-1936, and peaked at 30% in 1932. (24)

Income levels, an important factor in the demand for housing, were also lower between the wars than those of England and Wales. In the period from 1924 to 1949, Scottish income per head of population fluctuated from between 87% and 96% of the British average. In the depression years between 1929 and 1932, Scottish incomes declined by 22%, compared with a 15% fall in England and Wales. (25) However, regional differences in wage rates within Scotland largely disappeared in the 1930s. (26) Lower incomes, combined with the restricted percentage of income which Scots traditionally allocated to housing costs, limited the potential operations of builders of rented housing, who needed to be sure of being able to obtain an economic rent for their investment. This fact, in addition to the Ballantyne Commission legacy of denunciations of 'bad Scottish housing' and the political opposition to landlords, may have fuelled the growing strength of council housebuilding in the country between the wars, especially on Clydeside. For these reasons, council houses may have been acceptable to middle class Scots who might otherwise have chosen owner occupation, thus depressing the demand for speculatively built houses. (27) This certainly appears to have been the case in Glasgow.

Political constraints and differences

Where politics had rarely intruded directly on the laissez-faire housing system of the 19th century, now political demands and constraints were felt everywhere in the housing system. These were influenced not only by national factors, such as the different attitudes to council housing in Scotland and in England, but also by municipal political pressures; the post-Ballantyne system, after all, accorded local authorities a key role in influencing the supply of housing, and gave them some autonomy in determining the relative levels of council house and private sector building in their areas. The most important local political difference in attitudes to housing provision was that between Glasgow and Edinburgh. Although the former's population was more than twice that of the latter (1,088,461 in the 1931 census, compared with 439,010), there was in absolute terms substantially less interwar housebuilding by the private sector (especially by unsubsidised private enterprise) in Glasgow than in Edinburgh. This was largely because of the sharply differing political constitutions of the two cities; here we refer not to strict party politics but to a more general political-cultural ethos of the municipal ruling elites.

Within Glasgow Corporation, throughout the whole interwar period and indeed right up until the late 1970s, there was 'by-

and-large inter party agreement on the necessity for a strategy of large scale council house provision'. (28) The Corporation was dominated until 1933 by the Moderates, a non-socialist association of Liberals and Tories. The Liberal group, which was the main party in that alliance, believed in maintaining the tradition of municipal services provision which had been strongly established in Glasgow in the 19th century. (29) After 1933, when socialist councillors (in the form of a coalition of Labour, Independent Labour and Catholic Independent) gained the majority, the policy was only strengthened, as state housing was a central element of socialist policy. (30) The Labour Party controlled eighteen other Scottish burgh councils at this period, and had the same number of seats as the opposition parties in another four. (31)

In contrast, the growth of Labour representation in Edinburgh was slow. Although support for Labour in the city grew over the interwar period, the proportion of Labour councillors on the important Housing and Town Planning or Treasurer's Committees of Edinburgh Corporation never exceeded 28%, so that the party's influence on policy decisions concerning the supply of housing was limited; only for a brief period during the high-rise years of the 1960s was the Housing Committee eventually chaired by a Labour councillor, Pat Rogan. (32) The group which dominated local politics in the capital from 1930 until the 1970s was an anti-socialist coalition of Tories, Liberals and Independents which was given the label of 'Progressive'. Financial prudence was an important element of Progressive policy, and this ensured that the city's attitude towards building council housing was one of caution. In the view of David McCrone, 'These fairly loose coalitions kept alive the belief that local government was essentially a non-political business in which individuals were elected on their merits ... the appeal of the Progressives and moderates was particularly to small local businessmen who believed in apolitical administration by knowledgeable, essentially local, people like themselves.' (33) Property owners and landlords were in the majority on vital committees in Edinburgh, and their political ethos was strongly opposed to interventive, Glasgow-style municipal socialism. Because local revenues were raised by property taxes - 'the rates' - many small property owners, committed to preserve Edinburgh's rates at a lower level than those of other Scottish cities, sought election to the town council in order to control the level of public spending; this caution applied particularly to council housing, which was also seen as a competitor to the private rented sector. Protecting the interests of Edinburgh ratepayers was a priority, since maintaining a low level of rates was also seen as important in preserving the relatively successful industrial structure of Edinburgh and attracting new industry to the area. (34)

Local rates levels and speculative building

The system of local rates was seen by many as a factor inhibiting private housebuilding activity between the wars, because the liability was shared between occupiers and owners of housing; in 1956 it was eventually amended to apply only to occupiers (a system already established in England and Wales) by the Valuation and Rating (Scotland) Act. (35) This system was claimed to bear especially harshly on owner occupiers, who in effect were liable for two sets of property taxes. The Ballantyne Report argued that 'the classes on which the increase of rates has told most heavily are the occupying owners of houses of a good standard, many of whom have obtained their dwelling through building societies at the cost of prolonged effort, and who find themselves assessed for both owners' and occupiers' rates'. (36) The fact that owners' rates also had to be paid if a house was unoccupied also inhibited speculative building for owner occupation; indeed a 1945 command paper on the rating system claimed that this had affected not only demand, but also the supply of housing for owner occupation. (37) Builders who erected houses for sale owned the houses until they were sold. As owners, they were liable to pay not only the annual feu duty on the land, but also owners' rates on the houses that they had built. While a house remained unsold, the cost of these payments could not be passed on to the new owner and so the profits of the developer were eroded. This limited the level of private sector building both for renting and for owner occupation. The 1945 command paper expressed the problem in terms of an unfavourable comparison with England: 'With this to consider the speculative builder in Scotland naturally had to be more completely satisfied that there

B2.11. Piershill Barracks site, Edinburgh, a 342-dwelling flatted Corporation rental development built in 1936-38, on an open layout reflecting the government Highton Committee's study of Continental housing; the stone facing was recycled from the old barracks buildings. The two phases of the scheme were both built by separate-trades contracts, in both cases using W Arnott McLeod for demolition, excavation, mason and brick work. (RCAHMS B71032)

would be an immediate possibility of obtaining a purchaser than had his opposite number in England. As a result the tendency north of the Border has been to build only for an established market, and not in reasonable anticipation of demand - which has been the healthier practice adopted in England'. (38) Thus the setting of a high level of rates by an authority would discourage speculative private housebuilding in the locality, since rates formed a significant proportion of the annual costs of housing: 'in many of the towns and counties where houses are most needed the present rate per £ is far above the average, and the builder is consequently driven into other areas where the rating position is more favourable'. (39)

The decision about the relative proportion of the rate to be paid by owners and occupiers was the responsibility of each local authority, and it is significant that Glasgow Corporation not only tended to set a higher overall rate than Edinburgh, Aberdeen or Dundee, but also allocated a significantly higher proportion of rate poundage to owners, and a lower proportion to occupiers, than the other main Scottish cities. (40) Glasgow's high owners' rates policy was the result of attempts by working class ratepayers in Glasgow to get more of the burden of rates passed to owners. (41) The practical result of this high rates policy was that in Glasgow in 1934 the owner of an 'average' priced house of around £600, such as a newly built four-apartment bungalow, would have to pay an annual sum in owners' rates significantly greater than that paid on a similar house in Edinburgh; the difference was more than a full week's income for a white-collar worker. (42) This was an important contributory factor to the relatively low rates of building for owner occupation in Glasgow in the interwar period, and it was claimed that 'differences in rate poundages are undoubtedly an element in the situation to be taken into account by a builder who is estimating the possible market in various localities'. (43) In Edinburgh the priority was to keep rates, and particularly owners' rates, at a low level, while maintaining a high overall housing output.

The structure of the industry

The rate of housing provision was also powerfully affected by the structure of the building industry. This industry was smaller, in relation to population, than its counterparts in England and Wales; for example in 1932 there were only 16.1 insured building workers in the Scottish industry per thousand of population, compared with 19.1 in England and Wales. (44) Building in interwar Scotland remained a somewhat fragmented, casual trade, with the vast majority of building firms still small, separate-trades businesses; this was especially the case in the east of Scotland, including the Edinburgh area. In the period between 1923 and 1932, of the 78 Edinburgh building firms that employed more than ten workers, 22 employed an average of less than 25, 30 between 25 and 50, four between 100 and 200, and only three over 300. (45) Firms employing under ten men made up 19% of the total employed in the building trades, although such firms worked mainly on maintenance and repair work. In Edinburgh and the east, the net output per worker compared unfavourably with practically every other area of Scotland, England or Wales - including Clydeside. (46) This was due to a high proportion of manual labour and a lack of mechanised construction. But even within these limitations, the building industry in Edinburgh was the second most important in the city, employing 7.2% of all insured workers in 1923 and 9.7% by 1932/33. (47)

Some of the structural difficulties in the building industry, which between the wars continued to be dominated by Continental-

style multi-contracting amongst specialist craft trades, could have been overcome by single contracting on the English and American pattern. This was inhibited both by the weight of tradition and by opposition from the craft unions. However, throughout the 1930s, it seems that larger firms, which employed most of their own tradesmen but contracted out some specialised work when necessary, became increasingly important in building for both the private and public sectors, in contrast to the small-scale, fragmented housing projects typical of the previous century. Because few records of the Scottish firms engaged in housing work at that time have been available up to now, it has been difficult to obtain detailed information about private house building to substantiate this point. In Edinburgh, however, because 75% of the housing built for the private sector between 1918 and 1932 received assistance from the Corporation either in the form of loans or subsidies, details of changes over this period are available. To obtain subsidy, houses had to fulfil size and cost criteria, so it is likely that those that were built without subsidy were too large or expensive to qualify. An analysis of subsidy building showed a diminishing total of single applications by private individuals, relative to multiple applications by builders. This confirms that the 1920s and early 1930s in the capital, at any rate, was a watershed period, which saw the emergence of the modern system of speculative house construction by builders and developers. Single applications declined sharply throughout the subsidy period, so that although these made up 57.1% of the total in 1923, the percentage had fallen to 10.4% by 1927. From that year onwards it was mainly building firms who were applying to build under subsidy in Edinburgh and by 1932 only 0.8% of the houses built were individual applications. (48) Evidence by the City Architect indicated that houses around £600 (the cost price

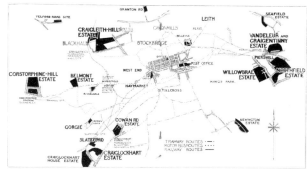

OUR SITES PLACE ONE WITHIN DIRECT ACCESS TO ANY DISTRICT IN EDINBURGH, AS SHOWN IN THE FOLLOWING DIAGRAM

B2.12. Edinburgh estate map from the 1934 edition of James Miller's brochure Home. *(James Miller Ltd)*

B2.13. Specimen bungalow-types and estate descriptions from Home. *(James Miller Ltd)*

B2.14. Miller bungalow built in 1935-36 in Davidson Road, Craigleith. (M Glendinning)

ceiling for a house eligible for subsidy) were the most popular properties with would-be purchasers in that year. (49) The increasing importance of speculative building allowed efficient firms to grow enormously in size, and in Edinburgh one builder, James Miller, came to dominate the provision of subsidy houses. Table 2 compares the numbers of subsidy houses built by Miller and the next nine builders, in descending rank order:

Table 2
Subsidised private sector building in Edinburgh, 1923-34

Name of builder	Number of houses
1. James Miller	1,922
2. T. S. Henderson	203
3. G. R. Black	96
4. Bangholm Building Company	90
5. Ford and Torrie	89
6. Edinburgh and Suburban Building Society	88
7. C. H. Dunlop	86
8. R. J. Robinson	83
9. Blyth Building Company	73
10. Anderson and Walker	68

Source: Edinburgh Corporation Treasurer's Committee Minutes, 1923-34.

Miller was only 23 when he completed his first big project, for 16 houses at Blackhall. These he advertised in the *Scotsman* in March 1927 as follows: 'It was, I believe, the first time such an advertisement had been put in the paper. The first pair were only being roofed. My first enquiry was at 10 o'clock in the morning. I hadn't time to eat or rest till after it was dark that night and practically every house was spoken for. These houses sold for £870 ... at the same time I got several enquiries for a smaller bungalow, and developed our A-type bungalow which was a best seller for the next 12 years'. (50) This firm's first subsidy application was for a modest 32 houses in 1927, at which time it was still a limited partnership involving James Miller and his two brothers. In 1932, after only five years in business, applications to build 1,224 houses were made, amounting to 64.4% of the total applications for subsidy houses in the city during that year. Overall, the total of 1,922 houses built by Miller between 1927 and 1934 accounted for 36% of all subsidy applications in Edinburgh. By the end of this period, the firm had become a limited company, James Miller & Partners, with capital of

£50,000. James Miller became a member of Edinburgh Town Council in 1936, his business having become 'well established and prosperous', and rose to be Lord Provost of Edinburgh from 1951 to 1954, and Lord Mayor of London in 1964. Of the Glasgow-based firms, Mactaggart & Mickel built a total of 19,391 houses in Scotland between 1922 and 1941, which was about 6% of all housing built in the country at this period. Of the 15,718 houses which they erected in Glasgow and the west, 3,148 were local authority houses built as contractors between 1922 and 1926, 4,524 were speculatively built for owner occupation between 1926 and 1940, and 8,046 were for the private rented sector between 1926 and 1934. Of the 3,673 houses completed by the firm in Edinburgh, 3,424 were for the private rented sector between 1933 and 1939, and 249 were for owner occupation between 1934 and 1940. (51)

In order to maximise the rate of building, availability of land was important. If this was not owned by the local authority, it was usually held in large tracts by 'landed proprietors, trusts, estate companies or the major local builders'. (52) Feuing restrictions regulated the development process, and ensured in general that the emphasis was on the building of medium-cost houses for owner occupation, since this type of development both enhanced the value of a feu superior's adjacent land holdings and, as a profitable form of development, served as insurance for the payment of feu duties to the superior. Of the larger builders, James Miller and Mactaggart & Mickel acquired extensive land banks. Miller had acquired 489 acres of land in 72 separate sites by the end of 1939, the peak year for acquisitions being 1934. Only ten of these sites were larger than ten acres and the largest site was 51 acres. The average area per site was 6.8 acres. (53). Later research by Bingham suggested that the company pursued a highly vigorous land acquisition policy, and exploited a little-used aspect of the feudal land tenure system, under which land could be acquired against payment of annual feu-duties only (rather than the usual system of an initial cash sum and annual feuduties). (54)

The high rate of building by firms like James Miller and Mactaggart & Mickel was achieved not just because they had an adequate supply of land, but also through economies of scale and efficient use of labour. Such firms tended to produce a limited range of inexpensive smaller houses which experience had shown were popular. Mactaggart & Mickel produced its high output by building mainly two types of three- and four-apartment houses; variety was added in the use of colour schemes and in minor differences in windows and roofs. As a large firm, it was also able to buy building materials cheaply and provide the relatively secure working conditions which helped it to retain building workers. (55) Since the traditional Scottish building material, prior to 1914, had been stone, there was an especially acute shortage of bricks and bricklayers between the wars. The major building firms tried to overcome shortages, and also cut costs, by the use of experimental materials such as concrete blocks and artificial stone; they were also innovators in building technology at this time, including the use of 'a steam powered bricklaying machine and plaster and cement guns'. (56) However, machines were expensive and only worthwhile on large-scale contracts for public housing, with their guaranteed income. Where organisation of labour was concerned, speculative housing developments appear to have been more efficiently organised than most public housing contracts, with one main builder and greater continuity of labour enabling faster progress. On public housing schemes, the separate trades system retained much of its popularity, owing to its alleged cost advantage of 5-10%; however, criticisms that it slowed the rate of building were increasingly voiced. In 1937, an Edinburgh

Corporation sub-committee on housing progress argued that the various trades 'will come forward with all sorts of excuses - frost, rain, strikes - any excuse is better than none. Each contractor standing for himself, one blames the other. Whereas if they were all in the one boat it would be up to them to organise the job properly'. (57)

The relationship between the publicly contracted and private speculative work was not just a matter of interesting academic comparisons, for there is evidence that, between the wars, there was growing competition for both materials and labour between the public and private sectors. This was especially the case from 1933 onwards, with the acceleration in the rate of building for owner occupation. In Edinburgh, all Corporation houses throughout the interwar period were built by private contractors and subcontractors (rather than by direct labour, as was an increasing proportion in Glasgow), and there was cut-throat competition for labour after 1935 between those building for the private sector and those on Corporation contracts. This adversely affected the production of council housing in the city, since contractors building houses for the private sector were able to pay more than the official rate, to entice building workers away from the local authority schemes. While this practice may have been necessary to ensure an adequate supply of labour for private sector construction, it was not an option for those building houses for Edinburgh Corporation, who were tied to fixed price contracts scrutinised by the Board of Health.

While the building firms were able to balance the potentially greater profits of the one against the greater security and continuity of the other, many among the workforce unambiguously preferred the higher pay of private contracts. The 1937 Edinburgh sub-committee painted a picture of low pay and low productivity on public housing contracts, a picture that (as we will see in the next chapter) would only become more accentuated after 1939: 'We have it on record that for six months as regards a man on commercial work and a man on [local authority] housing scheme work, the average wage of the bricklayer on the housing scheme was 25/- per week; the average wage of the man on commercial work, because the job was organised better, was 35/- ... The last job a man wants at present is a housing scheme job, run as they are run. Whenever a shower comes on, the whistle blows and everybody stops - not only here but elsewhere. Now if you can get a job somewhere else, you are not going to work on a housing scheme'. (58)

In 1937, this conflict between public and private building labour demands became a full-blown bidding war, when Glasgow Corporation introduced a new system which guaranteed work to its direct labour employees for 51 weeks in the year. The Corporation did not have significant direct labour projects until the 1930s, but between 1936 and 1939, 65% of the local authority houses in the city were built, or partially built, by direct labour, with only 35% completed by private contractors. (59) Because of the casual nature of the building trade, the certainty of a full week's work was a sufficient incentive to attract building workers to move to Glasgow, even from Edinburgh, in order to work for the Corporation: 'The men are all flocking to Glasgow because after they work a month they get the guaranteed week ... it is hurting the other work in Glasgow irrespective of housing because they are all rushing to housing ... I have no doubt the contractors in Glasgow are up against the Corporation'. (60)

Workers were willing to move to Glasgow to obtain some level of job security because employment conditions in the building trade between the wars were generally poor. Employees were engaged on an hourly basis, and workers below the grade of foreman had no guarantee of continual employment: they could be laid off at a day's notice. Building labourers were paid only for hours worked, and received no wages when time was lost because of bad weather. (61) Because accommodation for building workers on site was usually inadequate (a simple hut with no seating or cooking facilities), workers often had to go home when a job was interrupted by rain. Building workers' health was also affected by working in wet clothes. The average working week was 44 hours, except in December, when this was reduced to 41.5 hours. (62)

The influence of demographic and social change on housing demand

Although the changing structure of the building industry in Scotland between the wars was an important influence on the balance between private and public sector housing, demographic, economic and social change in the country were also significant factors in the growth of the private housebuilding industry. The key demographic change was the growth in the numbers of

B2.15. 1991 aerial view of Glasgow Corporation's Mosspark housing scheme (built by J A Mactaggart in 1921-24), a pioneer of large-scale garden-suburb developments of council housing. (RCAHMS B71293)

B2.16. 'Ribbon development' of bungalows along the south side of the main Glasgow Road in outer Edinburgh, built in 1933-38 by the Dunfermline and Edinburgh building firm of Hepburn Brothers and illustrated in the firm's 1934/35 brochure Ideal Bungalows. Between the wars, the firm developed a number of sites in outer Edinburgh; its house-types were designed by draughtsman Thomas Bruce of Inverkeithing. It also built, as main contractor, Edinburgh's first multi-storey blocks after World War II, at Westfield (1949-51) and Queensferry Road (1953-55). (James Miller Ltd)

separate households, which meant an increased demand for housing. The interwar years were also notable for the expansion in white-collar occupations with an income which could support homeownership, considered to be a minimum salary of £4 per week; for example, over this period, there was a three-fold increase in clerical workers. (63) The growth of real incomes for those in employment in the 1930s stimulated consumer demand, and new houses in the 1930s were as cheap as they would ever be again; it was then possible to buy a four-apartment house for 2.5 times annual income. (64) There was also an extension of owner occupation down the class structure to include more skilled and semi-skilled manual workers, who were also the main social groups to benefit from the provision of general-needs council housing. An analysis of the social class of owners in average-cost houses (i.e. with a selling price of around £600) in estates in Edinburgh built in the 1930s has shown that by 1939 about 40% were owned by manual workers, most of whom were in skilled occupations. (65)

The Ballantyne Report had condemned not only the private tenurial patterns of the prewar era, but also the tenements which had dominated its housing architecture. It thus helped to precipitate the replacement of the stone-built tenement by brick-built and harled cottages and low-rise flats, especially two-storey 'four-in-a-block' units. The design and layout of the new houses was influenced by the Tudor Walters Report on the standards of postwar local authority housing. This report, which was initially directed towards England but was later extended to Scotland, set layout standards for the whole of the interwar period, recommending the construction of low density suburban estates with a maximum of twelve houses to the acre to enable the

HEPBURN BROTHERS · COMPLETE HOUSE BUILDERS · EDINBURGH

3 Room Bungalow with Bathroom and Kitchenette, etc.
Semi-Detached, **£560**.   Self-Contained, **£585**.

B2.17. The cheapest bungalow in Hepburn's early 1930s range, a three-apartment house of which several examples were built at Glasgow Road. (James Miller Ltd)

HEPBURN BROTHERS · COMPLETE HOUSE BUILDERS · EDINBURGH

B2.18. The living-room from the most expensive bungalow illustrated in Ideal Bungalows, *the six-roomed 'D2' bungalow, costing £950 with a £95 deposit. (James Miller Ltd)*

penetration of sunlight into the houses even in winter. (66) In this it drew upon the earlier experience of philanthropic model housing and on the Garden City movement, by then ubiquitous among reformers across Europe. The generalised introduction of new house-types, such as bungalows in the private sector and four-in-a-block flats in the council sector, changed the appearance of the Scottish townscape over the interwar period, as the edges of urban settlements became colonised by spread-out council estates and areas of neat bungalows. Bungalows became the favourite type of low-cost Scottish housing, although they ranged from the cheapest semi-detached type to individual, architect designed houses, offering luxury to those who could afford it; around Glasgow, two-storey private houses and flats were also

popular. Most of the speculatively built bungalows were designed by builders themselves as variations on a standard plan; however, larger firms did use professional architects. Bungalows were cheap and simple to build, since they needed no heavy plant; although the Scottish tradition of building 'overhand' from trestles inside the house shell meant that there was no saving on scaffolding, construction was nevertheless much easier. There was a subtle continuity with the prewar years in these bungalow plans, as they resembled the layouts of large tenement flats, distributed singly at low density.

Suburban living, away from the perceived dirt and danger of cities, became fashionable in Scotland between the wars, and this was exploited by clever advertising. The larger building firms copied the marketing techniques of major English builders, and advertising material of the period stressed the safety and health-giving properties of the new housing areas, away from the danger and unhealthiness of the inner cities; this was part of the open air cult of the 1930s. Parental worries were exploited by advertisements which emphasised that the suburbs were the only setting for a safe and healthy childhood. Pride in owning rather than merely renting a house was also exploited and advertisements demanded: 'Are you handing a considerable portion of your hard earned income to a landlord for a house which will always be just on loan?' Perhaps the most important selling point was the modern fixtures and fittings of the speculatively built house, with its tiled bathroom and built-in bath, enamelled cooker instead of the old tenement range, and other labour-saving devices. Private sector builders tried to include features which would emphasise the differences in status between private and local authority housing, such as bay windows and the use of colour or other decorative features. The spread of homeownership, with its improved space and amenities, led to a more home-centred lifestyle, and increasing satisfaction was found in home-based activities such as gardening.

Many of the people buying houses in Scotland between the wars were new to owner occupation, so advertising material for low- and medium-priced houses included information about weekly costs, designed to show that owning a house might cost no more than renting. The fact that houses could be obtained on easy terms was made possible by financial arrangements between housing developers and building societies. In Scotland before 1914, the mortgage market had in general been personal, local and informal. Money to buy a house was usually provided by the savings of small businessmen channelled through lawyers. In the 1920s and 1930s, this informal system was superseded by an 'impersonal, national and formal market dominated by the building societies'. (67) This meant that the majority of purchases of new houses built by major developers over this period were funded by the larger English building societies, which began to open branches in Scottish cities after 1928.

The reduction of the initial deposit was done in several ways. One of these was the 'builders pool' system which operated mainly for large housing developments. (68) By 1938, up to half the business of some of the major English-based building societies was on this basis, under which housebuilders deposited a sum of money with building societies so that the societies would lend more than the usual percentage of the houses' value. (69) The initial deposit, which had previously been a lump sum of between a quarter and a third of valuation, was reduced; thus a purchaser had to find a deposit of only around £50 (7%) on a house costing £700; the amount of each repayment was also minimised by extending the period of the loan. If a purchaser defaulted on the loan the house reverted back to the builder rather than the building society; the builder then had to resell the property. The establishment of links between the larger building firms and branches of the building societies to reduce the cost of house purchase was an important aspect of the growth of speculative building for owner occupation in the interwar period, since this made house purchase more affordable for those on moderate incomes. Thus, in the 21 years following the end of World War I, modern methods of producing and funding housing were firmly put in place, and the private housebuilding industry in Scotland had constructed areas of housing which still compare favourably in popularity with those built in subsequent decades.

Conclusion

The role of private housebuilders in Scotland between the wars was a vital one. Not only did they build housing for the owner-occupied and private rented sectors, but (with the notable exception of Glasgow where a proportion of the local authority housing was built by the Corporation's direct labour organisation) they also built most public sector housing, usually under the contracting and subcontracting method. Because of the post-Ballantyne stigmatisation of pre-1914 private dwellings and their landlords, general-needs council housing was acceptable to middle class Scots who might otherwise have chosen owner occupation. This affected demand for owner occupation in the country between the wars, and appears to have been a contributory factor in the low overall level of housebuilding in the country. Yet private sector building seems, on the whole, to have been more efficient and productive than local authority contracts; indeed, contemporary evidence has indicated that rate of production on local authority housing schemes was often slow, owing to the difficulties of obtaining labour on the fixed price contracts which were then the norm.

The fact that local authorities in Scotland had the power to set a separate owners' rate increased the influence of municipal political factors on the tenure development of Scottish cities. For example, the way in which Edinburgh Corporation operated the rating system at this time, emphasising the setting of rates at a low level, meant that there was relatively little local authority funding for building general-needs council housing. Hence in Edinburgh between the wars a high level of loans and subsidies was provided to encourage private sector building, both for renting and owner occupation. Loans were also provided at low rates of interest to enable house purchase by individuals. Archival information on the attitudes of key officials of Edinburgh Corporation shows that the stated reason for the decision to restrict the amount of general-needs council house building in Edinburgh was because the building of a large number of local authority houses would depress the level of private house construction. This was not just because people could rent a Corporation house instead of buying or renting in the private sector, but also because too much simultaneous building would have meant an inevitable rise in prices as the public and private sectors were in competition for a limited pool of labour and materials. Of course, as many landlords and private sector housebuilders sat as councillors on key committees of Edinburgh Corporation, there was doubtless also a strong element of self-interest in this policy.

Although motives may not have been entirely altruistic, the policy does appear to have been successful in maximising overall housing provision in Edinburgh. This was in contrast to the situation in Glasgow where, in the absence of such initiatives and because of the policy of setting a high owners' rate in the city, building for the private sector was low. One further reason for the low level

of building for owner occupation in Glasgow was the relatively high level of general-needs council housing provided by the Corporation, which acted as competitor to the private sector. Thus although there were significantly higher numbers of white-collar workers in Glasgow than in Edinburgh, there was also less building for owner occupation.

Although the question of how a local authority should effectively and appropriately house all its citizens, including those who cannot afford an economic rent - the issue squarely posed in 1917 by Ballantyne - is beyond the remit of this chapter, in crude numerical terms it would appear that in order to maximise housing output between the wars a balance between public and private sector building was necessary. Whether or not this occurred was an important aspect of the local tenure differences which developed between Scottish cities. Cities which did not provide sufficient encouragement for private housebuilding, either by providing loans or subsidies or manipulating the rates system in favour of owner occupiers, appeared, in doing so, to depress their overall housing output level.

By the 1930s, the modern method of producing and selling houses, and funding house purchase, was in place, and social, political and economic factors combined to produce an unprecedented demand for cheap housing for owner occupation from many who previously would not have aspired to this tenure. The fact that builders had links with building societies, so that low-deposit mortgages were available to those purchasing houses, meant that owner occupation was extended down the class structure to skilled manual workers. The resulting expansion of the suburbs meant a fundamental shift both in the Scottish house form and in the appearance and layout of Scottish towns and cities.

Notes

1   Cd 8731, *Report of the Royal Commission on the Housing of the Industrial Population of Scotland Rural and Urban*, 1917. See also M Glendinning, 'The Ballantyne Report', in D Mays (ed.), *The Architecture of Scottish Cities*, 1997, 161-70

2   Cd 8731, 1917, paragraph 1938.

3   Cd 8731, 1917, *Minority Report*, paragraphs 2-3.

4   P Kemp, 'The transformation of the urban housing market in Britain 1885-1939', PhD thesis, University of Sussex, 1984, 237.

5   Central Housing Advisory Committee, *Private Enterprise Housing*, 1944, 8.

6   R D Cramond, *Housing Policy in Scotland*, 1965, 15.

7   Cramond, *Housing Policy*.

8   M Boddy, *The Building Societies*, 1980, 14.

9   Central Housing Advisory Committee, *Private Enterprise Housing*, 1944, 10.

10 R Issacharoff, *The Building Boom of the Interwar Years*, CES Conference Series, 19, 1978, 308.

11 M Bowley, *Housing and the State*, 1945, 266.

12 A O'Carroll, 'The development of owner occupation in Edinburgh', PhD thesis, Heriot-Watt University, 1994, 150.

13 N J Morgan and M J Daunton, 'Landlords in Glasgow: a study of 1900', *Business History*, 25, 1983, 256; O'Carroll, 'The development of owner occupation', 138.

14 E J Cleary, *The Building Society Movement*, 1965, 185.

15 M Swenarton and S Taylor, 'The scale and nature of the growth of owner occupation in Britain between the wars', *Economic History Review*, 38, 1985, 377.

16 City of Edinburgh, *Report on Survey of Housing Conditions*, 1948.

17 O'Carroll, 'The development of owner occupation', 366.

18 *Housing Problems in the City of Edinburgh*, Report by the City Chamberlain, March 1925, Edinburgh City Archives (ECA), Q.2/4.

19 *Housing Problems in the City of Edinburgh*.

20 A O'Carroll, 'The influence of local authorities on the growth of owner occupation: Edinburgh and Glasgow 1914-1939', *Planning Perspectives*, 11, 1996, 66.

21   G. Gordon, *Regional Cities in the UK*, 1986, 159.
22   Information provided by Mactaggart and Mickel.
23   O'Carroll, 'The development of owner occupation', 344.
24   S Damer, *A Social History of Glasgow Council Housing 1919-1965*, ESRC Research Project R000231241, 1991, 52.
25   A D Campbell, 'Changes in Scottish incomes 1924-49', *The Economic Journal*, 65, 1955, 231-240.
26   Cd 625, *21st Abstract of Labour Statistics*, 1934.
27   Cd 6595, *The Scottish Rating System*, 1945, 8.
28   Damer, *A Social History of Glasgow Council Housing*, 30.
29   Damer, *A Social History of Glasgow Council Housing*, 30; T Hart, 'Urban growth and municipal government: Glasgow in a comparative context, 1846-1914', in A Slaven and D Aldcroft (eds), *Business, Banking and Urban History*, 1982.
30   I S Wood, *John Wheatley*, 1990, 40.
31   I Donnachie, C Harvie and I S Wood, *Forward! Labour Politics in Scotland 1888-1988*, 1989, 59.
32   O'Carroll, 'The development of owner occupation', 210. On Rogan, see M Glendinning (ed.), *Rebuilding Scotland*, 1997, 66-74.
33   D McCrone, *Understanding Scotland*, 1992, 157.
34   T Stephenson, *Industrial Edinburgh*, 1921.
35   Cd 6595, *The Scottish Rating System*, 1945.
36   Cd 8731, Royal Commission on the Housing of the Industrial Population of Scotland, Rural and Urban, *Minority Report*, 1917, paragraph 58.
37   Cd 6595.
38   Cd 6595, 6.
39   Cd 6595, 17-18.
40   City of Edinburgh, *Epitome of the Corporation 1928-1939* (Edinburgh City Archives).
41   Donnachie *et al.*, 59.
42   O'Carroll, 'The development of owner occupation', 370.
43   Cd 6595, 7.
44   Bowley, *Housing and the State*, 226.
45   N Milnes, *A Study of Industrial Edinburgh*, 1936, 170.
46   Milnes, 174.
47   Milnes, 173.
48   Edinburgh Corporation, Treasurer's Committee Minutes, 1923-1933 (Edinburgh City Archives).
49   O'Carroll, 'The development of owner occupation', 269.
50   Notes from speech by James Miller, 29 March 1973 (McKean Archive, RIAS Library).
51   Figures provided by Mactaggart and Mickel.
52   P J Smith, 'Site selection in the Forth Basin', PhD thesis, University of Edinburgh, 1964, 307.
53   H M Bingham, 'Land hoarding in Edinburgh', MSc thesis, Edinburgh College of Art, 1974, 115.
54   Bingham, 115.
55   Unclassified file; statement by Mr Mickel to the Sub-committee on the Progress of the Housing Programme (Edinburgh City Archive, 3 February 1937).
56   N Morgan in R Rodger (ed.), *Scottish Housing in the Twentieth Century*, 1989, 132.
57   Evidence to Sub-committee appointed to consider the progress of the housing programme, 21 January 1937, unclassified file (Edinburgh City Archive).
58   Evidence to Sub-committee, 21 January 1937.
59   Corporation of Glasgow Housing Department, *Review of Operations 1919-1947*, 1948, 1-2.
60   Evidence to Sub-committee, 21 January 1937.
61   Milnes, 158.
62   Position of the Housing Programme, report, ECA Q 4/7 1937.
63   J Burnett, *A Social History of Housing 1815-1985*, 250.
64   Burnett, *Social History*, 252.
65   O'Carroll, 'The development of owner occupation', 257.
66   O'Carroll, 'The development of owner occupation', 257.
67   O'Carroll, 'The development of owner occupation', 223.
68   M J Daunton, *House and Home in the Victorian City: Working Class Housing 1850-1914*, 1983, 97.
69   P Craig, 'The House that Jerry Built? Building societies, the state and the politics of owner occupation', *Housing Studies*, 1 (2), 1986, 87-108; A McCulloch, 'A millstone round your neck? Building societies in the 1930s and mortgage default', *Housing Studies*, 5 (1), 1990, 43-58.
70   M Bowley, *Housing and the State*, 1945, 175.

PREFAB HOMES

The Years of Emergency, 1939-59

Miles Glendinning

Introduction

'Events since 1919 have shown that in housing it is necessary to run very fast simply to stand still.'
Scottish Development Department, 1969 (1)

In the three and a half decades covered in the two following chapters, the collectivist, state-orchestrated onslaught against laissez-faire individualism in housing reached its climax. During World War II and the thirty years that followed, the all-dominating theme seemed to be that of mass discipline, as expressed in the organisation of both demand and supply, and the relationship between them. Demand was co-ordinated and directed by the state; supply responded with mass provision. The reaction against the 19th century's free-market trade cycles and crises of excessive production reached its furthest extreme, in a system of politically directed demand and periodical crises of insufficient production. But this cycle, unlike the interwar years, was now driven not by depression but by three decades of almost uninterrupted economic growth - the decades referred to by the French as the *trente glorieuses*. The percentage of GDP represented by the building industry in Scotland rose dramatically, and vast, seemingly open-ended 'programmes' were undertaken. On the whole, the position of the building industry was generally similar across western Europe: the state became deeply involved in manipulating demand, but production was left basically in private hands (unlike eastern Europe). In the next two chapters, we deal with building firms mainly as contractors rather than as speculative builders. But this still remained overwhelmingly a private-owned industry. Where postwar Scotland differed from the rest of Europe was not in the production side of housing, but in the depth of state intervention in demand.

This was also a revolutionary period in the field of building construction and design. Although there had been dramatic changes in building technology before, it was only now that they began to be displayed openly and exuberantly in the architectural form of housing, especially in the linked but not identical movements of prefabrication and multi-storey building. For example, William Allen, the architect-acoustic collaborator of Robert Matthew at the Royal Festival Hall, proclaimed in 1954 that 'we are in a highly creative period, where we seek originality at every turn'. (2) It is because of that unprecedented originality that, in these two chapters, we must pay closer attention to the buildings themselves than in previous or following chapters.

The buildings produced in this period are, in many cases, the most distant in conception from the stereotypical single family house in a garden. From today's polemical anti-Modernist perspectives, it almost seems a contradiction in terms to apply the word 'home' to them. Yet that collective character is in some ways misleading. For these decades were arguably the period of greatest liberation of individuals from the coercion of previous bad housing conditions, with Modern housing blocks the means that made this possible. As one of the greatest of the tower block 'housing crusaders', Edinburgh's Pat Rogan, recalled, 'It was a magnificent thing to watch, as I did many times, whole streets of slum tenements being demolished - all those decades of human misery and degradation just vanishing into dust and rubble!' (3) That freedom of mass emancipation through collective political action, first legitimised by the 1917 Ballantyne Report, was taken to be a self-evident truth, almost to the end of the *trente glorieuses*. For example, as late as 1969, a Scottish Office booklet on housing policy argued that, over the remainder of the century, over 466,000 slum houses would need to be replaced, and that 30,000 further houses would become obsolete each year: as a result, over 45,000 houses, more than the maximum output so far attained, would have to be built for the foreseeable future. (4) Within a decade those open horizons would have vanished, and that type of 'mass freedom' would have become almost incomprehensible.

The correspondence of demand and supply over the three postwar decades was not exact. The overall trajectory of demand, and of the state's involvement, was a simple and linear one, following a downward path from initial forceful wartime intervention towards complication and decomposition, whereas the trajectory of the response of production was a more complex oscillation between revolutionary and evolutionary responses: the most extreme mass solutions, in the 1960s, actually came near the end of the period.

On the demand side, the gradual downward trend of state *dirigisme* was common to the whole of northern Europe. The wartime command economy was followed by the building of a highly directed welfare state, with emergency housing programmes supported by measures of control and rationing, such as rent freezes, general subsidies, commandeering of land, materials and labour, and imposition of mass standards. (5) In Scotland and England, the state intervened more directly in housing than elsewhere, but even so there was much continuity with what had gone before. In Scotland, the ground for mass building by local authorities had been laid by Ballantyne and the prewar work of Glasgow Corporation. Now it was a matter of generalising these across the country. Right across Europe, governments were also deeply involved in the housebuilding industry itself during this period: for example, in Scotland, by overriding the supply/demand boundary through direct labour building. (6) That era of the command economy came to an end during the later 1950s - a dividing line which separates Chapters B3 and B4. What replaced

B3.1. Mass housing, 1950s-style: Glasgow Corporation's Drumchapel township development, built in 1953-56, seen from the west in 1989. Unit 2, comprising 2,000 Lawrence crosswall flats and 1,310 direct labour conventional flats, is in the foreground; Unit 3, comprising 1,236 largely conventionally built dwellings, is in the centre. The Garscadden Policies tower blocks, added in the late 1960s by Truscon and the DLO, are at the right-hand side. The middle class suburban burgh of Bearsden is in the background. (RCAHMS B22001)

it was a mixed economy, in which the state exerted its influence more generally, by manipulating the economy indirectly through stop-go economics and through various conflicting built-environment agencies, such as regional planning and local authority housing. Conflicts grew as the economy became unbalanced, leading eventually to a further crisis in the 1970s and a move towards more openly capitalistic solutions, especially owner occupation, from the 1980s.

The repercussions of that pressure on the organisation of production, and what was provided, were indirect. Overall, after a substantial drop after World War I, the percentage of the national workforce accounted for by the building industry (9.7%) had almost recovered to the level of 1901. (7) But the way that those resources were employed had fundamentally changed. Where the 19th century had secured efficiency through the fluctuations of the unfettered market, now efficiency was to be sought by co-ordination and continuity, at times involving complex overlaps with demand. The most fundamental trend in the organisation of production resulted from an interplay between forces of concentration, to improve control, and fragmentation, to allow specialisation and raise productivity; the latter gradually gained ascendancy. In both cases, that gradual and fundamental process was concealed by more revolutionary but superficial changes. Of these, the most dramatic was the final decline of the separate-trades system of contracting, and the displacement of architects

from their previous control function by powerful single contractors and huge combine firms operating through negotiated and 'package deal' mechanisms. But this change was not all that it seemed. As the contractors assumed control, their own cohesion began to dissolve from below, with the growth of subcontracting in work such as demolition and excavation, structural steel or concrete, or services.

Technically, the revolutionary trends seemed at first glance even more dominant. As in the interwar period, each successive crisis of over-demand provoked a sudden burst of prefabrication and non-traditional mass building, which subsided as soon as it arose. Here, the most dramatic developments occurred late in our period, during the 1960s. But these revolutions were superimposed on longer-term evolutionary processes that were far less obvious, and were focused on more prosaic aspects of building. Just as in the case of the 19th century's prefabricated joinery, mechanisation made its most enduring impact on building in the field of supplies and 'rationalised traditional' construction. By the end of our period, in the 1970s, the cumulative effect of elements such as motor haulage and mechanised on-site equipment, or semi-traditional methods such as no-fines concrete or timber framing, was very considerable, yet unobtrusive.

The architectural form of the 'product' also seemed to be dominated by the 'revolutionary' bursts, the building of tower

225

blocks and heavy prefabricated 'systems'. But overall, there was a more long-term, evolutionary process at work in dwelling design - a more subtle egalitarianism, as public housing increased in size and equipment, and private housing was rounded down. Whether in semi-detached houses or tower blocks, there was a general convergence around the new dwelling of four or five rooms and 700-1,000 sq. ft, with fitted kitchen and central heating. Money saved by the architectural Modern Movement's omission of outside decorative ornament was reinvested inside. It could be argued that many of the developments in the industry represented a convergence with English norms since the 19th century, including the powerful single contractor, but in reality the latter's growing importance was a more general 'Anglo-Saxon' phenomenon, just as prevalent in North America. Other international comparisons are equally pertinent. Some of the most dramatic episodes of change in Scottish housebuilding organisation and construction were, in many ways, more comparable to those of France. There, a conservative industry, organised on separate-trades lines, was suddenly revitalised and mechanised from the late 1950s under the banner of industrialised construction.

Laying the foundations
prewar innovations

Organisationally and technically, our period really begins not in 1939 but in 1937, with the first of the great, state-orchestrated 'emergencies' which were to mark the building campaigns of the period. The emergency of World War II, the focus of this chapter, began to take shape in 1937, when the government rearmament drive began to have serious repercussions on housing. These repercussions were shaped, in turn, by the effects of the first national building emergency in the decade around World War I, an emergency which had severely disrupted the old building industry. In Chapter B2, we dealt especially with the builder as speculative builder between the wars. Now we must trace some of the changes in contracting during the same period.

In the categories of building dominated by stone construction, the catastrophic rise in quarrying and stone-working costs around World War I had, in effect, decapitated the separate-trades system, leaving it reliant on the new trade of the bricklayer and an uncertain supply of basic materials. The interwar years had failed to rectify that situation. Although brick production had been raised by 90% in the decade from 1924, there was still a need to import facing bricks from England. After a faltering revival in the 1920s, sandstone production had sunk back, by 1935, to a level only one-tenth that of 1902. (8) After 1935, the demands of rearmament and revived shipbuilding began to be felt. By 1937, there was a grave shortage of materials and labour, especially bricklayers and plasterers. Many schemes contracted for could not be started, and prices soared. For example, the price of bricks rose by a third between 1936 and 1937, and the price of a four-apartment house rose from £280 in early 1935 to £434 in late 1937.

That sharp rise in costs was not quite what it seemed. A committee appointed by the Department of Health for Scotland (DHS) to investigate the crisis (the Barr Committee) reported in 1939 that 50% of the rise was due to increased standards, especially the increase in the proportion of cottage houses from 10% of the programme in 1935 to 48% in 1938. (9) Of the remaining 50%, only two-thirds could be specifically attributed to higher materials and labour costs. The committee recommended the short-term remedies of extending brickworks

to raise production by a third. But long-term changes were also seen as necessary in both organisation and technology. The Barr Committee was especially critical of the separate-trades system, arguing that it was insufficiently flexible to deal with imbalances in materials and labour availability. They recognised that all-in contracting was not only more costly, by 5-10%, but was also familiar only to contractors of large, technology-intensive buildings. However, as we have seen in previous chapters, the single-contractor system was already well established in the 19th century for engineering works, and had begun to spread to housing.

The interwar speculative developers, such as Miller or Mactaggart & Mickel had shown a high degree of integration, and the later Sidwell Report on private housing production (1970) would argue that private housebuilding had been the 'common denominator' of convergence between Scotland and England. (10) The interwar trend to all-trades building had also been bound up with contracting work, such as Mactaggart & Mickel's building of the 1,500-dwelling Mosspark scheme for Glasgow Corporation as a single contractor - at £1,800,000, Glasgow Corporation's biggest interwar housing contract. (11) The same also applied at small scale: John Lawrence's first housing contract, for council houses at Shotts in 1924, was on an all-in basis. Elsewhere, there were hybrid methods, such as the longstanding Kilmarnock Bonus and Penalty Scheme, linked to anticipated rents of houses; here one trade acted as main contractor, and a good head of labour was necessary. The single-contractor system influenced the beginnings of state intervention in production, in the form of non-profit direct-labour building; an alternative experimental formula of non-profit-making building, through trade guilds, did not prove a long-term success. Direct labour in Scotland was pioneered by Glasgow Corporation, whose force was founded in 1921, and rapidly expanded under Labour control from 1933, accounting for 60% of production by 1938. The Laidlaw Report of 1938 on building costs hailed direct-labour building as better in standards, but more costly.

Longer-term remedies seemed equally necessary in the field of construction. Here, it was possible to build on the solid foundations laid earlier in the interwar period, following the materials shortages experienced during the 1919 Act building boom. From the beginning, there had been tension between the 'local' or 'municipal' on the one side and the 'national' on the other, with its provision for central government intervention. There was an energetic welcome to the possibilities of non-traditional production, especially using concrete blocks; it is not clear if this was partly the result of the previous stone-building tradition of thick walls and non-hand-portable building units, and partly the result of the crisis in the mason trade, which might have deterred attempts to develop facing brick production. A number of local authorities took a strong lead in constructional innovation using concrete, chief among them Glasgow Corporation, at the instigation of its first director of housing, Peter Fyfe. (12) Over 20% of the Corporation's general-needs houses built under the 1919-24 Acts (including some of Mactaggart's contract at Mosspark), and around 70% of its 14,000 'Rehousing' (slum clearance) tenements, were built using precast concrete. By 1938, the Corporation had constructed an experimental block of houses at Carntyne Road using 'foamslag' concrete, derived from power station waste. (13)

Clydeside's other major building-fabrication tradition, shipbuilding, gave construction in steel a potentially stronger hold on the public imagination than construction in concrete. At an experimental housing site sponsored by Glasgow Corporation at

Langlands in 1924 - the first of several such 'housing zoos' in 20th-century Scotland - several prototypes were built using steel sheeting. These included a type by G & J Weir of Cathcart, whose original proposal for erection by non-building labour stirred up memories of wartime conflicts. (14) Following this experiment, the government attempted to entice local authorities to build steel houses prefabricated by shipbuilding or engineering firms. But as a result of the Weir controversy, their response was so unenthusiastic that the government eventually, in December 1925, stepped in itself, setting up a mutually based housing company, the Scottish National Housing Trust, as an offshoot of the earlier company formed to build the wartime munitions town at Rosyth. The new trust built 2,552 houses in 1926-28, of which 1,500 were Weir steel houses.

What these earlier initiatives demonstrate is that, when it came to the search for long-term responses to the 1937 building contracting crisis, the principle was already established of direct intervention by central government through relatively spectacular experiments in construction, while local authorities pursued a more evolutionary approach.

The Scottish Special Housing Association

The mid-1930s began to see a growing policy of Keynesian state intervention to stimulate recovery from the depression, focused on industrial subsidy of depressed 'special areas'. By 1937, with the increasing pace of rearmament, there was a gradually mounting sense of national emergency. The initiative was seized by the new Secretary of State for Scotland, the reform-minded Walter Elliot. In a January 1937 memorandum to the Cabinet, he highlighted the distorting effect of shipbuilding and munitions manufacture on the building labour market, and argued that a new national organisation should be set up to build houses by non-traditional methods using non-skilled, unemployed labour; it should employ both private contractors and its own direct labour force. The organisation would be national and state-controlled, as both the private building industry and local authorities were considered inadequate for the strategic, redistributive aims now envisaged: henceforth no aspect of production would be tied to local interests. (15)

This new body, initially named the Scottish Special Areas Housing Association, was founded in late 1937 and almost immediately began to plan out a 5,000-dwelling programme. That programme was initially to be financed partly by ordinary Housing Act grants through local authorities, and partly by special areas economic development grants. The consultant architect was Rosyth garden city veteran A H Mottram, assisted by a panel of younger

B3.2. *Scottish Special Housing Association development of non-traditional construction, intended to circumvent the late-1930s resource shortages: solid-wall Canadian cedar houses in the rural Lanarkshire mining town of Forth, designed by Basil Spence and William Kininmonth in a Modernist style and built in 1938-39 by the Red Cedar Supply Company Ltd, Glasgow. (RCAHMS B32709)*

designers, including Sam Bunton, and Kininmonth and Spence; in 1938, Leonard Pond was appointed Master of Works. In the same year, to emphasise its national scope, the Association's competence was extended from the special areas to the whole country, and the word 'Areas' was dropped from its title.

In the choice of construction materials by the newly titled SSHA, steel seemed to be ruled out by rearmament demands. Eventually, poured concrete and solid timber were selected, and two prototype houses were built in Canadian timber at Carfin by the Red Cedar Supply Company, followed by others at Forth and Douglas. During the course of 1938, a shortage of joiners then re-focused attention exclusively on concrete, especially on 'no-fines' construction - a type of poured concrete pioneered in the Netherlands in the 1920s, using very coarse aggregate to enhance insulation and allow much simpler and lighter casting and shuttering equipment. Some poured concrete experiments were carried out by direct labour, including a 222-unit scheme at Carluke, built in 1938-39 in seven months. To emphasise the rejection of local or regional ties, the SSHA, in awarding its first really large contract, for 2,300 cavity-wall, dense concrete dwellings on six sites in various Clydeside towns in December 1938, selected a company, W Arnott MacLeod, which came not from Clydeside but from Edinburgh. By mid-1939, 750 houses were under construction or preparation at Kilmarnock, as were 700 houses at Coatbridge.

By that time, a total SSHA programme of over 30,000 houses had been authorised, and 3,390 houses were under construction or contract. The Association seemed set to become the overarching strategic authority for social housing in Scotland. Had that policy been realised, the interwar local authority drive would then doubtless have been seen, in the eyes of history, as a relatively brief phase in a trend towards ever greater state centralisation. In postwar Northern Ireland, an organisation set up in 1945 explicitly on the SSHA model, the Northern Ireland Housing Trust, succeeded in establishing precisely such a role; but in Scotland, with its deeply ingrained tradition of burgh government, the outcome was to be very different. (16)

Building and the war economy

The outbreak of war radically altered these equations. By taking emergency and dislocation to an extreme, it unleashed two competing forces. On the one hand, there was the demand for ever more strategic, centrally dictated solutions. On the other, there was the practical pressure for ad hoc, local, immediate solutions to urgent, even chaotic pressures.

On both these counts, the housing programme suffered severely. Local authority housebuilding was almost completely stopped, and only 1,714 houses of the SSHA programme were allowed to be completed. Throughout the whole war, only 32,000 houses were built. The implications for the speculative housebuilding industry were drastic, and had the effect of switching all activity from that sector into contracting. The specialist housebuilding firm, as such, disappeared for the duration of the war; firms moved into war contracting work, which, in many cases, generated rapid expansion and diversification, just as in the case of McAlpines in World War I.

For firms that had taken the first steps towards all-trades building, especially in the context of speculative housebuilding, war work gave the opportunity to expand and diversify into general contracting and other activities at government expense, freeing themselves from the prewar problems of dispersed management and capital tied up in land banks. Some of the large English speculative builders, such as Wimpey, under the leadership of Sir Godfrey Mitchell, made major breakthroughs in wartime civil engineering work. For Scottish firms, this often involved a new mobility between Scotland and England. For example, John Lawrence took on contracts for air-raid shelters and hospitals, and Thain built airfields and carried out bomb damage repairs in both Clydebank and London. Millers of Edinburgh, already engaged in building of beach defences before the war, now opened London and Birmingham offices and took over a firm of London contractors, L J Speight. In 1941, at government instigation, the firm also moved into opencast mining. (17)

At a slightly smaller scale, the association between war work and all-trades contracting gave some enterprising local firms the opportunity to develop regional hegemonies. In the north-east, the building firm of Alexander Hall & Son, founded in 1880 principally as a joiner's business, had taken the first steps in all-trades contracts from 1937, and from 1938 exploited a succession of War Department and Air Ministry contracts for anti-aircraft sites, air bases and camps to establish itself as the first and pre-eminent general building firm in the north and north-east. (18) But even as Scottish firms began to embrace all-trades contracting, the latter was being transformed by a series of government enquiries (especially the Simon Report of 1944) which undermined the competitive-tendering system and substituted negotiated serial or selective contracts. The mobility of the wartime years gave returning foremen and supervisors in such companies a dynamic outlook that could fuel rapid expansion in the postwar building drive.

There were attempts to maintain contact with the housing field, especially in fields of constructional innovation linked to wartime economy. Mactaggart & Mickel worked on a prototype 'woodless' house with Paisley Corporation in 1940, to allow completion of a housing scheme at Gallowhill, at the same time as undertaking war contracts for shelters, oil stores, and hospital buildings at Killearn and Buchanan Castle. And if speculative housebuilders were transformed into contractors for non-housing war projects, so too was the SSHA. From 1939 to 1941, its direct labour force concentrated on building timber camps for child evacuees and bombed-out workers, followed in 1943 by a hostel for 100 post office workers in Kirkwall, and family hostels in 1942-43.

For the housebuilding industry, the wartime command economy meant a large leap towards more socialised building conditions, and away from laissez-faire. Profit was replaced by quantity of output as the governing aim, almost regardless of cost; the sense of the discipline of the market almost disappeared. The ending of the boom-bust cycle and the new interdependency of government and building industry brought security for housebuilding as a whole, including both workforce and management. Conditions previously found mostly in direct labour organisations, for instance in Glasgow Corporation, where a guaranteed week for 51 weeks of the year had been instituted in 1936, were now generalised throughout the industry. A guaranteed 44-hour working week and payment by results were introduced in 1942, while in parallel to this the government allowed a vast expansion of trade-union recognition. (19)

From a contemporary social-democratic perspective, these changes seemed wholly beneficial. But they came at a considerable price. The prewar crises of production returned with a vengeance, with rises in material costs of 125% during the war, and a drop in the number of building operatives in Scotland from 26,000 in 1938

to only 3,600 by 1945. (20) They were compounded by new problems of poor productivity, with a workforce dominated by older or infirm substitute workers. Since it was no longer possible to stand off labour as before, there was an increase in overloading, indiscipline and inflexibility. As in the case of rent control in 1915, the acquiescence of the workforce to 'total war' was bought at the cost of long-term economic and social distortions.

When, in 1943, planning began for a postwar return to mass housebuilding, it was clear that the preferred vehicle for production would be a heavily controlled and socialised private enterprise, with demand channelled to a greater or lesser extent through the state. In this, Scotland and Britain were fairly typical of west/central European approaches, midway between the complete state control of supply and demand in the USSR and the dominance of both by private enterprise in North America. A roughly similar situation, in its tension between doctrinaire and pragmatic approaches, existed in Germany. There, prewar attempts by Robert Ley's German Workers' Front to construct a quasi-socialist production apparatus sidestepping private industry were replaced, under wartime pressures, by a more technocratic and collaborative approach, emphasising standardisation and mechanisation in partnership with private firms. (21) In the United States, too, the war years encouraged the housebuilding industry to turn to large-scale prefabrication, exploiting in this case the American tradition of timber-frame construction of detached dwellings: here there was no question of sidestepping the private industry, and most building firms remained small and local, with the exception of the huge business of Levitt & Sons Inc. (22)

In wartime Britain, as in Germany, the chief housing revolution was not to be in the ownership of the means of production, but in their organisational and constructional application. The influence of aircraft production began to win a more general acceptance of the Modern Movement view of building structure in scientific, rationalist terms. No longer should a building be the sum of a series of elements assembled in an ad hoc way, complete with generous excess tolerances. Rather, it should be an integrated concept, tailored exactly to its structural requirements. Again by analogy with aircraft, that integrated whole was understood in terms of a play between two complementary elements: a frame, to hold up the building, and infill, to keep out the weather. What was envisaged, as in most combatant countries, was a two-stage programme of housing provision. First, there would be transitional or temporary housing for displaced people or emergency needs; then would follow a return to permanent housebuilding, but under the new rationalised conditions. In contrast to some other combatant countries, such as France, there was to be no significant reliance in Scotland on collective types of emergency dwellings, such as barracks or hutted dormitories; self-contained 'homes' were, from the beginning, to be the rule.

The prefabs

As in most areas of war activity, the drive for mass production of emergency housing was characterised by a dichotomy between a rhetorical facade of extreme unity and discipline, and behind-the-scenes tendencies towards fragmentation and improvisation. To circumvent the calamitous shortage of building workers and materials, it was assumed from the start that production would have to maximise the element of factory prefabrication, again on the aircraft model. The concessions to organised labour ensured that there would be no workforce dissent at the use of non-

B3.3. The first consignment of AIROH bungalows leaves the Blackburn factory at Barge Park, Dumbarton, in 1946. (West Dunbartonshire Libraries)

B3.4. Kitchen of 'Seco' prefab bungalow at 1 Maxwell Road, Dirleton, photographed in 1981 immediately prior to demolition. (M Glendinning)

building labour, as there had been in the 1920s. Politically, while housing in general was a devolved matter for Scotland, this mass-produced prefabricated programme, with its close relationship to munitions production, was on the whole dealt with directly from London by pan-British agencies. During the war, some prefabricated dwellings for replacement of bombing losses were built on an ad hoc basis within Scotland, especially the 'Maycrete' - a programme of over 600 single-storey dwellings with prefabricated reinforced concrete frames and infill panels of compacted sawdust and cement, built in bombed towns such as Greenock by the SSHA. These developed severe structural problems and were all demolished after 1950. (23)

But the 'prefab' story proper began in 1943 in London, in a burst of imposing unity, in the announcement by the British Ministry of Works of a vast construction programme of one standard house-type, the 'Churchill' or 'Portal' house. This was to be a single-storey detached dwelling, constructed economically of pressed steel and incorporating a prefabricated kitchen-bathroom core; half a million were to be built across Britain immediately after the end of hostilities. A prototype was displayed in London in 1944. By then, however, the continuation of the war, and its insatiable demands for steel, had diverted attention away from this simple proposal: each Churchill House would have used five tons of steel.

The programme eventually set out in the Housing (Temporary Accommodation) Act of 1944 made use of not one but ten different agencies and construction methods. A range of standard single-storey houses was to be directly commissioned by the government from various consortia, using a range of materials and differing degrees of prefabrication. All of these would be of two rooms and kitchen and of 670 sq. ft (about 10% larger than the 616 sq. ft Churchill House). The main aspect of continuity with the Churchill House was that all the house-types would use a standard prefabricated kitchen-bathroom unit supplied by the Ministry of Works. The Ministry of Works set up a Directorate of Temporary Housing in July 1945 to oversee the programme; this operated until March 1949. Despite the highly centralised character of the programme, from the very beginning, there was an attempt to involve, rather than ignore, the local authorities. A simple rationing system applied: local authorities simply requisitioned as many as they needed, and merely had to pay for, and arrange, site preparation. House erection could be done either by local firms or by big all-in contractors. The houses had an expected life of ten years.

The 'prefabs' fell into two main types. On the one hand, at the cutting edge of constructional innovation, there was a completely prefabricated aluminium bungalow, the 'AIROH' house, each of which was made in factories and transported to the site on four lorries; it cost £1,589 - over 50% more than the government-estimated cost of an equivalent-sized prewar house with 1947 fittings (£1,041). (24) The remarkable AIROH programme is described in greater detail below. All the other kinds of prefabs involved a much lower level of prefabrication; they had in essence a panelised construction, assembled out of components that were designed and manufactured by various agencies and subcontractors, stored centrally in Ministry depots (mainly at airfields), and assembled on site. They were much simpler and cheaper, averaging £1,168 each, of which some £135 was accounted for by distribution and transport costs. Initially, the

B3.5. Rear of 'Seco' prefab at 3 Maxwell Road, Dirleton, showing shed made out of Anderson shelter. (M Glendinning)

prime contractors for the most important types tried to form a cartel, but this was turned down by the government, anxious to maintain even a small element of competition in the programme.

The panelised prefabs were supported by a wide variety of management and contractual mechanisms: all were based in England. One extreme was represented by the management-only operation of the ARCON project. This was a steel-framed house with asbestos exterior cladding and timber internal panels. It was designed in 1943 and co-ordinated by a group of 25 architects, with support from a consortium of manufacturers including steel firm Stewarts & Lloyds, and contractors Taylor Woodrow. Ten thousand were supplied to Scottish authorities; the first of Edinburgh's large quota was erected at Muirhouse in December 1945, on a layout prepared by German prisoners of war. (25) In strong contrast, the 'Seco' or 'Uni-Seco' bungalow was designed and directly built by a contracting organisation, originally formed in 1940 to build airbases: it had a timber frame with asbestos cement sheeting, and 5,000 were built in Scotland. Other timber-frame types included the 'Phoenix', and an imported type supplied by the U.S. National Housing Agency on a lend-lease basis. Prefabricated concrete-panel types included the Tarran, produced by a Hull-based firm, with 4,000 built in Scotland, and - an exception to the panelised pattern - a no-fines type built by Miller of Edinburgh in relatively small numbers. Altogether, 32,176 temporary prefabs were built in Scotland between 1945 and 1949, in 152 out of the 229 burghs and counties; the largest per-capita concentration was in Edinburgh, with 4,000. Temporary houses accounted for as much as 74% of Scottish housing output in 1946, falling to 26% by 1948.

The AIROH house was the only prefab-type built on a completely prefabricated and standardised basis, as had been the American TVA (Tennessee Valley Authority) house of the 1930s. After its conclusion, it was hailed by one American academic as 'the largest single industrialised house enterprise in human history: some 70,000 aluminium houses, all of one major design, were factory prefabricated under the direction of one managing agency within the space of about three years'. (26) The original motive for the programme was a desire on the part of aluminium and aircraft manufacturers, as the war approached its end, to use the vast accumulated stocks of aluminium to allow conversion of aircraft factories to civilian use. In February 1944, the Aluminium Development Association convened a meeting in London, at which housebuilders were also represented. With the endorsement of Sir Stafford Cripps, Minister of Aircraft Production, plans of the TVA house were obtained from America, and the Canadian Modernist architect Wells Coates drew up plans for an aluminium mock-up prototype.

After some modifications and simplifications to the prototype designs, initial contracts for 54,000 houses were given to four aircraft factories, one in Scotland (Blackburn of Dumbarton) and three in England (Bristol, A W Hawksley and Vickers-Armstrong). The entire AIROH project was co-ordinated, from 1945, by the Ministry of Aircraft Production, later renamed the Ministry of Supply. They financed production and let contracts for erection of the houses to fifteen building firms, of which George Wimpey accounted for the largest share. The Scottish programme was run as a self-contained operation entirely supplied by Blackburn. The Dumbarton factory of the Blackburn & General Aircraft Ltd was located at Barge Park, by the Clyde, and had been built as a rearmament project in 1937 by the Yorkshire-based firm at the instigation of Sir Maurice Denny. During the war, the 120,000 sq. ft facility had built over 200 light bombers, followed in 1940-45 by 250 Sunderland flying boats - aircraft which were 85 ft

long and as high as a three-storey house, and contained an exceptionally complex range of equipment. During late 1945, the factory was completely retooled for AIROH production at a cost of over £500,000; an initial batch of 50 houses was built in 1946 almost next door at Silverton High Mains, and a showhouse at Smollett Road. Over the following three years, the factory accounted for the whole of the Scottish element of AIROH production of temporary houses: 12,047 units, some 22% of the UK total.

Generally, the production rate at the Blackburn factory was 40 houses per day, but a maximum of 200 was reached briefly. Production was organised using the same flow techniques as for aircraft, from materials handling and fabrication through to assembly, painting and loading. In 1948, extending the aircraft analogy, the company set up a mobile contract maintenance unit to 'service' the completed houses, using three ex-navy vans. But by then, as we will see below, Blackburns had begun to follow the shift in government policy by throwing the emphasis of production onto permanent houses incorporating prefabricated elements: from then until eventual closure of the factory in 1961, the only genuine 'prefabs' manufactured there were for the armed forces ('Terrapin' mobile bungalows) and for colonial use ('Shipston' houses). (27)

The production process for the AIROH houses was completely mechanised. The bungalow walls were made of 57mm thick panels of aluminium with air-entrained grouting as insulation in the middle, and sprayed with two layers of bitumen inside; these methods, in the temporary prefabs, proved relatively ineffective, and there was serious condensation and corrosion. Partitions, floors, and roof trusses were also of aluminium, and the roof was felted and low-pitched. The houses were assembled in four front-back 'slices', each measuring 22'6" long by 7'6" wide, and complete with pre-installed fixtures and fittings. These segments were driven on trucks from Barge Park to the sites, the haulage firms being selected competitively, and assembled there by eight-man teams using mobile cranes. The *Architect and Building News* (20 December 1946) argued that the AIROH house, 'entirely non-traditional in its design and construction, represents ... the first large-scale application of Modern industrial techniques to problems of house building'.

The AIROH design was one of extreme complexity, requiring 4,000 different parts, supplied from 157 different firms. Arguably, it would have been much more economical, and would have performed better in the long run, if it had been built in steel and timber. But such a conclusion would be anachronistic, as the main motivation for the project at the time was that of rapid output, combined with safeguarding of military-industrial infrastructure; we should remember that rearmament started again as early as 1950!

Postwar government policy
public versus private

The gradual trend from unified centralism to complication and decentralisation became even clearer when the emphasis moved on from temporary to permanent houses. As early as 1942, the government had begun to give thought to this aspect of the housing programme. Here, too, to maximise production and speed up building, non-traditional methods would also clearly play a key role. In September 1942, an interdepartmental committee on house construction was established, under the chairmanship of Sir George Burt; the Department of Health for

Scotland (DHS) was represented on it, alongside the (English/Welsh) Ministry of Health and the (British) Ministry of Works. (28) The Burt Committee's task was to investigate non-traditional systems of building and to appraise and approve particular systems. From the beginning, there was a tension between state agencies and private building companies in the initiation and control of new building methods, with the initiative gradually passing from the first to the second.

Initially, the Burt Committee delegated much of its work in Scotland to the Scottish Special Housing Association. In the years of wartime coalition and command planning, the government-controlled SSHA had been the favoured partner for

B3.9. Prototype Swedish Timber houses, the first of a consignment of 200 for Glasgow, being built by the Corporation Housing Department at the Balornock scheme in November 1945. This view shows the fourth day of timber erection. The foundations and brick crosswalls were built by direct labour. (Glasgow City Archives)

B3.6. Prototype of the Weir Paragon steel bungalow, built by the SSHA in two weeks in July 1944 at Sighthill, Edinburgh. (M Glendinning)

B3.7. Living-room of the Paragon prototype. (M Glendinning)

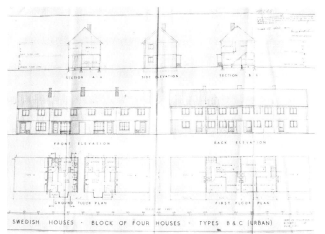

B3.8. Plans prepared in June 1945 by Robert Matthew's DHS team for terraced four-apartment Swedish Timber houses; the layout is comparable to that of Mactaggart & Mickel's 1920s terraced private housing. (Scottish Development Department)

postwar housing: in 1944, Secretary of State Tom Johnston had contemplated a ten-year SSHA programme of 100,000 in the large industrial towns. In the same year, a government-backed report on housing design, the Westwood Report (*Planning Our New Homes*) demanded not only a vast postwar programme of over 500,000 new dwellings, but made it clear that these should be designed on totally new lines. Of course, the houses would have to be larger and better equipped than prewar ones - that was a standard demand. But equally important was a new ethos of design and landscaping. The lines of repetitive blocks in prewar housing schemes were now branded bleak and utilitarian; what was called for now was a far more ambitious Modernist concept of layout and community planning. It seemed that a new housing revolution was about to erupt, which would sweep the municipal housing empires into the same oblivion into which they had consigned the private landlords after 1915. (29)

Preparations for this new era began immediately. Ambitious programmes of Modernist regional planning were set in train for the Clyde and Forth Valleys, as well as for the reconstruction of war-damaged Clydebank. In 1944, the SSHA was authorised to build an area of experimental house-types at Sighthill, in Edinburgh. For this site, ten houses of five types were designed by the energetic Sam Bunton, a prefabrication-minded member of SSHA's consultant architect panel, who was also, at the time, official replanning consultant for Clydebank. Later, a range of other types was added. The two main methods of construction at Sighthill were concrete and steel. The houses used a range of techniques, including no-fines and foamslag concrete, steel-framing, and 'Gyproc' - a type of compacted gypsum-based panel patented by Clydeside building contractor John Lawrence, an associate of Bunton's. The first house built at Sighthill was commissioned by the SSHA for its own use from Weirs of Cathcart: the 'Paragon', a four-apartment, flat-roofed bungalow built of steel external walls and Gyproc internal partitions, for use especially in mining areas at a unit cost of £950. Construction of the Sighthill prototype in July 1944 took only two weeks, and was followed by 100 elsewhere in Scotland. (30)

At this stage, the SSHA and the government seemed firmly in control of the process of innovation. The SSHA played a key role in the a major central government initiative just before the war's end to kick-start permanent housing production: the importation of several thousand prefabricated timber houses from Sweden and their erection throughout Scotland and rural areas of northern England, in a centrally planned manner which anticipated the slightly later prefab programme. The consignment

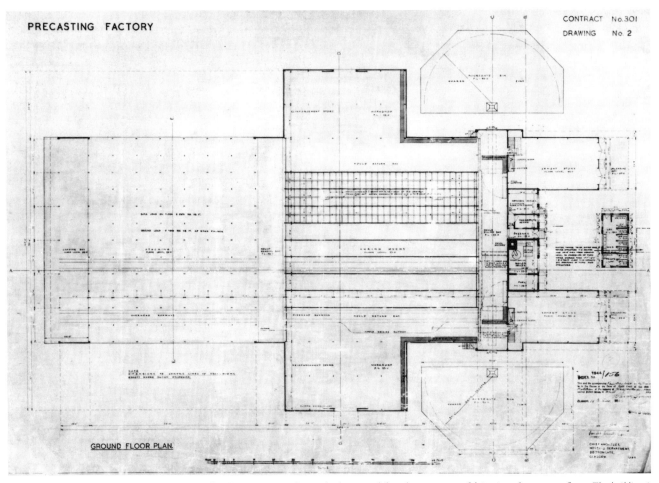

PRECASTING FACTORY

CONTRACT No. 301
DRAWING No. 2

GROUND FLOOR PLAN.

B3.10. 1944 plans for Glasgow Corporation's Amulree Street precasting factory for large-panel foamslag concrete prefabrication of two-storey flats. The building is organised in assembly-line fashion, from the storage and mould-filling areas on the right to the curing ovens in the middle and the store and loading bay on the left. (Glasgow City Archives)

was ordered after a visit to Sweden by Robert Matthew, chief architect of the DHS. Matthew travelled to Sweden on a wartime night flight from Leuchars, and was stranded in Scandinavia until VE Day; he designed the house-plans to conform to the guidelines of the Westwood Report. The one- and two-storey houses, which were of four apartments and 89-95 square metres, were constructed of timber-framed panels, with brick party walls. The work of erection was done by the reception local authorities: for example, the 200 houses supplied to Glasgow in 1945-46 were erected by direct labour. Of the initial Scottish consignment of 2,500, the SSHA built 1,000. A second large batch of over 1,000 Swedish Timber houses was ordered in 1950 for sites in the Highlands and Islands. The contract was divided between four firms, including both Miller and Hall.

But this picture of central control was to prove an illusion. An early pointer to an alternative outcome was provided by Glasgow Corporation's direct labour force, which during the war developed the foamslag-concrete construction of its prewar Carntyne prototype into a full-blown building system, and built a precasting factory to supply it. The system, which involved large, storey-height concrete panels, measuring 3.1m by 2.6m and 150mm in thickness, precast from foamslag and positioned by on-site mobile cranes, had first been devised in 1939 by Glasgow's chief housing architect, J H Ferrie. The £250,000 factory, at Tollcross, was delayed by wrangling with the Burt Committee, which insisted that a prototype 'four in a block' at Penilee should be built first (in 1944). Eventually, several hundred dwellings, in flat-roofed two-storey blocks, were built between 1945 and 1949, principally on sites at Priesthill, Maukinfauld Road and Cranhill. Construction, if completed to schedule, took up less than half

the labour resources and time of brick dwellings, but the programme was dogged by materials shortages and an inflexible on-site erection programme; it was calculated that it would only become cheaper than brick building above 700 dwellings a year, but the maximum actual rate was only 400. (31)

The autonomy demanded and obtained by the powerful production machine of Glasgow Corporation anticipated a more general, sudden decline in the authority of the centralised strategic programmes after the war's end. The postwar programme would represent a huge reinforcement of direct state intervention in housing, yet it would achieve this through a highly decentralised structure with numerous different and competing power sources. When the emergency wartime government coalition was replaced, in 1945, by a Labour administration closely bound up with municipal politics, the new Scottish housing minister, George Buchanan, began by redirecting the SSHA away from building in large towns, and drove home his point by sacking its entire board of management. The grand visions of armies of technocrats marching off in all directions from the Ministry had dissolved into thin air. What was now re-emerging from the wartime fog, reinvigorated with the new authority of the social state, was the local authority housing structure that had gradually grown up between the wars. (32) By 1951, only 14,500 SSHA dwellings had been completed since the war - well below the total anticipated by Johnston - and the Association settled down to building roughly 10% of the overall programme, running a substantial annual deficit even then.

It would be misleading to see this policy change as a cynical exercise in political patronage. (33) Rather, it was a new phase of realism in the constant balancing of strategic and pragmatic solutions, with the emphasis constantly and gradually shifting to the latter. To have begun one *tabula-rasa* housing revolution in 1915, in the heat of war, was a matter of understandable expediency; to have stampeded into another one, less than three decades later, when the first was not yet completed, would have been foolhardy in the extreme. Possibly, Johnston's wartime emphasis on the SSHA might have been another negotiating counter in his struggle to protect and extend administrative devolution from all-British agencies of command planning such as the Ministry of Works or the Ministry of Reconstruction. Once the war was over, talk of grand solutions could be replaced by greater realism, and a willingness to build on what already existed. The new policy was both radical and realistic. Radical, in that it proposed to carry to its logical extreme the Ballantyne revolution: public housing, previously unevenly spread across urban areas, was now to become the main provider in both urban and rural contexts. Realistic, in that it reverted to the previously dominant agencies, the local authorities, rather than new centralist agencies such as the SSHA or the Ministry of Works. The SSHA and other non-municipal bodies, such as the New Town Development Corporations, would play a role, as would, eventually, private enterprise, but this would be a strictly subordinate one.

This policy was almost unique in the developed world. In some other countries, private speculative builders proved able to sustain a vast output of government-subsidised small dwellings: in the postwar USA, houses subsidised by the Federal Housing Administration and the Veterans Administration through guaranteed mortgages accounted for 20-50% of total annual output. (34) In Belgium, too, the overwhelming emphasis was on government subsidy of owner occupation, as a result of the strong Catholic emphasis on family morality. In the communist countries, on the other hand, public housing programmes were dominant; but they were controlled by administrative-managerial organisations like the SSHA, rather than immersed in vigorous party political debate or civic life. The Scottish solution seemed to spring organically from the special power and prestige of municipalities in Scottish urban development since 1707. And, contrary to its monolithic image in hindsight, in fact the programme was highly decentralised and varied. (35) Correspondingly, central government would retreat from direct supply to a regulatory and subsidy-providing role. Initially, the centralised regulatory role was to be a very strong one, amounting to an extension of wartime rationing. But from the beginning, it would come up against the equally strong counter-force of the decentralised local authority building demands.

The foundation-stone for the new council housing drive was the 1946 Housing (Financial Provisions) (Scotland) Act, which nearly doubled subsidies for public housing. The result of this opening of the floodgates, in the postwar context of rationing, was to further compound the crises of supply which had accumulated throughout the war. Within a year there was a huge overload of materials and labour; by comparison with 1939, building costs had increased by 35%, and the cost of a four-apartment house by 167% (to £1,280). Whereas in 1939, roughly one house was under construction per building operative at any one time, by 1947 the figure had increased to 1.5; for example, in Edinburgh, bricklaying productivity had declined from the prewar figure of 700 bricks per man daily, to 300, and the average price of a four-apartment flatted house had increased from £420 in 1938 to £1,076. The first response was a simple reinforcement of rationing: in October 1947 the government froze work on all contracted houses other than those nearly completed, and reapportioned the resources freed. As a result, production rose

B3.11. Glasgow Corporation Housing Department canteen for the direct labour workforce building the Pollok development, 1947. (Glasgow City Archives)

B3.12. Direct labour building in the age of mass production: cartoon in Housing News *(the Glasgow Housing Department newsletter), December 1946. The cartoonist, Charlie Baird, was a plasterer in the maintenance section of the DLO. (Glasgow District Council)*

from 10,800 in 1947 to 19,700 in 1948. (36) In 1948, another report on building costs, the Laidlaw Report, was commissioned; it repeated the criticisms of the separate-trades system as a factor exacerbating shortages. In September 1948, there was a further government-imposed curb on new contracts, to concentrate labour and materials on houses already under construction. Gradually, the rationing measures took effect, until by October 1949 it could be claimed that it was rival, non-housing projects that were siphoning off labour: of some 700 bricklayers in Edinburgh, for example, only 200 were working on Corporation housing, and of the 20 bricklayers working on the Inch site, half had to travel in daily from Pumpherston, over 15 miles distant. (37)

As part of this structure of rationing, it was made clear that the building industry must largely confine itself, at this stage, to the role of contractor. The central control of building licensing would be used to prevent any revival of speculative housing, which might compete for resources with public housing, by placing a ceiling of 10% on the private contribution to total output. In 1947, Andrew Mickel attacked this 'attempt to eliminate building by private enterprise' and argued that it would 'mean dearer houses'. (38) As we saw above in Chapter A4, Mactaggart & Mickel had, in May 1945, built a demonstration bungalow pair at Broomhouse, Edinburgh, in 20 days using traditional brickwork at a cost of £550 each. Although this was far cheaper and quicker than the 'prefabs', when seen in the overall political-economic context of the time its achievement was almost completely beside the point: the main problem of mid- and late-1940s housing production was not one of cost but of resources, which ruled out building deregulation in what was still, in effect, a rationing-driven war economy. (39) In fact, the proportion of total output accounted for by private housing, far from reaching 10%, declined from 5.4% in 1948 to 3.3% in 1950. And non-socialist councils that had previously held out against council housing were forced into line. Whereas Edinburgh Corporation had built only one-third of the capital's total output in 1918-40, over the following 23 years its percentage contribution doubled, and by 1958 a quarter of all Edinburgh dwellings were council-owned. (40)

The curb on speculative housebuilding did not signal any large-scale move to the opposite extreme, of direct labour building, in which the local state dealt with both demand and production. Even in Glasgow, the direct labour organisation (DLO), which employed over 4,000 men in the late 1940s, accounted for only 50-66% of output at that time: what was as significant in the city was the trend towards negotiated - not competitive - contracts with a cartel of local all-in contractors. And the SSHA's DLO, feared from the municipal Labour viewpoint as a potential predator of resources, (41) was now redirected to concentrate on site servicing rather than housebuilding: during the shortages of 1947, the SSHA was gravely short of labour, with only 2,873 staff rather than the 5,013 needed for its programme. (42) Within the new, socialised system of housing production, security was a central feature - and so long as private industry accepted the role of contractors, its role was safeguarded.

Housing and the command economy
the 'permanent non-traditional' programme

The tension between radicalism on the one hand and pragmatism and decentralisation on the other also manifested itself in what was to be built. Of the 223,173 permanent houses constructed in the first postwar decade, 116,601 (52%) were built by 'non-traditional' methods: that proportion actually increased as the decade proceeded, from 33% in 1948 to 40% in September 1949: DHS Circulars 41/1949 and 28/1950 listed a wide range of approved methods. (43) But as the proportion of non-traditional building increased, the types of construction involved grew gradually less daring. There would never again be anything to rival the AIROH bungalow; in contrast to postwar prefabrication developments in America, in Scotland after 1949 no council house would ever again arrive at its site on a truck. And, in a further move away from the grand unitary solution, these methods were made up of a vast range of techniques, mostly under the control of private building consortia.

In 1948, as part of the trend back to 'normalcy', it was decided that private non-traditional building promoters should negotiate contracts directly with local authorities, with the Department of Health for Scotland (rather than the Ministry of Works in London) providing government oversight, working in conjunction with a newly established Scottish office of the Building Research Station at East Kilbride. The assumption of responsibility by the Scottish Office was justified by the fact that traditional building resources were scarcer than in England, and the demand for non-traditional building much higher. The technical expertise of the DHS had been greatly built up by chief architect Robert Matthew and his successor (from 1946) Robert Gardner-Medwin. The DHS and BRS closely collaborated with firms to develop particular systems: for example, the Scottish architect of Wimpeys recalls that DHS architects acted as their 'mentors' in the

development of no-fines construction. (44) Sam Bunton played an important impresario role in the middle ground which was opening up between the state and the industry; he displayed a frenetic dynamism in working with government and industry in devising numerous prefabricated 'systems'. In 1945, the SSHA experimental area at Sighthill had already been opened to private contractors for their proprietary designs; Glasgow Corporation also sponsored a small experimental area on its Garscube scheme. For each approved building system, the DHS would negotiate any additions to the basic subsidies. A special extra subsidy was agreed for non-traditional building in Scotland in December 1947. The DHS also gave approved firms a guarantee of orders for a certain number of houses.

The mainstream permanent dwellings were to have all the mod cons of the prefabs, but would be larger in area. Their planning and equipment was to conform to the demands of the Modern Movement for maximum light, air and convenience. But as the Westwood Report had made clear, Modernist-style high flats were only to be used exceptionally. The general rule would be the garden suburb of two-storey cottages. For non-traditional methods, this increase in height allowed the focus to remain on relatively lightweight building. But despite the growing tide of non-traditional systems, the largest single category of construction for permanent housing was still 'traditional' building. By this was now meant not stonework, but load-bearing cavity brick walling, externally rendered or possibly faced with terrazzo blocks. A wartime recovery in the level of Scottish sandstone quarrying, mostly for low-quality building rubble, had been followed, in 1945, by a crash to a lowest-ever production rate. (45) Despite new government grants for use of traditional facing materials in rural areas, the consequent rise in costs had forced back the load-bearing (as opposed to ornamental) use of stone into small redoubts clustered around remaining quarries. Aberdeen Corporation made vain attempts to maintain all-granite construction at its Kincorth scheme throughout the 1950s, while Dumfries Town Council had greater success in using local red sandstone throughout its developments of the 1950s and 1960s, such as Lincluden. Within traditional construction, the separate-trades system was gradually retreating in the face of all-in contracting, especially in the urban centres: for example, firms such as Thain and Miller were much involved with Edinburgh garden-suburb developments of the late 1940s and early 1950s such as Clermiston, while Pollok in Glasgow was divided out between the DLO and local firms, all strictly awarded through negotiated contracts.

A transitional episode which straddled the boundary of command production and proprietary production was centred on the Blackburn prefab works, which the government was anxious to keep open as a 'phantom' manufacturing facility. First, a special order of a permanent version of the AIROH bungalow was arranged with Blackburn in 1947. The permanent AIROH design, also built in quantity at the Hawksley factory in England, had 45% thicker metal walling panels (83mm) and more solid roofs and wooden floors with supporting piers; a small aluminium outhouse was also supplied. It required a £708 addition to the basic subsidy for that size of house. In Scotland, 2,504 were manufactured and supplied between 1947 and 1949, entirely at Blackburn's factory, who designated the house the 'Blackburn Mk.II'. In 1948, anticipating the end of this contract, a two-storey permanent house, the 'Mk.III', was designed by Sam Bunton for the firm; to appeal to conservative-minded local authorities, it combined a conventional 11 inch cavity wall brick shell with certain prefabricated features retained from the bungalow and delivered by truck, including the aluminium roof

B3.13. AIROH Mk.II Permanent Aluminium Bungalow, Moredun, Edinburgh, seen in 1993: part of a consignment supplied in 1949. (M Glendinning)

B3.14. A specimen pair of the Blackburn Mk.III brick and aluminium permanent non-traditional houses built in 1949-51 at the Moredun scheme, which also includes an aluminium school (visible at right background). (M Glendinning)

and chassis-mounted kitchen-bathroom unit, and the concrete infilling for partitions; internal wall linings were also prefabricated. A contract for some 5,300 of these houses, at a unit cost of £1,375, was arranged directly by the government, to the great irritation of mainstream building firms such as Crudens; in a further move towards conventional contracting, Blackburn was now to act as on-site builder itself. (46)

By early 1949, production of the two-storey Mk.III was about to begin, and in order to clear the last 120 permanent bungalows from Barge Park, what was probably the most spectacular prefab contract was arranged with Edinburgh Corporation for an outer-suburban site at Moredun, previously earmarked for a traditional garden suburb designed by J A W Grant. The 120 permanent bungalows were scheduled for delivery to a Clydeside town, but the site was not ready in time. After hurried telephone consultations between DHS and Edinburgh's housing chairman, and an emergency meeting of the Housing Committee, the consignment was accepted by the capital and deliveries at Moredun started the next week, at a rate of six bungalows daily; the contractors involved, Mowlem and Wimpey, could assemble a bungalow in just over half an hour from the time the four sections were hoisted up onto the site on gantries. (47) The Mk.III two-storey contract (which included a number of houses adjacent to the Mk.II group at Moredun) was completed between 1949 and the beginning of 1951. (48)

A wide range of private organisations developed their own responses and constructional methods, which combined concrete and metal construction in various ways. Building in steel frame or panels began as a strong contender, but was undermined after 1948 by rival industrial demands for steel, and after 1950 by rearmament. Predictably, the field was led by the firms involved in the steel experiments of the 1920s, above all Weirs of Cathcart,

who would build over 18,000 houses in various proprietary forms in 1945-55, using a special factory at Coatbridge. The Weir Housing Corporation had been asked by DHS in 1944 to alter its Paragon bungalow into a two-storey, four-apartment house more suitable for urban use. The resulting steel-clad type, the 'Weir Quality' house, was built in large numbers by both the SSHA (which built 2,700) and local authorities. Atholl Steel Houses Ltd of Craigton, Glasgow, modified its 1920s design into a new type for four-in-a-block houses. One thousand five hundred were authorised initially by the government in 1945 for building in mining and agricultural areas, but the economics of the type were undermined by the steel curbs of 1948, and a brick-clad, steel-framed design was substituted by the firm. To prevent closure of the firm's factory, it was exempted by the government from curbs on steel-framed housing. (49) Over 2,350 units of another steel-framed type devised by a Glasgow builder, Stuart & Sons, were built from 1946; these two-storey cottages and flats were clad in foamslag blocks or brick. These Scottish systems were rivalled by the BISF (British Iron and Steel Federation) House, a steel-framed and clad four-apartment semi-detached house designed by the architect Frederick Gibberd, and built by a special company (British Steel Homes Ltd). Out of a UK total of 36,000, some 4,900 were built in Scotland, with Sam Bunton acting as consultant architect.

With the gradual retreat from steel in housing, the cause of concrete construction advanced correspondingly. The enormous equipment costs and inflexibility of Glasgow's foamslag system demonstrated that heavy large-panel systems were fundamentally unsuited to the building of low-density two-storey houses, and attention focused largely on composite systems combining precast concrete blocks with frame-like elements - the general type of construction most similar to pre-1914 stone masonry and internal timber building. Here, owing to the more complicated constructional methods, the private promoters involved were not single firms but conglomerates and consortia, more like those that produced the prefabs. As in the case of the prefabs, some of the resulting systems were intended for design-and-build construction, others for licensing to smaller contractors - a method that would help disseminate the single-contractor system across the country, and which would help prepare the industry for greater organisational flexibility in the later phase of even greater constructional daring in the 1960s. The two most important umbrella organisations of the late 1940s and early 1950s phase - the Scottish Housing Group and the Cruden Group - were both national in scope, but were concentrated respectively in the west and the east. In general terms, they were similar, but the Cruden operation showed, from the beginning, a special innovativeness and discipline that was to mark it out for more rapid progress in later years.

The Scottish Housing Group (SHG) was a loosely organised cartel, grounded in the building industry of Clydeside. It was built up in the mid-1940s with DHS and Building Research Station help, and was managed from the office of Glasgow contractors Melville, Dundas & Whitson. It contained some of Scotland's largest firms - John Lawrence, Mactaggart & Mickel, John Bisset and William Tawse (both of Aberdeen), James Miller and W & J R Watson of Edinburgh, Charles Gray of Dundee. Lawrence, who was a member of the management board of the Scottish BRS, became chairman of the SHG, which was dedicated to the development of various non-traditional methods, and to supporting them with standardised tendering and contractual procedures. There was also an unspoken agenda of preventing English firms from exploiting the non-traditional programme to establish a presence in Scotland.

Typically, house-types would be devised by groups of architects, engineers and contractors (with Sam Bunton often playing a prominent role), and built out of combinations of various building and materials-supplies firms, and patented techniques under permutations of brand names, focusing mainly on concrete construction. One of the central threads in the bewilderingly rapid mutation of techniques and names was provided by the various gypsum and precast-concrete walling panels and blocks developed by offshoots of John Lawrence's organisation, in collaboration with Bunton, normally for use in framed construction: Bellrock, Gyproc, Gypunit, Wilson Block, Uniflat, Orlit-Bellrock, Hilcon Ex, and so forth. Some of the systems were intended for erection by the firms that had developed them, others for building under licence by local contractors.

One of the most prolifically built types developed under SHG auspices was the Whitson-Fairhurst house. It was based on a two-storey house-type with a precast concrete frame and foamslag panel cladding, designed in 1944 by Ayrshire county architect Robert Lindsay with the engineer W A Fairhurst of F A MacDonald & Partners, with help from Melville, Dundas & Whitson and the Ayrshire Dockyard Company of Irvine in developing the frame. An experimental block, with floor-plans based on the Westwood Report recommendations, was built in 1945 at Dalrymple. From 1946, Fairhurst developed this precast-frame system into the Whitson-Fairhurst type, of which over 3,350 were built across Scotland, either as flats or as cottages, by various members of the SHG consortium. The other precast-frame system built on a large scale by the SHG organisation - with over 6,200 built across Scotland - was the Orlit house, a system for two-storey cottages and two- or three-storey flats using precast outer walls, designed in collaboration with Sam Bunton. In a collaboration of 1949 with Blackburns, also orchestrated by Bunton, several hundred houses were built with Orlit frames and outer shells, and the standard Blackburn Mk.III prefabricated interior and roof. Blackburns claimed that each house could be erected in six months, and even agreed a penalty of £10 per house for late completion in the case of Edinburgh Corporation's Saughtonmains site, where 214 of these hybrid units were built in 1949, alongside 134 normal Orlit houses. The other Blackburn permanent types from Mk.III onwards were also built under SHG auspices. (50)

The Cruden Group was a rather different, and more tightly organised operation, which concentrated in a highly disciplined manner on the licensed-building method of operation. Like so many aspects of modern Scottish urban development, new towns and green belts among them, it was influenced in a subtle way by the earlier experience of colonialism and imperialism, here in the combination of an engineering ethos of efficiency combined with flexibility. Harry H Cruden, an engineering draughtsman who had worked as a coffee planter in Kenya and later in India in the 1930s, became involved in timber manufacture in Musselburgh during the war. Cruden was quite familiar, from the colonies, with the principle of kit-form buildings exported for erection elsewhere. In 1943, he converted his firm to a limited company with a capital of £1,000 and began work designing, himself, a building system suitable for large-scale building on a franchise basis, with special emphasis on the rural market. (51) The first postwar Cruden house was steel-framed, with external concrete panels and prefabricated timber-framed interior: a prototype was built in 1946 in Milton Road, Edinburgh. (52) Over the 1940s and early 1950s, the systems changed constantly in response to materials rationing, but the organisational method remained constant. A separate company, Cruden Houses Ltd, was set up by Cruden in alliance with a spread of builders all over the country,

to give the operation a strong regional flavour: Alexander Hall to cover the north-east and Highlands, Laidlaws to cover Glasgow and the west, Alliance Construction from Dundee, J Wright from Edinburgh. (53) The steel frames were produced centrally, and the member companies built the houses around them. Eventually, out of the 116,601 non-traditional houses built nationally in 1945-54, some 11% were accounted for by the consortium: Halls, for example, built over 600 houses from Aberdeen to Shetland.

The non-traditional programme was driven purely by rationing pressures, although there were frequent wild claims that it would dramatically speed up the building process: its main aim, and its substantial achievement, was that of spreading demand for materials more widely and thinly. Those hard facts were widely recognised almost from the beginning. For example, a report by Ronald Bradbury, Glasgow Corporation's Director of Housing, in November 1947, argued that 'there is no evidence that they produce completed houses more quickly than the normal techniques'; the only non-traditional houses in the city to have been completed were the Swedish Timber consignment. (54) And the Laidlaw Committee, the following year, claimed that non-traditional methods were successful in circumventing shortages of materials and labour for external building, although houses were often held up after that by shortages of materials for internal work, such as steel, cement, finishing materials and fittings. (55) The gains in production resources were also bought at the cost of problems in other areas. Almost all non-traditional houses were much more expensive, and their innovative methods led to widespread maintenance and structural problems: the SSHA had begun to criticise the condensation problems of its 'Weir Quality' houses as early as 1950.

Towards a mixed economy
the deregulation of building

The gradual easing of the postwar economic emergency allowed the post-1951 Tory government to begin the process of deregulation, and the construction of the mixed economy which would prevail from the mid-1950s to the late 1970s. In 1952, building restrictions were substantially eased, and in 1955 they were largely removed: within the field of non-traditional building, DHS Circular 82/1954 heralded the ending of all central controls as from June 1955. Speculative building was also in effect deregulated, but, largely because of the continuing legacy of working class hatred of the private landlords, the social and political climate was not yet ready for a wholesale revival of the private sector; we will explore later the limited private revival that did occur. The competition of housing solutions was, rather, within the public sector: it pitted against one another the post-World War I apparatus of decentralised, lightly regulated housing production under local political control, and the new post-World War II alliance of technocrats and strategic centralists committed to large-scale population and economic redistribution under the banner of regional planning.

The main task of the Scottish housebuilding industry was to work quietly yet innovatively as contractors, to exploit the often violently conflicting demands of these warring public bodies. Public housing offered large and small firms a safe haven in uncertain times. The collaborative relationship between private industry and government agencies was rapidly replaced by a clear separation. The producers themselves began to coalesce into more sharply defined businesses, and the single-contractor system approached a point of general breakthrough. The crucial issue was that of decision-making and control. Previously, the architect had performed the key role in co-ordinating the separate trades. But now the architectural profession, under the influence of the Modernist ethos, was becoming more interested in overarching social and technical ideas and less interested in directing tradesmen. In 1958, building-industry academic Norman Sidwell could still comment on the persistence of small single-trade firms, swarming over housing projects with their own improvised scaffolding and barely controlled by the architect's clerk of works. But only two years later, another commentator argued that separate-trades building was in terminal decline, owing to the withdrawal of architect control: 'the modern architect is letting his heritage go to the consulting engineer on the one hand and the main contractor on the other'. (56)

During the 1950s, the non-traditional systems became more obviously proprietary and commercially autonomous. But at the same time, with the easing of shortages of building tradesmen and mainstream building materials such as timber and bricks, and the rapid fall of prices of the latter, the structural distinctiveness of those systems from traditional construction, and from each other, became less and less. In constructional terms, the mid-1950s were clearly a transitional period between two phases of revolutionary innovation. What was important now was consolidation and the development of the more unglamorous but fundamental elements of building, such as materials supplies and site organisation.

This relatively conservative phase in Scotland, after a period of hectic innovation in the 1940s, contrasted with the enormous efforts devoted to system building and prefabrication research in some other European countries, including places with a strong separate-trades tradition of contracting. In Denmark and Sweden, the concern from the mid-1940s was to reconcile industrial modernity with a continuing high craft standard of building, and to ensure that systems consortia were led by professionals. (57) In France and the USSR, by contrast, the Fordist aspect of modernity was emphasised, and vast efforts were made in the 1950s to devise concrete panel prefabrication systems modelled on flow-line factory production. In the USSR by 1960, there were several systems of factory prefabrication and truck delivery of pre-assembled concrete flat units. (58) In France, another stronghold of separate-trades building, sluggish output immediately after the war provoked a revolution in housing production during the 1950s; the time taken to build one dwelling was slashed from 3,500 to 1,250 hours, and large greenfield sites were used for highly mechanised production of prefabricated flats. (59)

In the list of approved systems contained in DHS Circular 7/1954, we witness the last flowering of non-traditional methods, in the declining years of the movement. By then, owing to land shortages, the emphasis within urban housing was increasingly turning to flats, normally in the form of three- or four-storey

B3.16. 'New traditional' designs of cottages and low-rise flats by James Miller & Partners, as presented in an advertisement in the 1955 Scottish Municipal Annual. (James Miller Ltd)

tenements. There was also an increasing emphasis on variety of house sizes; the reign of the two-storey family house was coming to an end. The principal resource constraint was now not so much that of materials as of labour: some trades, such as plasterers, remained in extremely short supply. For cottages and two-storey flats, and in most cases also for tenements, promoters who had originally focused on wildly different constructional methods now converged on a similar formula. This used a traditional carcase, comprising rendered load-bearing walls of brick or precast concrete blocks with timber floors and ceilings, but combined it with non-traditional components and finishings, such as prefabricated kitchen units, concrete partition walls, standardised joinery, plasterboard linings. The greatest production benefit of these 'systems' was nothing to do with construction at all, but was concerned with organisation and marketing: systems were standard 'products' that simplified the process of promotion and building in any location.

On this basis, the industry settled down in the early and mid-1950s to a spell of steady, unglamorous public housing production. Some systems were still built on a completely nationwide basis. For example, Weir, having unceremoniously jettisoned steel construction altogether in 1949, first turned its Coatbridge factory over to a new no-fines concrete type (using the same prefabricated interiors as before), then built over 3,000 timber-framed houses across the country from 1952, followed (in 1954) by a new type of virtually conventional brick construction. (60) The Cruden programme continued at full steam, focusing from 1949 on a traditionally built but dry-lined house-type, the 'Dunedin'. However, at the opening of the

B3.15. The Hall Cottage, a single-storey version of the Dunedin house, designed by architect Ian Lindsay and built across the Highlands and Islands under the Cruden umbrella in the 1950s.

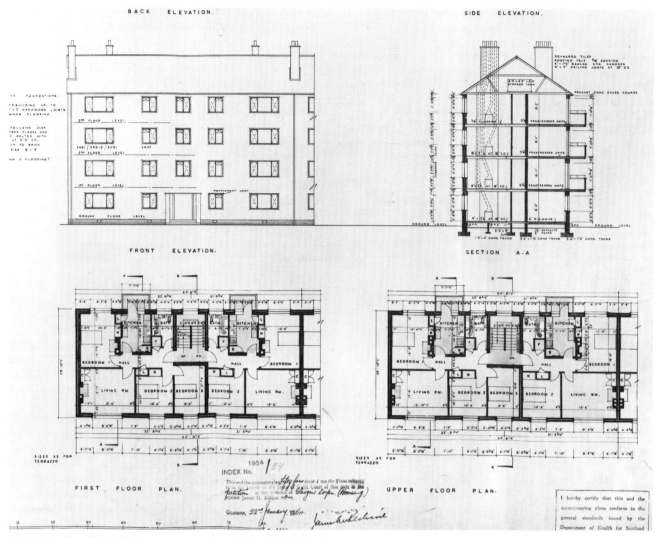

B3.17. *Type-plans of 1954 for four-storey tenement (type T/6/4) to be built by Glasgow Corporation direct labour at the Castlemilk township; construction was of brick faced with terrazzo, roughcast or blockwork, and the blocks contained two-, three- or four-apartment flats on each floor. (Glasgow City Archives)*

prototype in November 1949, in a scheme of houses for miners at Cuiken Burn, Penicuik, it was emphasised that the house had been built by Crudens itself as an all-trades contractor - a pointer to the firm's remarkable future. (61)

By 1960, over 25,000 Cruden houses, in various guises, had been built. (62) The other members of the Cruden group also began to develop their own separate strategies. Hall, for example, began by building the Dunedin house in large numbers; a serial negotiated contract was arranged with Aberdeen in the late 1940s with Tory housing convener 'Battling Baillie' Frank Magee. (63) At the same time, the firm introduced a single-storey variant designed by the Traditionalist architect Ian Lindsay, the 'Hall Cottage', for building across the Highlands and Islands under the Cruden umbrella, speading the ethos of single-contractor design-and-build into the remotest corners of the country. By 1960, Hall had developed its own precasting operation, with a system to match - the 'Kincorth', designed by engineers T Harley Haddow & Partners. (64)

In both Edinburgh and Glasgow, the consolidation of housebuilding operations in the 1950s was based around one dominant firm, which emphasised the manufacture of precast concrete blocks as a part of its operations. In Edinburgh, the Miller organisation, reinvigorated by wartime expansion and participation in the prefab and SHG programmes, made vigorous efforts to standardise the components of more-or-less traditional (or, as they were often styled, 'new traditional') house-types. They

took over one of Scotland's leading builders' merchants, and by 1950, they were employing a thousand workers at factories at Craigleith and Granton, producing standard joinery and precast concrete elements. In the early postwar years, especially in Edinburgh, over 7,250 Miller houses in various systems were built. These showed a diminishing element of prefabrication, but a continuing concern for systematised planning. Whereas in 1950/51, two-storey Miller cottages and flats featured brick or in-situ concrete walling, Gyproc plasterboard, metal floors, and prefabricated kitchen-bathroom and lighting units, the firm's 1954 type-plans for cottages and three/four-storey flats were of almost completely traditional construction. The Orlit organisation increasingly focused on the east of Scotland, renaming itself in 1954 the Scottish Construction Company (Scotcon), and devising systems for three- or four-storey tenements, using load-bearing precast blockwork.

In Glasgow, John Lawrence was now presiding over the largest private building organisation in Scotland, with extensive interests in the manufacture of gypsum products (such as the storey-high 'Bellrock' precast plaster panel, developed in 1946 and manufactured through the 1950s at Gypsum Construction Ltd's works, Dalmuir Dockyard) and precast concrete blocks for building construction, notably the hollow 'Wilson' block, made from 1945 by Wilson's Terrazzo Manufacturing Company of Glasgow. (65) Within Glasgow, the Corporation was, by the early 1950s, energetically developing the huge peripheral schemes (Pollok, Castlemilk and Drumchapel, followed by Easterhouse) with thousands of standardised three- and four-storey tenements. Negotiated contracts for these were divided up between the DLO and a consortium of local contractors within the SHG, including Lawrence alongside others such as Stuart and Mactaggart & Mickel. The DLO, having given up its own prefabricated system, had now returned to traditional building methods, although using numerous small precast components (such as window-sills) and cladding some blocks in terrazzo; after its wartime burst of innovation, it had slid back into a quiet reverie of featherbedding and inefficiency. Lawrence set about expanding his share of the Glasgow tenement market, in co-operation with the DLO, through limited elements of non-traditional construction, using Sam Bunton as a design impresario. In 1953, Bunton devised a rationalised variant of the standard Glasgow four-storey tenement plan using 'crosswall' construction, in which the load-bearing function was carried out by regularly spaced transverse walls, allowing front and back walls to be treated as light cladding. Several thousand of these flats, which used Wilson block cavity walling and Bellrock partitions, were built in extensive contracts under SHG auspices at Drumchapel and Castlemilk, and in Clydebank Burgh's war-relocation scheme at Faifley. Each crosswall tenement flat, at an average of £1,865, cost £80 more than comparable conventionally constructed flats, but construction times were faster: the first contract, for 2,000 flats at Drumchapel Unit 2, was built in 18 months from May 1953. (66) Lawrence, the chairman of Rangers Football Club, was a prominent Protestant unionist, and in the mid and late 1950s, his Ulster connections led him into some collaborative ventures with the Northern Ireland Housing Trust: for example, a factory to make Wilson blocks was built at Ballyclare in co-operation with Unit Construction of Liverpool.

Alongside these regional consolidation tendencies, with their anti-competitive overtones, several other key aspects of public housebuilding production during the early and mid-1950s pointed to the possibility of a return to revolutionary, rather than evolutionary, change again in the future. There was, after all, a general national rebuilding drive in progress, and any future imbalances and accelerations in that drive could bring shortages of labour or materials rapidly to the fore again. And the pattern of demand, on the part of the state housebuilding authorities, was also showing signs of instability. The conflict between the municipal-housing and regional-planning factions within local and central government was growing gradually more intense, as the planners devised more comprehensive ways to choke off Glasgow Corporation's land supply and force the city's Housing Committee to disgorge its population to the new towns and overspill areas. The riposte of the 'housers' seemed likely to be to build upwards: Glasgow, and some other towns, had begun prototype multi-storey blocks in the late 1940s and early 1950s, and a Glasgow delegation visited Le Corbusier's Unité d'Habitation in Marseille in March 1954. (67) The previous year, Sam Bunton and Lawrence had staked their claim to a leading

B3.18. Drumchapel Unit 2, Lawrence crosswall tenements under construction in 1954. (Glasgow City Archives)

position in any multi-storey drive by commencing a prototype nine-storey block at Melbourne Avenue, Clydebank, using a newly minted system of precast concrete blocks ('Multicon') developed with Lawrence. How would the Scottish building industry respond to a fresh resources crisis, combined with a demand for unconventional, multi-storey building?

Some possible answers were provided by two organisations - the Scottish Special Housing Association and George Wimpey Ltd - which stood outside the charmed circle of municipal politics and regional building interests. Both of them had decided to develop no-fines concrete, a 'wet' and simple constructional method which seemed very remote from the most extravagant factory systems, yet which was, in many ways, more flexible than any of them, as well as potentially cheaper: studies of 1946 had shown that no-fines houses built by Miller at Newtongrange had been £100 cheaper than equivalent traditional construction. (68)

The SSHA had not been idle since its expulsion from the urban centres in 1945 by George Buchanan - a policy which had been partly reversed in the late 1940s, although SSHA urban building remained subject to the goodwill of the town councils. Initially, its DLO had been largely confined to site servicing for proprietary systems, but from 1951, under chief engineer R Shiach and a new DLO manager, Ronald Macintosh, it embarked on a rapid phase of expansion and constructional innovation. By the early 1950s the organisation had 5,600 staff and built both for the SSHA's own programme and, occasionally, as a no-fines contractor for local authorities.

In contrast to the convulsive innovations of Glasgow's DLO force, the SSHA's policy was to develop its own no-fines system in a steady, rational manner. In 1950, a new, two-storey timber shutter was developed for use with on-site cranes, followed in 1951 by a steel shutter which would allow the building of the tenement blocks of three or four storeys that were increasingly demanded by the large towns. To ensure the stability of the top floor on four-storey no-fines blocks, a new type of precast floor wide-slab was specially designed and manufactured for the SSHA by Concrete (Scotland) of Falkirk - the first mention in this story of the 'Bison' construction that was to be so important in the 1960s. Using the new shutters, a 25-man squad, half of them unskilled, could pour ten dwellings a week. An annual SSHA DLO output of 276 houses in 1950/51 had increased within two years to 1,366; overall SSHA output by all methods in 1953 totalled 5,182. (69)

The SSHA then began to examine the possibilities of extending its no-fines construction upwards, into a multi-storey form. In May 1953, on a continental tour which also took in the original Dutch inventors of the no-fines technique, SSHA officials made contact with the German designers of a no-fines construction multi-storey students' hostel in Stuttgart, Professor Deininger and Ludwig Kresse. Deininger and Kresse were appointed consultants to the Association, and designed an experimental L-plan ten-storey point block, with three flats on each floor. Two prototypes were built at Toryglen, Glasgow, from 1955, followed by two more at Toryglen and eight in Dundee (four of these built by the DLO as contractors for Dundee Corporation). (70)

The SSHA had begun to point the way to the need for a national, rather than local or regional, scope of operations as the prerequisite for success in more troubled times; and it had shown how a relatively low-technology building system could be made suitable for the higher buildings that might be demanded in the future. But, for all its technical innovativeness, the Association was more constrained than private firms by the politico-economic context of public sector building. Given the large annual deficit under which the SSHA operated, the government had no compunction in using it as a regulator of the building industry. For example, in 1954, the Scottish Office asked the Association to reduce DLO annual output below 1,300, as part of a wider attempt to trim back economic growth. The contracting work of George Wimpey, as a firm with much greater resources than the SSHA, showed how the SSHA's technical and organisational ideas could be exploited much more effectively if those often arbitrary constraints were removed. And it also suggested that the 'threat' of incursions by large English firms, which was exploited by Scottish cartels such as the SHG, was more complex than it appeared. Owing to the separate system of building regulations and government housing administration in England and Wales, English firms wishing to operate successfully in Scotland had to set up autonomous divisions which, in effect, became 'Scottish' subsidiaries. Two of the Wimpey Scottish architects, whose recollections are included in this book (Ted Tysler and Tom Smyth), recalled entirely separate occasions when irate councillors demanded that 'good Scottish firms, like Wimpey' should be used, rather than 'English' ones!

In 1945, hoping to build on its wartime contracting successes, Wimpey commissioned an architect, Eric Collins, to investigate housebuilding techniques - metal, precast concrete, in-situ concrete - for possible adoption by the firm. As in the case of Cruden, it was the free-ranging ideas of a 'designer' which seem to have given this firm its innovative edge. Collins picked out no-fines concrete as the most suitable option, partly because the firm had a large amount of mobile equipment left from concrete-construction war work, and partly because of its good insulation qualities: a 10 inch no-fines wall had the same U-value (0.3) as an 11 inch cavity brick wall.

Because of its extensive use by the SSHA, it was natural that Wimpey, unlike other large London-based contractors, would aim to operate in Scotland as well as in England: between 1946 and 1955, Wimpey built 5,800 no-fines houses in Scotland. The firm kept a close eye on the SSHA's evolving techniques, but decided to use a more mechanised pouring technique, with large metal shutters that required cranes to move them about. This technique was well adapted to the building of flats. In the early 1950s, exploiting the early interest of Birmingham Corporation in experimental multi-storey building as a platform for its research, the firm devised several standard types of medium-rise no-fines blocks, including five-storey miniature point blocks of flats and maisonnettes for smaller authorities, and medium-rise Y-plan blocks of six or eight storeys, built first at Birmingham and then (from 1954) at Valley Gardens, Kirkcaldy.

Speculative building
beginnings of revival

During the early 1950s, private housebuilding had risen from its lowest point of 3% of total Scottish output, in 1950, to 17% in 1954. With the effective deregulation of the private sector from 1955, its contribution to overall Scottish housing output continued to grow steadily, if unspectacularly, to 23% in 1960 and 29% in 1962 (at which date the local authority proportion reached a temporary minimum level of 61%). What was clear was that no government, even a Tory one, could afford to change the overall orientation of government subsidy away from the public sector. There was no chance of the kind of vast subsidies for private building found in North America or Belgium. And the effect of those subsidies was compounded by local authorities'

ability to use the rates (local property taxes) to subsidise council rents. But whereas in the late 1940s central government policy, expressed through licensing, had held down private building fairly evenly across the country, the more decentralised system which emerged under Unionist rule in the 1950s ensured that private enterprise's contribution would be highly concentrated in some places.

Just as before the war, this concentration applied above all in Edinburgh, where the council had quietly and tenaciously maintained its policy of subsidising private building, and had nurtured a postwar housing stock which, by 1963, was one-third privately built. By that date, the Corporation had disbursed over £6,000,000 in this way, and a number of large firms, such as Miller, Mactaggart & Mickel and Thain, were engaged on developments of significant size - of over 2,000 dwellings, in the case of Mactaggart & Mickel's Broomhall. Millers returned to speculative building after 1955, with an expanded range of house-types: this side of the business was James Miller's own personal passion, and he controlled the programme personally.

In the Clyde Valley, by contrast, the large Labour authorities were determined not to allow any suburban land to pass to private builders, and so, as we saw above in Chapter A4, private development was squeezed out of the main urban areas into small burghs such as Bearsden and Milngavie, or areas outside burghs altogether, such as Newton Mearns. The fact that those sites that were zoned for private building were monopolised by relatively few firms depressed the level of competition, and pushed up prices further. During a brief period of Tory control of Glasgow Corporation in 1949-52, there was an attempt by the council to make good the deficiency itself, by selling to owner occupiers over 600 flats then under construction by direct labour at Merrylee, in a predominantly middle class area of the city; the proposal was delayed by mass protests by Corporation workers, and was eventually abandoned when Labour won back control in 1952. (71)

Architecturally, the new private developments rejected the bungalow pattern for a slightly denser, two-storeyed form, like their low-density council counterparts. In general matters of space, there was a convergence between the private and public sectors around the four-apartment (three-bedroom) house. As between the wars, private houses were set apart not so much by overall space standards as by slightly different relative room sizes and different layouts, with larger living rooms and smaller kitchens, a preference for two reception rooms in larger houses, and by higher levels of fittings and amenities. What was vital was to have small differentiations between types of similar size in order to emphasise the possibility of customer choice. In general, construction was traditional, although there was extensive use of concrete blockwork (especially internally); in 1955, Lawrence's gypsum construction subsidiary built a five-apartment show bungalow in a single week using storey-high Bellrock panels.

As an example of the late 1950s norm, we can take the two- and three-bedroom semi-detached cottage type houses advertised on Mactaggart & Mickel Edinburgh estates of 1960. These were similar in overall area to the corresponding standard council house-types offered by Miller as contractor to Edinburgh Corporation in the mid and late 1950s; the Mactaggart & Mickel houses, priced at £2,010 for two bedrooms and £2,250 for three, were conventionally built with roughcast brick cavity walls, joisted rather than solid concrete ground floor, and space for a garage. The divergence from the public sector in amenities and gadgets, and the potential for customer individualisation, was much greater

B3.20. Moss Heights, Glasgow: model of the three 10-storey slab blocks and low-rise flats, built in 1950-54 by English contractor Holland, Hannen & Cubitts; Glasgow Corporation's first large multi-storey project. (Glasgow District Council)

B3.19. Five-apartment show bungalow built by John Lawrence in 1955, using Bellrock gypsum panels.

in the larger house-types, such as a five-apartment cottage offered by Mactaggart & Mickel at Laurieston in 1960 for £3,740, which included a built-in garage; there was not yet any Scottish equivalent of the English attempts at small dwellings with luxury amenities, such as the 'Home of Tomorrow' showhouse opened in 1956 by Taylor Woodrow at Crawley New Town, offering an open-plan, lounge hall and warm-air central heating for £2,195. In fact, the closest comparison in terms of integrated fittings was the multi-storey flats beginning to rise in large numbers around 1960, but their much higher building costs vitiated any meaningful comparison: for example, an average dwelling in the 18-storey tower blocks designed by Robert Matthew at the Hutchesontown-Gorbals 'B' development in Glasgow, and built from 1958 onwards, cost £3,114 to build for 2.5 (average) apartments. (72)

B3.21. The Moss Heights project under construction in 1953. (RCAHMS A59636)

Conclusion

By the mid and late 1950s, a degree of normality seemed to have been restored to Scottish housing production. A range of public housing providers was engaged in mass programmes of fairly conventional dwelling-types, and the private industry was busy at work, as a contractor, on these secure and predictable tasks, as well as doing some speculative building on its own account once more. But that sense of stability was to prove deceptive. Within a few years, the public housing market was to find itself in revolutionary turmoil once again, as a new range of pressures and opportunities sprang into view. The reaction of some firms, such as Mactaggart & Mickel, would be to keep their eyes firmly fixed on their newly regained freedom to build on their own account. In doing so, they would largely forgo the growth opportunities offered by a fresh phase of convulsive public-sector production, but would ready themselves for the opportunities that eventually lay beyond. For the next two decades, the initiative would lie with a handful of firms bold enough to grasp at the colossal building tasks of the 1960s, yet sufficiently businesslike to avoid being consumed by them.

Site layout of 8-storey flats.

B3.22. Three 8-storey Y-plan blocks of council flats built by Wimpey in 1956-58 at the Esplanade, Kirkcaldy, using no-fines concrete construction. (George Wimpey Ltd)

Notes

1   Scottish Development Department, *Housing in Scotland* (typescript report), 1969 .

2   M Glendinning and S Muthesius, *Tower Block*, 1994, 73.

3   Glendinning and S Muthesius, *Tower Block*, 237.

4   Scottish Development Department, *Housing in Scotland*, 1969.

5   A Power, *Hovels to High Rise*, 1993, 5.

6   D Turin, *The Builder*, 31 March 1967, 516-17.

7   A Slaven and S Checkland (eds), *Dictionary of Scottish Business Biography*, 2, 1990, 126.

8   M Bowley, *The British Building Industry*, 1966; J Parry Lewis, *Building Cycles and Britain's Growth*, New York, 1965, 369.

9   Department of Health for Scotland, *Report of a Committee on Scottish Building Costs* (Barr Committee), 1939.

10 Scottish Housing Advisory Committee, *The Cost of Private Housebuilding in Scotland*, 1970, 46.

11 N Morgan, '£8 cottages for Glasgow citizens', in R Rodger (ed.), *Scottish Housing in the 20th Century*, 1989, 131-2.

12 Morgan, '£8 Cottages'.

13 N Hamilton (ed.), *From Spitfire to Microchip*, 1985, 59-66.

14 Morgan, '£8 Cottages', 137-44.

15 T Begg, *Housing Policy in Scotland*, 1996; Scottish Office Building Directorate (SOBD), *A Guide to Non-traditional Housing in Scotland*, 1987, 15; *The Scotsman*, 2 August 1939.

16 Glendinning and Muthesius, *Tower Block*, 286-303.

17 N Morgan, 'Sir James Miller', in Slaven and Checkland, *Dictionary*, 163-5.

18 J Fyfe Ltd, *Fyfe*, 1987, 20-4.

19 T Begg, *Fifty Special Years*, 1987.

20 Department of Health for Scotland, *Report of the Committee on Scottish Building Costs*, (Laidlaw Committee), 1948.

21 *Archis*, July 1997, 90; Gert Kaehler, 'Nicht nur Neues Bauen', in G Kaehler (ed), *Geschichte des Wohnens*, Volume 4, 1996, 436-50.

22 Ministry of Housing and Local Government, *Housebuilding in the USA*, 1966.

23 Begg, *Fifty Special Years*, 108-10.

24 H S Heavenrich, 'Housing in Great Britain', unpublished report for Albert Farwell Bemis Foundation of the Massachusetts Institute of Technology, Cambridge (Mass.) 1952, 62.

25 For prefabs in general see Heavenrich, 'Housing', and *Hansard*, 25 October 1945, column 414. For the Churchill House see *Building*, May 1944. For aluminium bungalows see *RIBA Journal*, July 1946; *Architect and Building News*, 20 December 1946; *The House Builder*, August 1946; *The Builder*, 6 April 1945. For Muirhouse ARCON see *Edinburgh Evening News*, 30 January 1946.

26 Heavenrich, 'Housing', 78.

27 A M Sherry, *The Blackburn*, Ochiltree, 1996

28 SOBD, *Guide to Non-traditional Housing*, 5-6; *Postwar Building Studies 1, House Construction*, 1943; *Postwar Building Studies 23, House Construction Second Report*, 1946.

29 Scottish Housing Advisory Committee, *Planning our New Homes* (Westwood Report), 1944.

30 Begg, *Housing Policy*, 28.

31 'Crathie Court and Moss Heights', Scottish Georgian Society Bulletin, 1982; Hamilton, *From Spitfire to Microchip*; Corporation of Glasgow, Housing Department, *Review of Operations*, 1948.

32 Begg, *Fifty Special Years*, 128-33

33 For this view see, for instance, Begg, *Housing Policy*, 161-3.

24 Ministry of Housing and Local Government, *Housebuilding in the USA*.

35 Begg, *Housing Policy*, 161-3.

36 Begg, *Housing Policy*, 96-105.

37 Department of Health for Scotland, *Report of the Committee on Scottish Building Costs*, 1948. On Edinburgh shortages, see *Evening Dispatch*, 5 October 1949.

38 *Sunday Mail*, 17 August 1947.

39 *Daily Express*, 19 May 1945; *Edinburgh Evening Dispatch*, 18 May 1945.

40 M Glendinning, 'The Modernist Era', *Rassegna*, 64, 1995, 5.

41 R Rodger and H Al-Qaddo, 'The SSHA', in R Rodger (ed.), *Scottish Housing in the 20th Century*, 1989, 195.

42 Begg, *Housing Policy*, 96-105.

43 Heavenrich, 'Housing', 140.

44 Interview with T Smyth, 5 July 1987.

45 Parry Lewis, *Building Cycles*, 369.

46 *Edinburgh Evening News*, 22 January 1948.

47 *Edinburgh Evening News*, 15 March 1949.

48 Heavenrich, 'Housing', 119-21.

49 SOBD, *Guide to Non-traditional Housing*, 6.

50 SOBD, *Guide to Non-traditional Housing*, 10. On Saughtonmains, see *Evening Dispatch*, 5 October 1949.

51 Morgan, 'Harry H Cruden', in Slaven and Checkland, *Dictionary*, 139-40.

52 SOBD, *Guide to Non-traditional Housing*, 9.

53 Morgan, 'Harry H Cruden', in Slaven and Checkland, *Dictionary*, 139-40.

54 Glasgow City Archives, Town Clerk's housing files, 'Foamslag' file; Hamilton, *From Spitfire to Microchip*, 60.

55 Department of Health for Scotland, *Report of the Committee on Scottish Building Costs* (Laidlaw Committee), 1948.

56 *The Builder*, 28 February 1958 and 29 April 1960.

57 M Kjeldsen, *Industrialised Housing in Denmark*, Copenhagen, 1976; Power, *Hovels to High Rise*, 261.

58 R M E Diamant, *Industrialised Building*, 1964, 123; R M E Diamant, *Industrialised Building 2*, 1965, 45.

59 Power, *Hovels to High Rise*, 44; *Architects' Journal*, 11 November 1970.

60 *Edinburgh Evening News*, 15 March 1949.

61 *The Scotsman*, 26 November 1949.

62 Morgan, 'Cruden', in Slaven and Checkland, *Dictionary*, 140.

63 W Mackie, *A Century of Craftsmanship, Alexander Hall & Son*, 1980, 31.

64 Mackie, *A Century of Craftsmanship*, 55.

65 Morgan, 'Cruden', in Slaven and Checkland, *Dictionary*, 140.

66 Glasgow City Archives, Dean of Guild reference 1953/74.

67 Corporation of the City of Glasgow, *Report of Visit of Deputation to Inspect "The Marseilles Block"*, 1954.

68 Begg, *Fifty Special Years*, 150.

69 Scottish Special Housing Association (SSHA), *A Chronicle of Forty Years*, 1977, 17; Begg, *Fifty Special Years*; SSHA, *Annual Digest for the Year ending 31 March 1974*, 1974, 17; SOBD, *Guide to Non-traditional Housing*, 13; R Macintosh, *The No-Fines Story*, n.d., 15.

70 Begg, *Fifty Special Years*, 168-75.

71 N Donaldson and L Forster, *Sell and Be Damned*, c.1991.

72 Glasgow City Archives, Town Clerk's files, *Comparative Costs of Multi-storey Flats*, reports by City Architect's Department, 13 September 1965, and City Chamberlain's Office, 18 January 1966.

PACKAGE-DEAL HOMES

The Years of Affluence, 1960-75

Miles Glendinning

Introduction

'The world's built on supply and demand - and, around 1960, the demand for high blocks was there, but the supply wasn't!'
Alec Mitchell (Concrete Ltd), 1987

The beginning of the 1960s brought a new crisis of production shortage - a crisis which, despite the vastly improved overall economic situation, was in some ways more intractable than that of the late 1940s, because the kinds of buildings now required were far more specialised and difficult to build. The years 1960-61 saw the start of a general building boom, whose effects were hardly alleviated by the 'Great Squeeze' on credit in 1961. Firms began to move out of housebuilding into more profitable industrial and commercial work. The most obvious result was a shortage of firms prepared to tender: for example, out of fourteen firms invited by the SSHA to tender to build four 26-storey tower blocks at Wyndford, Glasgow, in 1964, only two eventually did so.

This crisis in production was complicated, and in some ways made worse, by the fact that there was also a crisis of demand, caused by the mounting civil war within the state development apparatus: a conflict between the municipal and housing faction, who wished to solve the housing and slum problems of the old industrial towns by redeveloping and extending them in situ, and the planning technocrats, who aspired to redirect population and investment to new towns and growth centres. The policies of the planners, especially the green belts around some urban centres, had the effect of gradually choking off the land supply for council housing: annual output fell away from 24,210 in 1957 to only 16,245 in 1962. On its own, this cut in the land supply for new housing should have helped offset the building-industry shortages, but because it began to drive municipalities towards more specialised patterns such as multi-storey flats, it instead actually made the position worse. And this crisis happened at a time of growing public expectation that housing output should be generally rising, to reflect society's increasing affluence. After all, while the overall population had stabilised at around 5.2 million, the average household size was dropping, leading to a demand for slightly smaller homes. The detached family house in a garden suburb was no longer necessarily the ideal for all.

The result was a new burst of demand, channelled not into a unified flow but into the conflicting programmes of various competing agencies of the state. Although the government was Tory-controlled until late 1964, the continuing political and organisational difficulties of speculative building, and the low

B4.1. Mass housing, 1960s-style: Edinburgh Corporation's Muirhouse Temporary Housing Area project, a higher-density redevelopment of a prefab site from 1960, built adjacent to 1950s Scotcon tenements (at bottom right) and the late 1930s West Pilton area (at top right). At the centre of this view are medium-rise Wimpey and Smart flats of 1960-66, and at the bottom left, Wimpey and Scotcon tower blocks, along with the crowning feature of Martello Court (1962-64), a 23-storey point block built by W Arnott McLeod as a showcase of the local building industry. (RCAHMS B69850)

ideological status of private housing, ruled out any reliance on private enterprise as the main engine of revived output, as was being attempted in England. Public housing must, for the time being, continue in overwhelming dominance. The new public housing demand of the 1960s was for mass building in novel and unprecedented forms: the open-plan layouts, high tower blocks and unadorned forms of Modern architecture. In response, the industry entered a new phase of revolutionary innovation, developing the single-contractor formula into new and complex patterns of internalised decision-making, and attempting to combine the two innovative elements of high blocks and factory prefabrication in an efficient and profitable way.

On all sides, by both state and industry, this new phase was portrayed in the same language as the wartime 1940s campaigns, a language of concentration, co-ordination and discipline. Both demand and supply were described in terms of consortia, combines, conglomerates. But the reality of decision-making and organisation was far less tidy. During the 1940s, command planning, however unevenly implemented, was at least an overall aspiration. During the early 1960s, by contrast, the stereotypical

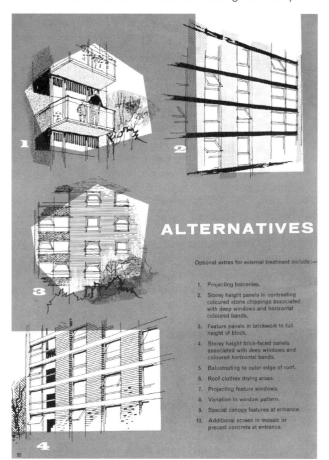

ALTERNATIVES

Optional extras for external treatment include:—

1. Projecting balconies.

2. Storey height panels in contrasting coloured stone chippings associated with deep windows and horizontal coloured bands.

3. Feature panels in brickwork to full height of block.

4. Storey height brick-faced panels associated with deep windows and coloured horizontal bands.

5. Balustrading to outer edge of roof.

6. Roof clothes drying areas.

7. Projecting feature windows.

8. Variation in window pattern.

9. Special canopy features at entrance.

10. Additional screen in mosaic or precast concrete at entrance.

B4.2. Illustration of alternative elevational treatments for standard Wimpey tower blocks, published in the company's 1965 brochure, Wimpey Rationalized Planning. *(George Wimpey Ltd)*

picture of postwar public housing as grey and monolithic becomes especially misleading. The governing ethos among public authorities was one of ideological and political competition, with some bodies, such as Glasgow Corporation, especially dominant and assertive, and others smaller and more passive. The response of the industry, and the power it exerted, was correspondingly variegated, leading to complex overlaps between demand and supply. The most powerful public clients could influence the industry's response, while conversely the most powerful contractors could shape the policies of smaller local authorities.

It was the open politicisation of the housing drive, and the conflict between powerful state housing and planning organisations, that was especially distinctive about Scotland. Even in England, which shared the same general organisation of government, the position was far more decentralised and less confrontational; there was no equivalent to Glasgow Corporation or the SSHA. On the Continent, housing was almost completely removed from immediate political conflict; there, figures such as the 'crusading' councillor or the council direct-labour boss did not exist. In West Germany, for example, the social housing system was decentralised to housing companies, and 'public authority housing' was almost unknown; even in the 1960s, there were comparatively few giant high-rise developments. In France, on the other hand, low-rent housing was kept in the hands of autonomous social 'HLM' organisations, at one remove from political controversy, and housing production and land supply were assured by technocratic command planning; from 1958, the state provided a limitless stock of greenfield 'Priority Urbanisation Zones' (ZUPs) around major cities, for industrialised development of high-rise slab blocks on vast, Versailles-like geometrical layouts. (1) In eastern Europe, there were highly varied structures of public

building - for example, in Czechoslovakia, national and regional building trusts with integrated design departments, and in Poland a three-way division between design bureaux, contracting trusts, and local or national government client bodies acting as intermediaries - but these structures were not the subject of openly expressed political controversy or representative-democratic control. (2)

During the early 1960s, the political weakness of Unionist (Tory) ministers on the housing question left them incapable of imposing any order on the decentralised, if not openly anarchic, situation that prevailed within Scottish public housing. It was only when the Labour Party returned to government in 1964 that a new and forceful Scottish Office housing minister, J Dickson Mabon, was able to begin to correct the vast imbalances between large and small authorities, and to dampen down the hostility between the municipal and the regional-planning strategies of building.

Burghs of barony
the patronage of
1960s public housing

The response of Scottish local authorities to the 1960/61 building crisis had two main stages. The first, short-term reaction was to begin seeking negotiated contracts, especially for multi-storey blocks and other large and complex housing projects. Although generally more expensive than competitive tendering, these gave both sides greater security. The second phase, from around 1962, focused more intensely on construction methods; as in the 1940s, a wide range of prefabrication 'systems' was employed in an attempt to circumvent shortages of labour and materials.

In those years, contractors and local authorities were gradually being drawn together. The old demarcation under separate-trades, with the architect holding the centre, had almost disappeared, although separate-trades contracts continued to prevail in some remoter areas such as Shetland throughout the 1960s. In general, however, the decision-making and design co-ordination process had now become highly fluid, and in effect 'up for grabs'. The labour shortage for public housing was a matter not just of building workers, but also of professionals and designers within the short-staffed local authorities. As a compensation for the continuing suppression of the speculative-building side of the private building industry, here, in contracting work, the industry was able to flex its financial muscle, attracting young designers away from the public authorities in droves.

In a late 1950s attempt to shore up architects' position, the Department of Health for Scotland (DHS) had tried to forbid negotiated contracts for high blocks direct with a building firm, and to insist on briefing and control by an architect, but the result had only been to stampede the largest authorities into complete design-and-build contracts, or 'package deals'. The flashpoint of this crisis had been an attempt of 1957-58 by Edinburgh Corporation to allocate package-deal contracts for up to 18 tower blocks on four sites to a 'panel' of contractors including Wimpey, Scotcon, Crudens, Laing and the SSHA's direct labour organisation (DLO). In response, Robert Woodcock, a senior DHS architect, thundered that 'neither now nor in the future is there a place for the promoter of the standard designed multi-storey block'; any nominated contractor 'should be confined to collaboration on the working details, organisation and building'. But resistance was futile, and eventually, in 1961, realising the cause was lost, DHS under-secretary J Callan Wilson ordered the complete lifting of restrictions on negotiated contracts. During the 1960s there were grumbling complaints about them, for instance by the 1964 Banwell Committee on tendering, but they were not seriously challenged. (3) Henceforth the government's regulatory role would be concerned with overall cost limits and conformity to design standards: its input into building organisation would be hortatory and advisory.

The emergence of the negotiated multi-storey contract allowed the development of a highly diverse range of client-contractor relationships, no longer mediated by the central state. With this devolution to a municipal level of decision-making about vast and complex programmes, the postwar decentralisation of public housebuilding reached its furthest extreme. What also reached its climax was the status within Scottish public housing enjoyed by the housing faction in Glasgow Corporation. This status derived not just from the Housing Committee's effective autonomy to act as it wished, but also from its power to influence national decision-making and act on equal terms with DHS. Ever since the early housing initiatives of Peter Fyfe after 1919, the government-Glasgow relationship in social housing had been a tense but mutually dependent one - like that between a neurotic parent and a dominant child. (4) In the 1930s and early 1940s, the power of the Housing Committee had waned for a while, with the arrival of younger rivals in the family: the SSHA, the regional planning movement. But now, with the government's determination to revive public housing output through the use of high blocks on limited sites, its dependence on Glasgow's 'housers' could only increase. As the city's chief planner, Ron Nicoll, complained, 'Glasgow Corporation was *the* power in the land - no minister sitting in Edinburgh could do much about Glasgow!' (5) As early as 1955, the Treasury had resigned itself to the likelihood that Glasgow would eventually try to break free into an unrestrained multi-storey building drive - in which case, they grimly predicted, DHS housing administrators would simply act as a postbox for the Housing Committee's spending demands. (6)

Glasgow's burgeoning power in the early 1960s could have led merely to a reinforcement of its somewhat defensive and inefficient production ethos of the 1950s, dominated by negotiated contracts with the DLO and the Clydeside contracting ring. Indeed, elements of low productivity and incompetence within the Glasgow production machine persisted into the 1960s: for example, the practice of launching into DLO contracts without proper costings or even subsequent 'remeasurement', or the administrative incompetence which led the Corporation to give Crudens, in the mid-1960s, a contract to build 20-storey blocks in Govan when the site for them had not yet been bought! (7) But overall, the 1960s housing drive in Glasgow brought about a remarkable rejuvenation of the city's production methods. This was largely due to two individuals: David Gibson, Convener of the Housing Committee until his death in 1964, and Lewis Cross, the official within the City Architect's department who was in charge of the housing drive.

Gibson's contribution, fuelled by a kind of secularised Presbyterian socialism, was to bring a messianic, moral driving force to bear on housing output, allowing him to drive headlong through the bitter opposition of the regional planning faction. He spoke of the Housing Committee's crash drive to construct tower blocks on gap sites across the city, as a crusade to build a City on a Hill: 'In the next three years, the skyline of Glasgow will become a more attractive one to me because of the likely vision of multi-storey houses rising by the thousand ... The prospect will be thrilling, I am certain, to the many thousands who are still yearning for a home. It may appear on occasion that I would

offend against all good planning principles, against open space and Green Belt principles - if I offend against these it is only in seeking to avoid the continuing and unpardonable offence that bad housing commits against human dignity. A decent home is the cradle of the infant, the seminar of the young and the refuge of the aged!' (8)

Gibson's charismatic and passionate career has been analysed in detail in several recent publications, and is touched on in several of the interviews by 1960s housing personalities, included in the appendices to this book. What is more directly relevant to the organisation of housing patronage (and also recalled in detail in the appendix interviews) is the activity of Lewis Cross. He revolutionised the way in which Glasgow dealt with housing contracts - and thus indirectly, through Glasgow's national status, shaped the course of housing production across the country. Cross, like Harry Cruden, was an engineer who had worked in the colonies. He brought to Glasgow an ethos of relentless managerial efficiency, which exactly complemented Gibson's fiery idealism. Unlike Cruden, Cross was not at all interested in the design or construction of buildings. What he enjoyed was negotiating and monitoring contracts, in a hard-headed way which ingeniously exploited the negotiated contract system so that it benefited the city, rather than hobbling production as in the 1940s and 1950s.

Cross realised that an authority of Glasgow's size and pulling power could turn the self-containedness of package-deal building to its own advantage, by dealing with a range of large contractors each in isolation, and by building up a secret land-bank of sites suitable for multi-storey building: the interviews with Crudens and Wimpey architects reproduced in the appendix show how close to his chest he held his negotiating cards! As Glasgow council house building, fuelled by unrestricted rate subsidies, was by then something of an open-chequebook affair, the aim of Cross's strategy was not so much to cut the cost of individual jobs as to encourage a glut of supply, and keep contractors on their toes: the overarching aim laid down by Gibson was not financial economy but maximum output. Especially with prefabricated building, a considerable investment in factories and equipment was necessary. By forcing the firms to compete with each other's package deals, Cross compelled them to make that investment themselves, at their own risk - with follow-on contracts entirely subject to their own performance. (9) For example, one English firm, Reema of Salisbury, built a precasting factory at Bellshill on the basis of a single order from Cross (for three tower blocks at Broomloan Road, in 1963); despite follow-on orders from Glasgow and Lanark County Council, their investment was never fully recouped.

In a way, Cross's system of package-deal competition and land-bank secrecy constituted a kind of laissez-faire 'market' - except that the governing ethos was not financial profit but maximum production efficiency. He was viscerally hostile to any 'anti-competitive' forces that might impede the free working of this 'market'. First and foremost among these was the building ring of Glasgow contractors and the DLO. Cross disliked consortia and cartels on principle. Using the unfamiliarity of high blocks as his lever, he set about tearing apart this cosy conglomerate with some relish, introducing contractors from outside to force its members to compete or fall behind. Here he had to fight many battles with Gibson and other councillors, arguing that, if output was the driving objective, socialist job protectionism would have to take second place.

Cross also opposed the traditional role of the architect as intermediary, believing that it fatally muddied the competitive process, and pointing to the colossal delays and overspending of early setpiece multi-storey schemes controlled by private architects, notably Basil Spence's Hutchesontown 'C' slab blocks. Making a virtue of the architectural short-staffing within the city, he delegated all design matters to contractors or their design teams: private architects, to be acceptable, had to work as part of an integrated contractual team. When he eventually left Glasgow to become the SSHA's general manager in 1965, his monitoring regime had raised the percentage of Glasgow multi-storey contracts running on time from 33% in 1961 to 83%, and his successor, James Kernohan, found himself in the fortunate position of having 'five large-panel-firms situated round the perimeter of Glasgow, all demanding the chance to build high flats - what Glasgow wanted, it got!' (10)

In the other cities and large towns, the decentralised housing system allowed a wide range of approaches to programme organisation and decision-making responsibility. Some authorities tried to maintain a degree of architectural control of the design process, while others followed Cross in delegating everything to package deals. Within the Central Belt, the relationships established by Cross in Glasgow spilled over into the general policies of other towns, as contractors who had ploughed large sums into equipment and infrastructure sought to recoup their investment. In 1963, Gibson tried to formalise that network of *auctoritas* by setting up a consortium of towns and cities dedicated to raising output by a further 10% through bulk-ordering of prefabricated high flats: the Scottish Local Authorities Special Housing Group (SLASH). It included many of his closest allies and admirers in other authorities, such as Pat Rogan, the housing chairman in Edinburgh, and Hutchison Sneddon, the Motherwell leader and housing convener. Some of the Central Belt towns, such as Falkirk or Kirkcaldy, channelled the 1960s output drive into highly structured planning and architectural frameworks, while others, notably Greenock, adopted the same hands-off approach as that of Cross.

Outside the Central Belt, some major centres were able to maintain a more or less self-contained regional 'housing economy' - for good or bad. In Dundee, some of the worst aspects of the local protectionism detested by Cross were displayed to the full. The short-staffed City Architect's Department was incapable of exercising the kind of overview maintained by Cross in Glasgow, and so local organised labour and elements of the local industry were able to maintain almost complete hegemony, setting out to 'bleed to death' most of the national contractors who ventured in. Of outside firms, only Crudens was able to break through this barrier on a significant scale, through the boldness of a series of massive multi-storey projects on the city periphery, including the huge slab blocks of Ardler (1964-66) and the honeycomb-plan Whitfield project of deck-access blocks (1968-72). (11) Aberdeen, in contrast, showed how a relatively closed regional contracting system could be made to work well, through relentless efficiency and incorruptibility, and could be combined with use of designs by the city architect without major loss of production impetus: package deals were virtually unknown in the Granite City.

The hierarchical structure of status among local housing authorities was clearest in the case of the small burghs, which made up three-quarters of the 234 housing authorities. If Glasgow's policies shaped what the contractors did, here it was the reverse, as building firms' public relations staff toured round, inciting burghs to compete with one another by building tower

blocks. These scattered and weak authorities constituted a major impediment to the housing drive as a whole: it was like a client equivalent of the separate-trades system, with each small tradesman coming to the site carrying his own makeshift bundle of scaffolding. In 1962, the government-sponsored Emmerson Report had argued that this could be overcome if small authorities combined in consortia to order serial contracts and package deals. (12) In 1964, Dickson Mabon made it one of his first priorities to cajole the smaller burghs to band together, overcoming old rivalries, for example between the Borders towns, to boost output. (13)

Unlike the 1940s, it was more difficult for the government to contemplate supporting these contracts with guarantees or direct subsidies: examples of such initiatives included the exempting of off-site prefabrication from Selective Employment Tax (introduced in 1966). What was principally on offer was advice from the National Building Agency, an organisation like the Burt Committee set up in 1963 to appraise and certify building systems. Not surprisingly, the actual progress of concentration of demand was halting, at best. In 1967, of 607 housing contracts approved by the Scottish Development Department (SDD), only 116 were for more than 100 dwellings. (14) Among the larger authorities, consortia often became a matter of rivalry and suspicion. In North Lanarkshire, for example, a consortium of large burghs (Motherwell, Coatbridge and Airdrie) was set up in the early 1960s to build a serial contract for 'Camus' prefabricated high and low flats. Lanark County Council's housing leader, Hugh Brannan, was pressured in 1965 by Mabon to join this consortium, but, jealously guarding the county's status, decided instead to make a separate package-deal order for 'Reema' tower blocks. (15)

In contrast to the unruly local authorities, the centrally-administered public housebuilding organisations, free of immediate political demands and governed more like colonial improvement trusts, pursued a more consistent patronage policy. (16) This took two main forms. The first was the old wartime-style procedure of emergency command planning, now used only for military or strategic projects such as the late 1950s project to build several hundred new houses in Thurso for incoming English workers at the Dounreay nuclear plant. Alexander Hall was awarded this job by UKAEA Risley as an extension of the contract for the plant, and undertook to have the first of the houses ready within four months; the contract included over 300 precast-concrete houses in Hall's 'Kincorth' system.

B4.3. A group of senior SSHA staff seen in 1970. Front row, from left: Harold Buteux, chief technical officer; A T Brown, assistant building manager; R H Macintosh, building manager; Lewis W S Cross, general manager. (Scottish Special Housing Association)

B4.4. '12M Jespersen' low-rise system-built flats constructed by Laing from 1965 at Craigshill South, Livingston New Town; a Jespersen factory was built by the firm at Livingston and opened in July 1965. (RCAHMS B21603)

The second, much larger and more important types of centrally run programme were those of the SSHA and the New Town Development Corporations. These organisations, as we have seen, formed part of the regional planning movement, and thus were regarded with suspicion or hostility by the large Labour municipalities. From around 1963, and especially under Dickson Mabon from 1965, the original anti-urban utopianism of the early new town movement was replaced by a doctrine of planned economic 'growth centres' set apart from the old industrial towns, and serviced by the housebuilding of the new towns and the SSHA.

The programmes of the five new towns - East Kilbride, Glenrothes, Cumbernauld, Livingston, and Glenrothes - were under the close control of their architectural and planning staffs, who insisted on careful integration of design and landscaping rather than maximum output. As the new town concept formed part of the regional planning ethos of reducing density, there was no question of massed contracts for multi-storey blocks, and tower blocks were used only selectively as landmarks. Negotiated contracts became increasingly popular, but almost always for designs by the authorities' own designers; for example, Wimpey built extensive low-rise developments for East Kilbride. Only at East Kilbride and Cumbernauld were large package-deal contracts awarded, for higher-rent executive tower blocks (to Wimpey and Bison respectively). At Livingston, the chief architect, Peter Daniel, was a passionate proselytiser of technocratic system-building, and succeeded not only in building a large contract for Laing '12M Jespersen' system flats to his own design at Craigshill (1965) but also in inducing Laing and Crudens to build precasting factories in the new town.

Within the SSHA, the position was very similar during the early 1960s: the designers were in overall charge of building policy. Throughout the previous decade, the main innovative force had been the constructional and engineering research centred on the DLO, and there was much use of standard low-rise systems by contractors. But in 1959, there was a decisive change, when a new Chief Technical Officer (i.e. chief architect), Harold Buteux, was appointed. Buteux had previously worked in Birmingham as deputy to city architect A G Sheppard Fidler, a passionate advocate

of the philosophy of designer-led housing production that ultimately stemmed from the London County Council (LCC) and the Arts and Crafts Movement. The LCC philosophy was grounded in the English public-sector tradition of competitive tendering by single contractors, working to the design of a local authority or consultant architect. This was a procedure which made sure that each project could be individually designed, but was grossly unsuited to maximising output at times of resource shortage, especially if large-scale prefabricated contracts were involved - as the LCC and Birmingham architects discovered to their cost in the early 1960s building boom. (17) Buteux explained his philosophy at length in the interview reproduced in the appendix to this book.

As the SSHA was free from driving local authority political pressure for output - and, indeed, was jealously excluded by some local authorities - Buteux could develop his ideas with greater freedom. He began by developing standard types, such as the 15-storey 'Mk.III' point block, derived from his designs for Sheppard Fidler in Birmingham. These were to be used as the basis for competitive tendering, and were built in the form of well-landscaped Modernist 'mixed developments' of high and low blocks, such as Wyndford, in Glasgow (1961-69). Buteux then attempted, with less success, to apply the same principle to prefabricated construction, in a series of contracts for point blocks from 1963 onwards, and a 1966 collaborative project for prototype medium-rise blocks at Anderston Cross, Glasgow, with SDD research and development architects.

From 1965, with Mabon's push for an expanded SSHA annual programme of 5,000 units in economic growth areas, and Cross's arrival as general manager of the Association, Buteux's design-led concerns were increasingly challenged by a demand for output. Cross modified his own approach to take account of the more stable programme of the SSHA and to allow for the use of Buteux's designs for low-rise housing, developed in collaboration with the SLASH group. The DLO was allocated half of the programme (with some agency work in addition), but was made to operate much more efficiently, and to collaborate with Wimpey - in view of their joint interest in no-fines construction. In the later phases of the economic-expansion drive, around 1975-77, the SSHA programme was reorientated towards the oil-development areas in Aberdeenshire, Shetland and the Moray Firth, and its technical and constructional expertise was freely shared with other contractors, such as Hall and Crudens. Here the Association's role was less as a patron of housing than as a member of a contractors' consortium, although Halls also built over 2,000 houses for the SSHA across the country. (18)

The management of innovation
organising the package deals

We discussed above, from the point of view of the public-authority clients, the accelerating stampede into negotiated and package-deal contracting in the early 1960s. But what did a package-deal contract actually mean for the people within the industry who organised and ran it? The term in fact covered a range of approaches, which looked roughly the same from the perspective of a councillor, but were organised very differently behind the scenes. The first alternative approach covered the whole works, namely the design and the whole building process, with subcontractors used for only subordinate tasks: the exemplar of this approach was Wimpey. The second was a design and management contract combined with finishing trades and general building, with the main structural work being delegated to a nominated subcontractor: the early multi-storey contracts of Crudens, including the gigantic Sighthill project in Glasgow, were of this type. The third was almost the reverse of the second, namely, a design, management and structural contract, with general building and finishing work dealt with by a local builder - an approach similar to the Cruden Group in the 1940s and 1950s, but, within 1960s multi-storey building, particularly associated with Concrete Ltd's 'Bison' system.

What did these approaches all have in common? It was certainly not their constructional or building organisation methods, which, as we will see in due course, differed widely. Rather, what they had in common was control - over building design and contact with the client, as well as over general decision-making on the running of the contract. The package-deal contractor, in other words, did exactly the same job that the architect and clerk of works had done under the separate-trades system: all that was left to the client's architect was the possibility of laying out the site, although in the case of Cross even that was delegated to the contractor. The resemblance to the old separate-trades situation was all the more uncanny because of the way in which the 'single contractor' or 'main contractor', although not even fully established as the mainstay of housing production, was already splintering into a myriad of specialised subcontractors, to cope with the growing complexity of large modern buildings like multi-storey blocks, boosting productivity in the process. Like the 'single-end' house, the separate-trades system was no sooner pronounced extinct than it was back again, in impeccably modern form. (19) The experimental low-rise housing of the 1940s and 1950s had already introduced various consultants and services specialists to the building site, but to build a 20-storey block of flats required as a matter of course the employment of subcontractors and/or consultant engineers for structure, heating, ventilation, lifts, erection, plant operation, and so on. What was not generally found in Scotland, in contrast to the far more overheated building industry in London, was 'the lump': labourers working as freelance 'subcontractors'. (20)

Thus the most crucial members of staff of a package-deal contractor were the design team, the negotiators and the co-ordinating managers. What was important - as Eric Collins, Harry Cruden and the ARCON designers had already demonstrated in the 1940s - was to be bold enough to grasp the huge opportunities suddenly thrust out by public housing, and to be able to manage the resulting growth. Where large, traditional firms focused on the business of building could have difficulty in adapting to the new climate - especially if they were also speculative builders, and emotionally tied by land-banks to particular localities - relatively small and highly mobile firms such as Crudens and Concrete Ltd could experience meteoric expansion.

The required combination of flexibility and discipline is demonstrated, for example, in the process of development of standard package-deal tower blocks, explained by Crudens chief architect, George Bowie, in the interview reproduced in the appendices to this book. As in the case of the individual buyer of a speculative house, the demand from individual local authorities was for overall reliability and predictability combined with a degree of flexibility in making customised, small alterations. From the firm's viewpoint, those demands had to be satisfied as economically as possible. Under the overall heading of demand also came the government regulations and standards laid down by DHS/SDD, which were of no intrinsic interest to the local authority but had to be constantly kept in mind by the designer. For example, the requirement for a minimum external wall area per flat potentially impeded the planning of tower blocks with

more than four flats on each floor. That obstacle was circumvented by Wimpey through a staggered, twin-tower design, and by Bowie's staff through inset 'lungs' in the block sides, an expedient which was constantly refined and made more economical. This type of fast-moving 'design' activity required an integration of architecture and engineering which was alien to the traditional architect's ethos, and beyond the staff capacity of the average practice. Wimpey's chief Scottish architect, Tom Smyth, recalls looking at drawings for a project by one Glasgow architect: 'I could see that the kitchens were too deep and I told him the scheme wouldn't pass. He didn't believe me, but that was just what happened!' (21)

The package-deal formula was further challenged in the early 1960s by the next stage in the boom, the sudden drive for industrialised building 'systems'. In general, the one-off contracts for non-prefabricated multi-storey blocks, which prevailed around 1960-63, had been highly profitable to contractors. To organise a housing package-deal required slightly more resources than the basic requirements of a property speculator - a desk, a chair and a telephone - but the principle was not dissimilar! (22) Prefabricated construction of high flats was a completely different matter; everything suddenly became deadly serious. The lightweight systems which had dominated the 1940s drive would be of no use, and thus substantial investment in heavy factory infrastructure would be necessary. How would this investment

B4.5. Contemporary montage of Pollokshaws Unit 2 redevelopment, Glasgow, built from 1961 and designed by Boswell, Mitchell & Johnston. The tower blocks had J Laidlaw as main contractor, with Concrete Scotland as structural subcontractor; the project was the prototype for large-scale use of Concrete's 'Bison' system. (Boswell, Mitchell & Johnston)

B4.6. Erection of Bison concrete cladding panels on the first high block of Pollokshaws Unit 2 in 1963. (Boswell, Mitchell & Johnston)

be paid for? The contractors who jumped on board the systems bandwagon thought it would be recouped by the large-scale orders which must inevitably come rolling in. The architectural establishment agreed, and drew their own, pessimistic conclusions. They denounced the likely monopolistic tendencies of heavy prefabricated systems, and unfavourably contrasted 'closed' contractor-controlled systems with a utopian vision of 'open' systems suitable for use in individual architectural designs. (23) But both were wrong; for the economics of system building, as we will see later in this chapter, turned out quite differently.

Insiders and outsiders
contractors of the 1960s

Let us now look more closely at the firms themselves that built the public housing of the 1960s boom: who were the losers and who were the winners?

Within the Central Belt, the clearest losers were the 'insiders', the local building interests: in fact, over the entire course of its multi-storey drive, Scotland was the part of the UK that built the lowest percentage using local firms (18%). In the west, the non-traditional leaders of the 1940s and 1950s at first made strenuous efforts to embrace the new patterns: even Blackburn designed its own tower block type and built three at Paisley, in 1958-59. Some firms, such as James Laidlaw, successfully made the transition to multi-storey building: following a huge initial Glasgow contract at Pollokshaws II awarded by Cross in 1961, Laidlaw became the preferred partner for Concrete Ltd's 'Bison' system in contracts around Glasgow. Other firms, such as A A Stuart and Hugh Leggat, had greater difficulty in satisfying Cross of their reliability. (24) The key was to establish a reliable design team and, where necessary, structural subcontractor. John Lawrence, tied to Sam Bunton as designer, met with mixed fortunes at the Blairdardie South tower-block project of 1960, with incessant demarcation disputes between Bunton and the city architect's staff. The same applied to the Glasgow DLO: by 1962 it had built 63% of the city's postwar housing, but the turn to high flats and system building cut its share of the programme from 84% in 1962 to 39% in 1967. Like all DLOs, the Glasgow force, despite its vast size, behaved like a small local builder, looking for continuity above all else. It attempted, with varying degrees of success, to establish a niche for itself in multi-storey building by providing a management-contracting and finishing trades service - a policy which went disastrously wrong, as we will see later, at the highly experimental Red Road project of 1962-69. Its most successful multi-storey venture was a much more modest eight-storey block, the 'Type 84', commissioned in

B4.7. Work in progress at the Pollokshaws Unit 2 site in 1963; the first 16-storey Bison block is visible in the background. (Boswell, Mitchell & Johnston)

B4.8. 19-storey point blocks designed by the Aberdeen city architect and built by Alexander Hall & Son Ltd at the city's Tillydrone-Hayton development in 1965-67. (RCAHMS)

1965 to provide bricklaying work and built all over the city. (25) In Edinburgh, likewise, some firms experienced problems in adjusting to multi-storey building. For example, Miller was awarded a large contract for tower blocks by the SSHA in 1963 at Whiteinch-Broomhill in Glasgow, but the contract was mismanaged (in the judgement of the SSHA), and overran schedule by a year. (26) And William Arnott McLeod had significant problems of overspending and time overruns in the building of Martello Court (1962-64), a 23-storey block in Edinburgh's Muirhouse, intended as a flagship of the local industry.

It was in Aberdeen, with its municipal efficiency ethos, that the regional industry made the most successful transition to the new patterns. Not coincidentally, the Corporation set its face firmly against prefabricated system-building for most of the 1960s, although the major Seaton project (1969-74) was built largely by Bison. Alexander Hall established a dominance in the field from the start, building the city's first high block at Ashgrove VIII (1959-61) and going on to build 41% of all its multi-storey dwellings. The north-east saw probably the most successful example in Scotland of a syndicate-style cartel, in the form of the Aberdeen Construction Group, formed in 1967; this merged Halls with the dominant regional civil-engineering contractor, William Tawse, as well as with precast manufacturer John Fyfe. (27) The Fyfe firm represented the north-east's response to the final collapse of the granite trade. Originally one of the main quarrying firms, they had diversified after 1945 into concrete-related products, and in 1957 commenced production of Fyfestone - a name borrowed from Peter Fyfe's earlier and unrelated experiments in Glasgow, but now denoting a kind of natural granite-faced blockwork in a range of different colours. By the early 1960s, Fyfestone had become the favourite ornamental facing material of public housing in the north-east, replacing the old grey homogeneity by what one local architect described as 'the aesthetic of a box of liquorice allsorts'. (28)

249

Polarised against the local industry was the constant threat, or perceived threat, of the outsiders - of predators from England. But, especially in view of the consolidation of the Scottish building regulation system as recently as 1963, it was not a straightforward matter for an English company to simply begin operations in this country. (29) Suppliers would not take a firm seriously unless it had opened an office, as the major London contractor Tersons discovered, when it took on a Clydebank multi-storey project in 1967, only to run into serious delays owing to non-delivery of cladding by a local supplier. Responding to an approach by a Birmingham firm in 1963, Glasgow's city architect, Archibald Jury, explained that 'there is a shortage of first-class experienced and able contractors in this area ... Success of a contractor in England or elsewhere outside Scotland does not necessarily ensure success of this order in Glasgow'. (30) And even some of the largest firms, such as Laings, came and went away again.

The three most successful firms of the 1960s boom era in Scotland - Wimpey, Crudens and Concrete Ltd (Bison) - all steered a middle way between the two extremes of the insiders and the outsiders. George Wimpey, founded in London in 1880, had expanded in three successive stages dominated by speculative housebuilding (1930s), war contracting (1940s) and property development (1960s); by 1970, with 9,000 staff it was by far the largest building firm in the UK, with a turnover of £225 million, more than twice that of its nearest rival. For Wimpey, public authority housing formed a secure backdrop to these more spectacular activities; although in 1960s Scotland there was relatively little speculative housing, property development provided a continuing entrepreneurial edge to the firm's work.

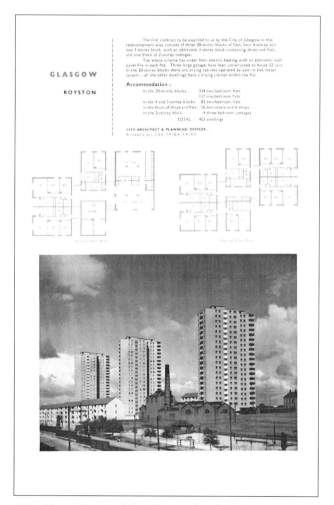

B4.10. *Type-plan of Wimpey's mid-1960s twin-tower '1001' block for local authority rental flats, as illustrated in the 1965 company brochure* Wimpey Rationalized Planning. *(RCAHMS)*

Under Eric Collins, the aim was to avoid rash or revolutionary changes, but to harness design innovativeness to the firm's prime selling points, reliability and punctuality. It exploited these to carve out a special niche with smaller authorities, who were often exasperated by the problems of co-ordinating separate-trades contracts. At the same time, it could win large contracts with cities like Glasgow, which hailed it as 'in a class of its own'. (31) In the interviews with company architect Tom Smyth and other colleagues (see appendices), we can trace the growth of the company's Scottish multi-storey market, from its prototype eight-storey block of 1954 in Kirkcaldy to its first breakthrough into the Glasgow market, through the rapidly constructed Royston A project of 1959.

In its internal organisation, the firm's size and complex structure imposed increasing overheads costs, which rose from 4% in 1944 to 5.5% in 1969, but allowed for extensive central support facilities. Wimpey's Scottish subsidiary made use of those supports, while maintaining an increasing operational autonomy; from around 1960, it was divided into east and west coast divisions. Type-plans for high flats were supplied by the headquarters in London, but were prepared by a special section familiar with the Scottish building regulations. Interestingly, whereas most English local authorities insisted on the use of one-off designs, including brick cladding, Scottish local authorities were more ready to use the standard Scottish variants of the type-plans. Wimpey's aim of bedding into the Scottish environment was furthered by its labour and subcontracting policy. Its no-fines system, in its most developed form, required a skilled pouring squad of no more than half a dozen men, comprising a mixer

B4.9. *Glasgow Corporation's first Wimpey package-deal multi-storey project, at Royston A, as illustrated in a 1961 company brochure. (George Wimpey Ltd)*

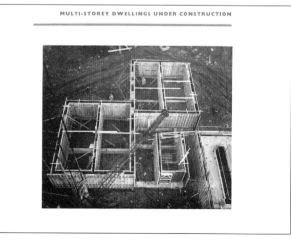

B4.11. *No-fines concrete casting in progress on '1001' block, from* Wimpey Rationalized Planning. *(RCAHMS)*

driver, shuttering joiners and gangers. All other building staff could be semi-skilled, and either drawn from the local workforce or supplied by Wimpey, whichever the local authority preferred. Subcontracts for finishing trades, and even for technical aspects of design, could also be offered to local firms. (32)

Crudens was a firm which, starting from a much lighter organisational base than Wimpey, emphasised mobility and agility to a far greater extent. In the late 1950s, Harry Cruden became aware that the market for his low-rise franchise operation was drying up, and that much larger building projects were looming over the horizon. With typical boldness, he decided on an almost complete organisational about-turn. From a licenceholder and supplier of lightweight frames for housing, the firm was to become an all-round public contractor that could build high blocks and other major projects itself, and embark on property development. Its skill in building up land-banks would also, on occasion, be useful in negotiating public housing contracts. In 1957, Cruden completely restructured the firm, increasing the share capital from £1,000 to £60,000, and brought in a new generation of management, headed by a 25 year old quantity surveyor, M R A Matthews; the latter became managing director, and Cruden became group chairman. (33)

A young chief architect, George Bowie, was engaged in 1960, and set to work immediately on a range of public sector housing types, including tower blocks. Eventually, in the late 1960s, his office would include several hundred architects, engineers and quantity surveyors, but at first, while the firm built up its architectural and engineering staff, the structural frames for tower

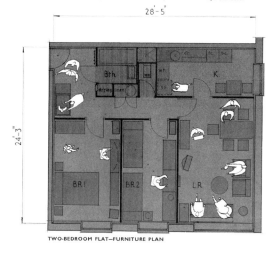

THE INSIDE

The internal areas of each of the flats are in accordance with the Manual prepared by the Ministry of Housing and Local Government entitled 'Flats and Houses' but at the same time the dwellings have been designed to allow extension to conform with the recommendations of the Parker Morris Committee contained in 'Homes for today and tomorrow' for those Authorities prepared to meet the extra cost.

In particular, as will be seen from the plan below, careful consideration has been given to the functional use of the space provided.

The basic specification includes electrical underfloor heating, but as an optional extra a gas heater can be placed in the corner of the living room with a balanced flue through the external wall and heating provided by hot air ducts.

The bathroom and W.C. are mechanically ventilated, the same system dealing with vapour from the electric clothes drying cupboard.

The basic specification includes a sink unit, dresser, brooms and food store for the kitchen.

Outside the flat a refuse chute is available from the ventilated lobby and the meters are grouped on the lift lobby.

It will be noted that the lifts discharge on to a landing which is free of the draughts associated with the permanent ventilation required for the Escape Staircase.

TWO-BEDROOM FLAT—FURNITURE PLAN

B4.12. Standard three-apartment flat layout and elevation details, from Wimpey Rationalized Planning. The manuals mentioned in the first paragraph were applicable to England and Wales, but the flats built in Scotland were generally similar. (RCAHMS)

B4.14. Casting of the concrete columns to support one of the massive 17-storey Crudens slab blocks at Ardler, Dundee, in 1965; the blocks were built of in-situ concrete and each contained 298 flats. (D C Thomson)

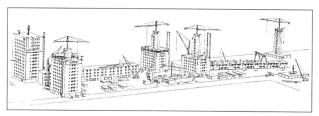

B4.15. Diagram of construction of the 'Skarne' system (licensed subsequently by Crudens) on an early 1960s Swedish site, showing the use of an in-situ core with tower crane as a base for panel assembly.

B4.13. 1964 view of Crudens tower blocks and lower flats under construction in Dundee Corporation's Menzieshill council housing scheme, Dundee. The picture was taken from the roof of the 15-storey Gowrie Court. (D C Thomson)

B4.16. 1998 view of the prototype Skarne tower blocks (1962) at the Näsbydal housing site, north of Stockholm; the blocks were arranged in a ring, and were linked by a small works railway during building. (M Glendinning)

blocks were subcontracted to Truscon. The first really large non-housing contracts, such as the Arts Tower designed for Edinburgh University by Robert Matthew (1960-63), were built at this time. From 1962, the firm began negotiating with foreign firms to obtain a licence for a prefabricated housing system, and eventually signed up with the Swedish Skarne system. Exploiting the potential mobility of precasting-based work, Crudens began building Skarne factories and opening branch offices elsewhere in Scotland and in England, seizing opportunities as they arose; for example, the sudden output demands that followed the formation of new and more powerful London boroughs in 1965 led to two massive contracts for Lewisham Borough Council (Evelyn Estate and Milton Court Road, from 1967), while the vast contracts from Dundee Corporation were dealt with by building a Skarne factory in 1966, with a planned output of 750 dwellings per annum. (34) As we will see later, Crudens's hectic expansion, by comparison with the more sedate progress of Wimpey, was to leave the firm in corresponding difficulties around 1970, when the systems boom turned to bust.

The third of the 'big three' mass housing contractors of the 1960s in Scotland, Concrete Ltd, represented in some important ways a high-rise equivalent to the earlier Cruden franchise and frame-manufacture operation. Concrete was basically a manufacturer of precast concrete components, marketed under the brand name 'Bison', which had extended its operations in either direction - into design on the one side, and building on the other - in order to offer a package-deal service. The firm was a conglomerate of different regional and national groups, headquartered in London; the Scottish subsidiary, Concrete (Scotland), was based in Falkirk. It had built its first multi-storey blocks in Barking, east of London, in 1956, but only in 1959 did its managing director, Kenneth Wood, decide to commission the firm's own system of large-panel construction, 'Bison Wall-Frame'. We will deal with the structural aspects of this system in greater detail below; what is important here is the way it was marketed and organised. The core of the firm's package deals was the design of the block-types and the building of the prefabricated structure: outside architects were normally needed for the layout, and local contractors for the finishing trades (although it often used its own architect for many English jobs, and sometimes acted as a main contractor for Scottish jobs, on occasion even competing against itself as main contractor and subcontractor!) (35)

Bison's first major Scottish breakthrough came just before the Wall-Frame system had been finalised, in its Pollokshaws contract of 1961, in partnership with Laidlaw as general contractor. The slab blocks used here were designed by architects Boswell, Mitchell and Johnston with engineers T Harley Haddow & Partners, and the Bison construction was adapted to them. (36) Once its system was fully in play, however, the firm tended to promote it not as a formula for grand-slam mass contracts, but as one specially suited to local interests and small contracts. Virtually any small builder could get a Bison contract, and almost unlimited plan variations could be made to the client's specification. Next to the West Midlands in England, where it was used for historically specific contractual reasons, Scotland was the place where Bison was most popular with local authorities. Its appeal was very like that of Wimpey - as a modern replacement for the separate-trades system, retaining much of the latter's local flexibility, but at a vastly increased level of productivity.

We can end our discussion of the contractors who built the 1960s high-rise boom, by glancing at a few figures which remind us of the main reason why Wimpey, Crudens and Bison were so popular: because of their reliability and efficiency. In 1965 and 1966,

B4.17. Official brochure of 1966 about the Anderston Cross housing scheme in Glasgow, a research and development project built by the SSHA and Glasgow Corporation to test whether high-density urban redevelopments could be achieved without tower blocks. For this project, the SSHA DLO acted as main contractor, while Concrete Scotland acted as structural subcontractor, using the Bison Wall-Frame system. (Scottish Special Housing Association)

Glasgow Corporation prepared some statistics on the cost and speed of the multi-storey contracts undertaken in the city since 1962. The projects were of roughly similar size and height, all above 16 storeys, but the differences in building performance between package deals and conventionally contracted and designed projects were striking. Whereas the cost of Wimpey projects ranged from £4.59 to £4.95 per square foot, that of Crudens projects from £4.61 to £5.02 and that of Bison from £4.87 to £5.04, those built by local Clydeside firms ranged from £5.07 to £6.25. And the same applied to construction times: between 14 and 18 months for Wimpey, 30 months for Crudens, and 19 to 34 months for Bison, but between 27 and 43 months for local firms; the position was even worse on the earlier Hutchesontown-Gorbals Areas B (Matthew) and C (Spence) projects, also conventionally tendered and contracted, which took 48 and 54 months respectively to complete, adding around 10% to the final cost through loss of rental and subsidy income. (37)

System built
the construction of 1960 housing

To round off our discussion of the production aspects of the systems boom, we need to glance at the new construction methods in their own right. In the ebb and flow of constructional innovation during the 20th century, this was the highest tide of all, in its combination of prefabrication and multi-storey building, although it should be remembered that the overlap was far from complete: 21% of high flats in Scotland were over 20 storeys tall, and 29% were in prefabricated construction. The Modern Movement conception of a building as a scientifically balanced, unified structure, in contrast to the pre-Modern idea of an assembly of massive elements, reached its greatest elaboration at this time: with very large and tall buildings, exact calculation of the stresses and strains, and the interaction of the parts, became obviously essential.

At first, the frame and infill principle continued its dominance, along with variants of calculated load-bearing wall construction: unreinforced no-fines concrete was a variant of the latter, as was the crosswall construction with blockwork used in Bunton's experimental tenements of the 1950s. For framed construction,

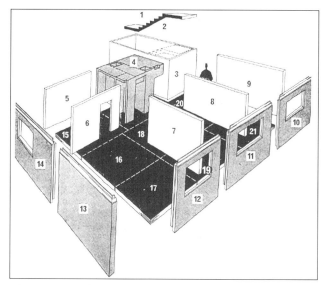

B4.18. Diagram of the 21 precast concrete parts required to assemble a two-bedroom Bison Wall-Frame multi-storey flat, as published in R Diamant, Industrialised Building, 1964. (Concrete Ltd)

steel was generally too expensive, and so reinforced concrete was the rule; the facing walls could be of brickwork or some other light cladding, while floors and inside walls were of thicker in-situ concrete. All of Crudens's early multi-storey projects fall into this category, while Wimpey's tower blocks combined their poured concrete walls with inserted reinforced-concrete columns, and other elements of a frame. By the early 1960s, the demand among architects and engineers was growing for an even higher degree of integration of the structure: these combinations of frames and load-bearing elements were beginning to seem somewhat untidy and insufficiently scientific. The solution was a cellular structure, in which the walls and floors themselves formed a strong and interlocking 'frame'. This pattern was normally called 'box-frame' construction, but Bison's brand name, 'Wall-Frame', was equally descriptive. Multi-storey box-frame construction seemed ideally suited to the prefabrication of large, storey-high concrete panels - the solution that had been found so wasteful and expensive by the Glasgow DLO at two storeys - and the prefabrication of service elements, as previously in the prefabs. What was not revived, in contrast to the contemporary USSR, was the prefabrication of entire units or flats, as had happened with AIROH. Precast box-frame construction, with its demand for precision, seemed tailor-made to the climate of scientific excitement in mid-1960s society: the most important element of the building seemed to be the joint, and much effort was devoted to finding the most precise and scientifically optimal solution, with greater prestige attaching to dry, rather than wet, or in-situ, joints.

But these highly integral structural concepts, inevitably, threw up their own drawbacks, above all their lack of flexibility: a local authority could not simply ask for an extra doorway half-way along a structural wall! In that respect, the most 'primitive' method on offer, no-fines, was in some ways the most client-friendly. Not surprisingly, therefore, Wimpey stuck doggedly to it, despite the unfashionableness of its messy wet construction, which was disliked even by some of its own designers; one regional architect recalls that he argued to colleagues that 'pouring concrete is not a "system" - it's just pouring concrete'. (38) The firm tried to compensate for this old-fashioned image by rationalising the planning of tower blocks around a central service core and introducing thin-plate floors and a sophisticated dry-lining system. The resulting type was marketed as the '1001 System', and countless housing committees were flown down to see the

prototype block at Manston Allotments, Ramsgate (completed in 1964).

In the sudden scramble for prefabricated systems, one of the most powerful driving forces was a realisation of the huge strides made during the 1950s by the countries that had chosen to develop (rather than, as in Scotland, abandon) system building in large concrete panels, namely, France and Scandinavia. The USSR, which had gone far further towards extreme mass solutions, was ruled out as an inspiration for ideological and organisational reasons. From around 1962, the race was on in earnest to 'sign up' a continental system on a licence basis, or to develop one's own variant. With the exception of Crudens, no Scottish firm had the resources to enter this field, but because of the effect of the separate Scottish and English building regulations, many of the English-based systems, such as Taylor Woodrow-Anglian's Larsen-Nielsen, were not used at all, or built only as isolated examples. (39)

In looking to the Continent, the inspiration of France was one of vast scale, with ZUP projects of up to 10,000 flats built using the full apparatus of tracked cranes and site factories. (40) The flats were usually medium-rise slab blocks rather than towers, and emphasised a kind of rough hardness rather than refinement of detail; cladding often used mosaic panels. The first French heavy-prefabrication system to begin marketing in Scotland was Camus, in 1959-60, but its bulk-order production method, requiring vast advance commitment, was frowned on by the DHS, who stopped Buteux from committing the SSHA to build a Camus factory. It commented that a government-financed body should not 'set up a private firm in a profitable line of business in which they could eventually charge monopoly prices'. (41) Only later did Camus build a factory in Lanarkshire, which supplied the needs of the Lanarkshire burghs consortium.

The example of Scandinavia, on the other hand, seemed better attuned to contemporary architectural opinion, emphasising technical precision in combination with meticulous crafts standards of building and orderly building-site management. In postwar Denmark, the separate-trades system, far from being abolished, was accentuated and modernised, but the resulting combines of specialist firms and professionals were, in functional terms, not unlike the teams of subcontractors and main contractors in Scotland and England. There was a tremendous effort to establish standard dimensions for all new housing, as a common framework for all these agencies, and from 1950 there were increasing efforts to extend this into concrete prefabrication.

B4.19. Perspective of the prototype Bison Wall-Frame multi-storey scheme at Hurcott Road, Kidderminster, England (built from 1963 by Bryant), as published in R Diamant, Industrialised Building, 1964. Local authority representatives from numerous towns, including many in Scotland, were taken to see these pioneering blocks. (Concrete Ltd)

(42) Bison Wall-Frame, although marketed as a 'British system', was fundamentally based on these Scandinavian concepts of precision and flexibility. It was designed in 1959-60 in collaboration with a prominent Danish engineer, P E Malmstrøm, as a development of the Larsen-Nielsen system, and a prototype group was completed at Kidderminster, in central England, in 1963. (43) In its basic form, the system comprised precast walls and floors, with each flat assembled out of an average of 21.5 units. The staircase and the lift housing were also precast, as was the seven-ton bathroom unit. Windows and ducting were cast into the walls, for which a very high U-value (insulation) of 0.15 was claimed. The joints between floors and walls were basically in-situ but with some dry insulating elements. Five Bison Wall-Frame casting factories were built, including one in Scotland at the Falkirk works; erection was carried out by teams of eight to ten men. The firm claimed that the system was economic for orders of as few as 24 dwellings. The first Wall-Frame contract in Scotland was Cumbernauld New Town Corporation's serial order of 1964 for point blocks. After severe problems with water penetration, it was realised that the English Wall-Frame designs were not suitable as they stood for Clydeside conditions, and they were redesigned with greatly improved jointing and insulation. The large Wall-Frame group built at Seaton in Aberdeen after 1969, on an exceptionally exposed sea-front site, had to have still further protection to the joints.

If teething problems like these could be experienced in adapting an 'English' system, the simple translation of continental systems to Scotland was an even less plausible proposition. That fact was demonstrated in the experience of Crudens with its adopted Swedish system, the Ohlsson-Skarne. As built in Sweden, for instance at the Näsbydal project north of Stockholm (1961-64), a Skarne tower block comprised a central, full-height core supporting a tower crane, around which precast walls and floors were built; the outer wall consisted of timber-framed cladding. (44) In the system as adapted by Crudens, and built from 1964 in a prototype three-storey block at Greendykes Road in Edinburgh, these distinctive features had vanished, leaving 'Skarne' as merely a particular design of precast slabs - or perhaps even just a marketing brand-name. (45) As George Bowie explained, '"systems" was and is a marketing vehicle. People would come and say, "We want your system", but they didn't get it! Lots of times when we were busy we got our precast elsewhere than in the Skarne factory. As the thing developed, I'd find us precasting ground-floor slabs in four-storey blocks, say at Whitfield in Dundee, and I'd say "That's rubbish!" Strictly

B4.21. 1988 aerial view of Red Road development. (RCAHMS A56760)

speaking, that was what the "system" involved, and so the engineers would automatically start doing it. But it didn't make economic sense to do it! ... Then very soon we said, "Skarne - so what! We won't precast the floors any more, just the walls!" It became delightfully vague, even in the terms of the contracts, where "Skarne" wasn't mentioned! After all, what does it really amount to - just casting large lumps of concrete!' (46)

The disparity between white-hot technological rhetoric and makeshift reality was seen at its clearest in a home-grown attempt at a package-deal 'system' by the regional building interests in the west: the Multi-Storey Consortium (MSC), a group of steel fabricators and contractors, in association of course with Sam Bunton as consultant architect. This syndicate operated under the same banner as Weir in the 1920s - that of bringing in outside resources to augment the building industry - but its motive was rather different. Rather than trying to break monopolies, this syndicate set out to extend the Glasgow DLO principle of building protectionism to a monumental level. Bunton's steel-framed towers and slabs, with metal 'Holorib' decking and concrete or asbestos cladding, were like vast nesting-boxes for Clydeside's industrial and labour interest groups: almost everywhere, for example, were lining panels and components made by Lawrence. (47) The most straightforward of these projects was a single 18-storey slab built at Parkhead Street, Motherwell, in 1963-64; the steelwork was divided between Flemings and Redpath Dorman Long, and Crudens, as management contractor, ensured that it was finished ahead of schedule. Another block was built by Lawrence in Paisley in 1965-67. But it was when the Glasgow DLO got its hands on the programme, and gave Bunton his head in a gigantic project of over 1,300 flats in 26-31 storey blocks at Red Road in Glasgow (built from 1963), that the steel-building syndicate came to grief. A previous proposal for modest crosswall concrete blocks based on Blairdardie South had been unceremoniously jettisoned. On this far larger and more experimental project, the DLO's lack of effective management contracting experience was exposed; Cross was excluded from any involvement with it. The contract slid into a chaotic situation of repeated structural redesign and uncontrolled overspending, and it was not completed until 1969. (48)

Design, Fabrication, and Erection of major portion of **Steelwork** by **Flemings**

B4.20. Glasgow Corporation direct labour department's steel-framed Red Road project under construction in 1966. (Glasgow Herald)

By the late 1960s, the wartime decline in productivity in the building industry had at last been reversed. But what was not clear was whether the spectacular multi-storey 'systems' had played a major role in this, or whether more modest improvements had been more important. Brick supply, for example, was substantially reorganised during the 1960s. Common bricks had been previously made in a somewhat ad hoc way with the National Coal Board the largest manufacturer; but in 1969 a new combine, the Scottish Brick Company, was formed.

Timber-framed housing, pushed out of the limelight by the heavy prefabrication systems, was making quiet but significant progress. The chief overseas inspiration was now no longer Sweden, but the vast timber housebuilding industry of North America, which was producing 1.5 million units annually; it showed how a wide range of external claddings could be built around a platform-frame internal structure. Although most US housebuilding was carried out in situ by small, local firms, prefabricated manufacturers accounted for some 22% of total output by 1964: the largest, National Homes, made over 20,000 timber-framed houses each year in seven different factories, the components being delivered to the sites by truck and assembled by local builders or owners. (49) Within these islands, the most enthusiastic initial pursuit of research into timber-framing took place in England, as a result of the widespread distrust of flats there. From 1960, research architects in the English government housing ministry had made energetic efforts to encourage timber-based 'systems' suitable for two-storey cottages. In 1961-62, a system of composite timber and steel frame construction and timber cladding for cottages, the '5M', was devised, and over 4,000 units were built by 1966; commercial systems such as Medway also made rapid progress. (50) By the early 1970s, many tens of thousands of timber houses were being built each year throughout Scotland and England. (51) Increasingly, timber-building began to appeal to speculative builders; for example, by 1976, Thain was using timber framing for much of its production. And a subtle trend towards concentration in Scotland began: in a 1980 trade list of UK timber house builders, nearly 30% were Scottish. Not long after, in a final ironical twist, timber framing would fall dramatically from fashion in England, while continuing to flourish in Scotland.

Speculative building in the 1960s

Throughout the 1960s, the private sector seemed becalmed. Its output in 1970 was only 6% higher than in 1962, and its perecentage contribution to total Scottish housing production had actually fallen, to only 19%. This situation seemed increasingly out of step with other west European countries. In some of them, after all - for instance, Denmark and West Germany - 'state housing' hardly even existed. And the contribution by the private sector was far higher everywhere: in 1964, for example, 66% in France, 86% in Switzerland, and 99.7% in Belgium. In some communist countries, the corresponding figure was also greater: in Poland, 29%, Hungary, 60%, Czechoslovakia, 74%. Even in the USSR, it was as much as 16%. (52)

What was the reason for this continuing low level of private output in Scotland? Two reports prepared for the Scottish Housing Advisory Committee in 1970 and 1972 analysed, respectively, the supply and demand sides of the industry. The 1970 report, by Norman Sidwell, argued that extra cost was not a decisive factor; the materials for a three-bedroom house actually cost 5% less in the Central Belt than in north-east England, and a Wimpey house-type selling for £6,765 in Greater London and £4,095 in

Yorkshire would cost £5,000 in Edinburgh or Clydeside. (53) What was more important was the continuing starvation of sites through local authority zoning, which continued to drive private housing away from the cities and accentuate social polarisation; only 4% of the 44,000 new houses built in Glasgow in the 1960s were private. The scarcity of land fuelled the anti-competitive tendencies within the market. In 1967/68, three-quarters of all Scottish speculative houses were built by only ten firms, and one firm alone accounted for 25%. That firm was Wimpey, which had carved out for itself a comfortable niche in this market, just as in public housing. These monopolistic tendencies were highlighted by the immediate comparison with England. There, Wimpey built only 5% of speculative output. A higher level of concentration was perhaps inevitable in a much smaller market, but on average, Scottish private housebuilders were twice as large as English ones and their sites were twice as big. As a result, there were far lower levels of owner occupation in each social grouping: 19% among foremen and supervisors in 1966 (47% in England), and 18% among skilled manual workers (41% in England). (54)

In any comparison with European countries, Scotland and England seemed to have much in common, in their polarisation between private owner occupation and state rental housing, and in their avoidance of the many intermediate solutions of social ownership and private rental. In comparison with the United States, on the other hand, the weakness and monopolistic character of the Scottish private housing industry seemed to stand out even more. Supported by massive mortgage guarantee and low-income ownership subsidies from the federal government, the highly decentralised, locally based American building industry was able to produce vast numbers of dwellings highly competitively. In 1966, the average new house in the USA was a single-storey, detached, five-roomed home of 1,100 square feet; at that date, only 16% of the average US income was devoted to mortgage repayment, housing tax and insurance, whereas the corresponding figure in Scotland, excluding insurance, was no less than 25%. And the lowest 20% of the market in the USA was catered for in an even more economical way, through demountable 'mobile homes'. (55)

To remedy this situation, the Labour government began to pressurise local authorities to unlock the land supply. In a key decision of 1965, Scottish housing minister Dickson Mabon refused a request by Edinburgh housing chairman Pat Rogan to develop a prime Edinburgh suburban site at Alnwickhill with council tower blocks, and encouraged the Corporation's Planning Committee to reallocate it to private builders. (56) As a consolation prize, the Housing Committee was given the less visually sensitive Wester Hailes site to develop instead. In a 1969 summary of state housing policy, the SDD observed, concerning this issue, that 'it is to be hoped that the message has been got across'. (57) The government also tried to stimulate demand, introducing in 1968 the option mortgage, designed to give lower-income owner occupiers the same tax benefits as the middle classes. The 1972 SHAC report argued that, although this method was still nearly £300 per annum more expensive than local authority renting, there was likely to be a big rise in demand for private houses by 1976. (58)

Architecturally, the 1960s and early 1970s saw a further convergence between the public and private sectors in the size and amenities of the 'average' new house. The latter was in itself, of course, a rather misleading term, as most new public sector houses in the 1960s were in fact flats, including those in tower blocks and other large housing complexes, requiring central heating, collective refuse disposal, fitted kitchen and other amenities as a matter of course. Among the semi-detached and detached two-storey homes that predominated in the private sector, a better comparison was with the low-rise housing which formed a minority of public authority output. There the difference was not so much in space standards as in architectural planning. The public housing was influenced by the highly complex open and split-level house-planning and 'low rise high density' layouts pioneered by Cumbernauld New Town Development Corporation and some private architects, whereas most private housing generally adhered to traditional layouts of small groups of homes and gardens along streets, and its internal planning made more limited concessions to open-planning ideas, remaining faithful to more segregated and smaller rooms. Construction, too, did not depart substantially at this stage from conventional cavity brickwork. The timber-frame revolution was yet to take hold in the 1960s, and surveys showed that Scottish speculative builders actually used a higher proportion of bricks (as opposed to blockwork) than their English counterparts. (59) There were some distinguishing marks: the provision of an integral garage was more and more common in the private sector, often in medium-sized houses and almost invariably in larger dwellings such as the 'executive houses' advertised in 1965 on the Balerno development of Edinburgh builder Thain, with their four bedrooms, two bathrooms, three public rooms, electric central heating, utility room and double garage.

The end of the drive

In the SDD's 1969 report on housing policy, triumphant satisfaction at the huge housing output was mixed with dire warnings of the need to maintain unbroken production. Nothing seemed to have changed since the Westwood Report in 1944; even the target was exactly the same: 'Half a million houses will need to be replaced in the near future'. The prospect was one of warlike campaigns, crusades and rationing crises continuing into eternity. (60) The private building industry seemed inextricably tied to the cause of the planned social economy. One Wimpey official recalled that 'Dr Mabon was manna from heaven for the contractors ... the building industry always reckoned, in those decades, that the Labour Party was the better party to be in power, because of its commitment to council housing'. But in Scotland, just as in France, the *trente glorieuses* were drawing to a close - an end that would be marked not quietly but by a storm of fireworks. And the collapse of the grand postwar reconstruction drive would bring down, along with it, the entire Ballantyne tradition of politicised and nationalised social housing.

This process was neither a smooth nor an even one, but a dramatic roller-coaster. The first harbinger of doom was the economic crisis of 1967-68, and the associated decline in the viability and prestige of multi-storey and system building. At Crudens's huge Killingworth development in north-eastern England, for example, Bowie recalled that 'the economics of the ... project were that we'd get the second phase - but we didn't! When the urban district council pulled out of the contract, I said, "Do you know how much money has been spent on designing the second phase?" They said, "Oh, don't worry!" I said, "What the hell do you think two dozen engineers have been doing for six months!"' (61) The abandonment of mass multi-storey building was under way across western Europe. In France, for example, ZUPs were phased out after 1972. From its 1970 maximum of nearly 35,000, Scottish public sector output would rapidly decline, to 16,000 in 1974 and 10,000 in 1978. The impact of this initial crisis was softened by Mabon's policy of redirecting public housing output

away from the dense urban areas towards the new towns and rural areas, where tower blocks and heavy systems were not required. In 1966, for example, at his instigation, Aberdeen County Council embarked on a five-year programme of over 3,500 houses, many in low-rise systems such as Dorran, Kincorth (Halls) or the Wimpey '6M'. (62) By 1977 the new towns were accounting for over one third of public housing output. The only exception to the end of multi-storey building was in Aberdeen, where the council embarked on a highly popular programme of sheltered-housing tower blocks for the elderly in the late 1970s; the last one to be built, an 11-storey Wimpey block at Jasmine Terrace, was completed in 1985.

The next wave of building-industry troubles, in the early 1970s, was more pervasive and debilitating. It formed part of the final

B4.22. Killingworth Township Contract B19 development, near Newcastle, north-east England, built by Crudens in Skarne industrialised construction in 1967-69; 1987 view prior to demolition. An example of the mobility of the boldest contractors at the height of the 1960s boom, and also of the problems of over-commitment implicit in public-sector industrialised building; a second phase, on which the economics of the project depended for Crudens, was cancelled by the local authority. (M Glendinning)

crisis of the planned mixed economy, exacerbated internationally by the impact of the 1973 OPEC oil crisis. Inflation accelerated, exceeding 20% in both 1975 and 1979, and the recovery in labour productivity was halted; building costs doubled between 1973 and 1978. A wage freeze in 1972 led to confusing anomalies and the migration of workers from one firm to another. Labour and materials shortages were felt unevenly across Britain, and bidding wars began, with contractors in overheated London bussing workers from Scotland. (63) Industrial unrest worsened across the economy, with a national building strike in 1972. The impact on private and public building organisations was one of constant chaos and improvisation. The SSHA's DLO, for example, reported in March 1974 that costs had been driven up 17% by inflation over the previous year, that there had been heavy losses on fixed price contracts, and that overall expenditure had risen by 23%; a severe shortage of men and materials was aggravated by the oil crisis, the miners' strike and the three-day week. (64) Within the building industry as elsewhere, these years would prove the swansong of the trade unions' power. Steep falls in membership since their heyday in the 1940s had been followed by amalgamations, including the formation of the Union of Construction and Allied Trades Technicians (UCATT) in 1968.

The only exception to this spreading depression was in the north-east and in Shetland, where the mid-1970s oil boom was stimulating substantial economic growth, and a demand for large-scale housebuilding by county councils and the SSHA. In a last phase of public sector planning activity, the strategy for this building campaign was laid down by bodies such as the North-East of Scotland Joint Planning Authority, which predicted in

B4.23. *Sound development, Phase 1 (Sandveien), Lerwick, Shetland, a low-rise high-density project built by the town council in 1969-73 to the designs of R & B Moira. As was usual in Lerwick even at this late date, separate-trades contracting was used for the scheme; the concrete blockwork and other mason work was carried out by local builder W Fraser. (M Glendinning)*

B4.24. *Norwegian timber houses at Brae, Shetland, built in 1973-74 by Zetland County Council, with Alexander Hall as main contractor and the SSHA as site servicing contractor. In contrast to the conservative contracting arrangements in Lerwick, this group formed part of a serial contract for essential oil-industry workers' houses on several landward sites. A contract of 100 conventionally built houses at Brae for the same purpose was carried out by James Miller in 1974-75 at a cost of £19,800 for each dwelling.*

1971 that oil development would create a shortage of 16,550 houses within 20 miles of Aberdeen - a prediction that would prove wildly excessive. (65) By now, the separate-trades system had disappeared even for rural housing, and had been replaced by a mixture of small local builders, and national firms for the large jobs. But the ruinous labour shortages now turned attention, yet again, to systems - in this case, for two-storey timber-framed houses. Under the leadership of a driving housing convener of the traditional kind, Sandy Rennie, Aberdeen County Council embarked on a further massive building drive in 1973-75, using

imported Norwegian and Swedish systems for nearly half the 2,770 houses under construction at one time. (66) Elsewhere in the north and north-east, the same applied. For example, Halls imported 600 timber kit houses from Norway to build in Ross-shire and Aberdeen, and the SSHA and Wimpey helped set up a Moray Firth housing consortium to build around Inverness.

Eventually, by the late 1970s, all factors began to converge around a final, irreversible decline in public sector building activity, including public housing. All over northern Europe, a general liberalisation of the housing market was under way, including a move to owner occupation and a scaling down of state-supported building programmes. In Scotland, the most important milestone in that process was the government's 1977 Green Paper on housing policy, which analysed the need for new public sector building, and pronounced that it 'appears very small indeed'; between 30,000 and 165,000 units would be needed in the decade to 1986. (67) In the event, what was actually built, at 94,000 units, split the difference. The Green Paper hailed the boom in rehabilitation of older houses, and argued that the owner-occupied housing stock, at 33%, should be boosted, chiefly by expanded private building output. Indeed, the latter rose from 8,220 in 1970 (19% of the total) to 11,529 in 1982 (70%). In 1979, a pioneering speculative housing development of low-rise brick cottages and flats was begun at Dalveen Street, Shettleston, in Glasgow's depressed east end, by Unit Construction. The advance guard of a tide of red brick in the following decades, this project formed part of the GEAR regeneration project (initiated in 1976), which envisaged owner occupation as high as 20%, and was intended to bring an end to the war between Glasgow and the new towns, by attracting young couples back from the latter to the city.

Conclusion

Less than ten years before the 1977 Green Paper, the Scottish Office had envisaged a state-sponsored housing drive of 45,000 new dwellings a year, stretching into the indefinite future, with houses torn down and replaced after a few decades of life. (68) By 1977, that vision of the 1960s was coming to seem as obsolete and historically remote as the dreadnought-building campaigns of the turn of the century.

Notes

1   A Power, *Hovels to High Rise*, 1993, 47, 127.
2   *The Builder*, 4 February 1966, 13 February 1970.
3   National Archives of Scotland (Scottish Record Office), file SRO DD6-2154, meeting of 3 July 1958; M Glendinning and S Muthesius, *Tower Block*, 1994, 201; Sir Harold Banwell, *The Placing and Management of Contracts for Building and Civil Engineering Works*, 1964.
4   N J Morgan, '£8 Cottages'.
5   Interview with R Nicoll, 1987.
6   C Carter and M Keating, *The Designation of Cumbernauld New Town*, 1986, 63.
7   Glendinning and Muthesius, *Tower Block*, 234. On Govan, interview with G Bowie, 1987.
8   1962 Glasgow Corporation Annual Housing Inspection, address by D Gibson, cited in Glendinning and Muthesius, *Tower Block*, 220.
9   Glendinning and Muthesius, *Tower Block*, 230.
10   Glendinning and Muthesius, *Tower Block*, 230, 246.
11   Interview with D Ross, 1987; Glendinning and Muthesius, *Tower Block*, 240.
12   Sir Harold Emmerson, *Survey of Problems before the Construction Industries*, 1962.
13   M Glendinning (ed.), *Rebuilding Scotland*, 88.
14   National Building Agency, *Continuity in Contracting for Housing Authorities*, 1969.

15   Glasgow City Archives, Lanark County Council Housing Committee Minutes, 9 November 1965; interview with H Brannan (former Lanarkshire Council Leader), 1987.

16   R Home, *Of Planting and Planning*, 1997, 170-4.

17   Glendinning and Muthesius, *Tower Block*, Chapters 24, 26, 27.

18   T Begg, *Fifty Special Years*, 1987, 204; Rodger and Al-Qaddo, 'The SSHA', 203.

19   For later criticism of separate-trades building, see also the *McEwan Younger Report*, 1964.

20   National Building Agency, *Continuity in Contracting*; E W Cooney, *Construction History*, 1993.

21   Interview with T Smyth, 1987.

22   Interview with P Lord (former senior manager, Wates Ltd), 1989.

23   Cement and Concrete Association, *Housing from the Factory*, 1962 (proceedings of conference, October 1962); *Architect and Building News*, 10 October 1962; *Architects' Journal*, 17 October 1962.

24   Glasgow City Archives, Town Clerk's files, letter of 21 July 1961, L Cross to Town Clerk.

25   Interview with J Kernohan (former Glasgow City Architect), 1987.

26   Interview with H Buteux, 1987.

27   Mackie, *Alexander Hall & Son*, 74.

28   Interview with Alex Mennie (of McCombie & Mennie, architects, Inverurie), 1984.

29   Building Standards (Scotland) Regulations, 1963.

30   Glasgow City Archives, multi-storey file, A G Jury letter to Town Clerk, 28 August 1963.

31   Interview with J Kernohan, 1987.

32   See, for example, Glasgow City Archives, Glasgow Corporation Housing Committee, Sub-committee on Sites and Buildings Minutes, 20 August 1965, Kirkton Avenue.

33   Interviews with H Corner (former architect, Edinburgh Corporation) and G Bowie, 1987; Morgan, 'Harry H Cruden', in Slaven and Checkland, *Dictionary*.

34   Glendinning and Muthesius, *Tower Block*, 243.

35   Port Glasgow Town Council Minutes, 14 October 1968. On systems in general, see K M Wood, 'The Bison Wall-Frame System', in *Housing from the Factory*, 87-94; R Diamant, *Industrialised Building*, 1964, 19.

36   N Johnston, 'The Corporation of Glasgow Comprehensive Development Area at Pollokshaws, Glasgow', in Cement and Concrete Association, *Housing from the Factory*, 95-102.

37   Glasgow City Archives, Town Clerk's files, *Comparative Costs of Multi-storey Flats*, reports by City Architect's Department, 13 September 1965, and City Chamberlain's Office, 18 January 1966.

38   Interview with T Tysler, 1987.

39   See Diamant, *Industrialised Building* 1 and 2, 1964 and 1965; *The Comprehensive Industrialised Building Systems Annual*, 1965. Cement and Concrete Association, *Housing from the Factory*; *Architect and Building News*, 10 October 1962; *Architects' Journal*, 17 October 1962.

40   Power, *Hovels to High Rise*, 49-51; Cement and Concrete Association, *Housing from the Factory*, articles by R Camus and R C Purdew.

41   National Archives of Scotland, file DD6-2201.

42   Power, *Hovels to High Rise*, 252-3, 262; Cement and Concrete Association, *Housing from the Factory*, 25-40.

43   K M Wood, 'The Bison Wall-Frame System', in Cement and Concrete Association, *Housing from the Factory*, 87-94; Diamant, *Industrialised Building*, 21.

44   Diamant, *Industrialised Building*, 67; *The Builder*, 28 June 1963.

45   *The Comprehensive Industrialised Building Systems Annual*, 1965.

46   Interview with G Bowie, 1987; Glendinning and Muthesius, *Tower Block*, 207.

47   Diamant, *Industrialised Building* 2, 36-7.

48   *The Builder*, 19 October 1962.

49   Ministry of Housing, *Housebuilding in the USA*, 1966, 7-12.

50   MHLG, *Designing a Low-rise Housing System*, Design Bulletin 18, 1970.

51   Timber Trade Federation of the UK, *Timber-Frame*, 1973.

52   United Nations, *Annual Bulletin of Housing and Building Statistics for Europe*, New York City, 1964 and 1966.

53   Scottish Housing Advisory Committee and Professor N Sidwell, *The Cost of Private Houses in Scotland*, 1970.

54   Scottish Housing Advisory Committee and Heriot-Watt University, *The Demand for Private Houses in Scotland*, 1972.

55   Scottish Housing Advisory Committee and Heriot-Watt University, *The Demand for Private Houses in Scotland*, 21, 26, 42, 45; Ministry of Housing, *Housebuilding in the USA*, 1966.

56   Interview with H Corner, 1987.

57   Scottish Development Department, *Housing in Scotland*, 5.

58   Scottish Housing Advisory Committee and Heriot-Watt University, *The Demand for Private Houses in Scotland*.

59   Scottish Development Department, *Housing in Scotland*, 5.

60   Glendinning and Muthesius, *Tower Block*, 1994, 145-7; M Glendinning

(ed.), *Rebuilding Scotland*, 1997, 115-24; Scottish Housing Advisory Committee and Professor N Sidwell, *The Cost of Private Houses in Scotland*.

61   Interview with G Bowie, 1987.

62   Grampian Archives, Aberdeenshire County Council Housing Committee Minutes, 28 January 1966.

63   W Mackie, *Alexander Hall & Son*. On the bidding wars, see interview with P Lord, 1989.

64   SSHA, *Annual Digest for the Year ending 31 March 1974*, 1974.

65   Grampian Archives, Aberdeenshire County Council Housing Committee Minutes, 28 May 1971.

66   Grampian Archives, Aberdeenshire County Council Housing Committee Minutes, 10 November 1972 and 4 November 1973.

67   Scottish Development Department, *Scottish Housing, a Consultative Document*, 1977, 19.

68   Scottish Development Department, *Housing in Scotland*.

REBIRTH OF THE MARKET

1975 to the Present Day - and Beyond

Kenneth Gibb

Introduction

Taking the last twenty-five years as a benchmark, this chapter draws out a number of themes, issues and challenges confronting the Scottish private housebuilding sector as the millennium approaches. The mid-1970s provide an apposite starting point for the chapter, as those years saw an international economic crisis affecting a new Labour government, and the beginning of the end of large-scale public spending and macroeconomic policy-making. This point of departure, symbolically at least, reflects a turning point between government support for public housing construction and a shift towards market demand and owner

B5.1. Demolition of troubled peripheral housing schemes began in the 1970s and 1980s: here Area C of Glasgow's Garthamlock development of 1952-56 (comprising three-storey tenements and type 'V' five-apartment terraced houses) is seen under demolition in 1981. (RCAHMS GW/3818)

B5.2. From the late 1980s, public sector demolitions were increasingly linked to subsequent mixed-tenure regeneration, in partnership with the private sector. In this episode of 1991, Edinburgh District Council undertook the regeneration of the Niddrie Marischal scheme in partnership with Wimpey Homes. This involved the 'blow-down' of two Bison point blocks, originally built in 1968-70 by Hart Bros. However, the towers failed to collapse as planned, so they eventually had to be pushed over by a giant battering crane. (RCAHMS)

B5.3. During the 1970s and 1980s, the decline in public housing output was at first reflected in a boom in tenement rehabilitation using improvement grants, both by individuals and by community-based housing associations. The pioneer was the Taransay Street project in Glasgow, carried through by the Central Govan Housing Association and the architects ASSIST in 1971-74. In this view, the Dundee builders Charles Gray are seen executing a more comprehensive follow-up improvement scheme in the area in 1989.

occupation as the main outlet for housebuilding. Of course, it took several years for these effects to be felt in Scotland, or to show the striking patterns in expenditure and construction that are now apparent in the 1990s. We traced the beginning of that process in the previous chapter, with its account of the breakdown of the system of public housing production and contracting-based building activity in the 1970s. In this chapter, we deal with the new, more wholeheartedly capitalistic system which emerged out of the ruins of its predecessor.

The years which followed the 1970s crystallised the divergent paths of housebuilding companies, between private developers who would purchase land and sell centrally designed homes, and the contractors who would construct the buildings. These differences were already apparent in the distinction between private speculative and public contracted housebuilding work, but through this period they also became the norm within the private sector, with the effective separation of development, design and marketing from the construction process. These issues, in combination with the growing private market and structural change in the process of housebuilding, in turn had a number of important implications for the industry's capacity to insulate itself from economic recession, and, in the longer term, to recycle its skills.

B5.4. The 1980s saw the first private-sector new-build interventions in areas previously dominated by public-sector building. The first postwar private housing project in the blighted east end of Glasgow was the Dalveen Street development, Shettleston: 134 brick terraced houses and three-storey flats, built in 1979-81. (RCAHMS B17737)

In this chapter, we will investigate these and related themes that emerge from a consideration of the past 25 years of Scottish private housebuilding. But we also look forward, and speculate on how the industry in its present position will face up to likely challenges in the future. The structure of the chapter is broadly as follows. The next section presents a summary statistical overview of private housebuilding in Scotland as it has evolved over the past two and a half decades. The following section discusses the underlying causes of these changes. The fourth part of the chapter isolates the major themes at work through the period; these include land release, centralised designs, business strategies, the advent of urban regeneration, social housing and related niche work, as well as the importance of economic cycles, the 'rationality' of the industry, and the relationship of the industry to housebuilding and housing policies enacted by governments. These themes are then extrapolated in the penultimate section to a consideration of the likely future of the private housebuilding sector as it faces a series of challenges in the present and likely future. The section also analyses the differences between the contemporary Scottish housebuilding sector and that of the rest of the UK. The chapter ends with a general conclusion.

A statistical profile

The overall level of private completions, even after accounting for cyclical changes, has grown appreciably over the period 1974-96, rising from levels of 10,000-14,000 in the earlier period to 17,000 or 18,000 in the last five years of the 1990s. However, this private sector growth in housebuilding has not been reflected in an overall growth of housebuilding in Scotland. Rather, total completions have fallen from levels comfortably above the 30,000 level in the mid-1970s to levels well below 20,000 in the early 1980s, and to levels typically of 19,000-21,000 in the recent period (apart from one appreciably stronger year - 1995). Thus this relative growth in private housebuilding has come about partly as a result of the decline in social housebuilding but also through higher levels of private demand. Table 1 illustrates this by demonstrating the rapid growth in the share of all housebuilding associated with private development - rising from less than 40% in the mid-1970s to more than 80% in the 1990s (although retaining some variability at these higher levels).

Maclennan points to an interesting trend in housing construction. (1) Taking quinquennial periods since the war, and excepting the periods 1956-60 and 1966-70, the proportion of private sector housebuilding relative to total Scottish housebuilding has risen steadily. In the first postwar period, private housebuilding was 6% of the total (1946-50) but rose to 22.6% in the first half of the 1960s. In the last 25 years, however, the growth has been more considerable, taking just over 50% in the 1976-80 period and exceeding 70% in each period after 1980. It is also noticeable that this proportionate growth has been accompanied by an absolute decline in output; for instance, the five years 1981-85 produced less than half the units built in 1966-70.

How does the Scottish experience of housebuilding compare with that of the remainder of the UK? While there is the same evidence of the private sector supplanting the social, particularly the council landlord, as builder, it is worth stressing that the fortunes of the building sector have been different in Scotland and England. Table 2 contrasts an index of total building completions for Scotland and the UK as a whole. This indicates that there was a common turning point after 1979/80, with subsequently much lower levels of completions in both Scotland and the UK. But Scottish and UK completions diverged between 1980 and 1992, with Scottish levels below the 1996 level and UK levels above their 1996 reference point. Then, the trends appear to have converged in the 1990s. The patterns in the data suggest that other parts of the UK had a better 1980s, and a worse 1990s, than Scotland in terms of output volumes.

In terms of what was built, Maclennan argues that Scottish dwellings were less likely to be semi-detached or terraced, more likely to be flats and, for the stock as a whole, to be newer than those in England, Wales or Northern Ireland. (2) Another way of looking at the performance of the industry is to examine the

Table 1
Scottish private housing completions, 1974-96

Year	Private completions	Private as a percentage of total
1974	11,239	39.7
1975	10,371	30.4
1976	13,704	37.6
1977	12,132	44.4
1978	14,443	56.0
1979	15,175	64.1
1980	12,242	59.1
1981	11,021	55.1
1982	11,529	68.4
1983	13,178	73.4
1984	14,118	74.9
1985	14,445	78.4
1986	14,843	79.8
1987	13,904	78.5
1988	14,179	77.6
1989	16,287	80.7
1990	16,461	80.3
1991	15,533	79.5
1992	14,389	78.0
1993	17,711	82.8
1994	17,753	82.9
1995	18,310	74.8
1996	17,813	86.1

Source: Housing and Construction Statistics, various issues

value of output (the annual value of contractors' output dedicated to new private housing) suitably deflated to account for the effects of inflation. The advantage of looking at these monetised data is that they take account of the different mix associated with housebuilding. The completions data may, after all, mask shifts in the type of housing being constructed, especially over a period in excess of 20 years.

Table 2
Building sector change in Scotland and the UK, 1974-96

Year	Scotland	Scottish index (1996 = 100)	UK	UK index (1996=100)
1974	28,336	138	279,582	149
1975	34,323	168	322,113	172
1976	36,527	177	324,445	173
1977	27,320	133	313,496	167
1978	25,759	126	288,091	154
1979	23,782	114	242,892	130
1980	20,611	101	241,986	129
1981	20,015	98	206,566	110
1982	16,429	80	182,819	97
1983	17,941	88	208,903	111
1984	18,841	92	220,265	117
1985	18,374	90	207,565	111
1986	18,610	91	216,592	115
1987	17,707	86	226,196	121
1988	18,272	89	242,324	129
1989	20,190	98	221,425	118
1990	20,362	99	202,688	108
1991	19,529	95	191,145	102
1992	18,443	90	179,638	96
1993	21,392	104	185,715	99
1994	21,404	104	192,969	103
1995	24,486	120	199,574	106
1996	20,754	100	187,546	100

Source: Housing and Construction Statistics, various issues

Table 3
Value of private new housing, 1980-96
(£m, and 1993-94 prices)

Year	Scotland cash	Scotland real	GB cash	GB real
1980	118	245	1,944	4,034
1981	145	274	2,013	3,808
1982	224	396	2,928	5,171
1983	316	533	4,078	6,881
1984	283	478	4,001	6,430
1985	322	518	4,555	7,158
1986	330	503	5,421	8,018
1987	306	483	6,441	9,045
1988	373	524	7,894	10,390
1989	526	692	6,497	7,993
1990	621	764	4,856	5,531
1991	548	624	4,552	5,185
1992	428	514	4,016	4,304
1993	532	548	4,874	5,023
1994	638	638	5,721	5,721
1995	548	537	4,905	4,809
1996	568	541	5,416	5,158

1993/94 = 100 (GDP deflator)
Source: as Table 2

Rebirth of the Market, 1975-99

Table 3 describes the changing value of new housing output for the private sector in Scotland and the whole of Britain from 1980 to 1996. Looking at the nominal figures first, it is evident that several years marked significant downturns in the value of new output from the private housebuilding sector (1984, 1987, 1991, 1992 and 1995 in Scotland; 1984, 1989, 1990, 1991, 1992 and 1995). It is striking that the significant reduction in the value of new output for Britain after 1988 was not mirrored in Scotland, although downturns were experienced in four of the years in both Scotland and Britain as a whole. In other words, the turning points were similar, but the structural downward shift in the value of output in England and Wales was avoided in Scotland. The figures presented in real terms are also significant. They show considerable growth in output between 1980 and 1990 in Scotland (more than three-fold), followed by a slump back by one-third within two years (1992) as a result of the recession, followed by major year-on-year fluctuations. This is in contrast to the wholesale collapse of the English housebuilding market in the early and mid-1990s; by 1996, the latter was only at a little more than half of its 1988 output level.

This period saw a marked convergence in the percentage rate of home ownership in Scotland and the rest of the UK. In 1979, less than 40% of Scots were home owners but this grew to just under 60% in 1996. Home ownership in the UK as a whole rose in the same period from the mid-50s to the high 60s percentages. Tables 4 and 5 also contrast Scotland and Britain - this time in terms of housing's share of all construction work in 1996 (Table 4) and the 10 year to 1996 growth rate in both countries for housebuilding. Private new-build as a proportion of all construction work was slightly less significant in Britain than in Scotland (10.1% compared with 11.4%) in 1996, while the growth rate of the Scottish sector has also outperformed Britain as a whole, both in 1996 and over the preceding ten years.

Table 4
Housing work and Scottish construction, 1996

Type of activity	£ million	Percentage of Scottish total	Percentage of GB total
Housing repair work	1,167	21.0	27.2
Private new-build	520	11.4	10.1
Social new-build	236	4.2	2.6
Total construction	5,568	100.0	100.0

Source: J Hamilton and K McKenzie, 'The construction industry in Scotland', *Scottish Economic Bulletin*, 1997

Table 5
Annual average growth rates in housing sectors of the construction industry, 1986-96 (%)

Activity	Scotland 1996	GB 1996	Scotland average 1986-96	GB average 1986-96
Housing repair work	- 3.3	0.0	1.5	2.3
Private new-build	4.6	- 0.2	1.6	- 2.6
Social new-build	- 1.6	-15.2	4.1	2.3
Construction total	- 0.9	1.1	2.3	1.7

Source: as Table 4

Explaining the trends

In general, therefore, it is evident that the market context of Scottish and UK private housebuilding has differed over the period under review. There are a number of reasons for this, and they help to explain the divergence in the statistics reported in the preceding section. The main points can be expressed as follows:

- Economically and socially, Scotland started from a different position in the mid-1970s, but subsequently has converged with the rest of the UK in a number of respects (e.g. home ownership). This does mean that exogenous shocks such as economic recession or financial deregulation would affect the Scottish economy and hence the housebuilding sector differently.

- A more stable housing market, in terms of lower rates of house price inflation, has moderated some of the worst excesses of speculation, and, despite the builders' claims to the contrary, the planning system has, in general, delivered sufficient land to meet new housing demand without the rapidly rising land and house prices of the sort experienced in south-east England. The 'UK' boom and bust side-stepped Scotland, where there was little if any negative equity.

- In the 1970s, builders could survive private sector recessions by switching to public-sector projects, including both housing and non-residential construction. Although this is now more difficult in the 1990s, subsidies and social housing have still played an important, albeit limited role in shoring up work for the private developer. The advent of subsidy mechanisms such as GRO-grant, and design-and-build projects with housing associations and tenant co-operatives, has provided work for a limited number of important developers (within a relatively small geographic marketplace).

- Fundamentally, the Scottish housebuilding sector has benefited from the release of pent-up demand for home ownership, which has grown from less than 40% to around 60% in the period examined. A large part of this growth is due to the 'Right to Buy' policy in relation to existing council property, but the more general long-term effect has been to widen significantly the market and demand for private housing, a demand which is, to a large extent, extensively for new rather than existing housing (particularly for the large number of urban dwellers who want to leave tenement housing).

It is worth elaborating a little on some of the above points. In the mid-1970s, compared with England and Wales, the Scottish economy was more dependent on its (declining) manufacturing base, and it had lower income per head, higher unemployment, fewer business start-ups and a greater dependence on (and acceptance of) council housing. This may have contributed to the observed phenomenon that the British economy has tended to perform better relative to that of Scotland in boom periods, while growing less quickly in economic slowdowns. Scotland's greater dependence on public sector activities, both in terms of employment and income (once the early 1980s recession is accounted for), may have acted as a buffer against recession, although it would also have impaired private-sector-led economic growth in the upswing.

While there has been a degree of convergence between Scotland and the rest of the UK in the intervening period, it remains the case that several of these broad patterns have persisted to the present day, particularly the counter-cyclical relationship in GDP growth. Discussions with industry participants over this period reveal an interesting paradox. Despite the figures suggesting that Scotland (particularly in the past eight years) has outperformed the rest of the UK, and has escaped recession as conventionally measured, the industry nonetheless points to fierce price competition, battles over market share and the absence of economic growth. Such counter-cyclical perceptions oddly echo the gloomy verdicts of building-industry observers in the 1890s, cited above by Richard Rodger (Chapter B1). Whether their recurrence today reflects myopia, the divergence between macro and urban markets or the spillover of other construction markets, is an issue to which we will return below.

The relationship between demographic trends and land-use policy has also shaped the Scottish context for the housebuilding sector. Household growth is projected to be at high levels, as a result of the growing significance of smaller household units, with clear implications for the building sector; something of the order of 200,000 to 230,000 new homes will be required over the next twenty years, primarily for single-person households, and often for more elderly people. The planning system and the land market will need to cope with these new stresses, and, in particular, 'brownfield' sites (sites reclaimed from previous uses, in contrast to 'greenfield' or 'virgin' sites) will be of central importance. The issue of land use is discussed further below.

The demand for new private housing largely depends on the wider demand for owner occupation. Despite the 'bust' of the early 1990s, home ownership remains the aspiration of the great majority of Scots, and the deregulated mortgage market has enabled long-term finance to be a relatively straightforward step.

Table 6
Trends in public spending on Scottish housing (£ million)

Type of expenditure	1989-90	1991-92	1993-94	1995-96	1997-98
Local authority capital (council)	486	476	475	579	299*
Local authority (private sector)	157	111	119	121	59*
Scottish Homes**	205	235	303	316	199*
Private finance	10	87	149	199	130*
Mortgage interest tax relief	470	420	300	200	not available
Local authority current subsidy	65	56	36	22	15
Housing Benefit (to local authority tenants)	364	446	524	562	586*

*estimate
**mostly capital grants to associations but some subsidy to developers (GRO-grant)
Sources: R Goodlad, 'Scottish housing policy', paper to Modern Studies Association conference, Edinburgh, November 1998; S Wilcox, *Housing Finance Review 1997-8*, 1997

High loan-to-value and high loan-to-income ratios require both high levels of employment continuity and the impact of inflation to erode the real value of debt (and therefore to sustain high household debt gearing). A major shift over the period in question has been the decline in traditional secure employment, and its replacement by more part-time, temporary and otherwise impermanent employment, alongside the more unexpected secular decline in the rate of inflation, which has paradoxically made the housing market less attractive to highly geared borrowers. Neither of these trends supports the long-term growth of home ownership and, allied with changes to government support for low-income mortgagors, suggests the likely retention of a significant level of arrears and repossessions problems in the housing market, a tendency which will be worsened in economic downturns.

Changes to the public sector environment have been very significant. First of all, council housing investment was sharply curtailed, leading to higher rents, which undoubtedly pushed many households into other tenures. Second, in the 1980s and early 1990s, housing association development became the alternative preferred way to build social housing. However, in the past few years, the pattern has shifted away from new development towards the transfer of council stock, and more limited packages of new development and rehabilitation on existing ex-council schemes. This fits in with the burgeoning role of housing development/rehabilitation within urban regeneration, and the use of implicit and explicit subsidy to encourage private investment, using direct subsidies but also cheap land.

Table 6 contains a summary of housing spending in the 1990s. Firstly, it emphasises the decline in the capital programmes of councils, both in relation to work on their own stock and to private sector grants (in terms of permissions to borrow). Second, it shows the increasing use of private finance in social housing, especially for transfers rather than new investment. And third, it shows the declining importance of both tax relief and conventional recurrent subsidy to council tenants. On the other hand, housing benefit (measured in terms of rebates to council tenants) has grown significantly, although the figures do not include benefit paid to private and association tenants. Table 6 does not account for inflation; the collapse of investment would appear even more precipitous if the effects of inflation were added.

The overall level of public expenditure directed towards capital housing projects has fallen significantly in real terms, even taking account of the growing element of private funding. Nevertheless, the impact of these changes has been mixed across the housebuilding sector, and has led to different strategic responses. Contractors were most exposed to the decline in council housebuilding; later, the growth of both design-and-build project solutions for housing associations and GRO-grant subsidised developments in the private sector led private developers to introduce 'social housing', 'partnership' and related offshoots, as they attempted to gain a niche in this new market. At the same time, contractors tried to compete for many of these projects, particularly during difficult market times.

In this section, the focus has been on the broad patterns that differentiate Scottish and British patterns and which help to explain the broad performance of Scottish private housebuilding in an era of large-scale socio-economic and political change. We will return later to the question of the distinctiveness of the Scottish housebuilding sector. In the following section, we consider processes under way within private housebuilding by focusing on specific key themes, including land release and the

builder/planner debate, centralised designs, business strategies, the advent of related niche work, as well as the importance of economic cycles and policy responses.

Themes and issues

It is striking, when looking back to the mid-1970s from the late 1990s, just how little the main themes and problems of the housebuilding industry seem to have changed. An article of 1977 by Gaskin set out the key factors which faced the industry in those years. (3) The main issues identified were (to paraphrase): the extent to which the construction industry could respond to housing policy initiatives; the challenge of increasing industry capacity and making it more flexible; the need to reduce volatility in construction output markets; the problem of skills shortages and mismatches; the task of increasing the competitiveness of the building industry, particularly at the local level; and the reorganisation of the supply of land to provide efficient quantities at reasonable prices in appropriate locations to meet demand, taking account of other planning objectives. Over twenty years later, this still remains a reasonable agenda for the housebuilding sector as it confronts the millennium. In the following section, we examine a number of these recurring themes in a little more depth.

Land release and the builder/planner debate
A fundamental issue for the industry is the release of adequate supplies of land of the required standard, in areas where the potential demand for private housing can be met. Historically, this need for land has been constrained by the planning system, as it juggles with a range of potentially conflicting objectives. Not only does the local planner have to weigh up alternative uses for land, including the sustainability/environmentalist position, but he/she also has to work within a controversial system of assessing likely future demand for private housing. Here, demographic projections of household formation and their tenure splits are used to produce estimates of how much land might need to be set aside for housebuilding. This has been criticised on the grounds that it takes insufficient account of the economic factors that drive housing demand, and that once the numbers are arrived at, the subsequent land allocations take insufficient account of the existence of housing sub-markets (meaning that some of the land provided for may actually have no likely demand and hence builders are unwilling to count it in as part of the allocation). As a result of this mechanism, there is considerable profitable scope for planning consultants and the like, as the

B5.5. During the mid-1980s, the Glasgow community housing associations began to extend their activities from tenement rehabilitation to new-build regeneration on strategic sites such as the 'Maryhill Corridor', initially using low-rise brick terraces. This view shows two projects by the Queens Cross Housing Association: on the left, the Queens Cross East development, built by Lawrence Construction in 1985, and on the right, the Queens Cross West group, built by Ogilvie Builders in 1987-89. Both projects were designed on an agency basis by Glasgow District Council's Department of Architecture. (RCAHMS B17735)

B5.6. In a pioneering effort to escape from Glasgow's small-scale brick aesthetic of the 1980s, the Maryhill Housing Association commissioned an architectural competition for a '21st Century Tenement' on a site at Stratford Street, Maryhill. The winning scheme (1984-89), by McGurn Logan Duncan & Opfer with Ken MacRae, used split-level planning, concrete blockwork facing and classical facade detail reminiscent of Alexander Thomson to create a sense of masonry monumentality. The contractor for the project was Laing Scotland, and the blockwork suppliers were John Fyfe Ltd (for the Kemnay Block front base and Creetown granite rear), and Boral Edenhall Ltd and Brand & Rae Ltd (for the upper front walling). The project was delayed by the need for repeated rebuilding of sections of wall, to obtain the required modular precision in the blockwork courses. (RCAHMS C38661)

B5.7. A number of 1990s projects of social housing developed the Maryhill block's innovative planning ideas. Reidvale Housing Association's U-shaped block of flats and shops in Duke Street (1992-93), built by Wimpey Construction using a JCT 80 form of contract, used split-level planning to create tall living-rooms facing the sheltered rear court. (RCAHMS C15570)

B5.8. A pioneer of private-sector new-build for owner occupation in the city centre: Barratt Glasgow's St. Vincent Court development of 1983-85, containing 194 brick-built flats in five storeys with attic. (RCAHMS A59848)

B5.9. Private builders increasingly exploited the revival in the prestige of the 19th-century tenement, by building 'new traditional tenements' of flats for sale. Here Traquair Court, a block of 23 flats, is seen under construction by speculative developer Kelvin Homes in 1989 at Wilton Street, Glasgow. The site building workforce comprised 18 men, expanded by 12 ancillary staff such as security men and technicians. The flats have an almost pre-1914 ceiling height of 3m; the walls were constructed of blockwork inside and brick on the outside, with stone mullions, and the floors are of precast concrete. (M Glendinning)

builders and planners fight over individual sites and planning permission for wider areas.

Within a single chapter, one cannot do justice to the range of issues encapsulated in the builder-planner debate, but a number of points can be singled out as key issues for the building industry. First, the drive to build primarily on brownfield sites is generally accepted across society, but it is unlikely that all of its implications have been fully addressed. In the first place, there is only a finite supply of brownfield sites, as there is of green space. Much of the desirable brownfield space has been built or is in preparation. Inevitably, the remaining space is more marginal, and will require more work to bring up to building standard (through decontamination and other regeneration work); someone has to bear the cost of that work. The development of brownfield land raises major questions about the future design and built environments of Scottish towns and cities, implying more planning input and delays to building - not the reverse. Secondly, the plan-led system, as well as the demise of the strategic regional local authorities, will only encourage a greater concentration of land ownership and land-banking by builders with sufficient capital to purchase land. In other words, the building-planning debate has implications for the overall structure and business objectives of the housebuilding industry in Scotland, a point insufficiently addressed by commentators.

Centralised designs

The evolution of speculative house designs in the private sector is affected by its own considerable tensions. On the one hand, the business production logic of scale economies and replicable working has pushed the industry towards a limited number of centralised design specifications, with UK-wide firms producing standard branded homes for use anywhere, their features dictated mainly by English cultural expectations. This can lead to the use of materials, designs and finishes which seem violently at odds with the Scottish environment: for example, the clumps of red-brick houses built mainly by English-based firms around the edges of our country's stone-built and harled urban environments. Running alongside those tendencies of homogenisation is an apparently conflicting, but in reality complementary trend towards design variation and cosmetic product changes within the centralised market system, driven by computer-aided design and the demands of marketing for homes suitable for customisation by buyers.

Business strategies

The Scottish housebuilding industry is distinct from the overall UK market in its considerable scope for growth, both in terms of home ownership levels and new demands coming through from household projections (subject to a number of caveats) for the next 20 years. However, there is little evidence that the building industry does, or indeed can, develop strategies for the long term. The industry is dominated by the construction cycle and, as a result, by its historical and projected land purchasing. All of the evidence suggests that the industry is conservative regarding innovation and new production processes and techniques, and it should not be surprising, also given the risks and uncertainties and delays inherent to the business, that reactive thinking tends to dominate broader business decision-making.

Niche work, and social housing

While it is true that opportunities to support speculative private work by publicly funded projects are now much reduced compared with the position in the early 1970s, there remains capacity to develop partnerships and to work with the social sector (and subsidised home ownership) in the field of urban regeneration.

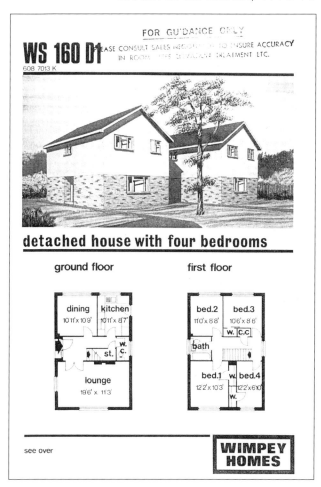

B5.10. Private-sector speculative volume building in Scotland during the 1970s was dominated by Wimpey, which exploited the nationwide spread it had established through its council contracts. The illustration shows a typical four-bedroom detached type of 1979, built in partly rendered load-bearing brick and featuring a side-entrance layout; including the optional garage and central heating, it cost £27,595 on an average estate in Stirling. (George Wimpey Ltd)

B5.11. An equivalent Wimpey 1998 house-type, of virtually identical rendered brick construction, and selling for £122,500 in a comparable location (the Sycamore Rise South development in Stirling). The garage is now integral to the design, the number of ancillary spaces (utility room, en-suite bathroom, etc.) and fittings has increased, and the facade is treated in a more busy, historicist style. (George Wimpey Ltd)

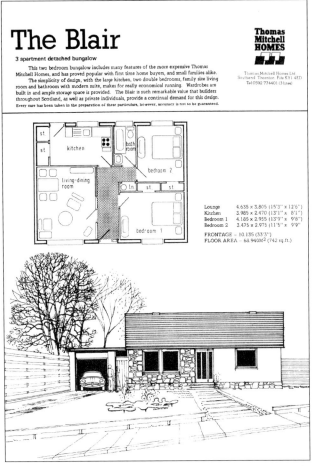

The Blair

Thomas Mitchell HOMES

3 apartment detached bungalow

This two bedroom bungalow includes many features of the more expensive Thomas Mitchell Homes, and has proved popular with first time home buyers, and small families alike.

The simplicity of design, with the large kitchen, two double bedrooms, family size living room and bathroom with modern suite, makes for really economical running. Wardrobes are built in and ample storage space is provided. The Blair is such remarkable value that builders throughout Scotland, as well as private individuals, provide a continual demand for this design. Every care has been taken in the preparation of these particulars, however, accuracy is not to be guaranteed.

Thomas Mitchell Homes Ltd.
Southend Thornton Fife KY1 4ED
Tel 0592 774401 (3 Lines)

Lounge	4.635 x 3.805 (15'3" x 12'6")
Kitchen	3.985 x 2.470 (13'1" x 8'1")
Bedroom 1	4.185 x 2.955 (13'9" x 9'8")
Bedroom 2	3.475 x 2.975 (11'5" x 9'9"

FRONTAGE – 10.135 (33'3")
FLOOR AREA – 68.940M² (742 sq.ft.)

B5.12. The popularity of timber-frame construction since the 1970s has sustained a substantial market for self-build 'kit' houses, as in some other countries (e.g. in Scandinavia). The timber framing is usually concealed by a masonry-style facade. This example is a two-bedroom bungalow-type offered in 1979 by Fife builder Thomas Mitchell Homes; supplied as a kit ex-works, it cost £4,075, and if built by the firm (excluding site cost), £11,100. (Thomas Mitchell Homes)

This is an increasingly important part of the building industry in Scotland, where considerable expertise has been established not just in the construction of homes but also in working with the public sector in a variety of scenarios. Experience in building low-cost home ownership housing, shared ownership housing, design-and-build new social housing, GRO-grant private housing and 'normal' build-for-sale on Scottish housing schemes since the late 1980s has made it possible to develop skills and to capture work associated with New Housing Partnerships and Social Inclusion Partnerships. This expertise can also be exported, as builders such as Millers have found with successful developments in England, capitalising on the lessons learned in Scotland.

Economic cycles and market volatility

Table 3 illustrates the volatility of the market, in terms of the value of work completed. Although Scottish building has historically been less volatile than that of the rest of the UK, this pattern is likely to diminish in the future as home ownership expands and the building sector becomes increasingly reliant on the fragile market for new owner-occupied housing. The housing market and the economy remain vulnerable to shifts in economic drivers such as world export demand and interest rates. The mortgage market relies on stable income from employment, but increasingly operates in a context of insecure employment and under-insured protection against income loss. When one also considers the supply inelasticity of the building industry, then the opportunity for the building sector to experience volatile shifts in activity remain significant. There is no evidence to suggest that this position will appreciably improve in the medium term.

The labour market and training

The industry is dominated by subcontracting and self-employment. Production processes within the housebuilding sector assume that such gangs of skilled and semi-skilled workers can be brought in and moved on to the next job. Training and the recycling of skills are therefore hampered by the economic logic of the building process. Why should a housebuilding firm train a worker who then becomes self-employed? In difficult economic times, training budgets are inevitably cut back. Twenty-five years ago, far more people entered the profession each year and were trained within the levy system. This operated under certain assumptions: for instance, that no one free-rode. But the advent of large-scale self-employment, the fiscal advantages of reducing direct employment for firms, and the growth in subcontracting by the industry, have fatally undermined the long-term recycling of construction skills. The consequences are high skilled wages, long commuting times for workers, product quality problems and the prospect of a declining supply of indigenous construction workers, supplanted by imported skilled labour. At worst, this threatens the future of a domestic industry; at best, it points to long-term increases in construction costs.

Government policy and the building sector

In the early 1970s, it was commonplace to conceive of the building industry as a regulator of economic activity. While these Keynesian notions are largely obsolete now, they are not completely so. One of the indirect effects of the GRO-grant programme in the 1990s was to provide considerable, subsidised, business to the Scottish housebuilding sector. Social housing activity, while much smaller in scale than public sector work in the 1970s, still remains significant. In recent years, the impact of government policy has been indirect but nonetheless important, in areas such as the following: redirecting the thrust of land release and land planning; shaping the physical element of area

Table 7
Market share of top 25 builders, Scotland and the UK, 1990-95

	1990	1991	1992	1993	1994	1995
Total revenue (£bn)	0.995	0.869	1.127	0.829	1.363	1.282
Top 25 sales market share	67%	66%	67%	58%	68%	72%
Top 25 revenue market share	68%	66%	67%	58%	68%	73%
UK top 25 market share sales	38%	42%	42%	43%	45%	46%

Table 8
Four-firm concentration ratios, 1990-95 (%)

Year	Scotland sales	Scotland revenue	Strathclyde sales	Strathclyde revenue	Grampian sales	Grampian revenue
1990	30	30	36	36	65	59
1991	31	30	37	37	62	60
1992	32	30	41	42	55	52
1993	25	22	31	29	43	42
1994	33	30	40	36	38	36
1995	31	30	37	34	49	49

Source: K Gibb, 'Regional differentiation and the Scottish housebuilding industry', *Housing Studies*, 1999

regeneration; promotion of home ownership; devising tax policy changes to reduce the level of 'self-employed' workers who tend to work for the same company; making changes to building regulations; and implementing more general macroeconomic policies.

Future challenges

In this penultimate section, two questions are considered. First, what does the most up-to-date information tell us about the fortunes of the Scottish private housebuilding sector? Second, what is the relationship between the Scottish and UK housebuilding industries?

The Scottish industry today

Table 7 outlines the market share of the top 25 builders in Scotland and the UK. It suggests that the Scottish housebuilding industry, just as in the 1960s and 1970s, remains much more concentrated than that of the UK as a whole, a fact confirmed in other measures of concentration at the Scottish national and regional levels; this may be due to the size of the Scottish market. To bring the story up to date, it is worthwhile to reflect on the results of a recent survey of the building industry. Towards the end of 1997, the University of Glasgow carried out a small survey (with 83 responding firms) of the Scottish housebuilding industry, on behalf of the Scottish House Building Association. The main findings from the survey were:

- The median turnover for all firms responding was £1.6 million, while the mean was £7.52 million. Firms in the bottom third of the distribution turned over less than £1 million; firms in the top third turned over more than £6 million. Subsequent analysis was categorised by firms into small, medium and large sizes, according to their distribution by turnover.

- The typical firm raised 50% of its turnover from housebuilding, but this increased to 73% for large builders. Small builders did as much as one-third of their turnover in refurbishment work and a further 17% from housing repairs. This emphasises the specialisation of larger building companies.

- The median annual level of completions was 10 units, but the mean was 103 completions. The impact of the volume housebuilders is indicated by the average annual completion rate for small firms (2 units), medium-sized builders (17 units) and larger builders (272).

- Output was distributed over a wide geographical spread of areas, although the largest quantities were built in areas of larger population (the cities, Lanarkshire, Fife, the Lothians, the rest of Greater Glasgow).

- Respondents largely drew their building materials from within Scotland; 71% of them sourced at least three-quarters of their materials from Scottish sources. However, large builders, often with UK-wide supplies agreements, were less reliant on Scottish materials.

- Some 71% of respondents thought that there was a skills shortage; in this, there was little variation by size of firm. The trades in which these problems were held to be most acute were joinery and bricklaying.

- More than half of respondents (64% of larger builders) had a land-bank for building purposes. Those with a land-bank had, on average, slightly less than four years' supply of land. The firms with land-banks had an average of 49.5% of their land on brownfield sites (a proportion which increased to 81% in the case of large builders).

- Fewer than one in five of the firms had been active in subsidised work (GRO, HAG, etc.) in the preceding year; those that had were predominantly large firms.

If we compare these results with a previous survey in 1994, then a few points stand out. (4) The average number of direct employees has fallen. Average turnover is unchanged at £7.5 million, as is the proportion of turnover devoted to housebuilding activity (51%). In 1997, 71% of respondents thought that there was a skills shortage, compared with less than two-thirds in 1994. However, the same trades, bricklaying and joinery, were emphasised as particularly problematic in both surveys. The distribution of construction work for different clients and tenures continues to favour the speculative-building market and, to a lesser extent, the housing association sector. In 1994, more than two in three firms had a land-bank; in 1997, that figure had fallen to just over half (53%) of respondents.

The relationship of the Scottish and UK industries

Six principal factors indicate the strength of differentiation of the Scottish housebuilding sector. (5)

Ownership of the industry

'Regional' subsidiaries are often party to centralised funding, design and purchasing constraints which can make them in effect a branch of an overall UK business. On the other hand, a subsidiary may have control over a supply chain which is largely Scottish, greatly reducing its dependence on non-Scottish decision-makers. There is evidence that some of the 'regional' offices of UK builders are constrained to use common purchasing policies, even though otherwise they have autonomy in their day-to-day actions. (6) The Scottish housebuilding sector is made up of a mix of wholly-owned subsidiaries and UK-wide players, along with a number of medium-sized Scottish housebuilders,

B5.13. A departure from the longstanding attempts of subsidiaries of English-based firms to 'blend in' to the Scottish scene was signalled by Birmingham-based builder Bryant. Seen in this view is Bryant's first Scottish 'regional' development, Pentland Gate, Craiglockhart, Edinburgh, opened in 1994. The four detached 'Victorian style' house-types, ranging in price from £127,500 to £180,000, were modelled on the red-brick 19th-century villas of English suburbs such as Birmingham's Edgbaston. The development excited a heated newspaper correspondence, with one Scotsman *letter-writer, Dr Bob Purdie, describing it as 'the case for Scottish independence built in red brick'. (*Scotsman, *14 February 1994, 11)*

construction firms and niche market builders; this position contrasts with the 1960s, when Wimpey was the only really large UK-wide firm seriously involved in Scottish private building. For 1995, it was possible to identify the antecedents of 23 out of the 25 top builders (as defined by market share). Twelve of the top 25 were Scottish vehicles or subsidiaries of UK builders, and represented nearly half of all of total output. Eleven of the top 25 were Scottish independents, but only two of these were represented in the top ten. Penetration by the UK volume housebuilders is thus considerable.

Nature of the product

Basic differences in the product will lead in turn to different labour and materials requirements. However, centralised designs tend to operate across the whole of the UK, as subsidiaries use a common set of property types. Furthermore, the Scottish independents tend to use their own centralised designs, which in some cases mimic those of English-based competitors. It is not in architectural design but in building construction that Scottish and English housing now differs most radically, in that the majority of new building in Scotland is dominated by timber-frame methods - a method rejected in England since the 1980s. In contrast to the position earlier in the century, when low-rise housing in Scotland and England was generally built in the same load-bearing construction (brickwork) but finished differently on the outside (with render in Scotland, and facing brick in England), this new divergence is concerned with the hidden, basic structure of the house, and not with its exterior skin - which can just as easily be of facing brick in Scotland as in England. Timber-framing not only produces large cost savings and environmental benefits, but it also changes the nature of the site management problem because of the quicker basic assembly it allows. As we saw in the previous chapter, timber-framing was at first a UK-wide development whose 1960s prototype stage was concentrated in England. However, following a media-led controversy focusing on alleged fire risks in the late 1970s and early 1980s, timber-framing in England became stigmatised, and there was a public outcry in that country for a return to 'traditional brick building'. As a result of this divergence, we now witness the practice in some cases of UK firms building homes of standard type-plans in England and Wales with brick and block, but with timber-frames in Scotland.

Structure of demand

The demand for new-build housing is part of the overall demand for housing, including second-hand housing and a large number of different product groups (defined by type, size location and other attributes) over which preferences are expressed by households. If the structure of demand is different in one part of the UK from the overall average, one may then expect to see different building industry outcomes in that area. However, one should distinguish between long-term differences and cyclical disturbances in demand. For instance, there appears to be a long-term set of geographical house price differentials in the UK which diverge during economic booms (the ripple effect) but converge during the downturn. Microeconomic evidence comparing Glasgow and Bristol suggests that there are structural differences in the amount that people borrow, their key lending ratios, the price they pay for housing and the overall stability of the local housing market (which is more volatile in Bristol). (7) English housing demand appears to be perceptibly different from that in Scotland, if to a matter of degree. The context within which Scottish builders work will not be the same as in other parts of the UK; local expertise and networks remain important to UK housebuilders operating in Scotland.

Contestability

The basic premise of contestability is that any market structure is compatible with an efficient competitive equilibrium, provided key conditions are met, namely, low entry barriers, low or zero sunk costs and relatively slow reaction time responses by incumbent producers. (8) If these conditions are met, the threat of potential effective competition by raider firms holds prices down to their competitive level (since that is the only way to deter entry). Contestability is an empirical question, but might apply to parts of the construction industry. Competitive contract tendering, keen profit margins, leasing markets which reduce sunk costs and low entry barriers suggest that the contracting part of the housebuilding industry may approximate to a contestable market. The more this is so, the less scope one would expect to have for the 'regionalisation' of housebuilding markets. However, contestability is unlikely to extend to developers, because of the time delays associated with land acquisition and building. The land market, and the capacity to develop land supply through banking, both undermine the conditions required for contestability.

Input and funding markets

Are there structural differences in input markets such as land, labour, finance or materials that may lead to systematic variations between Scotland and the UK building sector? Many of the building supplies industries are capital-intensive and relatively concentrated, chiefly operating at a UK level for the time being, but with a growing move towards a European scope. (9) In the labour market, craftsmen and labour-only subcontractors tend to operate within limited geographical market areas, with only site management being more likely to work across regions. For the present, most human relations issues are UK-wide in their competence (taxation, employment law, etc.). In short, labour supply tends to be localised but operates, for now, within a UK framework. The financing of housebuilding is dominated by ownership structure. Most of the UK firms operating in Scotland are publicly quoted and can therefore raise funds through equity financing, as well as the more traditional routes of bank lending and self-financing through retained earnings or phasing production. Furthermore, a Scottish division may be able to draw on capital from its parent, which acts as a banker to the regional subsidiary. Scottish independent developers tend to be family businesses or sole proprietor enterprises and not publicly quoted; they have to rely on the traditional financing routes. The contracting sector is much more heavily dependent on bank lending and hence on interest rates and credit availability.

Housing, legal and planning policy differences

Just as in the case of the 1960s contractors seeking to break into the council high-rise building market, non-Scottish firms seeking to break into today's private market have to deal with the autonomous housing, legal or land planning frameworks that have developed within the system of administrative devolution under the aegis of the Scottish Office. They also have to make provision for the additional transactions and sunk costs implied by dealing with this legal-political environment. The most pertinent aspects of these autonomous systems include building regulations and property law, some elements of land planning and subsidy incentives (including GRO-grant and higher HAG levels). These differences are likely to be expanded following 1999, with the transformation of administrative devolution into full legislative home rule. Though not insurmountable, and offering profit opportunities as well as problems, these additional transactions costs may well deter potential competition from outwith Scotland at the margin, particularly in the contracting market.

Scotland has a distinct housing market, and has a number of industry-specific features such as timber-framing, housing policy and legal differences, and a dominance of indigenous contractors and professionals in the industry. The Scottish building industry is developing a model within which developers are increasingly national in their approach and market share, while contracting and the professionals who work in the industry are dominated by local business in an increasingly competitive market environment.

Conclusion

This chapter has examined the Scottish private housebuilding industry as it has evolved over the past twenty-five years, with one eye on the future and the other concerned with the autonomy of the Scottish sector. Up until now, that autonomy has been defined in relation to the UK as the parent nation-state. But in

B5.14. Roadside advertisements for Taywood and Bellway developments, overlooking a newly completed extension of the A737 road at Howwood, Renfrewshire, in 1998. Estates such as these presupposed a constant extension of car transport, and sustained the road-building programme. (M Glendinning)

B5.15. Showhouse at one of the new developments in Howwood in 1998. (M Glendinning)

an economy increasingly dominated on the one hand by European and global trading forces in product and capital markets, and, on the other, by the new Scottish government at a national political level, that framework of comparison may change, with the role of the UK progressively squeezed from both sides. Housing policy, industrial policy and urban planning will be shaped by Holyrood, and economic policy may be influenced by Brussels and Frankfurt. Will this affect the positioning, opportunities and performance of Scottish housebuilding? And does this mean that the industry will now diverge from, rather than continue to converge with, that of England and the UK? This remains to be seen, but if a new Scottish national housebuilding sector can avoid some of the laissez-faire UK industry tendencies evidenced by writers such as Ball, that would be no small progress for building. (10)

In conclusion, it is worth returning to the questions posed by Gaskin in 1977, in response to the Green Paper on housing policy published in that year. (11) How does the performance of the Scottish housebuilding industry in the late 1990s measure up to these questions? Gaskin asked:

- *How well does the construction industry use its capacity to respond to housing policy initiatives?*
  Here the evidence from the GRO-grant experience is encouraging, although that was achieved in a period of some slack. It will be interesting to see how the skills learnt in the early 1990s are transferred to contemporary opportunities such as the New Housing Partnerships and similar joint ventures.

- *How can industry capacity be increased (and become more flexible)?*
  This remains a key question for the sector, especially in the context of rising household numbers and society's concern to keep house price inflation in check. Skills shortages and land release rigidities remain key sources of inflexibility.

- *How can volatility be reduced in construction output markets?*
  Ball advocates national housebuilding targets, but one must recall that volatility in the building sector to some extent mimics wider economic cycles - and no one has found a way to dampen their oscillations. (12) The lessons from continental Europe suggest that a more efficient industry can develop on the back of construction and building profits, with land development gain diminished as a source of profit. But

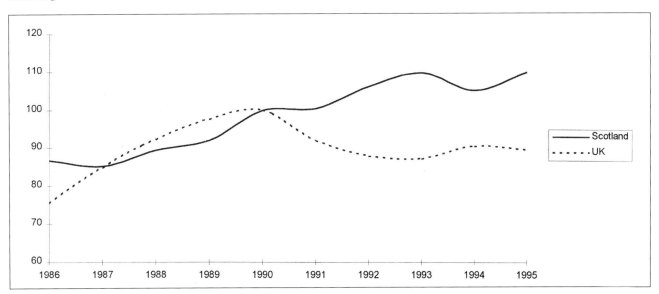

B5.16. Index of Scottish and UK construction between 1986 and 1995 (1990 = 100).

such a change, which would completely revolutionise the Scottish building industry, remains unlikely.

- *How can skills shortages and mismatches be resolved?*
  The training conundrum remains the critical problem for the industry; but this is an issue not just of increasing the funding for training, but also of encouraging sufficient supplies of potential workers into the industry. The Construction Industry Training Board points out that alternative careers and higher education courses absract much of the potential workforce away from the industry, which even today retains a mixed reputation.

- *How competitive is the building industry, particularly at the local level, and can it be made more competitive?*
  We saw evidence of concentration in the industry, even at local levels, and there is wider evidence of structural change favouring the national or volume house builders. (13) In Scotland, some of these 'big players' are Scottish firms - but the process of concentration is still apparent. Whether this leads to monopoly profits and inefficiency is a moot point, as many of the apparent sources of inefficiency seem to stem from more fundamental factors (such as subcontracting and land speculation).

- *How can the supply of land be suitably organised to provide efficient quantities at reasonable prices in appropriate locations to meet demand, taking account of other planning objectives?*
  Here we reach one of the most crucial issues. The operation of today's land market, with its processes of fragmented land ownership, land- banking and development gain, partly results from the system of planning permission and from the battle between builders and planners. Many economists argue that the present system confers few environmental benefits and land-use advantages; in their view, prices are too high, as are densities, and as a result the system generates at least as many harmful as beneficial effects. At heart, the issue is whether speculative profits are a suitable end for housebuilding, or whether the latter should instead be seen as a long-term business more closely linked to society's housing requirements. Arguably, the present-day planning system, particularly in heated markets, creates more incentives for the former than the latter.

Notes

1   D Maclennan, 'Housing in Scotland, 1977-87', in M Smith (ed.), *Guide to Housing* (third edition), 1989.
2   Maclennan, 'Housing in Scotland'.
3   M Gaskin, 'Housing and the construction industry', in D Maclennan and G Wood (eds), *Housing Policy and Research in Scotland*, 1977.
4   K Gibb, A McGregor and M Munro, 'Housebuilding in a recession: a regional case study', *Environment and Planning*, 29, 1997, 1739-58.
5   K Gibb, Regional Differentiation and the Scottish House Building Industry', *Housing Studies*, 1999 (forthcoming).
6   K Gibb and M Keoghan, 'Backward linkages from construction: exploring the economic development potential of Scottish building supplies', *Local Economy*, 13, November 1998, 6-23.
7   D Maclennan, *A Competitive UK Economy: The Challenge for Housing Policy*, York, 1994; D Maclennan, K Gibb and A More, *Fairer Subsidies, Faster Growth: Housing, Government and the Economy*, York, 1991; M Munro, *Beliefs, Perceptions and Expectations in the UK Owner Occupied Housing Market: Final Report to the ESRC Research Programme Economic Beliefs and Behaviour*, 1987.
8   W Baumol, J Panzar and R Willig, *Contestable Markets and the Theory of Industrial Structure*, 1982.
9   J Barlow and S Duncan, *Success and Failure in Housing Provision: European Systems Compared*, 1994.
10   M Ball, *Housing and Construction: A Troubled Relationship*, 1996.
11   Gaskin, 'Housing and the construction industry'.
12   Ball, *Housing and Construction*.
13   Ball, *Housing and Construction*.

Part C

MACTAGGART & MICKEL ARCHIVE

Summary Guide to Material in the National Monuments Record of Scotland

Introduction

The following list contains a summary guide to the Mactaggart & Mickel archive collection, which is at present being catalogued by the National Monuments Record of Scotland. It also functions as a provisional job list for all Mactaggart & Mickel developments from 1925 to the present day.

Detailed cataloguing of this unique collection is programmed for the next two years; after completion, archival information will be available through CANMORE, the NMRS database. The list below also includes references to drawings and other related materials which are not, at present, housed in the NMRS, but which will be deposited in due course. This summary guide is intended to provide an introductory overview to the collection, to highlight its breadth and diversity, to identify Mactaggart & Mickel developments in the central belt of Scotland, and ultimately to provide a future research resource for those interested in the history of private housebuilding.

The list is divided into two sections. The first section details the Mactaggart & Mickel holdings on specific owner-occupied and private rented schemes, and non-locational material; each entry can be interpreted with the help of a numbered key to the different categories of material. This first section also includes material relating to public housing contracts, including separate and all-trades contracts; these are all identified after the specific site name as follows: (CONTRACT). The

second section, arranged under archive type, summarises the small amount of non-Mactaggart & Mickel material within the archive; in each case a brief description of this material is given.

Key to categories of archive material

(1) **Drawings:** by contracted architects and in-house designers (from 1925 onwards) including the following types of material: survey plans, layout plans, house plans, elevations, sections, perspectives, construction details, patent construction type plans and details (see also under 1.4 for non-locational archive material), and plans for related buildings (offices, stores, and plant). The drawings may be in pencil, ink, coloured ink and wash, and on paper, linen, tracing paper or perspex. Where known, specific architects are listed under (1).

(2) **Photographs and negatives:** Black and white, and colour, photographs of house types, house construction, press and promotional events, staff, and other related activities from 1925 onwards.

(3) **Promotional material:** 17 large bound volumes of promotional cuttings relating to Mactaggart & Mickel developments, including advertising, promotional features, and newspaper and magazine articles relating to specific developments, 1932-97; sales brochures (including price lists), 1938-99; advertising display panels.

(4) **Other:** Specified under each individual entry. Where known, dates are given.

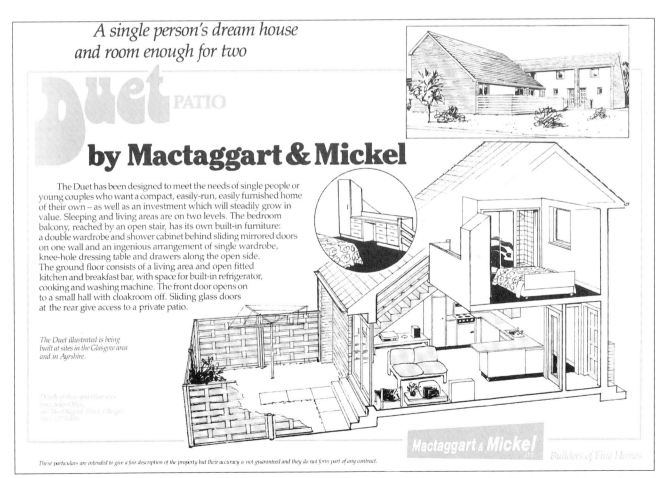

A single person's dream house and room enough for two

Duet PATIO

by Mactaggart & Mickel

The Duet has been designed to meet the needs of single people or young couples who want a compact, easily-run, easily furnished home of their own – as well as an investment which will steadily grow in value. Sleeping and living areas are on two levels. The bedroom balcony, reached by an open stair, has its own built-in furniture: a double wardrobe and shower cabinet behind sliding mirrored doors on one wall and an ingenious arrangement of single wardrobe, knee-hole dressing table and drawers along the open side. The ground floor consists of a living area and open fitted kitchen and breakfast bar, with space for built-in refrigerator, cooking and washing machine. The front door opens on to a small hall with cloakroom off. Sliding glass doors at the rear give access to a private patio.

The Duet illustrated is being built at sites in the Glasgow area and in Ayrshire.

These particulars are intended to give a fair description of the property but their accuracy is not guaranteed and they do not form part of any contract.

C1. *The 'Duet Patio', a one-bedroom Mactaggart & Mickel type designed by Buildings and Developments Manager Iain Drysdale in 1982, incorporated elements of open and split-level planning. As first built at Kingsburn, King's Park, the houses included integral garages. (MMC)*

C2. Cover of sales brochure for new phase of Mactaggart & Mickel's Higher Broom development, Broom North-East, c.1986. (MMC)

Mactaggart & Mickel archive

1.1 Glasgow

BALORNOCK 1948 (CONTRACT)
BARMULLOCH 1949 (CONTRACT)
BRAEHEAD 1952-54 ① John C C Munro;③
CARDONALD 1932-34 (CONTRACT)
CARNTYNE 1927-29 (CONTRACT) ①James Taylor, Joseph Wilson
CASTLEMILK 1955-56 (CONTRACT)
CASTLEMILK FUNERAL PARLOUR *c.*1952 (CONTRACT)
DRUMCHAPEL 1954-55 (CONTRACT)
GLASGOW GARDEN FESTIVAL, BROOM MILK BAR 1987-88 ①
②③
INGRAM STREET, RAMSHORN CHURCH ② small photograph album recording the refurbishment of the Ramshorn Church, Ingram Street, Glasgow, carried out by Mactaggart & Mickel, December 1991
KELVINSIDE 1926-59 ① John C C Munro, James Taylor; ②③
KELVINSIDE, ASCOT 1983 ③
KELVINSIDE, BEACONSFIELD 1960
KELVINSIDE, CHESTERFIELD COURT 1962 ③
KELVINSIDE, DORCHESTER, TERRITORIAL ARMY HOUSES 1954 (CONTRACT)
KELVINSIDE, DORCHESTER AVENUE, EARL HAIG FUND HOSPITAL 1951 ④ display panel, 1951
KELVINSIDE, DORCHESTER AVENUE/RIPON DRIVE, POLICE HOUSES 1952
KELVINSIDE, DORCHESTER COURT 1960-81 ②③
KELVINSIDE, HIGHFIELD DRIVE & CLEVEDEN PLACE 1963-70 ③
KELVINSIDE, NEW DORCHESTER 1981-82 ③
KELVINSIDE, SCOTTISH VETERANS GARDEN CITY ASSOCIATION 1949 ①
KELVINSIDE, WEYMOUTH COURT 1957 ③
KELVINSIDE, WHITTINGHAME COURT 1962-64③
KING'S PARK (CROFTFOOT) 1925-55 ① John C C Munro, William Ross, Joseph Wilson, James Taylor; ②③④ Douglas Mickel photograph album, 1929-31; log book listing prices and related costs of house types, 1931-34
KING'S PARK 1927-33 (CONTRACT)
KING'S PARK, BANKHEAD 1992-97 ③
KING'S PARK, CLUBHOUSE 1934① James Taylor
KING'S PARK, KILCHATTAN DRIVE 1971 ③
KING'S PARK, KINGSBURN 1979-82 ③
KING'S PARK, KINGSWAY COURT 1959③

KING'S PARK, SCOTTISH VETERANS' GARDEN CITY ASSOCIATION 1949 (CONTRACT)
KNIGHTSWOOD DEVELOPMENT 2 AND 3 1925-28 (CONTRACT)
LANARK STREET, HOMES FOR THE FUTURE 1997-99①Wren Rutherford ASL; ②③
LANGSIDE ROAD, PARKFIELD COURT 1992
POLLOK PRIMARY SCHOOL 1953 (CONTRACT)
SIMSHILL 1953-60 ①A Buchanan Campbell; ③
107 WEST REGENT STREET *c.*1960-90 ①

1.2 West of Scotland (except Glasgow)

AYR, BURTON 1976-86 ③
AYR, CASTLEHILL 1975-79③
AYR, DOONFOOT 1958-78 (INCLUDING EARL'S WAY AND ABBOT'S WAY 1962-64; KNOWEHOLM 1961-62; GREENAN ROAD AND CASTLE WALK 1969-78; GREENAN 1982-99) ③
AYR, DOONFOOT EXTENSION TO HMS SCOTIA CAMP 1943 (CONTRACT)
AYR, HEATHFIELD 1957-62 ③
AYR, MOUNT CHARLES 1969-78 ③
AYR, NETHER AUCHENDRANE 1975
BARRHEAD, AUCHENBACK 1949 (CONTRACT)
BROOM (ESTATE), AREAS A AND C 1934-39 ① P Abercrombie, James Taylor; ②③including *The Book of the Broom Estate*, 1938
BROOM B 1961-71③
BROOM 1-9 1957-74 ①②③
BROOM, BROOM COURT 1958 ②③
BROOM, BROOMBURN COURT 1958-61③
BROOM, BROOMCASTLE 1987-92 ③
BROOM, BROOMCLIFF 1966-71③
BROOM, BURNHOUSE BRAE 1998③
BROOM, CASTLE COURT 1961-62 ②③
BROOM, CASTLEFARM 1994-98 ③
BROOM, CASTLEFARM, GLENEAGLES GATE 1996-98
BROOM, THE DELL 1998-99③
BROOM, LITTLE BROOM 1967 ①②③
BROOM, LOCHBROOM COURT 1982-84②③
BROOM NORTH EAST (INCLUDING HIGHER BROOM) 1969-99 ②③
BROOM, ROBSHILL COURT 1978-83 ③
BROOM, SANDRINGHAM COURT 1938 ①W A Gladstone;③
BROOM, SHAWHILL CRESCENT 1957
BROOM SOUTH WEST (10, 11, 12) 1975-86③
BROOM, TOWNHEAD 1957-59 ③
BUCHANAN CASTLE EMERGENCY HOSPITAL 1940

(CONTRACT)
BURNSIDE, CRAWFURD GARDENS 1960
CLARKSTON, CAROLSIDE PARK 1934-60 ① James Taylor, ③
CLARKSTON, GREENBANK 1966-76 ③
CLARKSTON, GREENBANK COURT 1959-60 ③
CLARKSTON, GREENWOOD COURT 1957-58 ③
CLARKSTON, CARTSBRIDGE FARM 1975-76 ③
CLARKSTON, NEWFORD 1997-98 ③
DUMBARTON, BELLSMYRE 1947 (CONTRACT)
DUMBARTON, OVERTOUN ESTATE 1939-40 ① ③
DUMBARTON, GARSHAKE 1947-48 ① Joseph Wilson; ②
EAGLESHAM, ALEXANDER AVENUE 1963-66 ① ③
EAGLESHAM, HUMBIE ROAD 1966-72 ① ③
EAGLESHAM PARK 1994-97 ① A Buchanan Campbell; ③
EAGLESHAM, POLNOON 1970-84 ① ③
EAGLESHAM, RIVERSIDE 1960-67 ① ③
EAGLESHAM, RIVERSIDE COURT 1963-65 ① ③
EAGLESHAM, WATERFOOT/CRAIGLAW 1960-66 ① William
Vannan; ③
GREENOCK, AUCHMEAD 1954 (CONTRACT)
GREENOCK, LARKFIELD 1952 (CONTRACT)
GREENOCK, NEWARK STREET 1956 (CONTRACT)
GREENOCK, PENNYFERN 1953-57 (CONTRACT)
HELENSBURGH 1959-62 ③
INVERKIP, TERRITORIAL ARMY c.1955 (CONTRACT)
IRVINE, DREGHORN 1974-75 ② ③
IRVINE, MILL ROAD 1965-75 ③
IRVINE, PERCETON PADDOCK 1980 ③
IRVINE, WHITEHURST PARK 1975-78 ③
KILBARCHAN 1963-67 ① A Buchanan Campbell; ③
LARGS NO. 1 1935-38 ① James Taylor; ② ③
LARGS NO. 2 1939 ① ③
LARGS, BARR CRESCENT 1988-89 ③
LARGS, BRISBANE GLEN 1976-86 ③
LARGS, DANEFIELD 1955-57 ③
LINN PARK 1930-31 ④ log book listing prices and related costs of
house types, 1931-4
MAUCHLINE 1961-64 ③
MEARNSCROFT, 1986-96 ③
MERRYLEE PARK NO.1, 1931-34 ① Joseph Wilson, James Taylor;
② ③ ④ log book listing prices and related costs of house types, 1931-34
MERRYLEE PARK NO.2 1939-40 ③
MERRYLEE PARK 1948 & 1961 ① W A Gladstone; ③
MERRYLEE PARK, POLICE HOUSES 1960
MONTFODE 1984-98 ③
MOUNT FLORIDA, KINGSWAY COURT 1959 ③
MUIREND 1936-37 ① ③
MUIREND, DAIRSIE STREET 1985-86 ③
NETHERLEE PARK 1932-34 ① ③ ④ log book listing prices and
related costs of house types, 1931-34
OLD KILPATRICK AND DALNOTTAR, OIL STORAGE TANKS
1941 (CONTRACT)
ORCHARD PARK 1937-41 ① ③
ORCHARD PARK, HEATHWOOD 1977 ③
ORCHARD PARK, ORCHARD BURN 1982-83 ③
ORCHARD PARK, ORCHARD COURT 1959-61 ③
ORCHARD PARK, POLICE HOUSES 1939 ① C Davidson & Son
ORCHARD PARK, ROBSLEE DRIVE, FACTORY 1974-75 ①
A Buchanan Campbell
ORCHARD PARK, THORNWOOD COURT 1969 ③
ORCHARD PARK, TREEBURN 1985-87 ③
PAISLEY 1941 (CONTRACT) ①
PORT GLASGOW, ADMIRALTY NAVAL COMPLEX 1943-44
(CONTRACT)
PORT GLASGOW, BROADFIELD 1944 (CONTRACT)
RENFREW, COCKELS LOAN 1950 ①
ROUKEN GLEN 1931-33 ③ ④ log book listing prices and related costs
of house types, 1931-34
STEVENSTON 1939-40 ①
STEVENSTON, MAYFIELD 1962-69 ③
STEVENSTON, MEIKLEYARD 1952-61 ③
SYMINGTON 1970-72 ③
TROON, BARASSIE 1995-99 ③
TROON, LOANS 1969-78 ③
WEST KILBRIDE, GLENSIDE 1963-65 ③
WEST KILBRIDE, KIRKTONHALL 1966 ③
WEST KILBRIDE, OVERTON COURT 1959-63 ③
WEST KILBRIDE, SEAMILL, FULLARTON DRIVE 1965 ③

1.3 Edinburgh

ABERCROMBY PLACE 1993
BALERNO 1951-53 ① ③
BALERNO, JOHNSBURN 1987 ① ③
BALERNO, LOVEDALE 1979 ① ③
BONALY 1958-76 AND 1985-97 (INCLUDING BONALY BRAE
1974-75) ① William Vannan, L A Rolland; ③
BONALY, THE LOANINGS 1998-99 ① ③
BONALY, TORPHIN BANK 1995-97 ③
BROOMHALL 1952-55 ① ; ② Douglas Mickel photograph album,
1955; ③
BROOMHOUSE 1939-53 ① ②
BROOMHOUSE, 80-86 BROOMHOUSE ROAD 1944-45
CAIYSTANE 1958-64 ① ③
CAMMO 1956-65 ① ② Douglas Mickel photograph album, 1955; ③
CARRICK KNOWE 1936-37 ① Stewart Kaye
CLERMISTON DEVELOPMENT 1 AND 6 1953-55 (CONTRACT)
COLINTON 1937-38 ① Stewart Kaye
CRAIGCROOK 1976-90 ① ③
DRYLAW, LAWRENCE HOUSES 1952 (CONTRACT)
EAST CRAIGS 1980-82 ① ③
FORRESTER PARK 1965-78 AND 1974-78 ① ③
GILMERTON 1995-98 ① ③
GRACEMOUNT, DEVELOPMENT 3 AND 5 1956-57 (CONTRACT)
GRANTON, BUILDING TRADES TRAINING CENTRE 1945
(CONTRACT)
GRANTON, EAST PILTON 1933-36 ① Stewart Kaye
GRANTON, EAST PILTON, SHOPS AND HOUSING 1934-38 ①
Stewart Kaye
HILLPARK 1936-97 (INCLUDING HILLPARK LOAN 1973-75;
HILLPARK WOOD 1976-77; HILLPARK BRAE 1981-84; HILLPARK
COURT 1984-87; HILLPARK PINES 1989-98) ① W A Gladstone;
John Gray, Stewart Kaye, Rayack Construction Ltd; ② Douglas Mickel
photograph album, 1955; ③
MOREDUN AND OLD SAUGHTON, SHOPS 1950 (CONTRACT)
MUIRHOUSE, NORTHERN LIGHTHOUSE BOARD HOUSING
1952 (CONTRACT)
OLD SAUGHTON 1950 (CONTRACT)
PARSON'S GREEN 1934-35 ① Stewart Kaye; ③ ④ log book listing
prices and related costs of house types, 1931-34
PRINCESS MARGARET ROSE HOSPITAL 1939 (CONTRACT)
REDFORD ROAD, MARRIED OFFICERS' QUARTERS 1949
(CONTRACT)
SIGHTHILL, TEMPORARY OFFICES FOR MINISTRY OF WORKS
1947 (CONTRACT)
SILVERKNOWES 1935-74 ① John Gray, Stewart Kaye; ② photographs

C3. Sir John Arbuthnott, Principal of the University of Strathclyde (centre left),
seen with Lord Goold (centre right) and Mactaggart & Mickel site staff, outside
Ramshorn Church, Ingram Street, Glasgow, on the completion of its refurbishment
in December 1991. (MMC)

and Douglas Mickel photograph album, 1955; ③
SILVERKNOWES GLEBE 1996 ①③
SILVERKNOWES MAINS 1996 ①③
SOUTH GYLE 1979-97 ① L A Rolland; ③
STENHOUSE, SCOTTISH VETERANS' GARDEN CITY ASSOCIATION 1951 (CONTRACT)

1.4 East/Central/North Scotland (except Edinburgh)

BO'NESS, BLACKBURN HOUSES 1950 (CONTRACT)
BO'NESS, THE DRUM 1998-99 ① Wren Rutherford ASL
DALKEITH, WOODBURN ROAD 1948 (CONTRACT)
DOLLAR 1958-59
DANDERHALL, ATHOLL HOUSES 1947 (CONTRACT)
FALKIRK, LAURIESTON 1960-61 ①③
FALLIN, ATHOLL HOUSES 1947 (CONTRACT)
FORT WILLIAM 1932 ① bungalow, Stewart Kaye
GOREBRIDGE, ATHOLL HOUSES 1950 (CONTRACT)
KILLEARN EMERGENCY HOSPITAL 1939 (CONTRACT)
LOANHEAD, ATHOLL HOUSES 1947 (CONTRACT)
MILTON OF CAMPSIE 1953 (CONTRACT)
STONELEIGH 1956 (CONTRACT)
SOUTH MARKINHILL 1946 (CONTRACT)
WHITECROSS 1947 (CONTRACT)

1.5 Non-locational/other archive

Business correspondence

④ Letters, accounts, reports, and handwritten and official memos relating to Mactaggart & Mickel's building activities (and general housing issues in Scotland and Britain) from 1925 onwards; correspondence relating to the 'Ladies Syndicate', 1923-27.

Commemorative/anniversary-related material

④ '50 Years of Mactaggart & Mickel' folder containing advertising, newspaper cuttings, and promotional material, 1975.

Cuttings books

④ Three newspaper/magazine cuttings books, 1937-52, including cuttings on general housing issues (Scotland and Britain), and wartime and early postwar contracts carried out by Mactaggart & Mickel. Some general cuttings relating to housing are also interspersed in the main Mactaggart & Mickel advertising books; see above.

Douglas Mickel's personal archive

② Two photograph albums, dated 1929-31 and 1955, belonging to Douglas Mickel, including the following: student activities; family holidays; company offices; Mactaggart & Mickel staff; and site photographs (see also above under specific sites).

Exhibition-related material

①②③ Scottish Ideal Homes Exhibitions, 1955-57, ④ correspondence.

Plan types (non-traditional construction)

① Plans, elevations, and details of Patent Construction type; detail plans of timberless house, 1940; plan, cross section and elevations of Mansard timber construction three-apartment cottages, 1925, J Taylor; elevations cross-section and plan for type N3 (3 apartment) of patent Winget construction, 1927, James Taylor; full size details of Mactaggart & Mickel Patent Construction 5075/38, 1938; ② small photograph album showing Mactaggart & Mickel Patent Construction, 1948

Plan types (traditional construction)

① Plan types from 1925 onwards: plans, elevations, sections, and construction details of standard type plans (including executed, un-executed, un-identified). Architects/engineers: Alexander Buchanan Campbell; Iain Drysdale; L A M Fraser (Gratton & McLean); W A Gladstone; John Gray; Sydney T Gynn and Campbell Duff; Stewart Kaye; Derek Mickel; Bruce Mickel; William Ross; Stevenson & Fergusson; James Taylor; William Vannan; Williams & Williams Ltd.; Joseph Wilson; ② photographs and negatives of various house types, from c. 1927 onwards; ③ display panels of house types, from c. 1970 onwards.

Sales log books

④ Sales Department log book, March 1936 to October 1938; small log book listing prices, rates, down-payments, feu duties of various house types in Glasgow and Edinburgh (see also above under specific developments), 1931-34.

Scottish Veterans Garden City Association

① SVGCA housing ; ④ cuttings and memos relating to sites at: Earl Haig Gardens 1922-24, 31 houses; Liberton 1926, 5 houses; Muirhouse 1948-55, 86 houses; Corstorphine 1949, 2 houses; Stenhouse 1954, 5 houses; Juniper Green 1951-54, 2 houses.

Workplace views

② Photographs of offices, directors, employees, factory workers, and plant, from 1925; ① drawings of Shandwick Place office, Edinburgh, 1933, by Stewart Kaye; ① administrative office, Edinburgh, 1945, by W A Gladstone.

Section 2

Non-Mactaggart & Mickel archive

Andrew Mickel drawings

① Andrew Mickel drawings (including those for Andrew Mickel & Co.): block plan of houses at Stewart Drive, 1911; elevation, section and plan of eight terrace houses at Giffnock Road, Clarkston, 1914; plans of proposed terrace houses at Carolside Avenue, Clarkston, 1915; elevation and block plan of houses at Williamwood, 1915; block plan and plans of terraced houses at Carolside Avenue, Clarkston, 1918; elevation, section and plans of terraced houses at Giffnock Road, Clarkston, 1919; ④ small number of letters and memos relating to Andrew Mickel & Co, c.1911-19.

Western Heritable house types

① Plans, sections, elevations and cross-sections of eight house types by Joseph Wilson for Western Heritable Investment Co., 1933-34; estate layout plans, 1932-34, by John C C Munro.

Miscellaneous papers, plans, drawings

① Collection of Prestonplan Homes Ltd (Preston, Lancashire, England) drawings, 1970s, acquired by Mactaggart & Mickel following the take-over of Edward Ecrepont & Sons; proposed interwar bungalow design by J B Wright, for a site at Thorntonhall, for John Macdonald; Glasgow Corporation Housing Department house type drawings E, E1B, and N3, from 1929 onwards; copy of 1930s development plan of the Pollok estate for Sir John Stirling Maxwell; report and letters relating to the voluntary liquidation of J A Mactaggart & Co., 5 September 1925.

HISTORICAL INTERVIEW TRANSCRIPTS

Douglas Mickel

Statement to Edinburgh Corporation Sub-committee on the Progress of the Housing Programme, 3 February 1937 (Edinburgh City Archives)

The Committee chairman began by explaining that Mr Mickel had been invited at the suggestion of Councillor Horne, in view of his firm's successful experience in building houses.

The Chairman:
You have never up to the present tendered for any of our housing schemes?

Mr Mickel:
Not for Edinburgh schemes. We have done schemes for some of the largest authorities, but there were so many smaller people coming in and cutting prices to such an alarming extent (they have been finding it has not been a good policy) that we let the thing dry up a little bit and went on to this other system, and we have produced here in Edinburgh about 2,200 houses. We came over here on the Wheatley Scheme to begin with, because we had been the only people in Scotland who had been developing the Wheatley Scheme at all. We and our associated Company

have done 6,000 houses under the Wheatley Act, and it was that which first attracted us to Edinburgh. But we have been long established in Glasgow in the building trade, we are not a mushroom growth, and anything we take in hand we can see it through.

The Chairman:
I understand that your building in Edinburgh differs from ours, inasmuch as you have one specification?

Mr Mickel:
We have two types of houses - three and four apartment houses. We have variations in the construction of the oriel windows and the roofs, and you will find that our schemes have a considerable amount of sparkle about them in colour schemes. We have found that these two types of houses have been very attractive wherever we have gone, and people have clamoured to get into them. So we stuck to these particular types; there was no use experimenting with other types. It allows us to go ahead, our people get into the way of doing things, our men get into the way of working, and it becomes, as we say, a trick to get on with us.

The Chairman:
Your plan of organisation is very good, I understand?

Mr Mickel:
We have worked it up to a point now, even with our office establishment. We are of course not only letting houses, but selling houses as well all

C4. 1991 aerial view of East Pilton, Edinburgh, showing 1930s developments by Mactaggart & Mickel for private rental (in foreground) and by Edinburgh Corporation for public rental (in background). (RCAHMS B69852)

over the country, as you will see from our advertisements; so we have to have proper organisation, otherwise we would be in a state of chaos. I have an organisation here which I instituted when I came through to start in Granton first, and at times I have been very perturbed about not having something in front of me to keep that organisation going - perturbed in case I was not going to get land quick enough. Once I break up my organisation, it is a great business to gather it up again. We have drawn bricklayers into Edinburgh from all parts of the country, and that sort of thing.

The City Chamberlain:
You are still finding a demand for your private enterprise houses to let?

The Chairman:
Do you have any scarcity of bricklayers?

Mr Mickel:
I can produce the bricklayers if I get the work to do.

Councillor Trainer:
Have you many apprentices?

Mr Mickel:
The apprentices just now are somewhat lacking. Of course we ourselves are in no masters' association of any kind, and the masters have come to some arrangement for registering apprentices only through their association, and we are handicapped that way. We have very few apprentices. Now you have asked that question, the solution for bricklayers is a greater number of apprentices than we have got. I don't think the dilution of labour is a very good thing, but I think a greater number of apprentices should be brought in, because one can see from the number of houses you require, and that all the greater local authorities require, that we will be engaged for the next ten years building brick houses.

Councillor Trainer:
If you got the promise of five years' continuity of work and we guaranteed 3,000 or 2,000 houses, could you do it?

Mr Mickel:
Yes, if you do not delay in giving me the ground. Give me the plans, the ground, and the streets and roads into it if possible. I have already at Colinton spent £750 on sleeper roads, and I have only been there a few months, and they are crying out for more sleepers because they cannot get access to the place.

The City Chamberlain:
How many houses are you building just now under the Treasurer's Committee scheme?

Mr Mickel:
We are just finishing off about 1,144 at Gorgie now, and we are on a scheme in Colinton of three developments covering a thousand houses.

Councillor Banks:
What exact number could you build per annum of the type that we erect?

Mr Mickel:
Slum-cleared houses or two-storeyed houses? - Both.

Councillor Banks:
Suppose we asked you to give us 2,000, or 1,500, could you do it?

The Chairman:
Say we come to a thousand a year. Could you do it within a year, with the variation in the designs of the houses that we have here in Edinburgh?

Mr Mickel:
Would you give me a typical plan - how do you propose to deal with this? Not through schedules, but at a fixed price?

The Chairman:
Oh well, we have the Department of Health.

Mr Mickel:
But the Department of Health will take it the other way too - a fixed price. If you will give us a typical house, and your Director of Housing will say what he would like to pay for it, we will say whether we can give you it at that price, or we will give you a price. Then any under-building is paid for at schedule rates - that is a thing that varies - and any fancy 'frills', as the Department of Health call them, you pay for them. As we

all know just now, the cost of material is soaring, we do not know where it is going to end. The timber merchants had a meeting last week where they laid down the rule that unless you take up your contract within a certain period, they won't hold it for you, so we are getting worse and worse. If you care to fix a price - after that if you want so many houses per annum if prices go up or down we will meet you one way or other - we will make a basis, a dative line. But we can buy as cheap as anybody in the trade. Mr Crichton will tell you there has been no lack of bricks on our job. Has there?

The Depute Town Clerk:
Not so far as I know.

The Chairman:
Do you think the Department of Health would agree to that?

Mr Mickel:
I am sure the Department would agree, and be delighted.

Councillor Banks:
If you got contracts of that nature would it interfere with your private enterprise? Could you go on with both without one or the other suffering?

Mr Mickel:
Oh yes, I could go on with both.

Baillie Milne:
And with local bricklayers?

Mr Mickel:
I am not going to be tied down to local bricklayers, because of where they are.

The City Chamberlain
Where would you get the bricklayers?

Mr Mickel:
I will not tell you where I would get them.

The Chairman:
We would not like them to come from Ireland.

Councillor Banks:
Are there special inducements at the moment in the West, say Glasgow, for the bricklayers? Are they getting a guaranteed week?

Mr Mickel:
That is a thing I cannot answer, because I understand they have not got permission from the Department of Health to introduce it. We are waiting to hear of this. The Scottish Contractors' Association sent a representative to interview me last week, and asked what our view was on that. I said, 'I am not in favour of a guaranteed week, but I would be quite willing to consider any scheme that you care to put before us to get over this outcry against wet weather.' Because I may say I have every sympathy with the men in wet weather. But the great difficulty has been, who is to be the judge of wet weather?

The Depute Town Clerk:
That is what will bring it to grief in Glasgow.

Mr Mickel:
And if it was adopted all over, you would just come back to where you were.

The City Chamberlain:
Is not the fundamental thing that there is a shortage of bricklayers? There is more work going on in the country than there are bricklayers to do?

Mr Mickel:
I know a good many schemes would take more bricklayers if they could get them.

The Chairman:
If we gave you a thousand houses, would you have any difficulty in getting the labour for these houses?

Mr Mickel:
I will get the labour, but do not put any restrictions on me.

The Chairman:
If we get anything, it must be under Trades Union conditions.

Mr Mickel:
Oh yes, with Trades Union conditions. As a matter of fact, the Trades Unions will tell you that we are most helpful to them.

Councillor Trainer:
If you got five years' continuity of work, would that help?

Mr Mickel:
I would be quite willing with what the Convener suggests, 1,000 houses.

Councillor Trainer:
Would that not be an inducement to the men?

Mr Mickel:
I do not think it is a bit of an inducement. If there were any inducements in other places, they would go. There is a certain shortage, and you have to be very careful how you handle them.

The Chairman:
On your private enterprise jobs for us, is it the case that you have to pay extra for labour?

Mr Mickel:
We have to pay for travelling - we must give them their travelling money.

Councillor Banks:
At a fixed price, would you adhere to the City Architect's specification as to materials?

Mr Mickel:
I would adhere to the specification which you have got from the Department of Health, which is a printed circular, the standard specification.

The City Chamberlain:
Does that mean home materials?

The City Architect:
Yes.

Mr Mickel:
But there must be no laying down that you have to have home-made doors, for instance, because you are going to run yourselves into extra expense. We might put in home-made doors, or we might not. I have told Mr MacRae he has got to make up his mind to use alternatives; the material is not available. You will see that steel cannot be got now; the blast furnaces are going to shut down for want of scrap. A great deal of steel is used in the making of our rain-water goods. British cement has all gone up in price. You have to bring in the foreign stuff, even with the tariff on it, to keep down the other price. We are quite willing to use British stuff all along the line, but you will perhaps be stuck for certain things.

The City Chamberlain:
If you consider the building industry as a whole, if the work were rationed, the shortage of materials would disappear. If the Government said, munition factories are to be first, then housing, then schools and public buildings - if they did it that way, you would get that result.

Mr Mickel:
We tried that but we found it very poor with the DBMS.

The City Chamberlain:
We had experience of the DBMS too. But suppose all the Dean of Guild Courts in the country were told that they are not to pass plans for cinematographs and so on, you would achieve the same result?

Mr Mickel:
No, I do not think these things work at all. There would be all kinds of manoeuvres to get things passed - a hospital is very necessary, a church is very necessary, as are public health clinics and schools - what are you going to stop?

The City Chamberlain:
The Government are going into it at the moment. There are things you need not replace, you can keep them from replacing old schools and a lot of other things.

Mr Mickel:
You would need more new schools and clinics and hospitals. You cannot stop them. The more you look into it, the worse it becomes.

Councillor Trainer:
But you are quite sure you could give us these houses if you had a free hand?

Mr Mickel:
Yes, I think we could give you the houses.

The Chairman:
You have stated that you have first of all to get the lower part, and then we would be liable for any alterations that take place. Is that not complicated?

Mr Mickel:
No, it is not a bit complicated. There is the house as arranged, there is the house as built, there is the price. You have a line drawn, your damp-course or your wall-head. Underneath that it is just measured, at a rate that we have already fixed. A record is kept - No.1 house has three feet of under-building, and anything Mr MacRae wants in the way of a fancy dormer window or anything of that kind, he pays for it.

Mr Murchison:
That is more or less how we work at the present time. The Department of Health arrange that the house itself is paid for at a fixed figure, as brought out in a Schedule of Quantities, and there is a re-measurement of the foundations below a certain level.

Mr Mickel:
We do not want to go to the expense and trouble of a re-measurement of the main building.

Mr Murchison:
There is no re-measurement on any of our housing schemes.

Mr Mickel:
Well, what I would like to get - and I think it would be quite an easy matter - is for Mr MacRae to say, 'There is the house, there is the price we are willing to give you - can you do it?' Every day, prices are going up, and they won't cover you for timber just now at all. I have just been told that bricks are going up in price again.

Councillor Banks:
How many can a man lay a day?

Mr Mickel:
I am not going to say.

Councillor Banks:
How many houses per annum could he produce?

Mr Mickel:
I think it used to be said that one man could produce one house per annum. If we give you the goods, I don't think these questions arise.

The Chairman:
What are the capabilities of a bricklayer?

Mr Mickel:
I am not going to say; some will say 600, some 800, some more and some less. You had a very good example of that at the time of the war at Renfrew Aerodrome, where they were laying 80. They were indispensable, but they were laying 80 bricks a day. It depends on the type of man. I had one today who said he could lay two thousand bricks, but it all depends on the class of wall.

The Chairman:
You have explained, Mr Mickel, that if you had a thousand houses you could get the labour?

Mr Mickel:
Yes, if you adjust a price and a typical house. Not too many variations, because, when you come on to variations, you are slowing down; it makes all the difference. We can give variations in colour schemes, but variation in plan and design is a different matter. I would rather look after a scheme of 500 houses than possibly build a church, because everything there is detail. If we can help you in any way, we will be very pleased to do so.

C5. George Bowie (on right) seen with Glasgow Housing Convener David Gibson in 1962, inspecting a model of Cranhill Extension multi-storey development, a project pushed through to compensate for delays with the Sighthill site. (Glasgow Herald)

Interview 2

George Bowie,
former Chief Architect, Crudens Ltd

Interviews with Miles Glendinning, 3 November 1987 and 15 March 1990

Outline of own career

I trained at Edinburgh (Ian Arnott was in my year) and qualified as an architect in 1952. After a brief sojourn in Kirkcaldy, I went to work for two years (February 1953-February 1955) in the London County Council Housing Department, where I became a group leader. Then I worked briefly in the Coal Board for six months, followed by four years (1955-60) with Alison Hutchison & Partners, working on schools, where the firm had made its reputation: there I became an associate partner, and led the team that won the Paisley Technical College competition. Finally, I was approached by Crudens in February 1960, and joined as chief architect, a post I held until June 1982. Because of RIBA professional rules, I wasn't able to become a director at first, but eventually I was able to become chief architect and director at the same time.

Life at the London County Council

Life at the LCC was great fun. We all did as we pleased, there was no discipline or central control. You just ignored the design briefs and got on with designing what you, as an architect, thought was best for people! Thereafter, wherever you went, because you'd been at the LCC, you thought you were a bit special. It was easily the liveliest place in the UK, and to get in was quite difficult. My own work at the LCC included five-storey housing work near Bermondsey and King's Cross, and helping out as part of one of the Roehampton design teams for a couple of months.

Early days at Crudens

Harry Cruden, founder of the firm, had a vision of an organisational set-up which was fairly new at the time. This was that if you put all the professions under one roof and pulled them together, and combined them with contracting, and went out to work without being tied to the architect's or engineer's way of doing things, that this would be much more efficient. He saw that this was the way the market was going to go. During the 1940s and '50s, the firm had been occupied building a low-rise system, but by the late '50s, it was becoming clear that the time for that had passed. Cruden then turned to his new managing director and said, 'Let's find an architect!' Which was where I came in. When I arrived, the firm was a very small set-up, but in the early 1960s our workload went through the roof very quickly: I felt I was part of a brave new world! We had one pair of multi-storeys on the

drawing-board, at Whorterbank in Dundee. Gracemount, in Edinburgh, was already just under construction: there we were using Truscon, the reinforced concrete people, to help. At Whorterbank, we began by tendering to build two blocks to the design of the SSHA. The drawings supplied for our bid were given to me when I arrived, and they asked me, 'George, could you design something better than that?' I set to and got on with it, and, much to the chagrin of the previous designers, we were awarded that contract for our own designs.

Internal organisation during the 1960s

At our peak in the late '60s, I had a staff of about 75-100 architects, and getting on for 200 engineering staff, plus quantity surveyors. Our director of publicity was a quantity surveyor called Alec Gillies: he left the firm in the late 1960s. At our largest, we had offices in Edinburgh, Glasgow, London and north-east England (Peterlee New Town). Initially, everything was done in Musselburgh. Then, after a while, we set up an office in Glasgow and it did its share of the architectural work associated with the west of Scotland - although engineering work was always still done in Musselburgh. Then, finally, came the Peterlee and London offices.

The managing director was Malcolm R A Matthews, followed by Andrew Hughes (he had been the number two until then). Marketing in Scotland, from the late '60s, was dealt with by Harry Corner, previously chief housing architect in Edinburgh; marketing in England was the province of Wilfred Forgham. One of the most prominent quantity surveyors was Angus Gilchrist - now a director with Cruden Homes - who joined in 1959 and negotiated nearly every contract.

The main professional division within my department was between the architects and the engineers. Designing high blocks was often far more an engineering problem than an architectural problem: engineering for the foundations, for the roads, for the sewers, for the blocks themselves. For example, there was a sunlight rule that was specific to the Scottish regulations, and it was up to the engineers to sort that out. The architecture, bit by bit, became cosmetics, until a good engineer could say 'Could you not move this ...?' Suddenly, you'd find your engineers designing your whole block for you!

Relations with private architects, and own architectural preferences

Private architects and 'LCC types' were jealous about the work we were getting, but they couldn't touch us on efficiency! There's a going rate for any particular size of council house. Even if a local authority tried to push more things into that box, the going rate never changed. When the scheme went back up to the Scottish Development Department for approval, they assessed it in accordance with that figure - and all the additions were taken out again. We were sceptical about the architectural press: how a building was photographed, crisp or dreich, would depend on whether they were praising or condemning it!

My ideal concept of housing architecture around the time I started at Crudens was Roehampton, Roehampton, Roehampton! The memory of my brief stay in the Roehampton design team in the LCC had stayed with me. Ideally, I'd have gone for point blocks with four dwellings per floor, 15 or so storeys, concrete frame structure with repetitive cladding units clipped on, with some four-storey staircase or balcony access flats set around them, along with a few one-storey houses for old folks. Personally, I considered it was behind the times to be doing what we were

C6. The Sighthill site, Glasgow, seen in 1960 before reclamation. (Glasgow District Council)

C7. Crudens's Sighthill redevelopment of 1963-69, including ten 20-storey slab blocks. (RCAHMS A55620)

doing, building with straightforward cavity walls - and so that's why, when we moved into the Skarne large-panel system, I was a great enthusiast for it! Yet our cavity wall blocks have given next to no trouble in terms of water penetration or condensation.

Local government and housing

One important aspect of the postwar housing drive, especially the era of the multis, was that it all happened before local government reorganisation. The complexity was unbelievable! For example, North Berwick had its own burgh engineer and engineer's committee, and ran its own show. These disparities affected even large authorities, too. None of the cities we dealt with, including even Edinburgh and Glasgow, were fully equipped to deal with the building and proper management of large-scale housing work: the tendency was to let things ride, in one area or another. They might say, 'Well, gentlemen, this is a Wimpey appointment, a Crudens appointment or whichever, and if we want to hear more, we should call them'. There was a sense in some authorities that time didn't matter - so the sudden push, the 'we've got to build a lot of houses in a hurry!' caught them unprepared. I got the feeling from all three city architects I dealt with - Archibald Jury in Glasgow, Robert Dron in Dundee, Alex Steele in Edinburgh - that city politicians could knock some of the bounce out of the salaried officials. Alex Steele of Edinburgh was highly approachable, and the most go-ahead of the three. We got on fine, and in fact he treated me almost as his protege. In Dundee, I got on splendidly with Dron; he was a very nice old chap, but he just didn't have the technical staff to keep on top of things. Dundee was one of the very worst places of all, in terms of professional organisation. It always amazed me that here there was a substantial city, without a meaningful department of architecture at all. There was a city engineer and a city architect, with only half a dozen or so staff. So it had to dish out all its professional tasks to other people. Dron's involvement was in making recommendations to committee, in trying to slot away chunks of housing to various agencies.

In the late 1950s, with the growing pressure for output and high-density building, it became known among contractors that particular authorities were contemplating large programmes. We had marketing people going all over the country, and it wasn't difficult for them to find out these authorities' technical capability or otherwise. So it became obvious that this place or that place would be having to get things onto the drawing board, to QS stage, and then on to building. If it became known, for instance, as happened in 1958, that Edinburgh were wanting to get their programme under way with negotiated contracts for 14 blocks, it was our job to make sure we got our share! Some authorities were a bit different from the others, and wanted things very much their way. For example, at Clydebank, they wanted four flats per floor. But that was the exception rather than the rule.

In general, I avoided direct contacts with the politicians - my job was the technical side. There were other people in the firm who were in constant contact with them; but my only contact was usually at committee stage, and, funnily enough, despite the huge size of many of the projects, that was often a very brief contact indeed. What would happen was that you'd go along and present the drawings to the Housing Committee - other people would pontificate a bit, then someone would say, 'We've got Mr Bowie from Crudens here, who's going to explain about the scheme.' Then I'd say, 'There are three 20-storey blocks, with 120 three-apartment and 240 four-apartment dwellings', and so on. Then, 'Any questions?' 'How's it going to be heated?' 'That hasn't been decided yet.' 'Where's the children's play space going to be, Mr Bowie?' 'That'll be designed later.' 'Anything else?' 'No, that'll be all, thank you, Mr Bowie.' Then that would be it through! I used to joke, in Dundee for instance, that there was often far lengthier discussion about rebuilding public lavatories than about doing multi-storeys!'

The multi-storey drive

High flats came along for several reasons. I'll list them, not in order of importance. First, there was a need for housing in a hurry, linked to the misconception that multis can go up more quickly than other types - although, certainly, using point blocks is an easy way to develop small sites, so long as you aren't tied to other requirements like numbers of car parking spaces. Second, they were seen as a way to get rid of the old slums, and in the process free the ground for open space - the Corbusier vision. Third, Scotland is covered with 'multis' anyway, as a nation living in tenements since the year dot - so it wasn't such a big step. Fourth, and not least, there was prestige: if you were a councillor and you went trotting down to Glasgow or London, or were taken on a trip to the Interbau experimental housing area in Berlin, and saw impressive multi-storey blocks, prestigious buildings, you'd say: 'We must have a few of these!' You'd get places like Buckhaven and Methil: there's only one reason why there are multis there. They'd say, 'If Kirkcaldy and Dunfermline can have multis, by God we're gauny have a couple too!' In many respects, the builder would be happier building two-storey houses. At any level, politicians are influenced by what they see and what they're told. I might mention something about, say, Corbusier's architecture to a councillor at a committee meeting, and the next time I bumped into him, he'd proudly tell me, 'Do you know, George, we've got six multis on the go, standing on those - what d'ye call them - pilotis?' Sometimes multis were a spin-off from something else, such as a low-rise contract - for example at Niddrie in Edinburgh, where there were 700 walk-ups as well.

Evolution of package-deal multi-storey block types

The block type which was most popular with authorities had six flats on each upper floor. It was flexible because you could have four three-apartment houses on the

outside and smaller two-apartments in the middle. The first time we had built it was at Gracemount, in Edinburgh, before I started, and I then had to develop it as circumstances required. To take one example of that development: there was a building regulation which required that each flat should have slightly more than two-thirds of its perimeter on an outside wall, to get a kind of through-ventilation. The only way to get it, in the smaller flats, was by insetting into the sides. Wimpey did this by staggering the block, shunting the two-apartments, but as an architect, I preferred a simple rectangle, and creating insets, or 'lungs', in the side. We developed that feature steadily, for instance by introducing 'handed' lungs to reduce external walling and reduce thermal loss, or by manipulation of the building regulations and adding further identical block units to the plan, to eventually get 12 or 18 flats per floor. That continued into the Skarne era. For example, the Jackson Street Coatbridge blocks, built from 1967, got by with only two lungs; the only Skarne without lungs was at Clydebank.

That development process was a two-way thing. Long before the Gracemount blocks were built, we were already promoting them and, at the same time, evolving the design in response. Our marketing people were going round and saying to local authorities, 'If you come to Gracemount, you can see the frame coming out of the ground, and if not, here's a model, and some approximate costs'. And they were asking the authority whether they'd view kindly the same formula, or a slightly different permutation. That way the process of evolving the block type began. People have the idea that package deals were inflexible and repetitive. Nothing could be further from the truth. The whole process was one of interaction. There never was a completely standard block! No authority ever came and looked at anything we did and said, 'Can we have three of those?' - there were always ifs and buts! Having got yourself a contract, your marketing people would tell you, 'Here's another local authority, Falkirk want a scheme, why not bash on?' We'd say, 'If you can come, you can see the frame coming out of the ground, if not then here's a model, and some approximate costs'. Then the authority would say, 'We can start in four weeks'. We'd say, 'Here's the block'. The authority would look at it and say, 'We do like it, but we'd like the following things, only tiny wee things, like a slightly bigger kitchen and different windows, Mr Bowie - and can we have a clothes drying area inside the block, and a play area on the ground floor?' - and so on, and so on! Also our designers and engineers were getting cleverer and cleverer, so we incorporated improvements. It always annoyed us - every time we got a job, another set of working drawings always had to be done! Or the building regulations, say for sunlight and daylight, would change. Or, as at Sighthill in Glasgow and Ardler in Dundee, people would come along looking for bigger blocks, and we could stick two or three together in a line. People thought the blocks were the same, but they couldn't be: they were developing, they were being done more efficiently.

There's no doubt that the blocks did evolve through an attempt to 'improve' them, through a constant balancing of performance and economy. But that balance was different for the client and for ourselves. The authorities were concerned with usable floor areas, which had to conform to the standards set down, but had to avoid being much larger than the standards. Our aim was economy in a combination of floor area and wall area per room, within the constraints of the authorities' briefs and the building regulations. We would work out alternatives, and get our quantity surveyors to work to prove which was the best way from Crudens's point of view. The local authorities were not really concerned in such detail with 'value for money'. They had an 'acceptable figure' that they were prepared to pay the builder for, say, a two bedroom flat. If we could do that more efficiently than anyone else, that would mean a higher profit margin. And our sales drive, what we could offer people in the future, built on that. We'd say, for example, 'Let's cut out balconies in the next blocks, and instead go up a little higher, say to 23 storeys, but no more than that, or we'll have to put in more lifts'. Those were the kinds of factors we had to balance all the time.

Competitors

At the beginning, we never had the feeling that Wimpeys and ourselves were major competitors. They were far bigger, and were doing enormous numbers of walk-up flats in no-fines concrete. We were starting from a small base, and growing fast. So nobody in Crudens bothered two hoots about, say, Bison or Wimpeys. We were doing pretty well! I got the impression that Wimpeys were better than Crudens at persuading the local authority to accept a standard block. Often, when you got a brief, the only thing the local authority produced was a master plan - and these often contained distinctive block 'footprints', which might reflect the travels and visits of the housing committees and the company sales teams around the country. In the design brief, you're shown a nice layout, you'd get, say, Callendar Park, Falkirk, and you'd say, 'They've done our profile!' or 'They've done Wimpey's profile!' It was a clue as to whose salesmen had done the best job!

System building: Skarne

The big pressure to go for prefabricated construction systems began around 1962. The reason for it was certainly not, as is sometimes claimed now, to cut costs. In fact, people always knew they would cost more. The reason was the shortage of building resources, combined with the push to increase output, especially in the form of high blocks. I first really became aware of this movement at a big conference on prefabrication at the Cement and Concrete Association, 'Houses from the Factory', in late 1962, addressed by Cleeve Barr and others. At about that time, the Scottish Office and the English Ministry of Housing produced circulars which made very clear the pressure to push on and build more dwellings. And, what with the massive labour shortage, it was necessary to encourage techniques which reduced the labour content. So authorities would be allowed to negotiate contracts with a firm which had a reputable system. Prior to then, we'd avoided any attempt to be pioneers in construction; we had used Truscon to build our reinforced concrete frames for us, in early schemes like Cranhill in Glasgow. But right away, it became obvious we should acquire a system, and I and my opposite numbers shot off to Europe, to Denmark or Sweden and so on. In effect, it was the government, politically, that was shouting about low-labour factory-made multi-storey blocks, and they sent a lot of us chasing off to get something, almost anything, signed up on the Continent!

We nearly got the licence for Jespersen, but eventually we signed up with Skarne, a Swedish system. We paid the Swedish people to come over here and help us to set it up. Then we could begin going round the housing committees, telling them, 'We'd be happy to fly you to Sweden and see it'. For example, Harry Corner, then the chief housing architect in Edinburgh, might ring up and say, 'I'm very interested in your system.' I'd reply, 'There's none built in Scotland yet, but there's Stockholm! Do you want us to fix a trip, Harry?' He'd say, 'Well, let's say, take three or four people: the city architect, the housing chairman, and Councillor X or Y'.

Skarne, originally, was a technique using an in-situ core with precast walls hung off it. Projects fully under way before then were completely in-situ - for example, Sighthill in Glasgow. But even before Skarne we'd started building all our multis with an in-situ core, and precast walls - not precast columns, as those were still in-situ. Examples of that approach included Sighthill THA in Edinburgh. In the mid-1960s, there was a kind of half-way Skarne, excluding the cladding. Then by the time you got to, say, Jackson Street in Coatbridge, in 1967, the construction had become full Skarne. The first completely precast job was actually for two-storey houses, in Peterlee, north-east England. Then, using Skarne, we were able to become much bolder in where we looked for contracts. For example, from 1967 we built two big Skarne developments (Milton Court Road and Evelyn Court) in Lewisham, in London, totalling around a thousand houses.

Our first precast concrete factory was built in Livingston. We put it there because Peter Daniel, the first chief architect of the new town, had been on the Skarne trip, and he was determined to build the whole of Livingston in systems. Thereafter there was one factory in Dundee, one in Peterlee, one in Basildon. Suddenly we had a system, and life became very tough! Because nobody in central or local government, and I mean nobody, was prepared to contemplate buildings using the degree and scale of repetition required to make factory-based systems viable - as they did in the USSR. That meant that the average prefabrication system was a trap for the local authorities, who'd convinced themselves that it was far quicker than it really was: they'd been looking through rose-tinted spectacles. And, financially speaking, it was a trap for the builders, who went into it for the wrong reasons, as a marketing exercise. To start off with, precasting something took a tremendous amount of work anyway. The volume of drawing-board staff work for precast is 10 or 15 times that for in-situ, the cost of providing documentation is enormous compared to in-situ - and you always get mistakes! At its maximum in the late '60s, the engineering drawing-board staff in our office went up to 250 or 300 people, apportioned between various jobs. But changes multiplied this work even more. The tiniest of little changes, like changing the edge detailing, spat out all sorts of new requirements for redrawing! And some people in the National Building Agency tried to hammer us into designing in a grid, something which is utterly ludicrous when you're dealing with precast. We had to do two sets of drawings, one to satisfy the NBA and the other, real set for the use of the poor chap who actually had to build it. Really, builders aren't interested in centres, just in distances between faces!

When the craze for systems began, we had to acquire one - but 'systems' was and is a marketing vehicle. People would come and say, 'We want your system', but they didn't get it! Lots of times when we were busy we got our precast elsewhere than in the Skarne factory. As the thing developed, I'd find us precasting ground-floor slabs in four-storey blocks, say at Whitfield in Dundee, and I'd say 'That's rubbish!' Strictly speaking, that was what the 'system' involved, and so the engineers would automatically start doing it. But it didn't make economic sense to do it! At Whitfield, where the ends of the blocks are built into the ground, the ground floor would be in-situ, whereas the upper floors would go back to precast. And with the two-storey Skarne housing in England, I made a point of saying, 'Where the blocks sit into the ground, make it in-situ!' Then very soon we said, 'Skarne - so what! We won't precast the floors any more: just the walls!' It became delightfully vague, even in the terms of the contracts, where 'Skarne' wasn't mentioned! After all, what does it really amount to - just casting large lumps of concrete!

We hadn't thought the economics of the whole thing through - and we and many other firms paid the price when the systems bubble burst in the late '60s and early '70s, especially when the contractors started getting driven to the wall by inflation. The local authorities could just walk away, as happened in cases like Killingworth. We were left with the factories and the wasted investment!

Glasgow multi-storey projects

The first multis we did in Glasgow were at Cranhill, beginning in 1963. That particular site began, literally, as a dump! We had a very good relationship with Lewis Cross, the man at the top of Glasgow housing, the depute housing officer, in the city architect's department. He threw at us the challenge of negotiated contracting. We got those jobs, because of the shortage of high-calibre technical people in the architect's department. At Cranhill, we put in chemical engineers, and then put in a scheme, with special costs for the foundation work. And all the time, someone in our organisation was putting in a long hard look at a far bigger industrial reclamation site, at Sighthill.

In Glasgow, there was very little active guidance, in a planning sense, from the city. On the part of the planners, the most consistent theme was a concern to make the contractor-designed multis more interesting to look at, more like Basil Spence's

blocks at Hutchesontown. And, to be honest, some of the things Sir Basil did, I'd have liked to have done, too! But I'd got a lot of stick for the complexity of some of my early multis at Sighthill Neighbourhood Centre, Edinburgh, where I tried to make them more interesting with three-dimensional ramps and so on. There were divisions within the local authorities: you'd find that architect X didn't get on with planner Y. The chief planner in Jury's department, Ron Nicoll, was a very bright bloke, but he had some dreams for the city that didn't fit in with the aims of the housing faction! On the housing side, Lewis Cross was a superb, likeable chap. But I reckon, in his own, quiet, smiling way, that he was a pretty powerful person. If you didn't get on with Cross, you wouldn't get far. He gave the impression of having a high degree of integrity, yet he knew the right way to push on and get the results! I always got the feeling he was pro-Crudens - because we could perform. For the same reason, he was against the city's direct labour organisation. He was pretty scathing about some of the officialdom in the city, about some of the mistakes made - for example, about the fact that the city had awarded a multi-storey contract to Crudens at Govan when the Corporation didn't actually own the site, so that they found themselves paying vast sums to us every month. We didn't mind not building those blocks!

Sighthill (Glasgow)

One day, around 1961, two years before the eventual contract, my managing director came along with a piece of tracing paper, with what turned out to be the final shape of Sighthill on it, and a scale - it was ridiculous! - and he said, 'How many dwellings can you put on this site?' I replied, 'You've got access roads, daylight and sunlight to consider!' He said: 'Just put multis on it and some low rise.' So in a day I knocked together some thoughts, and then he asked, 'Could you make a model?' I said, 'There's nothing to make a model of!' But we put together this thing with matchboxes, and he went away with it. A few days later, he took me over to Sighthill in his Jag, and asked, 'What do you think?' I said, 'Jesus Christ!' The site was a vast chemical dumping ground, which would require huge reclamation work. So we had to do tremendous amount of site exploration work at our own risk. We proved it would work by undertaking a massive trial earth-shifting exercise. Sites like this were far more an engineering than an architectural matter. Quite soon we had a master plan knocked up - we had to alert everyone around the site. And then, beginning in 1963, construction of the project went on ahead, and when the first multis were done, providing we weren't naughty boys, there were several phases. So...[in due course] you'd say, 'It's about time we were thinking of Phase 3, Mr Cross'. He'd say, 'Just leave it with me,' then he'd ring up one day and say, 'If I were you, I should be putting in Phase 3 submissions now'. Because of massive financial constraints, the design frills disappeared bit by bit. And bit by bit, you got used to graffiti, vandalism - the heart slightly got knocked out of the original vision! To me today, the scale of Sighthill seems really too harsh.

Dundee

The unions were frighteningly influential in Dundee: we used to say that the unions' hourly rate was the sum of money they earned to come through the gate! - and thereafter they earned massively on bonuses. We succeeded there because we were prepared to take the large opportunities that were on offer, and run with them! Our two most spectacular developments in Dundee were Ardler and Whitfield. Ardler began with some high-density walk-up housing in the early '60s. Then the firm of architects who were designing the walk-up housing near Ardler were given a design brief for high flats on the site. They did a wildly impracticable proposal for a zigzag 'snake block' - that was why they eventually didn't get the job! Meanwhile, we'd bought some land by the site from a local golf club, and we approached the council. I was asked to take a look at the site, to see if we could develop it ourselves for the council. I shattered everyone by saying that the brief would require the equivalent of 18 of our standard tower blocks, and that under no circumstances should we put that number of blocks there! Instead, we devised a concept of six long slab blocks, each made up of three of our standard blocks put together, containing about 300 flats, with pedestrians feeding in from the top, and extensive community facilities. That was a £6 million contract, and we built it, starting in 1964, at one hell of a speed: because of cost cuts, all of those extras fell through. But I still think that, even in the reduced form in which it was built, it was a tremendous job. It's out in the country, it profiles well and looks well. [*Editorial postscript*: Dundee City council have commenced demolishing the Ardler blocks during the late 1990s]

Then the city architect came to us with a far larger site, also on the city edge, at Whitfield. We were asked how we might go about filling that vast site. We decided we couldn't do repetitive slab blocks yet again, and so we went in another direction altogether: the honeycomb pattern, which was built from 1968 onwards, was very much our idea. The credit for that layout belongs, to a large extent, to one or two bright young designers in our office.

Other Scottish local authorities

In Edinburgh, if they even had a city engineer at the time, I didn't even know about it. We had virtually no involvement with the planners. When you knocked together, say, a 750-house arragement, it was Alex Steele, the city architect, that you saw, or Harry Corner, as his chief housing architect. Further north on the east coast, our construction activity didn't go north of Aberdeen, or really even as far as Aberdeen - that was looked on very much as the territory of Wimpey or the local firms. In the Clyde Valley, Greenock had an almost complete lack of architectural control, whereas Motherwell had some very ambitious redevelopment plans.

Killingworth and the end of 'systems'

At the end of the 1960s, we did a contract for 900 houses in Skarne deck blocks at Killingworth, near Newcastle, for Longbenton Urban District Council. This was intended as a kind of mini new town, or township. At this stage in the game, even modestly sized places like Longbenton could put together a really good design team. Theirs was headed by Roy Gazzard, a super bloke with some very progressive ideas. But, with economic clouds on the horizon, cost was a growing obstacle. Roy would say, 'We want this, we want that ...' We'd reply, 'That's going to knock the price through the roof!' And sure enough, he wouldn't be able to get it through his QSs, and he'd have to come back to us. The entire project was to be deck access, which I thought was a tremendous idea in principle, allowing you to get the kiddies up off the street. A tremendous idea - so long as it was done right! But when the first phase eventually went up, from 1967 onwards, it looked pretty grim. Why was it grim? Because we were now in the middle of a national economic crisis, and, for cost-cutting purposes, all the cladding had to be straight off-the-shutter concrete. So you ended up with massive, crude structures. Then we ran into a more fundamental problem: system-building's basic lack of economic viability. The economics of the whole Killingworth project were that we'd get the second phase - but we didn't! When the urban district council pulled out of the contract, I said, 'Do you know how much money has been spent on designing the second phase?' They said, 'Oh, don't worry!' I said, 'What the hell do you think two dozen engineers have been doing for six months!'

C8. Harold Buteux (on right) seen with a colleague and Edinburgh's Lord Provost in 1961, inspecting a model of the SSHA's Wyndford redevelopment in Glasgow. (Scottish Special Housing Association)

Interview 3

Harold Buteux
former Chief Technical Officer, Scottish Special Housing Association

Extracts from interview with Miles Glendinning, 18 September 1987

Outline of own career

I began my career in the 1930s, working on the administrative side of London local government. In the war, after a spell doing rescue work as a pacifist, I became an observer in the Fleet Air Arm: only a quarter of our squadron survived. My pilot was a trainee dentist, and I was doing town planning: we were both optimists! That optimism and hope carried over after 1945, and eventually took me, in 1949, into the planning division of the London County Council, followed (in 1952) by Stevenage New Town Corporation, where I absorbed the ideals of good housing design and comprehensive planning. Between 1956 and 1959, I worked with Birmingham's city architect, A G Sheppard Fidler, as his deputy responsible for housing, until finally I was appointed to the SSHA post, which I held until 1978.

Housing design in Birmingham

Working in Sheppard Fidler's department, I had two main objectives. Firstly, to plan each area comprehensively, rather than in bits and pieces, and to use mixed developments of houses and point blocks, rather than just lines of high blocks. Secondly, to get away from the contractors' own standard blocks, because you had no control over their cost or design, and they prevented you from getting competitive tenders. To do that, you had to design everything yourself, or get a private architect to do so, which is a lot of work! In this policy, I got 100% backing from Sheppard Fidler: we were completely attuned, as we both had a new-town and mixed-development background. His main object was not numbers, but aesthetic and social quality; he wanted to achieve a truly 'urban' type of planning. In constructional matters, he was equally adventurous, and always wanted to be first in the field. For example, working with Wimpeys, we did 12-storey blocks in no-fines in the late '50s - the highest they'd ever built. We were the second city, we wanted to be the ones pushing the frontiers, so we gave Wimpey their head to press on with no-fines. In effect, we allowed them to do their development work at our expense!

Initial experiences at the SSHA

In general, my first task was to introduce to my new department the kind of philosophy of architectural variety that I'd experienced in Birmingham. Previously, what they were interested in doing was producing dwellings which were all the same. On my first day, there was a senior architect, a dear old boy, with no idea about planning. I asked, 'Let me see what you've got!' He got out stuff on about six schemes, and said, 'We get the engineers to put in the roads, and then give it to the contractors to build standard blocks.' He showed me type-plans for mainly two-storey houses, and three- or four-storey tenement-type flats. I said, 'We'll have to change this!' He said, 'Oh no, you can't!' So the first thing I had to do was to double the size of the office and then redouble it, and to do my own standard designs to negotiate from. But the trouble was, the local authorities kept asking us to use the old blocks. They were so popular!

More specifically, I had to address the issue of the design of high blocks and higher densities. The Association certainly wanted to get in on the multi-storey act, but they didn't have any positive idea of how to go about it. When I arrived, the general manager told me my first job was to go on with producing them. He said, 'You've got the experience, so just get on with them!' The very first problem which faced me as I sat down at my desk at the SSHA was concerned with multi-storey blocks. We were involved with Paisley Burgh Council in developing a big area on the south-east edge of the town, at Foxbar. They had built two already, to their own designs - the contractor was Blackburn, the aircraft and prefab manufacturer - and now they wanted us to build some as well. The resulting problems had been exercising the people in my department for nine months already. Paisley's design was a complex split-level thing; it was very expensive. But to avoid having some of one and some of another on the same site, I agreed to use their plans. This spurred us into designing a block of our own, which would do the same job, but much more economically. I'd learnt in Birmingham that, if you're going to use four flats per floor, then two-bedroom flats are the most economical plan you can use. As I had to design the block virtually overnight, I decided that we would use a proven type-plan, based on one of my Birmingham schemes, Hawkesley Farm Moat, using brick cladding. The result was the 'Mk.III', a 15-storey block which was one of our most popular designs. However, there was a problem with rain penetration in the cavities, something we hadn't experienced with the same detail at Birmingham, and which had to be sorted out. Later, the same basic plan, except a little wider, was used on the 26-storey blocks at Hutchesontown 'D'; we designed those with W V Zinn, a red-hot engineer, who sorted out the water and silt level of the Clyde, and advised that we should put the blocks on 100-foot deep piles.

Policy on housing types

My guiding rule was that the best housing possible is two-storey blocks, and that high blocks should be kept to a minimum, never built for their own sake. Occasionally we used them as landmarks, or for special reasons. For example, at Broomhill, in Glasgow [from 1965], the site was in some glorious woodlands, and high blocks were built there purely on aesthetic grounds, to preserve the trees - although the contract for those was not very successful, as Millers took over a year longer than they should have done. By the mid-1960s, we had become so restrictive on the use of multi-storeys that we turned down some sites where we would have had to use them. For example, in 1965-66, Glasgow Corporation tried to press us into building a line of point blocks on a narrow site at Sandwood Road, on the western edge of the city. I said no, so in the end the blocks were built by someone else, not by me! In our work in the Glasgow redevelopment areas, I felt the replacement density, 150 h.r.p.a. [habitable rooms per acre], was still too high, and behind the scenes I tried unsuccessfully to get it lowered to 120. I also tried to argue for the mixed development philosophy of different types of blocks for different types of households. That was often quite difficult in Glasgow, with the pressure for numbers, but we sometimes succeeded. For instance, at the Wyndford development in Maryhill, we tried to redress the imbalance against elderly people in our housing stock, by building half of the houses for one or two people. This meant we could minimise the number of children, and maximise the number of slender, high point blocks. At Hutchesontown 'D', Glasgow pressured our management into increasing the number of children in the scheme, so I had to build a nursery school on that site. My policy of minimising the number of large flats was completely supported by our housing manager, Jean Pollock. Polly was absolutely marvellous; she was someone who was absolutely dedicated to society, and fundamentally influenced by the Octavia Hill approach of careful management of people: at the end of the day, it was people who mattered.

We never built high blocks in our overspill programme, and almost never in the economic growth programme; the exception was Linwood, where we built two near the shopping centre so that the old people could be near the shops. At Linwood, we sat down with Rootes, who was building the car factory there; he wanted us to provide 2,000 houses, but we decided we could only offer 1,000.

Liaison with Glasgow Corporation

In our Glasgow work in the early 1960s, I would meet David Gibson, the housing convener, about once a month, to show him layout proposals for Glasgow projects that our governing council had approved. Sometimes he'd ask for changes, and I'd take them away and get the required adjustments made. Generally, the changes were a matter of detail, not general principle. Any disagreements were on small matters, as for instance in the case of the Wyndford project [from 1961], which was a redevelopment of the old Maryhill Barracks. As a socialist and pacifist, Gibson wanted to tear down all the walls of the old barracks - marvellous, massive rubble structures. When I first presented my plans, I put on a little historical exhibition about the place in the entrance hall, and he blew up! But eventually I argued successfully that they should be kept for practical reasons - as a way of controlling vandals and encouraging community. The chief housing engineer at that time was Lewis Cross: numbers were his sole concern. He had nothing to do with how the blocks were managed, just in building numbers. Glasgow Corporation's housing management was extremely poor. In 1965, Lewis Cross moved across to become our general manager. He tried to apply some of the same principles as in Glasgow - negotiated contracts and so forth - but in the end we were able to establish a *modus vivendi* with him.

Relations with central government

Dr Dickson Mabon, the Scottish housing minister from 1964, was an excellent leader of the national housing programme, standing head and shoulders above all his predecessors. He was also less imbued with socialist dogma than any other Labour minister. He gave us a huge programme - he boosted our annual targets by 2,500 - which gave us some organisational problems: we had to go out and buy the land, as fast as possible!

SSHA sponsorship of research and development

From 1960, we became closely involved, as a co-sponsor with DHS, with the government's experimental Joint Development Group on housing design. They were trying to work out alternative solutions of urban housing to the package-deal promoters' standard blocks. Although their projects, as experimental one-offs, were against my general policy, I felt that we were nevertheless the organisation that should work with them. I welcomed bringing them on board, because they were a force for good design, and a lot of their wilder arguments derived from inexperience. The first development group project, Fortrose Street, was for a single deck-access block. I wouldn't touch deck-access myself - I'd visited Park Hill in Sheffield, and thought it was a disaster, a recipe for housing management problems - but I was quite happy to let the development group try it out! At Dunbar, we worked on another R&D project with Sir Robert Matthew's housing research unit at Edinburgh University. There we tried to work out dense, low-rise solutions for a complicated sloping site, again rather than just plonking down standard blocks.

Our aim was to get good design and comprehensive planning, to get away from the contractors' standard solutions, to get away from the assumption you had to use high blocks everywhere - but without going overboard. As an example of what I mean by that, we very much admired what Hugh Wilson and his successor were doing at Cumbernauld New Town - they were very bold, they went for every new idea at the purely technical level, they made a terrific contribution to architecture and housing layout - but we were very cautious about following in their footsteps! You were also able to see the faults, only too clearly, especially in the town centre, where one felt they'd only been interested in the image of the architecture, and with solving the traffic problems of the centre, and had not been concerned with the problems that solution might create at a social level. The very different and more modest kind of thing we were pursuing was seen in the type-plans and rationalised planning which we pioneered under the aegis of the SLASH group from the early 1960s. That was an invaluable combine, which I put a lot of effort into helping establish and develop. It allowed us to pool our design ideas with the resources of the big local authorities.

System building

In the early '60s, we started to look towards prefabricated concrete systems, because the heights we were planning were unsuited to no-fines, and we wanted to put the blocks out to competitive tender. Ideally, I'd have liked to have done a flexible, open system, standardising the units that make up a house rather than standardising the entire house, or block.

Initially, I'd been one of the first to get enthusiastic about systems, and went with the engineer W V Zinn to inspect Camus, a French system that involved a high degree of mass production. We wanted to get it over here so we could try it out, and we were prepared to build a factory, but eventually the government squashed the idea. Sheppard Fidler was also keen to get Camus for Birmingham at that time, and, like me, he didn't succeed. After that experience, I became a lot more cagey, and decided that while I wanted to experiment with system building, it would be better to do it gently!

Eventually, we got started with a group of three eight-storey blocks at Wyndford, which ended up being built in Bison construction, from 1963. But that job was not altogether successful. After the first block had gone up, we were warned about water penetration, and we had to stop the job and pull down a section of the building. Bison experienced the same problems when its Wall-Frame system was introduced to Scotland, and they had to redesign it. Before long the trouble was sorted out, but it demonstrated the need for a terrific level of on-site supervision

on system-built contracts. With traditionally built blocks, like the 26-storey Laing ones at Wyndford, this was easier - you could inspect the cladding panels from the inside, and the construction was more predictable. But even this was not infallible: we had appalling problems with our mosaic facing on the Hutchesontown 'D' tower blocks, although we'd done six months of research on it! Eventually, under pressure from SDD to raise output, we had to give up the idea of competitive tendering for systems, and arranged negotiated contracts for high flats another French system, Tracoba. This was not an altogether satisfactory experience - we ended up having to use this heavy system to build four-storey blocks!

Relations with Wimpey

Wimpey was a special case for us, because we both used no-fines construction. During my time, we began to make increasing use of them, as they were one of the most reliable contractors around - if not *the* most reliable. They wanted work, and I wanted to use them! But I wasn't prepared to use their standard designs: Sheppard Fidler had laid that down in his dealings with Wimpey in Birmingham in the 1950s, and I stuck to the principle! From the late 1960s, to encourage competitive tendering, I tried an experiment of transferring our expertise in no-fines to a group of six firms, including, of course, Wimpey. We were unique in that we could design architecturally innovative work in no-fines, innovativeness which increased further after the founding of SLASH in the 1960s. So we and the firms worked closely, and learnt from each other. They learnt from our adventurous plans, our split-levels and all our other ideas, while we learnt from their constructional expertise.

C9. Aberdeen Corporation's only large package-deal development: Seaton Areas B, C and D development, built in 1971-74. The seven 19-storey towers are a special variant of Bison Wall-Frame, built by Concrete Limited as subcontractor working with local main contractor P Cameron; the three 10-storey blocks were built in conventional in-situ construction by Cameron. In the foreground are granite-faced council tenements of the 1930s. (RCAHMS B22237)

Interview 4

Alec Mitchell
former Sales Director, Concrete Scotland Ltd (Bison)

Interview with Miles Glendinning, 26 November 1987

Outline of own career

I was born in January 1924, worked as a joiner in Grangemouth, went to apprenticeship and evening classes in Falkirk, and worked as a shipwright in the navy in the war, followed by a training certificate at the Royal Technical College in Glasgow. In 1951-52, Bison asked me to join them, initially on the frame side of the drawing office, then working on outside sales. I was appointed sales director for Scotland in 1962, and only left that job in 1980, to work on business development with Barratts.

Bison and the begining of the 1960s boom

Around the early '60s, the political pressure to build council housing suddenly became much stronger - a political 'crash drive'. The statistics showed the old houses needed so much done to them. Housing is like a motor car - if it's not serviced, it'll deteriorate. The solution had to be quick - they had no choice but to go for multi-storeys. In Europe, ten- or eleven-storey blocks were already par for the course. It was a fashion. And this exposed a shortage of building resources. The world's built on supply and demand - and, around 1960, the demand for high blocks was there, but the supply wasn't!

The initial response to that problem was to build larger blocks of multis, but still purpose-designed for the site. Our first big multi-storey jobs in Glasgow, Pollokshaws II [from 1961] and Woodside A, were done in that way: they included blocks of up to 23 storeys. Laidlaw was nominated as main contractor to work with us for the Pollokshaws job. The architect (Boswell Mitchell & Johnston) and engineer had decided before the main contractor was appointed that they were going for precast for the whole development at Pollokshaws, and they came to Bison as nominated precast manufacturer. Once they got the package put together, we and the architects jointly did a presentation for the Housing Committee, and the project was approved. The blocks, structurally, were designed by Harley Haddow & Partners.

The next step in the response to the lack of traditional building resources was to build in systems. By 1961, the decision to develop our own system, Bison Wall-Frame, had already been taken, in England, by Sir Kenneth Wood. Prior to the late '50s, Concrete Limited had been basically a precast concrete components manufacturer. Wood began to see that high-rise would become a big market about 1958. He studied Continental systems and opted for a method based on the Danish Larsen-Nielsen system. In 1959, the firm appointed a prominent Danish engineer called Malmstrom, seconding someone first to his office. His staff then came and worked with our people in London, designing the Wall-Frame system on the same principles as Larsen-Nielsen. Prototype blocks were built in 1963 at Kidderminster: the firm was very strong in the Birmingham area, and a Birmingham architect called Miall Rhys-Davies played a key role in the design of Wall-Frame.

Here in Scotland, our first blocks, at Pollokshaws, weren't designed in Wall-Frame: for example, Wall-Frame never used cork or delta ties. In the later section of Pollokshaws, Area I, built from 1966, the blocks are Wall-Frame, and the architect was J L Gleave. The first development to go Wall-Frame was a series of point blocks built from 1964 for Cumbernauld New Town Corporation: Laidlaw was the main contractor there. Preparing for that project, I paid a visit to the prototype Wall-Frame blocks at Kidderminster with Alec Watson of our Building Inspectors Group, and a man called Wilson from the Building Research Station at East Kilbride. They detected weaknesses which wouldn't satisfy the damp west-of-Scotland climate. And they were right - the Cumbernauld blocks cost a fortune to sort out!

The Wall-Frame used in Scotland after Cumbernauld was a totally different construction from that used in England, which allowed us to avoid all the trouble they had there after Ronan Point in 1968. The only weakness in the Bison blocks in Scotland was the inadequate heating. They had a continuous damp course right round the building, full heavy-duty felt and PVC. Even then, we found that some of the blocks built in a very exposed position, as at Aberdeen's Seaton, had to have their open joints completely closed in. Crittalls had to make a different window for Aberdeen compared with everywhere else. The tower blocks at Glasgow's Pollokshaws Area I were early Wall-Frame, as were the six first SLASH blocks, built by Laidlaw, as part of Dickson Mabon's drive for homes - he cut the first sod for the ones at Greenock, in 1965.

Company organisation in the 1960s: general

The group headquarters was at Hounslow, in south-west London, and regional organisations were set up for the south of England (also at Hounslow), the north (at Leeds), the Midlands (at Lichfield); finally, there was our own Scottish subsidiary at Falkirk. Each one worked very much on its own area. The Wall-Frame details had to be changed where appropriate. For example, all the English factories worked with a face-down casting technique, whereas we used face-up. It gave you a better finish, more uniform - that was one of the best decisions we took! In any case, our Scottish building regulations were quite different from the English ones: for example, we couldn't finish a window against a party wall - we had to have a return. For the layouts of estates, we in Bison always brought in local authority or private architects. We had no architects of our own, as Bison was, basically, a manufacturing and engineering organisation (although many of the English estates were designed by Rhys-Davies). Some of those authorities made modifications to internal layout, walls, etc. For instance the blocks at Edinburgh Corporation's Wester Hailes Contract 4 were Wall-Frame blocks modified by an Edinburgh architect, called Naismith, of Frank Mears & Partners. We were nominated by the city and brought in by main contractor Hart Brothers to build the structures, from 1969.

We could manage small runs much more economically than some continental systems, who mass produced big panels, and used things like heavy-duty battery moulds. We used more individual moulds, which allowed us to make a large variety of small pieces: all the external panels were made up in individual moulds. Within our factory, we had different sections - we could build schools in one, Wall-Frame in the other. In some cases, Bison was nominated as the systems subcontractor, and the local authority selected the main contractor. In cases like that, we would give them all the same price, and what they added on top of that was their business; they would win the job on siteworks and finishing trades. For example, at Aberdeen Corporation's Seaton Phase I, in 1969, Betts were approved on a nominated contract agreed with the council, but Phase II, which followed three years later, had to go to competition. The three firms that quoted for that, using Bison, were: the winner, Cameron; second, Bett; and Loudon of Cleland third. The firms not using Bison for the Seaton tenders - Wimpey, Halls and Crudens - all came in more expensive. Sometimes, as with some one- and two-storey housing at Dunoon, or a low-rise job at Maybole, we had to work with a small local contractor. In other cases, we had to go in as main contractor: that was the local authority's decision, not ours. For example, that happened with the big Lanarkshire job for housing at Cambuslang, Tannochside, Orbliston and Bellshill - a very large contract, for well over a thousand houses.

Overall, our philosophy was that we didn't want to cut out the local industry. That was how we in Concrete Scotland saw it - I don't know how they looked at it in England. Our whole approach was flexibility, in both organisation and design. It was sound commercial sense for us to be seen to be all things to all men, to work with the local people - local builders, local architects - rather than trying to take all the cake. Throughout Scotland, what you'll find is that local allegiance went a long way in selecting builders - which was the factor we had to deal with. For instance, in Edinburgh there were Hart and Smart. In Glasgow there were people like Laidlaw, the firm we'd worked with from the beginning, at Pollokshaws II. Local allegiance went a long way. That applied especially strongly in Dundee - even the Chamber of Commerce there wasn't attached to any one! Bison Wall-Frame was the only fully industrialised system used in all the four cities of Scotland.

Our sales and marketing were very important to us. Wimpey and the others continued to build large amounts, but our literature and marketing gave us entry. We issued four standard Wall-Frame books, and sent them out to all local authority architects to promote our product. As sales people, our main line to the local authorities was that 'if you stick to the plans in the book, they're the most economical'.

Miscellaneous Wall-Frame contracts

At Belville Street in Greenock, a big project of seven point blocks and some low flats built on a steep hillside from 1965, we worked with Laidlaws under the architectural supervision of Burke Martin & Partners. At Kincardine on Forth, which is really a large village, a group of three multi-storeys had to be built in 1969, because they had to house a lot of people at once - staff who were needed for a new power station and mine nearby; because of all the older mine workings, they hadn't got the land to build low-rise on. We worked with Bett Brothers on that one. Anderston Cross in Glasgow, built from 1966, was a nominated job by the Scottish Office. It began as an experimental low-rise architectural research project, with architects like John Fullarton and Murray Graham involved there from the early days. At Seaton in Aberdeen, the local authority controlled the elevations, as did the SSHA at Carron Street and Wyndford in Glasgow. At Wyndford, we did a special small point block designed by the SSHA to fit in with Bison detailing; the Association still used their direct labour force for the finishing trades.

C10. Wimpey perspective of c.1960 of the originally intended layout for Edinburgh's Muirhouse Temporary Housing Area development. The main departure from this in the executed scheme was the substitution for a Wimpey point block of the 23-storey Martello Court, built by W Arnott McLeod in 1962-64 (see also illustration B4.1). (George Wimpey Ltd)

Interview 5

Donald H Ross
former Divisional Architect, Wimpey Ltd

Interview with Miles Glendinning, 3 June 1987

Outline of own career

I joined Wimpey in 1965; I'm an Aberdonian by origin, and was at college with Ian Ferguson. I had, previous to Wimpey, worked with Aberdeen Corporation in 1954-56, followed by Glenrothes New Town Development Corporation. Within Wimpey, I initially worked as deputy regional architect (east), and then as regional architect. Now [1987], I'm divisional architect to Wimpey Homes Holdings Ltd, here at the Barnton office in Edinburgh.

Company background

Wimpey was run by Sir Godfrey Mitchell, and Eric Collins, a far-sighted architect, was his right-hand man. Collins joined just after the war, in 1945; he became chief architect, and retired 10-12 years ago. He was a member of the influential Parker Morris Committee on English housing standards. A very forthright individual, who inspired a lot of respect: he could have been a director, if he hadn't wanted to remain a professional.

No-fines design and the '1001' system of the 1960s

When I joined Wimpey, the firm had just perfected the '1001' system. The '1001' took to an extreme the Wimpey philosophy, which was very different from some of the heavy prefabrication boys - almost the opposite, in fact. I should begin by saying a little about our basic system of construction, no-fines concrete. This was basically a very primitive technology - coarse-aggregate mass concrete with some reinforcement added - but we built it in a highly efficient way: we were selling high productivity and reliability. And it had some advantages already: for example it reduced water penetration. No-fines was originally devised in Holland and refined by the SSHA. But Eric Collins saw its future potential, and worked very hard at making it a success.

The '1001' went rather further than all our existing no-fines methods. It was a response to the 1960s stress on standardised or prefabricated 'systems'. It was a way of marketing a sophisticated interior lining method as a 'system': everything was dry lined, the services were tightly arranged, including a heating unit which was quite advanced for its time. In the building process, the machinery was arranged to get one floor poured per week; the 12" no-fines and the structural reinforcement columns were poured simultaneously, something which was much quicker than reinforced concrete frame and infill: the steel tube shutter for the dense concrete column was set inside the crude no-fines shutter, then the steel tube was pulled out to bond the two. Then, once you got the concrete pouring done, you could get on very quickly with the finishings. No plastering was needed: it was well ahead of its time. In general, our no-fines system depended absolutely on continuity of labour for a small group of roughly half a dozen key workers, that is, the pouring squad. This was made up of the mixer driver, shuttering joiners and the gangers. They followed us all over Scotland, and made our jobs work at the most basic level of building. These six or so men, because they were so essential to our system, earned very good money and had great security.

The '1000' type had preceded the '1001'. Its construction was basically the same. The '1000' was a beam and slab floor-type, and was thus slower to construct. The '1001' had a thin plate floor supported on a few columns or none; there were no beams, so internal planning was easier, with more free spaces. The '1001' drawings were all done in London. There were large foolscap books of standard details. The '1001' was based on standard plans for 'units' of dwellings - a central core, with things hung around it. The '1001/S' Scottish variant had an identical structure. The differences were in the detail, in response to the different building regulations; for example we had fire stair windows. In effect, we were saying, 'We've had multi-storey blocks for a few years, but we've revised our types, we've improved the productivity, and this is the result!'

The mid '60s was the height of the systems boom, but, rather than going in for prefabrication, we felt happier staying with this relatively crude, but strong, mass-concrete construction: we certainly looked with horror, for example, on the experimental tall blocks built in steel framing and sheet cladding at Red Road, Glasgow, in the mid-1960s. The architect, Sam Bunton, was the most commercial private architect in Scotland. I never met him, but he must have been an amazing bloke, because he invented his own systems! Our structural engineers had tried and tested no-fines to exhaustion. We've always been a belt-and-braces organisation: that kind of approach, that refusal to compromise our position as professionals, was one of the things that I most liked in my early days with the firm. It never occurred to me until Ronan Point that large-panel concrete could actually be unsafe; I was reassured some years later when there was a bad explosion in one of our blocks in Lancashire, and nothing happened! In the early 1960s, we did become worried about the elevational flexibility of no-fines: that was what eventually killed it, about 1982. There was also the elevation problem: with no-fines, we had to cover it all with porridge. We introduced mosaic panels, but that wasn't successful. But, when it came down to it, the decisive factor was that we reckoned we could beat the large-panel boys commercially any day. No-fines was a creature of volume. A lot of Wimpey's no-fines design was centrally co-ordinated from our Hammersmith Grove headquarters in London, by Adrian Carswell. He was originally from Edinburgh.

Prior to the mid '60s, we'd been dominant in large-scale Scottish mass housing. But by 1965, we faced two serious competitors in Crudens and Bison. They began to make a very large dent in our workload. We lost some big competitive-tendered jobs to Bison, who were able to rely on their links with local firms as main contractors for finishing work. For example, in the late '60s, there was Seaton in Aberdeen, a job involving seven 19-storey blocks. I thought we were likely to win that one. As an Aberdonian myself, with good contacts in the City Architect's Department, I was well aware that the department had a heavy workload. I thought that we, with our proven track-record, would be the clear favourites. So to find we'd been well beaten, on price, was a bitter blow.

During the boom years of the early '60s, our firm certainly did try to attract work. We tried to build up a reputation. We would show the housing committees our work: Tom Smyth and the marketing guys trailed all sorts of councils down to Ramsgate and Margate, where we had built our first '1001'. Our head of marketing, Brigadier Prentice, was a marvellous old guy. Of course, we were in the business to make money. But once we'd got a certain level of work, we didn't need to look for more. It was in no way a matter of 'free market competition'. The government, through the local authorities, was in effect doling out a continuous stream of work, and Wimpey's job was to get, and keep, a slice of it.

Wimpey never tendered for anything other than the complete works. We never did Bison-type contracts, tying up with another contractor for finishing works, although we obviously had to use specialist subcontractors for some aspects of a job. We were the cheapest when we had to fight to win a job. The ideal was a negotiated contract. Sometimes there was more money to be made that way, sometimes there was less, but there certainly was more security. Some firms saw it as a licence to print money, but the good local-authority architect would prevent that by specifying extras very precisely. When approaching a new council, the firm was always asked the delicate question, 'Will you employ local labour?' The answer they wanted varied from place to place, depending on their employment situation: some did want us to, others very definitely didn't. The answer of our PR men to that question was that we brought the handful of key men, but that the others could be either local or Wimpeys, as required.

Early Wimpey multi-storey schemes

Medium-sized towns like Kirkcaldy and Dunfermline had, per head of populations, quite big housing programmes. Our first multi-storey Scottish scheme was in Kirkcaldy. It was a tower block at Valley Gardens, built in 1954-55. They were a highly progressive council, and we had tremendous rapport with them. The officials were very good, including the housing factor, John Lees - the most progressive man I've ever met in housing management. This was reflected in the quality of the building; the standard of things like entrance halls was much higher than in, for instance, Edinburgh, with mosaics and murals. And the blocks were well cared for by the tenants. A lot of this attitude was down to this one man, Lees, who was a kind of benevolent dictator, encouraging the good tenants and pressurising the bad ones.

Out of all these towns, Falkirk was also special. It looked for a very high standard: the technical officials, especially Ian Ferguson, pushed for a high level of finish in the entrances and other public areas. It had a prime building site in parkland at Callendar Park, but this site was riddled with coal workings. This led to a decision to use 15-storey tower blocks. I joined Wimpey just after the company had been awarded our first two blocks there, in 1965; the contract was only just a piece of paper. Ian Ferguson, the burgh architect, and I had been students together in Aberdeen. We had to organise where the blocks would go, cut down enough trees for a site investigation. Then we had to move the site of the blocks, and cut down yet more trees. Crudens had won the big contract, for seven blocks. We had been a good second, and so they had given us two further blocks. Then there were two subsequent tenders - Sunnyside, never built, and Glenfuir, which we built, in 1969-70, and which was a super job, with two point blocks set in among old trees.

Another of our early Scottish multi-storey projects, from the late '50s, was in a medium-sized town - namely Perth. First, in 1958-59, we built Pomarium Street, which was made up of very ordinary blocks, and in a rather squalid location. Then, three years later, there was Potterhill, a complete contrast - a very handsome job in heavy landscaping on the other side of the river. Very often this kind of prototype high-flat scheme was negotiated, for reliability, but even so, at Pomarium Street there was a bizarre episode with our tender. The council never received it, and a duplicate had to be made up and submitted as a matter of great urgency. Some months later, the original documents eventually arrived in Perth, having first been to Australia. They were marked 'Try Scotland'.

Wimpey contracts in the big cities

Aberdeen were almost, but not quite, as well organised in the housing management field as smaller places like Kirkcaldy. Aberdeen eventually set up a new town-planning department, but the city engineer and city architect didn't get on very well with it. I don't recall any powerful 'housing' faction in Aberdeen, like the one in Glasgow.

The situation in the other cities was very different from the smaller authorities. For example, Edinburgh Corporation became very active in production from 1962 under Pat Rogan, who was a big, likeable guy; everybody was his friend. He, and the other housing chairmen before and after, had to balance our involvement in the programme alongside that of the local boys like Hart and Smart. They built the standard Wimpey kit as offered, and didn't want any embellishments. The Edinburgh housing management, in contrast to Kirkcaldy and Aberdeen, was terrible. Our last big scheme for them was the St Leonards redevelopment, which was to have been tall tower blocks but ended up, after many years of planning controversy, as medium rise. It started with Pat, but the discussions took so long that he was no longer chairman by the time construction actually started, in 1970.

Glasgow were the most choosy of all in the standards of construction and equipment they demanded, especially in the lifts, the sanitary arrangements, and the rooftop drying areas, which, rather than being left open as in other towns, they insisted on fully glazing-in, like a complete additional storey. They spent a lot more on that kind of thing than other authorities, because they had much higher calibre engineers and technical staff. The attitude to Glasgow on the part of contractors was, 'They're the biggest single customer we have, so whatever they want, they get!' In the City Architect's Department, the production strongman was obviously Lewis Cross, so we tried to ally ourselves to him - not always with complete success, as he was such an independent character! The housing management side of the city was a different matter. Glasgow, until a few years ago, was one of the most poorly managed housing authorities of all. It was incredible, the way in which one set of departments insisted on the very highest built quality in their blocks, up until completion, and then another department allowed them to fall into disrepair!

The reason we didn't work in Dundee was very simple: we didn't get on with the trade unions! At a previous job, a private housing development, the unions made it so difficult for us, and tried to coerce more money out of us, that we closed the site, and said we'd never build in Dundee again. Only now are we beginning to build there again for the first time, in the late 1980s, 25 years later - and even here, the development's being built for us by Taycon to ease our position. The unions were fearsome in Dundee. That applied especially when they got a national contractor in their sights: they thought they could bleed them to death! A case in point, during the 1970s, was a series of four factories we tendered to build for Michelin, including one in Aberdeen and one in Dundee. Aberdeen we got, which was just as we wanted, but although we'd priced the Dundee one deliberately high, we found to our horror that we'd only just escaped it by the skin of our teeth. The lucky winners were McAlpines, and the unions, of course, tore them apart!

Wimpey work for the new towns and SSHA

The new towns were a very different kind of market from the cities and towns. In the case of the tower block we built at Glenrothes in 1967-68, for instance, I was well aware, having worked previously in the Development Corporation's Architects Department, that they would have their own special requirements. Their block, at South Parks, was supposed to be a slightly special block, aimed at the young executive who wanted a flat not far from the town centre. Whereas the most economical block-type had six to the landing, the one we built at Glenrothes only had four. The only other example of that type we built in the east of Scotland during my time was an almost exactly contemporary project to Glenrothes, at Coillesdene in Edinburgh.

We did a vast programme of work for the SSHA from the mid-1960s: we built over 10,000 no-fines houses for them, mostly low-rise, but with some four- or five-storey blocks. Their general manager, from 1965, was Lewis Cross, who had moved from Glasgow. As before, he knew just what he wanted and made sure he would get it. Tom Smyth, our principal architect for Scotland, had become good friends with Cross during his time in charge of housing in Glasgow prior to 1965; Tom and Cross had worked on Glasgow high flats together. At the SSHA, we had a monthly progress meeting, chaired by Cross, where both our east and west regional architects were represented, as well as the regional managers; the eastern (or Edinburgh) one, who I dealt with in my work, was Roy Mason. The SSHA was represented by their chief architect, Harold Buteux, as well as by regional architects, who came in one by one to discuss cases. Most of this work was in negotiated contracts, but occasionally they invited contractors to tender against their own DLO. Buteux was a very interesting man, thoughtful and quite idealistic. He raised architectural standards in the SSHA from very low to very high. Sometimes his aims differed from Cross's. Cross wanted to get the maximum number of houses built - he listened to Harold, but made up his own mind. Thus his good relationship with Wimpey in Glasgow continued in the SSHA.

Consortia in the mid-1960s

Dr Dickson Mabon, the Labour housing minister from 1964, was manna from heaven for the contractors. He was set on radically raising production of houses. Although party politics didn't make a huge difference in housing, the building industry always reckoned in those decades that the Labour Party was the better party to be in power, because of its commitment to council housing. Mabon exploited the fact that smaller authorities largely built for prestige. That was how he got his housing drive going - he went round these places, stirring them all up! And he got them to join together into consortia, or groups, to make their orders big enough to make system building viable.

The first big consortium had been set up slightly earlier: SLASH (the Scottish Local Authorities Special Housing group). They tried to produce standard plans, and so forth. We tried to keep in with them, but never were fully on that particular bandwagon; whereas the precast merchants most certainly were! We felt slightly aggrieved at this upstart grouping coming along. But a lot of authorities just paid lip service to it, and continued coming to us. For example, at Glenrothes, we built adaptations of the SLASH plan.

After the main system-building period, when the oil boom started in the early 1970s, we set up a Moray Firth housing consortium (with Inverness the biggest participant) sponsored by the Scottish Development Department. John Fullarton, at that time the superintending architect with SDD, was appointed by them as the consortium's technical adviser. We were asked how many houses we could build in one year, and our response was, five hundred. We didn't have to compete for them, but on the other hand we could have been greedy and said twice as many as we did, but we didn't. We had a big labour problem, great difficulty in keeping good labour up there, and we didn't wish to compromise our record - one of the things that we were most proud of - that we never finished a job late.

Corruption in housing contracts

Generally, the largest contractors didn't need to tout for work during the systems era, so corruption wasn't a major factor. Our selling point in Wimpey was the very opposite, in fact: reliability and dependability. But with some other, smaller firms and smaller towns, certainly, there were occasionally some shenanigans. I remember one town in the Central Belt, in the mid-1960s, where one contractor was in favour with a faction in the town council, another contractor was being kept out, and we were just in, but as second-class citizens. In those days, the 'in' firm was a bit notorious for its dealings with councillors, with parties, lavish trips and all that kind of thing. In the case of one multi-storey project in this town, the firm's tender was ten minutes late in arriving, and the town clerk refused to have it opened, because he thought something untoward was going on - to be precise, the illegal opening of tenders to allow the favoured firm to undercut them. We in Wimpeys were the lower of the two that were left. So we got in by sheer accident, although the favoured firm would - surprise, surprise! - have been slightly lower still. Lewis Cross wouldn't have tolerated that sort of thing in his housing programme in

Glasgow! He was straight up and down - just as most local authority officials were, in fact. In this case it was a small-time, small-town crook who was involved. It was so blatant that, over a month later, even the local newspaper, rebelling against the 'in' faction, said, 'It's a month since the tenders were accepted, and you're still trying to get your pals in!'

C11. *Extract from Wimpey's 1961 booklet* A Problem Shared *depicting the firm's Royston Area A development, a pioneering package-deal project for Glasgow Corporation, built in 1959-61. (George Wimpey Ltd)*

Interview 6

Tom Smyth
former Principal Architect, Scottish Division, Wimpey Ltd

Interview with Miles Glendinning, 5 July 1987

General organisation of Wimpey architects in Scotland

Our design organisation in Scotland was as follows. I was principal architect, and at first dealt with all jobs personally, including liaison with people like Lewis Cross. From 1965, the structure below me was divided between new regional architect east and west posts. The eastern architect was Donald Ross, and in the west there was Tadeusz (Ted) Tysler, who left in 1969 to become assistant city architect in Glasgow, followed by Roy Scobie, who left in 1974, and became Glasgow depute city architect in the '80s: Ted was involved with projects like Townhead, and Roy with Battlefield.

Wimpey's position in the marketplace

In the 1950s, the task facing us was to adapt non-traditional building for the new types of housing coming in, especially high flats. Here we had a head-start with our no-fines technique of lightweight poured concrete. In any case, there was already a long history of mass-concrete building in Scotland - for instance in the Western Isles. In the early '50s, our main competitors seemed to be the firms linked with Sam Bunton, who had the whole of the west of Scotland tied up, and Scotcon in the east. Scotcon were only precast suppliers of panels, and worked with other contractors - we didn't know how exactly they made their money! Also complicating the position in non-traditional, and no-fines, was the SSHA. Our relations with them were complex, because of the overlap on no-fines. By the later '50s, we rather gave up on getting any work from them. There was some move to hand over to us part of their big redevelopment in Clydebank Central Area [built from 1960], but we never really got near to that. Especially after Harold Buteux

287

took over as their chief architect at the beginning of the '60s, there was no question of anybody except his department designing the SSHA's blocks. Prior to him, they'd been rather small in outlook, but he came along with grandiose ideas from Birmingham Corporation, and turned them into a big design-and-build, direct labour organisation - which cut off any spin-off for us from their no-fines work.

Our position in Scotland was quite unusual. By the late '50s, we'd been involved in housing for so long here that we looked on ourselves as a 'Scottish' firm. We were the only really large firm that had our own designs specific to the Scottish building regulations. Alex Steele, the Edinburgh city architect, once told me that a councillor had stood up in the Housing Committee and had said, 'We don't need English firms, we've got our own Scottish firms that can build high flats, firms like Scotcon, Miller - and Wimpey!' Alex said to me, 'Now you've really made it!' That didn't always protect us, as we found out for instance in Glasgow. Then, when systems came in in the '60s, the only Scottish firm that matched us for all-in contracts was Crudens. Other large English firms, like Reema or Laings, were never really that popular, and there was always resistance to them: they didn't understand the Scottish regulations, they didn't come with a ready-made product they could build tomorrow. Bison got round that problem in a different way from us, through the fact that they were precast suppliers, which appealed to the local building industry: any small builder could get a Bison contract. That's how, for differing reasons, we and Crudens and Bison were dominant in the '60s.

We had a highly standardised approach to package-deal designing. During my time, there was no way you could design for an individual site, although we architects would of course have liked to! It was a matter of fitting the standard types onto what was available. Our managing director said, for example, that there was no reason why people would want a different house in Glasgow or Aberdeen, or for that matter in Yorkshire. There was some dispute over the engineering input on our package-deal schemes: it carried legal implications. Around 1965, W A Fairhurst refused a contract to vet a Wimpey design, and we had a meeting about that with James Kernohan, the depute city architect in charge of housing. From then on, Glasgow looked on us as the design engineers: Tom Fleming, Glasgow's chief engineer, made that quite clear.

We were never happy about concrete prefabricated systems, we were very loath to try anything involving panels - although we were tempted! When I watched those big cladding panels going up on the Basil Spence blocks, I thought, 'How do you know that thing hasn't got damaged in some way?' And when the Ronan Point disaster happened in London in May 1968, I said to my wife, 'That's the end of multi-storey flats, then! I'll need to look for another job.'

Relations with central government

During the 1940s and early 1950s, the Department of Health were trying to encourage more non-traditional building (much as the NBA did later), and in the early days, we had very good relations with them, especially in the laying out of developments. They tended to act as our mentors - we took plans along there over and over again. Bertie Woodcock, their chief architect, was not at that stage in favour of package-deals, or design-and-build ideas. But he and his colleagues, like A Watson, were always very helpful on design matters. In the late '50s and early '60s, especially in the days of the SDD, there were more restrictions on contact, and we rather felt they'd withdrawn their positive collaboration. They kicked up a big row in 1958 when Edinburgh Corporation began dealing directly with contractors, and they were instrumental in getting Alex Steele, the city architect, down to the RIBA to explain himself. He had a word with our chairman beforehand to get some advice on what line he should take, and in the meeting he was quite uncompromising. We began to see the Department as a barrier. On one occasion, there was a decision held up on a scheme in Dunfermline, and we just couldn't get approval. Finally, our chairman spoke to a famous lawyer, Shawcross, and asked him to put on some pressure. I was sent for straight away at the Scottish Office, to a meeting with Bertie Woodcock in the chair, and we got permission there and then, that afternoon. On the whole, with the Department, the hold-ups weren't about the price - just look at the cost of the Spence blocks in the Gorbals, after all! - but about other things, like planning issues. In the Department, probably the strongest of the housing administrators we had to deal with was Gerard Kelly. He was quite a character, and had a lot to do with getting things done in housing production. If he got involved, there was never any indecision. I used to take him home from the club sometimes, and he'd get into the car and bark out directions, taking us back a very funny route through Pilrig because that was the way his bus went!

Relations with local authorities: marketing

In the early days, the housing committees made the decisions and got on with negotiating. Then, around 1961, it became obvious everything was getting much faster. Even in Edinburgh, it became obvious. The council architects and planners in large burghs told us what they wanted, especially in density, and increasingly that included high flats. Places like Dunfermline, Kirkcaldy, East Kilbride, Aberdeen went their own way. Certainly we didn't try, or need to try, to flog multis to them - they sold themselves! We were invited into those kinds of places. They wanted the architectural concept of high blocks in town centres, to recreate the role of the church spire. A lot of the smaller burghs just built multi-storeys for prestige. In some places, there were communist councillors who objected to new types of central heating systems because they didn't use coal. So we designed our first modern blocks to use chimneys - solidarity with the miners! - although one of our biggest mistakes was to get too committed to underfloor-heating systems. There was desperation to put people in new houses. There was never enough money to do it well. In Denmark, we saw £100 landscaping per house. We had about £6 or £7, if

at all! On one big visit to Sweden and Denmark in 1957 or 1958, we felt that they were behind us in construction standards and safety, but their finishes were more elegant.

Our selling point was absolute reliability and predictability. Many burgh architects would say, 'Thank goodness you're doing this job - that's one at least we don't need to worry about!' In small burghs, we did everything, whereas in larger towns, with bigger projects, private architects didn't have the resources to cope properly without making slips. For example, I remember once looking at a scheme designed by Jack Holmes of Glasgow for flats in Ayr. I could see the kitchens were too deep and I told him the scheme wouldn't pass. He didn't believe me, but that was just what happened! The same happened with a scheme by Frank Mears's firm.

Our head of marketing was Brigadier Prentice, a man who was very much an ex-army officer - he got the front door open to many town halls! He was a very respectable man, and the whole thing was all thoroughly above board - but nobody took him too seriously on technical matters. He didn't do a 'hard-sell', but arranged reasonably low-key professional presentations for various authorities, for example in the Central Hotel, with films and so forth. More usually, we were called into particular authorities by invitation. That would be the point at which I became involved, once the brigadier had made the introductions. Some other firms were very different, with more mixing of the technical and the promotional, and their publicity directors behaved, at conferences and so on, in a way that was little short of scandalous!

Early work in Glasgow

There were earlier schemes during the mid-1950s for blocks at Castlemilk, but these never got beyond the sketch stage. The Glasgow consortium firms and the DLO had low flats tied up, and we never had much hope of getting work in the city - until the swing began to high flats. My managing director took the design for our Kirkcaldy tower blocks of 1954 along to Archibald Jury, the city architect, but at first with no luck. The real breakthrough came in 1958. I went along to Glasgow one day with Brigadier Prentice. He knew Macpherson-Rait, an influential Progressive Party former housing convener, who felt that the city was having problems with its proposed multi-storey housing - it hadn't really got off the ground! The prototype scheme, Moss Heights, was plagued by problems and scandals, and the Glasgow consortium were ganging up to shut out other firms. Macpherson-Rait had already tried to get other firms into the consortium, but by 1955-56, it was beginning to break up anyway. His father had been a brigade major with Prentice in the war. Although he, as a Tory, had no direct weight himself, he was well-listened to and popular with all parties. In Glasgow, there was no 'them and us' split; what counted was whether you were for the city. Through Macpherson-Rait's good offices, we had an off-the-record interview with Jury. He asked us what we could do for Glasgow. So we did some work at our own risk, and designed a new point-block type. Then finally we were asked to submit a scheme for Royston A. Jury didn't really want us, but he was forced into high flats: Moss Heights had rather bounced back on him. Royston A was built in 1959-60 - three 20-storey blocks in no-fines - and because we built it so fast and reliably, it made a tremendous impression on the Housing Committee. It was followed in 1961 by Lincoln Avenue and Scotstoun House. They were the real trailblazers: the orders poured in after that. With gap sites, it was just 'Here's a sketch, get on with it!'

The convener of the Housing Committee from 1961, David Gibson, ruled the committee with tremendous power. He was a very genuine trade union man, a good socialist type of councillor, a very genuine man. And he got terrific support, even from the opposition, because he was getting things done. He and Cross had the most awful stand-up rows, but Cross, unlike Jury, could stand up to him. They were both good men, and worked together well, but Cross didn't allow Gibson to ride roughshod over him. Cross won most of their battles because of his administrative background. The Department of Health for Scotland were worried about Gibson, they saw him as a crusading angel, bulldozing through Glasgow, knocking everything down.

We used to think that Bailie Gibson was on our side, but we soon found out otherwise. Initially, he seemed to be all for us. He said, 'We're going to build hundreds more flats like Royston all round Glasgow'. He was a friendly man, a very positive sort of guy - but that soon changed! There was resistance to the fact that we were an English-headquartered firm, despite the company's policy of autonomy. We rather resented the feeling that some people, such as the direct labour force, who were taking work we'd have liked to have gone for, weren't nearly as competent as us. But there were other firms that could handle the pressure, firms like Crudens, who had a good team and a good architect. In competition with them, although we'd have taken more if we'd had the chance, we got our fair share: the commercial managers often complained, but I'd say, 'Come on - we've got enough!' Gibson died of a heart attack in 1964. His successor, Clark, was rather a cold fish, but a tough guy. To follow Gibson was a hard act, but Clark was very dour and strong. He wasn't any more pro-Wimpey than Gibson had been, though! It was funny how, despite all the mediocre characters on some of their committees, Glasgow often came up with a good Lord Provost and a good housing convener at the same time.

Lewis Cross

Archibald Jury, the Glasgow city architect, was in a difficult position, having as he did to balance the housing and planning interests within his department. On the planning front, he was under constant pressure from the professional bodies and the Scottish Office planners, while on housing, the councillors were all the time demanding maximum output. Jury himself was very much an administrator, defended by secretaries. He had two deputes under him. Lewis Cross controlled the housing programme, including sites, contracts and progress generally, while Ron Nicoll was in charge of planning.

Cross was the one we dealt directly with. He was an engineer by profession, and an extremely powerful personality. He had spent a long time in Kenya, as an officer in the Royal Engineers, building roads and drainage. There were two sides to him. On the one hand, he was a very affable, pleasant man, with a cultivated, slightly Yorkshire voice - he did everything with a laugh. He led a modest lifestyle, as he had an invalid wife with high blood pressure, which kept him out of social life. He hardly ever went out for lunch with contractors, as he had to go back home to see his wife. Just about his only social enjoyment was golfing. Cross had a very humorous way of speaking - a languid style. But it had steel beneath! You had to be on his side, and he wasn't really popular.

Lewis took the Housing Committee with him, though they didn't like it at times - an Englishman among Scots! But he had a dilettantish way of speaking, he made jokes with them. A very blunt man, but very charming - he could get away with telling them, 'You're a load of fools!' He made everything sound funny, in a way Jury never could - so Jury sent him to the committees instead! Nothing ever moved without his OK - you certainly didn't dare cut across his patch! What was very noticeable was, when he left to become SSHA general manager in 1965 and Kernohan took over, the way that output dropped.

Nicoll and Cross were always at loggerheads, and Jury couldn't control it. Cross was a very driving man - he didn't want any comments from his own designers or from Nicoll: his problem was to get houses built. He would hardly have the planners in the room. He'd say to you, 'Well, I suppose I'll have to get those idiots up here now - but don't pay any attention to what they say. It'll get built!' Interestingly, the planners later went from strength to strength under Jimmy Kernohan, when Cross moved to Edinburgh in 1965 to join the SSHA. Cross's relations with the architects and planners in the Scottish Office were just as difficult. He'd say, 'We're Glasgow, we're the biggest, we're not going to be shoved around by little tinpot architects in Edinburgh!' Then you'd get the Department's people taking the architect line back, standing on their dignity: 'Upstart Cross!', and so on. But Lewis was a man of action - he had no time whatever for people like that, and got on much better with the administrators, who spoke the same language as him. I remember once standing with Cross looking at the Glasgow Inner Ring Road being built. I said, 'You're creating havoc here!' And he replied, 'We've got to get this started or Glasgow will grind to a halt - it's nearly too late now! We can't afford to bother about your Greek Thomsons and Mackintoshes - to hell with these old churches, they've got to come down!' Although we kept out of his battles, instinctively we took Cross's side: the planners, by definition, always resented design-and-build work such as ours.

Cross's attitude to each project was to leave design totally up to you - he wasn't in the least bit interested in it. He'd give you an Ordnance Survey map and he'd say, come back in a month! Then all he did when I produced a layout with, say, five multi-storeys - he just looked at the box with the figures in the corner, took out his slide rule and if it was wrong he'd just finish a meeting there and then - he'd say, 'Come back when you've got it right!' You might say, 'What about the layout, Mr Cross?' But he'd reply, '*You're* the designers!' You didn't get that from his successor, Jimmy Kernohan, who was a capable designer in his own right, and became involved with the specifics of each case! But what it did mean, with Cross, was that you double-checked and triple-checked absolutely everything! Lewis would say, 'If you want work, you've got to get your finger out!' He was obsessed with the need to have all the factual information at his fingertips. Behind his desk, he had a filing system, and he'd spin around in his chair, reach in and get out his black notebooks - he compiled them at home, and kept them meticulously up to date - and he would say: 'It'll go to committee on such and such a date,' and so on. He was never stuck for an answer.

Cross told me once that on reliability grounds alone, he'd have had Wimpey build all his multi-storeys, because he got them on time and with no claims, but that, quite properly, he had to share the programme out. We would never have got half the number of contracts we did in Glasgow if there hadn't been a 'Cross' there. He argued on the basis of results. He often said, 'The fight I have to get your stuff through the committee, because there are a lot of people there against you!' He took a totally professional line, governed by only one thing: his target of 5,000 houses per annum. Cross didn't say an awful lot; he didn't give himself away. He dealt very much in compartments with people. 'He would never tell you he was negotiating with someone else about a job. Management would hit the roof and say, 'Someone else has got that big multi-storey job! How did that happen - you're in touch with Lewis Cross!' I'd say, 'He's the last person to tell me!' We never discussed any overall programme. Each site came out of the blue, and was almost a job by that stage. Cross would ring up: 'We've got a site, there's going to be multi-storeys on it, can you do it?' Once, when we were putting proposals together for one particular site, our general manager in Scotland, R W Marwick, complained to me that we didn't get enough notice from Cross, and asked me to fix up a meeting. So we had the meeting, we sat in a row, and Cross talked to me the whole time. At the end, he turned to Marwick and said, 'Now, Mr Marwick, to what do we owe this pleasure?' Marwick began to explain how we'd appreciate more notice, so we could plan better. Whereupon Cross cut him off and said, 'I've worked miracles for Wimpey in Glasgow! The trouble I've gone to, to get your schemes through - because you deliver! So don't, please, begin putting obstacles in the way!' Marwick hastily retreated, and excused himself: 'No, no - only a social call ...!' And when we got out, he promised me he wouldn't do that again!

One of Cross's difficulties was that the private architects who did design high blocks ran into problems. Spence and Matthew's Gorbals blocks, with their scissor and maisonnette plans, were twice as expensive as normal blocks: Wimpey wouldn't touch that sort of thing. And in both cases, the builders ran into financial problems, and had to go to Cross to ask for more money. Time after time, I used to meet them going to his office. He used to get pretty impatient with them - whereas we were the only ones who never came back for more. He tended to be a bit hard on private consultant architects from the efficiency viewpoint. After Spence and Matthew, he wasn't too keen on having more consultants in Glasgow. He said, 'They give me a headache; they come back with claims!' To avoid that, he steered it all in the direction of standard package-deal building from the major contractors.

One of the key figures among the Clydeside firms who were opposed to us was the architect Sam Bunton. He seemed to have a lot of business connections, but he had no status as a design architect. Cross didn't trust him, especially in view of his involvement with the consortium formed in the '40s by the Clydeside builders to get work. Cross disliked the whole idea of conglomerates or rings - he didn't want to deal with them. For Gibson, on the other hand, the fact that Bunton was from Glasgow was an advantage, whereas the fact that we were a UK-wide, indeed international, company based in London, with a Scottish office in Edinburgh, created a bit of hostility against us. The consortium was dominated by the contractor John Lawrence, who also ran Rangers Football Club. His chief engineer, J A MacGregor, had previously been burgh engineer in Paisley, and was a very strong man, another 'Cross' type, although more openly forceful. It was mainly through his efforts that Bunton got into the Red Road set-up. Before he moved to Lawrence, he ran everything in Paisley (as burgh engineer); he was one of these chaps with a red light at his door. The council architects were kept away from all decisions, and weren't allowed to come to meetings.

Cross made a more subtle impact when he moved to the SSHA. In Glasgow, the DLO had always been a thorn in his flesh: it just couldn't compete, but it didn't need to! There was also a powerful DLO at the SSHA, but Cross sorted it out by insisting that it tendered for all new work: eventually they had to close it down altogether. His relations with the designers were sometimes strained: on one occasion, the SSHA's programme of oil-related housebuilding up north was dragging out, and at one crucial meeting he took over proceedings first before the architects arrived, and got all the decisions through! While he was at the SSHA, he lived in Currie, in Cherry Tree Park, and he had a 50cc motor scooter to run about town. After he retired from the SSHA, he moved away from Edinburgh, and would come through to visit me in our Trinity villa - and he'd remark sardonically that architects don't often live in the kinds of houses they design for others!

Dundee

We never built in Dundee - nobody ever does! In particular, we fell out with the trade union bosses there in a big way, over a job we were doing in a jute works. As recently as the late '70s, I was told there was no future for us there.

Edinburgh

The key figure in the 1960s housing drive in Edinburgh was Pat Rogan, who was Socialist chairman of housing from 1962 to 1965. Pat and I got an awful lot done in Edinburgh, and it was mainly through Pat's driving force. A bricklayer by trade, he was a no-nonsense chairman who got things done, but also very much a sincere socialist, fighting for the people. Not like many councillors today, university lecturers and social workers, getting on to the council as a stepping stone to Parliament. Pat knew all the Glasgow people well, and everybody else in Scottish housing; even the Secretary of State would call him Pat. I first met him when we were showing people round our newly completed prototype high block at Valley Gardens, Kirkcaldy, around 1956, and I remember him as the person who asked all the right questions. With Pat, it was numbers above all else. He was very proud of the Muirhouse scheme, whose construction we were much involved with. Looming above the whole of that area was Martello Court, which was given to a local Edinburgh builder to do [in 1962], to show what the local industry could achieve. It had a unique arrangement of all-round balconies: we were all amazed to see this thing go up, perched on a minute site that had originally been earmarked for one of our blocks! Pat's special policy was to pull down the life-expired temporary prefabs and redevelop the sites with multi-storeys, gaining thousands of new dwellings. One of the biggest sites was at Moredun, where we built some point blocks in 1965-67. I was amazed when Alex Steele, the city architect, told me the required density. It was sheer luck there was a rocky outcrop running down the site, where we could build a strip of multis in a row - that was the only way we could achieve it.

In 1965, the Tories won back control of the Housing Committee, and Pat was replaced as housing chairman by Adolf Theurer. But the two of them collaborated extensively, and Adolf basically maintained Pat's policies. I remember going on a trip to Glasgow with the two of them. They had a great party-political argument all the way there, but at the end of it, we all agreed that what really mattered was that we, as individuals, were working to get the very best for the community. And then, driving up Maryhill Road, he pointed to the old tenements and exclaimed, 'Those people will never have a chance until we get houses like that down!' I said, 'Ach, come away, Pat ...!' That agreement among the personalities overrode party opposition.

The city architect in those years in Edinburgh, Alex Steele, was quite a dominant personality - very different from Jury in Glasgow. Like Cross, he had tense relations with the planners. On one occasion I watched him reading through some planning comments on a big scheme, and he scrawled across it, 'Pay no attention to this'!

Appendices

High blocks: motives, costs, management

One of the most driving motives for building high blocks, even in Glasgow, was prestige. That's why Glasgow Corporation, for instance, got us to build that tremendously prominent line of tower blocks at Ardencraig Road, on the skyline above Castlemilk [in 1963-65]. It would have been far more practical to build those high blocks in a hollow rather than on a hill, and I said to Cross, 'You're mad building them up there - we'll have to blast huge amounts of rock!' To get round that, we were allowed by DHS to turn the blocks off their daylighting axis: they told us to get on with it and not tell anyone! I'm sure that the Housing Committee felt that, by building lots of flats, they were being seen to solve their housing problem. There were also projects which were purely fantastic, and never intended to be built. For example, there was talk around 1963-64 of a 34-storey block at the Parkhead redevelopment area. It was too high, and could never have been economically built: an extra bank of lifts would have been needed to go up to 40 storeys.

Glasgow Corporation spent lots more than anyone else on any given type of block. They'd build our standard blocks, but put in lots more. For example, they always needed extra precautions in the lifts. They'd go for Otis when everyone else would go for Express. Whereas the same blocks, for Coatbridge, were much more basic. For example, at Parkhead Area A, the foundations were on silt, and we repeated to Cross that to put flats there would be horrendously expensive. He said, 'In Glasgow, we're so short of decent sites that we build on what sites we can, whatever the cost.' Any other town council would have said, 'We can't do that!' That was Cross's way. If he hadn't been there, they wouldn't have got built. But there were built - from 1967, after several years of negotiations, at a reduced height of 15 storeys. Those blocks are floating on a cavern with adjustable jacks - in effect, they're floating on mud!

Cross put large, three-bedroom flats into some of his multi-storey projects - for instance, the 20-storey ones we did at Scotstoun in 1962. That was appalling. The Department didn't want them, nor did we! It was a sacrosanct policy - no big flats in tall blocks. Yet Cross said, 'We are Glasgow, we have a problem, we want to be exempted'. And he got it - I couldn't believe it! The 'adult family' idea worked in Kirkcaldy, or in places like Glenrothes or East Kilbride, where there was first-class management. In the late '60s, SDD officials started telling me that multis were socially undesirable. We were more-or-less told we could forget building them in new developments. I used to argue back that it was the management that was at fault, and that you could go to Kirkcaldy and see well managed high flats, or to Glasgow and Edinburgh and see badly managed flats; where there's good management, they do well.

C12. Multi-storey redevelopments in central Motherwell, carried out under the council leadership of Hutchison Sneddon. The big 17-storey slab block, at Parkhead Street (1963-64) was a prototype of the 'MSC' steel-framed system designed by Sam Bunton. Behind it are five Bison tower blocks at Central Motherwell CDA, built in 1967-71 in conjunction with Loudon as main contractor; and behind those are the medium-height Wimpey no-fines blocks of Clyde Valley Street and Watson Street, 1961-65. (RCAHMS B22061)

Interview 7

Hutchison Sneddon
former Housing Convener and Leader, Motherwell and Wishaw Burgh Council

Interview with Miles Glendinning, 11 May 1988

Summary of own career

I grew up in Wishaw, and became a member of Motherwell and Wishaw Burgh Council in 1958 and Housing Committee convener and leader of the council in 1960. Politically speaking, I was Labour, but with reservations about many of the orthodoxies of the time, such as unrestricted general-needs building. I was very lucky, as I was only 31 years old when I became council leader, and began to be able to make things happen in my home town. My own background was as a structural steel engineer, so I wasn't one of those councillors who couldn't read a drawing! I stayed on the council through the years of transition until it became a

district council, and retired only in 1977; after that I was chairman of Cumbernauld New Town Development Committee for four years [1979-83].

General housing and redevelopment policy

When I became housing convener, I set out on a personal quest - simply, to remove all the substandard housing in the town. The clamour from people in slums was very heavy - councillors' lives weren't worth living! To begin that strategy, the first thing I felt we had to do was to get accurate information about the problem. So I initiated a door-to-door survey of all the substandard housing in the burgh. We asked them a series of questions: how many rooms, how many occupants, private owned or rented, does it have an inside WC and bathroom, and so on. The survey was done by sanitary inspectors, and it took 18 months to complete. We then looked at what we found, at the available housing and the land within the council's boundaries. We found that we didn't have any real open space, with the exception of one 25-acre site which was scheduled for industrial development. At that time, we were trying to diversify the town's industry from being totally dependent on steel, by bringing in component manufacturers.

At that stage, we then sat down and prioritised the most seriously substandard housing in the town, and produced a report which said that we would demolish specific areas in order of priority. We put monthly and yearly dates against each of the streets. We put closing order dates on, and dates for demolition to follow. We put the entire plan to the Scottish Development Department, who approved it, and we published it around 1961-62. We wanted, where possible, to avoid removing things piecemeal. We wouldn't just pull down one bad block, but would take the good, the bad and the indifferent together within any area. Our aim was to remove everything substandard, and, within the replacement housing, to cater for some special needs, such as tuberculosis sufferers, and so on. When I was driving the thing, I wasn't conscious of the specific elements of housing need that we were catering for.

To get started on the plan, we also depended on some vacant sites: of course we preferred virgin sites, and we'd have used them if we'd had more of them. We wanted to do two things: firstly, to build houses on the 25-acre industrial-zoned site, because companies weren't knocking on our door to build factories; and secondly, to seek an extension of the burgh boundaries from Lanark County Council, to take in Netherton and Gowkthrapple. We were successful in both of these, the second only after a public enquiry at which we were opposed by the county council. The county had just completed 300 houses in Netherton - probably built with the idea of stopping us from getting the extension. We then asked them to let us have them, because they'd have no use for them. They'd filled them with tenants from all over the county. We offered them that, for any empty houses they gave us, we'd repay them when our clearance programme started by taking their tenants from Carfin and Newarthill into houses in the burgh. Then we set about working out how many houses we'd need to build to achieve these targets. We rewrote the book of words, from the old annual target of 350 houses. I set about increasing this, over a five-year period, by moving to 500, then 750, and finally 1,000.

System building

The government, especially under Labour after 1964, was very anxious to step up the rate of removal of substandard properties, and increase the rate of building. About 400 systems of various sorts suddenly appeared on the scene. The government trailed the system-building cause around all the local authorities at the time, but there were far too many systems to make a rational choice. What happened was that big firms tried to establish an advantage. Crudens went and bought the Skarne system from Sweden. Wimpey developed their no-fines construction into a system. Concrete (Scotland) provided factory-built panels from Falkirk - and so it went on.

Multi-storey building

System building, in practice, was bound up with the drive to build multi-storey blocks. The fundamental argument was about the need to build higher buildings on less land. Although some people disagreed that there was a direct relationship between block height and land use, we in Motherwell generally accepted the argument that high blocks saved space.

Our multi-storey programme had two setpiece projects. The first was Glencairn Tower, a 17-storey slab block in Parkhead Street which we built from 1963, using steel-framed construction - something very unusual in housing. The main contractor was Crudens, but we used a consortium of the local steel firms to actually build the structure. The block was used for rehousing people from a big row of one- and two-apartment houses immediately adjacent, in Macdonald Street, houses without internal facilities. There were round about 160 houses in those tenements, and when we finished the 17-storey multi we found we hadn't gained a house!

The second setpiece project was Muirhouse. This was built from 1964, using no-fines construction, a method which had given Blackburn some problems a few years earlier, but which now, with Wimpey, was very much tried and tested, and was extremely reliable and successful. We built around 1,300 no-fines houses at Muirhouse. That enabled us to begin our redevelopment drive in earnest, pulling people out of tenements quickly, and beginning demolition and rebuilding on the same site straight away. In other words, in addition to and alongside our normal building for general-needs lettings during the year, we were able to start this full-scale demolition and decanting process.

The redevelopment process was not driven 100% by the results of our house condition survey. There was one significant exception, which stemmed from the fact that all the main roads into Motherwell and Wishaw entered the burgh through areas of substandard housing. So we took a conscious decision to deal with those areas out of strict order, to make sure the first housing the arriving visitor saw was modern, and let people know that the town was alive and actively renewing itself. That was a conscious decision. We built Stewarton Crescent and Terrace, for example, at the east end of Main Street Wishaw, on the approach from Lanark. We built new housing in Netherton, and on the Dalziel side of town. Forgewood was also a new scheme, but an unhappy one. It had an extremely high density, and walk-up blocks with open access-ways - the most unpopular house-type you could build in local authority housing, but also the most economical.

Consortia: SLASH

SLASH was an early consortium of Scottish authorities, set up in 1963. We attempted to pool the resources and expertise of large authorities for the benefit of the smaller ones, using cadres of city architects' staffs. We had quantity surveyors for examining ironmongery, heating systems and so on.

At first, SLASH was bound up with multi-storey blocks. The first big SLASH project began when the SDD suggested that several authorities order blocks based on the Bison system, and the Department would underwrite them. Glasgow, Edinburgh and Greenock opted to take two 15-storey blocks each - and there it stuck. The reasons those three places took the blocks were not altruistic. Glasgow's housing was then under David Gibson, and he would have taken anything, as he was so desperate for more houses by whatever means - it was at that time that he was plunging way ahead of all the rest of us, with schemes like Red Road. Edinburgh wanted to use this to get approval for a site that had been blocked by the planners. Greenock had an axe to grind too. That's typical of the way consortia worked. Everybody had their own individual motives.

When that first SLASH order for six Bison blocks was put together, Pat Rogan was the housing chairman in Edinburgh. After the meeting which authorised the contract, in Glasgow City Chambers, I had a blazing row in the corridor outside with Pat and Davie Gibson, bcause I wouldn't opt into the system. It was more expensive than our normal blocks, Wimpey or whatever - although one of the government's arguments for it was that it would end up cheaper. Davie and Pat's argument was that the government would offset any deficit. What I said to them was, 'You're off your heads - of course they won't!' And of course, in the end, they didn't! Glasgow, Edinburgh and Greenock had to stump up the difference themselves.

SLASH failed latterly only because architects tended not to tell their councillors that the designs were no longer new designs - they'd been more-or-less approved as standard for about 80% of the programme by around 1970. Members didn't understand why they were paying so much money to this organisation when they 'didnae get anything out of it!'

Central Lanarkshire consortium

The Central Lanarkshire consortium was a group of burghs - Coatbridge, Airdrie, and ourselves - who came together in the mid-1960s. The county council stayed out of it. The idea of grouping together was that we could buy the product cheaper. We, having examined a wide variety of systems, came to the conclusion that the Camus system, as built under licence by Mitchells, was the best option. This was for two main reasons: firstly, that they had the best joint design - something which is very important with prefabricated panel construction; secondly, that they could provide factory construction and employment in an area with plenty of unemployed labour available, because of mining recessions. As an engineer, one of my big concerns has always been in the joints, to ensure that they were the least likely possible to leak: in retrospect, I do feel we didn't put in anything like enough insulation.

Within the consortium, we embarked on a joint programme: Airdrie built Petersburn, a big low-rise high density project, and we built Gowkthrapple, which was mainly medium-rise with some small tower blocks. My opposite number as Labour Group leader at Coatbridge - Eddie Dowdalls, a technical college principal - was a key figure in that consortium, too. Motherwell then went on and built five multi-storeys on a site below Muirhouse. They'd previously built small multi-storeys on a site at Leven Street, which had been well received.

There was a vast difference of approaches among the various local authorities engaged in building housing. We saw ourselves as having a greater affinity to the biggest ones - Glasgow and Edinburgh. They were able to run ambitious programmes and big departments, whereas at the other end of the scale, there were some burghs that were so tiny that they had to put a penny on the rates every time the burgh engineer got a pay rise!

But one aspect of the Glasgow big-department approach we were determined not to copy was their no-expenses-spared spending on concealed equipment, while neglecting appearance and management. They used to insist on things like 150 gallons of water storage per house on the roof and a luxury electrical specification. If you stamped each ballcock, it used to cost 10s a time, and the electrical specification was another £70. All these added up to £200 extra per dwelling, which bought a whole lot of things, hidden behind skirting boards, that the tenant neither knew nor understood about. I examined the costs and benefits closely - how many bursts did they have per year, and was it worthwhile putting in grade 1 rather than grade 2 cylinders? And what we decided to do was to spend the money

saved this way on the appearance of the blocks, putting Portaflek on the walls, light rather than dark tiles on the floors, and spending a bob or two on timber in the entrance ways. That was successful - people polish their floors in Motherwell, whereas a man coming into one of my houses didn't say, 'My ballcock isn't stamped!'

That formed part of a wider management policy to safeguard our multi-storeys through a high standard of caretaking supervision, and through avoiding housing young children in the blocks. Only when the council relaxed that policy in the later blocks at Gowkthrapple, and reduced the caretaking levels, did we begin, later, to encounter management problems: that scheme wasn't very attractively located, with a major electricity installation right alongside it. In retrospect, there was a lack of defensible space, but in Scotland, we do have a tradition of roving where we like. In the 1960s, in Wishaw, a man used to regularly vault over my wall and walk across my garden to take a shortcut to his house, and he was quite indignant when I eventually asked him to stop!

We eventually realised that, with properly designed layouts, it was possible to obtain similar densities to multi-storeys without going above two storeys. But multi-storeys were still easier for officials to do, organisationally speaking. Pushing schemes through legal departments, redirecting services, meeting cost limits and so on, all these were easier with compact, concentrated blocks. Their members were screaming blue murder, the public was screaming blue murder, and the government was saying, 'We're doing the best we can'. You put multi-storeys and two- or four- storey blocks up, and that seemed like a balanced scheme. That was the easy way of doing it!

In our best year, we completed around 1,100 houses - the equivalent of 14,000 houses in Glasgow. Glasgow couldn't reach that per-capita level, because of building industry problems. They had a direct labour organisation which invariably seemed to finish blocks late, and some private builders who seemed to do so as well. Professor Cullingworth, who did the Glasgow report on houses of sub-tolerable standard, came to Motherwell after we'd produced the eight-year plan, and adopted it for Glasgow. The government used our eight-year plan as the basis for Glasgow's five-year programmes.

Housing management

In an owner-occupied house, the owner is the 'housing manager'. By 1975, I was looking at setting up a cyclical maintenance section. That initiative failed, because we didn't sell it properly to the people who would have to operate it.

Individual sites: Merry Street development

All our sites in the town suffered from underbuilding from old coal mines. That was a problem faced by towns all over Clydeside and the Lothians, of course, but in most cases they had enough land elsewhere to build on. We didn't! The worst case was the Merry Street multi-storey site, which we developed in 1967 with three 20-storey blocks by Crudens, and some lower housing. We found that there had been coal 70 and 200 feet down, and that the site was absolutely riddled with workings. We had a hell of a time finding a site for those blocks, because the council had decided in principle against using jackings. We bored holes all over the place, we spoke to men who had worked at Parkhead Colliery, and we looked at the booked totals of coal extracted. Despite all that, we kept coming across unknown workings. We eventually concluded that the stoops must have collapsed. Eventually, we built the high blocks, without jacks, on the bits of the site we were sure of. Their positioning then dictated the planning of the entire area: the rest had to be designed around them.

Brandon Street development

Right in the centre of town, we had a one-sided street with a wall and a goods yard on the blind side. The Co-operative had a fairly big group on the shop side of the street. A developer came along and made a deal with British Railways to buy the goods yard - where the shops now are. It wasn't offered to the local authority, which surprised me. It was formerly the site of the Duke of Hamilton's townhouse, so he didn't allow coal to be dug from under it. As a result, it was the one good site in the town for commercial development. The developers produced a plan, and immediately, the Co-operative produced a counter-plan; neither plan was very imaginative. So the Corporation turned both of them down, and decided, by turning the shops round and making the arcade face West Hamilton Street, to try to force the developer to change his plans, because we didn't have the money. They came back with a new plan, and, in our response to this, we said we didn't want the town centre to be dead at night, and we wanted the air space to build an economic-rental multi-storey block, with nice coloured bathroom suites, etc. The Brandon Street tower, as it was built, housed people who were prepared to pay a wee bit over the odds, people like a widow in a 14-room house in the Hamilton Road who couldn't maintain it, but was prepared to pay an economic rent.

Macdonald Street

The consultant architect, Sam Bunton, was known as a bit of a maverick, but he appealed to the council on this occasion because he was proposing to use the local product. It was an important place to try out some ideas of planning and construction. The block was very successful in the sense that it was popular with tenants - although there was disappointment that you went 18 storeys up and didn't come straight to your front door, but had to walk along an open gallery. But the main reason we didn't build any more of them was that many people didn't think that the block was aesthetically very nice-looking.

Appendices

Local authority relations: the land question

In the convention of Scottish burghs, theoretically everyone was the same: the Lord Provost of Glasgow had the same vote as the Provost of Portknockie. But, in reality, there was an accepted pecking order. Glasgow would lead, then Edinburgh, then Aberden, Dundee, Paisley and so on.

Relations between Lanark County Council and ourselves, the burghs, focused on the question of land for development. As a new town was being developed at East Kilbride, the county council people were interested in seeing that developed, rather than extensions of existing towns. Housing in Lanark County Council was controlled by Hughie Brannan, a very good councillor who came from the village of Forth: he became convener of the Labour Group and of the Housing Committee. They had a very big programme, but unfortunately they applied the same type of terraced system-built houses all over the county.

We were quite happy to participate in the Glasgow overspill programme. We approached Glasgow Corporation, offering to take overspill at the going rate. We felt it was a waste of money to create new services when we had existing services that could be used by more people, and we wanted to increase our population to give us a pool of labour; and we also felt that the thinning-out and revival of Glasgow was vital for the west of Scotland generally.

But on the other hand, I also kept on good terms with the main Housing Committee people in Glasgow, who were not so keen on overspill. I was good friends with the greatest of their housing leaders, David Gibson; in fact I knew him in the late '50s, before he became housing convener. He was very strict in respect of the morality of people living in terrible conditions - very ILP in his absolute sincerity. He saw the clear need that this had to be altered, and worked night and day to this end. Always agitated, always a cigarette in his hand - that was his style. Gibson set out to solve the immediate problem of bad housing, and the bad health which went with it. Other people could build a new city from the gaps he'd created, but first he'd make sure everyone had a bath and hot water. Gibson killed himself trying to solve Glasgow's housing problems! They used to say in Glasgow, 'If you're housing convener for three years, they send you to Gartnavel!' Gibson was perhaps the fieriest and most vigorous of the Glasgow conveners. His philosophy was an altruistic one which stemmed from his ILP background of Sunday-school socialism. His successor, Clark, inherited his ideas and was able to make things happen. Hart was an older man who just liked to get on with the job, without fuss; although he was a Tory, the Glasgow Labour Party treated him very well, and invited him to major events.

All these people were on very familiar terms - we were friends, we picked up the telephone, we talked - I was always invited by Davie to the Glasgow housing inspection, for instance! I was on close terms with all the Glasgow conveners of the 1960s, whether Labour or Tory - Gibson, Eddie Clark, McCrossan, Hart, Muir. I can recall Gibson trying to buy the 'Queen Mary' to house people. We had terrific arguments about Red Road - I said he'd gone overboard. And on the day we went to look round the Spence Hutchesontown 'C' blocks being built in the Gorbals, I told him that they were a disaster. He'd said, 'You must come, I've sent you a special invitation!' So I went along and went round the blocks - they were awful, with plasterboard and nails sticking out. Gibson said to me, 'What do you think?' I said, 'Come on, Davie, you don't really want to know'. He said, 'Come on, tell me!' I said, 'I think they're dreadful - I wouldn't live in them rent-free!' Then straight away he started passionately defending them - that was typical of him. He said, 'No, no, they're a completely new thing, it's the space and the lightness …!'

In Glasgow, there was a huge, running argument over the phasing of their redevelopment programme. It centred on the 29 Comprehensive Development Areas. The housing people argued that the planners, by designating all these areas without a firm plan for rebuilding, had sterilised a whole chunk of the city; and they wanted to build piecemeal in those areas. The planners, led in council by Bill Taylor, argued that you couldn't do that, because you mustn't prejudice all the longer-term changes that were needed - you must build around them, build to a master plan. As a smaller authority with more manageable problems, we in Motherwell were able to avoid that dilemma. We could have our cake and eat it. We could answer our immediate needs, and also build to a master plan. Arguably, Bill Taylor lost Glasgow 25 years. But equally, you could say that Gibson took the easy road out, and created more problems down the line.

In a major council like Glasgow, the chief councillors were as powerful, if not more so, than local MPs. If you've got a big pond with a lot of fish, then you get a lot more big ones. Glasgow Corporation was a big pond with a lot of big fish: it had a problem as to who was its most important person. Housing, because of its spending requirements, invariably assumed an importance out of all proportion to other departments. You get councillors clashing: some people don't emerge in debates, and they attach themselves to those who do. When they want something for their area, they'll speak to that guy sideways and he'll help, fixing a tenancy and so on. He then expects them to follow him in his wider cause - rebuilding Glasgow housing! In Glasgow, the city councillors were full-timers - unlike us burgh councillors. Gibson, for example, would have an office in the City Chambers, where he held his clinics with his constituents. That's the difference between the city and the burgh. In my part of Wishaw, I could knock on all these doors and know these people by name: I could just open the door and go in.

Archibald Jury was a very controlled man, and very efficient at delegating; I never saw a paper on his desk. When you saw him with people like Nicoll, there was never any doubt who the gaffer was. Yet he had a nice, smiling manner. He was abetted by a very good town clerk, Falconer. Glasgow was so formal, it wasn't true!

Labour municipal attitudes to private housing

People in Scotland didn't think about buying a house. In 1961-62, I was living in a house in York Street at a rent of 19s 2d per week. I thought I should be able to build my own house and leave this to someone else. But there was this dogma among Labour councillors, that housing was a public service and nobody should be encouraged to buy public property. In 1960, I began floating from the platform, in Motherwell, the need to sell council houses, and use the revenue to provide for maintenance -as it was lack of maintenance which brought the old tenements down, under rent control. To provide for this, I argued that houses should be sold with a sinking fund addition to the mortgage. I felt there was no sense in providing housing for people that didn't need the subsidy. In 1967, I was called in to the Scottish Office by the minister, who said, 'You've got to stop doing this sort of thing!' As late as 1978, house sales were still ignored in Labour's manifesto.

I live in Shand Street, Wishaw, now. Strathclyde Region have built a bypass, so it's much quieter. I live near a Safeway store. People can park on the road outside their houses. There's bingo round the corner. On a Saturday, it's like a fairground, and the rest of the week it's not too bad. The reason I live there is that it was the only site in my ward I could find to build a house! It's near shops, schools, a church - I've got everything on my doorstep - what I call 'God's little acre'.

Relations with central government

Labour's 1966 manifesto had said that we would build 50,000 houses in Scotland annually. I'd been working with SLASH, with the Central Lanarks consortium, and so I wrote to Dickson Mabon and said to him, 'If the manifesto is a serious commitment, I know how to do this now. If you can secure a two-year secondment for me from the Gas Board, I'll come and do this from the front!' Before long, I ended up on the SHAC as a 'thermometer'.

Willie Ross and I had a peculiar relationship. We were always fighting one another, but he kept on appointing me to things - perhaps at the instigation of Mabon, who I got on well with. Ross liked to lecture people on some occasions, but on others he tried to turn on a 'one of the boys' act: 'I'm telling you guys, because I've got problems'. One year in the late 1960s, Ross put the brakes on all local government tendering and spending, and called us all into St Andrew's House. It was a huge meeting, with a phalanx of officials there. Ross did his 'poor-mouth speech': he had a lot of problems, he wanted us to put the brakes on, and even if tenders were out, he didn't want them accepted. So I asked him to his face whether the government was holding back its own projects, because otherwise it would be difficult for me to tell my people they couldn't proceed with theirs. He blazed up at that - obviously I'd struck a tender nerve - and the meeting ended in disarray!

Life as a councillor

I used to come home at night to my house in a tenement in York Street - it's since been rehabilitated by Bield Housing Association. People would be queuing up the top of the stair and round again. I had one room, in a two-room flat, that was totally devoted to interviews. My wife and I, in our first house, hardly ever had a meal without a guest.

Unlike Glasgow, where the councillors were full-time, I had a job. But people just came to your house all the same - they came at 9 a.m., 9 p.m., whenever they wanted! Only Christians would come on a Sunday, on their way back from church. I interviewed thousands of people: it was always 'my problem'. And my wife interviewed more people than I did! Often the demands were strange ones: it's not funny when someone bangs on your door at 12 midnight, and four people tumble in and say, 'We've got a big problem', and their 'problem' turns out to be that they've been allocated a four-apartment council house, and they'd prefer a three-apartment one! In cases like that, I'd have to put my foot down and say, 'Get out of here and don't give me trouble!'

The attitude of some people then was, 'I'm entitled to anything that's going from the local authority'. For example, there were two back greens at York Street. The grass was cut by a man in the next block. He stopped doing it for some reason, and my wife asked me if I could do anything about that grass. I arranged for someone I knew to come and do it for £1, and everyone would contribute. But one man didn't pay, and when I asked him, he said, 'Oh, I thought it was being done by the council'.

I sat up one night - I had a drawing-board - and redesigned all the back staircases in that block, to add bathrooms on the back. But the burgh architect said it would be too expensive! We deliberately left around 1,000 substandard houses standing, for anti-social tenants - but it never worked out, as they always ended up in the more desirable spots!

The councillors

The traditionalist Labour councillors, never having been able to envisage housing at a rate of 900 houses annually, always worked on a local basis. They wanted council houses because, they thought, council houses produced Labour voters, and they could control letting procedures. My colleagues thought I was daft. I was at a meeting describing the Muirhouse project - the seven point blocks, and so on - when the councillor for that ward got up and said, 'All that sounds very nice, but Hutchie Sneddon's made it all up!' He was an older man, who didn't have much vision! Today, there's an even greater lack, or a loss, of idealistic drive in local government. I became a councillor because I felt I had a duty to put a voluntary effort into the town I'd been brought up in. Now, I see people who go into the council at the same age for much less urgent reasons - they could do stamp collecting, but they decide to become a councillor instead!

All important policy decisions were made at Labour Group meetings. But we never changed a policy without telling our opposition counterparts. We'd say, 'Tomorrow night, we're thrashing out our policy,' and then afterwards we'd go along and knock on their door, and tell them as much as possible before we went into council.

Some people in Motherwell today say that the Sneddons of this world were proved wrong by subsequent housing management problems. But, at the time, if you went round and knocked on doors, as I did all the time, you were only asked three questions: 'When am I going to get a new house?'; the schooling of their children; and general health amenities. Of course, everyone's desire would be for a detached council house in the country near a bus stop, within easy distance of the shops; but you can't get all those things!

We did put a lot of resources into housing management: we had 27 staff members working full-time on it in the late '60s. But I was a great believer in not breathing down their necks. With requests from constituents, I just passed them straight to the managers. So long as the councillor could deliver the new house, he felt that he had fulfilled his remit.

The idea that we should have kept all the old houses is a nonsense that's grown up, because the thing's eased itself. People didn't say, 'Can you rehabilitate this tenement?' They said, 'Can you get me out of this tenement - the roof's leaking - it's verminous!'

Motherwell officials

Our officers were variable in quality. The prime mover in virtually everything was our town clerk, a man called Alex MacIntosh. He was fired with enthusiasm for our programme, and harnessed the officers to keep up momentum in areas such as purchasing of properties. He was a potent force, and put the screw on everybody. The burgh architects were less important - first we had a man called Fyfe, followed by someone called Mandle, who died, and was then succeeded by his assistant, an architect named Hill. We didn't have a fully fledged architecture department during the boom years.

Relations with contractors

Because of the lack of a full architecture department, we tended to use package deals with contractors. In order to introduce an element of competitive tendering, we tried to group firms by size - to avoid having large firms tendering against small ones. We set up a banded list, and said that the smaller firms would be eligible for contracts below a certain size, which would be run competitively, while the big ones would be package deals. It was a parallel system.

Of the contractors we used, the most reliable were Wimpey and Crudens: both of them built on time. In some places. you used to have penalty clause contracts, and the contractors would build in all the extra before they started. In Motherwell, there was only one penalty clause: that if you didn't build on time, you wouldn't build again here! We only fell down once, with a firm called Pert from Dundee. They got two redevelopment jobs, almost fortuitously, having put in extremely cheap tenders in competition with local firms, although we had a gut feeling that they shouldn't have been put in. Their workmanship was not terribly good, and then, in the case of a block in Main Street, Wishaw, our surveyor went under the building and found there were no foundations! So we removed them from the lists, and didn't give them any more work until there was evidence they'd improved. Then they went bust - a narrow escape for us!

C13. *1990 aerial view of Wimpey's Townhead Area B redevelopment (in foreground) showing the simplification of Tysler's original interlocking layout concept, into a pattern of freestanding 25-storey slabs, built from 1967, and three storey walk-up blocks, added later. Crudens's much larger Sighthill development, with its ten 20-storey Zeilenbau slabs, is visible in the background. (RCAHMS B43564)*

Interview 8

Ted (Tadeusz) Tysler
former Regional Architect (West of Scotland), Wimpey Ltd

Interview with Miles Glendinning, 14 July 1987

Outline of own career

I joined Wimpey in 1959 as an architectural assistant. At the time, I wasn't qualified, and for my first year did not work on high blocks, but instead helped with the completion of the new eastern regional office at Barnton Grove. When I qualified in 1963, I was immediately promoted to depute regional architect forScotland, based at Barnton Grove. I began to come into contact with Glasgow Corporation at that time. Tom Smyth did most of the liaison: I occasionally got involved with Glasgow in his behalf, and sometimes spoke with Lewis Cross, the official in the city architect's department who dealt with housing. Early in 1965, when the west of Scotland became an independent region within the company, based at Bishopbriggs, I was sent here to become regional architect (west). Donald Ross became regional architect (east), and Tom Smyth was promoted to principal architect (Scotland). I left Wimpeys in October 1966 and worked with William Loudon Ltd for six years. In January 1973 I joined Glasgow Corporation as assistant chief housing architect. In 1975, on regionalisation, the housing section became two sections - rehab and new build. I became chief architect for rehab in May 1975, and now, in 1987, I'm DARS chief architect for Glasgow (North).

Ethos of the housing drive

In the 1950s and '60s, the push for houses was so great, with the desperation to get homes built for so many homeless families, that as soon as a site became available, the cry was, 'How many houses can we get on it?' As an architect, I had certain misgivings - it appeared a little bit indiscriminate, whenever a piece of land appeared, to shove a multi-storey block on it - but that was a private opinion. It was my bread and butter, and so I was naturally happy to build as many high blocks as possible. I agreed with some aspects of the theory behind them: that Scotland was a small country and we had to build high.

Indeed, I believe that the time for those kinds of solutions may come again, although not in this generation and definitely not in the precise way that we dealt with our problems. I have been to Poland on a number of recent occasions. There is a very acute housing shortage there now, and they are now doing what we did thirty years ago. My sister, who lives in Bydgoszcz, had to share a flat for years, and was absolutely delighted to be given a flat in a tower block on the periphery. When she first moved in a few years ago, I suggested that it might, in the long run, be a mistake, and she was very surprised. But since then, on subsequent visits, I have already begun to detect signs of deprivation - the enthusiasm was no longer as great as it had originally been. In any new multi-storey blocks built here in Scotland, some things would have to be different: for example, insulation. The 'U' value of the '1001' was 1.03, which was reasonably OK, but earlier ones were not up to today's standards.

Wimpey's reputation

When I went to see a burgh architect or engineer, I was quite proud to introduce myself as a Wimpey man. We felt our reputation was something based not on marketing stunts, but on clients' solid experience of our ability to deliver on time. The way it worked was illustrated by one of our successes of the mid '60s, with Clackmannan County Council. They needed some housing in a hurry, and so gave Wimpey two five-storey blocks to build quickly: they were just two of our standard five-storey maisonette and flat blocks, that you see in small towns all over Scotland. The county architect at first was very reluctant to give us the job, as he'd have preferred to carry on with the old rural separate-trades ways, rather than go for a package deal, which of course cost more. But when the blocks were finished his attitude had completely changed! He said he wouldn't have thought it possible for blocks to go up so quickly and so well, and to cause him so little trouble. He was quite converted, and after that, we built quite a number of low-rise developments for him.

Our emphasis on reliability also began to counteract the idea that we were outsiders, or an 'English' firm. There was one occasion, which I found very pleasing, and even comical. In the mid-1960s, I was at a committee meeting at which there was discussion of the possibility of some English builder trying to get into Glasgow, and a councillor said, 'Why should we allow such firms to get into our housing programme, when we have such good Scottish firms, like Laidlaw or Wimpey!'

Wimpey project design and management

The normal drill in the processing of a scheme up to start of work was that I went to meet the council architect first and established his requirements, then transmitted those to London. Then the layout and type-plans arrived from our Hammersmith head-office in due course. The relationship between Hammersmith and Glasgow was an uneasy one. Basically, all the multi-storey developments were designed by them, and, up to the early '60s, they had done what they liked in design matters more generally; our office were essentially messenger-boys between them and the client. At that time, the Scottish section down in London had a very good architect in charge of it, a forceful character called Cyril Saunders. He left around the time I started as Tom Smyth's depute, and was replaced by someone who didn't know the Scottish scene so well. So we could start extending our influence, usually on the pretext that our building regulations required this or that. Eventually, as we built up our Scottish architectural sections, we began to design the low-rise blocks completely, and to guide Hammersmith even on the high-rise. They would still do the layout, but we would make adaptations, negotiating with them by phone and telex and correspondence and visits. We were down there each month and they were up here about the same amount.

I was a bit worried about our standardised approach to every and any site, but that was offset by the need to produce good houses fast, and by the fact we were achieving that. Also, as the initiative in producing houses began to shift from Hammersmith to Scotland, we could begin altering things: I used to criticise their kitchens and even, eventually, their block layouts. And we were able to contribute to the evolution of variants of standard designs - for instance, the detailed Scottish alterations to the '1001'. Most significantly, low-rise house-types and layouts, from the mid-1960s a growing proportion of Wimpey's layout, were designed by us. When we wanted to alter a layout, we were a little bit devious: we could always tell London that was what the client wanted, regardless of whether or not he did! And when the client did want something different, we seized on that.

For example, whereas Cross, the Glasgow housing boss, accepted our standard designs without any qualms, Edinburgh city architect Alex Steele didn't always want standard blocks: he wanted not just units but designs. So on some occasions - for example, with the medium rise slab blocks at Multihouse - we had to design something special for him, and specific for the site. This necessitated a three-way debate between ourselves, Steele and Hammersmith - with us in the middle.

Marketing techniques

To keep the political side of the local authorities in touch, there was a constant effort of public relations by our head of marketing, Brigadier Prentice. For example, I'm sure that when the first prototypes of the '1001' - our rationalised-construction tower block type of the early and mid '60s - were built, he'd have seen to it that the Glasgow Housing Committee and those of other big towns were taken down south to Ramsgate to see them. Although Prentice, as a military type, could be a little bit forceful at times, he always kept methodically in touch with all the authorities and kept up their interest. We often attended these visits to explain the technical points - although our involvement was always kept distinct from the selling exercise.

Wimpey and system building

From the early '60s, the multi-storey market throughout the Central Belt was in full swing, although there were always fears of competition. I don't remember any kind of worry about running out of work. We were prepared and capable of building as much as we could get. Maybe in the boardrooms in Hammersmith, they had the usual commercial worries: 'Let's not expand too much!' But we in Scotland were itching to get on and get things done. At the height of the housing boom, we were building several schemes simultaneously. At the point of my departure, when we

were engaged in the design of my own biggest project, Townhead B in Glasgow, there wasn't much to look forward to in the city, apart from the low-rise. There was a kind of feeling that Glasgow was no longer our major field, and that East Kilbride and a few of the other towns had now taken over.

In sheer output terms, Crudens were regarded as our major competitor, because of the size of Sighthill, but increasingly the large-panel systems began to seem a more urgent threat. What did give the firm the most anxieties was not so much competitors or shortage of work, but the '60s government-sponsored push for large-panel system building. That's why Wimpey tried so hard, through the National Building Agency, to become listed as a system builder: all those negotiations were handled by Hammersmith.

I myself was thoroughly convinced by the systems philosophy. I remember saying in private conversations with Wimpey colleagues that we should get rid of no-fines and go to a proper system. Wimpey's sales pitch was that of building a basically old-fashioned system faster and more reliably, in a way that would impress people and maintain our reputation. My belief was: here we are in the 20th century, building cars and planes, and so why not build houses by the same methods? I used to argue, by the same token, that we had been producing windproof and rainproof railway carriages for decades, and yet we still could not do the same for houses, even though those were much more important. Thus, large-panel systems obviously seemed the answer to me then. Even today, I don't apologise for my philosophy of industrialised building. I said to colleagues, 'How can you justify a bloke standing outside in the rain and mud, laying brick on brick, spreading mortar, in just the same way people did thousands of years ago?' Within the company, I used to argue that pouring concrete is not a 'system', it's just pouring concrete; but nobody listened to me. I was in favour of a kind of Meccano set approach. My fascination with systems was based on the idea that the whole concept of erecting shutters and pouring concrete wasn't compatible with the new generation of jet travel and computers. In practice, I was wrong, as, although these ideas worked abroad, they didn't work in Scotland. Why, I don't know. We're now right back to square one - building in brick - which still goes against the grain for me. If there is, in the future, a reflation, we've been virtually standing still for a number of years in new building; eventually there's going to be a housing shortage, which will probably come out of the blue. Then, people will suddenly say that there's not enough bricklayers, and that we have to go back to some kind of system building.

Relationships with Glasgow Corporation

Glasgow Corporation's insistence on high specifications and high build quality was something that automatically benefited us. They insisted there should be no flats on the ground floor, and (apart from Royston A) a completely covered drying area on the roof. Apart from that, the only thing that was special, and which always gave us headaches, was the electrical side. It was their electrical side, rather than their architects or planners, who exerted a very strong and demanding influence on our projects.

Our normal procedure in Glasgow was a phone call from Cross, saying, 'We've got a site for you here - how soon can you fill it?' And if we could fit it in, then it was on to the brief, survey, off with proposals to Hammersmith, and on with the job! The chief housing architect, Tom Fleming, was very pleasant, but he was completely overpowered, metaphorically speaking, by Lewis Cross. He was mostly concerned with Glasgow's own designs. All that we exchanged were courtesies. We never discussed professional matters. There were two or three other architects who acted as liaison architects. However, some of the Corporation's architects must have cared about the design aspects of the programme, because just after I joined Glasgow Corporation in 1973, I mentioned the Balgrayhill deck-access blocks, designed by the housing architects ten years earlier, to one of my new colleagues as being a huge, rather inhuman development, and he gave me a very spirited defence of the design!

Specific Glasgow projects

The Battlefield development, built in 1965-66, was an example of our routine system in the mid '60s. It was pretty swift and automatic, a standard 20-storey solution. There were two blocks; there was very little choice. Hammersmith prepared the scheme, we submitted it to Cross's people, and it just went ahead. The only problem cases were Parkhead and Bridgeton-Dalmarnock CDA, because of the risk of subsidence caused by mining, and Ardencraig Road in Castlemilk, where we grossly exceeded the budgeted underbuilding costs.

Parkhead A and Bridgeton-Dalmarnock, both built in 1967-68, were hotly debated between our Glasgow regional office and the head office at Hammersmith Grove. The ground conditions were very poor. Hammersmith were dubious about the advisability of putting up multi-storeys. I was quite keen to get three multi-storeys up, but I couldn't persuade our engineers to agree. Eventually, I remember working out a solution with Bob Fleming in Engineering and Jim Kernohan, by then chief Glasgow housing architect. The three of us favoured a multi-storey scheme of a lower height, down to 15 storeys, and eventually we persuaded Engineers to build on rafts. There were problems with finding all the old pit-shafts in that area, and nearly a hundred bores were made to locate one of them. After we'd spent thousands of pounds, an old guy sitting on his doorstep told us where it was - under a washhouse!

The Townhead CDA Area B was really my baby. During the design stages in the mid '60s, I kept encouraging a low-rise solution which would act as a podium and, from that, here and there, a tower would rise. The whole thing would have been interconnected, giving closed courts and nice vistas. It would have been a thoroughly urban courtyard development with interlinked low-rise and towers, nicely landscaped, with pend-type links from each courtyard to the next, totally pedestrianised: looking along each vista, you would see a three-storey line culminating in a tower, with plants and greenery. But what finally emerged was not in accordance with that original concept. What happened was that the site was so big, and there were so many problems with acquiring all of it and phasing the development - to say nothing of some access problems with the design - that it was eventually agreed that the multis should go up first, from 1967 onwards, which to some extent destroyed the concept of a totally integrated scheme. The high blocks at Townhead B were more or less as I envisaged them. I was instrumental in suggesting that the blocks, which are 25-storey towers, should be on an eight-to-a-landing plan - I wanted to get away from the stereotype twin-tower Wimpey type-plan. Accommodation requirements also had something to do with it: being a central location, we wanted more two-apartments than we would normally get. I also wanted a design I could say to myself that I'd drawn up personally! The result was a simple slab. Now, in hindsight, they look a bit drab, a little bit overbearing.

East Kilbride New Town

At East Kilbride, they were very favourably disposed towards Wimpey. From 1965, they engaged us to build a series of what we liked to call 'luxury' multi-storeys, that is, standard point blocks much more lavishly equipped than usual. They primarily wanted four-to-a-landing blocks, all two-apartments - apparently there were queues of tenants for them! Although they had some very able architects, led by Scott, followed by Fraser, the odd thing was that they had such a high regard for Wimpey (as we'd already built low-rise so successfully for them, that we'd virtually solved their housing problem) that, apart from saying they wanted 'luxury' flats, they left us entirely to our own devices. They didn't want even to put a clerk of works on the job - I had to persuade them to do so! They had so much confidence in Wimpey that they were happy to give us the site and leave all the rest to me. They even exempted the scheme from the usual vetting by their own electrical and plumbing sections.

Work in other cities and burghs

Falkirk in the early 1960s had an architect, Ian Ferguson, who was extremely design conscious, and he imposed a number of high-quality features on our projects there. Paisley was a half-way house. An engineer, MacNaughtan, was in charge, and their special pride was a big district heating scheme. They more-or-less left Wimpey to our own devices. At Clydebank, there was only one block in my time, and that was the only one of our schemes which had severe problems. It was designed by a private architectural practice and built by us in no-fines. The architects didn't like inside bathrooms, and put them on the outside walls, so no internal ventilation was required; and this led to severe condensation. On the east coast, our experiences in Dundee and Aberdeen were of course very different. At Dundee, we were afraid our reputation would be tarnished as a result of the city's appalling building-industry and corruption problems. If we failed to deliver on time, it would be Wimpey that was blamed, not the labour - and Wimpeys always stand on their reputation. At Aberdeen, there were none of those problems, as everything was excellently organised and totally above board. The real problem there was getting into Aberdeen at all: with their spirit of civic pride and community, they were a hard nut to crack, as they firmly kept out outsiders.

STATISTICS ON HOUSING OUTPUT

C14. 1991 view of Mactaggart & Mickel's Hillpark development (with pre-1939 section at upper left). (RCAHMS B62319)

Table 1
Total numbers of houses completed in Scotland, 1919-44

Year	Total Public Sector	Total Private Sector	Overall Total
1919	-	-	-
1920	817	1,140	1,957
1921	4,342	2,237	6,379
1922	9,523	2,527	12,030
1923	6,462	1,667	8,129
1924	2,993	3,274	6,267
1925	4,822	5,227	10,049
1926	9,501	5,906	13,407
1927	16,923	5,484	22,407
1928	15,071	5,172	20,243
1929	14,316	5,199	19,515
1930	7,918	4,546	12,464
1931	8,315	4,153	12,468
1932	11,631	5,913	17,544
1933	15,808	8,155	23,963
1934	15,216	9,684	24,900
1935	18,814	7,086	25,900
1936	16,044	7,757	23,801
1937	13,341	8,187	21,328
1938	19,162	7,311	26,473
1939	19,118	6,411	23,329
1940	10,474	3,732	14,206
1941	4,714	692	5,406
1942	3,072	224	3,296
1943	2,717	92	2,809
1944	2,383	170	2,553

Source: Government quarterly and annual housing returns.

Table 2

Total numbers of houses completed in Scotland, 1945-97

Year	Public Sector					Housing Association Sector	Private Sector	All Sectors
	Local Authorities	New Towns	SSHA	Government Departments	Total Public Sector			
1945	1,351	-	77		1,428	-	141	1,569
1946	3,321	-	490		3,811		499	4,310
1947	8,919	-	1,854	2	10,775	20	1,354	12,149
1948	16,615	-	2,932	109	19,656	14	1,541	21,211
1949	20,004	60	4,116	493	24,673	72	1,102	25,847
1950	20,989	158	3,167	624	24,938	91	782	25,811
1951	17,971	120	2,906	647	21,644	139	1,145	22,928
1952	22,393	485	4,745	797	28,420	285	2,242	30,947
1953	29,719	1,316	4,957	946	36,938	217	2,393	39,548
1954	29,748	1,466	4,117	799	36,130	115	2,608	38,853
1955	24,210	1,323	3,745	1,137	30,415	31	3,523	34,069
1956	22,084	1,073	3,133	887	27,177	148	4,576	31,901
1957	24,239	951	3,136	493	28,819	105	3,513	32,437
1958	22,622	1,474	3,277	643	28,016	93	4,061	32,170
1959	18,665	1,551	2,493	348	23,057	4	4,232	27,293
1960	17,913	1,519	2,071	433	21,936	127	6,529	28,592
1961	16,823	1,265	1,453	489	20,030	53	7,147	27,230
1962	16,245	1,576	967	124	18,912	65	7,784	26,761
1963	17,699	1,649	1,816	399	21,563	32	6,622	28,217
1964	24,814	2,608	1,734	341	29,407	12	7,662	37,171
1965	21,823	2,996	1,765	825	27,409	154	7,553	35,116
1966	21,343	3,870	2,302	526	28,041	118	7,780	36,029
1967	27,092	3,941	2,189	557	33,779	181	7,498	41,458
1968	26,756	3,207	2,048	970	32,981	288	8,720	41,989
1969	27,497	3,656	2,779	187	34,119	183	8,327	42,629
1970	28,045	2,790	3,525	302	34,662	244	8,220	43,126
1971	23,125	2,394	3,058	260	28,837	332	11,614	40,783
1972	16,335	1,519	1,739	151	19,744	413	11,835	31,992
1973	14,432	1,589	1,328	224	17,573	245	12,215	30,033
1974	13,016	2,099	1,067	435	16,617	480	11,239	28,336
1975	16,086	3,636	3,062	402	23,186	766	10,371	34,323
1976	14,361	3,980	2,813	517	21,671	1,152	13,704	36,527
1977	9,119	3,167	2,042	314	14,642	546	12,132	27,320
1978	6,686	3,167	1,711	282	10,189	1,127	14,443	25,759
1979	4,755	2,018	1,084	206	8,063	544	15,175	23,782
1980	5,048	1,288	1,119	33	7,488	881	12,242	20,611
1981	3,770	1,516	1,779	1	7,066	1,928	11,021	20,015
1982	2,342	729	645	17	3,733	1,167	11,529	16,429
1983	2,311	667	508	6	3,402	1,271	13,178	17,941
1984	2,120	233	280	14	2,647	2,076	14,118	18,841
1985	1,989	201	621	17	2,828	1,099	14,445	18,374
1986	1,733	157	297	114	2,301	1,466	14,843	18,610
1987	1,710	107	678	139	2,634	1,169	13,904	17,707
1988	1,933	257	540	85	2,815	1,278	14,179	18,272
1989	1,474	409	400	-	2,283	1,620	16,287	20,190
1990	1,046	666	157	69	1,938	1,963	16,461	20,362
1991	1,016	550	166	-	1,732	2,264	15,533	19,529
1992	697	276	37	-	1,010	3,044	14,389	18,443
1993	502	456	-	-	958	2,723	17,711	21,392
1994	548	113	-	-	661	2,990	17,753	21,404
1995	499	674	-	-	1,173	5,003	18,310	24,486
1996	258	-	-	-	258	2,683	17,813	20,754
1997	108	-	-	-	-	4,507	17,065	21,680

Note: 1994-97 figures include some estimates; SSHA figures for 1990-92 refer to Scottish Homes.
Source: Government quarterly and annual housing returns and bulletins.

Table 3

Contractual arrangements for post-1945 multi-storey public housing (blocks of six or more storeys)

(a) Total numbers of dwellings completed within five-year periods

TYPE OF CONTRACTOR	1945-50	1951-55	1956-60	1961-65	1966-70	1971-75	Post-1975	TOTAL
Local/regional (within Scotland)	88	102	1,608	3,541	1,575	1,000	225	8,139
Scottish national main contractor (except Crudens)	-	32	-	2,045	281	-	-	2,358
Crudens (in-situ construction)	-	-	416	4,508*	3,950	552	-	9,426
Crudens (Skarne)	-	-	-	-	1,130	135	-	1,265
Wimpey	-	48	1,122	8,570	6,338	181	58	1,631
Other English main contractor (in-situ construction)	219	-	640	1,555	1,811	179	-	4,404
Bison (Concrete Scotland as main contractor)	-	-	-	467	916	-	-	1,383
Bison (Scottish main contractor)	-	-	-	1,111	2,698	1,019	-	4,828
Bison (SSHA/Glasgow DLO as main contractor)	-	-	-	532	415	-	-	947
Scottish main/English structural sub-contractor	-	-	-	-	208	-	-	208
Scottish main/European sub-contractor	-	-	-	-	677	117	-	794
Other English main contractor (large-panel prefabrication)	-	-	-	1,319	4,131	134	-	5,584
Glasgow DLO as main contractor (non-Bison)	89	-	308	3,784*	2,917	472	-	7,570
SSHA DLO as main contractor (non-Bison)	-	60	916	386	-	-	-	1,362

*including 161 flats by Crudens and 1,326 by Glasgow DLO with Multi-Storey Consortium (steel-framed) at Motherwell and Red Road (Glasgow)

(b) Overall numbers and percentages

Contractor	Number	Percentage of total
Crudens	11,299	18%
Wimpey	16,317	25%
Bison	7,158	11%
DLO (excluding Bison)	8,932	14%
All other main Scottish contractors	10,691	17%
All other main English contractors	9,988	15%
		100%

Source: M Glendinning and S Muthesius, Tower Block, 1994

GAZETTEER

General introduction

This gazetteer is an extract from *Tower Block - Modern Public Housing in England, Scotland, Wales and Northern Ireland*, by Miles Glendinning and Stefan Muthesius, published by Yale University Press in 1994. In that book, it formed part of a larger gazetteer of housing in Scotland, England, Wales, N Ireland and the Channel Islands. The gazetteer is made up of two separate parts. Section 1 is a list of all multi-storey developments erected or acquired by public housing authorities in Scotland since 1945, together with summary statistical information, including (especially importantly for our purposes here) the name of the contractor. Section 2 comprises brief periodical references concerning noteworthy developments of *c*.1945-70, whether or not containing multi-storey blocks.

Section 1 is subdivided alphabetically into individual local authorities and, within each authority, individual multi-storey developments, with additional locational information or cross-references to later estate names following in square brackets; any particular area may fall under several authority headings, as a result for example of local government reorganisation. The programme of the SSHA is listed after those of local authorities, and is subdivided under the relevant localities. The name of each individual development is followed in each case by committee approval or start date, number of blocks and dwellings in buildings of particular storey heights, and contractor's name. Thus, for instance, 'a1964, 6/17 (1788)' denotes a development of six 17-storey blocks containing a total of 1,788 flats, approved by committee in 1964. Individual contracts within a large staged development are separated by semi-colons; however, there are no statistics on non-multi-storey dwellings contained within the same contracts as the high flats. Some of the blocks listed have subsequently been demolished; where known, this is mentioned.

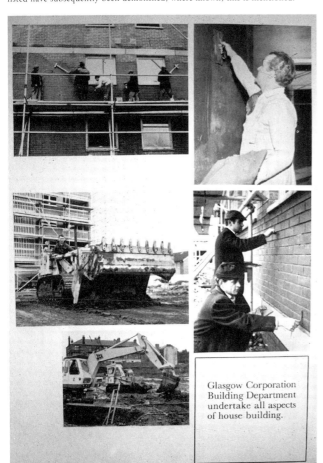

C15. Glasgow direct labour building: extract from a 1968 commemorative brochure produced by Glasgow Corporation for the opening of the city's '150,000th council house' (in a Springburn tower block) by Prime Minister Harold Wilson. (Glasgow District Council)

Section 2 is laid out in the same overall manner, with the authority's name followed by the development name: after these general headings, bibliographical references are listed, along with the names of architects (and, in some cases, other key individuals) involved in the design. Chief abbreviations are set out in the main abbreviations list for this book. It should be borne in mind that, in the early postwar years, there were no significant Scottish journals or periodicals devoted to building, as is, for example, *Project Scotland* today; the only coverage was that of the *RIAS Quarterly*. Thus these references are drawn mainly from architectural and building magazines published in London, which has the effect of slanting their coverage towards projects by those designers who were widely known in English architectural circles.

Section 1

List of public authority multi-storey developments, with contractual information

Local authorities

ABERDEEN BC (to 1975)
Ashgrove VIII [Gillespie Cres], s1959, 1/10 (40), A. Hall. Balnagask South Section 14 [Balnagask Circle], s1968, 3/14 (156), A. Hall. Castlehill Section 1 [Justice St], s1966, 1/19 (108), 1/9 (48), W.J. Anderson. Chapel St/Skene St Section 2 [Kidd St], s1961, 1/11 (75), W.J. Anderson. Cornhill-Stockethill Section I [Cairncry Rd], s1966, 1/17 (100), 2/16 (188), Wimpey; Section IV [Castleton Dr], s1967, 4/19 (288), W.J. Anderson; Section VII [Oldcroft Terr], s1968, 1/17 (100), Wimpey. Gallowgate II, s1964, 1/19 (126), 1/9 (72), W.J. Anderson. Great Northern Rd X [Printfield Walk], s1971, 1/10 (58), A. Hall. Great Northern Rd 'A' phase 2 [742, 768 G.N. Rd], s1974, 2/10 (112), A. Hall. Hazlehead I [Provost Graham Av], s1962, 4/12 (184), W.J. Anderson. Hutcheon St [Catherine St], s1973, 1/19 (144), 1/15 (140), A. Hall. Kincorth Section 49 [Tollohill Sq], s1963, 1/14 (52), A. Hall. Mastrick 1 [Mastrick Road], s1961, 1/14 (52), A. Hall. Mastrick 57 [Kingsford Rd], s1966, 1/10 (57), P. Cameron. Middlefield: Fowler Av, s1971, 1/10 (58), A. Hall. Rose St/Huntly St, s1973, 1/15 (126), A. Hall. Seaton 'A' [St. Ninian's Pl], s1969, 4/17 (296), Bett (Bison). Seaton 'B','C','D' [School Rd], Phase 1, s1971, 3/10 (170), P. Cameron; Phase 2, s1972, 7/19 (781), P. Cameron (Bison). South Mile End [Balmoral Ct, Holburn St], s1968, 1/10 (58), P. Cameron. Tillydrone-Hayton II [Pennan Rd], s1965, 1/14 (52), A. Hall; IV [Auchinleck Cres], s1965, 5/19 (360), A. Hall; XVI (A) [Gordon's Mill Cres], s1970, 1/10 (58), A. Hall. Upper Denburn CDA I [Gilcomston Park], s1971, 1/22 (120), A. Hall.

(CITY OF) ABERDEEN DISTRICT COUNCIL (from 1975)
Hardgate/Gairn Terrace, s1978, 1/11 (56), A. Hall. Hilton Rd/Rosehill Drive, s1976, 2/10 (113), A. Hall. Jasmine Place, s1983, 1/11 (58), Wimpey. Marchburn Drive, s1975, 1/10 (56), A. Hall.

AIRDRIE BC
Chapel St RD, a1970, 1/16 (94), Mitchell (Camus). Holehills, Thrashbush Rd, a1967, 3/8 (138), Mitchell (Camus).

AYR BC
John St [Riverside Pl], a1968, 3/14 (234), Concrete Scotland (Bison).

BARRHEAD BC
Blackbyres Rd [Glasgow Rd], s1968, 1/12 (47), J. Miller.

BUCKHAVEN & METHIL BC
Savoy Site [Swan Ct, Memorial Ct], s1968, 2/14 (148), Crudens.

CLYDEBANK BC
Central RDA [Kilbowie Rd], a1962, 1/12 (46), Wimpey. Dalmuir Gap Sites RD, a1963, 6/15 (528), Wimpey. East End RD [Glasgow Rd/Mill Rd], a1964, 3/16 (273), Crudens. Great Western Rd [Kirkoswald Dr], a1963, 5/13 (230), Wimpey. Littleholm [Mountblow], a1968, 3/16 (270), Tersons. Melbourne Av, a1953, 1/9 (32), Lawrence. Perth Crescent, a1962, 3/6 (78), A.A. Stuart.

COATBRIDGE BC
Blairgrove [Bank St], a1963, 2/15 (165), H. Leggat. Hutchison St Phase II [Henderson St], a1968, 1/8 (44), Crudens. Jackson St RD Phases I & II [Coats St], a1967, 2/18 (384), 1/17 (186), Crudens (Skarne). Ronald St, a1967, 2/15 (170), Wimpey. Whifflet [Calder St], a1963, 2/15 (165), H. Leggat. Wilton St, a1969, 1/15 (85), Wimpey. Woodside [Woodside St], a1965, 2/15 (170), Wimpey.

CUMBERNAULD NTDC
Carbrain 9 [Millcroft Rd], s1963, 5/6 (286), HHC. Kildrum 19 Phase 1 [Kenmore, Lammerton Rds], s1965, 2/7 (146), Concrete Scotland (Bison) [demol]. Kildrum 21 [Campsie View], s1967, 1/7 (66), Concrete Scotland (Bison) [demol]. Kildrum

22 [Burns Rd], s1967, 1/20 (73), 2/12 (89), Concrete Scotland (Bison). Muirhead 6 [Hume Rd], s1965, 3/12 (135), Laidlaw (Bison). Ravenswood 1 [Berryhill Rd], s1964, 3/12 (135), Laidlaw (Bison). Seafar 3 [Allanfauld Rd], s1964, 3/12 (135), Laidlaw (Bison). Town Centre Phase 1, s1963, 1/6 (35), Duncan Logan [penthouses in shopping centre: now converted to offices].

DUMBARTON BC
Central Area [Risk St], a1966, 2/6 (47), Atholl Homes (later Laidlaw). Howatshaws Rd, a1970, 4/16 (248), Crudens (Skarne). West Bridgend, a1969, 3/16 (186), Crudens (Skarne).

DUNDEE BC
Ardler Phase I [Birkdale Pl], a1964, 6/17 (1788), Crudens [partly demol]. Dallfield CDA 1st Devt. [Hilltown], a1964, 4/15 (336), Scotcon. Derby St CDA, a1967, 2/23 (374), Mitchell (Camus). Foggyley, 1st Devt, a1958, 4/10 (120), SSHA DL; 2nd Devt, a1962, 2/15 (168), Crudens. Kirk St CDA, a1967, 4/16 (480), Scotcon. Lansdowne Phase 2 [Coupar Angus Rd], a1962, 2/15 (168), Crudens. Maxwelltown CDA [Alexander St], a1965, 4/23 (440), C. Gray. Menzieshill 9th Devt., a1963, 5/15 (420), Crudens. St. Mary's Place CDA Block 4 [Lochee Rd], a1962, 1/15 (92), J. Miller. Trottick, a1966, 3/15 (171), Bett (Bison). Whitfield, Central Precinct [Lothian Cres], a1967, 2/16 (360), Crudens; Industrialised Phase I [Berwick Dr], a1968, 16/6 (288), Crudens (Skarne) [partly demol]. Whorterbank CDA 1st Devt, a1960, 2/15 (170), Crudens.

DUNFERMLINE BC
Broomhead Park [Pilmuir St], a1960, 3/12 (213), Wimpey.

EAST KILBRIDE NTDC
Calderwood 15, 16 [Bosworth Rd], a1966, 6/15 (522), Wimpey. The Murray 8(5), 9(2) [Dunlop, Lister Towers], a1965, 2/15 (145), Wimpey. St Leonards XI [Strathaven Rd], a1969, 1/20 (114), 1/19 (109), 1/16 (91), Reema Scotland. Westwood 2(14) [Fraser River Tower], a1965, 1/15 (87), Wimpey.

EDINBURGH BC
Citadel & Central Leith RDA: Cables Wynd Phase I, a1963, 1/10 (212), Smart; Couper St, a1961, 2/20 (153), Miller; Kirkgate, a1964, 1/18 (64), Token; Tolbooth Wynd Phase II, a1964, 1/11 (98), Smart. Coillesdene House [Seaview Cres], a1966, 1/11 (41), Wimpey. Comiston [Oxgangs Cres], a1960, 3/15 (240), Laing. Craigmillar THA [Craigmillar Castle Gdns] a1966, 2/15 (114), Concrete Scotland (Bison). Dumbiedykes [Holyrood Rd], a1958, 2/11 (182), Miller. Gracemount [Gracemount Dr], a1960, 3/14 (246), Crudens. Greendykes 3 THA [Greendykes Rd], a1964, 2/15 (172), Crudens. Leith Fort [Lindsay St], Stage I, a1960, 2/21 (152), Miller [demol]; Stage II, a1961, 1/7 (157), Smart. Lochend [Lochend Av], a1968, 2/15 (170), Smart. Moat Drive, a1957, 2/10 (120), Miller. Moredun Phase 3 [Moredunvale View], a1966, 2/16 (182), Wimpey. Moredun THA Phase 2 Stage 1 [Craigour Dr], a1965, 4/16 (364), Wimpey. Muirhouse: Phase II [Muirhouse Parkway], a1960, 2/15 (112), 2/9 (96), Wimpey, 2/11 (151), Scotcon; a1962, 1/23 (88), W. Arnott McLeod; THA II [Muirhouse Cres], a1963, 1/9 (49), 3/6 (75), Wimpey; THA III [West Pilton Bank], a1965, 1/16 (61), Wimpey. Niddrie Marischal [Niddrie Ho Dr], a1968, 2/15 (114), Hart Bros (Bison) [demol]. Portobello High St, a1966, 1/8 (60), J. Best. Queensferry Rd [Maidencraig Cres], a1953, 1/8 (42), Hepburn Bros. Restalrig House [Restalrig Dr], a1964, 2/13 (152), Miller. St Leonards CDA (Arthur St), a1970, 5/7 (125), 10/6 (256), Wimpey. Sighthill Neighbourhood Centre [Sighthill Bank], a1965, 3/17 (285), 1/11 (80), Crudens. Sighthill THA III [Calder Gdns], a1966, 3/13 (408), Crudens (Skarne). Spey St, a1955, 1/11 (60), Scotcon. Wester Hailes: Contract 4 [Hailesland Pk], a1969, 6/10 (519), Hart Bros (Bison) [three blocks demol]; Contract 5 [Westburn Gdns], a1969, 7/9 (442), Crudens [demol]; Contract 7 [Wester Hailes Pk], a1970, 7/9 (516), Crudens [demol]. Westfield Court [Westfield Rd], a1950, 1/8 (88), Hepburn Bros. West Pilton Grove, a1956, 2/10 (120), Wimpey.

FALKIRK BC
Callendar Estate [Callendar Rd], Phase 1, a1965, 5/15 (420), Crudens; Phase 2, a1966, 2/15 (168), Crudens; Section 4 [Corentin Ct, Breton Ct], a1967, 2/15 (170), Concrete Scotland (Bison); Site 3 [High Station Rd], a1965, 2/15 (170), Wimpey. Glenfuir Estate [Windsor Rd], a1969, 2/15 (170), Wimpey.

FIFE COUNTY COUNCIL
Kincardine 14th Devt. Phase A [Ramsay, Sandeman, Kincardine Cts, Kincardine-on-Forth], s1969, 3/16 (181), Bett (Bison).

GLASGOW BC (approval dates refer to Dean of Guild Court)
Acre Rd, a1969, 3/8 (96), 1/6 (24), Lawrence. Anderston Commercial Centre [Cadogan St], a1967, 3/16 (336), Myton. Anderston Cross CDA Phase III [St. Vincent Terr], a1967, 4/9 (124), 3/11 (115), 1/13 (48), SSHA DL (Bison). Anniesland Cross, a1966, 1/23 (126), DL. Archerhill Rd North [Archerhill Av], a1966, 5/8 (150), DL. Ardencraig Rd, a1963, 5/20 (570), Wimpey. Barfillan Drive, a1968, 2/8 (56), DL. Battlefield [Cathkinview Rd], a1965, 2/20 (228), Wimpey. Blairdardie South [Keal Dr], a1960, 1/15 (84), 1/14 (78), 2/13 (144), Lawrence. Blawarthill [Plean St], a1964, 2/20 (228), Wimpey. Bogany Terrace, a1966, 1/20 (114), Wimpey [demol]. Bridgeton-Dalmarnock CDA (Ruby St), a1967, 3/15 (252), Wimpey. Broadholm St, a1969, 1/8 (30), DL. Broomloan Road (Albion Site), a1963, 3/21 (285), Reema Scotland. Cleeves Rd [Nitshill Rd], a1969, 1/13 (49), F.G. Minter. Coll St, a1967, 3/18 (306), Reema Scotland [one block demol]. Cowcaddens CDA [Stewart St], Phase I [2, 6 Dundas Vale Court], a1968, 2/24 (274), Laing; Phase II, a1973, 1/24 (137), Laing. Cranhill Extension [Bellrock St], a1963, 3/18 (306), Crudens (Truscon). Crathie Drive, a1949, 1/8 (89), DL. Darnley [Glen Moriston Rd], Phase 2 Section 1, a1972, 1/8 (60), 3/7 (162), 6/6 (168), DL/Lawrence/Smart; Phase 2 Section 2, a1973, 3/6 (82), DL/Fairclough; Phase 2 Commercial Area, a1973, 1/8 (42), HHC [partly demol]. Dougrie Place, Castlemilk, a1960, 3/20 (233), Leggat. Dumbreck Av,

a1968, 2/22 (198), DL. Gallowgate CDA Area 'A' (Bluevale St), a1963, 2/31 (348), Thaw & Campbell. Garscadden Policies [Linkwood Dr], a1965, 1/23 (132), 1/22 (114), 1/18 (102), DL/Truscon/Scotcon. Govan CDA 'A' [Kintra St], a1967, 3/20 (342), Crudens. Hillpark I [Hillpark Dr], a1966, 5/8 (140), 3/6 (240), DL. Hutchesontown/Part Gorbals CDA: Area 'B' [Ballater St], a1958, 4/18 (308), DL/A.A. Stuart; Area 'C' [Old Rutherglen Rd], a1960, 2/20 (400), HHC [demol]; Area 'E' [Crown St], a1968, 2/24 (384), 12/7 (759), Gilbert-Ash Scotland (Tracoba) [7 storey blocks demol]. Ibroxholm [Ibrox Terr], a1962, 3/22 (297), DL. Kelso St [Halley Sq], a1965, 3/8 (90), DL. Kennishead [Kennishead Av], a1965, 5/23 (660), Laidlaw (Prometo). Kirkton Av, a1965, 5/24 (690), Wimpey. Kirriemuir Av, a1966, 3/8 (88), DL. Laurieston-Gorbals CDA [Gorbals St], Phase 1A, a1970, 2/24 (552), Crudens; Phase 2B, a1973, 2/24 (552), Crudens. Lillyburn Place, a1965, 1/8 (30), DL. Lincoln Av, a1962, 6/20 (684), Wimpey. Maryhill CDA Area 'B' [Rothes Dr, Duncruin St], Phase I, a1966, 3/21 (360), Reema Scotland; Phases II, III, a1967, 15/8 (451), DL. Milton North [Castlebay St, Scaraway St], a1966, 6/17 (576), Tersons. Moss Heights [Berryknowes Av], a1950, 3/10 (219), HHC. Mosspark Drive North [Tarfside Oval], a1962, 4/22 (396), DL. Northinch St, a1971, 1/21 (120), Wimpey. Northland Drive, a1966, 2/8 (60), DL. Paisley Rd West (Halfway), a1974, 1/18 (134), Taylor Woodrow. Parkhead CDA Area 'A' Phase 1 [Helenvale St], a1967, 3/15 (252), Wimpey. Pollokshaws CDA Unit 1 [Birness Dr], a1966, 2/22 (244), 1/20 (110), 1/18 (100), DL (Bison). Pollokshaws CDA Unit 2 [Shawbridge St], Phase 1, a1961, 3/16 (227), 1/20 (89), Laidlaw (Bison); Phase 2, a1962, 1/16 (75), Laidlaw (Bison); Phase 3, a1964, 3/23 (315), Laidlaw (Bison); Phase 4, a1968, 1/23 (105), Laidlaw (Bison); Blocks 28-30, a1971, a1971, 1/17 (134), Laidlaw (Bison). Prospecthill Rd [Myrtle Hill View], a1967, 3/8 (144), Lawrence. Queensland Drive, a1965, 2/20 (228), Wimpey. Red Rd, a1962, 6/31 (720), 2/27 (606), DL (MSC). Redpath Drive, a1968, 5/8 (154), DL. Royston RDA, Area 'A' [Garnock St], a1959, 3/20 (351), Wimpey; 'B' [Rosemount St], a1966, 2/25 (288), Reema Scotland; Area 'B' phase 2 (Millburn St I), a1969, 1/25 (144), Reema Scotland [partly demol]; (Millburn St II), a1970, 1/12 (140), Reema Scotland; Area 'C' [Charles St], a1969, 2/20 (228), Wimpey. St. Andrew's Drive, a1966, 7/8 (210), 9/6 (320), DL. Sandwood Rd Area 'B' [Birkhall Av], a1967, 8/8 (240), DL. Sandyhills House [Strowan St], a1964, 4/23 (528), DL. Scotstoun House [Kingsway], a1962, 6/20 (684), Wimpey. Sighthill [Fountainwell Rd, Pinkston Dr], Phase 1A, a1963, 4/20 (912), Crudens (Truscon); Phase 1B, a1964, 1/20 (228), Crudens (Truscon); Phase 2, a1964, 3/20 (684), Crudens (Truscon); Phases 2B/3, a1967, 2/20 (456), Crudens (Truscon). Smeaton St, a1965, 1/8 (30), DL. Springburn CDA, Area 'A' [Wellfield St] a1966, 2/26 (200), Reema Scotland; Area 'B' [Balgrayhill Rd], Phase 1, a1964, 2/26 (200), Reema Scotland, 7/6 (483), DL [partly demol]; Phase 2, a1966, 2/25 (192), Reema Scotland; Area 'C' (Elmvale St), a1971, 4/6 (117), Mitchell (Camus) [partly demol]. Summerfield [Summerfield St], Phase 1, a1963, 3/23 (396), Laidlaw (Prometo); Phase 1 Extension, a1965, 1/23 (132), Laidlaw (Prometo). Toryglen North [Prospecthill Circus], a1963, 2/23 (267), 1/21 (202), 2/6 (82), Laing. Townhead CDA Area 'A' (Ladywell Development) Phase 1, a1961, 1/16 (90), 1/15 (84), 1/13 (72), DL; Area 'B' [St. Mungo Dr], a1967, 4/25 (768), Wimpey. Woodside CDA [St. George's Rd], Area 'A' Phase 1, a1964, 3/23 (315), DL (Bison); Area 'B' Phase 3, a1970, 2/8 (203), Leggat.

GLENROTHES NTDC
South Parks 8th Devt [Raeburn Heights], s1967, 1/16 (61), Wimpey.

GOUROCK BC
Eastern School [Chapel St], s1968, 1/15 (87), Wimpey.

GREENOCK BC (to 1975; from 1975, see Inverclyde DC)
Carwood St/Sinclair St, a1965, 1/13 (49), H. Leggat. CDA 2 (Drumfrochar Rd/Ann St), a1968, 2/16 (182), Wimpey, a1969, 1/16 (89), Wimpey. CDA 4 Phase IIB [Belville St], a1967, 1/8 (30), 1/7 (33), 1/6 (36), C. Gray. CDA 4 Phase III [Belville St], a1965, 6/16 (492), 1/15 (76), J. Laidlaw (Bison). Duncan St, a1965, 1/15 (88), Wimpey. Grieve Rd, a1962, 3/16 (270), Crudens. Lady Octavia Phase I [John Wilson St], a1969, 1/18 (103), Crudens. Lynedoch St/Regent St, a1970, 2/18 (208), H. Leggat [Wates]. Neil St, a1965, 1/15 (57), Concrete Scotland (Bison). Old Inverkip Rd, a1965, 1/15 (57), Concrete Scotland (Bison). Ravenscraig Neighbourhood Centre [Cumberland Rd], a1969, 1/12 (44), J. Harrison. Regent St/Trafalgar St, a1970, 1/18 (71), Mitchell (Camus). Upper Bow Farm [Tay St], 1st Devt, a1964, 3/10 (165), Crudens; 2nd Devt, a1966, 2/10 (110), Crudens.

HAMILTON BC
Almada St RD, a1967, 1/14 (78), Lawrence. Duke St Phase 2 [Wyler Ct], a1968, 1/12 (70), Crudens.

INVERCLYDE DC
Kilblain St, a1975, 1/16 (61), Wimpey.

IRVINE BC
Fullarton St RD, a1966, 5/14 (275), Wimpey.

JOHNSTONE BC
High St/Dimity St Phase I [Provost Ho], a1972, 1/14 (72), Lawrence.

KIRKCALDY BC
Esplanade [Forth View], s1956, 3/8 (141), Wimpey. Pathhead [Mid St], Phase I, s1964, 2/15 (172), Wimpey; Phase II, s1968, 1/15 (86), Wimpey. Valley Gardens, s1954, 1/8 (48), Wimpey.

LANARK COUNTY COUNCIL
Cambuslang CDA No.2, Central Area [Allison Dr]: a1963, 1/14 (96), 1/6 (22), Laing; a1967, 3/13 (216), Reema Scotland. Lightburn [Hamilton Rd, Cambuslang], a1967, 1/13 (72), Reema Scotland. Springhall [Cruachan Rd, Cambuslang], a1967,

1/13 (72), Reema Scotland. Whitlawburn, Cambuslang [Western Rd], a1968, 6/13 (432), Reema Scotland.

MOTHERWELL & WISHAW BC
Brandon St/Merry St Area: Railway Site, a1967, 1/20 (106), Loudon (Bison). Central Motherwell CDA: Phase I [Anderson St], a1967, 2/17 (134), Loudon (Bison); Phase II [Thistle St], a1970, 3/17 (201), Loudon (Bison). Clyde Valley St & Leven St, a1961, 3/12 (140), Wimpey. Flemington Area: Burnside St Phase I, a1966, 5/18 (520), Wimpey; Phase III [Doonside Tower], a1968, 1/20 (116), Wimpey. Main St, Wishaw (Burgh Chambers Site), a1964, 1/6 (25), Scott (Builders). Merry St (Dalziel St to Wilson St), a1967, 3/20 (351), Crudens. Muirhouse Area: Phase III [Shields Dr], a1964, 7/18 (735), Wimpey. Netherton Area: Main Site (Gowkthrapple) [Castlehill Rd], a1968, 3/12 (210), Mitchell (Camus). Parkhead St/Macdonald St, a1963, 1/17 (161), Crudens (MSC). Watson St Area: Phase III [Elvan Tower], a1964, 1/12 (46), Wimpey.

PAISLEY BC
Blackhall [Cartha Cres], a1958, 2/15 (112), Blackburn. Foxbar 1st Stage [Montrose Rd], a1958, 3/15 (168), Blackburn [partly demol]. Gallowhill [Montgomery Rd], a1968, 3/15 (270), Wimpey. George St/Canal St, a1958, 1/15 (56), Blackburn. George St Stage 2 Phase II [Maxwellton St], a1965, 1/18 (102), Lawrence (MSC). Great Hamilton St, Phase I, a1963, 3/16 (270), Wimpey; Phase II, a1965, 2/16 (180), Wimpey. High Calside, a1967, 2/16 (180), Wimpey. Lacy St RDA, a1967, 1/15 (88), J. Miller. Millarston East [Millarston Dr], a1967, 3/15 (270), Wimpey. Nethercraigs/Gleniffer Rd, a1965, 2/15 (114), Concrete Scotland (Bison).

PERTH BC
Market St & Caledonian Rd, a1973, 3/9 (104), Bett (Bison). Pomarium St, a1958, 1/11 (44), 1/8 (45), Wimpey. Potterhill [Gowrie St], a1961, 1/8 (48), Wimpey. Strathtay Rd, a1966, 9/6 (99), C. Gray.

PORT GLASGOW BC
Bay Area RD [John Wood St], s1968, 3/15 (170), Concrete Scotland (Bison).

RUTHERGLEN BC
Regent St [Greenhill Ct], a1973, 3/9 (135), Crudens (Skarne).

SALTCOATS BC
Glebelands 2nd Devt. [The Glebe], a1966, 2/12 (94), J. Miller (Bison).

STEVENSTON BC
Central RD, Phase 1, Part A [The Riggs], s1964, 2/6 (20), J. Moulds.

Scottish Special Housing Association

Clydebank: Central RDA, Radnor Park, a1960, 7/15 (392), DL.

Dundee: Lansdowne Phase I [Dryburgh], a1958, 4/10 (120), DL.

Glasgow: Anderston Cross CDA Phase II [St. Vincent Terr], a1967, 1/18 (128), DL (Bison). Carron St 1st Devt [Carbisdale St], a1961, 4/15 (224), Wight; 3rd Devt [Carron Pl], a1964, 3/8 (93), Concrete Scotland (Bison). Fortrose St, a1961, 1/9 (53), DL. Gorget Av, a1965, 3/8 (93), Gilbert Ash Scotland (Tracoba). Hutchesontown-Part Gorbals CDA Area 'D' [Caledonia Rd], a1963, 4/24 (552), 3/8 (96), Gilbert-Ash Scotland (Tracoba); 5th Devt, a1968, 3/8 (96), Gilbert-Ash Scotland (Tracoba). Langlands Rd, a1960, 2/15 (112), DL. Maryhill CDA Area 'A' [Collina St], a1968, 1/19 (113), Gilbert-Ash Scotland (Tracoba). North Kelvin CDA Area 'A' [Wester Common Rd], a1967, 4/19 (452), Gilbert-Ash Scotland (Tracoba). Toryglen [Prospecthill Cres], 6th Devt, a1955, 2/10 (60), DL; 10th Devt, a1957, 2/10 (60), DL. Whiteinch-Broomhill [Broomhill Dr], a1963, 5/17 (510), Miller; 2nd Devt area 'D', a1965, 3/8 (93), Gilbert-Ash Scotland (Tracoba). Wyndford [Wyndford Rd/Glenfinnan Rd], 1st Devt, a1961, 5/15 (280), DL; 3rd Devt, a1963, 7/8 (217), DL (Bison); 4th Devt, a1964, 4/26 (600), Laing; 5th Devt, a1965, 1/9 (53), DL.

Paisley: Foxbar, 2nd Stage [Heriot Av], a1958, 2/15 (112), DL.
Renfrewshire, Linwood: [Belmar, Asbury Cts], a1970, 2/16 (174), Crudens.

C16. Airdrie Town Council's Holehills development of 1967-69, an industrialised project which formed part of the Lanarkshire burghs consortium order of Camus prefabricated dwellings, the main contractor being Mitchell Ltd. (RCAHMS B21595)

Section 2

Bibliographical references to key housing projects, c.1945-70

Local authorities

ABERDEEN BC: *TCP* 6-1967 284-5; *S* 5-10-1973 49-50. Ashgrove *MJ* 9-1-1953 37-41 (A.B.Gardner LA). Kincorth *IB* 4-1964 26-8 (Harley, Haddow & Ptrs). Rosemount Sq *ABN* 18-2-1949 138-9; *AJ* 17-2-1949 155 (A.B.Gardner LA).
AIRDRIE BC: *ABN* 24-8-1966 320-1.
CLYDEBANK BC: *OAP* 2-1944 72-3; *B* 18-1-1952 120; *MJ* 15-2-1952 333-41. Littleholm *AR* 1-1967 30-1 (J.Vaughan LA). Melbourne Av Mountblow Hs *S* 21-8-1954 713-14; *AJ* 26-8-1954 250; *MJ* 15-10-1954 1493-5 (S.Bunton Assoc).
CUMBERNAULD NTDC: *S* 7-6-1958 577-8; 3-9-1960 999-1001; 3-7-1965 33-6; *TCP* 9-1961 355-6; *ABN* 29-3-1961 407-26; 5-12-1962 824; *JTPLI* 5-1964 195-200; *AR* 2-1964 93-9; 1-1964 14-15; *AD* 9-1960 352; 1-1962 20; *HR* 7/8-1963 120-3; *MJ* 5-4-1963 982-4; *JRIBA* 5-1964 206; *AJ* 5-12-1962 1248, 1279-88; 8-1-1964 65-6; 31-1-1968 293-310; *JRIBA* 5-1964 191-206; *IB* 7-1965 32-5; *AY* Vol 10 1962 99-103; Vol 11 1965 231-64.
Abronhill South *AR* 1-1966 48 (D.R.Leaker LA). Abronhill T 49 Hs *AJ* 6-7-1966 16 (Rothwell Perrin Ltd, Portland Ontario). Carbrain 1,2 *AR* 1-1961 30 (L.Hugh Wilson LA). Carbrain 13,14 *AR* 1-1967 29 (D.R.Leaker LA). Muirhead 3 *AR* 2-1964 95-9 (L.Hugh Wilson, D.R.Leaker LA). Park 3 West *AR* 1-1964 15; *IB* 5-1966 33-4 (Edinburgh Univ., ARU). Park 4 *AR* 1-1965 54 (D.R.Leaker LA). Ravenswood 5 *AR* 1-1965 54 (D.R.Leaker LA). Seafar 2 *AR* 1-1961 31; 2-1964 95-9 (L.Hugh Wilson, D.R.Leaker LA).
DUMBARTON BC: Central Area RD *B* 8-7-1960 48-52 (J.Rae, D.Preston, S.Garner, W.Strebel). Cardross Rd *B* 6-3-1953 380 (A.D.Holmes).
DUNBAR BC: Fishermen's Cottages *ABN* 15-4-1949 334-7; *B* 2-11-1951 581-5; *MJ* 5-9-1952 1642-5; *AJ* 18-9-1952 339-41 (B.Spence & Ptrs).
DUNDEE BC: *TPLR* 7-1972 275-85. Ardler Courtyard Housing *AJ* 4-3-1964 537-46; 14-1-1970 89-100; Decade 21 (Baxter, Clark & Paul).
EAST KILBRIDE NTDC: *B* 7-11-1952 657ff; *S* 11-8-1956 583-4; *TPLR* 1-1964 306-16. Brouster Pl Quebec Drive *MJ* 18-1-1957 129-30 (F.C.Scott LA).
EAST LOTHIAN CC: Prestonpans Inchview Dev *AD* 9-1960 351; *AR* 1-1961 28-9; *AJ* 24-5-1967 1217-27 (Edinburgh Univ. ARU, R.H.Matthew).
EDINBURGH BC: *B* 15-11-1946 508-10; 20-6-1952 913-30; *ABN* 26-6-1952 732ff. Couper St Leith Phase I *AJ* 28-12-1966 1607-18 (Alison & Hutchison & Ptrs). The Inch Nether Liberton *B* 15-11-1946 508-10; 20-6-1952 913-19; *MJ* 24-9-1954 2276-8 (A.G.Forgie LA with D.Stratton Davis). Leith Fort *B* 31-1-1958 214-23; 7-2-1958 261; *AJ* 6-2-1958 205-16; 7-4-1965 837-48; *AR* 1-1961 32-4; 3-1965 218-23; P.Whiting, *New Single-Storey Houses*, 1966, 166-9 (S.Stewart, Baikie & Perry). Muirhouse Demonstration Maisonettes and Houses *AJ* 7-3-1957 356-7;

Appendices

MJ 22-3-1957 645-50; *OAP* 12-1957 175-9; *AD* 4-1957 145 (T.A.Jeffryes of DHS). Muirhouse 2 Martello Ct *ABN* 22-9-1965 535 (R.Anderson, Kininmonth & Paul). Newhaven Annfield *B* 12-5-1961 886-7 (Sir B.Spence Ptrs). Queensferry Rd *MJ* 16-3-1951 607; *B* 20-6-1952 932; *Concrete* 1-1954 58-9 (A.G.Forgie LA). Sighthill 3-storey flats *B* 30-7-1954 169-71; *MJ* 18-6-1957-60; *S* 8-5-1954 377-8; 10-8-1957 833-5 (Archit. Sect. DHS and Min.of Works). Westfield Ct *B* 20-6-1952 930-1 (Williamson & Hubbard).
GALASHIELS BC: Church St *ABN* 22-6-1966 1125-8 (P.Womersley).
GLASGOW BC: M.Horsey, 'Crathie Court and Moss Heights', *Scottish Georgian Society Bulletin* 1982; idem. 'The Story of Red Road Flats', *TCP* 7/8-1982 177-9; idem, 'Multi-Storey Council Housing in Britain, *Planning Perspectives*, 5-1988, 167-96; idem, *Tenements and Towers*, 1990. *Building Industries and Scottish Architect* 11-1945 22-3; *Building* 2-1946 54-5; *AJ* 15-9-1949 283-94; *BHPR* 2/3-1951 60-1; *S* 21-8-1954 713-14; *ABN* 18-3-1954 326-8; *B* 9-4-1954 627-8; *AJ* 4-2-1960 196-205; *IB* 9-1960 32-7; *OAP* 2-1961 65-72; *Concrete* 11-1963 449-56; *B* 8-5-1964 953-8; *JTPLI* 1-1965 3-8; *S* 1-7-1967 29-33; 23-4-1971 30-2; *TPLR* 1969 319-34; *OAP* 1-1972 33-7. Calfhill Ct, Pollok *B* 18-9-1953 427-9; *MJ* 9-10-1953 2187-90 (A.G.Jury LA). Cranhill Ext *OAP* 2-1963 116-17 (A.G.Jury with G.Bowie/Crudens). Hillpark *OAP* 10-1962 619,631; *IB* 9-1962 35; *S* 8-9-1962 1111-12 (A.G.Jury LA). Fyvie Av *B* 7-11-1952 672 (A.G.Jury LA). Hutchesontown/Part Gorbals CDA *MJ* 23-4-1954 899-902; 15-3-1957 588-9; *OAP* 5-1954 225-7; 6-1956 277-80; *AJ* 18-4-1957 570-3; 4-9-1958 326; *OAP* 10-1958 469-72; *S* 2-3-1957 197-8; 6-9-1958 890; 26-3-1960 301; *B* 5-9-1958 282-3; *HR* 11/12-1958 184-5; *ABN* 10-9-1958 350-1; 27-5-1959 678-9; 15-1-1970 26-9; *AR* 1-1959 9-11; *B* 7-7-1961 32; *S* 13-5-1961 615-16; *Building Industries and Scottish Architect* 11-1962 40-6; *AJ* 15-4-1964 857-72; *AR* 11-1967 348-9 (Area B: R.Matthew & Johnson Marshall; Area C: Sir B.Spence Ptrs). Hillpark *B* 19-10-1962 769-70 (T.S.Cordiner). Liddesdale Rd Milton *MJ* 29-4-1955 1151-3 (A.G.Jury LA). Moss Heights *MJ* 22-9-1950 2281; *B* 12-6-1953 910-11; *AR* 5-1954 342; *ConcrQ* No 19 7/9-1953 16-19; *AJ* 25-2-1954 250 (A.G.Jury LA). Pollokshaws CDA Unit 2 *IB* 11-1961 36-9; *OAP* 3-1958 126-9 (Boswell, Mitchell & Johnston). Red Rd *B* 19-10-1962 769-70; *JRIBA* 2-1967 46; *AR* 11-1967 343; *SBD* 5-1967 50-3; *International Asbestos Cement Review* No 44 10-1966 21-5 (S.Bunton Assoc). Royston RDA *S* 10-91-1960 1019-20; *All Electric Flats Royston Glasgow*, 1961 (A.G.Jury LA). Sannox Gdns Flats for Single Women *BHPR* 8/9-1951 152 (R. Bradbury LA). Sighthill *IB* 4-1963 11; *S* 23-3-1963 337-8 (Crudens). Summerfield [Dalmarnock] *IBSC* 4-1967 9-11 (Parry & Hughes). Springburn CDA *OAP* 8-1963 867-9 (A.G.Jury LA). Toryglen North *IB* 9-1963 24 (Laing). Townhead CDA *IB* 9-1962 35; *OAP* 9-1962 535-7; *S* 6-1-1962 11 (A.G.Jury). Woodside CDA *IBSC* 10-1964 71 (Boswell, Mitchell & Johnson/Bison). See also below, under SSHA.
GLENROTHES NTDC: *MJ* 20-3-1959 804-6. Auchmuty, Woodside *MJ* 18-1-1957; A Cleeve Barr, *Public Authority Housing*, 1958, 243 (P.Tinto LA). Caskieberran Tanshall *IB* 1-1966 32 (Laing 12 M Jespersen).
KIRKCALDY BC: Valley Gdns (Templehall Estate) *ABN* 21-7-1955 97; *B* 9-9-1955 432-5; *ConcrQ* No 38 7/9-1958 23-4; Cleeve Barr 255 (M.R.Meldrum LA). Dysart *AJ* 14-2-1962 338; *HR* 7/8 1967 107-10; *AR* 4-1967 277-9 (A.Wheeler of Wheeler & Sproson).
LESLIE BC: Bowery Dev *MJ* 20-12-1953 2759 (H.Anthony Wheeler).
LIVINGSTON NTDC: Craigshill 1 *AR* 1-1965 45; *B* 15-5-1964 1035-6; *IB* 5-1964 20-1; *AJ* 10-1-1968 83-100 (MHLG P.Daniel, later W.Newman Brown LA with Laing 12M Jespersen). Craigshill 2 *Concrete* 4-1967 132 (Messrs J. Parr Ptrs with Siporex/Costain).
PAISLEY BC: *MJ* 9-1-1953 42-3; *S* 10-10-1959 823-4; 5-6-1965 33; *B* 14-10-1960 698; *OAP* 11-1959 512. George St Phase II *S* 5-8-1967 39 (Lawrence (MSC)).
PRESTONPANS see East Lothian CC.
SELKIRK BC: *ABN* 26-3-1948 290-3.
STIRLING BC: Baker St *OAP* 4-1954 160-2 (Sir F.Mears & Ptrs).

Scottish Special Housing Association

GENERAL: *ABN* 20/27-12-1967 103-6; *OAP* 8-1968 1030-4; *S* 3-4-197038-41; *JRIBA* 9-1951 415-22; 2-1971 68-72. SPECIFIC LOCATIONS: Erskine New Town: *S* 14-11-1969 63; 7-5-1971 19. Glasgow. Anderston Cross CDA *OAP* 8-1968 1034 (SDD/SSHA Joint Dev. Unit). Whiteinch-Broomhill *AJ* 7-12-1966 1405; *ABN* 20/27-12 1967 1003 (H.Buteux SSHA). Fortrose St *IB* 5-1964 18-19 (SSHA/SDD Joint Dev. Unit). Toryglen *Prefabrication* 1-1954 22-4; *B* 25-1-1957 185-6; *MJ* 8-2-1957 299-300; *ConcrQ* 36 1/3-1958 38-9; Cleeve Barr 241 (J.Austen Bent SSHA). Wyndford *B* 22-1-1965 220 (H.E.Buteux).
West Calder: Parkhead Est *S* 21-5-1971 26-9.

ABBREVIATIONS

This table includes important and frequently used abbreviations in the text and notes of Parts A and B, and all abbreviations, including journal references, in the gazetteer section of Part C.

a	date of committee approval or Dean of Guild Court approval
AAJNL	*Architectural Association Journal*
AB	*Architecture and Building*
ABN	*Architect and Building News*
AD	*Architectural Design*
AF	*Architectural Forum*
AIROH	The Aircraft Industries Research Organisation on Housing
AJ	*The Architects' Journal*
AR	*The Architectural Review*
ARU	Architecture Research Unit (University of Edinburgh)
AY	*The Architects' Yearbook*
B	*The Builder*
BC	Burgh Council
BHPR	*British Housing and Planning Review*
BRS	Building Research Station
CC	County Council
CDA	Comprehensive Development Area
Concrete	*Concrete and Constructional Engineering*
CQ	Concrete Quarterly
DC	District Council
DHS	Department of Health for Scotland
DLO	direct [municipal] labour organisation
DOO	A O'Carroll, 'The development of owner occupation in Edinburgh', 1994
DR	*Daily Record*
DSBB	Slaven and S Checkland (eds), *Dictionary of Scottish Business Biography*, 1990
EAAYB	*Edinburgh Architectural Association Year Book*
ECM	Edinburgh Corporation Minutes
EN	*Evening News* (Edinburgh)
ET	*Evening Times* (Glasgow)
GCM	Glasgow Corporation Minutes
GH	*Glasgow Herald*
H	*Housing*
HC	Housing Committee
HFF	Cement and Concrete Association, *Housing from the Factory*, 1962
HHC	Holland Hannen & Cubitt
HR	*Housing Review*
IB	*Interbuild*
IBSC	*Industrialised Building Systems and Components*
ILA	O'Carroll, 'The influence of local authorities on the growth of owner occupation', *Planning Perspectives*, 11, 1996
JRIBA	*Journal of the Royal Institute of British Architects*
JTPLI	*Journal of the (Royal) Town Planning Institute*
LA	local authority
MAP	Ministry of Aircraft Production
MHLG	Ministry of Housing and Local Government (England and Wales)
MJ	*Municipal Journal*
MM	Mactaggart & Mickel
MMA	Mactaggart & Mickel Archive
MMAD	Mactaggart & Mickel Archive drawings
MMAEPB	Mactaggart & Mickel Archive estate prices book
MMASB	Mactaggart & Mickel Archive sales books
MOW	Ministry of Works
MPBW	Ministry of Public Building and Works
NBA	National Building Agency
NHTPLCY	*Yearbook of the National Housing and Town Planning Council*
NTDC	New Town Development Corporation
OAP	*Official Architecture and Planning*
Planning our New Homes	SHAC, *Planning our New Homes*, 1944 (Westwood Report)
QRIAS	*Quarterly of the RIAS*
R&D	research and development
RC	reinforced concrete
RD	redevelopment
RDA	redevelopment area
RIAS	Royal Incorporation of Architects in Scotland
RIBA	Royal Institute of British Architects
RMJM	Robert Matthew, Johnson Marshall
s	date of start of construction
S	*Surveyor*
SBD	*Systems Building and Design*
SBCEY	*Scottish Building and Civil Engineering Yearbook*
SDD	Scottish Development Department
SHAC	Scottish Housing Advisory Committee
Sites	Glasgow Corporation Housing Committee, Sub-committee on Sites & Buildings
SLASH	Scottish Local Authorities Special Housing Group
SRA	Strathclyde Regional Archive
SRO	Scottish Record Office (National Archives of Scotland)
SSHA	Scottish Special Housing Association
Sub	Sub-committee
TCP	*Town and Country Planning*
TPLR	*Town Planning Review*
TVA	Tennessee Valley Authority
White	R B White, *Prefabrication*, 1965

C17. *Cover of James Miller's 1934 speculative housing brochure* Home. *(James Miller Ltd)*

BIBLIOGRAPHY

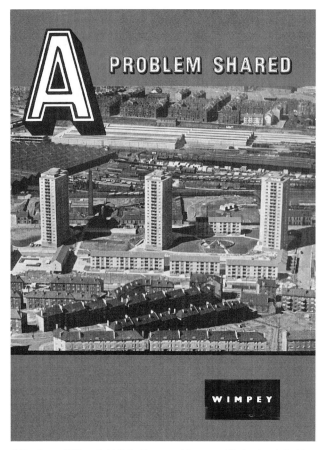

C18. Cover of Wimpey's 1961 booklet on multi-storey public housing, A Problem Shared. The illustration shows the Royston Area A development in Glasgow, 1959-61. (George Wimpey Ltd)

Scottish housing and its cultural context: general accounts

T Begg, *Housing Policy in Scotland*, 1996.
M Bowley, *The British Building Industry*, 1966.
DHS/SDD, *Housing Return for Scotland* (quarterly; various dates).
T Devine and R J Findlay (eds), *Scotland in the 20th Century*, 1996.
J S Gibson, *The Thistle and the Crown*, 1985.
M Horsey, *Tenements and Towers*, 1990.
M Keating and A Midwinter, *The Government of Scotland*, 1983.
J P Lewis, *Building Cycles and Britain's Growth*, 1965.
W Mackie, *Alexander Hall & Son, A Century of Craftsmanship*, 1980.
S Merrett and F Gray, *Owner-Occupation in Britain*, 1982.
T Newson (ed.), *A Housing Bibliography*, Birmingham University Centre for Urban and Regional Studies, 4th edition, 1982.
G Pottinger, *The Secretaries of State for Scotland*, 1979.
C G Powell, *An Economic History of the British Building Industry*, 1980.
R Saville (ed.), *The Economic Development of Modern Scotland*, 1985.
Scottish Municipal Annual (various dates).
A Slaven and S Checkland (eds), *Dictionary of Scottish Business Biography*, Volume 2, 1990. Includes articles on Harry Cruden, Sir John Mactaggart, Andrew Mickel, Sir James Miller, William Tawse, R A Whitson (all by N J Morgan), and J Lawrence (by C C Lee).
P A Stone, *Building Economy*, 1966.

Pre-1939 housing

M Bowley, *Housing and the State*, 1945.
W Chambers, *Report on the Sanitary State of ... the Old Town of Edinburgh*, 1840.
E J Cleary, *The Building Society Movement*, 1965.
S Damer, *A Social History of Glasgow Council Housing 1919-1965*, ESRC Research Project, 1991.
M J Daunton, *House and Home in the Victorian City*, 1983.
Department of Health for Scotland, *Report of the Scottish Architectural Advisory*

Committee on the Incorporation of Architectural Quality ... and the Erection of High Tenements*, 1937.
Department of Health for Scotland, *Report on Working-class Housing on the Continent* (Highton Report), 1935.
J Frew, 'Ebenezer Macrae', *St Andrews Studies* ii, 1991.
Glasgow Municipal Commission on the Housing of the Poor, *Evidence*, 1904.
M Glendinning, 'The Ballantyne Report', in D Mays (ed.), *The Architecture of Scottish Cities*, 1997.
R Issacharoff, *The Building Boom of the Interwar Years*, 1978.
P Kemp, 'The transformation of the urban housing market in Britain', PhD thesis, University of Sussex, 1984.
C McKean, *The Scottish Thirties*, 1987, Chapter 10.
G C Mooney, *Living on the Periphery: the Rise and Fall of Pollok Estate*, 1983.
N J Morgan, '£8 Cottages for Glasgow citizens', in R Rodger (ed.), *Scottish Housing in the Twentieth Century*, 1989.
N J Morgan and M J Daunton, 'Landlords in Glasgow', *Business History*, 25, 1983, 256.
R J Morris and R Rodger (eds), *The Victorian City*, 1993.
S Muthesius, *The English Terraced House*, 1982.
A O'Carroll, 'The influence of local authorities on the growth of owner-occupation', *Planning Perspectives*, November 1996.
A O'Carroll, 'The development of owner occupation in Edinburgh', PhD thesis, Heriot-Watt University, 1994.
R Pipes, *The Colonies of Stockbridge*, 1984.
Report of a Committee of the Working Classes of Edinburgh, 1860.
Report of the Royal Commission on the Housing of the Industrial Population of Scotland (Ballantyne Commission), 1917 (Cd 8731; includes Wilson Report).
Report of the Committee appointed by the President of the Local Government Board and Secretary for Scotland to consider questions of building construction in connection with the provision of dwellings for the working classes (Tudor Walters Report), 1918.
R Rodger, '"The Invisible Hand": market forces, housing and the urban form in Victorian cities', in D Fraser and A Sutcliffe (eds), *The Pursuit of Urban History*, 1983.
R Rodger, 'Speculative builders and the structure of the Scottish building industry', *Business History*, 21 (2), 1979.
R Rodger, 'The Victorian building industry', in M Doughty (ed.), *Building the Industrial City*, 1986.
Royal Commission on the Housing of the Working Classes, *Report*, 1884/85.
J B Russell, *Life in One Room*, 1888.
J B Russell, 'The house in relation to public health', *Transactions of the Insurance and Actuarial Society of Glasgow*, 5, 1887, 5-10.
Scottish Office Building Directorate, *A Guide to Non-Traditional Housing in Scotland*, 1987.
M A Simpson, 'Glasgow', in M A Simpson and T H Lloyd (eds), *Middle Class Housing in Britain*, 1977.
P J Smith, 'Slum clearance as an instrument of sanitary reform', *Planning Perspectives*, 9, 1994, 1-27.
W Thompson, *Housing Up-to-Date*, 1907.

1939-60 housing

W M Ballantine, *Rebuilding a Nation*, 1944.
T Begg, *Fifty Special Years*, 1987.
M Bowley, *Housing and the State*, 1945, Appendix.
J Burnett, *A Social History of Housing 1815-1970*, 1978/1986 Corporation of Glasgow, *Report of Visit of Deputation to inspect "The Marseilles Block"*, 1954
Corporation of Glasgow Housing Department, *Review of Operations 1919-1947*, 1948.
S Damer, *A Social History of Glasgow Council Housing 1919-1965*, ESRC Research Project, 1991.
Department of Health for Scotland (DHS), *Housing Handbook* (various dates).
Department of Health for Scotland, *Report of a Committee on Scottish Building Costs* (Cd 5977; Barr Committee), 1939.
Department of Health for Scotland, *Report of the Committee on Scottish Building Costs* (Laidlaw Committee), 1948.
N Donaldson and L Forster, *Sell and be Damned*, 1991.
A Gibb, 'Policy and politics in Scottish housing', in R Rodger (ed.), *Scottish Housing in the Twentieth Century*, 1989.
H S Heavenrich, *Housing in Great Britain*, Cambridge, Mass, 1952 (report for Bemis Foundation).
W S Hilton, *Building by Direct Labour*, 1954.
M Horsey, 'Postwar council housing in Glasgow', in Design Council, *From the Spitfire to the Microchip*, 1985.
A G Jury, *Housing Centenary*, 1966.
G Kaehler (ed.), *Geschichte des Wohnens*, Volume 4, Stuttgart, 1996.
R H Macintosh, *The No-Fines Story*, 1974.
Ministry of Works, *House Construction* (Burt Committee, Post-War Building Studies No.1), 1943/44.
Ministry of Works, *House Construction Second Report* (Burt Committee, Post-War

Building Studies No.23), 1946.

Ministry of Works, *House Construction Third Report* (Burt Committee, Post-War Building Studies No.25), 1948.

G C Mooney, *Living on the Periphery: the Rise and Fall of Pollok Estate*, 1983.

F J Osborn and A Whittick, *New Towns*, 1977.

R Rodger and H Al-Qaddo, 'The Scottish Special Housing Association', in R Rodger (ed.), *Scottish Housing in the Twentieth Century*, 1989.

Royal Institute of British Architects, *Symposium on High Flats*, 1955.

B Russell, *Building Systems, Industrialization and Architecture*, 1981.

Scottish Housing Advisory Committee, *Design and Workmanship of Non-Traditional Houses*, 1951.

Scottish Housing Advisory Committee, *Planning Our New Homes* (Westwood Report), 1944.

Scottish Housing Advisory Committee, *Modernising Our Homes* (McTaggart Report), 1947.

Scottish Office Building Directorate, *A Guide to Non-Traditional Housing in Scotland*, 1987.

Scottish Special Housing Association, *A Chronicle of Forty Years*, 1977.

A Sherry, *The Blackburn*, 1996.

R B White, *Prefabrication*, 1965.

Post-1960 housing

M Ball, *Housing and Construction: a Troubled Relationship*, 1996.

Cement and Concrete Association, *Housing from the Factory*, 1962 (see especially papers by J F Munch-Petersen and T Gerholm on Scandinavia, W E Reed on Reema, K M Wood on Bison Wall-Frame, N Johnston on Bison/Pollokshaws).

A F L Deeson (ed.), *The Comprehensive Industrialised Building Systems Annual*, 1965.

R M E Diamant, *Industrialised Building*, 1964.

R M E Diamant, *Industrialised Building 2*, 1965.

B Finnimore, *Houses from the Factory*, 1989.

M Gaskin, 'Housing and the Construction Industry', in D Maclennan and G Wood (eds), *Housing Policy and Research in Scotland*, 1977

A Gibb, 'Policy and politics in Scottish housing', in R Rodger (ed.), *Scottish Housing in the Twentieth Century*, 1989.

K Gibb, 'Regional differentiation and the Scottish house building industry', *Housing Studies*, 1999.

K Gibb and M Keoghan, 'Backward linkages from construction', *Local Economy*, 13, November 1998, 6-23.

K Gibb, A McGregor and M Munro, 'Housebuilding in a recession', *Environment and Planning*, 29, 1997, 1739-58.

M Glendinning and S Muthesius, *Tower Block*, 1994.

A G Jury, *Housing Centenary*, 1966.

D Maclennan, 'Housing in Scotland, 1977-87', in M Smith (ed.), *Guide to Housing*, 3rd edition, 1989.

D Maclennan, *A Competitive UK Economy*, 1994.

D Maclennan, K Gibb and A More, *Fairer Subsidies, Faster Growth: Housing, Government and the Economy*, 1991.

Ministry of Housing (England), Design Bulletin 18, *Designing a Low-Rise Housing System*, 1970.

Ministry of Housing (England), *Homes for Today and Tomorrow* (Parker Morris Report), 1961.

National Building Agency, *Continuity in Contracting for Housing Authorities*, 1969.

A Rennie, *Twa Legs is Better than Nane*, *c*.1982.

D S Robertson, 'Scottish Home Improvement Policy 1945-75', *Urban Studies*, 29 (7), 1992.

R Rodger and H Al-Qaddo, 'The Scottish Special Housing Association', in R Rodger (ed.), *Scottish Housing in the Twentieth Century*, 1989.

B Russell, *Building Systems, Industrialization and Architecture*, 1981.

Scotland's New Homebuyer, from 1992.

Scottish Council (Development & Industry), *Inquiry into the Scottish Economy*, 1961 (Toothill Report).

Scottish Development Department, Annual Reports (from 1963).

Scottish Development Department, *Building (Scotland) Act, 1959, Building Standards (Scotland) Regulations, 1963; Explanatory Memorandum*, 1964.

Scottish Development Department, *Central Scotland*, 1963.

Scottish Development Department, *The Older Houses in Scotland*, 1968.

Scottish Development Department, *Housing in Scotland*, 1969.

Scottish Development Department Circulars, 6/1963 (*Co-operation among Housing Authorities*), 3/1965 (*Housing: the National Building Agency*), 11/1967 (*Use of Industrialised Systems*).

Scottish Housing - A Consultative Document, 1977 (Cd 6852).

Scottish Housing Advisory Committee, *Scotland's Older Houses* (Cullingworth Report), 1967.

Scottish Housing Advisory Committee, *The Demand for Private Houses in Scotland*, 1970.

Scottish Housing Advisory Committee, *The Cost of Private Houses in Scotland* (Sidwell Report), 1972.

Scottish Special Housing Association, *A Chronicle of Forty Years*, 1977.

R B White, *Prefabrication*, 1965.

George Wimpey Ltd, *A Problem Shared*, *c*.1961.

George Wimpey Ltd, *Redevelopment in Wimpey No-Fines Concrete*, *c*.1957.

George Wimpey Ltd, *Rationalized Planning in No-Fines Construction: Series 1001*, *c*.1963.

International comparisons

J Barlow and S Duncan, *Success and Failure in Housing Provision: European Systems Compared*, 1994.

M J Daunton (ed.), *Housing the Workers - A Comparative History 1850-1914*, 1990.

R-H Guerrand, *Une Europe en Construction*, 1992.

S Lowe and D Hughes, *A New Century of Social Housing*, 1991.

Ministry of Housing, *Housebuilding in the USA*, 1966.

C G Pooley (ed.), *Housing Strategies in Europe 1880-1930*, 1992.

A Power, *Hovels to High Rise*, 1993.

INDEX

This index is largely drawn from the main text of the book (Parts A and B), with selected names included from the Appendices (Part C). Where appropriate, estates and other particular locations are grouped together under town headings; for individual Mactaggart & Mickel estates, readers should also consult the archive list in Appendix I.

Index

Index

Ministry of Labour, 118
Ministry of Works, 109-10, 117-8, 229, 234
Mitchell, Alec, 284-5
Mitchell, Sydney, 207-8
Mitchell, Thomas, 266
Moderate Party, *see* Tory Party
Modern Movement, 86, 89, 134, 187, 228, 231, 243, 252
Morgan, T, 11
Morris, David, 164
Motherwell, 290-3
Multi-Storey Consortium, 254
multi-storey flats, 4-5, 39, 116, 128-30, 142-3, 158, 161, 164, 169, 224-5, 239-41, 244-5, 252-3, 258
municipal housing, *see* public housing
Munro, John C C, 22, 52, 86
Murray, Douglas, 164

National Building Agency, 246
National Building Society, 107
National Federation of Building Trades Operatives, 23, 36-7
National House Builders Registration Council, 153-4, 169
negotiated contract, *see* contract type
Netherlee Park, 52, 57, 60, 62, 64-9, 73, 166
Newburgh, 169
Newford, 143
Newton Mearns, 98, 128, 143-4
new towns, 247
no-fines concrete, *see* concrete construction
Northern Ireland, 227, 239
Northern Lighthouse Board, 124
Norwich, 169

Oban, 205
Old Kilpatrick, 11, 109
Orchard Park, 42, 47, 59, 62, 97-101, 103, 109, 117-9, 165, 172, 184
Orlit, 238
Oswald, J W Gordon, 14
overcrowding, 194, 203, 210
owner-occupation, 3, 5, 12, 16, 18, 24-5, 34, 37, 39, 47, 49, 52, 57, 60, 79, 82, 84, 166, 212-7, 220-1, 257, 258-70

package deal, *see* contract type
Page & Park, 187
Paisley, 97, 114, 120
Paragon, 231
Parrot, Bonney, 140-2
Paterson, Jack, 112
Percival, David, 169
Plumstead, Derek, 118
Pollock, Robert, 13
Poole Committee, 111
population, 193, 199, 220, 243, 262
Port Glasgow, 109-10, 114
Powell, C C, 122
prefabrication, 4-5, 22, 34, 36, 42, 113-4, 119, 158, 167, 224-9, 232, 234, 237, 239, 244, 249, 252-3, 257
prefabs, 114, 116, 119, 229-30, 234-5, 253
private rental housing, 3, 12, 16, 25, 34, 37, 39, 49-50, 57-8, 64, 73, 76-8, 118, 122, 166, 183, 203, 211, 215, 217, 221-2
productivity, 228, 233, 255
Progressive Party, *see* Tory Party
public housing, 1-2, 5-6, 9, 18, 21-5, 28-9, 34-7, 57-8, 110, 113, 117-8, 169, 173, 206, 211-6, 221, 224, 233, 243-4, 257-9, 260, 263, 265

Rangers Football Club, 153
rates (local property tax), 217-8, 222
Rayack Construction, 171
Reema Ltd, 167, 245-6
Reith, Lord, 111
Renfrew, 120, 174, 183
Renfrew County Council, 60, 62, 73, 100, 109, 117-8, 143, 160, 165
Rennie, Sandy, 257
Ritchie, I, 189
rent restrictions, 18, 34, 107, 112, 166, 211
Roberts, Dr and Mrs George, 177
Rogan, Pat, 155, 217, 224, 246, 255, 289
Rolland, L A, 169
Ross, Donald, 285-7
Ross, W, 56
Rosyth, 209, 227
Rouken Glen, 52, 60, 62
Royal Incorporation of Architects in Scotland, 167, 189
Russell, J B, 204, 206
Rutherford, R, 153, 185, 187-9

Sandringham Court, 47, 95, 103, 108, 118, 147, 164
sanitation, *see* domestic facilities
Scotcon, 238
Scotsman, 116, 120, 122
Scottish Board of Health, 21-2
Scottish Builders Group, 116, 119
Scottish Building Contractors' Association, 165
Scottish Development Department, *see* Department of Health for Scotland
Scottish Educational Journal, 61
Scottish House Builders' Association, 119-20
Scottish Housing Advisory Committee, 255
Scottish Housing Group, 120, 235-6, 239
Scottish Milk Marketing Board, 177
Scottish National Federation of Building Trades Employers, 160
Scottish National Housing Company, 76
Scottish Special Housing Association, 113, 117-8, 120, 125-6, 167, 231-4, 239-40, 244, 246-9, 252-3, 256-7, 283-7
Scottish Veterans' Garden City Association, 114, 125
Seco, *see* prefabs
separate trades, *see* contract type
service apartments, *see* apartment blocks
Shetland, 256-7
Short, J, 195
showhouses, 58, 60, 68-9, 82, 130, 132, 136-142, 147, 149, 154, 157, 161, 163-4
Sidwell Report, 165, 255
Sinclair, John, 205
single contractor, *see* contract type
Skarne, 251-2, 281-2
slum clearance, 21, 27, 37, 205, 212
Smith, George, 50, 98
Smyth, Tom, 248, 287-90
Sneddon, H, 246, 290-3
socialism, *see* Labour Party
Span, 169
speculative building, 5-6, 14, 16, 18, 27, 30, 37, 85, 98, 110, 117-21, 123, 130, 142-3, 149, 152, 173-4, 185, 211, 213, 218-20, 226-7, 233-4, 255, 259-70
Stamperland, 166
Steel, James, 22, 195, 199-200
steel construction, 120, 158, 227, 230-1, 235-6, 254
Stevenston, 47, 101, 104, 109, 120, 122, 144, 149, 160
Stewart, Archibald, 16